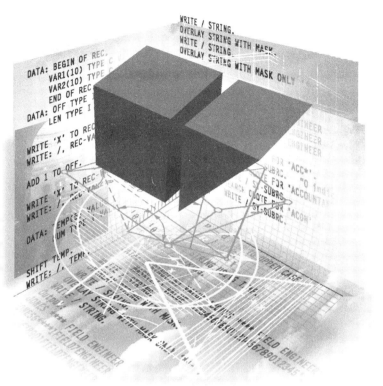

GW00994724

ALE, EDI, & IDoc
Technologies for
SAP™

Arvind Nagpal

SERIES EDITORS:
Gareth M. de Bruyn
Robert Lyfareff

A Division of Prima Publishing

A Division of Prima Publishing
Prima Publishing and colophon are registered trademarks of Prima Communications, Inc. PRIMA TECH is a trademark of Prima Communications, Inc., Rocklin, California 95765.

"SAP" is a registered trademark of SAP Aktiengesellschaft, Systems, Applications and Products in Data Processing, Neurottstrasse 16, 69190 Walldorf, Germany. The publisher gratefully acknowledges SAP's kind permission to use its trademark in this publication. SAP AG is not the publisher of this book and is not responsible for it under any aspect of press law.

R/2, R/3, SAP Business Workflow, ABAP/4, SAP EarlyWatch, SAP ArchiveLink, R/3 Retail, SAPPHIRE, SAP Solution, and ALE/WEB are either trademarks or registered trademarks of SAP Aktiengesellschaft, Walldorf, Germany.

Windows, Windows Explorer, and Microsoft are registered trademarks of Microsoft Corporation.

Prima Publishing and the author have attempted throughout this book to distinguish proprietary trademarks from descriptive terms by following the capitalization style used by the manufacturers.

ISBN: 0-7615-1903-3

Library of Congress Catalog Card Number: 98-68139

Printed in the United States of America

99 00 01 02 03 HH 10 9 8 7 6 5 4 3 2 1

Publisher:
Stacy L. Hiquet

Associate Publisher:
Nancy Stevenson

Managing Editor:
Dan J. Foster

Sr. Acquisitions Editor:
Deborah F. Abshier

Project Editor:
Kevin W. Ferns

Assistant Project Editor:
Estelle Manticas

Development Editor:
Chris Haidri

Copy Editor:
June Waldman

Technical Reviewer:
Ron Herrmann

Interior Layout:
Marco Sipriaso of CWA, Inc.

Cover Design:
Prima Design Team

Indexer:
Sherry Massey

I gratefully dedicate this book to my dear wife, Ritu, my little darling, Anika, and both our parents. Ritu, I could not have done this without your full cooperation, support, and persistence. Dear Anika, winter is almost over but I hope we can still catch some snow and make that snowman you wanted. To our respected parents, your continuous encouragement, belief in me, and blessings have made this book a reality. I could not have asked for a better family. I love you all; thanks for making my dream a reality!

Contents at a Glance

Contents

Chapter 11   Monitoring the Interface **213**

Acknowledgments

Doing a book of this magnitude requires a team effort. First of all, I want to thank Matthew Carleson and Debbie Abshier of Prima Tech for giving me an opportunity to do this book and share my knowledge with the SAP community. Hats off to Kevin Ferns and Chris Haidri for giving this book a professional look. Your excellent comments and suggestions were invaluable. I still think you guys should write a book called *How to Write a Book*. Thank you to June Waldman for keeping me straight on my corky English. Ron Herrmann, your technical review was a big help in ensuring the correctness of this material.

I want to take this opportunity to thank several other individuals who have guided me in building my SAP career thus far. Thanks to Dr. Mike Spano of IBM, for introducing me to the world of SAP; to Dr. Thom Hodgson of North Carolina State University, for your expert advice on my masters thesis on SAP EDI; to Mike Perroni of BFI Houston and Jeff Cassel of AMP Inc., for keeping me challenged with real-world problems; to Hari Adusumilli and Paul Leing for giving me an opportunity to teach at SAP America; and to all my students whose questions, input, and appreciation guided me along the path of writing this book.

Finally, I would like to thank SAP America.

About the Author

Arvind Nagpal is an active leader in the ALE/EDI community today, and he has over ten years of experience in the IT industry and four years of SAP experience. An independent consultant and instructor, he consults with several Fortune 500 companies and teaches at SAP America. His in-depth knowledge has helped companies implement successful and scalable ALE and EDI systems.

Mr. Nagpal enjoys the continued support and admiration of his clients and students, most of whom still call on him for advice in such SAP cross-application technologies as ALE, EDI, Business Framework, Internet commerce, and Workflow. He has recently launched a company through which he plans to help businesses leverage their investments in SAP and extend their reach to consumers and businesses via the Internet.

About the Series Editors

Gareth de Bruyn's background includes chemical engineering, UNIX site administration, and network installations. His experience with SAP began shortly after the technology became available, and he currently works as an independent SAP consultant with a Fortune 50 company. A native of South Africa but raised and educated in the United States, de Bruyn believes SAP technology is revolutionizing international business. He plans to earn a law degree to unite his technical and international business skills to capitalize on this global opportunity.

Robert Lyfareff is a veteran of several successful SAP installation teams over the past four years. Coupled with his formal training in computer science and electrical engineering, this unique SAP experience enables him to write about real-world business situations and issues. What excites and challenges him about his work is the integration and modification of business practices with the new technology. Currently, he works as an independent SAP consultant and author.

About Prima Tech's SAP Series

The demand for SAP programming and support expertise is exploding. Prima Tech's SAP series is designed to prepare IT professionals for a successful career using the world's leading ERP application. From ABAP/4 programming to preparing an effective organizational structure for the support of an SAP installation, to providing guidance on becoming an SAP consultant, Prima Tech's SAP series is the most comprehensive resource available for IT professionals. For more information on this and other SAP books and resources, see Prima Tech's Web site at **www.prima-tech.com**.

Foreword

Over the past several years, we have seen dramatic growth in the number of companies who have embarked on the implementation of ERP systems. This phenomenon continues to be driven by both the need to cut costs from critical business processes and the availability of high quality, affordable computer hardware and software. While there are a number of software vendors offering ERP solutions, it is generally recognized that SAP is the market leader. With over 20 years' experience developing, deploying, and supporting main frame-based ERP systems, SAP was well positioned to capitalize on the advent of large scale client/server hardware systems introduced to the marketplace in the early 1990's. By migrating their highly successful R/2 main frame product, with its proven business processes, to a client/server environment, SAP was able to offer a mature, stable product which embodied world-class business processes and new, user-friendly functions.

Global Fortune 500 companies, eager to improve processes and reduce costs, were quick to endorse the R/3 client server system, and many launched large, global efforts to implement the system. The smaller companies followed a similar approach. While each SAP installation has its own unique challenges, there are thousands of commercial concerns today that have successfully implemented the SAP R/3 system.

R/3 is designed to operate as a tightly integrated system, with all functional modules interfacing directly and immediately with all other applicable modules. By design, the standard R/2 system expects the various components (Sales and Distribution, Finance, Production Planning, etc.) to reside on a single computer system. When entering an order, for example, the Sales and Distribution system expects to be able to make direct updates to the Financial system. While a single system architecture offers simplicity of design, it introduces complexities when trying to formulate a strategy for deploying R/3 across a large organization.

Today's client/server hardware is approaching main frame capabilities. Still, the idea of trying to support several thousand global users, spread across 24 time zones, on a single client/server configuration, does not yet have widespread support. The risks involved with outages, combined with the difficulties of scheduling worldwide operations, makes the single computer approach less than desirable. Rather, system architects are looking for ways to deploy R/3 on a multitude of client/server systems without sacrificing the tight integration inherent in the product.

The scope of R/3 is both broad and deep. Yet, it would be unusual to find an SAP customer who uses SAP products exclusively. Normally, SAP must peacefully coexist with legacy systems which remain in place after R/3 is installed. Most often it is necessary to develop an interface mechanism such that information can flow freely between SAP and those legacy systems. This can be a costly, time consuming task which introduces a high level of risk into the project.

These two requirements, hardware scalability and interfaces to external systems, cry out for a rationalized approach to distributing R/3 functionality. What's needed is a way to deploy R/3 across multiple client/server systems and at the same time interface R/3 with non-SAP systems. Enter ALE, Application Link Enabling, which is designed to help address those requirements. With ALE, planners are able to construct a large, integrated solution which encompasses R/3 deployed over multiple systems and interfaced with the top third-party systems or legacy systems. SAP offers ALE as part of its standard Cross Application suite of products delivered with the basic product.

ALE has several facets. On the one hand it can be used to bring to life the standard ALE scenarios delivered by SAP, such as running FI/CO on one system and logistics on another, or it can be used to develop brand new scenarios, unique to particular customers. In either case, ALE is a tried-and-true product used by dozens of large corporations in deployment of their production systems. This is not pie-in-the-sky technology. It is standard, delivered software which is used in production by many Fortune 500 companies. Going forward, ALE plays a central role in SAP's component architecture strategy.

An important aspect of ALE technology is the lengths to which SAP has gone to insulate the application systems from ALE. When implementing ALE, it is crucial that the various application modules (Sales and Distribution, Finance, Cost Accounting, etc.) not be adversely impacted. The designers of ALE envisioned an environment where the SAP components could be distributed across multiple physical systems and linked together via ALE without the need to reconfigure or restructure those components. The method they selected was to employ a special Intermediate Document (IDoc) that would carry information between the various components. The concept of IDocs is central to ALE processing. In the delivered ALE design, the application systems themselves are not even aware that IDocs are being sent and received across system boundaries by ALE. There is no need to make adjustments to the SAP application systems.

IDocs are also used to facilitate SAP's EDI interfaces. As incoming EDI traffic arrives, EDI software translates the EDI messages into Intermediate Documents and then passes those IDocs along to the ALE layer for further disposition. On the outbound side, SAP application programs can be instructed to create outbound IDocs for certain transactions, such as Purchase Orders or Invoices, which should be sent to trading partners. These outbound IDocs are then forwarded to the EDI subsystem where they are translated into the appropriate EDI structures. Because both ALE and EDI use the same IDoc formats, the SAP applications employ a consistent inbound and outbound interface regardless of whether they are interacting with ALE or EDI.

These three technology components (ALE, IDocs, and EDI) are all interrelated, and it is important that planners and implementation teams understand how they interact with one another. Even if an implementation is being planned without the use of ALE, it is probable that there will be EDI trading activity and, if this is the case, you must understand how to deploy IDocs, EDI, and portions of ALE.

In this text, you will learn how ALE can be used to address real-life business issues. You will learn how R/3 can be configured to run on multiple systems, how to interface R/3 with third-party and legacy systems, and how to use ALE functionality to enable EDI partner trading. You will also learn how to extend existing IDocs and create entirely new IDocs to address your unique business requirements. Finally, you will learn how to create new functionality which may be required to process your new IDocs.

If you or your company are involved with or are planning an SAP implementation, you should take the time to become acquainted with the concepts and capabilities covered herein. There is no better single source of information than Mr. Nagpal's book. If you're serious about SAP, you will have to deal with these technologies sooner or later, and this book will give you the knowledge you need to chart a clear course and execute with confidence.

Jeffory A. Cassel

Director, International ALE Users Group

Manager, SAP Distributed Architecture, AMP, Inc.

Harrisburg, Pennsylvania

Introduction

In any SAP implementation, integration between business processes within a company and across companies is very important for a successful implementation. Within a company integration needs include interfacing with legacy systems, communicating with third party products, and integrating business processes across distributed SAP systems. The two most commonly deployed technologies for this type of integration are ALE (Application Link and Enabling) and EDI (Electronic Data Interchange) technologies, which make use of the popular IDoc (Intermediate Document) interface for exchanging data.

EDI provides business process integration across companies by exchanging business documents such as purchase orders, invoices, and shipment notices in electronic form, using industry standard formats such as ANSI X.12 (American National Standards Institute) and EDIFACT (Electronic Data Interchange For Administration, Commerce, and Transport).

ALE, which is SAP's proprietary technology for integrating distributed business processes within a company, has been available in SAP since release 3.0. ALE was designed to link one SAP system to another SAP system, but the ALE architecture lent itself to being used in linking SAP systems to non-SAP systems without any modification. The flexibility of ALE technology has proliferated into several application areas, and today most third-party products use it to exchange data with SAP. ALE technology is also the basis for SAP's Business Framework architecture, introduced in release 4.0.

The underlying architecture of the ALE and EDI technologies are quite similar. Both make use of SAP's proprietary IDoc interface, which defines the format and structure of the data that is exchanged between two systems. Although ALE and EDI are the two biggest users of the IDoc interface, this interface can also be used by any two applications that need to exchange data. For example, it can be readily used to integrate SAP with Web applications.

As cross-application technologies, ALE and EDI are used in various modules of SAP such as SD (Sales and Distribution), MM (Materials Management), and FI (Financials). The wide-ranging application of these technologies has created an ever-increasing need for ALE, EDI, and IDoc skills. Mastery of these skills is a necessity for anyone involved in the technical or functional side of an SAP implementation.

Who Should Read this Book?

Because ALE, EDI, and IDoc are cross-application technologies, a wide audience can benefit from this book. EDI and ALE team members, support providers, data-interfacing and workflow experts, EDI and ALE programmers, aspiring EDI and ALE experts, e-commerce experts, and curious readers alike will find useful information in this book.

◆ **EDI team member.** This book provides you with a good foundation by explaining the concepts behind EDI and IDoc technologies. Tips throughout Part 3, "Configuring the EDI Interface," show you how to tweak certain parameters to achieve a particular effect without doing an enhancement. Message control is used very widely in the EDI process. You learn to customize the message control component and set up workflow for error handling. If you cannot satisfy business requirements by configuring the existing components, then you need either to enhance those components or to build from ground zero. Section III, "IDocs," covers all the steps required to extend or create IDocs, along with programs to support the extensions and configuration to make these components known to the system.

◆ **ALE team member.** This book provides you with a good foundation by explaining the need and concepts behind ALE and IDoc technologies. You learn about the various configuration components involved in enabling any ALE process. Tips throughout Part 8, "Configuring the ALE Interface," show you how to tweak certain parameters to achieve a particular effect without doing an enhancement. Master data distribution and Distributed business processes are explained with real-world business scenarios. You learn how to set up workflow for error handling. If you cannot satisfy the business requirements by configuring the existing components, then you need either to enhance the existing components or to build from ground zero. Section III, "IDocs," covers all the steps required to extend or create new IDocs, along with the programs to support the extensions and configuration to make these components known to the system.

◆ **Support provider.** If you are or anticipate being in a support role for the ALE and the EDI process, then Part 4, "Operating and Administering the EDI Interface," and Part 9, "Operating and Administering the ALE Interface," will be especially useful in understanding the various tasks and challenges that you will face in a live environment and the various kinds of problems that you can expect. These parts of the book also provide common remedies to those problems. In addition, you learn about utilities that help you accomplish your everyday tasks.

◆ **Data-interfacing expert.** If you are a systems analyst and are contemplating various technologies for integrating external systems, you have several choices. Your decision does not rest simply on the capabilities of the various technologies; it also concerns ongoing support and maintenance, as well as restart and recovery options. This book helps you in making an informed decision as to whether ALE and IDoc technologies are appropriate alternatives for your environment. Section III, "IDocs," is a great place to start.

◆ **Complementary software partner.** You either have a complementary product or are developing a product that will interface with SAP. Most third-party business systems (external warehouse management systems, EDI translators, production planning optimizers, and so on) interface with SAP via ALE and IDocs.

◆ **Workflow expert.** You are an expert in developing complex business workflows and have been given the task of setting up the workflow system for error handling in ALE and EDI. To understand various points in the ALE/EDI process where workflow is triggered and to familiarize yourself with various workflow tasks, turn to Chapter 9, "Configuring Workflow."

◆ **EDI/ALE programmer.** You are part of the technical team. You are responsible for writing or modifying ABAP/4 programs used by the IDoc interface. These programs have a certain structure, organization, and flow that is important to integrate seamlessly with the various components of the ALE or EDI process. You will find details about the structure of these programs in Section III.

◆ **Aspiring EDI and ALE expert.** You have been programming in ABAP/4 for a long time and want to jump to the next step without forsaking your technical roots. You can easily turn yourself into an EDI/ALE programmer as long as you understand how these programs fit in the overall process; this book provides the knowledge you need, such as locating and developing user exits in the EDI/ALE process and developing new programs from scratch.

- **Curious reader.** You have heard a lot about the ALE, EDI, and IDoc technologies, but have never found any book that described them in simple language yet provided all the details. You can use this book to learn at your own pace, moving from a very high-level overview of the process into a detailed description of each component. You can select the level of detail that you are comfortable with. If you have access to the SAP system, then you can try out some of the example EDI and ALE scenarios discussed in this book.

- **E-commerce expert.** If you have worked on EDI projects in the past, you won't have any trouble grasping the EDI concepts in SAP. Section I of this book explains how SAP carries out the EDI process and is an excellent guide to help you build on the knowledge you've gained by working with EDI in other systems.

What This Book Covers

This book covers the full breadth and depth of ALE, EDI and IDoc technology. You will learn the concepts behind these technologies and then configure some commonly used business ALE and EDI scenarios. You'll develop custom scenarios by either extending or developing new IDocs from scratch for different business situations. You will learn how to utilize user-exits for the extended IDocs and develop new programs for custom IDocs.

Part 1—EDI Basics

Part 1 begins with a discussion of general EDI technology and then moves on to the basics of SAP EDI architecture. The goal is to provide a high-level overview of the various components used in the EDI process, benefits of EDI, and EDI's advantages to corporations.

Part 2—The SAP EDI Interface

Part 2 examines the more advanced technical and functional details of the inbound and outbound SAP EDI process, including the interface with the EDI subsystem. Although this part is mainly for technical people, functional users can also benefit from this material. You will grasp the contents quickly with the aid of the flowcharts included throughout the chapters.

Part 3—Configuring the EDI Interface

An SAP EDI process uses several components to generate and process EDI transactions. These components are highly configurable to meet the varying needs of several corporations. Part 3 provides the technical details of the concept, role, and options available for each component in the process; this material is designed for readers who are responsible for setting up the EDI interface. In a step-by-step manner, you learn to do the complete setup, which includes setting up the basic EDI infrastructure, building partner profiles, configuring Message control, and setting up the workflow component for error handling. The steps are illustrated with screen shots, tips, and tricks to make the learning process more fun.

Part 4—Operating and Administering the EDI Interface

Part 4 covers the operational aspects of the EDI interface. After you have configured the system, you need to test your process inside and out to make sure it works as desired. You learn about various testing techniques and tools that you can use. After testing the interface, you can start running the process. The various monitoring tools available in the system and how to interpret the information logged in the system is also discussed. Sooner or later you will run into problems and need an efficient way to troubleshoot them. The troubleshooting process is described in detail. A set of flowcharts has been provided to help you quickly get to the cause of a particular problem and then fix it. Finally, you'll also be involved in managing the performance and throughput of the system. The various ways to manage performance and throughput at the same time are discussed.

Part 5—EDI Scenarios

In Part 5, you will apply the knowledge that you have gained in the previous chapters to create actual outbound and inbound EDI transactions using real-world business scenarios. For outbound, you learn the complete setup required to send purchase orders to your vendors via EDI, and to send payment orders and remittance advice to your bank via EDI. For inbound, you learn the complete setup required to bring sales orders into the system via EDI, and sales order changes via workflow. The primary focus of this part is to present a methodology so that you can tackle any EDI transaction.

Part 6—ALE Basics

In Part 6, you are introduced to the ALE process, why it was invented, why some of the existing technologies do not suffice, its architecture, and its benefits. This is a general introduction and provides a high-level overview of the capabilities of the ALE process.

Part 7—The SAP ALE Interface

Part 7 is an advanced technical and functional reference section for inbound and outbound ALE processes. You will grasp the contents quickly with the aid of several flowcharts included throughout the chapters.

Part 8—Configuring the ALE Interface

The material in Part 8 is designed for readers who are responsible for setting up the ALE interface. First you learn how to set up the basic ALE infrastructure required by all ALE processes. Then you learn about one of the most widely used application of ALE—the distribution of master data. You learn about the various distribution techniques, business issues, and strategies used by large organizations to keep master data under control. The material master data is used as an example to illustrate the various points. Another major application of ALE, the distribution of business processes, is described in complete detail using the distributed purchasing process.

Part 9—Operating and Administering the ALE Interface

Part 9 covers the operational matters of the ALE Interface. Once you have configured the system, you need to test your process to make sure it is working as desired. The various testing tools and techniques are discussed. Once you have tested the process, you can start executing it. The monitoring tools described in the EDI section are used for ALE processes. The monitoring tools describe how to interpret the information logged in the system. Sooner or later you will run into problems, and you need an efficient way to troubleshoot the problem and restart the process from the point of failure. A set of flowcharts has been provided to help you quickly get to the cause of the problem. Last but not the least, you will be involved in managing the performance and throughput of the ALE system. The possible approaches to manage performance and throughput are described.

Part 10—IDoc Basics

In Part 10, you will be introduced to the basics of the IDoc from an end-user perspective, and then you'll move into the more technical details required in the development and design of IDocs. The concepts cover data transfer via IDocs versus data transfer using flat files. This simple analogy will help you become an expert in a very short time.

Part 11—Customer Modifications to the IDoc Interface

A good understanding of the IDoc development process and programming of the IDocs is one of the important skills needed in an SAP implementation. In this part of the book, you will learn about the enhancement process to the IDoc interface. The enhancement process is effectively a three-step process. First you create new IDocs or extend existing IDocs. Next you develop programs for the new and extended IDocs. Finally you customize the ALE/EDI interface layer to recognize the IDocs and their programs. There are three chapters in this part devoted to each step of the enhancement process.

Part 12—Archiving in the IDoc Interface

When your system is operational and in production, the number of IDocs and workflow run-time logs can grow quickly. If your transaction volume is high, you need a strategy to archive IDocs. SAP provides archiving programs and deletion programs for several documents in the system, and you'll learn how to archive IDocs and delete work items and work item history.

Appendix—FAQs, User Exits, and Miscellaneous Resources

The appendix provides answers to frequently asked questions, a cross-reference chart for EDI transaction-to-SAP messages, a list of standard user-exits in the system, a comparison between release 3.x and 4.x systems, and other miscellaneous resources such as useful Web sites and Internet discussion groups.

Conventions Used in This Book

To comfortably absorb the information this book presents, you should be familiar with the teaching tools you'll find throughout.

Most notably, there are many SAP screen images, which help you to follow along with the instruction on an active SAP session of your own. Using the screen images, you can determine the pace at which you would like to progress, assuring yourself that you can clearly identify each activity being described.

Throughout the text, you'll encounter several explanatory techniques that will make the lessons easier to understand and apply. These techniques will help you quickly determine what action needs to be taken or which keyboard functions are required for the execution of each task. When you need to go through more than one menu to get where you're going, the **path** shows up as a series of monospaced words separated by commas.

You'll also see some special typographical devices to call your attention to certain points in the text:

 TIP

Tips present helpful information in an attention-getting format. These tips reinforce key concepts and explanations, making them easier to remember and use.

 NOTE

Notes provide additional related information, alternatives, or commentary that might help you better understand the topic under discussion or lead you to additional sources of information to make you more successful in SAP usage.

 CAUTION

Cautions warn of potential hazards and pitfalls you should be aware of.

These conventions will serve as your signposts throughout this text. Use them to help you identify critical elements and information about SAP. The lessons throughout this book will increase in pace and relative complexity to match your growing knowledge, and the conventions described will help you keep up.

Contacting the Author

You will learn something new about SAP practically every day, and working through this book probably won't be enough to make you perfectly comfortable with every SAP function you may need to use. If you find you can't locate the information you seek in SAP's help utilities, feel free to contact me via e-mail at **anagpal@bacusa.com.** I hope to help you become more proficient with SAP, and I'll strive to apply my experience in ways that will help you achieve SAP proficiency at a faster rate. Good luck!

SECTION I

EDI

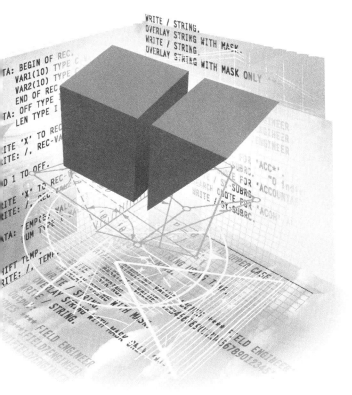

PART

1

EDI Basics

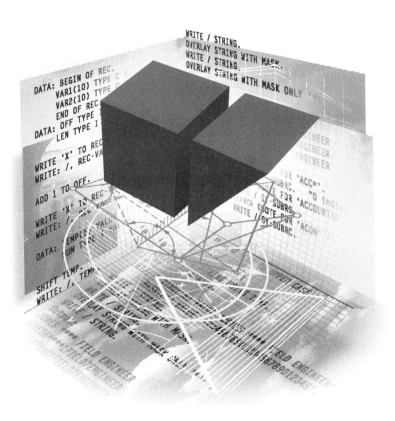

Chapter 1

Introduction to the EDI Process

EDI (Electronic Data Interchange) has been around for several years. The goal of this chapter is to provide a high level overview of the EDI process: what it is, how it started, why companies implement EDI, EDI's benefits to corporations, and various components used to build the EDI process. The material here is particularly important for someone who is new to EDI technology.

What Is EDI?

EDI is the electronic exchange of business documents between the computer systems of business partners, using a standard format over a communication network. EDI is also called paperless exchange.

This definition very nicely sums up the whole process in a few words, but the actual implementation of an effective EDI system requires considerable effort and support.

The Evolution of EDI

Consider a very simple business scenario. A customer who wants to purchase an item creates a Purchase order and then faxes or mails it to the vendor. The vendor receives the Purchase order and manually keys in a Sales order. The vendor's system generates a confirmation date that is sent back to the customer via fax or mail. The vendor then ships the goods via a carrier. The carrier delivers the products to the customer. When the goods are shipped, the vendor invoices the customer. The customer makes the payment by check, and the vendor deposits the check in the bank. Finally, funds are transferred from the customer's account to the vendor's account.

This simple scenario requires the exchange of various documents between several business partners at different times. There are some inherent problems with this scenario, in that it:

♦ Is highly inefficient and laborious
♦ Cannot be tracked easily
♦ Gives no visibility into the process
♦ Has a very long lead time
♦ Includes redundant data entry at various points

To circumvent some of the trouble spots, the business partners started exchanging data electronically via floppy disks and other storage devices, which meant that the business partners had to adopt standard formats. An ANSI committee was formed to define the standards. Ultimately, the electronic exchange of business documents in a standard format gave birth to what is now known as EDI.

EDI is not a recent invention; it has been around for more than 30 years. The transportation industry pioneered this technology and is thus responsible for its current architecture, but most industries have realized the benefits of using EDI. Today almost any industry or organization can take advantage of EDI. The retail and automotive industries are major EDI users, and the technology is used in several other large industries, including health care, government agencies, real estate, and education. In fact, EDI can be implemented not only between organizations, but also within an organization, an area that is gaining strength these days.

Benefits of the EDI Process

Implementing EDI benefits both the sender and the receiver. It is a mutual effort, and its benefits are maximized by sharing information in a timely manner. The benefits include the following:

◆ **Reduced data entry errors.** EDI does not involve data entry at multiple points. In the traditional system a sender creates a purchase order on their system, prints it, and then faxes or mails it to a trading partner. The receiver then rekeys the same information on their computer. The process is prone to data entry errors. This procedure is repeated when invoicing takes place. With EDI, data goes directly from one computer to another without involving a human being.

◆ **Reduced processing cycle time.** The biggest advantage is the reduced processing time of the complete cycle. As soon as orders are entered into the system, they can be processed on the receiving side in seconds. There is a considerable saving in the processing time of document transfer.

◆ **Availability of data in electronic form.** Data from EDI is in electronic form, which makes it easy to share across the organization. For example, a purchasing department can use the data to evaluate vendors, or a marketing department can use it to analyze the trends and demands of customers.

◆ **Reduced paperwork.** The entire EDI process can be handled without using a single piece of paper. Some companies believe that they must have appropriate paperwork for audits and legal issues. In its Paperwork Reduction Act, the IRS recognizes the electronic form as a valid legal document as long as the vendor or supplier can prove the origin and show complete trails on how data was generated. A company needs to have controlled processes to handle data flowing in and out. This ruling has created some tough auditing requirements, but meeting them is worth the effort.

◆ **Reduced cost.** Time is money. Any savings in time are directly linked to savings in money. The initial cost of an EDI setup is certainly higher as compared to the paper process, but over a long period it is very cost effective. In the long term, the overall cost of exchanging business documents in paper form can cost anywhere from $10-$15 per transaction. If the process has to be repeated for some reason, for example if an invoice is lost, it can cost around $45. On the flip side, the average cost of an EDI transaction is close to $2.

◆ **Reduced inventories and better planning.** Companies do not have to keep a safety stock for the time taken with order processing. Changes to planning schedules can be communicated instantaneously. MRP (Material Requirement and Planning) can take into account a shipment in transit as soon as an Advance ship notice (EDI 856) transaction is received.

◆ **Standard means of communication.** Because EDI enforces standards on the contents of data, uniform naming standards and field sizes have emerged. Such consistency leads to clearer communication and less ambiguity.

◆ **Better business processes.** Compared to traditional methods of exchanging business documents, EDI is certainly a better way of communicating with your trading partners. Companies are willing to share information and participate in interorganizational issues. This environment enhances supply-chain management.

◆ **Competitive advantage.** In many cases, companies that have implemented EDI have an advantage over their competitors, especially when dealing with government agencies or large corporations. For example, potential vendors must use EDI to bid for certain government contracts. The procurement divisions in government agencies publish their RFPs (Request for Proposal) on the EDI network. In addition, large retailers and corporations discourage doing business with a business partner if the partner cannot send EDI transactions. The same holds true for the auto-motive industry. To be a certified auto-industry vendor, an organization must be able to communicate electronically. Trying to clear goods through customs is truly a nightmare if the necessary documentation is not in EDI format and has not been sent in advance.

Business Process Using EDI

In the process of buying and selling goods, business documents are exchanged at various points in the process with various partners. Figure 1-1 depicts some common business documents that business partners exchange.

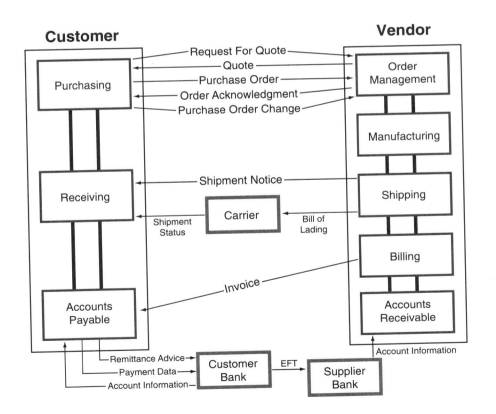

FIGURE 1-1

Typical business documents that business partners exchange

Documents Exchanged with Customers

Between a customer and a supplier, it is the customer that typically drives the EDI requirements. The following are some of the key business documents exchanged between a customer and supplier:

- Customer requests price catalogs
- Customer requests quotes
- Customer places blanket purchase orders
- Customer authorizes delivery against its blanket orders
- Customer places an order
- Customer expects an order acknowledgment
- Customer expects a delivery schedule
- Customer wants to know the status of the order
- Customer may cancel an order
- Customer may change an order
- Customer expects an order
- Customer requires a ship notification
- Customer receives goods
- Customer notifies supplier that goods have been received
- Customer wants authorization to return goods
- Customer wants to return goods damaged in transit
- Customer is an international customer
- Customer receives an invoice

Documents Exchanged with Carriers

A carrier is a party that undertakes the transportation of goods from one point to another. The following documents are exchanged during the transportation process:

- Shipper requests a carrier pickup
- Carrier responds with a pickup date
- Carrier prints a bill of lading
- Carrier informs the receiving party of the shipment
- Receiver tells carrier where to unload the goods

◆ Shipper requests tracking for a particular shipment

◆ Carrier informs the shipper of the status of shipment

◆ Carrier bills the shipper through an invoice

◆ Carrier receives payment

Documents Exchanged with Financial Institutions

Financial institutions act as agents for payers or as guarantors or advisors in matters involving letters of credit. The following documents are exchanged in business transactions with financial institutions:

◆ Banks receive authorization to transfer funds from buyer's account to seller's account

◆ Customer may request account information

◆ Banks have to send account summary

Documents Exchanged with Insurance Institutions

An insurance institution writes insurance policies for freight and pays claims for items damaged in shipment. The following documents are exchanged in business transactions with insurance institutions:

◆ Establish insurance policy

◆ Inform the insurer of the goods being transported

◆ Process a claim for goods damaged in transit

◆ Settle claim

Documents Exchanged with Government Agencies

A government agency is a regulating agency at the federal, state, or local level that has policies regarding shipments. For example, the Customs Department is involved when shipping or receiving goods across a national boundary. The following documents are exchanged with the Customs Department in international trade:

◆ Provide customs with manifest data on cargo

◆ Obtain cargo release and clearance information from customs

◆ Obtain rejection or approval notice from customs

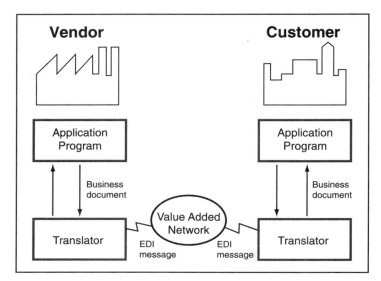

FIGURE 1-2

*Components of the
EDI system*

Components Used in the EDI Process

This section describes the various components used in an EDI process (see Figure 1-2).

Trading Partners

Parties involved in a business transaction are called trading partners. The trading partners can be any combination of organizations or business types. For example, customers and vendors are trading partners.

Business Documents

A business document is a legal document that defines the transaction conducted between trading partners. The legal boundaries for these transactions are defined by trade agencies, trading partners, and the ISO (International Standards Organization). The trading partners are bound by the terms and conditions of these documents. Numerous business documents are in existence today. Examples of some typical business documents are the following:

- ◆ Requests for a quote
- ◆ Purchase orders
- ◆ Purchase order changes
- ◆ Purchase order acknowledgments
- ◆ Invoices
- ◆ Remittance advice

EDI Messages

The transportation industry pioneered the exchange of business documents in electronic form. However, there was no commonly adopted standard among the companies involved, which resulted in multiple documents for the same business document. Multiplicity of business documents was carried over to the new environment, so the industry eventually saw a need for standardization. A committee named ANSI X.12 was formed in 1975 to address this issue. The X signified its relevance to the computer industry, and the number 12 was the next sequential number in the list of numbers assigned to each committee. The committee published its first standards in 1979. The standards defined various EDI messages which govern the rules, format, and content of data in a transaction. A one-to-one correspondence exists between the components of a paper-based document and an EDI message. The terminology may vary from one standard to another. The standards also determine the format of the transmission packet.

The formation of common standards has many advantages:

- ◆ Standardization allows representation that can easily be processed by a computer system.
- ◆ Standardization allows companies to exchange information that is independent of the application software.
- ◆ Third-party applications can provide EDI translation and thus relieve the application of having to keep up with evolving standards.

The choice of standards is mainly based on the industry and standards used by a company's trading partner. It is common for a company to use multiple standards because its customers use various standards. Two widely used standards are ANSI ASC X.12 and EDIFACT.

ANSI ASC X.12

The ANSI X.12 standard is dominant in North America, New Zealand, and Australia. The committee comprises representatives of major organizations, government bodies, and EDI software companies. The X.12 committee is divided into several subcommittees (see Table 1-1) that are responsible for developing standards for a specific industry sector. The approval process is based on a consensus of all the subcommittees.

Table 1-1 ANSI X.12 Subcommittees

Subcommittee	Primary Focus
X12A	Education administration
X12C	Communications and controls
X12E	Product data
X12F	Finance
X12G	Government
X12H	Materials management
X12I	Transportation
X12J	Technical assessment
X12K	Purchasing
X12L	Industry standards transition
X12M	Distribution and warehousing
X12N	Insurance

Technical Structure of a Business Document

The structure of a business document in ANSI X.12 standards can be described using the following three-tier hierarchy: transactions, segments, and data elements (see Figure 1-3).

◆ **Transaction.** A transaction is the electronic equivalent of a business document. A transaction is usually divided into three areas: header area, detail area, and summary area. The header area consists of segments that apply to the entire document and is usually mandatory. For example, in a purchase order, vendor number and vendor address are part of the header segments. The detail area contains document details. The items being ordered and their quantity are considered detail segments. The summary area consists of data that summarizes the entire document, and the total amount and taxes are part of the summary segments.

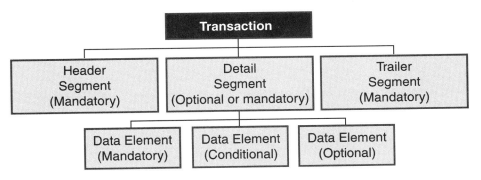

FIGURE 1-3

Technical structure of a business document in EDI format

- ◆ **Segment.** A segment is equivalent to a record in a document. A data segment has the following attributes: A unique ID, a name, a flag indicating whether it is optional or mandatory, and a number of occurrences. A group of segments can be combined to form a loop, which can also be mandatory or optional, and nested as well. Segments are contained in a segment directory (X12.22). A segment consists of a sequence of logically related data elements. Data elements are separated by a data element separator, and can be mandatory or optional. Some data elements are conditional, or mandatory in certain conditions.
- ◆ **Data Elements** Data elements are the smallest unit of information in a transaction, and are defined in the data element dictionary (X12.3). A data element is identified by a data element reference number, data type, and min/max length.

Technical Structure of a Communication Packet

It is common to bundle several EDI messages in one packet before transmitting it over the network. The communication packet as transmitted over the network has a hierarchical format, as shown in Figure 1-4.

Each message (a purchase order, for example) is wrapped in a transaction set header (ST) and a transaction set trailer (SE). Several messages of similar type can be combined into a functional group. For example, if an EDI message contains three purchase orders, they will be combined into one functional group. Each functional group is wrapped with a functional group header (GS) and functional group trailer (GE). An EDI transmission can contain several functional groups,

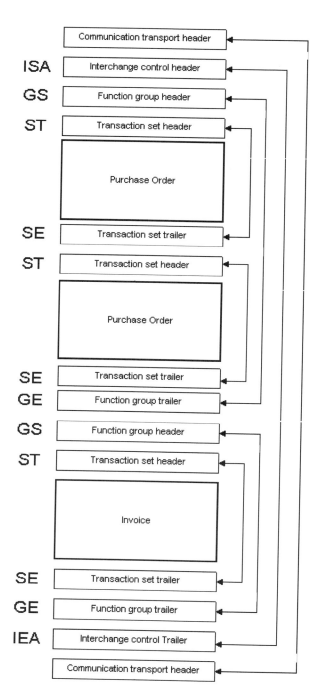

FIGURE 1-4

Structure of an ANSI X.12 message

which are bundled together and wrapped with an EDI header and trailer, also called the interchange control header (ISA) and interchange control trailer (IEA). The communication network wraps yet another header and trailer on the EDI message.

UN/EDIFACT

UN/EDIFACT (United Nations EDI For Administration, Commerce, and Transport) formed in 1985, using the ANSI X.12 and UNTDI (United Nations Trade Data Interchange) as the base standards. The purpose of the standard was to develop an international standard to meet the needs of a global economy. Most companies are moving toward adopting EDIFACT because of its international recognition. EDIFACT is quite similar to ANSI X.12 with some minor differences in terminology and layout.

◆ EDIFACT calls business documents **messages**, and represents them by a name such as **ORDERS** for a purchase order, whereas ANSI X.12 calls them **transactions** and represents them by a number such as 850 for a purchase order.

◆ EDIFACT uses the same segment in multiple places, whereas ANSI has a specific use for each segment.

◆ EDIFACT has additional segments that apply to international trade.

◆ EDIFACT uses different terminology for fields. Conditional fields of EDIFACT are the same as optional fields in ANSI X.12.

Application Programs

Application programs are responsible for generating and processing data in the business documents. These application programs are part of the application suite commonly referred to as ERP (Enterprise Resource Planning). ERP systems (an example of an ERP system is SAP) meet a broad range of a company's business needs. Most ERP vendors recognize the business needs for EDI and thus enable their software to support EDI processes. An ERP system must do the following:

◆ Support standard EDI transactions in the business area of interest. For example, if the focus of a company is shipping and distribution, the software must support basic shipping transactions.

◆ The data necessary for EDI messages should be readily available.

◆ The EDI processes and functionality must be well documented.

- The system needs to be flexible enough to incorporate business requirements within the existing process.

- Provide support for enhancing existing transactions.

- Contain easily configurable and manageable systems.

- Contain a sufficient number of control points to meet business needs.

- Exhibit a disciplined approach for controlling the flow of documents, from error handling to the approval process, within the organization.

- Be integrated with EDI translation software vendors.

- System limits and performance measures are important if a company expects a large volume of EDI transactions.

SAP meets all of these business requirements. Starting with the next chapter, you learn about the capabilities of SAP.

Translators

The traditional approach to EDI implementation was to incorporate the conversion of application data to EDI standards as an integral part of the business application. The problem with this approach was that a separate program existed not only for each transaction but also for each trading partner to meet its unique requirements. Another problem was keeping up with the changing standards. Programs had to be modified every time a trading partner adopted a newer version of the standards.

This approach has changed with the development of third-party translation software, which has become a key element of the EDI process chain. The translator is responsible for mapping application data to the EDI standard format and vice versa. This technology frees the application software to concentrate on the business logic.

 NOTE

The business applications do have to be EDI-enabled, which means they should be capable of interfacing with the translation software, whether through a flat file or transactions.

Value Added Network

Communication networks, often called VANs (value-added networks), provide a means of transmission for EDI transactions between trading partners. The VAN provides a mailbox on the network to each trading partner. This mailbox is polled periodically for messages. The mailboxes are marked as incoming or outgoing mailboxes. The VAN picks up outgoing messages and delivers them to the incoming mailbox of the receiving trading partner. The application software does not need to be connected or running at the time of message exchange. VANs enable trading partners with different internal communication networks to communicate with each other.

The following criteria can be used in evaluating a VAN:

◆ Round-the-clock availability of the network

◆ Reach of the network (national versus international boundaries)

◆ Performance characteristics

◆ Flexibility of cost structure (flat rate versus per document versus number of characters)

◆ Retransmission of failed documents

◆ Gateway to link to other VANs

◆ Availability of audit reports and error reports

◆ Security of data transmitted over the network

The major drawbacks with VANs are the ongoing cost of network services and cost associated with each transmission. If the volume of transactions is high, the total cost could be substantial. Several companies are currently using direct links (via modems) with their trading partners to avoid the cost of a VAN. The only problem with this system is that any new partners must follow similar standards.

A new trend involves using the Internet to transmit EDI documents. The use of the Internet has several advantages: there is no cost for each document, it is available to everyone very cheaply, and it is available 24 hours a day.

Summary

In this chapter, you learned about the basic features of EDI, how it can benefit small and large organizations, and which components are used to build an EDI system. By now you should have a good understanding of the overall EDI process and the terminology used in the process. This background will enable you to understand the equivalent terminology in SAP when the SAP EDI process is introduced in the next chapter.

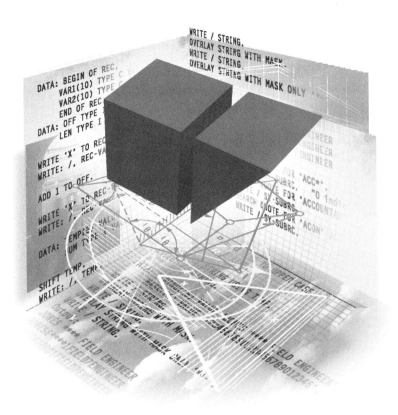

Chapter 2

Introduction to SAP EDI Architecture

In this chapter, you learn the basics of SAP EDI architecture and get a high-level overview of its various components. This chapter shows you how SAP supports the EDI process, what it means to be EDI-enabled, and what support SAP provides for creating new processes. You also learn the boundaries of SAP EDI in the big EDI picture.

SAP EDI Boundaries

Chapter 1, "Introduction to the EDI Process," presented a general overview of the EDI process. It is important to understand which components are supplied by SAP. Figure 2-1 illustrates the SAP EDI boundaries. SAP provides the application logic, application data and the format for the data contents. Third-party software vendors supply the other pieces.

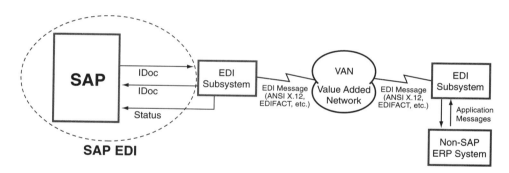

FIGURE 2-1

SAP EDI boundaries

EDI-Enabled Applications in SAP

EDI-enabled applications in SAP are either capable of generating IDoc data from an SAP document or can read IDoc data and create application documents. The application must understand the syntax and semantics of the data in the IDoc format. In the case of outbound processes, a separate selection program exists that reads application data and creates an IDoc, as shown in Figure 2-2. Similarly for inbound processes, IDoc data is read by a posting program to create an application document.

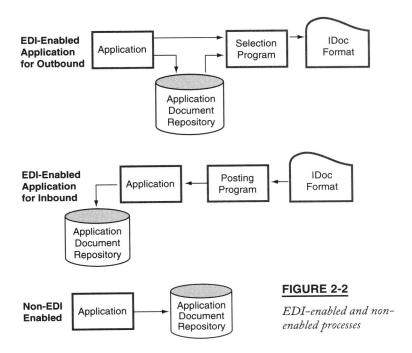

FIGURE 2-2

EDI-enabled and non-enabled processes

Chapter 1 also introduced some of the common documents that business partners exchange at various points during the process. Your tendency might be to think that SAP would support almost every EDI transaction because SAP is the enterprise system and has data in a single repository. This assumption is not completely valid. In the standard SAP system, several EDI-enabled applications in various modules are capable of generating and processing IDoc data, but all EDI documents are not supported. It is very likely that SAP supports the business process, but not the creation or processing of IDocs. With every release of SAP, the list of supported IDocs grows considerably.

A complete list of EDI documents supported in the standard process as of release 4.0B is included in the appendix.

 NOTE

An application that is not EDI-enabled can be enabled by developing the selection and posting programs and IDoc structures. This is an important aspect of any SAP EDI project. SAP provides a comprehensive set of tools for developing IDocs and programs. Refer to Section III, "IDocs," for details on how to enable an application for both inbound and outbound processes.

Process Overview

The SAP EDI process comprises two distinct processes:

- ◆ Outbound process
- ◆ Inbound process

Outbound Process

The outbound process sends documents from the SAP system to a business partner (vendor, customer, bank). Figure 2-3 shows the outbound process at a very high level. The outbound process consists of six steps.

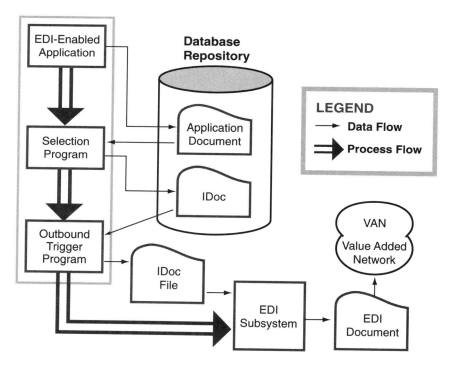

FIGURE 2-3

Process flow and data flow in an outbound EDI process

1. **The application document is created.** The first step in the outbound process involves creating an application document such as a purchase order or sales order and saving it in the database tables. This step is no different from the way in which these documents are normally created. It is the following steps that have relevance to EDI. The document is created and leaves some hooks for the EDI process to begin.

2. **The IDoc is generated.** The application document just created is now formatted to an IDoc format. At this point you can think of IDoc as yet another format in which the application document has been represented. For example, think of how a date can be stored in different formats—imagine a date as a document with three components: day, month, and year. In one case you may represent it as MM/DD/YYYY, a standard American way of representing date. But to make it meaningful for a German partner, you may have to represent it as DD.MM.YY. IDocs follow a similar concept of representing information in different ways. The data in the application document format is suitable for the application modules, screens, and internal programs. A document in an IDoc format is suitable for processing by EDI components, as later sections explain in more detail.

3. **From SAP to operating system layer.** The IDoc created in step 2 resides in the SAP database repository. This IDoc document must be passed down to the operating system layer for processing by the EDI subsystem. In step 3 the IDoc is transferred to the operating system as a text file. The document is still in an IDoc format. The only difference is the medium of storage.

4. **IDoc to EDI standards conversion.** The IDoc format is an SAP proprietary format. For EDI purposes the document in IDoc format has to be converted into an EDI standard format. Third-party software, called translators, carry out the transformation process and reports status back to the SAP system. SAP refers to these translators as EDI subsystems and has certified several subsystems for connectivity to SAP. SAP takes no responsibility for translation. Thus from SAP's perspective, after the IDoc has been delivered to the subsystem, SAP does not have control over the process , but it maintains the status reported by the EDI subsystem.

 CAUTION

SAP does not restrict you to using certified systems, but doing so adds assurance of connectivity and compatibility. Because there are several technical and business issues to worry about, I do not recommend exploring noncertified systems.

5. **EDI document transmission to business partner.** After the document is converted to an EDI standard format, it is transmitted to a trading partner based on the partner's settings. This step is not part of the SAP EDI architecture, but is mentioned here to describe the complete process from a business perspective.

6. **EDI subsystem reports status to SAP.** Once an IDoc is under the control of the EDI Subsystem, the subsystem can optionally report the state of processing at various milestones back to the SAP system. This mechanism is always recommended because it provides complete visibility of the process from within SAP, and the user does not need to be involved with the intricacies of the EDI subsystem.

Inbound Process

The inbound process is the opposite of the outbound process and simply reverses the steps of the outbound process. The inbound process receives an EDI document (such as a purchase order response, sales order, or payment information) from a business partner (vendor, customer, bank) and creates SAP documents from it. Figure 2-4 shows the inbound process at a very high level. Complete technical and functional details are provided in Chapter 4, "The Inbound EDI Process."

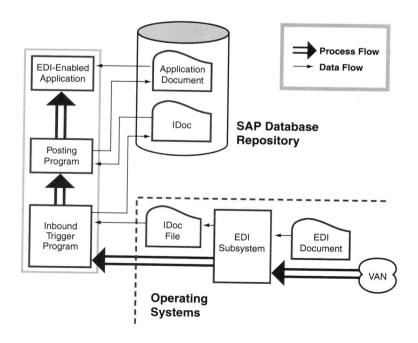

FIGURE 2-4

Process flow and data flow in an inbound EDI process

The inbound process consists of the following five steps.

1. **The EDI transmission is received.** EDI documents are received from a business partner over the VAN. These documents are in one of the EDI standard formats. The documents are deposited in a common repository for the subsystem. This part of the process is not part of the EDI architecture.

2. **From EDI document to IDoc conversion.** The EDI-specific headers and trailers are stripped off, and the document is converted into an IDoc format that is suitable for SAP applications. The process is carried out at the EDI subsystem level.

3. **Transfer of IDoc to SAP layer.** The IDoc created in step 2 is stored in a text file at the operating system layer. The subsystem starts an inbound program in the SAP layer. This program reads the IDoc file and creates an IDoc in the SAP repository for further processing.

4. **The application document is created.** The IDoc received from the subsystem is passed to a posting program. This program creates an application document such as a sales order, purchase order acknowledgment, invoice, or shipment notice.

5. **View the application document.** The application document created via EDI is the same as any document created manually in the system: The document can be viewed using standard application transactions. For example, if an incoming sales order was created via EDI, you can view the sales order document via transaction VA03.

Exception Handling via Workflow

The preceding steps described the success path. Exceptions can occur at any point in either the outbound or the inbound process. These exceptions can be of different types, depending on where they occur. Exceptions can be caused by technical problems, such as network connectivity failures, file system problems, or data-related problems.

Workflow provides a very sophisticated method for managing the exception handling process. The type of error points to the person responsible for the error. Workflow provides the flexibility to inform the right person in a timely manner. This person will be able to diagnose the problem and fix it. After the problem is fixed, the process can be restarted from the point of failure. Chapter 9, "Configuring Workflow," provides complete details on how to set up workflow and manage the error handing process.

IDocs Explained

An IDoc is a container that can be used to exchange data between any two processes. The document represented in an IDoc is independent of the complex structure used in SAP to store application data. This feature enables SAP to rearrange its internal structure without affecting the existing interfaces.

The word IDoc is used very loosely in the IDoc interface. An IDoc represents an IDoc type and IDoc data, depending on the context in which the word IDoc is used. An IDoc type defines the structure and format of the data that is being exchanged. For example, the IDoc type INVOIC01 defines the format of an invoice document. IDoc data can be seen as an instance of an IDoc type. For example, an actual invoice received from a vendor in electronic form is converted into an IDoc.

IDoc Type

IDocs types are based on EDI standards (ANSI X.12 and EDIFACT). They are closer to the EDIFACT standards than to ANSI X.12. The size and format of data elements in an IDoc type are derived from these standards wherever applicable. The IDoc format is compatible with most EDI standards.

An IDoc structure consists of several segments, and segments consist of several data fields. The IDoc structure defines the syntax of the data by specifying a list of permitted segments, arrangement of the segments, and optional versus mandatory segments. Segments define a set of fields and their formats.

IDocs

An IDoc is an instance of an IDoc type. Each IDoc is assigned a unique number for tracking and future reference. An IDoc serves as a focal object for tracking the state of the process that generated it. An IDoc consists of the following three types of records (see Figure 2-5):

♦ One control record

♦ One or many data records

♦ One or many status records

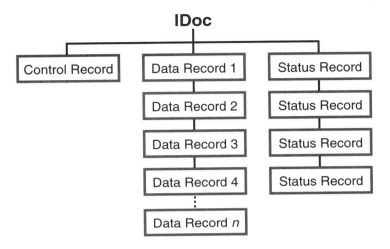

FIGURE 2-5

Internal structure of an IDoc showing the control record, data records, and status records

- ◆ **Control record.** There is only one control record per IDoc. The control record contains all the control information about an IDoc: IDoc number, sender and receiver information, and other control information such as the message type it represents and IDoc type. The structure of the control record is the same for all IDocs and is defined by SAP. The field values, of course, can be different.

- ◆ **Data record.** An IDoc can contain multiple data records, as defined by the IDoc structure. Segments translate into data records. Data records store the application data such as purchase order header information, purchase order details lines, and other relevant information.

- ◆ **Status record.** Multiple status records are usually attached to an IDoc. Status records are attached to an IDoc throughout the process as the IDoc achieves different milestones. A status code, date, and time are assigned at every milestone.

In the outbound process, after the IDoc is passed from SAP to the subsystem, the status records are generated by the subsystem and passed back to SAP. For the inbound process, the status records are generated by SAP because once an IDoc is generated, it stays in the system. Status records help you determine the status of the process and whether an IDoc is in error or not.

SAP provides tools to view the IDoc structure and IDoc data. Chapter 11, "Monitoring the Interface," provides complete details on various tools available in the system for monitoring the IDocs.

Multiple Messages per IDoc

A message represents a specific type of document that is transmitted between two partners. Orders, order responses, order acknowledgments, invoices, and shipment notices are examples of messages. An IDoc in SAP can be used to represent several messages or several business documents. Of course, the messages must be logically related. For example, in Figure 2-6, an IDoc type exists to represent all possible information about an employee. This IDoc is being used to send two separate messages to two separate applications. One message is the Employee Salary Information; the other is the Employee Security Information. The difference between the two messages is the set of segments used.

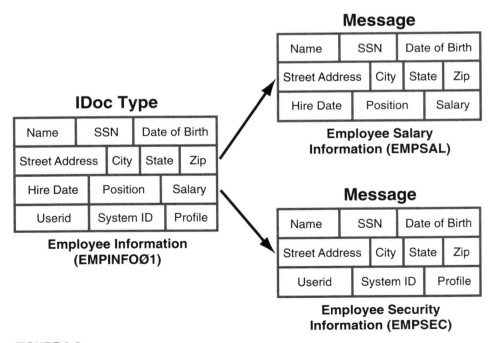

FIGURE 2-6

Multiple messages derived from the same IDoc type

SAP uses a single IDoc type for several logically related messages. For example, the Orders IDoc type (ORDERS02) is used for several messages like Order (ORDERS), Order Response (ORDRSP), and Order Change (ORDCHG).

Independence of EDI Standards

Several EDI standards are in use today, and these standards are continuously evolving. Different companies are using different versions of the standards. SAP decided not to chase the standards and instead came out with its own proprietary format, the IDoc format. The responsibility of maintaining compliance with EDI standards was left to companies that develop translators. Hence the architecture of EDI in SAP is completely independent of the EDI standards used by any other company.

Another reason for keeping the translation and conversion out of SAP is the computing-intensive nature of the translation process. It is a logical piece that can be handled separately without having any impact on the process flow.

Configuration Tools

The flexible SAP EDI interface meets the varying needs of many different companies. The processes can be operated in real-time mode or batch mode. The components used in the interface can be customized to implement customer-specific business scenarios. For example, if one vendor accepts EDI transmission and the other vendor accepts only faxes, the process can be configured to produce different outputs depending on the vendor. The standard scenarios are preconfigured. If you develop new EDI scenarios, the system allows you to configure the EDI interface to recognize your custom scenarios, as explained in Section III, "IDocs."

Support Tools

Several tools are available to meet everyday needs for working with the EDI interface. An area menu (Transaction WEDI) has been defined for EDI. You can access most of the tools from this location. The following section introduces you to the types of tools available in the system.

Documentation

IDoc structures are thoroughly documented. You can view the documentation of IDoc structures in a report format, which can be printed and downloaded to a file. The report can be used to understand the functionality of an IDoc. The use of segments and their fields is clearly documented.

Monitoring

IDocs can be viewed using standard tools. Several tools enable you to view the IDoc information in different ways. For example, you can get a complete list of IDocs in the system or you can limit it to IDocs that are in error. These tools are described in full detail in Chapter 11, "Monitoring the Interface" and in Chapter 12, "EDI Process Troubleshooting and Recovery."

Testing

Several tools enable you to test the inbound and outbound processes. In addition, tools that simulate the process as if the subsystem were installed enable you to test the system without having an EDI subsystem installed. Several utilities make the testing process easy by creating IDocs on the fly, copying existing IDocs, or simulating error conditions. These tools are described in full detail in Chapter 10, "Testing the EDI Interface."

Enhancing the Standard Processes

If the standard process does not meet your requirements, you can enhance the scenario. You can extend the standard IDocs and enhance the standard programs to meet your business needs. SAP provides user-exits at strategic points in the IDoc process to add your custom code. For example, if your customer requires you to supply their Engineering part number on a sales order response, you could extend the ORDERS02 IDoc to add a segment containing the Engineering part number and write custom code to populate a value in the Engineering part number. Enhancements are supported when you upgrade your SAP system. SAP guarantees the location of the user exit and the context in which it is invoked. Section III, "IDocs," provides programming examples for extending IDocs.

You can also develop new scenarios from scratch. You can create new IDoc structures and programs to create or process those IDocs. After you develop the IDoc and the programs, you can configure the interface to recognize your newly created programs and IDocs. The standard monitoring and testing tools can be used for custom-defined scenarios.

Summary

SAP supports the EDI process by providing EDI-enabled applications that are capable of sending and receiving IDoc messages. IDocs are SAP's proprietary format for exchanging data between business applications. IDocs are based on EDI standards and have a very flexible structure to accommodate business rules for representing data. These IDocs are mapped to an EDI standard format by EDI subsystems, which are third-party tools certified by SAP for their connectivity and ability to handle IDoc messages.

One IDoc can be mapped to one or more business transactions. SAP provides a complete development and enhancement environment for extending and creating new IDocs. Various tools configure, monitor, and troubleshoot the system.

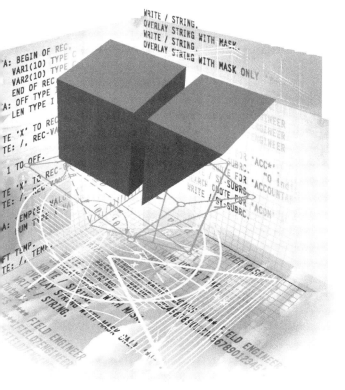

PART

The SAP EDI Interface

2

Chapter 3

The Outbound EDI Process

The outbound process uses several components, including the IDoc Type, Message control, Partner profile, Port definition, Selection programs, Service programs, and Configuration tables. You'll get a quick overview of these components and then you will learn how the outbound process uses these components to generate an IDoc for EDI transmission. Although this chapter mainly covers technical issues, functional users can also benefit from this material. If you have scratched your head several times asking why SAP is behaving in a certain way, then this chapter should be your savior.

Components Used in the Outbound Process

The outbound process uses IDoc Type, Message control, Partner profile, Port definition, Selection programs, Service programs, and Tables to generate an IDoc. A brief description of these components follows. A detailed description and the various configuration options available within each component appears in Part 3, "Configuring the EDI Interface."

IDoc Structure

The EDI document to be generated has an equivalent message type defined in the SAP system. The message type is based on an IDoc structure. For example, if you are going to generate EDI transaction 850, which is a purchase order, the message type ORDERS is assigned in SAP to purchase order. This message is based on IDoc type ORDERS01 and ORDERS02. A list of IDoc types and their equivalent messages in EDIFACT and ANSI X.12 standards is provided in the appendix, "FAQs, User Exits, and Miscellaneous Resources."

 TIP

The list in the appendix is valid as of release 4.0. This list is evolving, so check with SAP for the latest list.

The IDoc is the most important component in the EDI process. A good understanding of the IDoc is necessary for working with the EDI Interface. See Chapter 29, "IDocs from the Outside," and Chapter 30, "IDocs on the Inside," for complete details on the benefits and architecture of IDocs.

Selection Programs

Selection programs, which are typically implemented as function modules, are designed to extract application data and create an IDoc. A selection program exists for each message type. The programs are generally named with the following naming convention:

```
IDOC_OUTPUT_<message type>
```

CAUTION

The naming convention mentioned above is not a rule, but it is a common practice for naming the outbound programs. You will find certain discrepancies in the names.

These function modules have a standard interface for input and output parameters. A process code is assigned to each selection program that executes under Message control. Because process codes are flexible, you can assign any processing option to a process code. A process code can point to a function module or a workflow. In the standard system, process codes always point to a function module.

For example, the selection program for message type ORDERS is IDOC_OUTPUT_ORDERS. A four-character process code ME10 has been assigned to this function module. You can see a list of outbound process codes and their corresponding function modules by executing the following transaction:

Transaction: WE41

Menu Path: From the area menu of EDI (WEDI): Control, Outb. Process Code

You can develop your own custom function modules. See Chapter 32, "Programming in the IDoc Interface," for details on the structure of these programs and how to write a new program.

Message Control

Message control is a cross-application technology. It is used in pricing, account determination, material determination, and output determination. The Message control component allows you to encapsulate business rules without having to write ABAP/4 programs. In the EDI process the Message control determines and processes the various outputs associated with an application document (for example, EDI, printed output, fax, confirmation, and mail). The Message control component is described in full detail in Chapter 8, "Configuring Message Control," where you learn how to build business rules in the message control. In a nutshell, Message control separates the logic of generating EDI documents from the logic of the application. A list of applications supporting Message control is also included in Chapter 8.

Port Definition

A port is used in the outbound process to determine the name of the EDI subsystem program (if installed), the directory path where the IDoc file needs to be created at the operating system level, the IDoc file names, and the RFC destination. Port definitions are described in full detail in Chapter 6, "Configuring Basic EDI Components."

RFC Destination

RFC (Remote Function Call) destination is the term used to define the characteristics of communication links to a remote system on which a function needs to be executed. In EDI, it is used to specify information required to gain access to the system on which the EDI subsystem is installed. The various parameters and options in the RFC destination definition are described in Chapter 6, "Configuring Basic EDI Components."

 NOTE

This process in EDI is different from the ALE process, where the RFC destination is used to specify parameters to log on to the remote SAP system.

Partner Profile

A Partner profile specifies the various components used in an outbound process (Partner number, IDoc type, Message type, Port, Process code); the mode in which it communicates with the subsystem (batch versus immediate); and the person to be notified in case of errors.

A Partner profile is created for each business partner, and a record exists for each outbound message sent to a business partner. For example, if two outbound messages (purchase order and purchase order change) are being sent to vendor number VEN001, then a Partner profile must exist for VEN001 and two outbound records (one for each message type) must exist in the Partner profile. Partner profile is an important and frequently-referred-to component. The various attributes of the Partner profile are described in detail in Chapter 7, "Configuring Partner Profiles."

Service Programs and Configuration Tables

The asynchronous outbound process can be seen as a sequence of several processes that work together. Service programs and Configuration tables are provided by SAP to link the various components and provide various customizing options for an outbound process. The process flow for the outbound process describes the role played by each Service program and Configuration table.

Types of Outbound Processes

By now you should be able to list the components that are used in the outbound process. This section describes how the components are used and explains the function performed by each component. The outbound process has two distinct paths for creating IDocs:

◆ With Message control
◆ Directly—without Message control

Outbound Process with Message Control

Most of the SD (Sales and Distribution) and MM (Materials Management) applications use message control. The FI (Financial) applications do not use the services of the message control component.

The outbound process can best be described by explaining the processing that occurs at each layer, as shown in Figure 3-1. The corresponding technical flow is shown in Figure 3-2 to aid you in understanding the technical components such as programs, table entries, and parameter values that are used.

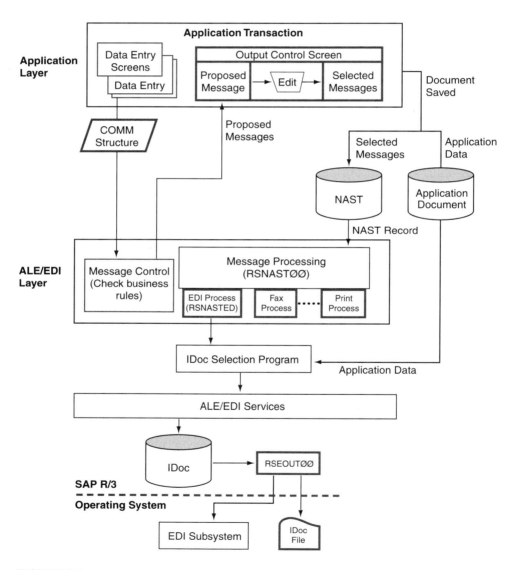

FIGURE 3-1

Details of the outbound process with Message control

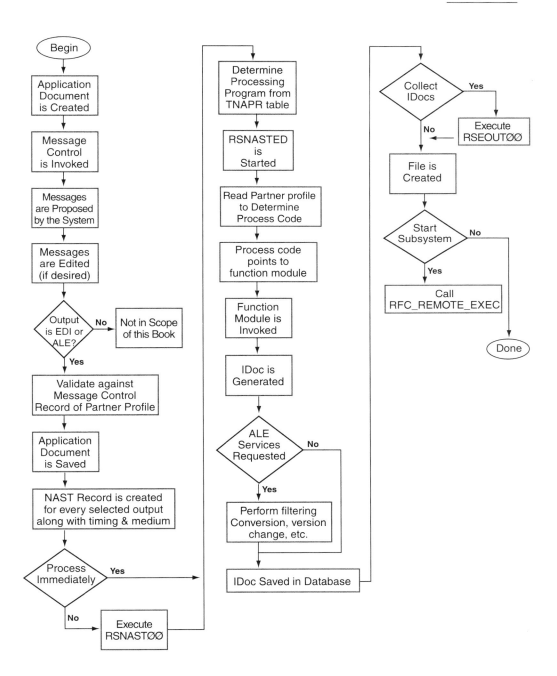

Processing in the Application Layer

An application document is entered via a transaction; for example, a sales order is entered via VA01. Before an application document is saved, the message control component is invoked. An application passes several key elements of the application data to the message control component via communication structures.

Processing in the Message Control Layer

The message control component checks various business rules defined in the Message control configuration. Based on the business rules, the message control proposes output types (sales order response, internal notification, and so on); timing (immediate, batch); medium (EDI, ALE, printout, mail, fax, and so on); and language of the message. Multiple outputs are possible from message control. Each output is processed independently. A simple example of a business rule is to send a sales order response immediately via EDI for a sales order from customer 1111 and generate an internal message for the production department.

The proposed outputs can be seen on the output control screen of the transaction. Some applications provide output control both at the line-item level and at the header level. In most applications, the output control screen can be reached in one of the following ways on the application transaction screen:

- By choosing Header, Messages
- By choosing Header, Output

For example, the output control screen for a purchase order is reached by selecting Header, Messages. For a pales order, the output screen is reached at the header level by selecting Header, output and at the item level by selecting Item, Output.

The output proposed by the message control component can be edited. The user can delete, add, or modify any of the outputs proposed on the output control screen.

When the application document is saved, the outputs proposed on the output control screen are saved as a record in the NAST table. An entry in the NAST table stores the key of the application document, output type, timing, processing status, and language.

If the timing for an output is set to 4 (Immediate), the processing of the output type is started immediately by the system by executing the RSNAST00 program. If the timing is set to 1 (Batch Mode), the entries are processed when the RSNAST00 program is executed explicitly. The RSNAST00 program is usually scheduled to run on a regular basis. The RSNAST00 program selects entries that can be processed based on their status and calls the appropriate program for the selected medium. Each output medium (EDI, ALE, fax, printed output, and so on) has a corresponding program to generate the output in the required medium. SAP provides standard processing programs for each output medium.

In the case of EDI, the processing program is a form routine: EDI_PROCESSING in the RSNASTED program. This program is a generic program for all EDI outputs. This program reads the partner profile configuration to determine the selection program for a particular message.

In the case of ALE, the processing program is a form routine: ALE_PROCESSING in the RSNASTED program. This program is a generic program for all ALE outputs. This program reads the partner profile configuration to determine the selection program for a particular message.

Processing in the Selection Program

The selection program is specified in the partner profile with a process code. The RSNASTED program calls the appropriate selection program.

One of the parameters for these function modules is the NAST entry, which contains the key of the application document. These programs extract application data, format it into an IDoc format in an internal table, and then pass control to the ALE/EDI layer.

Processing in the ALE/EDI Layer

The ALE/EDI layer is responsible for creating the IDoc in the SAP database. By now a tangible IDoc that can be viewed using the various monitoring tools has been created in the system. The IDoc gets a status record with a status code of 01 (IDoc Created).

The IDoc, before being saved in the database, goes through a syntax check and other validations. If there are no errors, the IDoc gets a status of 30 (IDoc ready for dispatch to ALE service).

Dispatching the IDoc

The next step is to pass the IDoc to the operating system layer. The settings of the Output Mode field in the Partner profile is read to determine the timing of this step, and the Port definition is read to determine the directory location in which the file will be created. If the mode is set to Do Not Collect IDocs, the IDoc is immediately passed to the operating system layer automatically, using program RSEOUT00. If the field is set to Collect IDocs, the IDoc is buffered in the system until RSEOUT00 program is executed explicitly. The RSEOUT00 program is scheduled to run on a regular basis. If IDocs are collected, then RSEOUT00 creates a single file with all the IDocs in it. After the IDoc file has been created successfully, the IDoc gets a status code of 03 (Data Passed to Port OK). The timing of this step is important from a performance point of view. See Chapter 13, "Managing EDI Process Performance and Throughput," for details.

Now the system determines whether the subsystem is to be started or not. This parameter is also specified in the Partner profile in the Output Mode field. If the value is set to Do Not Start the Subsystem, the process ends here. If the flag is set to Start the Subsystem, the subsystem program name is read from the port definition and the subsystem program is started. The name of the IDoc file is passed to the EDI Subsystem Program. If the subsystem is started successfully, the IDoc gets another status code 18 (Triggering EDI Subsystem OK).

Processing in the EDI Subsystem Layer

The control of the IDoc process has now been transferred to the subsystem layer. The subsystem takes the IDoc file as input and translates it into an EDI standard format. The subsystem reports the status of the process at various milestones to SAP, thus providing complete visibility into the process from within SAP. The status reported by the subsystem is attached as a status record to the IDoc in the SAP database.

To report status back to the SAP system, the subsystem creates a status file at the OS level and calls the function module EDI_STATUS_INCOMING in SAP, passing the status file name as an input parameter. For this, SAP provides a standard program called startrfc at the OS level to execute any RFC-enabled function module in SAP. The layout of the status file is shown in the appendix, and the syntax of the startrfc command is described in Chapter 6, "Configuring Basic EDI Components."

Outbound Process without Message Control

The biggest advantage of the message control component is the flexibility in proposing the outputs based on business rules and conditions and in controlling the timing of IDoc creation.

Nevertheless, the following conditions may steer you away from message control:

◆ Message control may not be available for your application document. In this case, you have no choice. Applications are programmed to make use of the message control service, so it is not automatically available for every application. The FI applications, for example, do not use message control. The REMADV message is generated by the Payment Run program, which does not use Message control. Most of the ALE processes do not use Message control.

◆ The message control component is quite intricate because of its generic technology of building business rules without coding ABAP/4 programs. I have come across situations in which a client did not want to maintain message control because of its complexity and decided to bypass message control completely. This is not a configuration option. The client had developed custom programs to select IDoc data and pass it directly to the ALE/EDI layer.

The outbound process can be best described by explaining the processing that occurs at each layer, as shown in Figure 3-3. The corresponding technical flow, shown in Figure 3-4, points out the technical components such as Service programs, Configuration tables, and parameter values that are used.

Processing in the Application Layer

The application document is entered by way of a transaction; for example, the Payment Run program (RFFOEDI1) is executed via SE38. The business rules for selecting objects for EDI output are established through a selection screen or a dialog box. The data-extraction logic, which is built into the application, is implemented as a separate function module but is still a part of the application logic. This concept is different compared to outbound with Message control, in which the data-extraction logic is not part of the application logic. The application builds the IDoc and passes control to the ALE layer. The interface to the ALE layer is through the function module MASTER_IDOC_DISTRIBUTE.

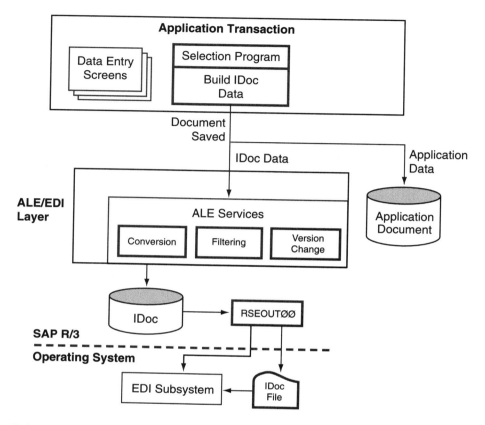

FIGURE 3-3

Details of the Outbound process without message control

Processing in the ALE/EDI Layer

The ALE/EDI layer checks for the sender and receiver fields. If they are not supplied, then the ALE distribution model is consulted to determine the recipients. The ALE distribution model is used to model the messages exchanged between the systems. A message can have multiple recipients.

After the set of receivers is determined, the IDocs are processed for filtering, data conversion, and version change. An IDoc is generated for each partner identified in the distribution model. These IDocs, called communication IDocs, are then saved in the SAP database. At this point a tangible IDoc has been created in the system and can be viewed using the various monitoring tools. That IDoc gets a status record with a status code of 01 (IDoc Created).

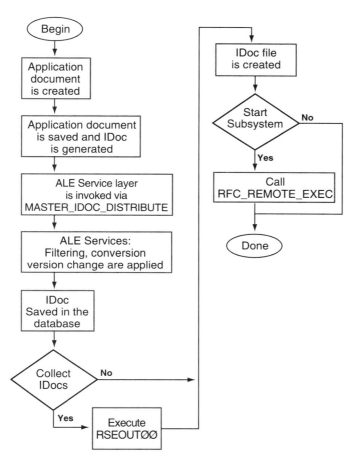

FIGURE 3-4

Technical flow of the outbound process without Message control

The IDoc goes through a syntax check and other validations. If there are no errors, the IDoc gets a status of 30 (IDoc Ready for Dispatch to ALE Service).

 NOTE

Dispatching of IDocs is exactly the same as described for the outbound process with Message control. Processing in the EDI Subsystem layer is also exactly the same as that described for the outbound process with Message control.

Exception Handling in the Outbound Process

The process flows described so far in this chapter show the success path. Nevertheless, the system can experience problems at any stage of the process. Workflow is integrated in the outbound process to handle exceptions. If an error occurs at any stage, a specified user is notified. Complete details on the various points of failure and how the system reports those problems are described in Chapter 12, "EDI Process Troubleshooting and Recovery."

The system uses the Person to Be Notified field in the partner profile to send the error notification. An error may occur when an IDoc has not yet been created, when the partner profile cannot be read, or in the subsystem. In these situations the EDI administrator specified in the EDIADMIN table is notified. The complete details of Workflow and how to set it up are discussed in Chapter 9, "Configuring Workflow."

Summary

In this chapter you learned how an outbound process works with and without the use of the message control component. First an application document is created. Next the message control provides the flexibility to propose outputs automatically, using various output media. Applications that do not use message control provide a selection screen to limit EDI output to selected business partners. A selection program formats the application document into an IDoc format. The IDoc is then passed to the ALE layer for filtering and conversion, and is eventually passed to the operating system in a text file format. The subsystem can then be triggered to start the intended processes. If errors occur at any point in the process, a previously designated person responsible for handling the errors is notified via workflow.

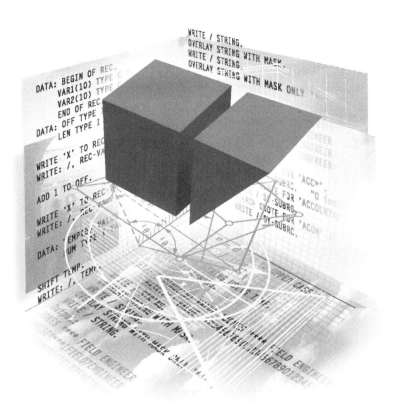

Chapter 4

The Inbound
EDI Process

In Chapter 2, "Introduction to SAP EDI Architecture," you got a high-level overview of the inbound process. This chapter describes the technical and functional details of the inbound process. Like the outbound process, the inbound process uses several components such as IDoc type, partner profile, port definition, posting programs, and service programs. This chapter explains how the inbound process uses these components to create an application document from an IDoc file. Although this chapter focuses mainly on the technical aspects of the process, functional users can also benefit from this material.

Components Used in the Inbound Process

The inbound process uses the following components to post an application document from an IDoc: IDoc type, Port definition, Posting programs, Service programs, and Configuration tables. The various components used by an inbound process are specified in Partner profile and Configuration tables. An overview of each component is provided here. For detailed descriptions and the various configuration options available within these components, see Part 3, "Configuring the EDI Interface."

IDoc Types

The EDI document to be posted has an equivalent message type defined in the SAP system. The message type is based on an IDoc structure. For example, if you are going to post EDI transaction 850, which is a sales order, the message type ORDERS is assigned in SAP to the document. This message type can be based on IDoc type ORDERS01 or ORDERS02. A list of IDoc types and their equivalent messages in EDIFACT and ANSI X.12 standards is provided in the appendix, "FAQs, User Exits, and Miscellaneous Resources."

TIP

The list in the appendix is valid as of release 4.0. This list is evolving, so check with SAP for the latest list.

The IDoc is the most important component in the EDI process. A good understanding of the IDoc is necessary for working with the EDI Interface. See Chapter 29, "IDocs from the Outside," and Chapter 30, "IDocs on the Inside," for complete details on the benefits and architecture of IDocs.

Posting Programs

Posting programs are implemented in the system as function modules. A posting program exists for each message type. The programs are named with the following naming convention:

IDOC_INPUT_<message type>

These function modules have a standard interface for their input and output parameters. The function modules can handle one IDoc or multiple IDocs of the same type simultaneously.

A process code is assigned to each posting program. Because process codes are flexible, you can assign any processing option to a process code. A process code can point to a function module or a workflow. In the standard system, process codes always point to a function module. The option of assigning a workflow to a process code for inbound processing is covered in Chapter 17, "Inbound via Workflow—Sales Order Changes."

For example, the posting program for message type ORDERS is IDOC_INPUT_ORDERS. A four-character process code ORDE has been assigned to this function module. You can see a list of inbound process codes and their corresponding function modules by executing the following transaction:

Transaction: WE41

Menu Path: From the Area menu of EDI (WEDI), choose Control, Inbound Process Code.

You can develop your own custom function modules. See Chapter 32, "Programming in the IDoc Interface," for details on the structure of these programs and how to write a new program.

Port Definition

In the inbound process, the Port definition specifies the name of the input IDoc file and the directory path where the file is located. Port definitions are described in full detail in Chapter 6, "Configuring Basic EDI Components."

NOTE

These parameters are used only if the subsystem does not pass this information to the SAP inbound process. If the subsystem provides this information, then the Port definition is not used.

SAP Business Workflow

SAP Business workflow represents a sequence of customized steps (dialog and background) that are to be carried out for a process. The workflow management system is used to model the sequence, the information required to carry out the various steps, and the person responsible for the dialog steps. In workflow terminology, if there is only one step in a flow, it can be implemented using a single Step Task. If there are multiple steps, it is implemented as a Workflow that contains multiple Single Step Tasks.

Partner Profile

A partner profile specifies the various components used in an inbound process (Partner number, Message type, Process code); the mode in which it communicates with the posting program (batch or immediate); and the person to be notified in case of errors.

 NOTE

You may have noticed that IDoc type is not specified in the Partner profile for an inbound process. This omission does not mean that IDoc type is not needed. The link between the IDoc type, Message type, and function module for the inbound process is maintained in the EDIFCT table. This table is maintained via IMG (Implementation Guide). The only time you need to maintain this table is when you are developing your own customized inbound process. Details on maintaining the EDIFCT table are presented in Chapter 33, "Customizing the Interface for New or Extended IDocs."

A partner profile is created for each business partner, and a record exists for each inbound message received from a business partner. For example, if two inbound messages (sales order and sales order change) are received from a customer number CUST001, then a partner profile must exist for CUST001, and two inbound records (one for each message type) must exist in the Partner profile. Partner profile is one of the very important and frequently referred to components. The various attributes of partner profiles are described in full detail in Chapter 7, "Configuring Partner Profiles."

Service Programs and Configuration Tables

The inbound process is asynchronous and can be seen as a sequence of several processes that work together. Service programs and Configuration tables are provided by SAP to link the various components and provide various customizing options for an inbound process. The process flow for the inbound process describes the role played by each service program.

Inbound Process via the Function Module

The inbound process also has two distinct paths for posting the application documents from the IDocs:

◆ Via Function module

◆ Via Workflow

In this process the IDocs are transferred from the EDI subsystem to SAP and then are passed to the posting function module to post an application document.

The inbound process can best be described by explaining the processing that occurs at each layer, as shown in Figure 4-1. The technical flow shown in Figure 4-2 explains the technical components such as programs, table entries, and parameter values that are used.

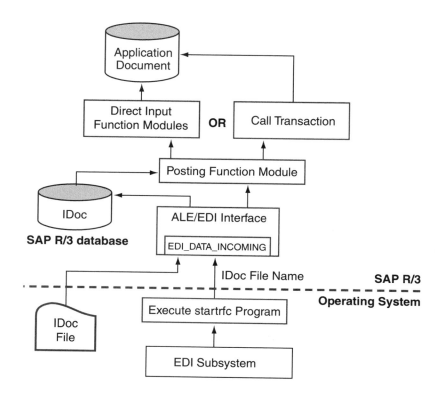

FIGURE 4-1

The inbound process using a posting function module

Processing in the EDI Subsystem Layer

The inbound SAP EDI process begins at the subsystem layer with an EDI document converted to an IDoc format. The IDoc is stored in a text file at the operating system layer. The IDoc file is then passed to the ALE/EDI interface layer via the file port using the startrfc program.

The startrfc program is a standard SAP program at the OS level to call any RFC-enabled function module in SAP. The startrfc program calls the function module EDI_DATA_INCOMING, which acts as the entry point for inbound processes, to trigger the inbound process. The name of the IDoc file is passed as an input parameter to this function module.

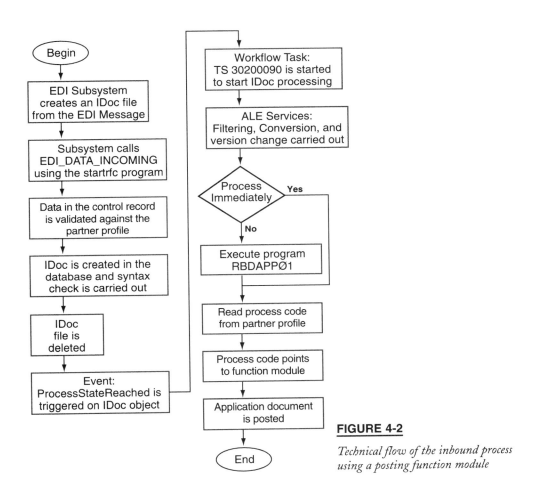

FIGURE 4-2

Technical flow of the inbound process using a posting function module

Processing in the ALE/EDI Layer

The EDI_DATA_INCOMING function module reads the IDoc file into an internal table. The IDoc is first checked for integrity by doing a syntax check. Then the standard ALE services such as version change, filtering, and conversion are applied if necessary. The ALE/EDI layer creates an application IDoc in the database. At this point a tangible IDoc, which can be monitored via one of the monitoring transactions, is created in the system. The IDoc gets a status code of 50 (IDoc added). If the IDoc passed the syntax check process earlier, it gets a status code of 64 (IDoc ready to be passed to application), signifying that the process can continue.

CAUTION

After the IDoc has been created in the database, the IDoc file is deleted even if the IDoc itself has errors. If for some reason the IDoc file cannot be deleted, SAP creates an entry in the EDFI2 table with the file name to mark it for deletion. This technique prevents the same file from being processed multiple times

Next the Processing flag and process code are read from the partner profile table. If the value of the Processing field is set to Process Immediately, the IDoc is passed to the posting program using the RBDAPP01 program. If the field is set to Background Processing, the IDocs are buffered in the system until the RBDAPP01 program is executed explicitly. RBDAPP01 is usually scheduled to run on a regular basis or it can be started as a result of an event raised by the subsystem after the IDoc file has been loaded into the SAP system.

NOTE

Starting with release 3.1, the process of creating IDocs in the database was disconnected from the process that posts the application document. This modification improves the efficiency of creating IDocs from the text files and logically separates the two processes. A workflow task handles the coupling between the process that creates the IDocs and the posting process. This process should not be confused with the inbound process via workflow, which is explained later. The configuration of this coupling process is described in Chapter 6, "Configuring Basic EDI Components."

Processing in the Application Layer

The posting function module either calls a standard SAP transaction, using the call transaction command for posting the document, or invokes a direct input function module.

NOTE

Direct input function modules are preferred to the call transaction approach because of inherent problems of screen sequence associated with call transactions. The screen sequence may change with every release. Nevertheless, it is easier to debug inbound processes that use the call transaction method, as explained in Chapter 12, "EDI Process Troubleshooting and Recovery."

TIP

To see whether a standard inbound process uses call transaction or direct input, you can execute transaction BD51 and inspect the entries in table TBD51. Entries with a value of 1 or 2 in the Input Type column use the call transaction method, whereas entries with a value of 0 use the direct function module.

The results of the execution are passed back via the function module's output parameters. If posting is successful, an application document is created. The IDoc gets a status code of 53 (Application document posted). If errors occur, then the IDoc gets a status code of 51 (Application document not posted). A complete list of status codes is included in the appendix, "FAQs, User Exits, and Miscellaneous Resources."

Inbound Process via Workflow

The inbound process via workflow is similar to the inbound process via function module, as described earlier, except for the difference in the processing that occurs in the Application layer. The IDoc, instead of being processed by a posting program, is processed by a Single Step Task or a multi-step workflow. In the system this option is configured by pointing the Process code to a workflow.

Workflow allows human intervention in the process, which may sometimes be necessary. A typical example where this scenario can be used is the sales order change transaction coming in via EDI. Someone may need to review any change from a customer before the change can be accepted; if you have already begun production, you may not be able to accept a change in quantity or delivery date. This process gives you the option of reviewing the changes and taking appropriate action.

NOTE

In the standard system, the inbound processes use posting function modules for posting the document. Although no process uses workflow by default, you can customize the interface to start workflow. Refer to Chapter 17, "Inbound via Workflow—Sales Order Changes," which provides an example on how to use SAP Business Workflow for an inbound process.

The inbound process can best be described by explaining the processing that occurs in the Application layer because processing in the EDI Subsystem layer and the ALE/EDI layer is similar to the inbound process via function module (see figure 4-3).

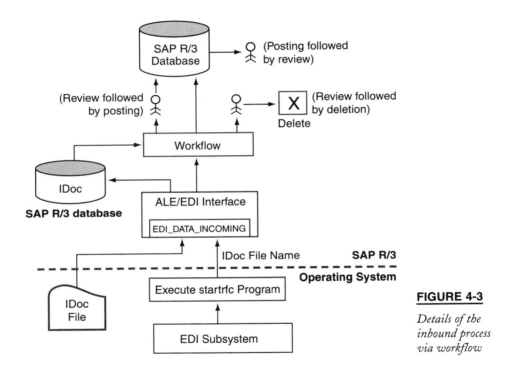

FIGURE 4-3

Details of the inbound process via workflow

Processing in the Application Layer

The posting module in this case is a workflow task. The workflow task can be designed to accommodate any customized processing such as reviewing an incoming order change transaction followed by posting or posting an incoming order change document followed by review.

If a complex business process is associated with an incoming document, then you can use a multistep workflow to map that process. As an example, invoices greater than $5,000.00 coming into the system may need an approval for payment. You may want to route the invoices to more than one person. This step can easily be accomplished via workflow. Basically, workflow is a development environment, and you can build any functionality you need. The standard EDI processes do not use this path.

 CAUTION

The use of workflow may seem like a useful method for processing inbound EDI transactions, but it adds additional load to the system, especially when you have high-volume EDI transactions. It also blocks the process unless someone processes the workitem, which may cause unnecessary delays.

Exception Handling in the Inbound Process

The process flows described in this chapter show the success path, but the system can experience problems at any stage of the process. Compared to the outbound process, the inbound process has more opportunity for error because data originates outside the SAP system. SAP validates the data using the same business rules as if the document were entered online.

The workflow system uses the Person to Be Notified field in the partner profile to send the error notification. For example, an error might occur before an IDoc is created or because the partner profile cannot be read; in any case, the EDI administrator specified in the EDIADMIN table is notified. Complete details of workflow and how to set it up are discussed in Chapter 9, "Configuring Workflow."

Summary

In this chapter you learned how an inbound process posts an application document from an IDoc file. The subsystem starts the inbound process by passing an IDoc file to the ALE/EDI interface layer. The IDoc is read by the system, and an IDoc is created in the SAP database. The new IDoc is passed to the posting module, which can be either a function module or a workflow. In the standard system, the posting module is a function module. The posting module then creates the application document using either a standard call transaction method or a direct input function module. If errors occur at any point in the process, a previously designated person responsible for handling the errors is notified via workflow.

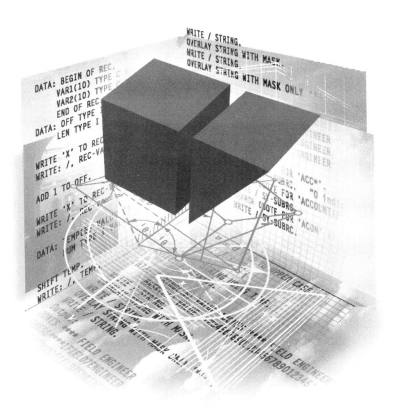

Chapter 5

The EDI Subsystem

Although SAP does not provide the EDI subsystem, it plays a key role in the SAP EDI process. In this chapter you learn about the various functions carried out by the subsystem and take a quick look at typical subsystem architecture. Then you are introduced to the mapping process, which is one of the key functions provided by an EDI subsystem. Finally, you learn about the certification process that ensures the compatibility of the EDI subsystem with SAP.

Overview of the EDI Subsystem

The EDI subsystem carries out the task of converting an EDI document in a standard EDI format to an IDoc file and vice versa. As you may have observed, the conversion process is one of the key tasks in SAP EDI architecture. SAP does not supply the EDI subsystem because several EDI standards are in existence and each standard has multiple versions. To further complicate the process, these standards are still evolving. Hence this task is best carried out by EDI vendors who stay current with the standards.

EDI vendors have developed translators to help with the conversion of application-specific messages—IDocs in the case of SAP—to standard EDI format. Any translator software product is completely independent of the SAP software and resides outside the SAP system. The translator can be installed on the same hardware as the SAP system or can stand alone on another computer. The operating system environment of the EDI subsystem can be different from the SAP operating system environment. If the SAP system is installed on a UNIX platform, the subsystem could reside on a separate platform that operates on Windows NT or another platform.

SAP certifies several EDI subsystems for compatibility with the EDI interface. Because the IDoc interface has changed with every release (2.2 to 4.0), the certification is applicable only for a specific release of SAP. Check with your third-party vendor for the release level of its certification. You can obtain the latest list from SAP's Web site at **www.sap.com.**

Responsibilities of the EDI Subsystem

The subsystem has several responsibilities in the EDI process chain. They are listed here in order of importance from the SAP perspective.

Data Mapping

The conversion of a business document in IDoc format to an EDI standard format (and vice versa) is the most important task performed by a subsystem from SAP's perspective. This process is quite resource-intensive and hence is better done at the subsystem level than within SAP. The following conversions and translations are carried out:

◆ **Creating control record for inbound.** An inbound IDoc must have a control record. The control record is built by the EDI subsystem using the information stored in its local repository or from the SAP repository.

◆ **Stripping control record on outbound.** The control record in the IDoc file is used for housekeeping functions such as locating the trading partner profile. The control record is not needed on the EDI documents. It is thus stripped out by the EDI subsystem.

◆ **Translating data from IDoc format to EDI format.** For an outbound transaction, data in the IDoc format is converted to a suitable EDI format by the EDI subsystem.

◆ **Translating data from EDI format to IDoc format.** For an inbound transaction, data in the standard EDI format is converted to IDoc format by the EDI subsystem.

◆ **Bundling and unbundling IDocs.** If several IDocs are passed to the EDI subsystem in one file, then the subsystem separates them into individual documents. Similarly, on the inbound process the subsystem can bundle multiple IDocs into a single file to improve performance.

Maintaining the Partner Profile

A partner is defined as the business partner with whom you conduct business and exchange EDI documents. These partners are not necessarily the same as the partners in the partner profile of SAP. However, the concept is quite similar. In SAP the partner profile maintains parameters specific to the IDoc process, and in the subsystem the partner profile maintains parameters specific to the EDI process. Some of the typical attributes in a partner profile are:

◆ Unique partner number

◆ Partner type (Customer, Vendor)

◆ Standard used (EDIFACT, ANSI X.12, and so on)

◆ Version of the EDI standard

◆ EDI message exchanged (850, 860, ORDERS, ORDCHG)

◆ Functional Acknowledgment flag

Triggering the Inbound Process

After receiving an inbound EDI transmission and creating an IDoc file, the subsystem is responsible for triggering the inbound process. SAP provides a program called startrfc to start any RFC-enabled function module from the operating system level. For the EDI process, the subsystem uses the startrfc program to trigger the function module EDI_DATA_INCOMING. The complete details and parameters of the startrfc program are provided in Chapter 6, "Configuring Basic EDI Components." The results of execution are logged in the subsystem.

Reporting Process Status to SAP

In an outbound process, after an IDoc has been transferred from SAP to the subsystem, SAP loses control over the process. However, SAP maintains visibility into the process by requiring the subsystem to report on the status of the process. SAP provides a file interface for the subsystem to send a status report at every milestone. The subsystem reports the status codes in Table 5-1 to SAP, depending on the state of the process.

When the subsystem has status information to send to SAP, the subsystem creates a status file and uses the startrfc program to trigger the SAP system. The status file contains the IDoc number, which is used to identify the IDoc to which the status record is to be attached. The startrfc program calls the EDI_STATUS_INCOMING function module to start the processing of the status file in SAP.

Table 5-1 Status Codes Reported by the EDI Subsystem to SAP

Status	CodeDescription
04	Error within control information of EDI subsystem
05	Error during translation
06	Translation OK
07	Error during syntax check
08	Syntax check OK
09	Error during interchange handling
10	Interchange handling OK
11	Error during dispatch
12	Dispatch OK
13	Retransmission OK
14	Interchange Acknowledgment positive
15	Interchange Acknowledgment negative
16	Functional Acknowledgment positive
17	Functional Acknowledgment negative
22	Dispatch OK, acknowledgment still due
23	Error during retransmission
24	Control information of EDI subsystem OK
36	Electronic signature not performed (timeout)

Handling Functional and Interchange Acknowledgments

An Interchange Acknowledgment is the message that the VAN sends to the subsystem to inform it about the results of the transmission. A Functional Acknowledgment (ANSI X.12 transaction 997) acknowledges the receipt of data by the receiving system. This transaction verifies the successful receipt of an EDI document, but does not guarantee successful data processing. The subsystems are responsible for generating this document on receipt of an EDI transmission.

For an outbound process, the status codes that the subsystem reports to SAP depend on the results of the acknowledgment. Status codes 14, 15, 16, 17, and 22 are returned to SAP (see Table 5-1).

Performing a Syntax Check

The EDI standards have a rigid structure. The segments and fields have various characteristics:

◆ Optional or mandatory

◆ Conditional or nonconditional

◆ Data format

◆ Data length

◆ Loop counts

◆ ID codes (similar to SAP IDoc qualifiers)

These characteristics form the basis for a syntax check. If any of the rules are violated, the document processing can fail. To avoid wasteful transmissions, the subsystem checks the documents for conformance to the standards defined by the standards committee. The results of the syntax check are sent back to SAP using status code 07 or 08 (see Table 5-1).

Handling Partner-Specific Processing

The subsystem also handles partner-specific processing. For example, business partner A sends all purchase orders bundled as one huge purchase order. For business partner B, you may need to break the single purchase order down by shipping location and create several smaller purchase orders.

Several data elements in the EDI transactions have not been assigned a definitive meaning. Companies can freely use those fields to mean different things. If you are a vendor, you will end up accepting whatever data your customers send you and will send them any specific data that is relevant only to them. The subsystem can handle this partner-specific processing.

 NOTE

Sometimes it may be necessary to retransmit EDI documents because they are either lost or have errors at your trading partner's end. The subsystems provide tools to retransmit a document.

Handling Errors

In the outbound process, the subsystem is responsible for reporting to SAP any errors, including translation errors, syntax errors, transmission errors, and connectivity issues.

In the inbound process, until an IDoc is created, the subsystem is responsible for reporting and managing the errors. The subsystem provides the necessary monitoring and recovery tools. Once an IDoc is inside SAP, then SAP has full responsibility for handling errors.

Communicating with Business Partners

Business partners may provide a direct connection to their network or may subscribe to a VAN. The subsystem is responsible for establishing and terminating connections with the business partner's network or VAN to send and receive EDI transmissions. The subsystem is also responsible for processing acknowledgments from the VAN and communicating those to SAP.

Attaching EDI Headers and Controls

EDI transmissions have several header and trailer segments that act as control information (for example, the ISA and GS headers and trailers). The subsystem is responsible for attaching these segments to the document.

Archiving

All important documents, such as payment stubs or remittance advice transmitted to the trading partners, may need to be archived for auditing purposes and liability issues. The subsystems provide data archiving and management options.

Subsystem Architecture

In one way or another, all EDI subsystems carry out the responsibilities described in the preceding section. The basic subsystem architecture does not vary much from one software vendor to another. This section does not describe the architecture of any particular subsystem; rather, the architecture presented here can be applied to any EDI subsystem product.

When you buy a subsystem, it has two major components:

◆ Definition component

◆ Execution component

Definition Component

The definition component is where mapping definitions between EDI and IDoc formats are created. This component can run without any connection to the SAP system or to its server module. The maps are platform independent. The definition component carries out the following functions:

- ◆ Defines the source structure and destination structure
- ◆ Maps fields in the source structure to fields in the destination structure
- ◆ Compiles maps for other platforms
- ◆ Tests maps
- ◆ Provides utilities to download and upload IDoc structures, document structures, and maps. (Software vendors usually license this component on a per-user basis.)

 NOTE

The structure of standard EDI documents for commonly used standards (ANSI X.12 and EDIFACT) are shipped with most EDI subsystems.

Execution Component

Maps created in the preceding step are executed on the server, which is known as the execution component. The execution component is where the complete environment for executing the maps, trading partner relationships, and other server-related functions are performed. The execution component is usually licensed on a per installation basis. The following list shows some of the common tasks performed on the server and the features commonly found in EDI subsystems:

- ◆ Execution of maps
- ◆ Maintenance of trading partner agreements
- ◆ Configuration of the environment
- ◆ Maintenance of log information
- ◆ Archiving
- ◆ Tools for monitoring the process
- ◆ Tools for restart and recovery of failed transactions
- ◆ Scripts for connectivity with VAN

Mapping Concepts for IDocs and EDI Document Formats

The most important function of a subsystem is data transformation, or mapping. A map is created for every message that is exchanged with a business partner. Thus if you receive sales order data from 10 customers via EDI, you are likely to have 10 maps. Even though the data format has been standardized, only the syntax is standardized. The syntax rules were described earlier. The company using the data still needs to interpret the meaning of the data, and several data elements do not have a definitive meaning and are open to interpretation by a company. The result can be a document that is slightly different for each company. Mapping an IDoc to an EDI format requires the following steps:

1. **Download the SAP IDoc structure.** In this step the IDoc structure is downloaded into the definition component. SAP provides a program named RSEIDOC3 that generates a structured report of the IDoc structure. The report is downloaded to a file and can then be copied to the PC on which the definition component is installed.

2. **Define the IDoc structure.** The output file can be imported into the definition component to make the IDoc format known to the system. The software vendors provide a utility program to automatically import the file to create the IDoc structure. The IDoc structure will have a control record structure and several data record structures.

3. **Define the EDI document structure.** Software vendors usually provide the structure of the standard EDI documents. For example, if you are interested in the sales order document of ANSI X.12 version 3050, you do not need to build the structure from scratch. Vendors provide formats for various standards and versions. This information is their bread and butter.

 TIP

Most software vendors also provide special maps that are designed for particular companies. For example, if you are going to accept sales orders from a large corporation such as Ford or Wal-Mart, you can buy maps that define the syntax and semantics used by that company. Access to these maps can reduce your development time considerably.

4. **Define the maps.** Mapping is the process of linking source fields to destination fields. Mapping can be a simple operation (for example, one-to one mapping in which a field from the source structure is directly copied to the destination structure), or it can be a complex process. In complex mapping, values from several fields of the source structure are manipulated in different ways to generate an output value for a field in the destination structure. The systems usually allow manipulation using functions, external program calls, and so on. You will need to check with your software vendor about the sophistication of the mapping process.

5. **Compile the maps.** Maps need to be compiled before they can be executed. The compilation process is fairly simple. The system checks the syntax of the map, consistency of business rules used in the map, and source and destination data elements in the map. If compilation is successful, the map is ready to be executed.

6. **Test the compiled maps.** The maps can be tested on the definition system using some test data. An input file is processed through a map to generate the output. The output should be verified manually: the data should be in the correct location and in the correct format.

7. **Transport the maps.** The definition component can usually compile maps for use on other platforms. Thus if the execution engine resides on UNIX while the definition component is on a PC, the system can generate a compile map for the UNIX system. The compiled map can then be transported to the EDI server system via any file transfer techniques.

8. **Execute the maps.** The maps can then be executed on the server. During production the system executes maps on the server.

Certification and Test Scenarios

The certification process is an endorsement by SAP regarding (1) the connectivity between the SAP system and the subsystem and (2) the ability of the two systems to exchange data in an IDoc format. The internal structure of the IDoc has changed with every major release, so SAP certifies the subsystems on a per release basis. A subsystem certified for release 3.0 IDocs is not necessarily going to work with release 4.0 IDocs. Check with the subsystem vendor for certification information.

Certification requires the subsystem to pass the following tests:

◆ Connectivity
◆ The ability to process IDoc format
◆ The ability to report status back to SAP

SAP has developed standard test scenarios that have been recorded using the CATT (Computer Automated Test Tool) system. These tests are played and the results are verified. The test scenarios are described in the following sections.

Test Scenarios for Connectivity

An outbound IDoc is created, and the shell script provided by the subsystem vendor to start the EDI Subsystem is executed. If the shell script executes successfully, the test of outbound connectivity is successful.

To test inbound connectivity, the subsystem calls the startrfc program to pass an IDoc file or a status file to the SAP system. The program calls the EDI_DATA_INCOMING function module for IDoc files and EDI_STATUS_INCOMING for status files. If the function modules are started correctly, the test is considered successful.

Test Scenarios for Handling IDoc Format

Two business scenarios are implemented in SAP to test the subsystem's ability to handle IDocs:

◆ Send out purchase orders and receive purchase order acknowledgment

◆ Receive sales orders and send out a sales order acknowledgment

The steps are as follows:

1. SAP creates a purchase order for a vendor. This purchase order is passed to the subsystem as an IDoc file. The subsystem converts the IDoc into an EDI standard format and then reports the status of the IDoc to SAP.

2. The outbound purchase order is sent to SAP as a sales order from a customer.

3. A sales order response is created in the SAP system. This sales order response is passed to the subsystem as an IDoc file. The subsystem converts the IDoc into an EDI standard format and then reports the status of the IDoc to SAP.

4. The outbound sales order acknowledgment is sent to SAP as a purchase order acknowledgment for the purchase order created in step 1.

These steps are repeated for several vendors and for different types of purchase orders (single-line item and multiple-line item). If the results are positive, the subsystem is certified. Complete details of the certification process can be obtained from SAP's Web site at **www.sap.com.**

Summary

The subsystem is a key component in the SAP EDI architecture. This component is not provided by SAP, but works very closely with the SAP system. The subsystem carries out the conversion from IDoc format to EDI document and vice versa. The subsystem is also responsible for other tasks such as providing status reports to SAP and handling IDoc structures. SAP certifies the subsystems for their connectivity to SAP and their ability to handle the IDoc format. Although it is possible to work with an EDI subsystem that is not certified, it is not recommended because you cannot be certain about the connectivity.

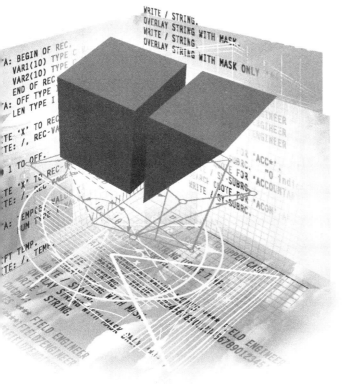

PART 3

Configuring the EDI Interface

Chapter 6

Configuring Basic EDI Components

The EDI interface right out of the box cannot be used to generate IDocs. SAP cannot possibly know your business partners and the messages that you want to exchange. You need to set up the various components before you can get an IDoc out of or into the system. Before you start you must have a good understanding of the inbound and outbound process flow and of the roles of various components, especially the IDoc, used in the process.

The SAP EDI process is built and supported by two types of components:

◆ Components specifically designed for the ALE/EDI process (for example, port definition, partner profiles, process codes)

◆ Flexible cross-application technologies that are deployed in the EDI process and can be adapted across multiple applications (for example, message control and workflow).

These components are highly flexible and can be adapted to meet a variety of customer needs and requirements. The next four chapters provide full technical details of the concept, role, and various options available for each component in the process; this material is designed for readers who are responsible for setting up the EDI interface. Although the following presentation has been designed for first-time users of the EDI interface, this is not introductory material. Readers should be conversant with the SAP system and able to navigate it. In this chapter you learn about the components that are solely designed for use in the EDI/ALE process. You learn about the basic IDoc settings, which are mainly one-time settings, and communication settings, which define the link between the EDI subsystem and the SAP system.

The Configuration Settings

The various configuration settings for the EDI process are done in the IMG (Implementation Guide) and in the Area menu of the EDI system. Explanations of these elements follow:

◆ **Implementation Guide (IMG).** The various EDI customizing settings (see Figure 6-1) are available under the following headings in the IMG: Cross-Application Components, IDoc Interface/Electronic Data Interchange, and IDoc Interface—Basis.

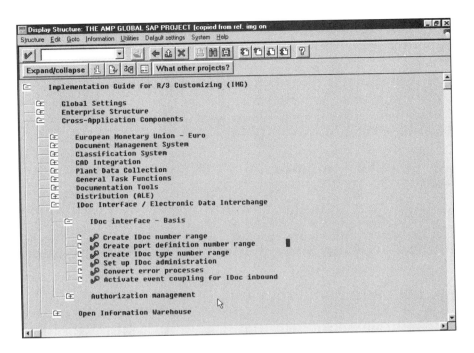

FIGURE 6-1

The area in the IMG where you make EDI settings

◆ **The Area menu of the EDI system.** Some of the commonly used settings are also reached via the Area menu of EDI. The path to get to this Area menu is as follows:

`Transaction:` WEDI

`Menu Path:` Tools, Administration, Administration, Process Technology, Idoc,
Idoc Basis

Basic Settings for IDocs

This section describes the basic settings required for the IDoc interface used in the EDI process. They need to be established only once for the whole system and are rarely changed.

Number Ranges for IDocs

Path: EDI settings in the IMG, Create IDoc number range

Every IDoc created in the system, inbound or outbound, is assigned a 16-digit number that uniquely identifies an IDoc in the system. The IDoc number range is already defined. You normally do not need to maintain this number range, but theoretically you can exhaust the number range and then have to reset it.

CAUTION

Be careful when resetting the number range. Make sure that old IDocs with the number range to which you are resetting have been archived and deleted from the system. Otherwise, the system will not be able to create IDocs in the number range that has been initialized.

NOTE

If you change the number range, you will have to manually transport the number range interval to your production system because number range objects are not automatically recorded for transport. To manually record a number range interval for transport, select Interval, Transport from the number range maintenance screen.

EDIADMIN Table

Transaction: WE46

Path: From the Area menu of EDI, choose Control, IDoc Administration

In the EDIADMIN table you assign values to the global variables used in the EDI process. The table consists of two columns; the first represents the parameter name, and the second represents the value assigned to that parameter (see Figure 6-2).

NOTE

The screen to maintain global parameters has changed in release 4.0. Please see the Appendix.

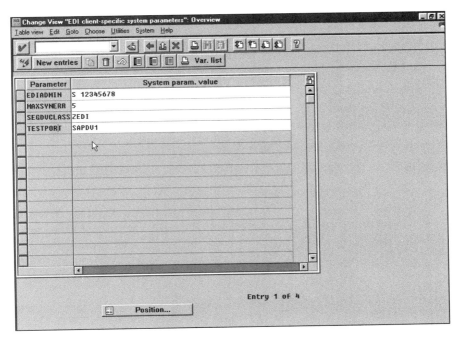

FIGURE 6-2

EDI Settings in the EDIADMIN table

 CAUTION

The system validates the parameter values only if the parameter name is correct. If the parameter name is incorrect, the system does not validate the parameter values. Hence there is a chance of error if someone types a parameter name incorrectly. Be extra careful when entering these values.

◆ **EDIADMIN.** This parameter specifies the administrator for the IDoc interface at run time. This person is responsible for the integrity of the overall IDoc interface. The format for the value assigned to this field is XXCCCCCCCC. XX is the two-character ID representing the object type (for example, US—User ID, S—Position, O—Organization unit). If the object type is a single character, it must be followed by a space. CCCCCCCC is the eight-character object identifier. See Chapter 9,

"Configuring Workflow," for details on all the different types of objects that you can specify here. For example, if the position with position number 12345678 is assigned as the administrator, then the value of the parameter in the EDIADMIN field will be S 12345678. If a user with user ID AN000001 is the administrator, then the value of the parameter in the EDIADMIN field will be USAN000001. This parameter is used by the Workflow system in either of the following situations:

A technical error occurs in the EDI interface layer, for example, an error in deleting an IDoc file after successfully creating an IDoc.

An application error occurs in processing an IDoc. In this case workflow first attempts to send a notification to the ID specified in the partner profile. If the error is such that the partner profile cannot be read, then notification is sent to the IDoc administrator.

NOTE

Normally, these situations should not occur, because the EDI administrator has overall responsibility for the interface and cannot handle application-specific errors. During development and testing, the EDI administrator usually gets several workitems, but in a production system it should not be as frequent.

TIP

It's wise to avoid a user ID in the EDIADMIN field. You should use more abstract object types such as position, job, or organization unit. This approach saves you the headache of changing the entry when the user leaves the company or changes jobs. Compared to users, other organizational objects such as positions, jobs, and organization units tend to be more stable.

◆ **MAXSYNERR.** This parameter sets the maximum limit on the number of status records created for syntax errors—a good recommendation is five. If your IDoc gets more than five syntax errors in a production environment, then something is terribly wrong. Setting this number higher usually does not help you in debugging the problem; at that point you would need to investigate the process more deeply at the source of data.

◆ **SEGDVCLASS.** This parameter is the development class used when developing new segments.

◆ **TESTPORT.** This setting is used for testing purposes only. It defines the port name that will be used for assigning default parameters during inbound testing. The naming convention used for this port is SAP<xxx> where xxx is a three-character ID assigned to your SAP instance. For example, if the name of your development instance is DV1, then the port name will be SAPDV1. This port must be defined in the port definition.

TIP

Instance ID is the 3-character name shown in the status bar which appears at the bottom portion of any SAP screen. However, if the status bar is turned off, you can also determine the instance ID by executing transaction SM51. The three characters following the first underscore under the server name is the instance ID.

◆ **INBOUND.** Starting with release 3.1G, for the inbound process the creation of IDocs from the input file was disconnected from the processing of the IDocs for posting. However, if you want to maintain the old style, you can use this parameter and set the value to OLD. See the next section for details on why the two processes were disconnected and the settings required to connect the two processes.

CAUTION

If this field is not used or left blank, then it uses the new processing style. If the configuration described in the next step is not maintained, IDocs are not transferred to the processing layer, and they stay in status 50.

Coupling IDoc Creation to IDoc Processing

Path: EDI settings in the IMG, Activate event coupling for IDoc inbound

The process of creating IDocs from the input file was disconnected from the processing of the IDocs for posting for two reasons:

◆ To improve the efficiency of the process of creating IDocs from a file
◆ To logically separate the process of posting an IDoc from the process of creating an IDoc, because they are two independent processes

However, the two processes need to be coupled for EDI process flow. Coupling is accomplished by using the Workflow concept of publish and subscribe, as shown in Figure 6-3. The link is maintained via an event-linkage table. When an IDoc is created, it raises an event, which is the publishing piece, to inform the system about the creation. The subscriber is the process that processes the IDoc. The subscriber starts automatically when the corresponding event is published.

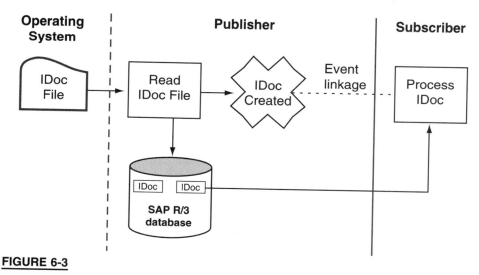

FIGURE 6-3

Coupling IDoc creation and IDoc processing

Communication Settings

This section describes the technical settings for linking the subsystem to SAP. These settings are made one time. They are independent of both the transaction and the business partner.

Setting an RFC Destination

In this section you'll learn how SAP uses an RFC destination to link to the subsystem program. If you do not have a subsystem installed yet, you can skip this step and go to the next step on configuring the Port definition. This will not affect the EDI functionality in SAP. By skipping this step you only lose the automatic start of the subsystem when an outbound IDoc file is created. In fact some companies skip this step completely and schedule the subsystem program to run periodically and process the IDoc files. However, if you are planning to implement a real time EDI scenario, you will require these steps. The section below starts with an introduction to the RFC concept followed by details on maintaining an RFC destination.

What Is an RFC Destination?

An RFC destination is a logical name used to identify a remote system on which a function needs to be executed. In the RFC destination, you specify the characteristics of the remote system, such as the host name and program containing the function to be executed. An RFC destination is used for the subsystem because the subsystem is an external system from SAP's perspective, no matter whether it resides on the same system as SAP or a separate system. The following two prerequisites apply when executing a function remotely:

◆ The systems should be accessible to each other via TCP/IP or one of the supported network protocols. An operating system level SAP user ID should be able to start a program remotely on the destination system. This feature requires configuration at the operating system level.

◆ The program that implements the functions must use RFC protocols to communicate with SAP. RFC protocols are implemented via a set of APIs (Application Programming Interfaces) that are used by both the sending and receiving programs.

 NOTE

The RFC destination is used in several applications besides ALE and EDI. For example, it is used to access external print programs, fax programs, tax programs, and barcode readers. In fact, the RFC destination is used to start the online help program on your computer when you select Help, R/3 library from any menu in SAP.

How the EDI Interface Uses an RFC Destination

The subsystem is considered a remote system because it is not an SAP program. It can be installed locally on the SAP box or on an external system. Hence any communication between SAP and the subsystem requires the RFC destination (see Figure 6-4).

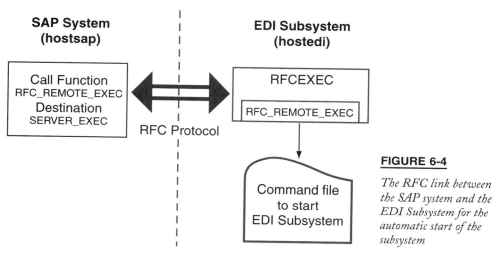

FIGURE 6-4

The RFC link between the SAP system and the EDI Subsystem for the automatic start of the subsystem

For connectivity to occur, two prerequisites must be met:

♦ The first requirement of connectivity is met by connecting the systems via TCP/IP and maintaining a "trusted user ID" on each system so that each can execute programs on the other system.

♦ The second requirement is that the subsystem vendors need to write their subsystem programs using RFC protocols. You can circumvent this problem by using the rfcexec program shipped with the standard SAP system. The rfcexec is a program at the operating system level that acts as the RFC server and can respond to SAP's RFC requests. When SAP needs to start the subsystem, SAP calls the function RFC_REMOTE_EXEC, which is implemented in the program rfcexec (see Figure 6-4). SAP passes the name of the shell script for the subsystem, and the RFC_REMOTE_EXEC function executes the shell script. This strategy means that the EDI subsystem program does not have to use RFC protocols.

NOTE

SAP uses <xxx>adm as the ID to access the operating system files and commands, where xxx is the instance of your SAP system.

TIP

RFC_REMOTE_EXEC is a function in the rfcexec program and hence cannot be seen in the function library on the SAP system via SE37.

The trusted user setting is necessary to allow the SAP system to trigger rfcexec remotely. Assume you have two systems, one running SAP and the other running the EDI subsystem. Assume the TCP/IP host names of the two systems are hostsap and hostedi.

Before you proceed with any settings, make sure that the systems are configured at the TCP/IP level to see each other. You can execute the ping command at the OS level to verify that the two systems are connected and can see each other. After you verify the connection, proceed as follows:

1. Set up a user ID on the hostedi system; give that user ID the same name as the SAP user ID at the OS layer on the hostsap system, which is <sid>adm. Thus if your SAP instance is dv1, then the user ID will be dv1adm.

2. Create a home directory for this user on hostedi; the directory should be the same as the home directory on hostsap.

3. Create an .rhosts file in both systems. This file allows you to create trusted users. The permissions on this file should be 600, which is read and write for the user ID only. Setting permissions to any other value will not work.

4. In the .rhosts file on hostedi, enter hostsap, and in the .rhosts file on hostsap, enter hostedi. This step completes the configuration for trusted users.

You can verify the trusted user setup by executing the following command at the OS level:

◆ Execute **remsh hostedi date** from hostsap. This command should return the date from the hostedi system.

◆ Execute **remsh hostsap date** from hostedi. This command should return a date from the hostsap system.

How to Set Up an RFC Destination in SAP

Transaction: SM59

Path: Tools, Administration, Administration, Network, RFC Destination

There are several types of RFC destinations. EDI uses type TCP/IP to connect to the subsystem. A default RFC destination (SERVER_EXEC) is shipped with SAP; that RFC destination starts the rfcexec server program on the SAP application server on which the process is executing. You can change this destination to suit your needs or create a destination from scratch. The attributes and their meanings follow (see Figure 6.5).

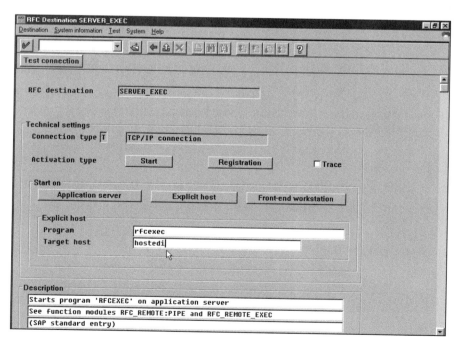

FIGURE 6-5

Attributes in a TCP/IP RFC destination

◆ **RFC Destination.** This attribute is a unique name for your RFC destination.

◆ **Connection Type.** Use type 'T' to indicate TCP/IP.

TIP

Pressing Enter after you put in the type and description of your RFC destination enables the fields necessary for connection type TCP/IP.

◆ **Activation Type.** Press the Start button. The Registration button is used only when your EDI subsystem is registered with a gateway. This technique is used only for RFC-enabled EDI subsystems. You are not assuming an RFC-enabled EDI subsystem.

◆ **Start On.** Select either Application Server or Explicit Host, depending on where the subsystem is installed. Check with your Basis people for this installation. If you select Explicit Host, then the system lets you enter the TCP/IP host name of the system on which your EDI subsystem is installed.

CAUTION

If you select the Application Server and have multiple application servers installed, then you must make sure they share the file system through some technique. A commonly used technique is NFS (Network File System) that allows a file system to be shared across multiple systems.

TIP

You can view the list of application servers running in your instance by executing transaction SM51.

◆ **Program.** Enter the RFC server program name rfcexec in this field.

CAUTION

The program name and the server name are case-sensitive.

TIP

You can test the connectivity to the rfcexec program by clicking on the Test button. If the result is successful, then you have successfully connected to the system that has or will have the EDI subsystem.

Local versus Remote Subsystems

If the subsystem is installed locally on the SAP box, you will have very few problems, because SAP and the subsystem operate under one environment and share a common file system. IDoc files created by the SAP system are automatically available to the subsystem. However, this configuration is not always advisable because of the additional load created on the system. Thus it's sometimes necessary to install the subsystem on a separate box.

If the subsystem is installed on a separate box, then you need to make sure that IDoc files created by SAP are accessible to the EDI subsystem and vice versa. The two options are NFS mount and remote copy. Check whether the subsystem can NFS mount the same directory where IDocs are created by SAP (the Basis staff can help you with NFS mounting). If so, the IDoc files are accessible.

Companies sometimes restrict the number of mount points for a file system. In this case the subsystem does not have visibility into the IDoc file created by SAP. If the two systems are completely separate and have only a TCP/IP connection, then you need a mechanism to copy the file from the SAP system to the subsystem. The subsystem is responsible for providing this functionality. Typically, some remote copy command (such as an rcp command in UNIX) provides this functionality, or an FTP (File Transfer Protocol) mechanism is put in place.

Port Definition

Transaction: WE21

Path: From the Area menu of EDI, choose IDoc, Port Definition.

The port defines the technical characteristics of the connection between SAP and the subsystem. The port defines the medium in which data is exchanged between the two systems.

In the EDI process, IDocs are transferred to external systems via ports. Four types of ports are available in release 4.0, as shown in Table 6-1.

Table 6-1 SAP Release 4.0 Ports

Port	Function
tRFC port	Used for ALE communication
File port	Used by EDI
R/2 system port	Used to communicate with an R/2 system
Internet port	Used to connect with Internet applications

The EDI process uses the file port. The type of port that can be used also depends on the receiving side. If the receiver cannot accept data in the medium used by a port, then the port cannot be used. For example, the tRFC port cannot be used for EDI unless the receiving subsystem has support for tRFC. Check with your vendor for the port supported. All vendors support the file port, so don't pick up your phone unless you are interested in using another port.

A port is a client-independent object. The following parameters are specified in a port definition. Figure 6-6 shows an example of how to specify the various attributes in a port definition.

- ◆ **Port Name.** The port name is any meaningful name to uniquely identify the port.
- ◆ **Description.** Any meaningful description of the port. This parameter is for documentation only.
- ◆ **Version.** You can control the release level of the IDoc being generated by SAP. In SAP the internal structure of the IDoc has changed in every major release. For example, in release 4.0, the IDoc name can be up to 30 characters. To support backward compatibility, you can set the version

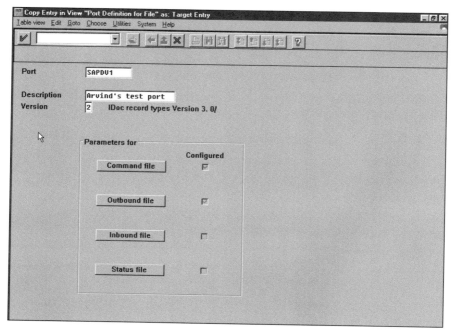

FIGURE 6-6

Attributes in a file port definition

of the IDoc to be generated. Consider a scenario in which you have upgraded to SAP release 4.0, but your subsystem is still working with IDocs of SAP release 3.0. You can use this field to specify the version to be generated, using the following values:

        1—Format for R/2.2 IDocs

        2—Format for R/3 IDocs

        3—Format for R/4 IDocs

Command File

The command file parameter specifies the path to get to the command file for the subsystem. This file is usually in the form of a shell script or batch file provided by your subsystem vendor. The various fields in the command file window (see Figure 6-7) are as follows:

    ◆ **Automatic Start Possible.** This flag specifies whether the subsystem can

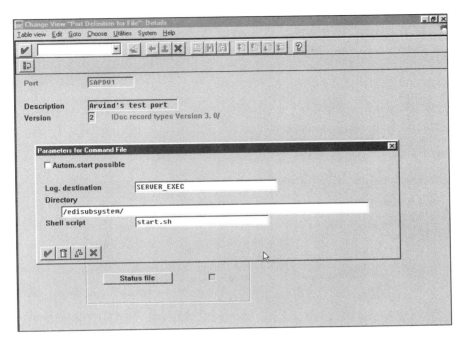

FIGURE 6-7

Attributes of the command file used to start the subsystem

be started by SAP or not.

◆ **Logical Destination.** Name of the RFC destination defined in previous step. This field locates the system on which the subsystem is installed. If the subsystem is not installed then you can use the default RFC destination SERVER_EXEC here.

◆ **Directory.** Fully qualified directory path where the subsystem shell script is installed.

◆ **Shell Script.** Name of the shell script supplied by the subsystem vendor. It is case-sensitive for UNIX.

 TIP

The directory path must end with a forward slash (/) for UNIX or a back slash (\) for PC-based systems.

Outbound File

This option specifies the name and location of the IDoc file generated for an outbound process. The various fields in the outbound file window (see Figure 6-8) are as follows:

◆ **Directory.** This field is the fully qualified directory path where the IDoc file is to be generated.

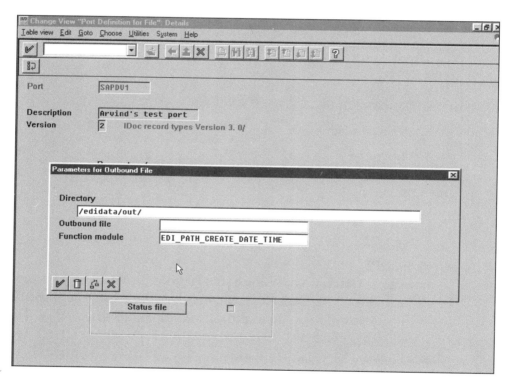

FIGURE 6-8

Attributes of the outbound IDoc files created by SAP

CAUTION

The directory path must be accessible to the SAP user ID <sid>adm. The sid is the system ID or the instance ID. Access to directory path is usually not a problem for <sid>adm because <sid>adm is set up as a superuser.

TIP

If you are using a port for testing and do not know of a directory path to put your IDoc files or are having permission problems, use the /tmp/ path on UNIX systems. This path is always present, and any user can write to this directory.

◆ **Outbound File.** You can specify a fixed file name for your outbound IDocs. This file name is used for all outbound IDocs and overwritten every time you create an outbound IDoc using this port. This option is useful during testing only—in a production environment you leave this entry blank and use dynamic file names as described next (generated via a function module).

◆ **Function Module.** By using the function module field, SAP provides a dynamic file naming option, which generates a file name at runtime. Several of these function modules ensure that a unique file is created for every IDoc that uses this port. You can select the function module that fits your needs. If these standard function modules do not meet your needs, then you can create your own function module for naming the files. Execute transaction WE55 to add your custom function module for naming the files.

CAUTION

If you use the function module field, then the Outbound File field should be blank.

TIP

If you are going to write your own function module, it's easiest to copy and modify an existing function module.

Inbound File

Entries for the inbound file are optional. The entries specify the name and location of the IDoc file for an inbound process. The values are typically not used because the subsystem provides a fully qualified path name and file name when it triggers the inbound process via startrfc. If the subsystem does not provide other values, then these specified values are used. These values are also used during testing, so it may be worthwhile to specify this option for the test port. The various fields in the inbound file window (see Figure 6-9) are as follows:

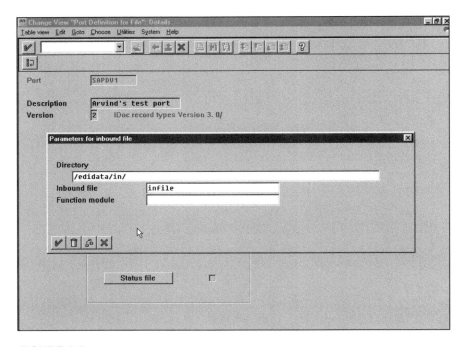

FIGURE 6-9

Attributes of the inbound IDoc files imported into SAP

◆ **Directory.** A fully qualified directory path where the IDoc file will be present.

CAUTION

The directory path must be accessible to the SAP user ID specified in the startrfc command on the inbound process.

◆ **Inbound File.** You can specify a fixed file name for your inbound IDocs. This file name is used for all inbound IDocs. This item is useful during testing only. In a production environment, you leave this entry blank and use dynamic file names.

◆ **Function Module.** SAP provides a dynamic file naming option, which ensures that a unique file name is used for every file.

Status File

Entries for the status file are optional. This setting specifies the name and location of the status file used to pass status information for an outbound IDoc. Again, the values are typically not used, because the subsystem provides a fully qualified path name and file name when it triggers the process via startrfc. If the subsystem does not provide other values, then these specified values are used. The various fields in the status file window (see Figure 6-10) are as follows:

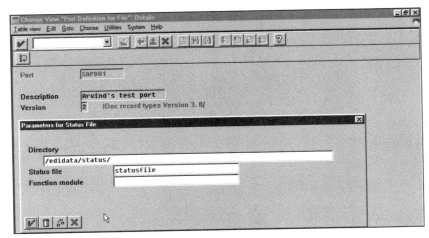

FIGURE 6-10

Attributes of the status files imported into SAP

◆ **Directory.** A fully qualified directory path where the status file will be present.

CAUTION

The directory path must be accessible to the SAP user ID specified in the startrfc command.

◆ **Status File.** You can specify a fixed file name for your inbound status file. This item is useful during testing only. In a production environment, you leave this entry blank and use dynamic file names.

◆ **Function Module.** SAP provides a dynamic file naming option, which ensures that a unique file name is used for every file.

Strategies for Building Ports

The port is not simply a parameter that you have to complete—some strategies can be used in port definitions. You may need to define multiple ports in the following situations:

◆ If you need to communicate with two separate systems and they use different IDoc formats (one uses 3.0 IDocs while the other uses 4.0), you have to create a separate port for each type.

◆ You must also create a separate test port for testing the process.

◆ You may want to separate the IDoc files to separate directories based on the type of EDI transaction. For example, you may want outgoing invoices to be in a separate directory from the outbound sales order response.

Triggering the Inbound Process by the Subsystem

The subsystem triggers the SAP system in two situations (see Figure 6-11).

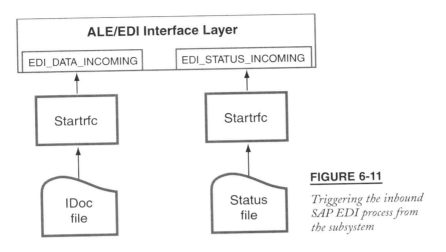

FIGURE 6-11

Triggering the inbound SAP EDI process from the subsystem

- ◆ The EDI subsystem has converted an EDI document to an IDoc file format for an inbound process. This file needs to be passed to the SAP system to start the inbound process in SAP.

- ◆ An outbound IDoc was passed to the subsystem in a file format. The subsystem has converted the file into an EDI document and transmitted the EDI document to the business partner. The subsystem now needs to report the status of the process at every milestone to SAP so that SAP has visibility into the process after it leaves the SAP boundaries. The subsystem creates a status file to report the status to SAP.

These two tasks are carried out using startrfc, a generic program supplied by SAP. This program resides on the operating system and can trigger any RFC-enabled function module synchronously. SAP provides two function modules that act as entry points for an inbound process, specifically for the two tasks described above. The function modules are

- ◆ EDI_DATA_INCOMING
- ◆ EDI_STATUS_INCOMING

The syntax for the startrfc command follows. When you read the syntax, keep in mind all the information that is generally needed for anyone to log on to the SAP system:

> **startrfc** -3 –d <system id> -u <userid> -p <password> -c <client> -l <language> -h <App. Server> -s <system number> -g <gateway host> -x <gateway services> -t –E <file name> -E <port name> -F <function module name>

◆ **-3** indicates to log on to the R/3 system.

◆ **system ID** can be determined by looking at the status bar on your SAP screen. This three-character identifier is assigned to your SAP instance. You can also execute transaction SM51 to determine the instance ID. The instance ID comprises the two characters following the underscore.

◆ **userid** is the ID used to log on to the SAP system. This user should be a background user or a CPIC user. This ID has SAPALL permission.

◆ **password** is the password for the logon ID used to log on to the system.

◆ **client** is the SAP client.

◆ **language** of the logon ID.

◆ **App. Server** is the server to which the user will log on to connect to the SAP system.

◆ **system number** is the two-digit system number. Use SM51 to display the application servers. The last two digits in the application server name provide the value for the system number.

◆ **gateway host** is the name of the host on which the gateway service programs are executing. The gateway host is used for all RFC communications which use CPIC communications behind the scenes. In a simple installation, this entry is the name of the application server host, but the gateway services can be installed separately. Check with your Basis staff for the gateway server.

◆ **gateway services** as defined in the services file at the OS level. From within SAP, you can execute program RSPARAM and on the output screen, look for an entry with rdisp/sna_gw_service in the parameter name column. The value displayed in the user-defined column is the value to be entered in the gateway services parameter.

◆ **-t** is the option that turns on trace. If this option is used, then a trace file named dev_rfc is created in the current directory.

Summary

In this chapter you learned about general EDI settings and communication settings used in the EDI configuration. These configuration items are one-time settings that must be done at the beginning of the project. The Basis group is likely to carry out some of the configurations because they involve setting up communication components. The parameters discussed in this chapter have a major impact on the overall performance and operation of the interface and must be set correctly before you can proceed with other EDI components.

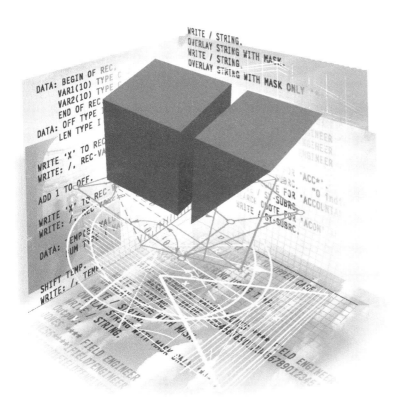

Chapter 7

**Configuring
Partner Profiles**

In this chapter you learn about the partner profile component in complete detail: the use of partner profiles, the various views, how the characteristics are defined, and the significance of those characteristics. A large corporation can have hundreds of partners and therefore needs a way to maintain partner profiles (other than entering them manually online). In this chapter you learn how to use various effort-reducing techniques to streamline that process. At the end of the chapter are advanced tips and tricks that can help you address some common problems without having to write ABAP/4 programs as workarounds. A partner profile is defined for every business partner with whom you exchange business documents. In EDI, a partner can be a customer, vendor, bank, or any entity with which your company does business. In ALE, a partner is a remote SAP system or legacy system with which you exchange data. A partner profile specifies the various characteristics of data that you exchange with a business partner, the mode of operation, and a person responsible for handling errors for that business partner.

Four Views of a Partner Profile

Transaction: WE20

Path: From the Area menu of EDI, choose IDoc, partner Profile

A partner profile has four views in which different characteristics for a partner are maintained (see figure 7-1):

◆ General view

◆ Message Control view

◆ Outbound view

◆ Inbound view

The values are stored in four different tables. The partner number and partner type bind all the views together.

General View

The General view contains some very basic information about the partner, such as partner number, partner type, and partner status. This information is maintained only once for each partner. Figure 7-2 shows the fields that are maintained in the General view. These values are stored in table EDPP1.

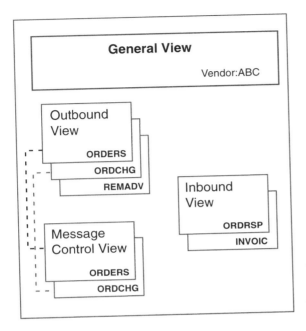

FIGURE 7-1

Structure of a partner profile showing the various components

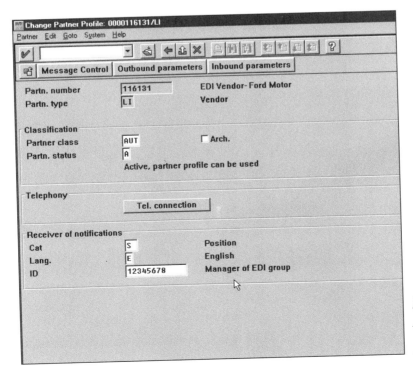

FIGURE 7-2

Attributes in the General view of a Partner profile

The following attributes are defined in the General view:

◆ **Partn. number.** In EDI, the partner number can be a customer number, vendor number, or bank ID. In ALE, it is the logical name assigned to the partner SAP system or legacy system. The standard system validates the partner number against the customer master, vendor master, or bank master data, depending on the type of business partner.

◆ **Partn. type.** The partner type represents the type of your business partner. For example, in EDI it is customer (KU), vendor (LI), and bank (B). In ALE, it is the logical system (LS).

◆ **Partner Class.** This field is for documentation only and has no intelligence behind it. You can use this field to classify your partners. For example, if you want to classify automotive vendors versus railroad vendors, you could enter particular codes representing automotive or railroad.

◆ **Arch.** This field is also for documentation only. It represents whether a partner agreement exists or not. Partner agreement is an EDI term that refers to legal documents used to define each partner's responsibilities in a business relationship.

◆ **Partner Status.** This field makes a partner active or inactive. If a partner is deactivated, no documents are passed to it.

TIP

If you maintain Partner profiles in the production system, then you can use this field to indicate that the Partner profile is under construction until the Partner profile has been completed. After a Partner profile is complete, you can activate it to mark it ready for use.

◆ **Receiver of Notifications.** This field represents the workflow object (for example, user, position, organization unit) used for notification. This object is notified when a corresponding outbound or inbound record is not found for a message that is being sent to or received from this business partner. See Chapter 9, "Configuring workflow," for details on how the system sends workflow notifications for errors. For example, if a person with position ID 12345678 is responsible for handling errors for this business partner, then the value of the various fields are as follows:

Cat. S
Lang. E
ID. 12345678

TIP

Avoid using a user ID in this field. You should use more abstract object types such as position, job, or organization unit. This approach saves you the headache of changing the entry when the user leaves the company or changes jobs. Compared to users, other objects such as positions, jobs, and organization units tend to be more stable. However, during the development phase you can use your user ID for a quick start.

Message Control View

Message Control view is maintained for those outbound messages (for example, purchase order, sales order response, invoice) that make use of the Message control component to generate IDocs. If an outbound message (for example, Remittance advice) does not use Message control, then this view is not maintained. The values in the Message control view are stored in table EDP12.

In the Message Control view, you specify the Message control components that are used in the process to generate IDocs. See Figure 7-3 for the various fields maintained in this view. The various attributes defined in Message control view are as follows:

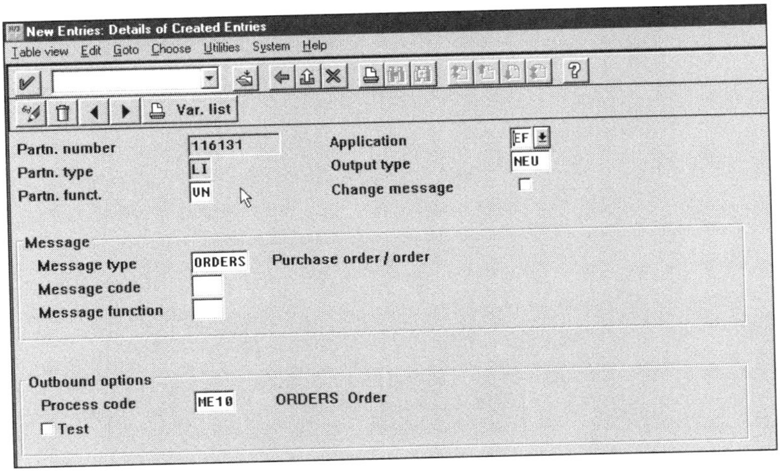

FIGURE 7-3

Attributes in the Message control view of a Partner profile

◆ **Partn. Number.** Same values as specified in the General view. In fact, the system automatically copies the values from the General view when you maintain the Message control view.

◆ **Partn. Type.** Same values as specified in the General view. In fact, the system automatically copies the values from the General view.

◆ **Partn. Funct.** In SAP a business partner can have multiple roles. For example, a customer can have ship to, sold to, and bill to functions. This field describes the partner function being used for this message.

◆ **Application.** Each Message control application (Sales—V1, Purchase Order—EF) is assigned a two-character ID. This field identifies the application generating the outbound message. See Chapter 8, "Configuring Message Control," for more detail on the application ID.

◆ **Output Type.** Message control assigns a 4-character Output type (for example, BA00 for Order response, NEU for Purchase order) to the various messages exchanged between business partners. Enter the appropriate output type in this field. See Chapter 8, "Configuring Message Control," for more details on the output type.

◆ **Change Message.** Set this flag if the output represents changed output for a document that was sent earlier. For example, if an Order change message (ORDCHG) is being sent, then this flag is turned on.

◆ **Message Type/Message Code/Message Function.** These three fields together represent the SAP Message type assigned to the EDI transaction being sent to a business partner. The Message type field has been derived from the EDIFACT messages, but a one-to-one equivalence is not guaranteed. The Message type is independent of the ANSI X.12 or EDIFACT standards. The Message code and Message function fields are not commonly used. Refer to the appendix for a cross reference list between SAP Message type and the EDI messages.

 TIP

The Message code and Message function field can be utilized to create a variation of the same message by assigning different values in these two fields. Details are presented in "Using the Partner Profiles," later in this chapter.

◆ **Process Code.** A process code points to a function module that reads application data and formats the data into an IDoc format. These function modules are commonly referred to as selection programs or data extraction programs. A selection program exists for each outbound message generated via Message control. Execute transaction WE41 and look under Outbound with ALE service, With function module Version 3 for a list of process codes for outbound messages. You can double click on any process code to view its details.

◆ **Test.** This flag indicates whether the system generates a test IDoc before generating an actual IDoc. This option is not available for all messages. It is available for certain FI related messages such as Remittance advice and Payment orders. It helps you verify the data contents before transmitting the actual message. This attribute is also a directive for the subsystem not to transmit these messages to the business partner.

 CAUTION

This flag is part of the key and therefore you must create two entries (with and without the test flag) for your message type to generate a test IDoc and actual IDoc.

Outbound View

The outbound parameters define the characteristics of an outbound message to your business partner and how SAP transfers the IDocs to the subsystem. A record is created for every outbound message to a business partner regardless of whether it uses Message control or not. The outbound attributes are stored in table EDP13. The following characteristics (see Figure 7-4) are specified on an Outbound view:

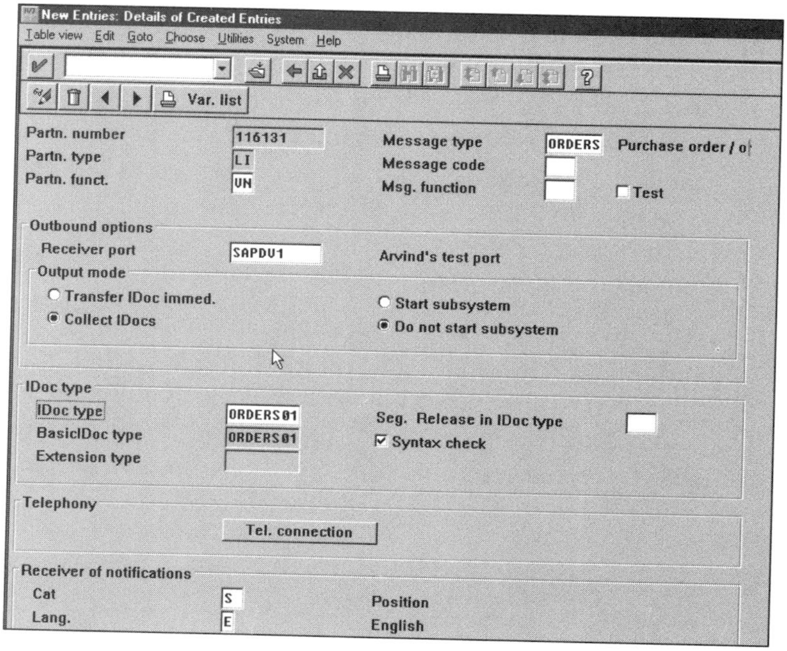

FIGURE 7-4

Attributes in the Outbound view of a Partner profile

◆ **Partn. Number.** The same values as specified in the General view. In fact, the system automatically copies the values from the General view when you maintain the Outbound view.

◆ **Partn. Type.** The same values as specified in the General view. In fact, the system automatically copies the values from the General view.

◆ **Partn. Funct.** In SAP a business partner can have multiple roles. This field describes the partner function being used for this message.

◆ **Message Type/Message Code/Msg. Function.** These three fields have the same meaning, as described earlier in the Message control view.

CAUTION

If your outbound process uses message control, then the combination of Message type/Message code/Message function must match the one specified in Message Control view.

◆ **Test.** This flag has the same meaning, as described earlier in the Message control view.

CAUTION

If your outbound process uses Message control, then the flag must match the settings of this flag in Message control view.

◆ **Receiver Port.** This field contains the port to be used by your outbound process. In EDI this entry is the file port explained in the "Port Definition" section of Chapter 6, "Configuring Basic EDI Components." Port defines the directory location and file name for IDoc files and the name of the subsystem program (if installed). In ALE the receiver port is of type tRFC, as explained in the "Port Definition" section of Chapter 22, "Configuring the ALE Infrastructure."

◆ **Pack Size.** This field is specific to ALE processes and is only visible if the port used in the partner profile is of type tRFC. This field defines the number of IDocs that are bundled in a packet for transmission to a partner system. The value in this field affects the performance of the system. Initially you can select defaults proposed by the system, but read Chapter 28, "Managing ALE Process Performance and Throughput," for details on how to calculate the value to be entered in this field.

◆ **Output Mode.** Output mode controls when the IDocs are transferred to the subsystem and whether or not the subsystem is to be started. The settings you make here affect the performance of the system. See Chapter 13, "Managing EDI Process Performance and Throughput," for details on how to set these values.

The following subfields are defined in Output mode:

Transfer IDoc immed. If this flag is turned on and each IDoc is passed to the subsystem layer immediately upon creation as an IDoc file.

Collect IDocs. If this flag is turned on, the IDocs are collected in the system. A program RSEOUT00 must be executed to transfer the collected IDocs to the subsystem.

Start subsystem. If this flag is turned on, the subsystem is started as soon as IDocs are transferred to the subsystem.

Do not start subsystem. If this flag is turned on, the subsystem is not started. This flag is useful if you do not have a subsystem installed.

◆ **IDoc Type.** This field contains the IDoc type used in the process. A message type can be assigned to multiple IDoc types. You select the IDoc type that is relevant for your process. The IDoc type is Basic IDoc Type + Extension Type. For standard SAP scenarios, the IDoc type is the same as the Basic IDoc type. If you extend an SAP IDoc, then the IDoc type will not be same as the Basic IDoc type.

◆ **Basic IDoc Type.** This field contains the Basic IDoc type used in the process. When you enter the IDoc type, the system automatically enters this value for you. This value is known to the system based on the IDoc type you entered.

◆ **Extension Type.** This field contains the name of the extension you are using in your IDoc. When you enter the IDoc type, the system automatically enters this value for you. This value is known to the system when you create an IDoc extension.

◆ **Seg. Release in IDoc Type.** A segment gets a new definition when new fields are added to it. The standard SAP segments have different versions depending on when they were enhanced by SAP. If you want to use the latest segment definition in an IDoc, you must leave this field blank. However, if you are interested in a specific version of a segment, you must enter the version of the segment here.

◆ **Syntax Check.** This flag controls how the system behaves when a syntax error is found in an IDoc. If this flag is checked, the system stops the IDoc processing and sends a workflow message to a user. If this flag is not checked, the processing continues and a workflow message is sent to indicate that a syntax error has occurred. See "Syntax Rules for an IDoc" in Chapter 30, "IDocs on the Inside," for a list of syntax rules checked in an IDoc.

◆ **Receiver of Notifications.** This field defines the workflow object (for example, user, position, organization unit) that is notified when an error occurs in the outbound process for a message being sent to the business partner. The type of values that can be specified in the three fields (Cat., Lang., and ID) are the same as described in the General view earlier.

◆ **EDI Settings.** These settings define the EDI standards being used and the EDI message type or transaction number, along with the version. These values are for use by the subsystem only; SAP does not have any functionality behind these fields and you can leave them empty. For example, if you were sending out purchase orders via ANSI X.12 version 3050, then the values would be as follows:

```
EDI standard. E

Message type. 850

Version. 003050
```

Inbound View

The inbound parameters define the characteristics of an inbound message coming from your business partner and how the IDoc is processed by SAP. A record is created for every inbound message (for example, sales order, purchase order acknowledgment, invoice) from a business partner. The values are stored in table EDP21. The following characteristics (see Figure 7-5) are specified on Inbound view.

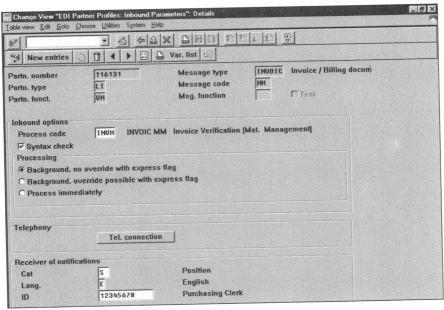

FIGURE 7-5

Attributes in the Inbound view of a Partner profile

- **Partn. Number.** The same values as specified in the General view. In fact, the system automatically copies the values from the General view when you maintain the Inbound view.

- **Partn. Type.** The same values as specified in the General view. In fact, the system automatically copies the values from the General view.

- **Partner Function.** In SAP a business partner can have multiple roles. This field describes the partner function being used for this message.

- **Message Type/Message Code/Msg. Function.** These three fields have the same meaning as described earlier in the Message control view.

- **Test.** This flag indicates whether the message is a test message or real message.

- **Process Code.** A process code points to a posting program that is implemented as function modules. A posting program exists for each inbound message type. Execute transaction WE42 and look under Inbound with ALE service, Processing by function module for a list of process codes for inbound messages. You can double-click on any process code to view its details.

- **Syntax Check.** This flag controls how the system behaves when a syntax error is found in an IDoc. If this flag is checked, the system stops the IDoc processing and sends a workflow message to a user. If this flag is not checked, the processing continues and a workflow message is sent to indicate that a syntax error has occurred. See "Syntax Rules for an IDoc" in Chapter 30, "IDocs on the Inside," for a list of syntax rules checked in an IDoc.

- **Processing.** The Processing field controls when the IDocs are transferred to the posting modules. The settings you make here affect the performance of the system. See Chapter 13, "Managing EDI Process Performance and Throughput," for details on how to set these values. The following subfields are defined in the Processing box:

  Background, no override with express flag. If this flag is turned on, the IDocs are not passed to the posting module immediately. The RBDAPP01 program is executed to process the IDocs.

  Background, override possible with express flag. If this flag is turned on, the IDocs are not passed to the posting module. But if the express flag is set in the control record, the IDoc is passed immediately. This flag can only be set in the subsystem before an IDoc is passed to SAP.

Immediate. If this flag is turned on, then the IDoc is immediately passed to the posting module upon creation.

◆ **Receiver of Notifications.** This field defines the workflow object (for example, user, position, organization unit) that is notified when an error occurs in the inbound process for a message received from a business partner. The type of values that can be specified in the three fields (Cat., Lang., and ID) are the same as described in the General view earlier.

Tips for Maintaining Partner Profiles

Partner profile is an important element in customizing the ALE/EDI interface. You will be frequently involved in creating, changing, or adjusting values in the Partner profile. An incorrect partner profile can lead to hours of debugging and frustration. In this section you learn some simple techniques that can make it easier to maintain partner profiles.

Consistency Check

A standard program RSECHK07 is available in the system to carry out the following checks on the values specified in the partner profile:

◆ Process code

◆ User to be notified

◆ Consistency of Message control parameters with outbound parameters

You can execute the RSECHK07 program via transaction SE38 or from the menus of the initial partner profile screen. The output is a color-coded report that details any problems.

Although a check is carried out when the partner profile is initially created, some parameters can eventually become invalid. For example, if a user ID specified in the Receiver of Notifications field in the partner profile no longer exists, this report will flag it as an error.

Copying Partner Profiles

The copy function is very useful in maintaining partner profiles, especially if you have partners who look similar. You can create a sample partner profile with all possible messages, copy it for a new trading partner, and then delete the unwanted components. Deleting extraneous components is much easier than creating the whole partner profile from scratch.

Copying Partner Profile Views

If you've created a record (inbound or outbound) with incorrect key values, the only way to change it is to delete it and create it again. However, the copy function can be very useful in this case. Assume that you've forgotten to enter a partner function and have created everything else correctly. Instead of deleting the record, copy it, change the key values, save the new record, and delete the original record.

Automatic Generation

In release 4.0, the IMG contains a tool to set default parameters for each message for a partner type. Then you can build your partner profiles using these defaults. This tool will quickly create your partner profile using the defaults set for each message. See the apppendix for more details

However, if you are still using release 3.0, you can use an ALE tool (Transaction: BD82) to generate partner profiles automatically for ALE partners based on the ALE distribution model. This tool is mainly designed for ALE, but you can use it to build a basic partner profile structure with some default values for EDI. You must edit the entries to adjust certain parameters such as ports, so this tool is for expert users only.

 CAUTION

Transaction BD82 can interfere with your existing ALE configuration, so use this tool only if your site is not using ALE or if you know exactly what you are doing.

Programming to Maintain Partner Profiles

If several hundred partner profiles are already being used in your legacy environment, then you can build an interface to create your partner profiles in the

SAP system. You can use the following options to create your partner profiles:

◆ Write a BDC (Batch Data Communication) program

◆ Use standard function modules

Several function modules are available in the system to maintain partner profiles without going directly to the database. The function modules are present in function group EDI6.

Moving Partner Profiles to the Production System

Until release 3.0F, partner profiles were treated as configuration tables, which meant that partner profiles could not be created or modified in the production system. They had to be modified in the development system and then transported to the production system. This approach was unacceptable to customers who wanted to change partners in the production system and could not wait for the profile to be transported from development systems.

SAP has provided a temporary fix for this problem for customers who are still on release 3.0F or prior releases. Check OSS note 0049758 for details on how to fix this problem. The note essentially changes the delivery class of the table from customizing to master data. This modification allows changes to be made in the production system.

In release 3.1, the partner profile tables have been changed to class Master Data. This modification allows companies to maintain partner profiles directly in the production system.

Alternatively, you can maintain partner profiles in the development system if you maintain very few partner profiles, if they do not change frequently, or if your company prefers that method. In this case you must manually transport the partner profiles. From the initial partner profile screen, choose partner, Transport. The system prompts you for a change request.

Using the Partner Profiles

This section mentions some tricks that I have used or learned in the past to solve certain problems without writing any ABAP/4 code or to otherwise make particular tasks a little easier.

Problems in Communicating with the Subsystem

If you have set up your EDI subsystem on a system other than the SAP system, you already know the pain involved in getting all the links to work. You may have called your EDI subsystem vendor to come in for a day and enable that link—especially the piece where the SAP system cannot find the subsystem. You constantly see your IDocs going into status 20 (Error triggering the EDI subsystem). Problems in linking the two systems at the OS level cause this error. The setup for RFC destinations was described in Chapter 6, "Configuring Basic EDI Components," but following is an alternative that does not require that complex setup.

The solution approaches the problem by first understanding what you are trying to do with this remote link. You are trying to make sure that when an IDoc file is written, the subsystem can pick up the file for processing.

The solution is to execute the two processes independently. In the partner profile, enable the Do Not Start the Subsystem flag. After the SAP EDI process creates the outbound file, SAP will not attempt to start the subsystem. Next have the subsystem poll the outbound directory for any new files on a periodic basis. You can control the timing of this job to suit your needs. After processing the file, the EDI subsystem can report the file's status to the SAP system as usual. This trick saves you from trying to figure out why the subsystem could not be started. Because the EDI process is asynchronous, operate the SAP to EDI subsystem connection using this approach, unless you want a near real-time behavior with certain transactions

Workflow Notifications

A typical problem in large organizations is the need to route workflow notifications in EDI to a different person depending on the business conditions. For example, consider the following situations:

- ◆ You have a staff that handles errors in the processing of incoming Sales orders via EDI. You want to assign different people the job of handling workflow notifications for different types (Customer order, Internal order) of incoming sales orders.

- ◆ You want to assign different people the job of handling workflow notifications for incoming Sales orders for different sales organizations.

The Inbound and Outbound views of the partner profile have two fields (Message Code and Message Function) that are part of the key but are usually left blank. These fields can be utilized to address the two business situations mentioned above. Create two variants of the ORDERS message by assigning a three-digit code to the Message Code field based on the order type or on the sales organization, respectively. The incoming IDoc originates in the EDI subsystem, so you must make the that control record contains the appropriate codes in the Message code and Message function field.

Now you can create two entries in the partner profile for the same message with the two variants. You should be able to assign a different workflow object type in the Receiver of Notifications field.

Summary

In this chapter you learned about the partner profile component, which defines the characteristics of the messages exchanged with a business partner and the mode (batch versus immediate) in which an IDoc is processed. partner profile has four views: General, Message Control, Outbound, and Inbound. The General view defines the basic attributes of a business partner such as partner number and type of partner. The Message Control view is only used in outbound processes that use Message control and is used to specify the Message control objects in the process. The Outbound view defines the components used in the outbound process and how SAP hands over the IDocs to the subsystem. The Inbound view defines the components used in the inbound process and how IDocs are passed to the posting module for processing.

SAP provides various tools to help you maintain partner profiles. You can build an interface program for creating partner profiles, and you can use the basic copy function to speed up the process.

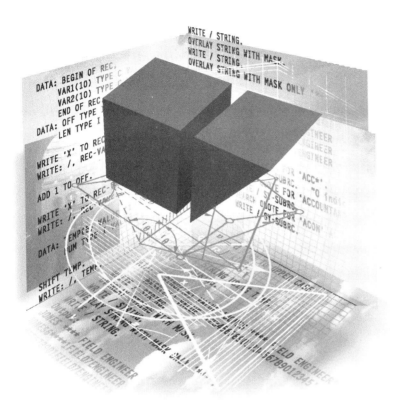

Chapter 8

Configuring Message Control

In this chapter you'll learn about the Message control component that is used in the outbound process. It is important to note that Message control is not built specifically for the EDI process. It has applications in various areas such as account determination, material determination, and pricing. Therefore, the terminology of Message control is not related to EDI terminology. You will discover several new terms that you should get accustomed to. This chapter introduces the concept of Message control—what it is, how it is used in EDI, the architecture of the whole process—and then describes the steps for using the standard Message control components. The chapter also discusses how to develop new Message control components.

Introduction to Message Control

Message control is also sometimes referred to as output control or conditioning techniques. Message control is a cross-application component that is used as a service program in several areas. The biggest application is in pricing, but Message control is also used for output determination in EDI and account determination and material determination in the SD (Sales and Distribution) module.

The basic concept behind Message control is to generate and manage various outputs from an application and control their timing and medium of exchange. For example, you may want to create the following outputs when a sales order is entered in the system (see Figure 8-1):

- Internal mail message to the production control staff immediately
- Sales order response to the customer via fax immediately
- Printed output for warehouse personnel when necessary
- Sales order response to the customer via EDI at night
- Workflow notification to quality engineer at the end of the day
- Sales order to another system via ALE

 NOTE

If this is your first encounter with message control, skip ahead to "Setting Up Standard Message Control."

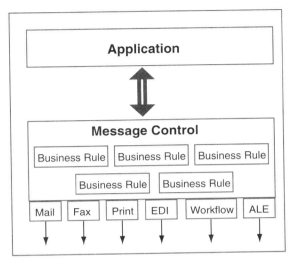

FIGURE 8-1

Outputs managed by Message control

The outputs may require certain business conditions to be met before they are proposed. For example, send out the EDI message only when the customer number is 3000009. Otherwise, send a printed output. Print the output in German if it is for a customer in Germany; for customers anywhere else, print the output in English. The Message control encapsulates such if-then business rules without having to write ABAP/4 programs. The Message control technique has proven to be quite useful and provides a consistent way of generating outputs from several applications. Most of the SD and MM applications are enabled to use the Message control component.

Benefits of Using Message Control

From an EDI perspective, Message control has the following advantages. Some of these advantages will become more apparent when you start using the Message control component.

 ◆ **Disconnecting the process of creating an application document from the process of generating outputs.** For example, the sales order transaction VA01 does not have any logic in its code to generate IDocs for the EDI process. Creating application documents and generating IDocs are two separate processes. The separation helps keep errors in one process from affecting the processing of the other component.

◆ **Automatic proposal of output based on business rules specified in Message control.** Rules can be very generic or very specific. After the business rules are encapsulated in the Message control, the output is proposed only when the business conditions are met.

◆ **Capability to override the automatic proposal.** Although you can set up the system for automatic proposal, the system allows for the outputs to be edited before they are sent. For example, an EDI message is sent to vendor 300009 for purchase orders. But the vendor has reported some problems temporarily and does not want to accept EDI for a certain time period. You can delete the proposed output, and the system will not send the EDI document.

◆ **Capability to manually select an output.** Some business rules require human intelligence and therefore cannot be encapsulated in the Message control. For example, an internal notification is to be sent to an MRP (Material Requirement Planning) planner when the delivery date proposed by the sales system is unacceptable to a customer and the customer is a major one. In this case the concept of "major customer" requires human intelligence and cannot be adequately encapsulated in a business rule. Hence the sales order clerk entering the order can manually select the Output type for internal notification.

◆ **Capability to generate multiple outputs.** For example, printed output and order response via EDI at the same time. The system can propose any number of desired outputs.

◆ **Capability to control the timing, medium, and language of the output messages.** As part of the configuration, you can specify all these parameters. For example, EDI can wait until the end of the day for transmissions, but the internal notifications can be printed immediately.

◆ **Capability to retransmit an output.** If a printed output is lost or if an EDI transmission fails at the subsystem level and it is necessary to retransmit the output, the system can resend the output without having to duplicate the application document.

◆ **Capability to monitor the results of execution.** The results of processing an Output type are logged in the system, and they can be monitored from the application document.

Applications Enabled for Message Control

Most of the SD and MM applications use Message control for output determination. Thus if you enter a sales order, quote, scheduling agreement, purchase order, invoice, or other business documents in the SD or MM module, the EDI output can be controlled using Message control. A complete list of applications that currently use Message control can be reached via transaction NACE.

Message control is a service module, and applications call the Message control services using standard function modules of the Message control. A list of applications commonly used in the EDI process that are enabled for Message control follows:

> Sales
>
> Shipping
>
> Billing
>
> Transportation
>
> Request for quote
>
> Purchasing
>
> Purchasing outline agreement
>
> Delivery schedule

The Architecture of the Message Control

First the various components that make up the Message control architecture are described. Then you'll learn how the Message control process uses these components to propose various outputs and process them.

The Components of Message Control

To understand the Message control process, it is important to clarify the terminology and identify the various components. The terminology associated with Message control can be confusing because several terms can be used for the same thing, depending on the particular application area. In other cases, two terms that seem similar can have two very different meanings. Such ambiguity can be a problem for beginners as well as for seasoned consultants. Take note of the following terms:

◆ Output types are also called Messages, Message types, or Condition types.

◆ Procedures are also called Message schemas.

◆ Condition type and Condition record are two separate things.

Figure 8-2 shows the relationship between various components that make up the Message control system and reusability of components. Components are reusable within an application. For example, a condition table can be used in more than one Access sequence. Components are related to each other via one-to-one relationships or one-to-many relationships. In a one-to-one relationship a component can have only one component linked to it. For example, an Output type can have only one Access sequence associated with it. In one-to-many relationships, a component can be associated with more than one component. For example, an Application can have more than one Procedure associated with it. You can execute the transaction NACE and select the Expert mode button to access the various Message control components for various applications.

Application ID

Applications that are capable of generating various outputs are assigned a two-character Application ID in Message control. For example, the ID for the purchasing application is EF, and the ID for the sales order application is V1. Figure 8-3 shows a complete list of Application IDs. Application IDs serve as the starting points to drill down into the various Message control components used by an application.

TIP

A quick shortcut to access various Message control components for the SD and MM applications is to use transactions VOK2 for SD and VOK3 for purchasing.

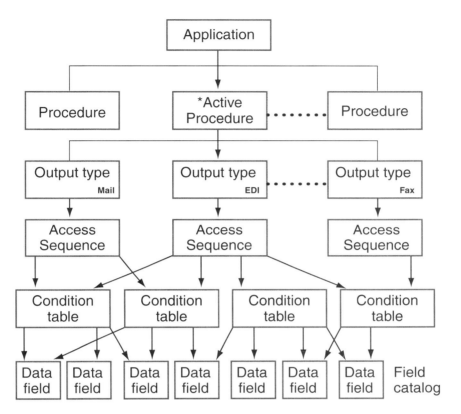

FIGURE 8-2

The components used in Message control

Communication Structures

Communication structures pass application information to the Message control. Thus, the Communication structure acts as a container. Each application has its own application structure. The Communication structure for output determination uses the naming convention **KOMxByy**, where **x** can be **K** or **P. K** means the header structure, **P** means line-item structure, and **yy** is the two-character Application ID. Hence **KOMKBV1** is the Communication structure for sales order header information.

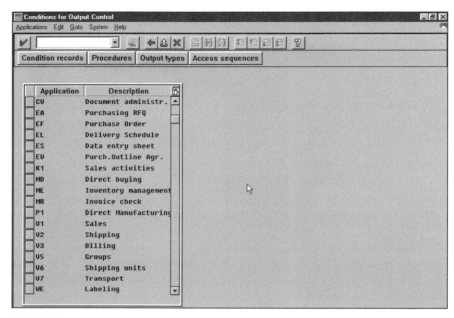

FIGURE 8-3

Two character Application ID's assigned to applications that support Message control

Procedure

A Procedure defines a set of possible outputs for an application. A Procedure is assigned a six-character name. An application can have several Procedures defined for it, but only one can be configured as active. A list of Procedures for an application can be seen via the IMG. A Procedure has three main attributes that affect the proposal of an Output type, as shown in Figure 8-4.

- ◆ List of Output types
- ◆ Requirement field
- ◆ Manual flag

 NOTE

Fields in a Communication structure can be viewed using transaction SE11. Communication structures can also be extended by using append structures. If a Communication structure is extended, the extended fields need to be populated in a user exit to pass those values to the Message control. User exits are available for populating the extended fields in a Communication structure.

The list of Output types represents a set of outputs that are possible for an application. It does not mean that they will be proposed. It simply means that the system evaluates these outputs for proposal. An Output type that does not exist in a Procedure cannot be proposed. Examples of certain Output types applicable for a sales order are:

◆ Sales order response

◆ Internal message

◆ Hard copy output

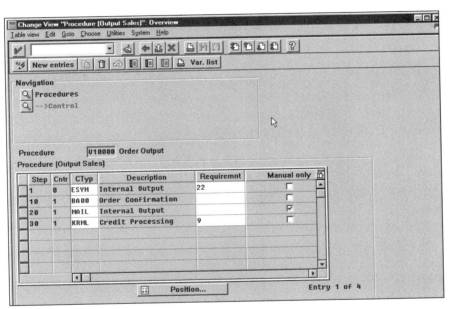

FIGURE 8-4

Attributes of a Procedure

Each Output type can have some preconditions defined for it. For example, a sales order response should not be sent out unless the sales order is complete. These preconditions are captured in the Requirements. A Requirement is implemented as an ABAP/4 program and assigned a number. A list of Requirements defined in the system can be viewed using transaction VOFM. A Requirement is optional, but if desired, it can be specified for each output used in a Procedure.

An Output type can be marked as manual in a Procedure, meaning that the system does not attempt to propose that output automatically. This output can only be selected manually by a user. This type of output can be important when you do not want an automatic proposal or because the business rules are based on human intelligence and cannot be encapsulated in an ABAP/4 routine.

NOTE

New Procedures, Output types, and Requirements can be created to suit your needs.

Output Types

An Output type defines the characteristics and attributes of the output itself, as shown in Figure 8-5. Examples of Output types available for a sales order are BA00 (sales order response), ESYM (internal output), and MAIL (mail).

The following attributes are defined for an Output type:

◆ A name with up to four characters. Examples of Output types are NEU and BA00.

◆ Access sequence, which is basically a set of business rules.

◆ Condition Access flag. If this flag is selected, the values for the output medium and timing are determined from the Condition records using the Access sequence. For the Output types used in the SD modules (sales, shipping, and billing), if this flag is not selected, then the values for the output medium and timing are not determined from the Condition records. Instead, those values are determined from the customer master data. In the customer master data, an output view exists in the sales area data to specify the values for the output medium and the language. Specifying the values in the customer master is useful when you do not have any complex rules and the values for the output medium and timing are based on the customer number.

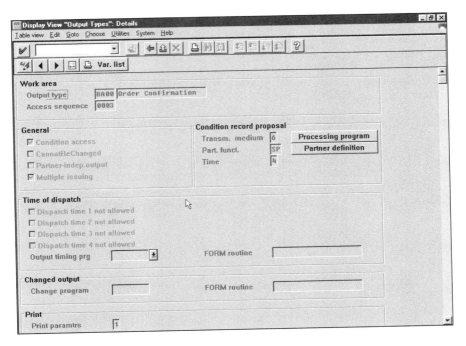

FIGURE 8-5

Attributes of an Output type

- ◆ Default medium for transmission (EDI, print, SAP office mail, workflow, ALE).
- ◆ Default timing (immediate or batch).
- ◆ Whether multiple outputs are permitted.
- ◆ Whether the output can be edited.
- ◆ Program for changed output. This program determines whether changes made to the document are relevant for sending the output in a change mode.

This list of attributes that you can assign to an Output type is not complete, but covers the most commonly used attributes for EDI.

Access Sequence

An Access sequence defines a sequence in which business rules are checked for proposing an Output type. A business rule is checked by comparing the values passed in the application data to the values defined in the Condition records of the condition table. If a match occurs, then a business rule is considered satisfied. After a business rule is satisfied, the output values from the Condition record are used for the Output type.

An Access sequence is given a four-character name, usually a number, and has the following attributes:

◆ A set of business rules or conditions

◆ A sequence in which they are checked

◆ A requirement that checks for business rules using ABAP programs

◆ Exclusive or inclusive

Figure 8-6 illustrates two business rules. Business rule 1 is based on Doc.Type/Sales Org./Customer. Business rule 2 is based on Sales Organization/Customer Number. Each business rule is effectively a set of fields defined in a condition table.

Each business rule can also have some preconditions, which are implemented in Requirements. The concept is the same as the concept used in the Procedure, but provides a more granular control at the business-rule level. For example, an output message is to be sent to the credit department only if there is a credit block on the

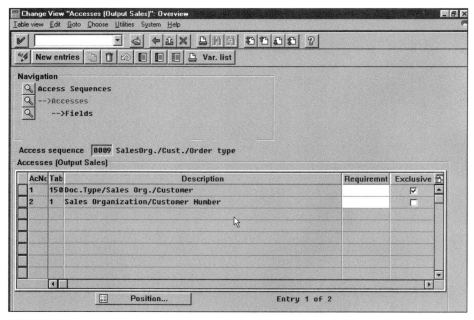

FIGURE 8-6

Attributes of an Access sequence

sales order. These preconditions are captured in the Requirements. A Requirement is implemented as an ABAP/4 program and assigned a number. A list of Requirements defined in the system can be viewed by using transaction VOFM. A Requirement is optional, but if desired, it can be specified for each business rule used in an Access sequence.

The exclusive or inclusive strategy specifies whether the system should exit after the first match of the business rule against the Condition records or continue to process other business rules in the Access sequence.

If the exclusive strategy is used, then the system exits on the first match. In the case of inclusive strategy, the system continues to validate the rest of the business rules. The reason for an inclusive strategy is to have an Output type proposed multiple times. However one of the attributes (partner function, partner number, or language) must be different. The system does not allow two Output types to have identical values.

For example, the inclusive strategy can be used when you have to send a purchase order to your business partner via EDI and also to another SAP system via ALE. In this case the output is the same, but the partners are different. Any number of business rules can be defined in an Access sequence.

Condition Tables

Condition tables specify the key fields for a business rule. If a business rule requires you to send EDI based on sales organization and customer, then the key for the business rule is Sales Organization (VKORG) and Customer Number (KNDNR). Thus a business rule is formulated by specifying the fields that are to be used in decision making, as shown in Figure 8-7. This key is used to access the Condition records for output values like output medium, partner function, partner number, language, and time for the message.

If the standard condition tables supplied in the system do not meet your Requirements, then new condition tables can be created. The keys for condition tables must be derived from the field catalog, which is a subset of the Communication structure. This added layer helps you to manage fields. You can select all the fields from the Communication structure in your field catalog.

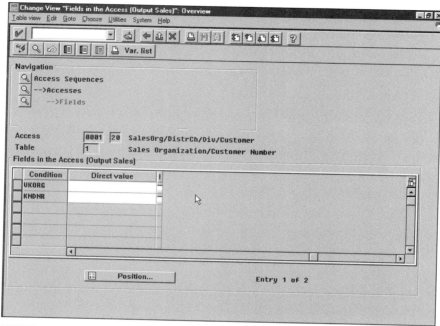

FIGURE 8-7

Key fields in a condition table

Condition Records

Condition records are inserted in the condition table. Condition records contain the actual data against which the business rules are checked to propose an output. Figure 8-8 shows that customer number is used as a rule to propose the output. A Condition record has two pieces:

- ◆ Key values of the business rule by which a Condition record is accessed. In Figure 8-8, customer number is the key value.

- ◆ Output values (output medium, language, partner function, partner number, and timing), as shown in Figure 8-8.

Condition records are considered master data and are maintained by customers. If you are using standard pieces of the Message control, then the only components that you need to create are Condition records and Message control parameters in the partner profile.

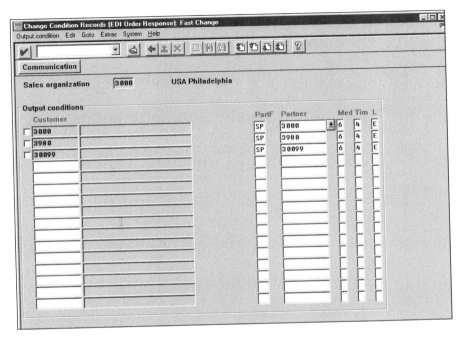

FIGURE 8-8

Condition records for a condition table

Processing Programs and Tables

Several programs and tables are part of the Message control. For EDI you will frequently deal with the following tables and programs:

- **NAST.** This table stores an entry for each Output type created for an application document.
- **TNAPR.** This table has an entry for the processing program used for an Output type.
- **RSNAST00.** This program is used to process entries in the NAST table.
- **RSNASTED.** This processing program exists for each output medium. EDI_PROCESSING is a routine in the RSNASTED program to process EDI outputs. The relationship between an Output type, output medium, and processing program is established in the TNAPR table.

Understanding How Message Control Works

Message control is a three-step process:

1. **Output proposal.** Message control checks various business rules and proposes various Output types.

2. **Output editing.** The user can accept or change the proposed Output types.

3. **Output processing.** The system processes the final list of Output types to produce the actual outputs.

The various components used in the process are shown in Figure 8-9 and the technical flow is described in Figure 8-10.

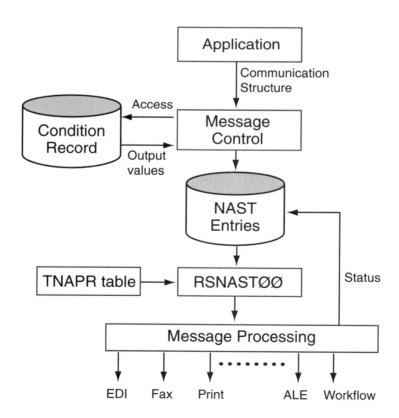

FIGURE 8-9

Components used in Message control to propose various outputs

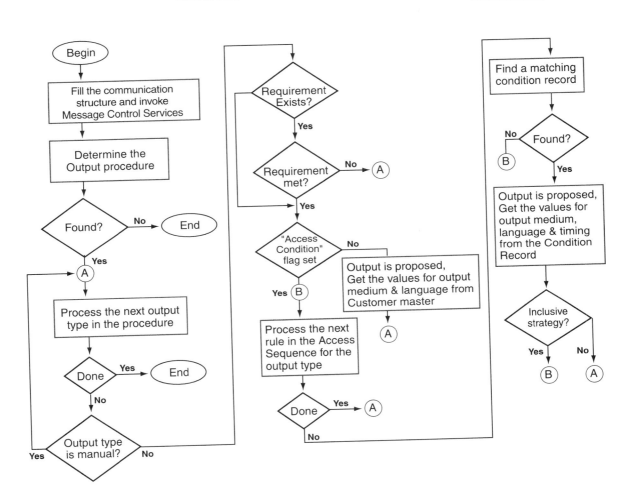

FIGURE 8-10

The process for proposing an output

Output Proposal

The process begins when an application document is created or changed. The application program fills the Communication structure with values from the application data entered on the screen. This Communication structure is passed to the Message control along with the Application ID and the Procedure.

The various Output types defined in a Procedure are processed one at a time. They are mutually independent, so results of one do not affect the other outputs.

An Output type marked as manual in a Procedure is not used for an automatic proposal. This output can only be selected manually by the end user. This approach can be important when you do not want an automatic proposal or when business rules are based on human intelligence and cannot be encapsulated in an ABAP/4 routine.

The processing of Output types that are not marked as manual is described here. If a Requirement is specified for an Output type in the Procedure, then the code behind the Requirement is executed to see whether the Output type meets the Requirements or preconditions. If Requirements are met, then further checking continues as described in the following steps. If the Output type does not meet the Requirements, then the next Output type in the list is processed. For example, a sales order response should not be sent out unless the sales order is complete. After parsing the list of Output types in a Procedure, the system "short lists" the Output types that meets the Requirements or preconditions.

In the case of Output types for the SD modules (sales, shipping, and billing), the system checks whether the Access Condition flag is set for an Output type. If the flag is not set, then the values for the output medium and timing for the Output type are determined from the customer master data. If the flag is selected, then processing continues for determining the output medium and timing as described next.

For each Output type in which the Access Condition flag is set, the Access sequence associated with the Output type is used to access various business rules and determine which of these business rules are satisfied. A business rule is satisfied if the application values passed in the Communication structure result in a Condition record being found using the keys of the business rule. The process is as follows:

◆ The first step is to validate any Requirements that may exist for a business rule. If the result is negative, then the current business rule is skipped and the next business rule in the sequence is checked.

◆ If a business rule passes the Requirement check or a Requirement is not specified, then the condition table for that business rule is accessed for any Condition records that match the application data passed in the Communication structures.

◆ If a match is found, then the values of the partner function, partner number, output medium, language, and timings are copied for that Output type and the Output type is considered as proposed.

◆ If the business rule uses exclusive strategy, then the process ends here and the whole processing starts from the very beginning for the next Output type.

◆ If an inclusive strategy is used, then the next business rule in the Access sequence is processed. The purpose of an inclusive strategy is to propose multiple outputs of the same type to different partners. Two instances of the same Output type cannot have identical output parameters.

TIP

You can display the logic used to evaluate the various outputs. From the output control screen, choose Goto, Determination Analysis from the menu to see the logic used.

Output Editing

After the output proposal process is complete, the list of proposed outputs is shown on the output control screen of an application, as shown in Figure 8-11. The output control screen is usually available at the header level but in some cases at other levels; for example, with sales orders it is available at the sales order header and at the sales order item level.

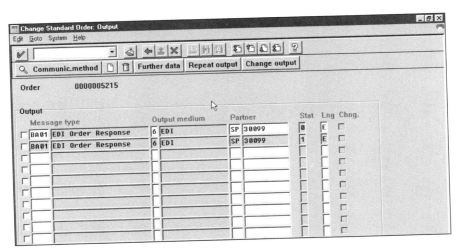

FIGURE 8-11

Output control screen showing the various outputs proposed for an application document

To reach the output control screen of an application, follow these steps:

1. Go to the application document that you are working with (sales order, purchase order, delivery, or billing document).

2. Look for Header, Output or Header, Messages on the menu, depending on the application area. At the line-item level, you can look for Item, Output.

The initial status of these outputs is 0 (not processed). The user entering the application document can carry out the following editing operations:

◆ Delete proposed outputs

◆ Change timing

◆ Select new outputs from the list. The same output cannot be listed twice in status 0.

◆ Copy a previously processed output for reprocessing.

If the output medium is 6 (EDI) for an output, then the partner number in the proposed output is validated against a partner profile entry. If an entry does not exist in the partner profile table, then you cannot save the output.

Output Processing

When the final selection of the outputs is complete, the application document can be saved. A record for each proposed output is saved in the NAST table with the following values:

◆ Application ID

◆ Application document key (prefixed with zeros if less than 10 characters)

◆ Output type

◆ Output medium

◆ Timing

◆ Status code with value 0 (not processed)

A complete list of fields in the NAST table can be seen via transaction SE11.

The RSNAST00 program processes entries in the NAST table. This program is started immediately for NAST entries whose timing is set to immediate. For other NAST entries, this program has to be scheduled. The selection list for this program allows you to specify various parameters.

After RSNAST00 selects a record for processing, it checks the TNAPR table for the processing program associated with an output medium. For EDI a standard routine, EDI_PROCESSING, exists in the RSNASTED program.

The EDI_PROCESSING routine reads the Message control record in the partner profile and determines the process code. The process code points to a function module. The function module has a standard interface for its input and output parameters. One of the input parameters is the NAST record. This function module then has all the information it needs to read the application document data and formats the document for the message to be generated, using the IDoc format. The output parameters of the function module are the IDoc data and the control record.

The EDI_PROCESSING program creates a physical IDoc from the data passed back to it from the function module. Then the IDoc is ready for the ALE service layer, where it goes through version change, filtering, and conversion, and is subsequently sent to the operating system through a file port. Refer to Chapter 3, "The Outbound EDI Process," for details on process flow using Message control.

TIP

The results of processing an Output type are logged in the system. To view the results, select the Output type from the output control screen and click on Goto, Processing Log.

Setting Up Standard Message Control

This section describes the steps for using the standard Message control component for an application document.The standard system ships with a complete suite of Message control components for each application. These components can be used as is, or they can be modified to suit your needs. If your objective is to use the standard components, then all you need to do is create Condition records to enable your application to use Message control. If you plan to build some of the components such as a new condition table, then you have to carry out some configuration steps as described in this section.

Creating Condition Records

Creating Condition records is specific to each application. You can reach the screen to create Condition records via the application menu or use transaction

NACE. The steps are as follows:

1. Execute NACE to display the various applications.

2. Choose the application that you're interested in and click on the Condition Record button.

3. Specify the Output type for which you want to create the Condition records.

4. Pick the business rule (condition table) for which you want to maintain the Condition records.

5. Enter values for the key fields and specify the output medium, output timing, partner number, and partner function for each record.

6. Save your entries.

Creating a New Condition Component

If the standard Message control functionality does not meet your requirements, you can build the necessary pieces in Message control. The following information explains how to create a new Condition type or business rule. These steps are intended to be a guideline; you will need to use the knowledge you've gained from previous sections to carry them out.

An area presented here sends out an order response via EDI for customer group 01 and sales organization 3000. Standard components are used wherever appropriate.In the analysis of the standard system, Output type BA01 is used for EDI output. It points to Access sequence 0003, which lacks a business rule based on customer group and sales organization. Therefore, a new business rule will be created and added to an access sequence.

The customer group number is available on the header portion of the sales order. An analysis of the existing condition table shows that there is no condition table based on the customer group and sales organization combination.The steps to build the components for the SD applications can be reached from the Area menu for SD Message control. The transaction is VOK2.

 NOTE

You don't need to extend the Communication structure if the customer group is a field in it. If a field does not exist in the Communication structure, you can extend the structure by appending user-defined fields. In such cases the customer-defined fields have to be filled in a user exit, defined for the Communication structure.

Field Catalog

Transaction: V/86

Menu path: From the Area menu for SD Message control, choose SD Document, Sales Document, Condition Table, Field Catalog.

Make sure the Customer Group field is selected in the field catalog. If it is not, insert the entry in the field catalog.

Create Condition Tables

Transaction: V/56

Menu path: From the Area menu for SD Message control, choose SD Document, Sales Document, Condition Table, Create

You establish the key for your business rule in this step. For the scenario, the key fields are Customer Group (KDGRP) and Sales Organization (VKORG).

Use table numbers 900 and above. Numbers lower than 900 are reserved for SAP. Enter a description for your business rule and select the sales organization field and the customer group field from the field catalog. After you create your condition table, you need to generate it so that it will be available for later steps.

Define New Requirements

You can create new requirements if necessary; the current scenario does not require this step. You can create new requirements by executing transaction VOFM.

Create Access Sequence

Transaction: V/48

Menu path: From the Area menu for SD Message control, choose SD Document, Sales Document, Access Sequence.

A new Access sequence does not have to be created, because you can modify the existing Access sequence 0003 being used in the Condition type BA01. Because the Access sequence can be used in several Output types, you should build a new Access sequence to avoid conflicts with other Output types.

You can begin by copying an existing Access sequence, or you can create a new sequence using the transaction specified above. Start your Access sequence with a

Z to distinguish it from the standard Access sequences.

Create Output Type

Transaction: V/30

Menu path: From the Area menu for SD Message control, choose SD Document, Sales Document, Condition Type

The new Access sequence can be assigned to BA01 (order response), or a new Output type can be created. If a new Output type is to be created, the best option is to copy BA01 as ZB01 (order response). Select BA01 and click on the Copy icon.

Add Output Type to a Procedure

Transaction: V/32

Menu path: From the Area menu for SD Message control, choose SD Document, Sales Document, Output Determination Procedure

If a new Output type was created in the previous step, then it needs to be added to the standard Procedure. You can also create a new Procedure to keep your entries separate from the SAP entries. The Procedure for sales order is V10000. To add an Output type to this Procedure, select Procedure V10000 and add an entry for the new Output type.

Assign Procedure at the Header Level

Transaction: V/43

Menu path: From the Area menu for SD Message control, choose SD Document, Sales Document, Assign, Header

Creating a new Procedure is generally not necessary, but if you decide to do so, then the new Procedure needs to be assigned to the application at the header level, using the preceding transaction. Select the order type and assign your newly created Procedure to it.

Create Condition Records

The last step is to maintain the Condition records for your newly created condition table. The steps are the same as described earlier in "How to Set Up Standard Message Control."

Building Message Control

Following are tips for building Message control:

◆ Two Area menu transactions are available for SD and MM Message control. The necessary configuration components for the respective modules can be reached from their Area menus. The other path is via the IMG. To reach the SD Message control maintenance, you can execute VOK2; to reach the MM Message control maintenance, you can execute VOK3.

◆ A Message control wizard is also available for building the various components for the Message control. The wizard walks you through the various steps using workflow. When you execute the NACE command, it asks whether you want to use the system in the expert mode or to use workflow.

Summary

The Message control module, through its various components, provides a great deal of flexibility and enables the application to generate and manage various Output types associated with it. You can use Message control to determine the timing and the medium of the output at run time. The various outputs can be generated conditionally depending on the business rules. Various business rules can be encapsulated in the Message control to meet business needs.

Each application is associated with a Procedure that defines the various Output types. These Output types are processed one at a time to determine whether they are valid for proposal. The proposed outputs can then be edited, and the edited outputs are saved in the NAST table. A program RSNAST00 processes each NAST entry and generates the output. The results are logged in the processing log.

In the standard Message control, several condition tables have been predefined. If the intent is to use the standard components, then all you need to do is create Condition records for using the Message control system. If your business needs cannot be met using the standard components, then you can enhance the Message control component accordingly.

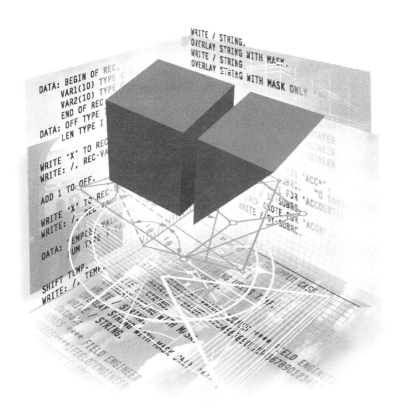

Chapter 9

Configuring Workflow

Workflow technology is a cross-application component used in various areas, including the ALE/EDI interface. I have found that Workflow is a big mystery for most ALE and EDI users. This chapter introduces the concept of workflow—what it is, how it is used in ALE/EDI, the various elements of the workflow module, and the configuration of various components used by the ALE/EDI interface. At the end of this chapter you should have a good handle on the workflow process.

The section on design tips at the end of the chapter contains various tips and techniques that you can use to handle everyday issues with ALE/EDI and workflow.

 NOTE

If you're interested in the bare minimum configuration required to enable the workflow for error handling in the standard system, you can go directly to "Setting Up Workflow for Exception Handling" later in this chapter.

Introduction to the Workflow Management System

This section provides a high-level overview of the workflow module. You'll learn about the basic theme behind workflow, why it was invented, what problems it solves, and how it's used in the ALE/EDI process.

Understanding the Workflow Management System

The workflow management system provides procedural automation of various steps in a business process. A formal definition has been prepared by the WFMC (Workflow Management Coalition), which is a nonprofit organization devoted to the development of workflow standards to ensure compatibility between various workflow software products. WFMC defines workflow as "the automation of a business process, in whole or part, during which documents, information, or tasks are passed from one participant to another for action, according to a set of procedural rules."

A business process can consist of several steps. Historically, the tasks have been coordinated manually or by some informal means of communication (sticky note, e-mail, shouting, and so on). The common problem in these approaches is inefficiency; each lacks a way to trace where a task is, who executed (or is executing) it, and how much time it required. In contrast, the workflow management system ensures that the right work is sent to the right person at the right time in the right sequence with the right information.

CAUTION

Workflow does not add any new business functionality when coordinating business processes! If a business function is not available in the system, then Workflow cannot execute it. Contrary to some companies' belief, workflow does not fill in gaps identified in a business process.

In the early days of workflow, it was mainly viewed as document management software, but recently the popularity of off-the-shelf ERP systems has blessed the use of workflow in managing everyday business processes. SAP embraces workflow as a cross-application technology for use in all modules. SAP provides a full development environment to model and implement your business process via workflow.

Workflow development can be viewed as a programming environment. The workflow development environment is a true object-oriented development environment. The basic component in workflow is a business object on which various operations are carried out. These operations are implemented as methods. BAPIs (Business Application Programming Interfaces) are special methods implemented in the business objects. Events, which are part of the business object, are triggered for changes in the state of the object, which can cause other processes to begin.

workflow uses the organization structure to determine the person responsible for executing a task. The organization structure is modeled by using the PD-ORG (Personnel Planning and Development) component of the HR (Human Resources) module.

Benefits of Using Workflow

From an operational perspective, workflow provides several benefits. With workflow the entire process is completely traceable and auditable. Some of the key benefits of using the workflow module follow.

- **Business process integration.** The actual time spent executing a task is far less than the time from when it becomes available for execution to the time it is completed. When a task is ready for execution, workflow eliminates unnecessary waiting by sending it directly to the right person to execute it.

- **Intelligent routing.** Tasks are often routed to the wrong person because the person who originally carried out the task is no longer with the company or has moved to another division. workflow has a built-in module to determine the right person for the job dynamically at run time. workflow takes into account the dynamics of the organization and ensures that the right person is notified.

- **Flexible task assignments.** Using workflow, you can set the person to be notified at a level that is more abstract than user ID. Assigning a task directly to a user has several disadvantages. The user may leave the company or change jobs. On the other hand, positions and jobs tend to be relatively stable. It is more likely that a user would leave a job than that a company would eliminate a job. Thus, if tasks are assigned to a position or a job, whomever holds that position in the company at any given time is assigned the task

- **Proactive approach.** The responsible person does not have to constantly look for problems. If a situation requires the user's attention, he or she is notified via a work item in his or her SAP Inbox. This system is also called active monitoring.

- **Substitution and backup facility.** Substitution and backup are built into the workflow system. You can assign a backup for each position on an as-needed basis. When the primary person for execution of a task is unavailable, work can be automatically routed to a backup.

- **Process monitoring capability.** Several tools are available in the workflow system to monitor the current state of a process and to determine workloads by users, positions, and so on.

◆ **Deadline monitoring.** Tasks in a business process can be assigned a time limit for completion. If the task is not completed within the time frame, someone else—such as the person's supervisor—can be notified.

◆ **Statistical analysis.** The monitoring tools also provide statistical information for fine-tuning the business process. You can identify bottlenecks in the process and take corrective measures.

Applications of Workflow in ALE/EDI

The ALE/EDI interface mainly uses workflow for exception (or error) handling. You can also use workflow for handling notifications in other areas.

Error Notification

Error notification is the primary use of workflow in the ALE/EDI interface. Figure 9-1 illustrates the process for error handling via workflow. When exceptions are raised in the outbound or the inbound process, workflow is started and a user responsible for handling the error receives a notification in his or her SAP Inbox. After the problem is analyzed and fixed, the process can be restarted from the Inbox. If the problem is severe enough to require the process to be restarted from the beginning, then the process in error can be purged to avoid any further processing.

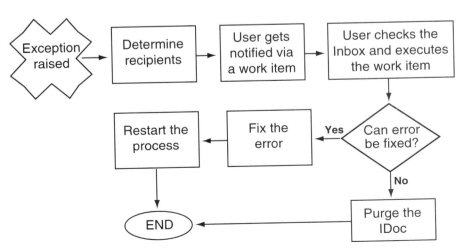

FIGURE 9-1

The error handling process using workflow

Errors are intelligently routed to the right person based on the type of error. Errors have been grouped into various categories. A person can be responsible for handling multiple types of errors or several users can be responsible for resolving a single type of error. The system can be configured in various ways to handle errors, depending on the size of your company. Technical details of the error notification process are described in "The Error Notification Process" and steps to configure workflow for error notification are described in "Setting Up Workflow for Error Notification" later in this chapter.

Active Monitoring

Active monitoring allows you to specify threshold values for the state of the system. If the system crosses the threshold limit, a person responsible for system problems can be notified. A threshold can be set on the number of IDocs in error or the time limit in which a process must complete. For example, you could have someone notified when the number of failed invoice IDocs in the system crosses 50. A complete set of options and how to set up the system for active monitoring is described in "Setting Up Active Monitoring" later in this chapter.

Rule-Based Inbound Flow

This application of workflow in ALE/EDI does not fall under the category of exception handling. Workflow can be set up to handle processing of an inbound IDoc. Figure 9-2 illustrates how workflow can be used to process an IDoc. Normally an inbound IDoc starts a function module that invokes the posting program to create an application document from the IDoc. In contrast, if a workflow is used, then it can be set up to do whatever is needed for your business process. SAP does not provide standard Workflows for the inbound ALE/EDI processes, but you can develop your own Workflows and tie them to the ALE/EDI process. Refer to Chapter 17, "Inbound via Workflow—Sales Order Changes," if you are interested in using workflow to process an incoming IDoc.

Consider the example of an inbound order change transaction that allows a customer to modify a previous order. Whether order changes are passed to the system with or without verification is a business issue. In such a situation, it may be essential to review the changes before allowing them to be posted. This step can be accomplished via workflow. An incoming order change IDoc can be routed via workflow to a person for review. If the changes requested by the customer are acceptable, then the IDoc can be posted. If the customer's changes are not acceptable, then the IDoc can be rejected and an IDoc can be generated to send a response to the customer.

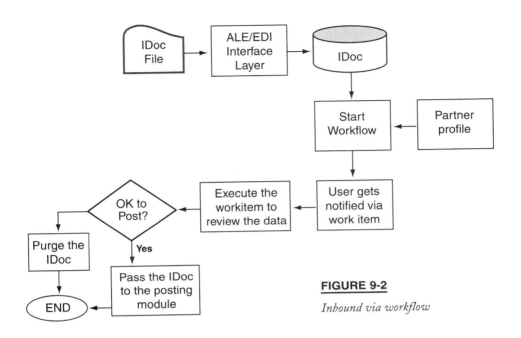

FIGURE 9-2

Inbound via workflow

As a simple example, the customer might request a change in the quantity or delivery date that is not acceptable, possibly because production has already started or because of the lead time required to procure material. The workflow system can also be designed to handle complex business processes.

Notification of Successful Posting

The system can notify a person of a successful posting of an IDoc. This feature can be useful when critical documents are posted in the system. Notification after successful posting is not used in the standard ALE/EDI processes, but the system provides hooks to achieve this functionality for custom scenarios without doing any ABAP/4 development. Refer to "Setting Up Notification of Successful Posting."

Architecture of ALE/EDI Workflow

This section describes the terminology and components of the workflow module as used in the ALE/EDI interface. This material is intended for readers who want detailed knowledge of how the workflow component works in ALE/EDI.

To understand the ALE/EDI workflow process, you'll need to learn the workflow terminology and the concept behind the various components. The components used in workflow fall into two categories: PD-ORG objects, and workflow objects, as shown in Figure 9-3. These components can be viewed and maintained by using standard transactions, which can be reached via the Area menu for workflow as described below:

Transaction: SWLD

Menu Path: From the Area menu for Workflow, choose Tools, Business Engineering, Business Workflow, Development

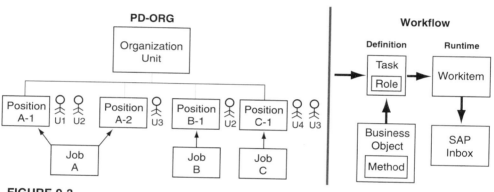

FIGURE 9-3

Objects used in the workflow process

PD Organization Objects

PD-ORG objects are used to represent the organization structure of a company in SAP. SAP provides several types of PD-ORG objects such as positions, jobs, organization units, and workcenters. These objects are assigned a one-character or two-character ID to represent the object type. In the following sections, you'll get a basic understanding of these objects, their significance, and how you can use them in building your organization structure. The type of object is shown in parenthesis wherever applicable.

Organizational Plans

An organizational plan represents the complete information about a company's organization structure. The main elements of an organizational plan are as follows:

◆ **Hierarchy among various organization units**. A company can have several organization units broken down by function. For example, a company can have several divisions such as engineering, manufacturing, and finance. A division could be broken down further. For example, a manufacturing division could contain several plants.

◆ **Various jobs performed in a company.** For example, purchasing clerk, sales order clerk, design engineer, programmer, secretary, and manager.

◆ **Various positions held by employees in the organization and the reporting structure.** For example, purchasing clerk for plant 1000, manager of the accounting department, and secretary to the CEO. The reporting structure or chain of command might be that the manager of the accounting department reports to the head of the finance division, and so on.

Organization Unit (O)

An organization unit is responsible for a specific function in a company. For example, an organization unit can represent a department, a physical location, a division, a subsidiary, or a project team. An organization unit can contain other organization units. Organization units are linked in a hierarchical fashion to form the entire organization structure. An EDI department is an example of an organization unit.

Jobs (C)

From a workflow perspective, jobs represent a flexible means of identifying a user responsible for handling errors. A job describes a set of tasks that are performed by a person holding a position to which that job is assigned. Although individual tasks can be assigned directly to a position, it is advisable to group tasks together in a job and to assign the job to the position. This approach helps in reducing the maintenance effort. EDI administrator, manager, secretary, and engineer are jobs. The job of an EDI administrator could be to handle all the technical errors associated with the EDI interface.

Positions (S)

From a workflow perspective, a position is another flexible means of finding a person responsible for handling errors. A position in a company represents a rank.

For example, a level 1 manager represents the first level of management. Positions are linked in hierarchical fashion to represent the chain of command in a company. A user is assigned to a position that represents his or her rank. If an employee is promoted, that person leaves his or her current position and is assigned to another position. Positions are thus more stable entities than are employees in a company. Positions are assigned jobs to represent the tasks performed by a position. Tasks can be assigned to a position directly or via jobs.

TIP

The system allows multiple users to hold a position or a single user to hold multiple positions. It is advisable to set up one person per position. Doing so eases the maintenance effort when a person changes positions or when a user is assigned to a vacant position. Sharing a position by multiple users also has a complicating affect on HR reporting of resource use.

Workcenter (A)

Workcenters represent a physical location where a set of activities is carried out. In the case of workflow, you can use workcenters to represent one or more groups in the EDI department.

Users (US)

A user is a person who has been granted access to the SAP system to use its various functions. A user in the system is identified by a user ID.

Workflow Objects

Workflow objects model a workflow process. Workflow objects are also assigned a two-character ID to represent the type of object. The following sections describe the various workflow objects used in an ALE/EDI process. The type of object is shown in parentheses wherever applicable.

Business Objects

Transaction: SWO1

Menu Path: From the Area menu of Workflow, choose Definition Tools,
Object Repository

A business object represents a business entity that has a definite state and various properties. You can carry out various functions on the object. A business object encapsulates the entire functionality of an object. A business object is given a name in SAP. For instance, a material is assigned the name BUS1001; it has various properties such as material number, description, and material type. These properties are represented using attributes of the business object. The various operations that can be carried out on an object are implemented with methods. For example, if you want to create a material, you can call that business object's Create method. An object also has different states. It exposes its various states by publishing events. For example, the material object has a created event that is published whenever a new material is created.

Several business objects are defined in the system and organized in the BOR (Business Object Repository). Objects are implemented as a series of inherited objects starting with a generic object to a very specific object. The various objects designed for the ALE/EDI process are as follows:

- ◆ **IDOC.** The IDOC object represents a generic IDoc. This object is not used directly in the process but provides a generic implementation of the various attributes and functions associated with an IDoc.

- ◆ **IDOCAPPL.** The IDOCAPPL object represents a generic application IDoc used in ALE and EDI. It is inherited from the IDOC object and acts as the main object from which application-specific objects are inherited. Most of the functions and attributes used in an IDoc are implemented in this object. The various components of the IDOCAPPL are shown in Figure 9-4.

- ◆ **IDOC<message_type>.** This object is derived from the IDOCAPPL object and represents an application-specific object. Although no additional functionality is added after inheriting the IDOCAPPL object, it is the application specific object that is referenced in the configuration tables.

- ◆ **IDOCPACKET.** This object represents a packet of IDocs.

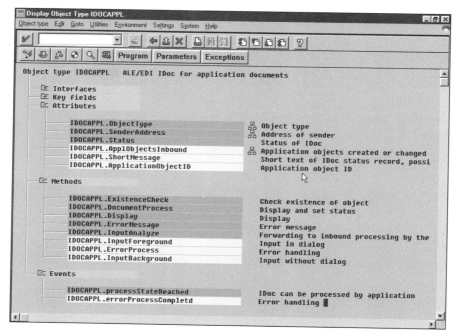

FIGURE 9-4

The attributes, methods, and events in the application IDOC object (IDOCAPPL)

◆ **IDPK\<message type\>.** This object represents a packet of specific types of IDocs. For example, IDPKORDERS represents a packet of IDoc orders. The IDPKORDERS object is inherited from IDOCPACKET.

Each IDoc-related object has several attributes, methods, and events. When a work item is executed, it executes one of the methods encapsulated in the object.

Tasks (T or TS)

Transaction: PFTC

Menu Path: From the Area menu of Workflow, choose Definition Tools, Tasks.

A task defines a piece of work that can be executed and tracked in the system. Technically, a task points to a method of an object, as shown in Figure 9-5. In addition, a task defines the text describing the purpose of the task, the triggering event based on which the task is started, the terminating event that marks the completion of a task, and a role that contains the rules to identify the person who is responsible for executing the task. A task can be started in response to an event triggered in the system.

Tasks are categorized as standard tasks (TS) or customer tasks (T). Standard tasks are provided by SAP and are client-independent, whereas customer tasks are client-dependent and developed by customers.

In the ALE/EDI process, tasks are mainly used for error handling. A task has been defined for every standard message and for each type of error in the process. The tasks for a message are named as <message type>_Error. The tasks for errors in the process are shown in Table 9-1.

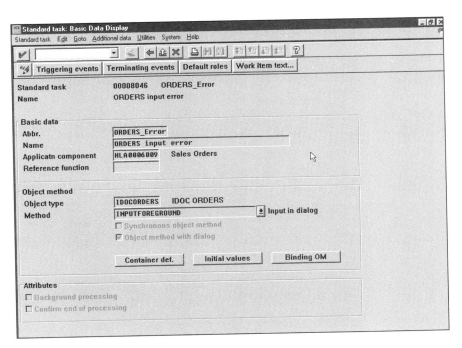

FIGURE 9-5

Standard task Orders_Error

Table 9-1 Error Tasks in the EDI Process

Process Code	Task Number	Description
EDIM	TS00007988	No IDoc created yet
EDIO	TS00007989	Error in the outbound process
EDIX	TS00008070	Syntax error—outbound
EDII	TS00008068	Error in the inbound process
EDIY	TS00008074	Syntax error—inbound
EDIS	TS30000078	Error in the subsystem

Customers can change the following attributes of a task:

◆ Work item text

◆ Triggering events

Roles

Transaction: PFAC

Menu Path: From the Area menu of Workflow, choose Definition Tools,
Standard Roles.

Roles are workflow objects used to determine the actual person responsible for
carrying out a specific task. Each task has a role assigned to it.

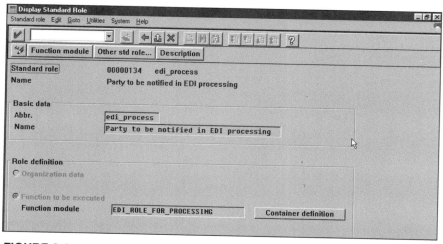

FIGURE 9-6

Standard Role for ALE/EDI errors

Roles for the ALE/EDI process are implemented as function modules in the system (see Figure 9-6). These function modules can read any information stored in the SAP system. The interface for these function modules is set by SAP. The return parameters of this function module are the object type and object ID.

Work Items

A work item represents an instance of a task that needs to be executed. A work item has text describing its purpose (see Figure 9-7) and can have various states that govern the operations allowed. The various states of a work item and its affect on the usability are described in Table 9-2.

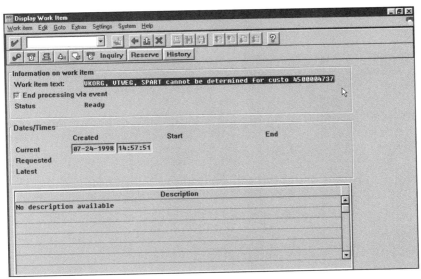

FIGURE 9-7

Work item describing the cause of an error in the ALE/EDI process

Table 9-2 Work Item States from Inception to Completion

Status	Description
Ready	Work item is created and is visible to all selected agents.
Reserved	Work item has been reserved by a user and disappears from other selected user's Inbox.
In Process	Work item is being worked on and can only be seen in the Inbox of user who started working on it
Completed	Work item is complete and cannot be seen in the Inbox of any user.

SAP Inbox

Transaction: SO01

Menu Path: From the Main menu, choose Office, Inbox.

The SAP Inbox is an interface to manage work items and SAP office documents. Figure 9-8 shows a list of work items in a user's Inbox. It can be compared to the Inbox of regular e-mail systems that you use at work. The SAP Inbox contains separate buckets for office documents and work items. Office documents are the e-mail documents, whereas work items are workflow items. The work items can be displayed and executed from the Inbox. The Inbox interface is highly configurable.

A detailed description of the SAP Inbox appears in Chapter 11, "Monitoring the Interface," as part of the discussion on monitoring tools.

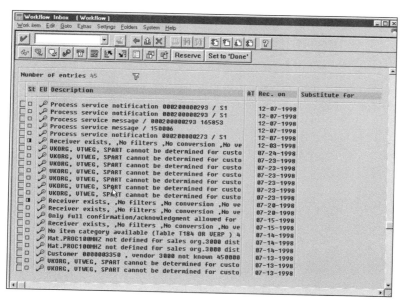

FIGURE 9-8

Worklist in the SAP Inbox

Understanding the Error Notification Process

This section describes how the various workflow components are used in the error notification process to inform the right person about an error situation and how this person gets the right information to execute the process in a timely fashion. Errors can be encountered at various points in the inbound as well as the outbound process. Errors are routed to responsible agents (also called selected agents) via workflow. The selected agents find a work item in their Inbox. The work items can be executed to examine the details of the error. After the problem is fixed, the process can be restarted from the point of failure.

The error notification process comprises the following steps:

1. Determining the task to be started
2. Routing the error to a responsible agent as a work item
3. The responsible agent processes the work item

Determining the Task

Errors are classified into categories, depending on the type. A task is started in response to an error. The error-handling process for each type of error is unique and defined in a task via the method that gets executed. A role is also defined for each task to identify the person responsible for it. The following sections describe the error categories.

General Errors (EDIM—TS00007988)

General errors are encountered in the process before an IDoc is created. In the inbound process, these errors are related to reading or deleting the IDoc file at the OS level or to any internal errors in processing an incoming IDoc file. In the outbound process, these errors are related to processing an output type from the NAST record. If the object specified in the NAST record cannot be found, then the error is classified as a technical error.

This task (TS00007988) is initiated by the system. The EDI administrator specified in the EDIADMIN table is notified.

Syntax Errors During Inbound Processing (EDIY—TS00008074)

After an inbound IDoc has been created successfully in the system, the IDoc goes through a syntax check. When syntax errors are found in an incoming IDoc, they are logged in the IDoc with a status code of 60 (Error during syntax check—

inbound). Syntax errors usually occur during testing; frequent syntax errors in a live system suggest a lack of testing. Refer to "Syntax Rules for IDocs" in Chapter 30, "IDocs on the Inside," for syntax rules checked in an IDoc.

This task (TS00008074) is initiated by the system. The person identified in the partner profile for the IDoc message is notified.

Errors in the Inbound ALE/EDI Interface (EDII—TS00008068)

Errors other than syntax errors can occur from the point at which a physical IDoc is created in the system to the point at which the IDoc is delivered to the application posting program. These errors are mainly due to configuration problems in the partner profile or to information passed in the control record that does not find a matching partner profile. These errors are logged with a status code of 56 (IDoc with errors added).

This task (TS00008068) is initiated by the system. The person identified in the General view of the partner profile is notified. If a partner profile cannot be read at all, then the EDI administrator is notified.

Errors in the Application Posting Program

After an IDoc is passed to the posting program, errors reported by the posting program are considered application errors. These are logged in the IDoc with a status code of 51 (Application document not posted). Such errors are usually related to data in the IDoc and are among the most common errors seen on an inbound process.

A standard task exists for each incoming message. The naming convention is <message type>_Errors. These tasks are initiated as a result of an error event (InputErrorOccurred) triggered by the system on the application IDoc object. The person identified in the Inbound view of the partner profile for that message is notified. For example, the task for incoming orders is Orders_Error (TS00008046). This task is started when the InputErrorOccurred event is raised on object IDOCORDERS. The linkage between an event and the task can be seen in the event linkage table using transaction SWE2.

Syntax Errors during Outbound Processing (EDIX—TS00008070)

After an outbound IDoc has been created successfully in the system, the IDoc goes through a syntax check. This task is started for syntax errors found on an outbound IDoc. Errors are logged in the IDoc with a status code of 26 (Error during syntax check—outbound). This error usually occurs during testing, and frequent syntax errors in a live system suggest lack of testing.

This task (TS00008070) is initiated by the system. The person identified in the partner profile for the IDoc message is notified.

Errors in the Outbound ALE/EDI Interface (EDIO—TS00007989)

Errors other than syntax errors can occur from the point at which a physical IDoc is created in the system to the point at which the IDoc is delivered to the EDI subsystem. These errors are mainly due to configuration problems in the partner profile or occur when receivers for a message cannot be determined. These errors are logged with a status code of 29 (Error in ALE service).

This task (TS00007989) is initiated by the system. The person identified in the General view of the partner profile is notified. If a partner profile cannot be read at all, then the EDI administrator is notified.

Errors in the Subsystem (EDIS—TS30000078)

This error is only relevant for outbound IDocs. When an IDoc leaves the SAP system and is transferred to the subsystem, errors encountered in the subsystem or processes thereafter are reported to SAP. These errors start a workflow that sends a notification to the EDI administrator.

This task (TS30000078) is also started by the system. The person identified in the General view of the partner profile is notified. If a partner profile cannot be read at all, then the EDI administrator is notified.

Routing to a Responsible Agent As a Work Item

After an error has been classified into one of the above categories, the task associated with the error is started. The user responsible for the task is determined via the role defined at the task level. A work item is created for the task and sent to the person identified using in the role.

The workflow concept behind resolving a person responsible for an error is interesting. The system defines various types of agents, and each type has a specific objective. When you work in the workflow module, you may have trouble at first figuring out who gets notified, why work items seem to disappear automatically, why sometimes everyone in the SAP system receives a work item in his or her Inbox, what happens if a person does not exist, and so on.

Possible Agents vs. Selected Agents vs. Actual Agents

A task has three types of agents: possible agents, selected agents, and the actual agent (see Figure 9-9). Possible agents represent persons who can possibly execute a task. Not all the possible agents get a work item when a task is started.

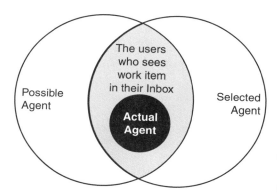

FIGURE 9-9

Various agents applicable to a work item in Workflow

Possible agents are configured in the system by assigning a task to several HR objects (job, position, organization unit, and so on). A task can be set to General Task, which means it can be executed by anyone. If you define a task as a General Task you do not need to assign a task specifically to an HR object.

CAUTION

Setting a task as a General Task is useful if the possible agents cannot be identified any other way. The only drawback is that workflow sends a work item to possible agents if it cannot determine selected agents, meaning everyone in the SAP system will get a work item in their Inbox. Such a situation indicates that the EDI administrator field in the EDIADMIN table is not set up correctly.

Selected agents are the users who actually get a work item in their Inbox. Selected agents are determined by the role resolution logic. Selected agents must be a subset of possible agents. If the selected agents are not a subset of possible agents, then the status of the work item is set to Error and the work item is routed to the workflow administrator.

If the selected agents cannot be found, then the work item is sent to all possible agents. In the ALE/EDI process, the selected agents are configured in the partner profile and the EDIADMIN table.

The actual agent is the person who actually executes the work item from the Inbox. A work item can have several selected agents, but only one actual agent. When a selected agent executes a work item, the actual agent for the work item is established and the work item immediately disappears from the Inbox of other selected agents. However, if an actual agent realizes that he or she cannot resolve the problem, the user can replace the work item, causing it to reappear in the selected agent's Inbox.

Agents in the ALE/EDI Process

In Chapters 6 and 7 you were introduced to four placeholders (EDIADMIN table, General view of Partner profile, Inbound view of Partner profile, and Outbound view of Partner profile) where you can specify the agent responsible for handling errors in the ALE/EDI process. This section summarizes what happens when a specific agent is notified. The agent for each type of task was described in the task categories earlier. The EDIM and the EDIS categories of errors are reported directly to the EDI administrator. The remaining errors, EDIX, EDIY, EDIO, and EDII, have three levels of support for reporting the error (see Figure 9-10).

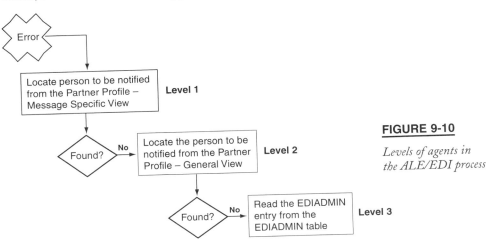

FIGURE 9-10

Levels of agents in the ALE/EDI process

◆ **Level 1.** If a partner profile is located for that problem, then the organization object specified at the message level (inbound or outbound) in the partner profile is notified.

◆ **Level 2.** If level 1 cannot be identified because of a problem in locating the record, then the level 2 organization object specified in the General view of the partner profile is read.

◆ **Level 3.** If neither level 1 nor level 2 can be identified, then the system reads the EDIADMIN table for the EDI administrator and sends a notification.

Processing by the Responsible Agent

A selected agent can access the work items from the Inbox. Executing a work item establishes the actual agent of the work item and causes it to disappear from the view of other selected agents. After the work item has been processed completely, it also disappears from the actual agent's Inbox. The steps necessary to fix an error for which a work item is generated are as follows:

1. Execute work item to display the error. Examples of errors include problems in the control record, errors in the IDoc data, and incorrect configuration.

2. The cause of the problem can usually be determined from the error message. If applicable, additional error information is also available for certain types of errors (for example, application errors).

3. After the cause of the problem has been determined, it must be fixed outside of workflow (or in some cases within workflow). The recovery procedure depends on the nature of the problem:

    ◆ If the error is in the IDoc data, the IDoc can be edited and then reprocessed from workflow.

    ◆ If the error requires restarting the process from the beginning, then the IDoc has to be marked for deletion to stop it from further processing and to clear the work item from the Inbox.

    ◆ If the error involves an IDoc that has not been created yet, then the work item merely informs the person about the error. The work item is deleted when the user exits the display screen. In some cases the user is prompted to acknowledge that he or she has completed the processing. For such cases the work item stays in the user's Inbox until the user acknowledges that processing is complete.

Setting Up Workflow for Error Notification

Although the workflow component seems very intricate and involves several components, don't worry. Most of the components and configuration for the standard components have already been done in the standard system. You do need to carry out steps that cannot be supplied by SAP, for example, the organization structure and identifying the users responsible for error handling. The workflow settings that you need to be aware of are described below.

Basic Workflow Settings

`Transaction: SWU3`

`Menu Path: From the IMG, choose Basis, Workflow, Basic Workflow Settings.`

Before any workflow configuration can begin, a set of basic workflow settings must be maintained in the system. If you have a workflow team, these settings are probably already done for you; otherwise the Basis team can help you with them. If an application is using the workflow module for the first time these settings will most likely be missing. The steps to carry out the Basic workflow settings are not in the scope of ALE/EDI settings, but you'll need to verify that these settings are maintained. These settings establish a basic infrastructure for the various workflow components.

At the bottom of the screen there are two set of lights: one for the definition components and one for the runtime components of workflow. A green light indicates that all the necessary settings are correct. However, a red light does not necessarily mean that workflow will not work; that depends on the item that is not configured correctly. You can use the Autocustomizing button, but you must be logged on with the highest authorization level. A Basis person is usually the best person to execute Autocustomizing because his or her ID should have all possible authorizations.

Setting Up the EDI Organization Unit

As a person responsible for ALE/EDI customizing, you are responsible for either maintaining the organization unit for the ALE/EDI department or providing your input to the HR group that maintains the PD-ORG. You must first develop a strategy for your ALE/EDI organization and then carry out the steps to enter the information in the system.

Developing a Strategy

Your objective is to design the organization structure so that the right person is notified and the workload can be managed efficiently. The following steps will help you build a strategy:

♦ Develop a list of messages that are being used in the ALE/EDI process. Identify the tasks associated with each message.

♦ Develop a list of users who will handle application errors for each of the identified messages. When selecting a user, make sure you select a business person and not a technical person, because most errors that occur during production are data related and business people are the best equipped to fix data errors.

♦ Identify a key technical person who will handle technical problems with the interface. This person becomes the EDI administrator; he or she does not need detailed functional knowledge.

♦ Identify the number of positions that will be required to handle the ALE/EDI process. This number depends on the complexity of the organization, number of EDI messages, and volume of EDI transactions. It is usually best to define a position for each business function; for example, one position can handle all messages related to the purchasing cycle, and another position can handle messages related to invoicing. Your organization may require one person per message type.

♦ Identify backups for each user.

After the various objects such as positions, tasks, and users are identified, you can start building the PD-ORG for the EDI group.

Building an Organization Unit

Transaction: PPOC

Menu Path: From the Area menu of Workflow, choose Definition Tools, Organization Plan, Create.

The organization unit can be maintained via the Simple maintenance tool or the Detail maintenance transactions. The Simple maintenance tool was specifically designed for workflow users. It's easy to use and provides a visual perspective of the organization structure in a tree format. The various objects are color coded to differentiate one from another. Although the Simple maintenance tool is easy to use and intuitive, it doesn't provide all of the functions available in the PD-ORG; therefore, you may need to maintain certain components and relationships via the Detailed maintenance tool.

To build an organization unit, follow these steps:

1. Start the simple maintenance tool by using transaction PPOC.

2. Assign an abbreviation and name to your organization unit and click on the Create button.

3. Double-click on the name of the organization unit to get to an area where you can create positions and assign users.

4. Create the various positions as required. You can leave the job description blank for now. Assign an abbreviation to the position and give it a meaningful name. Repeat this step for all positions identified earlier.

5. Assign users to these positions. Click on the position and then click on the Assign Holder button. You can now enter a user ID. Repeat this step for all positions.

Your organization unit is now complete. Figure 9-11 shows what an organization unit consisting of a position for the EDI administrator and several positions for the application areas may look like. Your organization structure might be totally different.

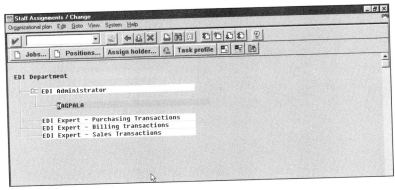

FIGURE 9-11

An EDI organization unit

Assigning a Task Profile

As discussed in the previous section, it is important to define the possible agents for each error task that will be used in the ALE/EDI process. To do so, you'll need to assign the task to various positions that can possibly execute it. Keep in mind that the possible agents are not necessarily the selected agents. You can adopt either of the following strategies for assigning the possible agents to a task:

◆ Possible agents = Everyone

◆ Possible agents = Certain positions only

In the first case, you simply need to specify the task as a General Task, which means that anyone can execute it. This technique can be used for ALE/EDI messages. The only drawback is that if the workflow system cannot determine selected agents for a task it will send the work item to all possible agents. In such a case, every user of the system sees this work item in his or her Inbox until one person elects to execute it. However, the chances of this particular situation occurring in the production system are slim because it implies an incorrect ALE/EDI configuration, or that a user has been deleted from his or her position. Therefore, in most cases the General Task assignment is the best approach. The steps are as follows:

Transaction: PFTC

Menu Path: From the Area menu of Workflow, choose Definition Tools, Tasks.

1. Enter the task number. Click on Display.
2. From the menu, choose Additional Data, Agent Assignment, Maintain. Click on the task and press the General Task button. Check the General Task check box and save the values.

In the second strategy for assigning agents, you specifically assign each task to a set of positions that you have identified. The steps are as follows:

Transaction: PFTC

Menu Path: From the Area menu of Workflow, choose Definition Tools, Tasks.

1. Enter the task number. Click on Display.
2. From the menu, choose Additional Data, Agent Assignment, Maintain.
3. Click on the task and click on the Create button. Select the Position radio button and then enter the position number. You can repeat this step for all positions that are to be assigned to this task.

NOTE

You can also use the simple maintenance tool to create the task profile. To use this method, you start at the position level and assign all the tasks for a position.

Setting Up Active Monitoring

Active monitoring sends a work item when the state of the system exceeds a predefined threshold state. For example, if the number of error IDocs for invoices exceeds 100, then you can have the system send a work item to a user or position.

SAP provides a report program RSEIDOCM that you can schedule to run on regular intervals or execute online. The selection parameters for this report allow you to specify the threshold values and the person to be notified (see Figure 9-12). You can restrict the report by IDoc type, groups of messages, and several other parameters. The system starts a single-step task (TS30200088) when it exceeds the defined threshold.

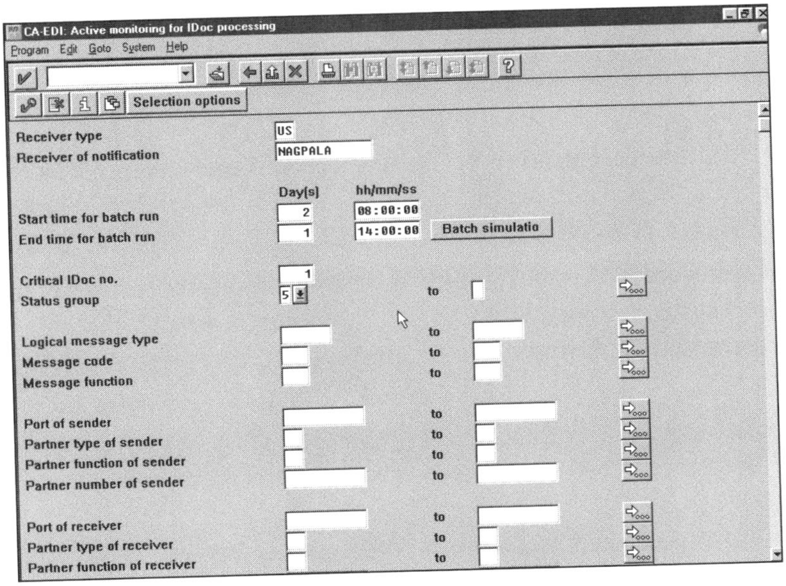

FIGURE 9-12

Selection parameters for the active monitoring report

Follow these steps to run the report online:

1. Create a task profile. Like any other task, you need to define the possible agents for the task (TS30200088). You can use the two strategies discussed in the previous section: making the task a General Task, or specifically assigning the task to certain positions, jobs, or organization units.

2. Execute the report (RSEIDOCM) by using transaction SE38. Refer to Figure 9-12 for the selection parameters.

3. Specify the responsible PD-ORG object on the selection screen. This object could be a user, position, job, or an organization unit.

4. Define threshold values. The selection parameters allow you to specify threshold values. Most of the parameters on the selection list are self-explanatory. The following parameters may need some explanation:

   ◆ **Status group.** The various status codes associated with an IDoc have been categorized in status groups. This arrangement allows you to monitor the state based on a status group. For example, group 5 represents errors in the IDoc interface for outbound IDocs. The various status codes in this group are 02, 20, 21, 26, 27, 29, and 34. You can see the grouping in table TEDS3.

   ◆ **Critical IDoc no.** The value in this field specifies the threshold value that is checked for sending a work item. If the state of the system exceeds this value, a work item is sent.

   ◆ **Start time for batch run.** From the current date and time, specify the number of days, hours, minutes, and seconds in the past from which the run should be executed.

   ◆ **End time for batch run.** From the current date and time, specify the number of days, hours, minutes, and seconds up to which the run should be executed. This value should be less than the start date.

Click on the Execute button to start the report. If the system state exceeds the threshold, then the person specified in the report will receive a work item. Executing the work item generates the IDoc statistics report, and you can drill down to see a list of IDocs that were selected.

Setting Up an Inbound Process via Workflow

Transaction: WE42

Menu Path: From the Area menu of EDI, choose Control Inb. Process Code, Inbound with ALE Service, Processing by Task

In the standard system, the inbound process is implemented as a function module that calls a posting program for an IDoc. The standard system can be configured to start a workflow or a single-step task for an incoming IDoc. This approach of using a workflow or a single step task can be useful when you want someone to review the IDoc data before it's posted in the system. For example, you can use this approach for incoming sales order change transactions to review changes to quantity and delivery dates before they are applied.

The steps to process an incoming IDoc via single step task or workflow are as follows:

1. Identify a standard task, a customer task, or a workflow that needs to be started. In the standard system, none of the processes are configured for starting a task or a workflow for inbound. You have to develop a custom workflow to implement your business process.

2. Create a new process code and point the process code to the new workflow by using transaction WE42.

3. In the partner profile for the inbound message, make sure the inbound message uses the new process code.

Setting Up Notification of Successful Posting

The ALE/EDI interface can be set up to raise an event when an IDoc posts successfully. This option is provided in the settings for an inbound process code. You can attach a single-step task or a workflow to be started when the event is raised.

Follow these steps to set up notification of successful posting:

1. Identify the application object that is created by the IDoc. You can view the setting in table EDIFCT, or execute transaction SALE and select Extensions, Inbound, Allocate function module to logical message. A link is defined between a message, a business object, and the function module.

2. Identify the event in the application object that needs to be raised.

3. Execute transaction BD67, select the process code used for the inbound process, and go to the details. In the application object, enter values for the Object Type and Start Event fields as identified in step 2.

4. Identify an existing task or create a new task or a workflow that should be started based on the event.

5. Define the event linkage between the event and the workflow. This step can also be performed from the task itself by activating the triggering event.

Setting Up Advanced Workflow

The simple organization unit described above will get you started, and you'll soon see the workflow system sending each error notification to the right person. In the long run, though, you'll need to understand some advanced workflow concepts. This section addresses some of the common issues faced with the workflow process and proposes some techniques and solutions to address resulting problems.

Setting Up Backups

From a security point of view, workflow acts very much like an e-mail system. If a work item is not meant for you, then you cannot see or execute it. In the real world you'll need some way of assigning the responsibility of fixing errors to multiple people, or an ability to define backups for various reasons:

- The workload is too much for a single person.
- The person who normally handles the problem has called in sick.
- The person who normally handles the problem is on vacation.

Multiple Users to a Position

The first solution is to use a position as the organization object to which errors are directed. You can assign multiple users to a position so that all users assigned to the specified position receive a work item in their Inbox. The users can examine the work item by looking at the description and decide whether to start processing. As soon as someone starts processing a work item, it disappears from all other Inboxes. This step automatically resolves issues two and three listed above.

Assigning multiple users usually works, but some organizations have rules requiring one user to each position. Or you simply might not want to assign multiple users to a position because doing so doesn't enforce any rules for a specific user to process the work items. In such cases, you can use the substitution capability.

Substitution by User

Substitution is the capability to designate another position as a backup to execute your work items. The process has to be initiated by the person who wants to assign someone else as his or her substitute.

Assume that John and Mary are in the EDI department. When John is away, Mary will handle all the EDI problems that are normally routed to John. To define a substitute, John has to initiate the process from his Inbox. The steps are as follows (assume you are John):

1. Go to Office, Inbox.
2. Choose Extras, Substitute.
3. Click on the Create Substitute button.
4. Enter the user ID of the person who will substitute for you and enter the date(s) on which you'll be gone in the validation period.

If John sets the substitute option correctly, Mary can log on to the system with her ID and select John's work item as follows (assume that you are Mary):

1. Go to Office, Inbox.
2. Select Extras, Substitute For.
3. From the list of users who have assigned you as the backup, click on John. You should see John's work items.

The rightmost column in the worklist has the name of the person for whom you are substituting.

Substitution by the System Administrator

What if John had to leave town on very short notice and did not get a chance to set the substitute? In this situation the system administrator can set a substitute in the HR module. Typically, the manager of the EDI department can be given authorization to execute this transaction. The steps are as follows:

1. Execute transaction PO13. From the menu, choose Human Resources, Planning, Organization, Detail Maintenance, Position.

2. Enter the position of the person who needs a substitute. Click on Relationship and the Active check box. Click on the Create button.

3. Use A255 in the Type of Relationship field. Enter S for the Type of Related Object and enter the position of the user who will be the substitute in the ID of the Related Object field. Save your entry to define the substitute.

Executing Subordinate and Peer Work Items

The ability to see and execute work items of subordinates and peers can be useful for managers and peers. In certain situations a manager may want to view the work items of their subordinates, or a person may need to share the load of their peers and should be allowed to process specific peers' work items on an as-needed basis.

This setup requires some detailed knowledge of evaluation paths in the HR module. An evaluation path defines an access path to navigate from one organization object to another.

The setup consists of the following steps:

1. Define an evaluation path that starts at the user level and ends in a position or a user ID. Use transaction OOAW.

2. Create a view using transaction SWLV and assign it the evaluation path created in step 1.

3. Go to Inbox, Select Extras, Choose View. The name of the view you created in the last step is displayed. At the prompt, select the organization object whose work items you want to see. Click on the Select button to see the worklist in your Inbox.

Connecting the SAP Inbox to a MAPI-Based E-mail Client

When using workflow you may want to receive work items through your company's regular e-mail system. The ability to do so is useful to infrequent users of the system who don't want to log on to the SAP system and view their work items on a daily basis. These users can view their work items via regular e-mail system if the e-mail system is MAPI compliant.

SAP Labs, a subsidiary of SAP AG, has developed a MAPI connector to link the SAP Inbox to a MAPI-based client such as Microsoft Outlook or Exchange. The free connector can be downloaded from the SAP Labs Web site (**www.saplabs.com**). Instructions on how to install the product are included.

During the installation process, the system records the SAP server name, client number, user ID, and password for the SAP system. This information is used to automatically log on to the system to retrieve work items into the e-mail client on a periodic basis.

After the software is installed, a new folder for SAP is created in the e-mail client Inbox. You can click on this folder to view the work items. There are no settings to be made on the SAP system. Work items continue to reside in the SAP system as well. When a work item is executed, the system automatically logs on to the SAP system and takes you to the screen you normally use when you execute a work item from the SAP Inbox.

NOTE

Use of MAPI connector does not prohibit you from executing the work items directly from the SAP Inbox.

TIP

In large organizations it's a huge undertaking to install and maintain new software on every PC. Therefore, organizations are often reluctant to use this tool. As an alternative, corporations use SAP server to e-mail server connections. At present there is an Exchange connector available from SAP to link Microsoft Exchange server with the SAP server. This will allow you to receive an e-mail in your regular e-mail system telling you that you have a work item in SAP. You must apply note number 131795 for this process to work.

Using Tips and Techniques

The following tricks and tips can help you in certain situations.

Changing Work Item Text

The work item text that appears in the user's Inbox can be customized to the needs of your users. This modification is considered a customizing change and will be supported on upgrade. The text can be changed as follows:

1. Go to the task for which the text needs to be modified.
2. Click on the Workitem Text button.
3. Choose Display->Expand button.
4. Change the text to suit your needs. The text can include substitution parameters from the workflow container fields. Put an ampersand in the text and click on the Assign Cont. Elements button to select parameters from the container.

Using Workcenters Instead of Organization Units

Using workcenters instead of organization units is an interesting business scenario. For example, a client was implementing the HR module and enforced the following rules:

◆ Single user to a single position.

◆ EDI functional users were already assigned to a position in their respective organization units.

The problem was that EDI group was not allowed to create additional organization units but wanted multiple users to be able to receive the same notification.

The solution was to create a workcenter for each functional area. For example, workcenters were created for the purchasing group, sales group, and FI group. The positions held by users in their respective organizations were each assigned to a workcenter. The workcenter was used in the partner profile as the party to be notified. This technique provided a clean solution without interfering with the required HR functionality.

Summary

In this chapter you saw the various applications of the workflow module in the ALE/EDI process. The biggest application of the workflow module is exception handling. Errors are intelligently routed to a user, job, position, or organization unit. The workflow module uses the PD-ORG component of the HR module to determine users from positions or jobs. Within the ALE/EDI process, the workflow module has several other applications, for example, processing incoming IDocs and actively monitoring the state of the system.

Solutions to some of the everyday problems of backups and substitutes are designed into the workflow module. Work items can be transferred to your company's e-mail system as long as it is MAPI compliant.

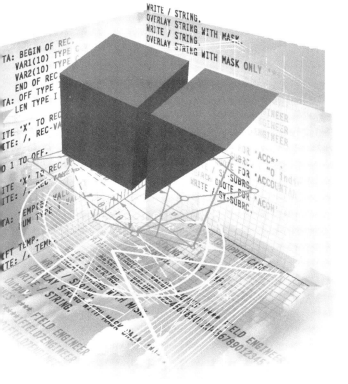

PART

Operating and Administering the EDI Interface

4

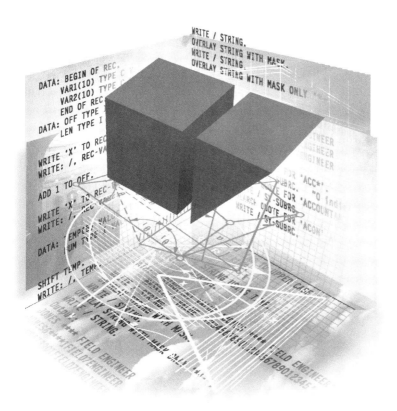

Chapter 10

Testing the EDI Interface

After you have completed all the necessary steps to configure the EDI interface, you need to test each component to make sure the configuration settings work as desired. This chapter introduces the utilities and techniques used in testing an inbound and an outbound EDI process. The standard system provides several utilities and tools, and every release includes both new tools and enhancements to existing tools. If you are working with a release of less than 3.1G, then some of the inbound tools mentioned here may not be available to you.

TIP

In designing the test utilities, SAP assumes that a subsystem may not be installed at the time of testing.

You want to make sure that all the steps of EDI configuration have been carried out correctly. If you developed some of the components of the EDI interface from scratch to meet your business needs (for example, Message control, IDoc structure, or IDoc programs) testing each individual piece thoroughly before deploying it in production is especially important.

This chapter describes the various tests for the outbound and the inbound processes. The following items are mentioned for each test wherever appropriate:

◆ Steps to carry out the task

◆ Where to look for problems

◆ Possible causes of the problem(s) (to help debug)

◆ How to verify the successful execution of the test

The focus of this chapter is on the testing methods and techniques. On several occasions you will need to refer to Chapter 11, "Monitoring the Interface," for details on the various monitoring tools, and to Chapter 12, "EDI Process Troubleshooting and Recovery," for details on the troubleshooting process.

Testing the Outbound Process

The outbound process is relatively simple to test and requires the least simulation because the process originates in SAP and all the major components reside in

SAP. The best approach for testing an outbound process is to first test each component and then the whole process. Descriptions of the utilities available for testing and complete details of testing each component follow.

Types of Test Utilities

SAP provides two types of test utilities:

- Utilities for a sanity test
- Utilities to test the process

The first type performs a basic sanity test on the configuration of EDI objects such as partner profile, port definition, and RFC destination parameters. A sanity test allows you to test a component without executing the actual process. For example, you do not need to execute the purchase order process to test the accuracy of settings in the partner profile. These utilities are accessed from within the maintenance screens of the objects.

The outbound process can be tested using the actual components that are involved in the process. The only piece that can be missing is the subsystem. A utility in the standard system simulates the functionality of the subsystem, which is to report the status of the process to the SAP system. This utility is described in "Testing the Steps in an Outbound Process" later in this chapter.

Prerequisites for Testing an Outbound Process

The outbound process is composed of various programs that are linked to run one after another. To test each component separately, you have to make the following settings to ensure that the components are disconnected from each other and do not start the next process immediately.

- If your application uses Message control, then the timing of the output type should be set to 1 (Run with the next selection of RSNAST00) in the condition records. This setting causes the RSNAST00 program to not run immediately after creating an entry in the NAST table.
- In the partner profile, set the Collect IDocs flag and the Do Not Start the Subsystem flag. These settings cause the RSEOUT00 program to not run immediately after an IDoc is created in the system.

Performing a Sanity Test of the Configuration

This section describes the basic sanity tests available for individual objects such as partner profile, RFC destination, and Port definition. Sanity tests check for the validity of various attributes in the objects without executing the process. Although you may have carried out some of these tests while configuring the various components, the tests are mentioned here with complete details.

Testing the Partner Profile

Partner profiles can be checked to make sure the parameters specified are still correct. The following checks are carried out:

- Process code
- User to be notified
- Message control consistency with outbound parameters

You can execute the program RSECHK07 to check the consistency of Partner profiles. You can execute this program via transaction SE38 or from the menus of the initial Partner profile screen. The output is a color-coded report that shows the details of any problems that were found.

Although a check is carried out when the partners are created, some of the parameters can become invalid over time. For example, if a user ID was specified in the Partner profile that no longer exists, this report flags the invalid user ID as an error.

Testing the RFC Destination

This test confirms the connectivity between the computer system on which SAP is running and the system on which the subsystem is or will be installed.

Execute transaction SM59. Click on the RFC destination being used in the process. The destination is typically SERVER_EXEC, but confirm your RFC destination by viewing the details of the Port definition that will be used for outbound processes. Click on the Test button. If the results are positive, then the connectivity is working correctly.

If the test connection returns negative results, the message should indicate the problem. If the message is not self-explanatory, then you can turn on RFC trace to log every step of the RFC test. This log is slightly cryptic. Knowledge of CPIC (Common Programming Interface Communication) is necessary to understand the trace information.

The problem is basically the connectivity between the two systems. The possible causes of errors are:

◆ The RFC destination may be using an explicit host name to reach the destination system, which may have been misspelled.

TIP

If the problem persists, you can try to use the IP address of the host on which the EDI subsystem is or will be installed. If this test works, then the problem lies in the TCP/IP configuration. Check with your Basis staff.

◆ The RFC server program (typically rfcexec) is unreachable; perhaps this program does not exist on the destination server, or the path is unreachable or inaccessible. Keep in mind that path name and program name are case sensitive. The ID used to access the files is <sid>adm, where sid is the system ID. If you are using separate systems for SAP and the subsystem, refer to "How the EDI Interface Uses and RFC Destination" in Chapter 6, "Configuring Basic EDI Components."

◆ Although the network is rarely at fault, make sure the physical links and network links are working. You can execute the ping command at the OS level to make sure that the link is up.

Testing the Port Definition

This test confirms access to the directory location where the IDoc files will be stored for the inbound and the outbound process.

Execute transaction WE21. Select your Port definition and then click on the Outbound File button to view the directory location where IDoc files will be stored. Click on the Check button on this screen to test accessibility to the directory. If the check is successful, then the Port definition is correct. Perform a similar operation for the inbound process and the Command file.

If the test connection returns negative results, the message should indicate the problem.

◆ The problem involves access to the directory location. Make sure the path is spelled correctly. It is case sensitive, and the directory name must end with a slash.

◆ If access to the file system is via NFS (Network File System), the NFS mounts should be verified from the Application server that you are logged on to.

Testing the Steps in an Outbound Process

The outbound process is essentially a sequence of several subprocesses that link together to form the total process. Five subprocesses are tested in the outbound process (see Figure 10-1):

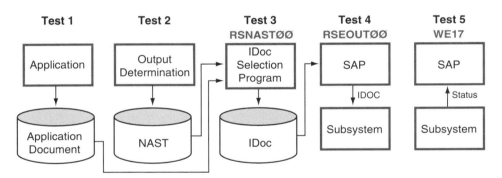

FIGURE 10-1

Testing various outbound components

◆ Successful creation of an application document
◆ Proposal of output by Message control
◆ Generation of IDocs
◆ Connection between the SAP system and the subsystem
◆ Status reporting by the subsystem

Verifying the Successful Creation of an Application Document

In this test you want to make sure that your application document can be created successfully. The steps to execute the test and verify the results are as follows:

Execute your application transaction (for example, VA01) to create a sales order or ME21 to create a purchase order. Make sure the application document is created successfully. This step usually works without any problem. However, this step can fail completely, in which case a document is not created, or fail partially, in which case the document is marked incomplete.

 CAUTION

In certain situations the system reports that the document was created successfully, yet when you go into the display mode, you do not see a document. In this case the problem lies in the IDoc selection program. Make sure the timing in the condition record is set to 1 as described in the prerequisites.

The system reports any problems to you immediately on the application status bar. You can click on the problem reported in the status bar to get additional details. You can also use extended help (if available) to view the online help in that context.

The application configuration can have a variety of problems. For example, pricing has not been maintained, a credit block is on the customer, or the vendor has not been maintained in the desired company code. You will need to work closely with the business team to resolve this type of problem.

If this step is successful, you should have an application document in the system. Verify it by going into the display transaction and making sure you see the document and that it is complete.

Verifying the Proposal of Output by Message Control

If your output (EDI, ALE, or fax) will be proposed automatically via Message control, then you must make sure that all the desired outputs are proposed with correct values.

This component is tested by executing the application transaction. No tool is available to test the Message control component by itself. The only option is to create an application document and go to the output control screen. In some cases (for example, order change), you need to go to the change document transaction instead of the create document transaction.

Verify the following on the output control screen:

- ◆ If output was to be proposed automatically, make sure an output record exists in the output control screen. If output is to be entered manually, pull down the list of output types and select your output.

- ◆ Accuracy of output medium, timing, and language.

TIP

Press Enter on the output control screen to validate the values.

If your desired outputs (such as EDI, ALE, fax, and Print) are not proposed, then go to the menu bar on the output control screen and choose Determination Analysis to view the output log, as shown in Figure 10-2.

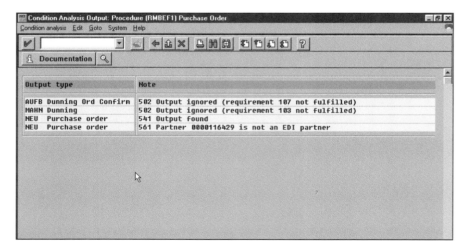

FIGURE 10-2

Determination Analysis log showing the steps used in proposing an output type

The output log displays the reason for the problem. This log is slightly cryptic, but it is the only alternative. If you understand the Message control concept, then you should have no problem reading the log. For example, the last line in Figure 10-2 indicates that partner profile does not exist and therefore the system did not propose the output type NEU.

The following list identifies some of the common problems that can prevent the output record from being proposed. This list is not complete, but it should help you resolve some of the common problems:

◆ The condition record is missing.

◆ The Message control record of the Partner profile is missing.

◆ Output type is set to manual.

◆ One of the prerequisites for the conditions was not satisfied in the requirement logic of the Message control.

If the output proposal is working correctly, you must make sure that a NAST entry is created for each of the outputs. To see the NAST entries, execute transaction SE16 or SE17, and enter NAST in the table name. Enter your application document number in the object key field, click on the Execute button, and verify that a record exists for each output proposed on the output control screen.

TIP

If the application document number is less than 10 characters, you must prefix it with leading zeros; otherwise, the record will not be located.

Verifying the Generation of IDocs

In this step you verify the process of generating IDocs from the application document. If you have extended the IDoc selection program via user exits, modified it, or created a new one, then this step allows you to debug your program logic.

Transaction: WE15

Path: From the Area menu of EDI, choose Test, Outbound from NAST.

This step is tested by executing the RSNAST00 program via transaction SE38 or by directly executing transaction WE15. The selection screen for this program is shown in Figure 10-3. This step processes the NAST entries that you have created in the previous step and calls the selection program for that message. For example, IDOC_OUTPUT_ORDERS will be called for message type ORDERS.

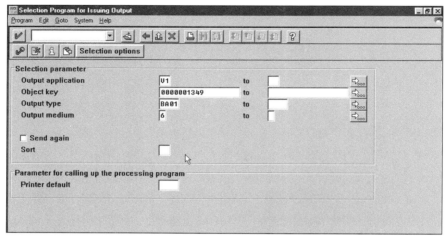

FIGURE 10-3

Selection screen for the RSNAST00 program

TIP

After a NAST record has been processed successfully, the record can be resent either by selecting the Send Again check box without creating a new document or by going into the application document again. You must make sure that the timing of the output was set to 1 or 2 as mentioned in the prerequisites.

If an error occurs during the execution of RSNAST00, it creates an output log that is displayed on the screen. Extended help on each record of the log is also available by clicking on the Documentation button.

Another possibility is that syntax errors have been found in the IDoc. The IDoc will be in status 26 (Error during syntax check of IDoc). Transaction WE02 is used to display IDocs in the system. The status record in the IDoc tells you whether syntax errors were generated for the IDoc.

If you are testing a standard SAP supplied program, then errors at this stage are rarely due to program logic. The possible causes of the errors are:

◆ The Partner profile may have an incorrect process code. You can perform a syntax check on the Partner profile.

◆ The application document may have been deleted. Display the application document to confirm that the document exists.

◆ The application document may contain an inconsistency. For example, partner functions may not have been defined.

◆ The program logic may have errors. If you have developed your own selection program or extended the standard program via user exits, then check the program logic for errors.

If this step works correctly, then a success message should appear in the output log window. You can then use transaction WE02 to display the IDoc. It must be in status 30 (IDoc ready for dispatch).

TIP

If you cannot figure out the problem, try debugging the program. Set a breakpoint at the start of the function module. You can set additional breakpoints, depending on the problem. For example, if you are getting an error message, then set a breakpoint on the keyword message to quickly navigate to the code where the error is being generated.

TIP

Click on the Documentation button in the output log window to view the IDoc number.

Verifying the Connection between the SAP System and the Subsystem

The connection between the SAP system and the subsystem is one of the major culprits in the process. This connection is responsible for the greatest number of problems, because it crosses the boundary from SAP to the OS layer. If you successfully tested the components as described in "Performing a Sanity Test of the Configuration," then you should not experience any problems here.

Transaction: WE14

Path: From the Area menu of EDI, choose Test, Outbound from IDoc.

If the sanity tests were successful, there is very little chance of error in transferring IDocs from the SAP system to the operating system. The IDoc must be in status 30 (IDoc ready for dispatch) to be passed to the subsystem. Execute program RSEOUT00 via transaction SE38 or execute WE14 to transfer IDocs to the subsystem, as shown in Figure 10-4. The selection screen allows you to select an IDoc based on various criteria. You can enter the IDoc number as generated in the previous step, "Verifying the Generation of IDocs."

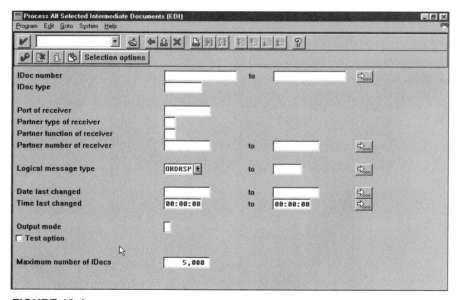

FIGURE 10-4

Selection screen for the RSEOUT00 program

If this step does not execute successfully, you have a problem, so check the last status record of the IDoc. See the list of errors explained in the sanity test in "Testing the Port Definition."

- ◆ This step is verified by checking the status of the IDoc. If the RSEOUT00 program executes successfully, the status of the IDoc will change to 03 (Data passed to port OK).
- ◆ An IDoc file will also be created at the OS level with a name specified in the Port definition.

TIP

If you do not have an account at the OS layer, you can execute transaction AL11 to view the IDoc file.

Verifying Status Reporting by the Subsystem

In this step you test the process of status reporting by the subsystem, but the subsystem is not required. SAP provides a utility to test this step.

Status codes can be of type success or failure. In either case a status record is attached to the IDoc. If a status code represents an error, then a workflow is also started (Column Workflow contains Yes in Table 10-1).

Table 10-1 Status Codes Passed to SAP by the Subsystem

Status Code	Workflow	Description
04	Yes	Error within control information of EDI subsystem
05	Yes	Error during translation
06	No	Translation OK
07	Yes	Error during syntax check
08	No	Syntax check OK
09	Yes	Error during interchange handling
10	No	Interchange handling OK
11	Yes	Error during dispatch
12	No	Dispatch OK

13	No	Retransmission OK
10	No	Interchange Acknowledgment positive
15	Yes	Interchange Acknowledgment negative
16	No	Functional Acknowledgment positive
17	Yes	Functional Acknowledgment negative
22	No	Dispatch OK, acknowledgment still due
23	Yes	Error during retransmission
24	No	Control information of EDI subsystem OK
36	No	Electronic signature not performed (timeout)

Transaction: WE17

Path: From the Area menu of EDI, choose Test, Inbound Status File.

You can use a standard system tool to test the process without having an actual subsystem installed. First you use this tool to import a status file with any success status code from Table 10-1. You do not need to test every success status code. Then you can test each individual error status code from the subsystem by importing a separate file each time. Figure 10-5 shows the selection screen of this test tool where you can specify the input file name. A sample file for testing inbound status processing is shown in Listing 10-1. The second line gives you a reference for the position and is not part of the file. This file adds a status record with a status code 16 to an IDoc number 1184 with a date of December 16, 1998, and a time of 10:10:03. This record contains the minimum amount of information required to append a status record. You can certainly include additional information (for example, message and message text).

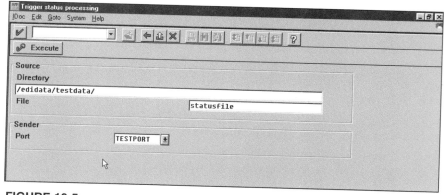

FIGURE 10-5

Processing the inbound status file

The results are displayed on the screen itself. This process does not experience many problems. The main reason for failure is that the format of the status file is imported into the system, or the IDoc number specified in the file is incorrect.

 NOTE

Because the format of the file has changed with every major release of SAP, the file should conform to the revision in use.

Listing 10-1 Sample inbound status file

```
EDI_DS          00000000000011841998121610100316

12345678901234567890123456789012345678901234567890
```

The results can be verified by viewing the last status record in the IDoc. You can view the IDoc by using transaction WE02 (Display IDocs). If the status code represents an error, then the EDI administrator as identified in the EDIADMIN table will also be notified via workflow. The Inbox of the EDI Administrator should be checked for an error message.

Testing the Inbound Process

The inbound process is different from the inbound because the inbound originates outside the SAP system. If the subsystem is not installed, then you need to use the inbound utilities to start the inbound process. Several utilities simulate the start of the inbound process. The actual processing is carried out by the real components. The best strategy for testing an inbound process is to test each component separately.

SAP provides two types of test utilities:

◆ Utilities for the sanity test
◆ Utilities to test the process

The first type performs a basic sanity test on the configuration of the EDI objects (For example, Partner profile and process codes). These utilities are accessed from within the objects' maintenance screens or through special programs.

The second type tests the process. The inbound process can be tested using the actual components that are involved in the process. The only piece that can be missing is the subsystem. The standard system includes several utilities to simulate the functions of a subsystem, including creating an IDoc and simulating the start of the inbound process.

The inbound process comprises various programs that are linked to run one after another. To test each component separately, set the Background to No Override with Express flag in the partner profile. This setting ensures that all the components are disconnected from each other and do not start the next process immediately.

Performing a Sanity Test of the Configuration

The various configuration components defined for the inbound process can be tested with tools provided in the standard system. These tools help in doing a basic sanity test of the configuration settings without executing the process.

Partner profiles can be checked to make sure the parameters specified are still correct. The process is the same as defined for the outbound process in "Testing the Partner Profile."

The ALE system provides a tool to test the consistency of inbound parameters for error handling. You can use this tool to test all the process codes together or one process code at a time. The output is a color-coded report that displays the possible cause of any problem.

You can run this report for all process codes by using program RBDMOINF via transaction SE38. Alternatively, you can run program RBDMOINC to test an individual code.

The results are displayed on the output screen. The report is a color-coded report showing different problems. You can double-click on a problem to get additional details.

◆ The link between the process code and the function module is not defined.

◆ The object type for this message's IDoc is missing. If the object is present, it checks for the presence of a triggering event (INPUTERROROCCURED) and a terminating event (INPUTFINISHED). This error is more likely to occur for custom processes.

◆ The object type for this message's IDoc packets is missing. If the object is present, it checks for a terminating event named MASSINPUTFINISHED.

◆ The task for error handling has not been defined.

◆ The linkage between the task and the triggering events is inactive or undefined.

◆ The linkage for the terminating events is undefined or inactive.

◆ The roles for the task are undefined.

Most of these settings are related to workflow settings for a new process. SAP already provides these objects for standard messages. The test for inbound settings is useful for custom processes. See Chapter 33, "Customizing the Interface for New and Extended IDocs," for details on the settings required for new inbound processes.

Utilities to Start the Inbound Process

One of the major components for the inbound process is the IDoc itself. If a subsystem is not available, then you need a way to create an IDoc and start the inbound process. Several utilities are available to address this problem.

Utility 1: Start the Inbound Process by Copying an Outbound IDoc As Inbound

Transaction: WE12

Path: From the Area menu of EDI, choose Test, Inb.modif.outb.file.

The SAP IDoc architecture does not differentiate between the structures of an inbound IDoc and an outbound IDoc. Utility 1, which is also called the turnaround utility, uses that principle to copy an outbound IDoc file as an inbound IDoc file and to start the inbound process. This utility is useful if you already have an outbound process that is generating an IDoc type that you want to use for your inbound testing. For example, if you want to test the inbound sales order process and you are already generating outbound purchase orders, you know that the IDoc type for purchase orders (ORDERS02) is the same as the IDoc type for sales orders (ORDERS02). You can use the turnaround utility to make the outbound purchase order file come in as a sales order and start the inbound process.

You start this utility via transaction WE12. The selection parameters allow you to change the sender and receiver fields as well as the message type, as shown in Figure 10-6. However, this utility does not allow you to change the actual data contents. You must make sure that data in the outbound IDoc can be used for an inbound process. After you enter the parameters, click on the Execute button. The system displays the following message:

```
Transfer to ALE carried out.
```

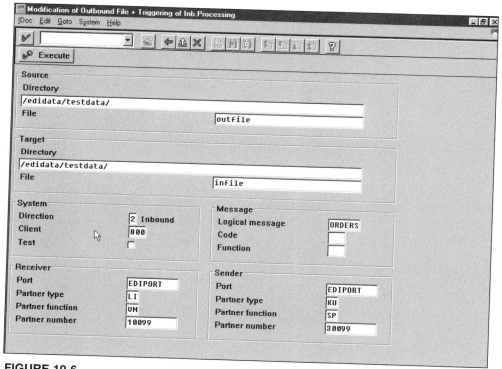

FIGURE 10-6

The turnaround utility to copy an outbound IDoc file as inbound

TIP

The default parameters for this utility are built from the Port definition specified in the TESTPORT parameter in the EDIADMIN table.

CAUTION

You must make sure that the outbound IDoc file you are using has the correct IDoc type. I have seen a static outbound file name for the test port many times, which means that the file is overwritten every time an outbound process is executed. The tester thinks that he has the correct file but someone else may have executed an outbound process using the same port and overwritten the file with his own IDoc type. For example, consider that you are using a test port in which the outbound file name is static. Assume that the name of the file is outfile and that you want to test the inbound process for sales orders. You have been generating purchase orders using this port. Now someone else in the team generates an outbound invoice using the same port, and the invoice IDoc overwrites the IDoc containing the purchase order. If you are unaware of this situation, you could waste a lot of time wondering why your process is failing. Using a dynamic file name that is based on your user ID prevents accidental overwriting by another team member.

Utility 2: Start the Inbound Process from an Inbound Text File

Transaction: WE16

Path: From the Area menu of EDI, choose Test, Inb.orig.inb.file.

If you do not have any outbound process configured, then you cannot use the turnaround utility. Also, you may have noticed that there is no facility to save a variant for the utility. If you are involved in testing an inbound process over and over again using the same data, specifying the parameters repeatedly becomes a nuisance.

You can use utility 2 to start the inbound process from an inbound file. But first you need to build an inbound file. You can build an IDoc file in several different ways, depending on your needs, the situation, and the amount of effort you want to expend. The options are listed from easiest to hardest:

1. Copy an existing inbound IDoc in the system and save the IDoc to a file via transaction WE19 by selecting an existing IDoc number and clicking on the Create icon. On the next screen, you can change the values and then click on the Execute button. Then click on the Generate an IDoc Inbound File button, enter the file name, and deselect the Start IDoc Inbound Processing of File Immediately flag. Click on the Execute button again, and an IDoc file is created for you.

2. Copy an outbound file and modify it to look like an inbound file. Alternatively, if you have an outbound file, you can set a breakpoint while executing the turnaround utility. Set the breakpoint where it has copied an outbound file, modified it to look like an inbound file, and is ready to start the inbound process. At that point you can end the session. Now you should have an IDoc file that you can use for your inbound process.

   If you copy an outbound IDoc file manually, then you need to change certain fields (listed in Table 10-2) in the control record. Refer to the structure of the control record (structure edi_dc) for the position and data length of these variables.

Table 10-2 Required fields in the control record of an inbound IDoc file

Field	Value
outmod	Spaces
docrel	Spaces
docnum	Spaces
mandt	Client that you are going to test in
direct	2
rcvpor	Your test port or any valid file port
rcvprt	Receiver partner type
rcvpfc	Receiver partner function
rcvprn	Receiver partner number
sndpor	Sender port: any valid file port
sndprt	Sender partner type
sndpfc	Sender partner function
sndprn	Sender partner number
mestyp	Message type
mescod	Message code
mesfct	Message function
test	Test flag

3. Use WE19 to create an IDoc on-the-fly, based on IDoc type or message type. Before you click on the final Execute button, save the IDoc to a file as described earlier.

4. This option should be your last resort, but you can use a text editor to create an IDoc from scratch. Refer to the EDI_DC and EDI_DD structures for the position and length of each required field. Good luck!

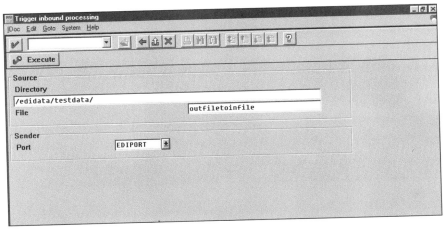

FIGURE 10-7

Start inbound processing from a file

 CAUTION

After the system successfully reads a file, it is deleted. If you plan to use the file again, you must make a copy of it before you execute this process.

After you create the IDoc file, you are ready to start inbound processing using utility 2. The selection parameters of this program allow you to specify the file name for the inbound IDoc file, as shown in Figure 10-7. Then click on the Execute button to start the inbound processing.

Utility 3: Start the Inbound Process with the Inbound Test Tool

Transaction: WE19

Path: From the Area menu of EDI, choose Test, Test Tool, Inbound.

This tool is a two-step process. In the first step, you create an IDoc using one of the four methods (see Figure 10-8): copy an existing IDoc, create an IDoc based on the IDoc type, create an IDoc based on a message type, or create an IDoc with no template. You will modify the IDoc data as needed, as shown in Figure 10-9.

In the second step, you process your newly created IDoc (see Figure 10-10). You can call the inbound process using the normal path, in which case the process goes through the checks as if it had been sent in by the subsystem, or you can pass the process to a function module directly. In this case the system bypasses the checks for Partner profile and hands the IDoc data to your inbound function module directly. This approach is useful for testing an inbound process without having to maintain any inbound configuration. You can also start the function module in debug mode and select the processing option for your posting module. Finally, you can choose to save the IDoc in a file, as described in utility 2.

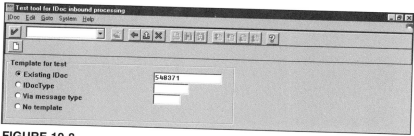

FIGURE 10-8

The various options to create an IDoc

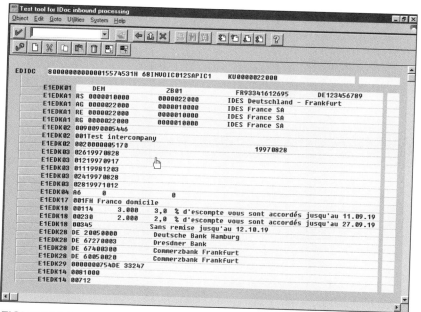

FIGURE 10-9

The data entry screen to modify the IDoc before it is saved in the system

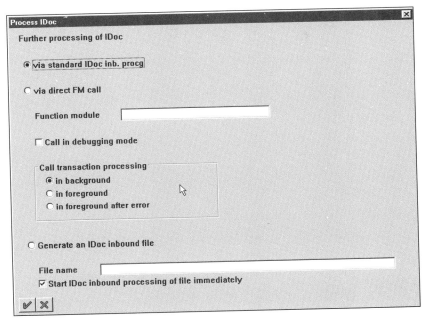

FIGURE 10-10

Select one of the many different ways to start the inbound process with the Process IDoc dialog box

Testing the Steps in an Inbound Process

Now that you have selected a method to start the inbound process and have met the prerequisites, you need to understand the various components that you will test on the inbound process (see Figure 10-11):

- ◆ Inbound triggering process
- ◆ Successfully creating IDocs in the database
- ◆ Posting the application document

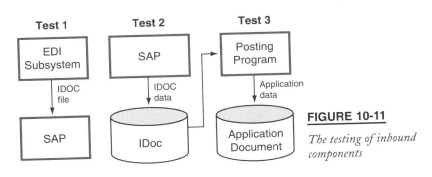

FIGURE 10-11

The testing of inbound components

Verifying the Inbound Triggering Process

This step tests the connectivity between the subsystem and the SAP system. Although you may not have a subsystem, you can start the startrfc program from the command line. The subsystem uses the same technique to start the SAP system.

This test requires the process to begin at the OS layer using an IDoc file. Use one of the utilities described earlier to create an IDoc file for the inbound process. At the OS level, execute the startrfc command, using the syntax described in "Triggering the Inbound Process by the Subsystem" in Chapter 6, "Configuring Basic EDI Components."

The results of executing the startrfc command will be displayed at the command line where you started the program. The errors are usually from message class E0. If you see a message with E0, then you can use transaction SE91 to look up the details of the message. If the error message is unclear, you can turn on the trace when executing startrfc to view detailed information.

Problems are very common in this test. Use the following list to troubleshoot problems:

- **Permission problems in executing the startrfc command.** You must have proper authorization to execute operating system commands.
- **Problems with input parameters.** The parameters must be specified according to the syntax. Typically, the user ID and passwords have problems. You can use your logon ID to test the process.
- **Problems with the gateway services.** You can use transaction SMGW to check the status of your gateway services. Gateway services are used for every CPIC communication, and RFC is implemented using CPIC protocols. Check with your Basis staff for appropriate gateway service values.
- **Problems accessing the inbound file.** The file system if NFS mounted may not be available or SAP does not have authorization to read the file.

If this step is successful, an IDoc created should be created in the SAP database. You should not be concerned about errors in the IDoc at this stage. The scope of this test is limited to making sure the triggering process works.

Verifying the Creation of Successful IDocs

In this step you use the information in the IDoc's control record to verify that a Partner profile is found and that the IDoc is created without any structural errors. This step is useful for custom IDocs when you want to make sure that the incoming IDocs are structurally correct.

Start the inbound process with one of the utilities described earlier. This time the process does not have to start from a file.

The results are logged in the status records of the IDoc. The status records can be displayed using the IDoc display utilities. If an error occurs, the IDoc gets a status code of 56 (IDoc with errors added) and an error workflow is started. The person notified in this case depends on whether a Partner profile could be read or not. If a Partner profile was found, then workflow is sent to the person specified in the Partner profile. If a Partner profile entry could not be read, then the message is sent to the EDI administrator specified in the EDIADMIN table.

Common problems in this step are related to data in the control record and to syntax errors in the IDoc. The parameters in the control record must match the key of the Partner profile record for that inbound message. The various causes of syntax errors are described in "Syntax Rules for an IDoc" in Chapter 30, "IDocs on the Inside." The status records should give you the specific details. If this step is successful, you should see an IDoc that has a status code of 64 (IDoc ready to be passed to application).

 TIP

If you are seeing some strange segment names that you think do not exist in the IDoc, then the problem lies in the process that created the IDoc. Remember that SAP treats the incoming file as a stream of data. It parses the data by position so that if any field is off by even one position, you will see these problems. For example, you might have accidentally deleted a character in the data records.

Verifying the Posting of Application Documents

Transaction: BD87

The logic for posting an application document is coded in inbound function modules. Verifying the logic of the inbound function module is the most important step for custom function modules. You verify not only that the posting function module is working correctly but also that the logic and interface of the function module is correct. If problems exist, you may also want to debug the process one step at a time.

The IDoc created in "Verifying the Creation of Successful IDocs" is used to test this process. To start, execute program RBDAPP01 via SE38, or execute BD87. Then enter your IDoc number and start the process. The selection screen for the RBDAPP01 program is shown in Figure 10-12.

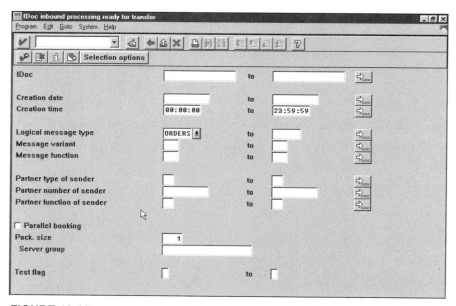

FIGURE 10-12

The selection screen to pass an IDoc to the posting program

Errors in this step are mainly related to data errors and are logged in the status records of the IDoc. The status records can be displayed using the IDoc display utilities. The IDoc gets a status code of 51 (IDoc with errors added). A multitude of errors can be related to data errors. Detailed information about a specific error is also logged in the status record, and an error workflow is started to notify the person responsible for handling the error. If your posting program uses call transaction to post the document, then you can step through every screen to determine the exact location of the error.

The common problems in this step are either data related or are in the application configuration, so you need to make sure the data values are correct in the various fields of the data record. Check your program logic for any errors.

If this step is successful, an application document is created and the IDoc gets a status code of 53 (Application document posted). The document number is logged in the status record. For example, if an incoming IDoc creates a sales order number 10000, then this number is seen in the last status record.

Testing the Workflow Exception Process

After you have tested the inbound and outbound processes, you can specifically test the workflow component's exception-handling process. One obvious method is to create an error in the process and check for a work item in the Inbox of the responsible user. However, this approach requires you to build error data, which may be difficult at times. You can test the workflow component by itself using the simple procedure listed below. This procedure applies to all error workflows for the outbound and inbound process.

Transaction: SWUS

Menu Path: From the Area menu of Workflow, choose Runtime Tools, Start Workflow.

In this step your aim is to test the exception-handling process and to make sure that the correct person is notified when an error occurs. You start the error process manually using transaction SWUS. In an actual process, the system starts the error process based on the type of error. The steps are as follows:

1. Identify the workflow task that is started for a particular exception. Refer to "Tasks" in Chapter 9, "Configuring Workflow," for a list of error tasks.

2. On the selection screen (see Figure 10-13), enter the task number in the Task field and click on the Input data button. On the next screen, press F4 and enter an IDoc number.

3. Click on the back arrow and click on the Start button. This step should start a workflow process.

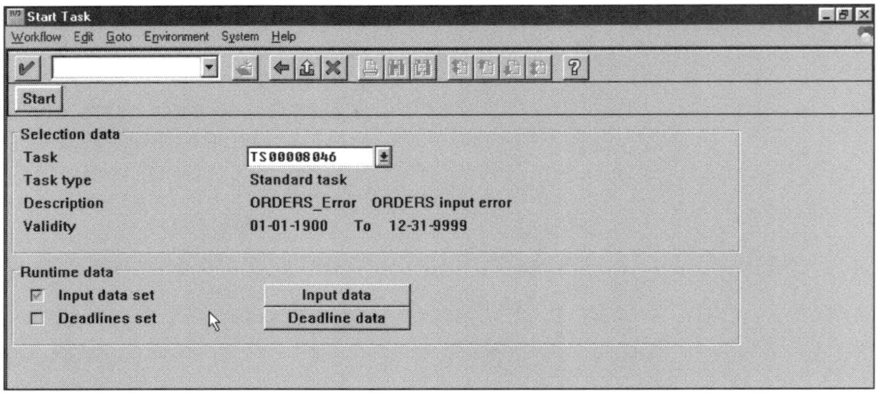

FIGURE 10-13

Starting an error task manually

Errors in this step are communicated in the status bar. You can click on the message to get additional details. The common problem in this step is related to workflow configuration. If the system reports that you are not one of the possible agents, task profile has not been maintained or there is a problem with your PD-ORG setup. Refer to Chapter 9, "Configuring Workflow," to create a task profile. If this step is successful, the responsible person for the task should receive a work item in the Inbox.

Summary

In this chapter you learned about tools and techniques for testing an outbound and an inbound process. An outbound process during testing uses the same components as a real process except that the test does not require the subsystem. A test utility simulates the logic of the subsystem, passing status records to SAP. The outbound process is split into five steps to test each component separately.

Several utilities enable the inbound process to generate an IDoc in the database or an IDoc at the OS level in the form of a text file. An IDoc can be generated by using one already in the system or by building one on-the-fly. After an IDoc is created, each component of the inbound process goes through a three-step test. The results of each step are verified before proceeding to the next step.

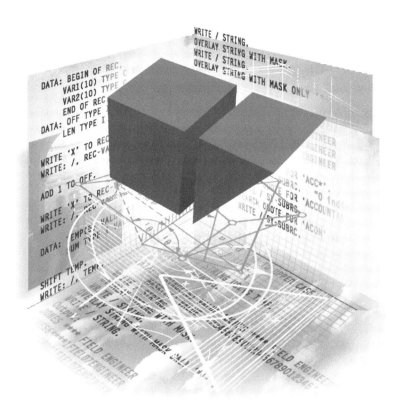

Chapter 11

Monitoring the Interface

Monitoring tools are used in two situations: to display errors and to get an overview of the state of the system. For example, you may want to know why an IDoc was not generated for a purchase order, how many EDI orders were received in a certain time, or how the ALE data transfers are progressing. In this chapter you learn to operate various monitoring tools used in the ALE/EDI process. You'll learn about the significance of various error logs, where to look for key information that will help you debug problems, and how to interpret the information displayed in the logs.

SAP provides extensive logging features at different milestones in the ALE/EDI process. The main component used for logging information is an IDoc; however, processing occurs before an IDoc is created, which means that you must monitor the process at other points. Errors not directly related to the IDoc are logged in places other than the IDoc. At times the system can experience severe errors, such as system dumps, and it doesn't get an opportunity to log an error. It's important to monitor the process at several points. This chapter outlines all the areas where SAP logs information for ALE/EDI processes.

The first section of this chapter describes how to operate the SAP Inbox and process various workitems. Over time, you will become adept at working with these tools. The troubleshooting guide in Chapter 12, "EDI Process Troubleshooting and Recovery," should help you decide which log to review for a given problem or situation in EDI. The troubleshooting guide in Chapter 27, "ALE Process Troubleshooting and Recovery," should help you decide which log to review for a given problem or situation in ALE.

The tools that you use depend on your role in the company. If you are an end user, you may be interested in looking at the application log and IDocs, but if you are a system administrator for the ALE/EDI interface, you will use system level tools such as the tRFC log or update log. For each tool you will find a mention of the user group that uses the tool. It is best to experiment with these tools to get a feel for how and where they display the required information.

 NOTE

The tools described in this chapter are applicable to both the ALE and EDI processes. However, in certain cases a tool may be used specifically in the ALE or EDI process. In such cases you will find some mention of the specific use of the tool.

Monitoring Errors via the SAP Inbox

Workflow is useful for detecting errors that are infrequent, have unpredictable timing, and are meant for a specific group of people.

For example, assume you are in charge of handling errors with purchase orders going out to your vendors via EDI. Several purchasing clerks can create purchase orders in the system. You might try to stay up-to-date with the problems by displaying a list of purchase orders created in the system every hour, looking for purchase orders that go via EDI, and then checking the status of each output to make sure the EDI part is correct. You could devote your entire day to monitoring the system manually and not find a problem. Or you might be busy doing something else and end up being accountable for an unresolved error.

The SAP ALE/EDI interface handles most of the errors via workflow. When an error occurs, an event is raised which causes workflow to be started. If you are responsible for handling errors, you receive a workitem in your SAP Inbox. The SAP Inbox is a common interface for all messages that are sent to you by any ALE/EDI process via workflow. Thus you can monitor errors from one place.

Understanding the SAP Inbox

Transaction: SO01

Path: Office, Inbox

The SAP Inbox is an interface to view and process workitems and SAP office documents (see Figure 11-1). It is similar to the inbox of any e-mail system. The SAP Inbox contains separate buckets for the office documents and work items. The office documents are e-mail documents, and the work items are workflow items. It is almost an offense to call a work item an e-mail message because the workflow system was specifically designed to circumvent the inherent problems of communicating via e-mail.

The number next to each bucket indicates the number of items in the bucket. New buckets can be set up with criteria of your choice. For example, you could set up a bucket to represent work items that are in the In Process state. To set up a new bucket, choose Settings, Configuration from the menu.

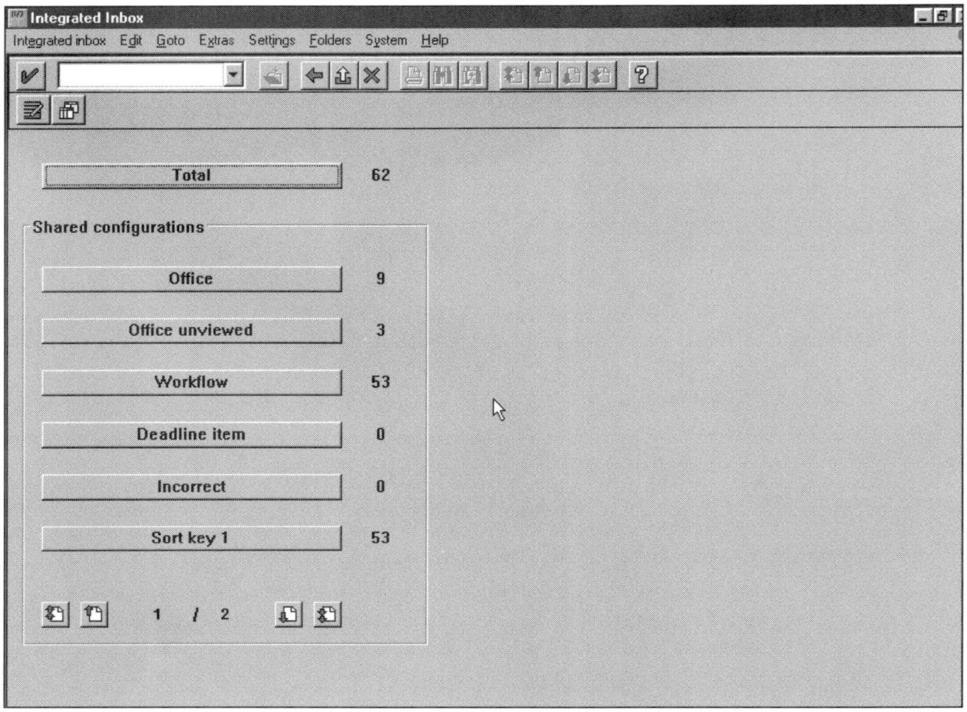

FIGURE 11-1

The SAP Inbox interface

Understanding Work Items

A work item represents an instance of a task that needs to be executed. For example, a Workflow task (Orders_Error) handles application errors in the orders IDoc. When a sales order IDoc has application errors in posting, a work item representing this task gets instantiated. A work item has a short text describing the purpose of the work item (but a separate long text can also be specified when necessary). A work item is executed from the Inbox to carry out the task. A work item can have more than one status that governs the operations allowed on it. The statuses you most commonly see in a work item are shown in Table 11-1.

Table 11-1 Work Item Status

Status	Description
Ready	The work item is visible to all selected agents.
Reserved	The work item has been reserved by a user and disappears from other selected users' Inboxes.
In Process	The work item is currently being worked on and can only be seen in the Inbox of the user who started working on it.
Executed	The work item has been executed at least once.
Completed	The work item is complete and cannot be seen in the Inbox of any user.
Error	The work item itself has gone into error status due to an internal problem with Workflow. This is a very rare situation.

As part of the ALE/EDI interface, the following items can appear in the SAP Inbox. Because work items are intelligently routed to the person responsible for them, the type of work item determines who is notified. You can expect to see work items for the following items:

◆ Errors in the outbound ALE/EDI interface

◆ Errors in the inbound ALE/EDI interface

◆ Syntax errors in an IDoc for the outbound process

◆ Syntax errors in an IDoc for the inbound process

◆ Application errors in posting an IDoc on the inbound process

◆ Errors reported by the EDI subsystem

◆ Technical errors in the EDI interface with reading and deleting IDoc files for the inbound process

◆ Number of IDocs exceeding a predefined threshold state. For example, someone is notified when at least 10 sales order IDocs are not posted because of application errors.

◆ Inbound EDI processes routed via workflow. For example, someone needs to review an order change IDoc before it is posted.

◆ Successful posting of an application document. For example, you want to view invoices whenever they are successfully posted in the system via EDI.

These scenarios are part of the standard SAP ALE/EDI functionality; refer to Chapter 9, "Configuring Workflow" for details on setting them up. The last three scenarios mentioned above are available in the system but are turned off or require some additional configuration before you see their work items.

Viewing a Worklist

A worklist is a list of work items sent to your SAP Inbox. Click on the Workflow button to see a list of all of the work items for which you have been selected as the responsible person. The default list has seven columns (see Figure 11-2).

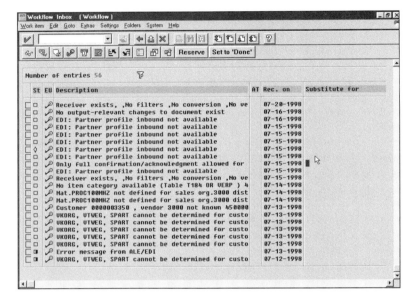

FIGURE 11-2

A list of work items in a user's SAP Inbox

◆ **Column 1.** Shows a checkbox that allows you to select a work item. You can select multiple work items by clicking in this column for each item. This feature is useful for carrying out mass operations on work items.

◆ **Column 2.** Indicates the status of a work item. If the box is empty, then the work item has never been processed. If the box is half black, then the work item has been executed at least once but has not been completed yet. If the box is all black, then the work item has been completed.

◆ **Column 3.** A Check icon. You can double-click on this icon to start execution of the work item.

◆ **Column 4.** Gives a short description of the work item.

◆ **Column 5.** Indicates whether an attachment is associated with this work item. An attachment can be a file, note, business document, or any other object that the system supports.

◆ **Column 6.** Indicates the date on which the work item was received in your Inbox.

◆ **Column 7.** Indicates the ID of the person for whom you're substituting, if you're substituting for another person and viewing that person's work items.

The SAP Inbox interface is highly configurable. Some common customizing options are listed later in this chapter in "Personalizing the SAP Inbox."

The worklist includes a short description of the work item. To see additional details (such as status, long text, terminating event, selected agents, IDoc number) of a work item, double-click on its Description entry (see Figure 11-3).

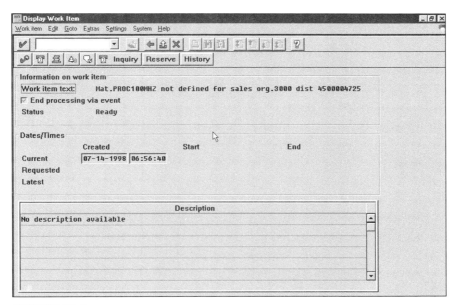

FIGURE 11-3

Details of a work item

The Description box in the Display Work Item screen is usually blank. As part of workflow customizing, you can change the text that appears in this box. From the menu options on this screen, you can get additional information about a work item. For example, to find out who else received this work item, choose Goto, Agent, Selected Agents. You can also find technical data, such as the task number, for a work item. Another important piece of information is the IDoc number, which you can find by choosing Work item, Object, Display.

Processing a Work Item

There is a standard procedure for execution of any work item. On the worklist screen, you can double-click on the Check icon in the second column, or you can click on the Execute button on the work item detail screen. When you click on the Execute button, you are automatically established as the owner of this work item and the work item disappears from the Inbox of other selected agents.

Executing a work item starts the task behind it. You do not need to know the transaction or the underlying data. Executing a task automatically takes you to a screen with all the information filled in. From this screen you can execute the task steps. This screen is different for every task, but the concept behind executing any work item is the same.

The work item in Figure 11-4 represents an application error in an incoming Sales order. From this screen, which displays the last status record of the IDoc, you can analyze the error. After you fix the error, you can restart the failed process by clicking on the Process button.

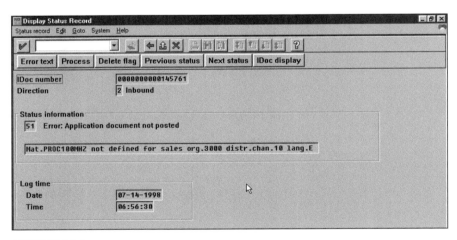

FIGURE 11-4

Results of executing a work item for sales order errors

 NOTE

If a work item is sent to multiple users, then each user can see an entry in his or her Inbox. As soon as one user looks at or executes the work item, it is considered reserved and disappears from the other Inboxes.

TIP

If the user who first looks at the work item decides not to work on it, he or she can replace the work item into the pool by executing the Replace function from the Inbox. This step returns the work item to the original Inboxes.

Marking a Work Item as Complete

Work items are automatically removed from the Inbox when the task they represent is completed. Work items can be classified into two categories:

◆ Work items requiring a terminating event

◆ Work items not requiring a terminating event

Terminating events are raised from within applications. The workflow management system then automatically removes the work item from your Inbox. For example, work items for application errors associated with an IDoc are completed by the terminating event ErrorProcessCompleted. After you fix the error and restart the process and the document posts successfully, the work item automatically disappears. The advantage of this method is that the task can be executed outside the workflow system and the work item will disappear from the Inbox. However, such work items cannot be deleted from the Inbox unless a terminating event is raised.

TIP

To find out whether a work item requires a terminating event, display the work item details by double-clicking on the workitem text. This screen has a check box to indicate whether the work item requires a terminating event.

Work items of the second type are completed upon an explicit input from a user, indicating that the task is complete. SAP uses this approach for tasks in which it cannot determine the completion of a task. For example, if the task is to write a letter, the system cannot know when you are done. In the SAP ALE/EDI process, tasks that are only for information—for example, technical errors in the IDoc interface—use this approach. The system displays the error. Upon exiting, the system asks whether you want to complete the task or not. If you click on the

Complete Processing of Step button, the work item is considered complete and disappears from the Inbox. Note that the system cannot validate what you have done to logically complete the task outside workflow. If you click on Cancel, the work item stays in your Inbox and you can reprocess the work item later.

Executing Additional Operations on a Work item

Besides executing a work item, you can carry out several other operations on a work item. Following are some of the common operations:

◆ **Forwarding.** You can forward a work item to another person to work on it as long as that person is one of the possible agents. See Chapter 9, "Configuring Workflow" for configuring possible agents.

◆ **Reserving.** By reserving a work item, you can take ownership of the work item task without executing it. This step makes the work item disappear from other Inboxes.

◆ **Replacing.** If you start working on a work item that was sent to multiple agents, it disappears from other Inboxes. If, however, you decide the work item is not for you, you can replace it into the pool. It will then be available to you as well as to the other original recipients.

◆ **Setting an item to done.** Any work item that does not have a terminating event can be completed by setting it to done. This step removes the work item from your Inbox.

◆ **Resubmitting.** If a work item does not require your immediate attention, you can make it disappear temporarily. It will reappear in your Inbox upon expiration of the specified time. For example, if you receive a work item and decide that you will work on it two days later, you can use the resubmit option to make the work item disappear from your Inbox for two days.

Personalizing the SAP Inbox

The Inbox interface is highly configurable. It can be configured to do the following:

◆ View work items by sender
◆ View work items by task ID
◆ View work items of a user who has designated you as the substitute
◆ View unviewed work items in a separate bucket

The Inbox can also be used to set substitutes, automatic forwarding, sorting, filtering, and do other customization.

NOTE

The configuration settings for personality the SAP Inbox were described in "Setting Up Advanced Workflow" in Chapter 9.

Displaying the Processing Log for the Output Type

The processing log is maintained in the message control component to provide details of the processing of an output type. This log is available only for applications that use message control to send an output. The log is useful for end users who create application documents and want to know the status of the output. For example, a purchasing clerk who created a purchase order for a vendor might want to find out whether or not a message was successfully processed.

Follow these steps to view and interpret the output log:

1. Go to the output control screen of the application document. You can usually reach this screen by choosing the menu option Header, Messages or Header, Output. The output list in Figure 11-5 shows the various output types for this document. The list is sorted by time, so if you have multiple output types of the same kind, the latest output type is at the top.

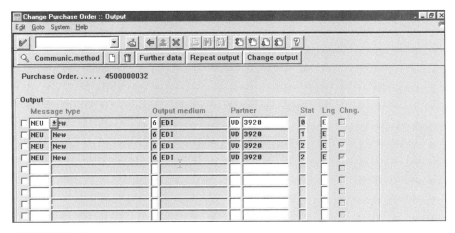

FIGURE 11-5

Various outputs proposed by the system as visible on the Output control screen

2. Look at the Status column (column 7) for your output type. The various values are as follows:

0—The processing has not started yet. The timing of the output was not set for immediate processing; it's waiting for the next run of the RSNAST00 program. If you want to start the processing immediately, you can click on the Further Data button, set the timing in the Send Time field to 4, and save your document. It should start the processing.

1—The output was successfully processed. You can find additional details such as the IDoc number generated for the output by selecting your output type and then choosing Goto, Processing Log from the menu (see Figure 11-6).

2—Errors occurred in processing the output type. You can find additional details about the error by selecting the output type in error and then choosing Goto, Processing log from the menu. The log should display the error message. The long text for the message can be viewed by clicking on the Documentation button (see Figure 11-6).

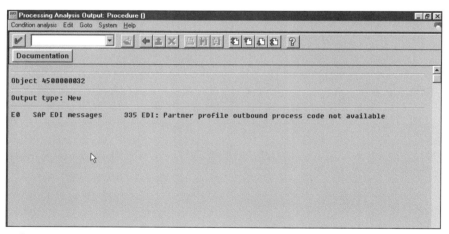

FIGURE 11-6

Processing log for an output type

3—The output type has been deactivated in the message control configuration. This entry prevents an output type from being processed. You should check your message control configuration.

Displaying Information in the IDoc Tables

The tools described in this section provide three different ways to retrieve the IDoc data stored in the tables, but the information is the same. Each tool has a purpose, so you'll end up using all these IDoc display tools according to your needs at a given moment.

IDoc Display

Transaction: WE02

Menu Path: From the Area menu of EDI, choose IDoc, Display IDoc.

The IDoc Display tool is one of the most commonly used tools to view the status of an ALE/EDI process. This tool generates a list of IDocs that match your selection criteria. As mentioned earlier, after an IDoc is created in the system all of the status information at various milestones is recorded in the status records of the IDoc. Everyone who works with the ALE/EDI interface uses this tool. The selection parameters of this program (see Figure 11-7) allow you to restrict the number of IDocs that are selected.

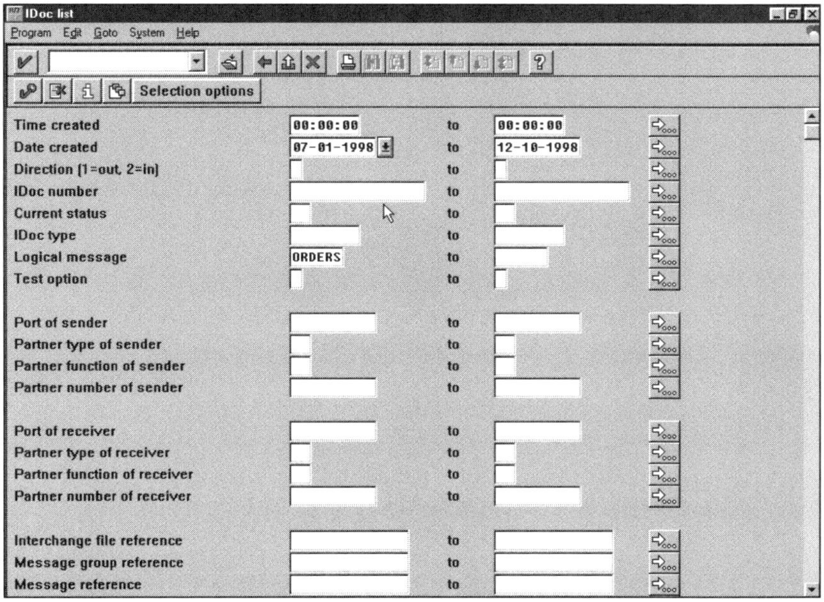

FIGURE 11-7

Selection parameters for the IDoc Display program

The output is a list of IDocs sorted by date and time, as shown in Figure 11-8. You can double-click on any line to display the specific IDoc. If the selection results in exactly one IDoc, then the system displays the IDoc directly without going through the intermediate step of listing the IDoc.

IDoc list Date	Time	Di	IDoc number	Log.messag	Test	Partner	Status
07-07-1998	07:02:32	2	0000000000144745	ORDERS		KU SP 30019	56 IDoc with err
07-11-1998	13:41:33	1	0000000000145745	ORDERS		LI UD 3001	03 Data passed t
07-12-1998	07:21:28	1	0000000000145746	ORDERS		LI UD 3001	03 Data passed t
07-12-1998	07:26:35	2	0000000000145747	ORDERS		KU SP 3980	51 Error: Applic
07-12-1998	21:32:36	1	0000000000145748	ORDERS		LI UD 1500	03 Data passed t
07-13-1998	07:38:21	1	0000000000145749	ORDERS		LI UD 1500	03 Data passed t
07-13-1998	11:34:55	2	0000000000145750	ORDERS		KU SP 3350	51 Error: Applic
07-13-1998	11:39:18	2	0000000000145751	ORDERS		KU SP 3350	51 Error: Applic
07-13-1998	11:43:21	2	0000000000145752	ORDERS		KU SP 3350	51 Error: Applic
07-13-1998	12:33:57	2	0000000000145753	ORDERS		KU SP 3350	51 Error: Applic
07-13-1998	12:40:01	1	0000000000145754	ORDERS		LI UD 1500	03 Data passed t
07-13-1998	16:20:58	2	0000000000145755	ORDERS		KU SP 3350	51 Error: Applic
07-13-1998	16:33:24	2	0000000000145756	ORDERS		KU SP 3350	51 Error: Applic
07-14-1998	06:22:54	1	0000000000145757	ORDERS		LI UD 3001	03 Data passed t
07-14-1998	06:47:10	1	0000000000145758	ORDERS		LI UD 3001	03 Data passed t
07-14-1998	06:49:43	2	0000000000145759	ORDERS		KU SP 3980	51 Error: Applic
07-14-1998	06:54:55	1	0000000000145760	ORDERS		LI UD 3001	03 Data passed t
07-14-1998	06:56:17	2	0000000000145761	ORDERS		KU SP 3980	51 Error: Applic
07-14-1998	07:05:28	1	0000000000145762	ORDERS		LI UD 3001	03 Data passed t
07-14-1998	07:06:19	2	0000000000145763	ORDERS		KU SP 3980	51 Error: Applic
07-14-1998	07:10:41	1	0000000000145764	ORDERS		LI UD 3001	03 Data passed t
07-14-1998	07:10:50	2	0000000000145765	ORDERS		KU SP 3980	53 Application d
07-15-1998	07:52:45	1	0000000000145767	ORDERS		LI UD 3001	03 Data passed t
07-16-1998	08:55:24	1	0000000000145779	ORDERS		LI UD 3001	03 Data passed t

FIGURE 11-8

List of IDocs sorted by date and time

> ### TIP
>
> The transaction WE02 uses program RSEIDOC2. You can call this program in your custom programs to display a specific IDoc.

The IDoc display screen, shown in Figure 11-9, lists the various components of an IDoc such as the control record, data records, and status records. You can display the output in a tree format or a normal screen format. You can change the display format from the IDoc display screen by choosing Goto, Configure, and you can double-click on a record type to display the details.

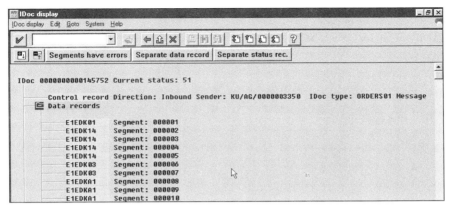

FIGURE 11-9

IDoc shown in a tree format with control record, data records, and status records

The control record screen (see Figure 11-10) displays some commonly used information about a control record. You can get additional details—such as technical details, EDI details, and address information—by selecting the appropriate option from the menu.

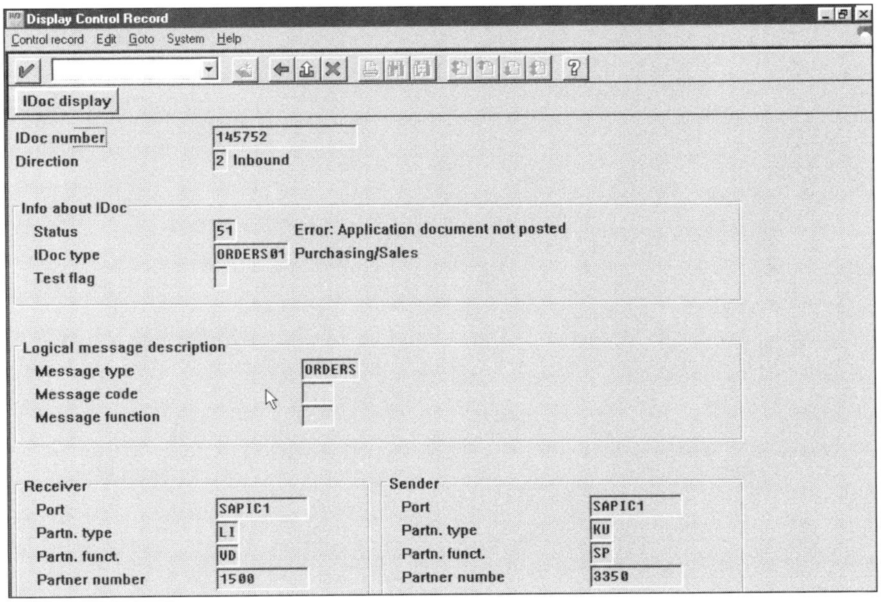

FIGURE 11-10

Details of a control record in an IDoc

The data records portion of the IDoc (see Figure 11-9) displays the data records sequentially. The hierarchy of the data records is visible only in the tree format display. You can select a data record and then double-click on the data record to see the fields in that data record (see Figure 11-11).

CAUTION

In the non-tree display format, you must first select the desired data record. Simply double-clicking on any data record displays the previously selected data record only.

NOTE

If a data element is blank in the IDoc, it does not show up on the screen.

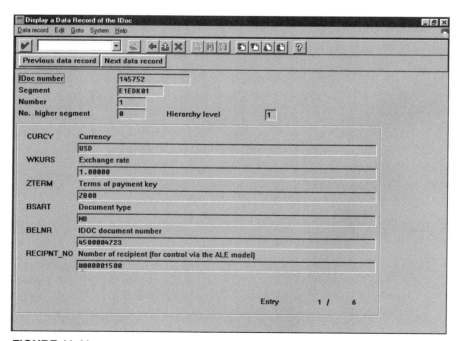

FIGURE 11-11

Details of an IDoc data record

The status records portion of the IDoc (see Figure 11-9) displays the status records sequentially. A plus sign in front of a status record indicates that a message is available in the status record. You can double-click on the message to view its long text. Double-clicking on the record displays additional details of the status record such as the date and time (see Figure 11-12). If a status record contains application error information, then you may also see a segment number and field that is in error. This information is displayed only if the application that processes the IDoc has logged this information.

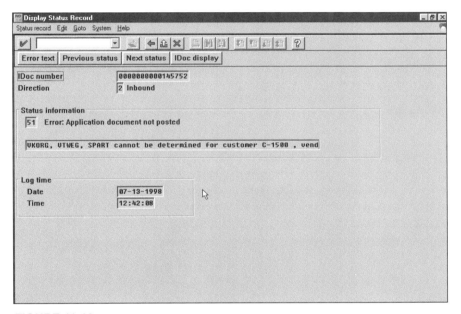

FIGURE 11-12

Details of the IDoc status record

IDoc List

Transaction: WE05

Menu Path: From the Area menu of EDI, choose IDoc, IDoc List.

The IDoc List program is another commonly used ALE/EDI interface tool for viewing the status of an ALE/EDI process. This program generates a list of IDocs that match your selection criteria. The selection parameters of this program (see Figure 11-13) allow you to restrict the number of IDocs that are selected.

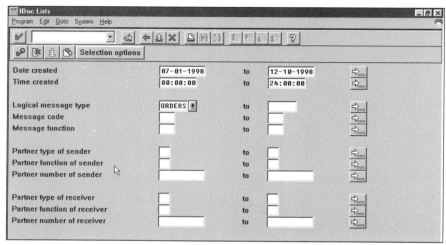

FIGURE 11-13

Selection screen for the IDoc List program

The output is a color-coded list of IDocs sorted first by direction (inbound or outbound) and then by status codes (see Figure 11-14). IDocs in error are displayed in red, IDocs with a warning are in yellow, and successful IDocs are in white. You can double-click on any line to display the IDocs with that status code.

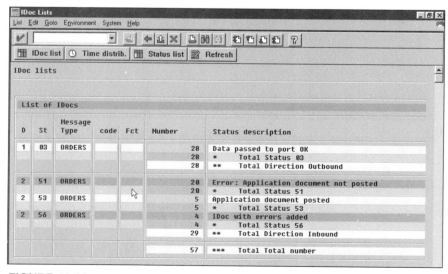

FIGURE 11-14

Output of the IDoc List program

IDoc Statistics

Transaction: WE07

Menu Path: From the Area menu of EDI, choose IDoc, IDoc List.

The IDoc Statistics program provides an excellent report on the overall status of all the IDocs in the ALE/EDI interface. This program generates an output of IDocs that match your selection criteria. The selection parameters of this program (see Figure 11-15) allow you to restrict the number of IDocs that are selected. The default is all IDocs.

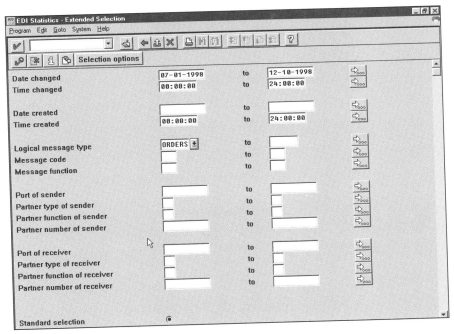

FIGURE 11-15

Extended Selection parameter list for the IDoc Statistics program

The output is a report of all the IDocs by status groups. A status group is a number that represents a list of status codes that have been grouped together to represent a particular type of error. For example, status group 6 represents errors in the subsystem. In table TEDS3 you can see a list of various status groups and the status code included in each group.

By looking at the output of this report (see Figure 11-16), you can tell how many IDocs are in the EDI subsystem, how many are in error, how many are awaiting dispatch, and so on. You can double-click on any box to display the list of IDocs in a particular status group. From the list you can drill down to a specific IDoc.

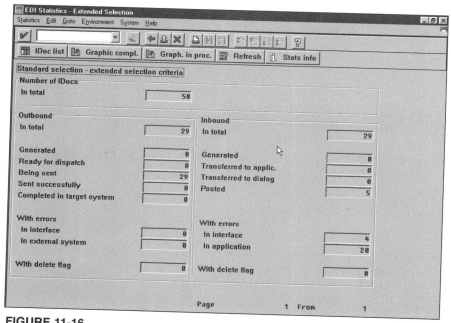

FIGURE 11-16

Output screen of the IDoc Statistics program

Displaying the Workflow Log

The workflow management system maintains an extensive log of all the activities carried out in the workflow system. From the time a work item is created to when it's completed, it goes through several steps. A log documents each step, along with any vital information. The two tools described next help you retrieve the logged information in a useful and presentable format. The tools are mainly used by the EDI administrator to view the state of work items and the duration of the process (how long it took to resolve the problem). This report can help in identifying bottlenecks and the source of any major problems.

Work Item Analysis

Transaction: SWI2

Menu Path: From the Area menu of workflow (SWLD), choose Reporting, Work item Analysis.

The work item analysis report is a comprehensive report for determining the state of work items in the system. You can execute this report for the following information:

◆ Number of work items created in the system and their status

◆ Time it took to resolve the problems

The work item analysis report can be used in place of the IDoc reports if you're interested in an overview of the ALE/EDI processes that have errored out in the past. Compared to IDoc reports, the work item analysis provides better information because the IDoc reports are based on the current status of the IDocs. For example, if you want to analyze the cause of problems in the ALE/EDI interface, you need to know what processes have errored out in the past. The IDoc report does not show this information unless you drill down into each individual IDoc.

The selection parameters list (see Figure 11-17) allows you to restrict the number of entries returned to you. You can restrict them by time or type of process. For example, if you're only interested in sales order IDocs that have failed in the past month, then you can use the task number for order IDoc as the restricting criteria. You can press the F4 key on the task field and enter the task abbreviation (Orders_Error). The system will return the task number.

You can choose the desired output by pressing the appropriate button on the toolbar. You will be mainly interested in the Frequency and Process Duration options. The other options are mostly used for SAP business workflow processes.

The output of the frequency report is a list of work items that have been generated in the system based on your selection criteria. You can drill down to display the status of these work items, as shown in Figure 11-18. You can drill down further to each work item to get the details , such as the person who has it and the IDoc number associated with the work item.

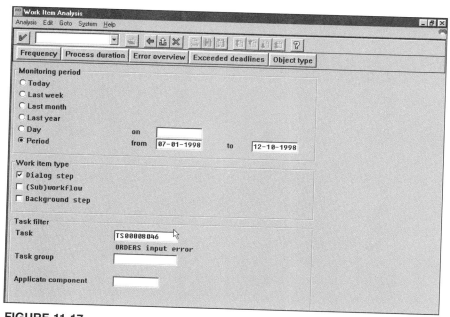

FIGURE 11-17

Selection parameters for the work item analysis report

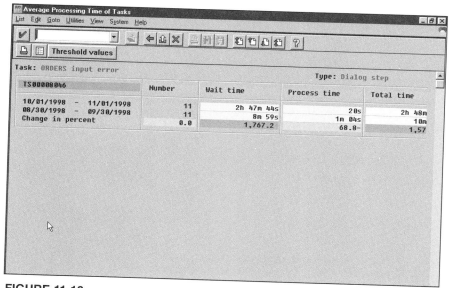

FIGURE 11-18

Details of the frequency report

The output of the process duration report is a time analysis of the work items for the selected period. You can toggle between average values and threshold values on the output report. The threshold values report provides a breakdown by percentage (10%, 50%, and 90%) of items completed in the given time period, as shown in Figure 11-19. A value of zero means that the IDoc was processed in a negligible time period. This report should give you an idea of how long it took to fix an error from the time the user saw the error until it was finally resolved.

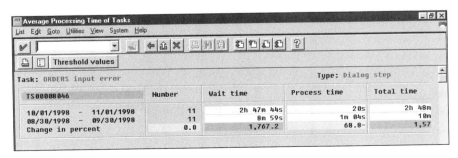

FIGURE 11-19

Work item report showing the percentage of items completed at various milestones

The average values report provides a breakdown by waiting time and processing time, as shown in Figure 11-20. Waiting time is the elapsed time from when the work item was created in the system by workflow to when a user actually looked at the work item. Processing time is the elapsed time from when the user looked at the error until it was finally resolved.

FIGURE 11-20

The work item report showing average values for waiting time and processing time

The process duration report also draws comparisons with work items from a previous interval of the same value. Thus if you selected the output for the last week, the system will draw a comparison with values from a week before that and show you the change in processing times.

Workload Analysis

Transaction: SWI5

Menu Path: From the Area menu of workflow (SWLD), choose Reporting, Workload Analysis.

The workload analysis report monitors load on an organization object such as user, position, job, or workcenter. The only restriction is that work items must have been executed and completed from within the workflow. If they are completed outside the workflow, the system does not have visibility into the person who carries out the task. The selection parameters of this report (see Figure 11-21) allow you to restrict the output by type of organization object, task, and completion date. The output is a report (see Figure 11-22) showing the work items that have been completed by the user.

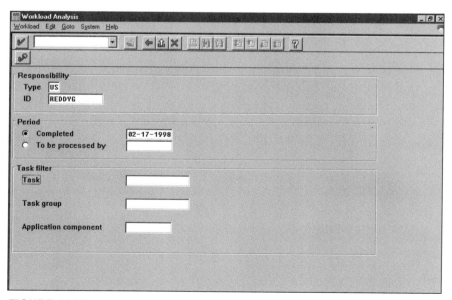

FIGURE 11-21

Selection parameters list for the workload analysis report

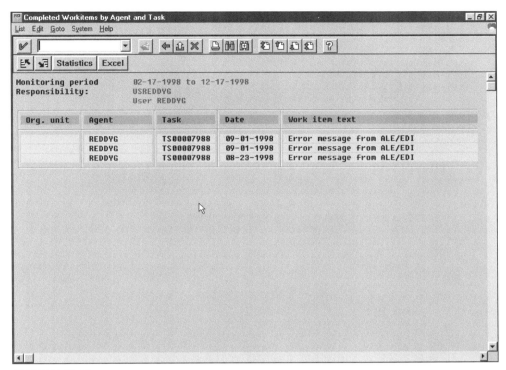

FIGURE 11-22

Workload analysis report showing work items completed by a user

Displaying System Level Logs

The system maintains log information for critical errors that are related to technical problems, such as problems with the network or the file system. A functional user is not involved in analyzing or resolving these errors. The main users are the system administrators who are responsible for maintaining the system. The EDI administrator will most likely be involved with these tools at some point. The ALE/EDI programmers may also interact with these tools during the development and testing phase.

Input File Log

Transaction: WE08

Menu Path: From the Area menu of EDI, choose IDoc, Display File Status.

A file log is maintained in the EDI process to log any problems in reading or deleting IDoc files on the inbound process. The inbound process maintains this log to avoid processing the same file twice in case of an error. Figure 11-23 shows an example of entries in the file log. The EDI administrator is notified when entries are created in the file log.

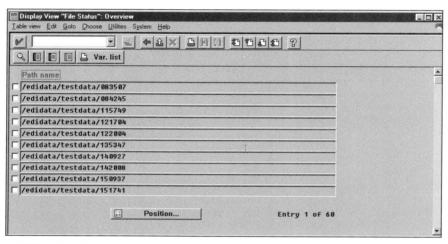

FIGURE 11-23

Log of files that failed during input

The system maintains the file name and the last record read successfully from the IDoc file. The system also records the last IDoc number generated from the file. The EDI administrator has to edit the incoming file manually by looking for problems near the record number recorded in the log, copying into another file the records that have not been processed yet, and then starting the process again.

Asynchronous Update Log

Transaction: SM13

Menu Path: From the main menu, choose Tools, Administration, Monitoring, Update.

Most applications use an asynchronous update method to speed up the response time for end users. When an application document is saved, the data is stored in intermediate storage and then transferred to the database by asynchronous update processes.

For outbound ALE/EDI processes, the IDoc selection program in many cases is started in the update routine. Syntax errors in the selection program or other hard errors may cause the update process to fail and result in a dump. In this event, the system maintains an update log (shown in Figure 11-24). This log is mainly monitored by the Basis group or by a programmer who is testing an IDoc selection program. You can double-click on the error line to get detailed information.

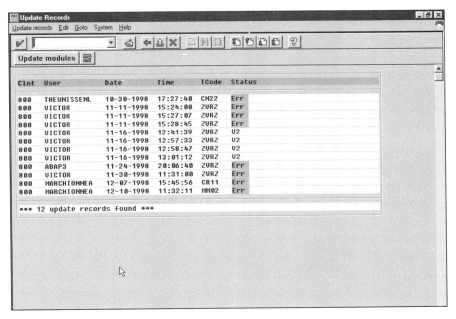

FIGURE 11-24

Example entries in the asynchronous update log

An express mail is also sent to the user informing him or her about the error. If you have written IDoc selection programs for the ALE/EDI interface, then you probably remember getting an express mail saying that the update was terminated when an error occurred in your selection program.

Dump Analysis

Transaction: ST22

Menu Path: From the main menu, choose Tools, Administration, Monitoring, Dump Analysis.

This log maintains a list of dumps, that is, a log of program crashes. You can view this log to resolve any dumps described in the previous step. The dump report is highly technical and used mainly by a programmer developing IDoc programs. I tend to use it when the system behaves mysteriously and everything looks fine. The reason for the mysterious behavior is obvious: the program crashed and did not get a chance to log any information. The dump analysis report in the SAP system is far superior to similar reports in any other system that I've used. The report provides several leads to help you determine the cause of the problem and also shows you the line of code where the failure occurred. Figure 11-25 shows the typical options available in the dump report.

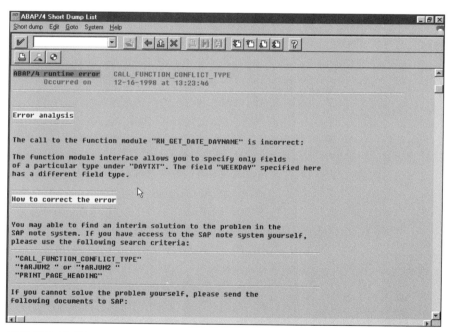

FIGURE 11-25

Options available to analyze a dump analysis report

System Log

Transaction: SM21

Menu Path: From the main menu, choose Tools, Administration, Monitoring, System Log.

The system log is a very comprehensive log maintained on each application server and possibly copied to a central log. This log records all system events such as starting the system, shutdown, process terminations, system errors, and communication problems. This universal log is used by all the application modules and is typically monitored by the Basis administrators. Because of the universal nature of this log, the entries are slightly cryptic and are best analyzed by a Basis person in conjunction with the application person.

If you experience any unexplainable behavior in the ALE/EDI system there is a good chance that something has gone wrong and is logged in the system log. An example of entries in the system log is shown in Figure 11-26.

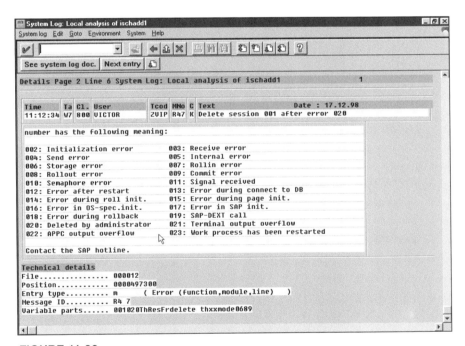

FIGURE 11-26

An example entry in the system log report

Displaying the Transactional RFC Log

Transaction: SM58

Menu Path: From the Area menu of ALE (BALE), choose Monitoring, Transactional RFC

Transactional RFC (tRFC) is SAP's enhanced asynchronous communication concept in which delivery of data is guaranteed. If network problems or any other conditions prevent data from being transferred, SAP holds the data and information about the remote system in the tRFC tables and attempts to deliver the data based on the configuration settings in the tRFC destination. This tool is used mainly in the ALE process. The tRFC settings are discussed in Chapter 22, "Configuring the ALE Infrastructure." A standard program RSARFCRD (Transaction SM58) is provided to display entries in the tRFC log. On the selection screen, the user name field defaults to your user ID, but you can clear it to see tRFC entries for all users. The output report (see Figure 11-27) shows entries that are in error. The following columns should be of interest to you:

TIP

Transactional RFC is a general technology, and therefore you may see entries from other applications (such as workflow) if they have failed. Entries that have INBOUND_IDOC_PROCESS in column 2 are ALE-related errors.

- ◆ **Column 1 (caller).** The caller is the user who initiates the ALE process.
- ◆ **Column 2 (function module).** This entry identifies the RFC function module that is to be invoked on the destination system. The RFC function module for ALE processes is INBOUND_IDOC_PROCESS.
- ◆ **Column 3 (target system).** This entry specifies the name of the destination system.
- ◆ **Column 4 (status text).** This column contains a short description of the problem. You can double-click on this text to get extended information. In most cases the problem is due to an incorrect user ID or network connection. Check your tRFC destination.

There are some additional fields that are not visible on the screen (you need to scroll to the right to see them) that display administrative information such as date, time, and name of the calling program. This information is only useful for identifying the process that made the tRFC call. It does not have any value in debugging the problem.

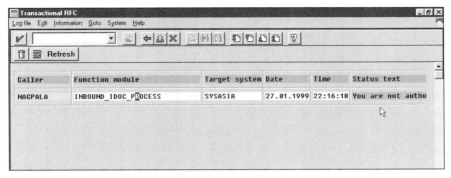

FIGURE 11-27

Entries in the transactional RFC log

Statistical Analysis of the Audit Log

Transaction: BDM7

Menu Path: From the Area menu of ALE, choose Monitoring, Audit Analysis

The audit analysis for a destination system allows you to:

◆ Monitor the processing state of IDocs from the sending system

◆ Monitor IDocs currently being processed on the sending system

---

 NOTE

The statistical analysis of the audit log process does not come pre-configured. You need to set up the process. Configuration of the audit process is described in the advanced settings portion of Chapter 22.

A standard program RBDAUD01 (Transaction BDM7) is provided to display entries in the audit log. On the selection screen of this program, you can choose the logical system name of the destination system, message type, and creation date of IDocs. The output report (see Figure 11-28) shows IDocs in process on the current system for the destination system and IDocs in process on the receiving system. You can double-click on any line to display detailed statistics.

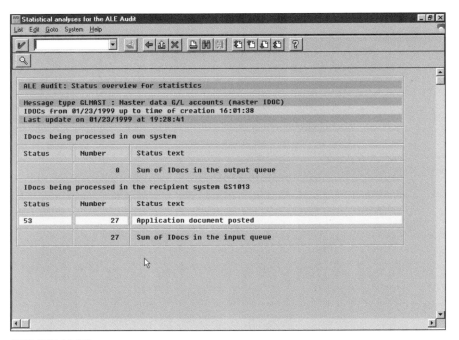

FIGURE 11-28

Viewing the audit log of IDocs processed on the receiving system

To Use or Not to Use the SAP Inbox

You will notice that when you execute a work item, it takes you to a log that you can also view without using workflow. For example, if you have a work item for an application error in the IDoc, it takes you to the IDoc display screen where you can look at the error. By now you're probably wondering why you use workflow when you can get to the IDoc display directly using the transaction WE02 or WE05.

Workflow notifications are useful for error situations that can be predefined, but where the timing of errors are unpredictable. For example, the problem with the file log is very rare, so the system administrator will not be monitoring the log on a regular basis. Workflow monitoring is also suited for people who are not frequent users of the system. The advantages of using workflow are timeliness and accountability for resolving the problems.

System administrators are interested in the overall state of the system and are more tuned to using the tools directly for everyday repetitive tasks. For example, the EDI administrator will most likely be monitoring the IDoc list for errors to get a global view of the problems in the system. The information that administrators need cannot be defined concisely. Also, they need to monitor a wide range of errors.

Summary

The ALE/EDI interface provides several tools to monitor the overall health of the system, display IDocs, process work items in the Inbox, display message control logs, display system level logs, and display workflow logs. IDoc monitoring tools (WE02, WE05, and WE07) are the most commonly used tools because the IDoc is the main component in an ALE/EDI process. The status records in an IDoc provide details of the process at various milestones. Errors in the ALE/EDI process are reported via workflow whenever possible. The SAP Inbox serves the interface to view work items that are sent to a user as part of the error handling process via workflow. Workflow is best suited for infrequent, predefined problems that are addressed to a specific group of people. System administrators use the system level tools to monitor update logs, file logs, and system logs. A great deal of statistical information can be derived from the workflow logs, which helps you analyze trends in the types of errors that occur in your environment. There is a wealth of information available in the system and a wealth of tools available to view that information.

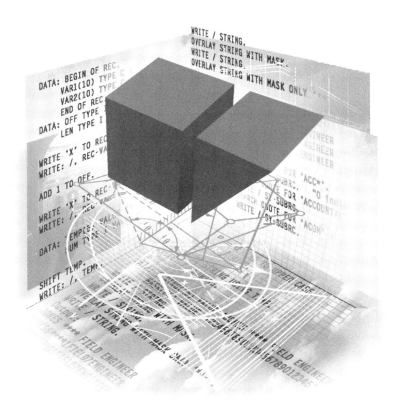

Chapter 12

EDI Process Troubleshooting and Recovery

Even if you carry out all of the configuration steps detailed in Chapters 6 through 9 and test all the components thoroughly, the system will experience problems at some point. In this chapter you learn how to identify a successful process execution, how to troubleshoot the system when it fails, and how to restart the system from the point of failure. Chapter 12 extends the coverage of Chapter 11, "Monitoring the Interface," and shows you how and when to use the various system-monitoring tools introduced there. In the following section, you learn how to logically navigate to the location of an error or a problem so that you can correct it quickly.

The best approach to troubleshooting any process is to understand the process, learn what the points of failure are, and then determine how the system reports problems. (This chapter assumes that you already understand the outbound and inbound processes.)

Follow this simple approach to troubleshooting:

1. Determine whether a failure has occurred.

2. For a given symptom, use the troubleshooting chart (Figures 12-1 to 12-16) as your guide to quickly get to the root of the problem.

3. Use the appropriate monitoring tools as described in Chapter 11, "Monitoring the Interface," to read and interpret the appropriate log. Use the information in the log to help you analyze the problem.

4. Fix the cause of the problem.

5. Determine the point of restart as suggested in the troubleshooting chart. Depending on the problem, you may restart the process from the point of failure, or you may have to restart from the very beginning.

6. Use the technique most suitable for restarting the process. You can restart it from within workflow (if applicable) or use one of the ALE/EDI tools for restarting the process.

Troubleshooting the Outbound Process

In this section you learn how to troubleshoot an outbound process, find the cause of a problem, fix it as necessary, and restart the process using an appropriate technique.

Points of Failure in the Outbound Process

The outbound process is a sequence of asynchronous processes. Failure can occur within any process. The points of failure on an outbound process are as follows:

◆ Error in creating the application document

◆ Error in proposal of Output type

◆ Error in NAST processing

◆ Error in processing of the Output type

◆ Error in the ALE/EDI interface layer

◆ Error in the IDoc (syntax errors, conversion, and so on)

◆ Error in sending the IDoc to the EDI subsystem

◆ Error in triggering the subsystem

◆ Error in the subsystem

◆ Unknown errors or mysterious errors

Reporting Problems

When problems occur in the outbound process, the system uses the technique most suitable at that point to report the problem. The main technique used is the workflow component, but workflow is not started until you are interacting with the system in a dialog mode. After control is passed to the SAP system for processing, the system logs the problems and reports them via workflow. The mechanism used to report problems at different points of failure is as follows:

◆ When an application document is created, the output control screen displays the proposed outputs. For any problems at this point, use the Determination Analysis option from the menu to determine the cause of the problem. No workflow is necessary.

◆ After the document is saved, control passes to the SAP system, and the processing of the Output types starts asynchronously. The NAST table is processed for Output types. Errors in managing the NAST entries are logged in the Message control table, but no workflow is started. Errors in managing the NAST table are very rare.

 NOTE

With release 4.5, a workflow is created for errors with processing of NAST.

◆ The Output type for EDI messages is processed by calling the IDoc selection program. Until an IDoc is created, the system cannot log the problems in the IDoc; therefore, problems at this point are logged in the Message control tables. For applications that use Message control, this log can be viewed from the output control screen. If an error occurs in the IDoc selection program before an IDoc is created, the system sends a workflow message to the EDI administrator.

◆ After an IDoc is created, the system logs every problem in the status records of the IDoc and then uses the workflow component to send a workitem to the responsible person (as identified in the Partner profile).

◆ The system performs some basic integrity checks on the IDoc, as well as a syntax check. If an error is found, then the IDoc gets a status code of 26 (Error during syntax check of IDoc outbound). A workflow message is sent to the responsible person (as identified in the Partner profile). Up to this point any errors discovered in the system are categorized as ALE/EDI interface errors.

◆ The IDoc is then passed to the OS. Errors can occur for several reasons, and are reported with a status code of 02 (Error passing data to port). A workflow message is generated for the responsible person (as identified in the Partner profile).

◆ After an IDoc is passed to the OS and the subsystem is installed, the system tries to start the subsystem. Errors can occur for several reasons and are reported with a status code of 20 (Error triggering the subsystem). A workflow message is generated for the responsible person (as identified in the Partner profile).

Determining Whether an Outbound Process Is Successful

Problems can occur at any point in the process, as noted earlier in the chapter. Your objective is to receive a success message. Knowing what is considered successful will help you achieve your goal. If everything works as desired, then there is no need to dig into the troubleshooting process. The final success milestone depends on whether or not the subsystem is installed:

◆ **Subsystem not installed.** If the subsystem is not installed, then the process is considered a success when the IDoc generated for your process gets a status code of 03 (Data passed to port OK).

◆ **Subsystem installed.** If the subsystem is installed the final status code depends on the various status codes reported by your subsystem. The subsystem could have been set up to send one final confirmation at the end, or it may report status at every milestone, in which case there can be several status codes in an IDoc. From SAP's perspective the process is successful if you get a status code of 18 (Triggering EDI subsystem OK). If the subsystem reports any of the status codes in Table 12-1, then the process is considered a failure on the subsystem.

Table 12-1 Subsystem Error Codes

Status Code	Description
04	Error within control information of EDI subsystem
05	Error during translation
07	Error during syntax check
09	Error during interchange handling
11	Error during dispatch
15	Interchange Acknowledgment negative
17	Functional Acknowledgment negative
23	Error during retransmission

Troubleshooting Guide for Outbound Errors

The best way to troubleshoot an outbound process is to first check the output control log for errors and then check the IDoc or the SAP Inbox.

The flowcharts shown in Figure 12-1 through 12-9 depict the logical sequence of the troubleshooting process. They also tell you which log to monitor and identify the point of restart.

You always start at the top of Figure 12-1 and then navigate to the cause of problem using the decision boxes. Figure 12-1 shows the troubleshooting process when your desired output type is not proposed correctly on the output control screen. Figure 12-2 walks you through the troubleshooting process when your output types have been proposed correctly but an IDoc is not generated. Figure 12-3 guides you to look for severe errors in the system if the system confirms that an IDoc was generated but an actual IDoc does not exist. If an IDoc exists, then depending on the IDoc status, you will navigate to the respective diagrams as described.

Refer to Figure 12-4 for IDoc status 02 (Error passing data to port). The cause of the problem is probably the port settings. Refer to Figure 12-5 for IDoc status 03 (Data passed to port OK). This status usually indicates success unless you have a subsystem installed and the subsystem was not started. Figure 12-6 describes the troubleshooting process when the IDoc goes into status 18 (Error triggering the subsystem). This is mainly caused due to connectivity errors between SAP and the EDI subsystem.

Figure 12-7 helps you in locating the cause of syntax errors in an IDoc (status 26— Errors during syntax check). Figure 12-8 helps you analyze errors in the ALE service layer (status 29—Error in ALE service). In most cases it is a problem with partner profiles. Figure 12-9 describes a situation in which an IDoc is stuck in status 30. It could be related to a configuration error or could be some other severe error.

 NOTE

The set of Figures 12-1 through 12-9 should be viewed as one logical figure. But like any other flowcharting technique, you will find suitable connectors that allow you to navigate from one figure to another.

Restart Points for Outbound Errors

The restart can be carried out from the very beginning, or you can restart from the point of failure (see Figures 12-1 through 12-9). The following sections explain the steps for restarting from various points.

Restart from the Application Document

In this case you must re-create the application document, following the same steps you used the first time. This time the error should be gone. If you run into problems again, follow the troubleshooting guide to find the cause of the problem.

Restart from Message Control

The restart from within the Message control can be carried out for applications that use Message control. The following sections describe three techniques for this type of restart, depending on the configuration of the Message control component and your preference.

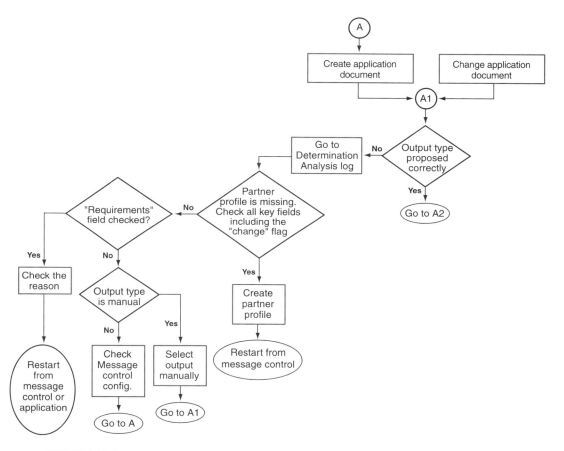

FIGURE 12-1

Troubleshooting chart for outbound errors—error in proposing correct output type

Automatically

You can restart the outbound process from within the application document by going to the output control screen. You go into the document in change mode. Some Output types are configured to be proposed every time you enter the document this way. A new entry will exist with a current status of 0, indicating that the entry has not been processed yet. The document can now be saved. The timing of the Output type determines when processing will start.

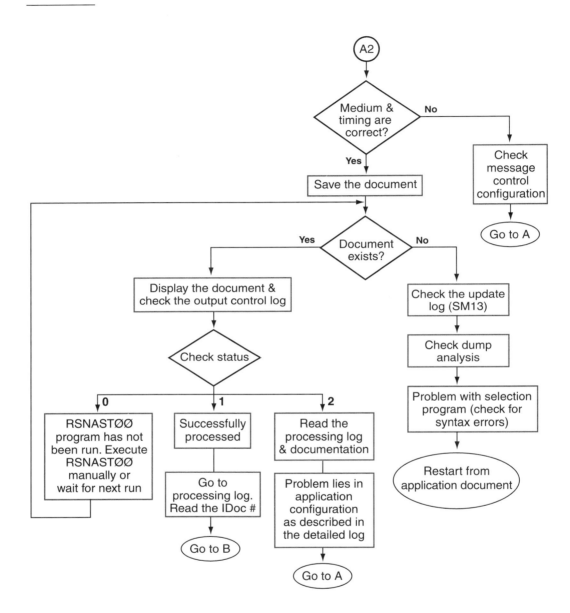

FIGURE 12-2

Troubleshooting chart for outbound errors—errors in processing an output type

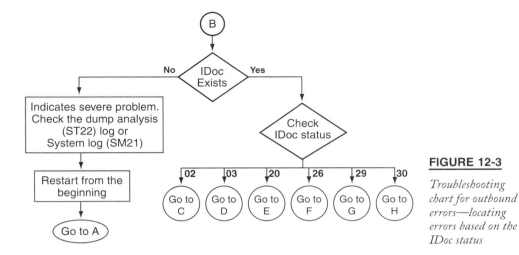

FIGURE 12-3

Troubleshooting chart for outbound errors—locating errors based on the IDoc status

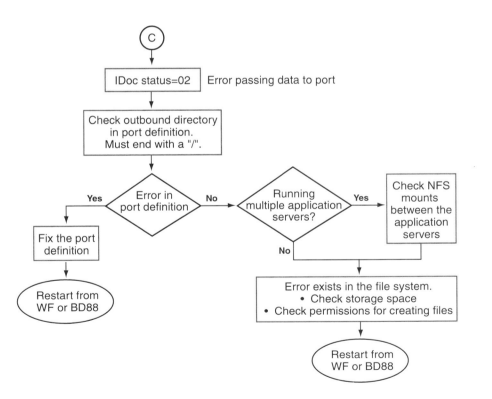

FIGURE 12-4

Troubleshooting chart for outbound errors—IDoc status 02

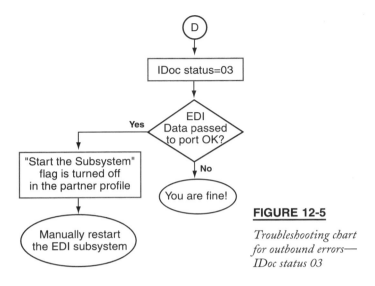

FIGURE 12-5

Troubleshooting chart for outbound errors— IDoc status 03

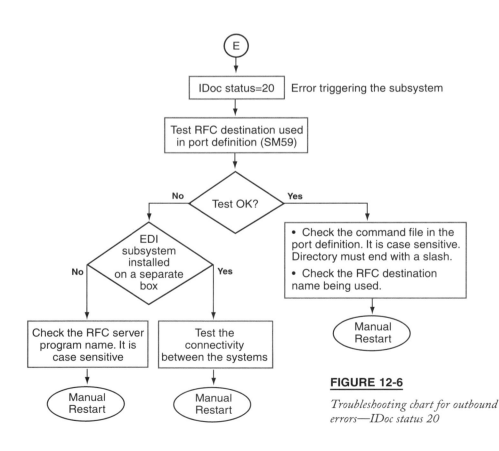

FIGURE 12-6

Troubleshooting chart for outbound errors—IDoc status 20

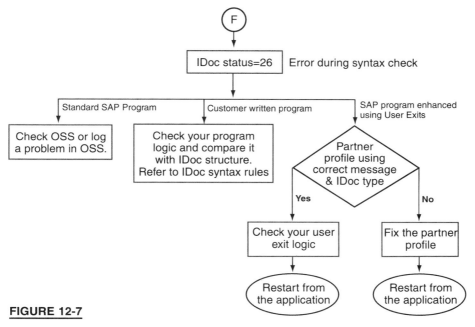

FIGURE 12-7

Troubleshooting chart for outbound errors—IDoc status 26

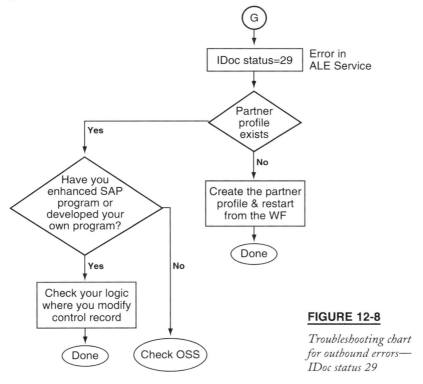

FIGURE 12-8

Troubleshooting chart for outbound errors— IDoc status 29

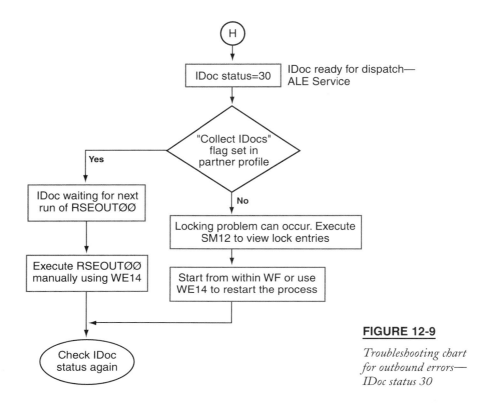

FIGURE 12-9

Troubleshooting chart for outbound errors— IDoc status 30

TIP

To see whether an Output type is proposed every time you go to change a document, go to the settings of the Output type. If the Condition Access and Multiple Issuing flags are checked, then the Output type is configured for proposal every time. However, the output may still not be proposed if Condition records and Requirements are not satisfied. Refer to Chapter 8, "Configuring Message Control" for details on Output type, Requirements and Condition records.

Repeat Output

If your output is not proposed automatically, then you can manually repeat the output from the output control screen by selecting the previously failed output and then clicking on the Repeat Output button in the toolbar.

This step should create a new entry in the Output type list. After you save the document, the timing of the output determines when the processing will start.

Output from NAST

You can also start the process from a NAST entry. This approach is possible only for entries that were once successful and were sent with a timing of 1 or 2 in the Output type. This technique is useful when you have to send an output because it was lost or when you have to repeatedly test an Output type. In this case if you use the output control screen, it fills up very quickly and looks quite messy. This is a personal choice; if you feel comfortable with the first technique, then you can ignore this option.

To start the processing, you execute the RSNAST00 program via SE38 or directly by executing transaction WE15. Enter the object key, which is your document number (prefixed with zeros if it is less than 10 characters) and select the Send Again check box. Click on the Execute button to restart the outbound process.

Restart from the SAP Inbox

If a workflow message was generated for the error, then you have the option of restarting the process from within workflow. However, for some errors the workflow message is merely an FYI message, in which case you cannot restart the process from workflow. Such processes are either restarted manually or restarted from outside the SAP system. You can easily tell whether a work item allows restart by executing it. If the resulting screen has a Process button, then restart is possible from within workflow.

Restarting from the SAP Inbox saves you the trouble of remembering the application transaction and data values. Remember, workflow brings the right task with the right information to the right person at the right time in the right sequence. You can simply execute the work item to start the process.

 TIP

If the error was such that several IDocs failed for the same reason, then it is convenient to use one of the ALE/EDI tools to start the process, as described in the next section.

Restarting Using ALE Tools

Transaction: BD88

Menu Path: Logistics, Central Functions, Distribution, Periodic Processing, ALE
Outbound IDocs

This method is an alternative to restarting the process from the SAP Inbox and
is commonly deployed for mass errors, but you can also use this approach for
single errors. Using this tool instead of the workflow tool has merit in certain
cases. Consider the following situation: If the file system has some problem—say
it's full or inaccessible—then the dispatch program will fail in passing the IDocs
from the SAP system to the EDI subsystem. A work item will be generated for
every IDoc that fails. The number of such work items can be enormous
considering the number of IDocs that are typically exchanged in a company. After
you fix the problem, you can use the outbound ALE tool to restart all the failed
IDocs in one step without having to execute a workitem for each failed IDoc in
the SAP Inbox. Transaction BD88 is used to bail out IDocs that are in error. It
works for IDocs that are in the status codes shown in Table 12-2.

Table 12-2 Status Codes Processed by the ALE Outbound Tool

Status	Status code	Status text
IDocs in ALE/EDI error	02	Error passing data to port
	04	Error within control information of EDI
	05	Error during translation
	25	Processing despite syntax error (outbound)
	29	Error in ALE service
IDocs with syntax error	26	Error during syntax check of IDoc (outbound)
IDocs ready for dispatch	30	IDoc ready for dispatch (ALE service)
IDocs that have been edited	32	IDoc was edited

This tool allows you to process the IDocs from the point of failure without having
to restart the process from the beginning. The steps are as follows:

1. Execute Transaction BD88.
2. From the screen displayed (see Figure 12-10), select the appropriate radio
    button based on the status of your IDoc.

3. On the next screen, you can further restrict the number of IDocs to be processed. After you enter the parameters, click on the Execute button to start the processing.

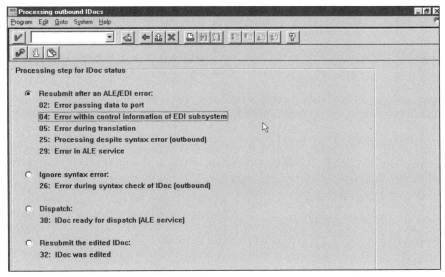

FIGURE 12-10

Selection screen for restarting outbound IDocs

Manual Restart

This technique is useful when an error has occurred outside the SAP system or a strange error occurs in the SAP system. If the error occurs in the EDI subsystem, the SAP system can only resend the IDoc for the following status codes:

◆ 04 (Error within control information of EDI subsystem)

◆ 05 (Error during translation)

In other cases you'll have to fix the problem within the subsystem. For unexplained errors within the SAP system, it is best to restart from the application document. For example, if you create an application document for which an Output type is proposed with a timing of 1, the system will wait for the RSNAST00 program to execute and process the Output type. However, in the meantime someone could delete the application document, and the RSNAST00 program will be thoroughly confused. I call this type of event a "strange error," or an error the system cannot handle. You will get a work item, but SAP cannot restart the process. In such a situation, you'll have to find the cause of the problem and manually fix it. You'll most likely end up restarting the process from the very beginning.

Purging the Outbound Process

The recovery process doesn't always mean getting the IDoc to the final success milestone. In certain situations corrupt data may prevent you from fixing a problem and force you to start the process from scratch. If the process in error has created an IDoc, then you don't want to leave the IDoc in limbo. You must make it impossible to accidentally reprocess the IDoc.

You can purge the IDoc that is not going to be used. An erroneous IDoc can be purged from the work item generated as a result of this error or from one of the ALE tools discussed earlier. The only other means of getting rid of an IDoc is via the archiving process.

The steps to purge an IDoc from a work item are straightforward. First you need to identify the work item that was sent to you for the error situation that you want to purge. Execute the work item and look for the Delete button. After you click on the Delete button, the IDoc is marked for deletion and gets a status code of 31 (Error—no further processing). This step prevents the EDI or ALE tools from accidentally reprocessing the IDoc.

Troubleshooting the Inbound Process

In this section you learn how to troubleshoot an inbound process, find the cause of problem, fix it as necessary, and restart the process using an appropriate technique.

Failures in the Inbound Process

The inbound process is a sequence of asynchronous processes. Failure can occur within any process. The points of failure on an inbound process are as follows:

◆ Error in triggering the SAP system from the EDI subsystem

◆ Error in creating the IDoc

◆ Error in the ALE/EDI interface layer

- ◆ Error in the posting function module
- ◆ Unknown or mysterious errors

Reporting Problems

When problems occur in the inbound process, the system uses the technique most suitable at that point to report the problem. The main technique used is the workflow component, but workflow is not started until an IDoc file is passed to the SAP system. After control is passed to the SAP system for processing, the SAP system logs the problems and reports them via workflow.

The EDI subsystem handles problems encountered in processing an inbound EDI document on the EDI subsystem. You'll have to check with the subsystem vendor for a troubleshooting guide. However, you can design your EDI subsystem to send a TXTRAW message to the SAP system to report problems. This message can be directed to the EDI administrator.

The mechanism used to report problems at different points of failure is described below:

- ◆ Errors that occur in triggering the SAP system from the EDI subsystem are logged in the system log and are reported to the subsystem as RFC errors. No workflow is started until this point. Thus errors up to this point have to be monitored at the EDI subsystem level.
- ◆ From the point when an IDoc has been passed to the SAP system to the point it gets created in the database, errors are logged in the EDFI2 table (File log). A workflow message is also generated to inform the EDI administrator.
- ◆ After an IDoc is created, errors are logged in the status record of the IDoc and problems are reported via workflow.
- ◆ The system performs some basic integrity checks on the IDoc. After the basic checks, the control information is matched against a Partner profile. If a partner profile is not found, then the IDoc gets a status code of 56 (IDoc with errors added) and a workflow message is sent to the EDI administrator.
- ◆ After an IDoc is created, a syntax check is done, the IDoc goes through version change, and conversion occurs. If an error is found, then the IDoc gets a status code of 60 (Error during syntax check of IDoc inbound). A workflow message is sent to the responsible person (as identified in the partner profile).

◆ Up to this point, any errors discovered in the system are categorized as ALE/EDI interface errors.

◆ The IDoc is then passed to the posting module. If the posting module returns an error, the IDoc gets a status code of 51 (Application document not posted). A workflow message is sent to the responsible person (as identified in the Partner profile). There are several reasons for failure of an application document. In most cases the problem is with the data.

Determining the Success of an Inbound Process

Errors can occur at several points in the inbound process as noted earlier in the chapter. Your objective is to receive a success message; knowing the measure of success will help you achieve that objective.

When an incoming IDoc is successfully posted, it gets a status code of 53 (Application document posted).

Troubleshooting Guide for Inbound Errors

The best approach for troubleshooting an inbound process is to first check the SAP Inbox. If there is no error message check the IDoc list for any problems.

The flowchart in Figures 12-11 through 12-17 will help you with the troubleshooting process. The chart depicts the process in logical sequence, tells you which log to monitor, and helps you determine the correct point of restart.

You always start at the top of Figure 12-11 and then navigate quickly to the cause of problem using the decision boxes. Figure 12-11 shows you the steps for locating problems when the inbound process is started but an IDoc is not present. If an IDoc was created, use Figure 12-12 to branch to the next figure that corresponds to the IDoc status. Figure 12-13 helps you resolve IDocs stuck in status 50. This is mainly due to a configuration error.

Figure 12-14 describes the troubleshooting process for the most common errors found in inbound IDocs—the application errors. Refer to the next section, "Resolving Application Errors," for details on how to resolve the errors. Figure 12-15 shows you the possible cause of errors in the ALE/EDI layer, which results in an IDoc getting stuck in status 56. Figure 12-16 helps you in debugging the cause for syntax errors in an incoming IDoc. Figure 12-17 helps you in locating the reason for the IDoc in status 64. This is usually a configuration error in the partner profile, but if the partner profile configuration is correct, it indicates a severe error or another problem that may have been fixed by SAP. You need to consult OSS in this case.

 NOTE

The set of Figures 12-11 through 12-17 should be viewed as one logical figure.

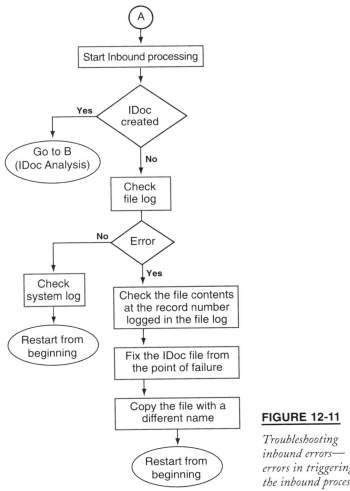

FIGURE 12-11

Troubleshooting inbound errors— errors in triggering the inbound process

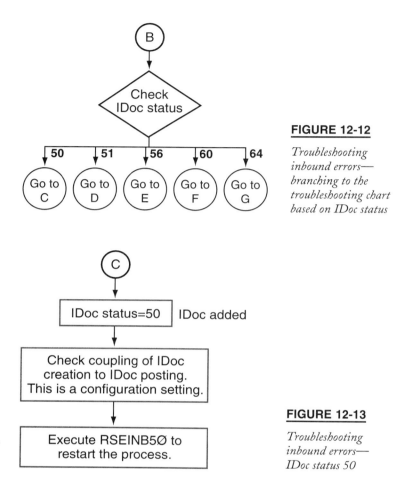

FIGURE 12-12

Troubleshooting inbound errors— branching to the troubleshooting chart based on IDoc status

FIGURE 12-13

Troubleshooting inbound errors— IDoc status 50

Resolving Application Errors

Application errors are by far the most common errors on an inbound process. Because data originates outside the system, you may always have some data-related problems to resolve. Problems within SAP will eventually cease as you find fixes or make appropriate changes. The following tips can help you resolve application errors.

◆ **Executing Failed Processes in Foreground Mode.** If the posting program in SAP uses CALL Transaction, you can restart the process in foreground mode and step through each screen until you find the problem. To see whether your posting program uses CALL Transaction, execute transaction BD52. Entries with a value of 1 or 2 use CALL Transaction.

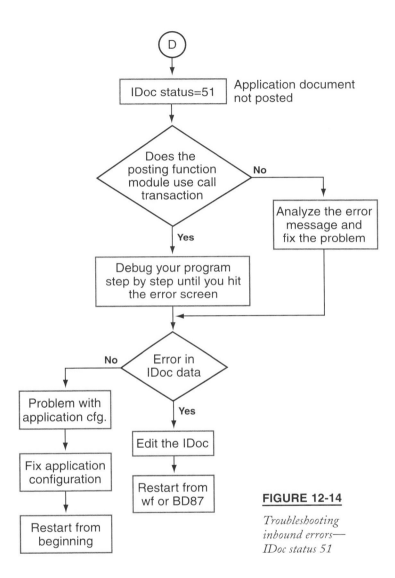

FIGURE 12-14

Troubleshooting inbound errors—IDoc status 51

◆ **Editing Failed IDocs.** Editing a failed IDoc is a quick fix for data-related problems. For example, if your vendor sent in a wrong material number, you can change the value in the IDoc. You can then restart the process, and the document should post. SAP makes a backup copy of the original IDoc and assigns it a status of 70 (Original of an IDoc that was edited). You should not use this technique as a permanent fix, however, because doing so only addresses the symptoms, not the cause of the problem.

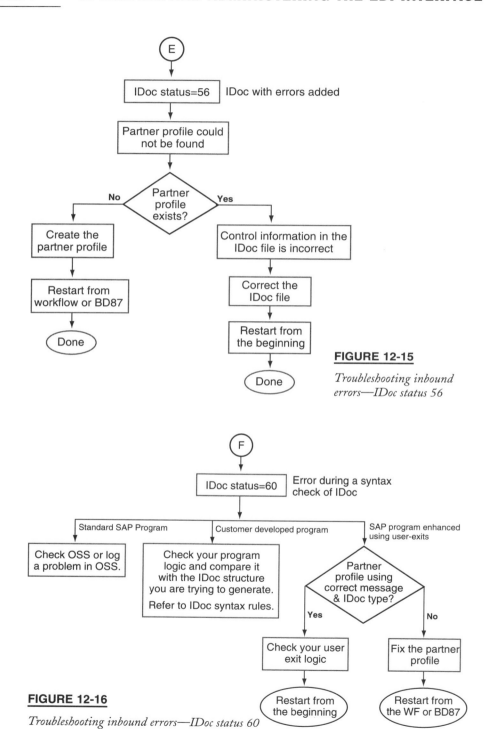

FIGURE 12-15

Troubleshooting inbound errors—IDoc status 56

FIGURE 12-16

Troubleshooting inbound errors—IDoc status 60

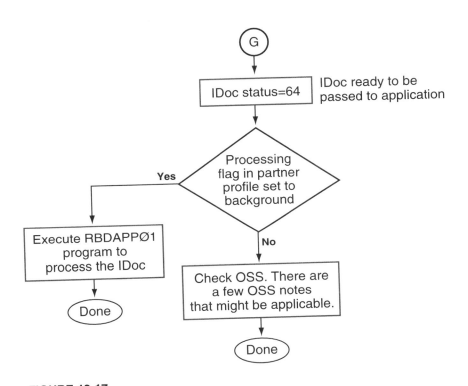

FIGURE 12-17

Troubleshooting inbound errors—IDoc status 64

Restart Points for Inbound Errors

Restart can be carried out from the very beginning or from the point of failure. The restart point should be determined from the troubleshooting chart. The following sections explain the steps for restarting from various points.

Restart from the EDI Subsystem

In this case you resend the IDoc file from the EDI subsystem to the SAP system. You can use the startrfc command or one of the inbound utilities. Refer to "Testing Utilities to Start the Inbound Process" in Chapter 10, "Testing the EDI Interface."

Restart from the SAP Inbox

If a workflow message was generated for the error, then you have the option of restarting the process from within workflow. However, for some errors, the workflow message is merely an FYI message, as with an error in reading or deleting the inbound file. Such processes are meant to be restarted manually or from outside the SAP system.

TIP

You can easily tell whether a workitem allows restart by executing it. If the resulting screen has a Process button, then restart is possible from within workflow.

Restarting from the SAP Inbox saves you the trouble of remembering the application transaction and data values. You can simply execute the work item to restart the process.

If the error caused several IDocs to fail for the same reason, then it's convenient to use one of the ALE tools to start the process, as explained in the next section.

Restart Using ALE Tools

Transaction: BD88

Menu Path: Logistics, Central Functions, Distribution, Periodic Processing, ALE Inbound IDocs

This method is commonly deployed for mass errors, but you can use it for single errors. Using this tool instead of the workflow tool is advantageous in certain cases. For example, if several orders are received from a customer and a small glitch occurs in the customer master record, the orders will not post successfully. These IDocs are now in status 51 (Application document not posted), and the system sends a workflow message. You could certainly go into the SAP Inbox, execute the workitems one at a time, and fix the problem, but it is more convenient to use the ALE tools to restart the failed IDocs in one step.

You can use transaction BD87 to bail out IDocs that are in error. This technique works for IDocs with the status codes in Table 12-3.

Table 12-3 Status Codes Processed by the ALE Inbound Tool

Status	Status code	Status text
IDocs in application error	51	Error: Application document not posted
Error in the ALE/EDI interface layer	56	IDoc with errors added
	61	Processing despite syntax error
	63	Error passing IDoc to application
	65	Error in ALE service
IDocs with syntax errors	60	Error during syntax check of IDoc (inbound)
IDocs ready for posting	64	IDoc ready to be passed to application
IDocs have been edited	69	IDoc was edited

This tool allows you to process the IDocs from the point of failure without having to restart the process from the beginning. The steps are as follows:

1. Execute Transaction BD87.

2. Select the appropriate radio button based on the status of your IDoc (see Figure 12-18).

3. On the next screen, you can further restrict the number of IDocs to be processed. After you enter the parameters, click on the Execute button to start processing. The results are logged in the status record.

Purging the Inbound Process

Just like the outbound process, you can purge the IDoc that's not going to be used. An erroneous IDoc can be purged from the work item that was generated because of this error or from one of the ALE tools discussed earlier. The only other means of getting rid of an IDoc is via the archiving process.

To purge an IDoc from a work item, you need to identify the work item that was sent to you. Execute the work item and look for the Delete button. After you click on the Delete button, the IDoc is marked for deletion and gets a status code of 68 (Error—no further processing). This step prevents the EDI or ALE tools from accidentally reprocessing the IDoc.

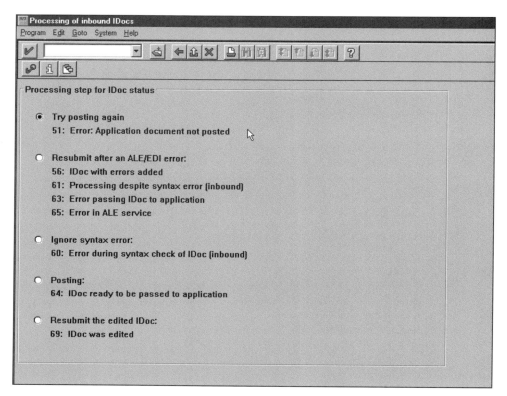

FIGURE 12-18

The selection screen for restarting inbound IDocs

Summary

Errors can occur at various steps in the outbound and inbound processes. SAP provides extensive log information at various points. Until an IDoc is generated, SAP logs the error in the application initiating the process. After an IDoc is generated, the IDoc becomes the main vehicle for any log information, and errors are routed via workflow to the right person.

Because errors are possible at various points, knowing where to look can reduce the time required to fix them. The troubleshooting process follows a simple approach: Determine whether an error has occurred and then use the troubleshooting flowchart to track down the problem. After you find the cause of the problem, fix it; then restart the process from the point of failure if the system permits a restart. If not, you must restart the process from the very beginning. In some cases you can restart the process, but you may opt to start from the beginning because data is corrupted. In those cases, you must ensure that the items in error are purged.

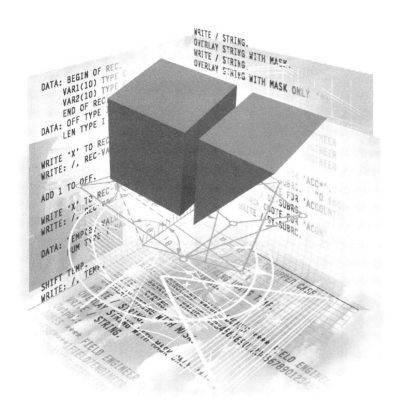

Chapter 13

Managing EDI Process Performance and Throughput

In this chapter you'll learn how to manage the performance of your EDI interface so that it provides the necessary throughput without causing the other processes to slow down. This chapter focuses on ways to manage performance at the application level by controlling the execution of processes; the focus is not on performance-tuning procedures used for program and database tuning. The later procedures are part of an overall performance-tuning strategy that applies to all modules.

Performance is a relative term. A system that is executing fast enough for one user may not be fast enough for another. Luckily, you don't have this problem because the EDI process is inherently asynchronous, meaning that the user does not have to wait for the process to complete. For example, if you create a purchase order document, you do not have to wait for a response from your business partner. After you create a document, the system carries out the EDI process behind the scene.

EDI processes consume a lot of system cycles, which can hamper the performance of the system for other users. Each time an outbound IDoc is created, the system extracts application data, creates an IDoc, extracts the IDoc data, and creates an outbound file. On the inbound, an application document is created from an IDoc. If the inbound transaction uses CALL Transaction, then the process is very much like a user entering data online. A huge EDI transaction volume can slow down the system performance considerably.

You need to manage your EDI processes so that outbound IDocs are created when the system is not heavily loaded; the same applies to application documents for incoming IDocs. This guideline is not a suggestion to run everything at night. Some transactions such as advance shipment notices and delivery schedules are designed to support a JIT (Just in Time) environment. You can configure the interface to run these immediately as described in the following section.

Managing Performance of Outbound Processes

The outbound interface can be run in near-real-time mode or in batch mode. The benefits and drawbacks of each approach are discussed next.

Real-Time Outbound

The EDI process in SAP is implemented as a series of application programs. An asynchronous process can be operated in a near-real-time mode by executing the various programs in a coordinated fashion so that as soon as one program completes, the next program starts instantaneously.

In near-real-time mode, as soon as the application document is created, the IDoc is generated and passed to the subsystem and the subsystem is started. This sequence gives a real-time feel, which is useful for critical EDI transactions. Criticality is a relative term and has a different meaning for each organization. In some businesses outgoing invoices are critical; for JIT partners advance shipment notices are critical transactions. This option should not be used for high-volume and noncritical transactions, as it will cause performance problems.

The configuration option allows you to control the output at a very granular level. You could have a partner enabled for all messages to go in real-time mode or for only specific messages to go in real-time mode. The outbound interface can be seen as a link of the following programs:

◆ **Application Transaction.** The application transaction creates the application document. For example, VA01—Create Sales Order, ME21—Create Purchase Order.

◆ **RSNAST00.** Starts the process of generating IDocs from the application document.

◆ **RSEOUT00.** Transfers IDocs from the SAP database to the OS and starts the subsystem.

Figures 13-1 and 13-2 show the settings necessary to achieve the near-real-time behavior. The following settings are required to achieve the near real-time behavior:

◆ In Message control, the timing of the output type should be set to 4 (Immediate). On the output control screen, you can reach this setting by clicking on the Further Data button (see Figure 13-1).

◆ In the Partner profile for the outbound message, the outbound mode should be Transfer IDoc Immediately and Start Subsystem (see Figure 13-2).

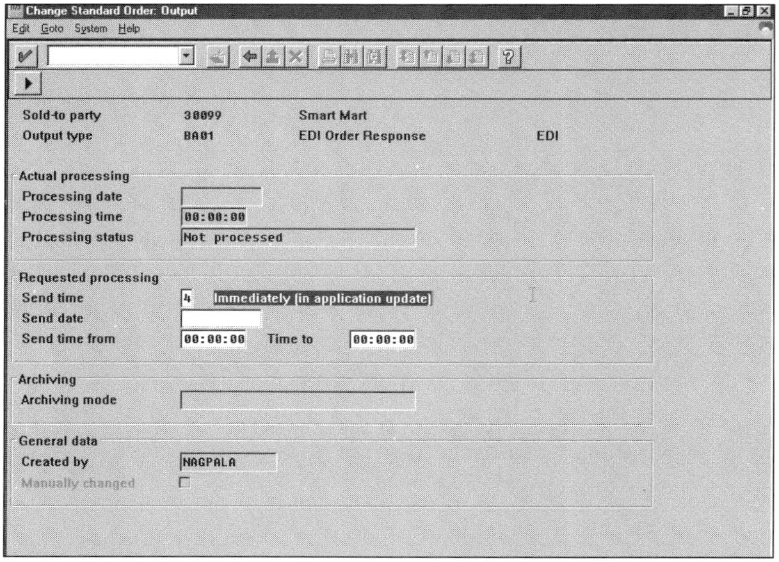

FIGURE 13-1

Settings of an output type for immediate processing

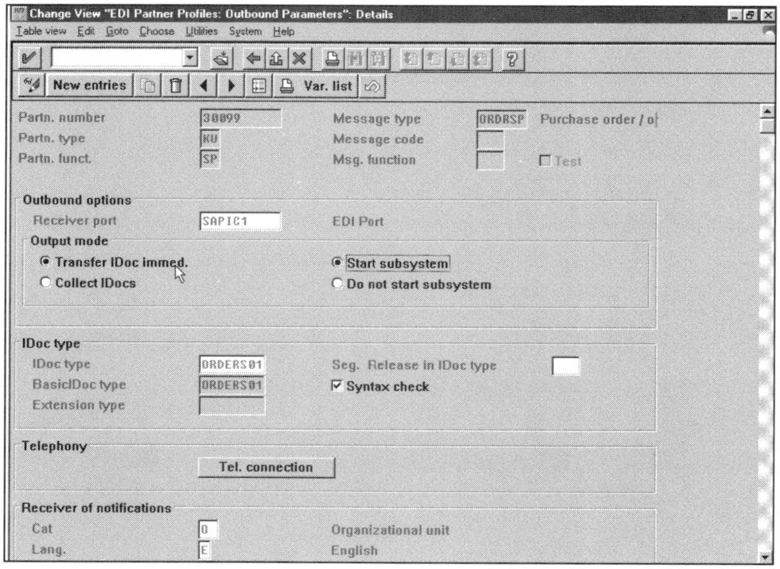

FIGURE 13-2

Partner profile settings for immediate processing

Outbound in Batch Mode

Batch mode is appropriate for noncritical and high-volume transactions. This mode is useful from a performance perspective because output is not generated immediately upon the creation of the application document.

The process can be controlled at two stages, depending on the needs of the company. The first point of control is at the Message control level. When an application document is created, the process to start creating the IDocs can be batched by setting the timing in the Message control output screen to 1, as shown in Figure 13-3. In this case a record is created in the NAST table with the application document number. Buffering IDocs at this stage provides the highest performance benefits because there is no load on the system from an EDI perspective. The process can be scheduled to run when the system is not loaded, such as at night. The only drawback with this approach is that any errors in the outbound process will not be discovered until the process is executed. The program used at this stage is the RSNAST00 program to start the process of generating IDocs. Several instances of this program can be scheduled with different variants to achieve the desired results.

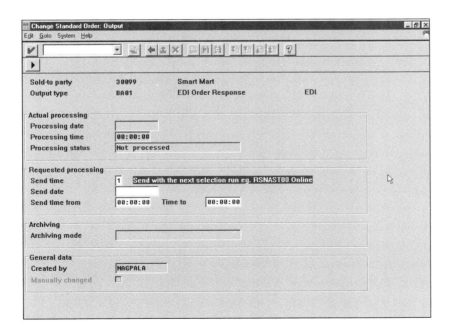

FIGURE 13-3

Settings of an output type for batch processing

As an example, suppose outbound purchase orders and invoices are buffered. A decision has been made to send purchase orders once every day at night, while invoices must go out within four hours of their creation. Two instances of RSNAST00 can be scheduled: one to run every night, at 11:00 p.m. to process the purchase order documents and the other to run every four hours to process the invoices.

The second point of control is when IDocs are transferred to the OS layer. This feature can also be controlled by setting the output mode in the Partner profile to Collect IDocs, as shown in Figure 13-4. There are two advantages of buffering IDocs at this stage. First, the IDocs have been generated, and any errors in the outbound process should have been discovered. The second advantage is that performance is improved by collecting IDocs and thus creating a single file bundled with several IDocs.

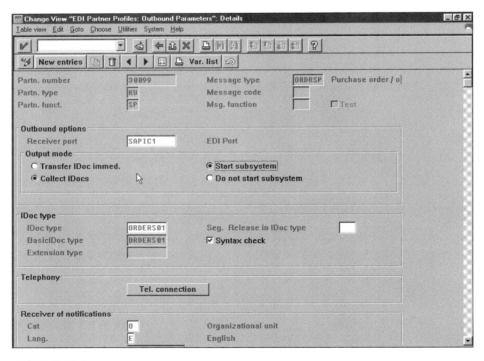

FIGURE 13-4

Partner profile settings for collecting IDocs

The RSEOUT00 program transfers buffered IDocs in the database to the OS. This program must be scheduled on an as-needed basis. Several instances of this program can also be scheduled to send the buffered IDocs to the OS layer.

Outbound Process with and without ALE Services

When IDocs are created from the application document, they are passed to the ALE/EDI interface layer. The ALE interface layer handles any formatting, filtering, and data conversion that may be applicable for the IDoc. In an EDI process, these functions can be better handled in the subsystem layer, and thus an IDoc does not need to go through the ALE services layer. This approach also improves performance to a certain extent. In the standard system, the IDocs generated in the EDI process go through the ALE services layer.

To prevent the process from using the ALE services, the process code needs to be moved from its current location (use ALE services) to a new location (without ALE services), as shown in Figure 13-5.

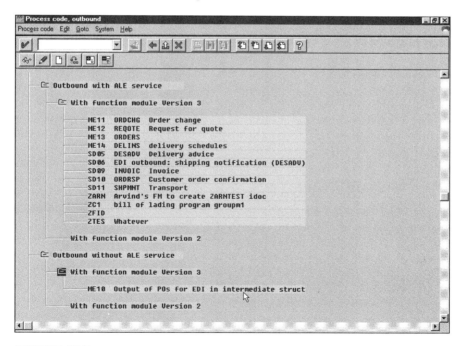

FIGURE 13-5

Settings for the process codes for EDI processes
without the ALE service layer

The steps are as follows:

Transaction: WE41

Menu Path: From the Area menu of EDI, select Control, Outbound Process Code.

1. Delete the process code from its current location under Process Code, Outbound; Outbound with ALE Service, With Function Module Version 3.

2. Add the process code to Process code, Outbound; Outbound without ALE Service, With Function Module Version 3.

 CAUTION

This procedure is not supported on upgrade, so make a note of it in your to-do list for upgrade items.

Managing Performance of Inbound Processes

The inbound interface can be run in near-real-time mode or in batch mode. The benefits and drawbacks of each approach are discussed in the following sections.

Real-Time Inbound

In near-real-time mode, when an IDoc is passed to the EDI Interface layer, an application document is created almost immediately. Although the process is asynchronous, the system gives the feel of a real-time system. This mode is useful for critical EDI processes such as order changes and advance shipment notices. This option should not be used for high-volume and noncritical transactions.

The execution of the following programs is controlled for achieving near-real-time behavior:

◆ **Startrfc.** This program is at the OS layer and starts the inbound process. The inbound process creates an IDoc.

◆ **RBDAPP01.** This program passes the IDoc to the posting program, which creates the application document.

The settings shown in Figure 13-6 are necessary to achieve the near-real-time behavior.

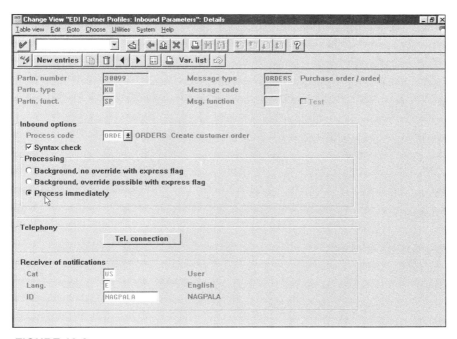

FIGURE 13-6

Settings in the Partner profile for immediate processing

 NOTE

Keep in mind that startrfc should be started as soon as an IDoc file is created, and that in the inbound record of the message in the partner profile, the processing option should be set to Process Immediately.

Inbound in Batch Mode

The batch mode is used for noncritical and high-volume transactions. This mode is useful from a performance perspective. The application document is not created as soon as an IDoc is created, but is batched to support mass processing.

The process can be controlled at the subsystem layer and within SAP. The subsystem can bundle several IDocs into one file to improve the performance of creating IDocs in the database. In the SAP system, the IDocs can be batched until the system is not busy (such as at night) to pass the IDocs to the posting programs.

The Processing Option field in the inbound record of the Partner profile should be set to Background, no override with express flag or Background, override with express flag, as shown in Figure 13-7.

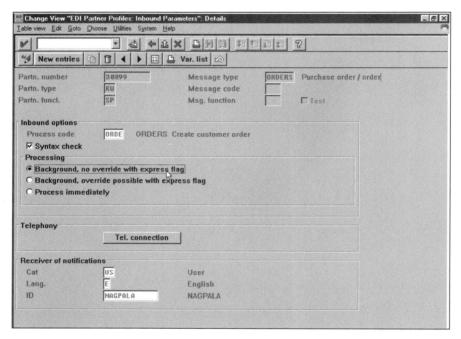

FIGURE 13-7

Settings in the Partner profile for batch processing

The RBDAPP01 program passes buffered IDocs in the database to the posting program. This program must be scheduled on an as-needed basis. Several instances of this program can also be scheduled to send the buffered IDocs to the posting program based on the IDoc type. Each instance can be scheduled with a different variant.

By way of example, suppose inbound sales orders and invoices are buffered. A decision has been made to process sales orders once every hour, whereas the invoices can wait until the end of the day. Two instances of RBDAPP01 can be scheduled: one to run every hour to process sales orders and the second to run at 10:00 p.m. to process the invoices.

The RBDAPP01 program can pass the buffered IDocs in a single-threaded or multithreaded mode. In single-threaded mode the program passes one IDoc packet and waits for the process to finish before the next IDoc packet is sent. The packet size can be set in the selection list of the RBDAPP01 program. A general rule cannot be established for the packet size because the value will vary depending on the memory, processor size, and load on the application server. You'll need to experiment with different values and it's an iterative exercise to determine the optimal packet size.

In multithreaded mode the IDoc packets are passed to the inbound process simultaneously. If there are several IDoc packets, then the system keeps dispatching until it runs out of packets or the number of processes is exhausted.

Improving Performance

In addition to the methods suggested earlier for improving performance, you can adopt the following strategies for both inbound and outbound processes.

EDI Subsystem on a Separate Server

Placing the EDI subsystem on a separate server is an easy way to achieve high-performance benefits. The EDI subsystem is not part of the SAP system and can be installed to run stand-alone on a separate server. Depending on the EDI transaction volume, you can house the EDI subsystem on a UNIX-based or a PC-based system. The systems can be configured to share a file system to avoid complications with file sharing.

Dedicated Application Server for EDI Processes

If you run the inbound IDoc processes in a parallel mode, the programs have a tendency to take up as many sessions as are available on the application server. On a large inbound set, such behavior can cripple the system and bring it to a halt.

However, you do want the parallel processing to achieve the throughput you need. It is advisable to have a server group established for EDI processing, to limit the number of processes allocated to a server group. The server group is also a parameter that can be specified on the RBDAPP01 program for inbound IDocs. For outbound processes you can schedule the RSNAST00 and RSEOUT00 programs to run on the dedicated application server.

Performance of ABAP/4 Programs

IDoc programs contain a fairly large amount of executable code. Some sections of the code are not necessarily optimized for batch input, which causes a long processing time. Several patches are available in the OSS (Online Service System) to improve the efficiency of individual programs.

Tuning the Database

Database access can be improved by creating index on table fields that are frequently used to access the table. Adding an index improves the performance considerably, especially if a table has large number of entries. This exercise is performed by your Basis group as part of the overall strategy to improve performance of the system.

Summary

The performance of a system is usually measured by the response time of a user transaction. When a user creates a document or runs a report, the time it takes for the process to complete is used as a starting measure to improve the performance. The asynchronous EDI process does not have this problem, because users are not waiting for the process to complete. Nevertheless, the EDI processes can take up a major chunk of system cycles. The best way to improve performance is to install the EDI subsystem on a separate server. Another approach, useful for high-volume transactions, is to batch the generation of IDocs and to perform parallel processing. You must schedule the processing programs, such as RSNAST00, RSEOUT00, and RBDAPP01, with appropriate variants to process the buffered IDocs. Low-volume and critical transactions can be set up to run in near-real-time mode.

PART 5

EDI Scenarios

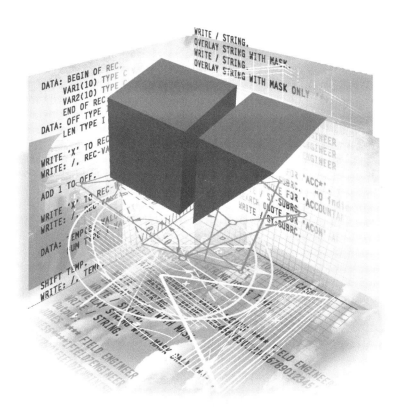

Chapter 14

Outbound with Message Control— Purchase Orders

In the next four chapters you'll apply the knowledge that you've gained in the previous chapters to create some outbound and inbound transactions. This chapter explains the steps you need to follow to build an EDI transaction. In Section III, "IDocs," you learn about ways to modify the process, such as extending the IDocs and programs that create or receive the IDocs.

The technical details are not repeated here, so for any technical matters, please refer to Part 3, "Configuring the EDI Interface."

In the case of outbound transactions, there are two paths to create an outbound IDoc: (1) via Message control and (2) without Message control. This chapter uses an outbound purchase order transaction to illustrate the methodology for creating an outbound transaction using Message control. The next chapter provides an example of an outbound process without using Message control. The purchase order transaction was chosen because you're probably familiar with this process, and because it's the most commonly deployed transaction in a company. The concept will apply to all outbound EDI transactions that use Message control, so what you learn about purchase orders is also applicable to, say, outbound advance shipment notices or outbound invoices, because they also use Message control. The values and parameters vary from transaction to transaction, but the concept remains the same.

Overview of the Purchase Order

The purchase order transaction is a business document sent by a customer to a vendor to procure materials or services. The purchase order document has been assigned number 850 in the ANSI X.12 standards.

The formal definition of the ANSI X.12 850 transaction is as follows: "This transaction set provides for customary and established business and industry practice relative to the placement of purchase orders for goods and services."

In this example you are using EDI to order 10 units of 100MHz processors from Computer Mart Corporation (the vendor). The methodology to create an IDoc for an outbound process uses a simple approach. First you analyze the business requirements and compare them with what SAP provides (analysis phase). Then you identify various parameters used in the process (preparation phase). Next you configure the EDI components and build the necessary master data (setup phase), test the setup (test phase), execute the process (execution phase), verify the results (verification phase), and celebrate if they look good! In the following sections you will learn the objectives and tasks involved in each phase (see Figure 14-1).

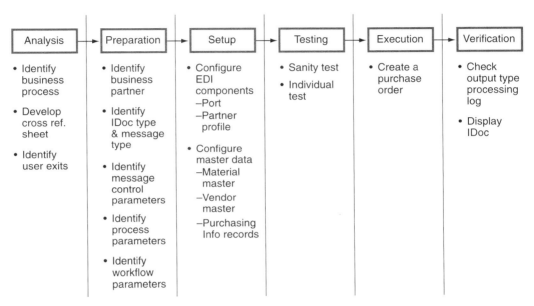

FIGURE 14-1

Phases for an outbound EDI process

The Analysis Phase

The analysis phase consists of analyzing business requirements and comparing them with the standard functionality of SAP. It's useful to have a good understanding of the SAP business process, because in several cases gaps can be filled by customizing the system. If gaps cannot be filled via customizing, then you should explore the use of user exits to meet your business needs (before you decide to build the process from scratch). The tasks in the analysis phase are described next.

Identifying Business Processes

Identify the SAP business process that supports the EDI transaction you are interested in. In some cases the lingo in SAP may be different from what you are used to. The online help will be very useful at this stage. You'll need to identify the SAP transaction from which you can initiate the process. For example, the purchase order transaction is part of the Materials Management module. The transaction is ME21 for creating new purchase orders. This information, although not tricky, helps you understand what business process will be used and at what stage you initiate the process. For example, if you are going to send out an advance shipment notice transaction, you could carry it out at the time of creating a delivery or you could do it after a goods issue process. Thus identifying a business process helps you understand your company's business rules.

Developing a Cross-Reference Sheet and Performing a Gap Analysis

In the analysis phase, you identify the gaps between the SAP-provided functionality and the business needs. Customers develop a cross-reference spreadsheet that maps the IDoc data fields to the SAP data elements and the EDI standards. A template is provided for reference (see Figure 14-2). This cross-reference list helps in identifying gaps that exist between your business needs and the standard system. Every company develops the cross-reference sheet in one form or another for each transaction.

TIP

Helpful resources in this area are user groups, such as the EDI user group under ASUG (America's SAP User Group) at **www.asug.com.** You can consult with member companies for this information. A cross-reference sheet is also provided as part of the EDI configuration guide when you attend the SAP EDI course CA210 at SAP.

You can develop this cross-reference sheet from the documentation of the IDocs. The fields in the IDocs have been derived from the data dictionary and use the same data elements as the application whenever and wherever possible. The only time application data field is not used is when the internal SAP format is not character based. The fields in the IDocs are always character-based. Several unused fields in the IDoc are available for your own purposes. It is possible, however, that SAP may use those fields in the future.

Name of the transaction:_____

Description: _____

IDoc Type: _____

Message Type:_____

EDI Standard:_____ Version:_____

Segment Description: _____									Business Partner Requirements			
IDoc segment name	IDoc field name	Field length	Qualifier	Qualifier description	IDoc field description	EDI segment field	SAP table field	Screen field	Partner A	Partner B	Partner C	Notes & Gaps

FIGURE 14-2

Template for developing a cross-reference list between IDoc fields, SAP application fields, and EDI segment fields

Identifying Available User Exits

As part of the gap analysis, you would have discovered gaps between your business needs and the standard SAP functionality. If the gaps cannot be filled using one of the customizing options, then you can use one of the user exits. User exits allow you to formally add customized code to an existing SAP process. They have been provided at strategic points in the process and are supported during an upgrade. You can browse the list of user exits by using the CMOD/SMOD transactions. Refer to "Locating User-Exits" in Chapter 32, "Programming in the IDoc Interface" for details on locating user exits for the IDoc processes.

The user exit for the outbound purchase order transaction is MM06E001. To view a list of all user exits and their purposes, execute transaction SMOD, enter the enhancement name **MM06E001**, click on the documentation button, and select display. A reference list of the user-exits for the commonly used EDI transactions is included in the appendix.

The Preparation Phase

In this phase you do all of the groundwork and identify all of the parameters needed for your transaction. Identify the business partner (vendor) to whom you are going to send the business document. The business partner will be an entry from your vendor master data.

Identifying the IDoc Type and the Message Type

Identify the IDoc type and the message type to support the process: ORDERS02 and ORDERS (from the reference chart). You may wonder why there are two IDocs—ORDERS01 and ORDERS02—and which one to choose. The last two digits represent the version. ORDERS02 is a newer version, which means it still has all the segments of the previous version, ORDERS01. ORDERS02 supports configurable materials. Always use the latest version of an IDoc type unless you specifically need the older version. Each IDoc type is thoroughly documented. Execute transaction WE60 to look up IDoc documentation.

Identifying Message Control Parameters

The next step is to identify the Message control parameters. For each application there is an application ID from which you can drill down to other components of the Message control. You'll need to determine the Application ID and Output type used in the process. Refer to Chapter 8, "Configuring Message Control," for complete details on the significance of each of these components and how to locate the list in the SAP system. For the purchase order transaction, the values are as follows:

`Application ID:` EF

`Output type:` NEU

Identifying Process Parameters

In this step you determine the process code for your IDoc type and message type combination. Execute transaction WE41 for a list of process codes available in the system. The process code for generating the ORDERS message using the ORDERS02 IDoc is ME14.

Identifying the Workflow Parameters

In this step you identify the organization object (user ID, position, workcenter, and so on) responsible for handling errors associated with this EDI transaction.

You can choose from several different types of organization objects. Refer to Chapter 9, "Configuring Workflow" for details on the different types of objects. To begin with, you can use your user ID for this step.

The Setup Phase

Once you have identified the parameters, you'll verify the one-time settings, set up the EDI components that are required for each transaction, and set up the master data needed from an EDI perspective.

EDI Configuration Components

You should have already carried out the one-time EDI setting required by all EDI transactions. The settings include:

◆ Basic Settings for IDocs
◆ Communication Settings

You will find the information in Chapter 6, "Configuring Basic EDI Components," helpful in performing the setup.

Partner Profile: Creating Message Control and Outbound View

Transaction: WE20

A partner profile is created for every business partner that sends or receives EDI documents. In the partner profile, a Message control record and an outbound record are created for each outbound message, as shown in Figures 14-3 and 14-4.

Create a partner profile if it does not exist. Add the Message control record and outbound record for your message. The necessary parameters were identified earlier in the "The Preparation Phase."

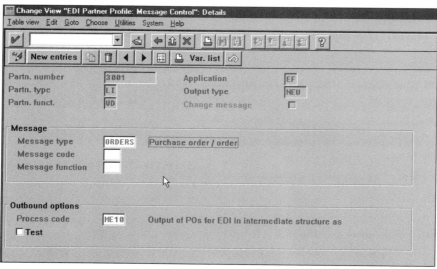

FIGURE 14-3

Message control parameters in the partner profile

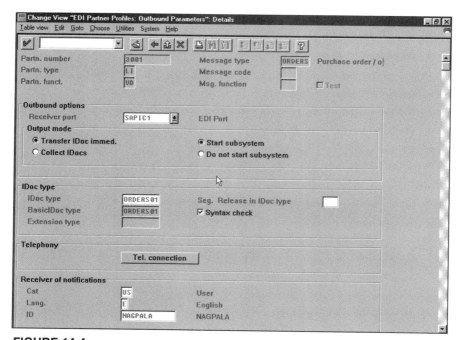

FIGURE 14-4

Outbound parameters in the partner profile

Message Control: Creating Condition Records

Transaction: MN04

Create a condition record for the output type identified in the preparation phase. The condition records are used to define the conditions under which the output type should be proposed. When you create a condition record, you choose the business rule on which you want to create your condition records, as shown in Figure 14-5. To start, you can be very specific, so choose a business rule that has vendor number as one of the fields. Specify the values for the medium as 6 (EDI) and the timing to suit your needs. Initially you can specify the timing as 4 to indicate immediate (see Figure 14-6).

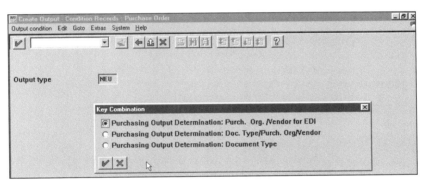

FIGURE 14-5

Selecting a business rule when you create condition records

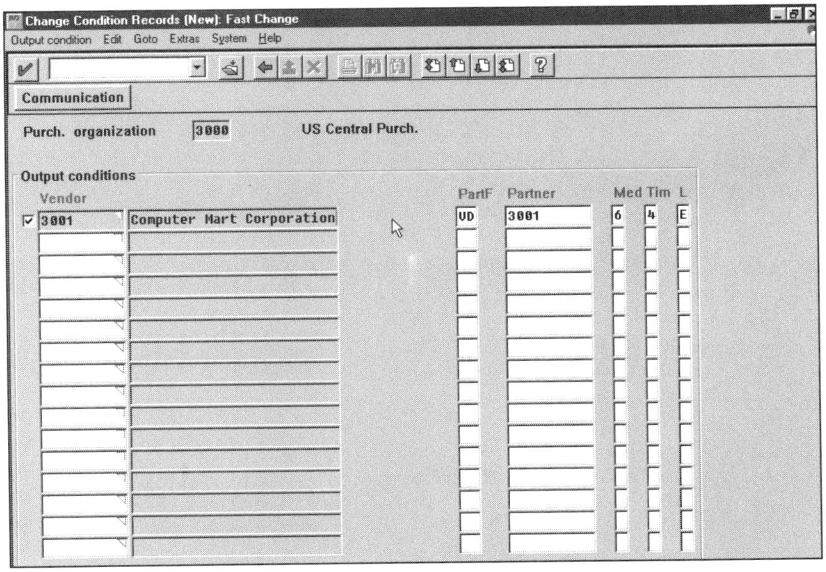

FIGURE 14-6

Entering output values when you create condition records

Workflow Settings: Create Task Profile

This section assumes that the workflow configuration has already been done. Please refer to "Setting Up Workflow for Exception Handling" in Chapter 9, "Configuring Workflow," for details.

Outbound messages require the following workflow settings:

- ◆ Verifying basic workflow settings
- ◆ Setting up the organization unit
- ◆ A task profile for the error tasks

TIP

To get started quickly, you can make the error task a General task. Doing so fulfills the requirement for the task profile. You can use your user ID as the person responsible in the partner profile in which case you do not require the setting up of the organization unit.

Master Data Requirements

The type of master data and the required fields from an EDI perspective in the master data vary for each transaction. Your task is not necessarily to maintain the entire master data, but you should be aware of the fields that are required from an EDI perspective. These fields may not be required fields otherwise in the master data. The values in these fields are used to populate critical information in the IDoc, or they are absolutely required fields in the EDI standards. For example, the Account at Vendor field in the vendor master data populates the Sender field in the control record of the IDoc. The cross-reference sheet will be helpful in identifying the fields that must be filled for your business needs.

The following section covers the basics of the master data concept in SAP. You can skip this review if you are familiar with the concept of master data in SAP. The master data required for the purchase order transaction is described after the introductory material.

Master Data Basics

This section is meant for those who are not familiar with the concept of how master data is implemented in the SAP system. This section is an introduction to the concept of master data as implemented in SAP, not an introduction to any specific master data.

The master data in the SAP system represents the characteristics of the business entities or the business objects used in the system, for example, material, customer, and vendor. These are stored in Material Master, Customer Master, and Vendor Master tables. SAP also has various SAP organization objects that represent the various organization entities. These entities have a defined business responsibility and are used to represent the company's structure in different forms, such as the purchasing organization, sales organization, and company code.

 NOTE

There is a distinction between organization object and SAP organization object. Organization objects are entities like users, positions, jobs. SAP organization objects are company codes and sales organizations. They were named SAP organization objects because of their relevance to the SAP system.

When master data is created in the system, you define views for each SAP organization object depending on the master data. For example, when you create a vendor you will create a separate view for each company code and purchasing organization that deals with the vendor, as shown in Figure 14-7. A view holds information specific to the respective SAP organization object. Similarly, if you were creating a customer master, you would have a separate view for each sales area, which consists of a sales organization, distribution channel, and division. For the material master, you have views that are based on plants, storage locations, sales organizations, and so on.

This concept is important to understand when you are creating transactional data, such as purchase orders and sales orders. You cannot create a purchase order for a vendor that has not been defined for your purchasing organization. You cannot order a material for a plant if the material has not been created for that plant. This setup can take a long time. As an EDI person, you aren't responsible for maintaining it, but you must be aware of the structure of your company and its materials before you can create a purchase order or sales order.

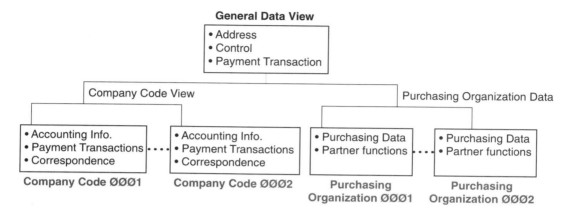

FIGURE 14-7

Structure of master data for a vendor

Material Master Data

Transaction: MM01, MM02

Menu Path: Logistics, Materials Management, Material Master, Material, Create (general), Immediately

A material master is created for materials that you procure from a vendor. You must create a view for the plant to which the materials will be delivered. Although these are not EDI requirements, you will not be able to create a purchase order without this information.

Vendor Master Data

Transaction: XK01 and XK02

Menu Path: Logistics, Materials Management, Purchasing, Master Data, Vendor, Central, Create

A vendor master is created for vendors from whom you procure material. Maintain the vendor for each purchasing organization that can procure from this vendor. The following fields must be entered in the vendor master for EDI in their respective views. The various views to be selected are shown in Figure 14-8.

◆ **General data, Address.** The address information must be filled out. Fig-

ure 14-9 shows an example of address information fields filled out for the
vendor Computer Mart Corporation.

◆ **Company code data, Accounting information.** The reconciliation account
must be filled out. Figure 14-10 shows an example of accounting information for Computer Mart Corporation.

   ◆ **Correspondence.** In this view you fill in the Account at Vendor
   field. This field is used in the Sender field of the control record. This
   field defines how the vendor recognizes your company in their system. Figure 14-10 shows an example of correspondence information
   for Computer Mart Corporation.

◆ **Purchasing organization data, Purchasing data.** Order currency, terms of
payment, and Incoterms must be filled. Incoterms define the commonly used
trading terms established by International Chambers of Commerce. If they
are not filled, then they need to be filled when creating a purchase order (see
Figures 14-11 and 14-12).

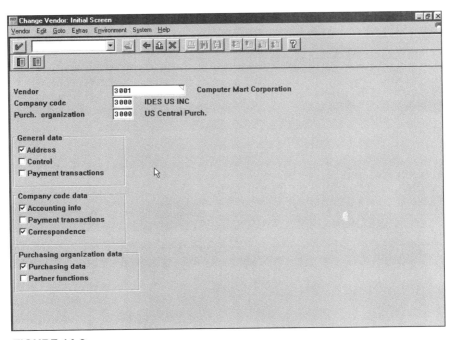

FIGURE 14-8

Vendor master—views required for EDI

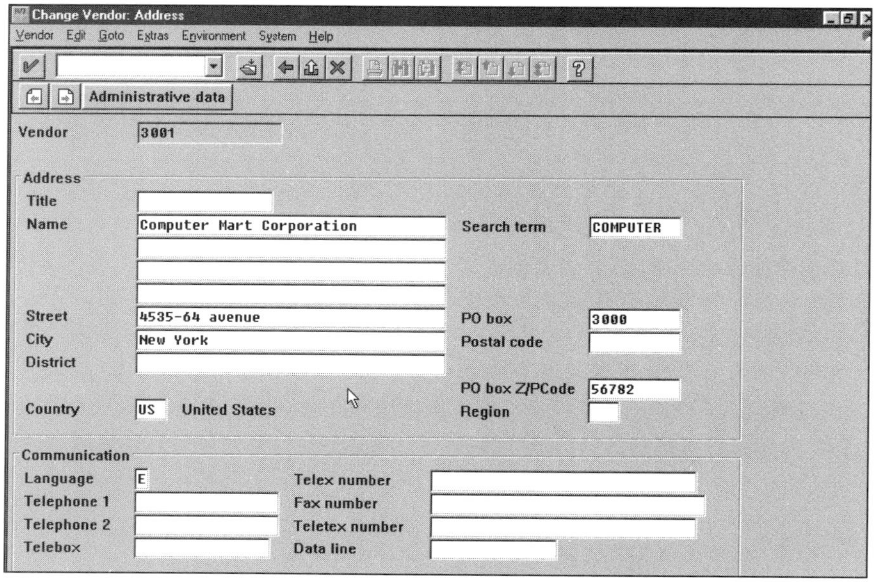

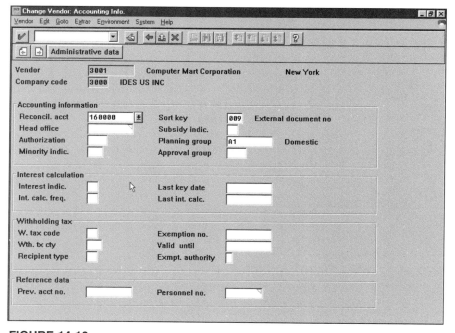

FIGURE 14-9

Vendor master—address information

FIGURE 14-10

Vendor master—accounting information details.

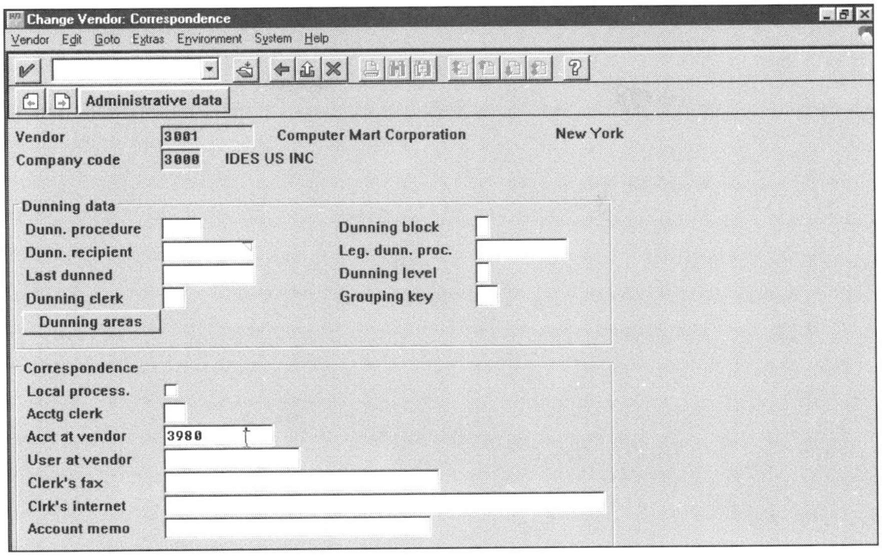

FIGURE 14-11

Vendor master—correspondence information

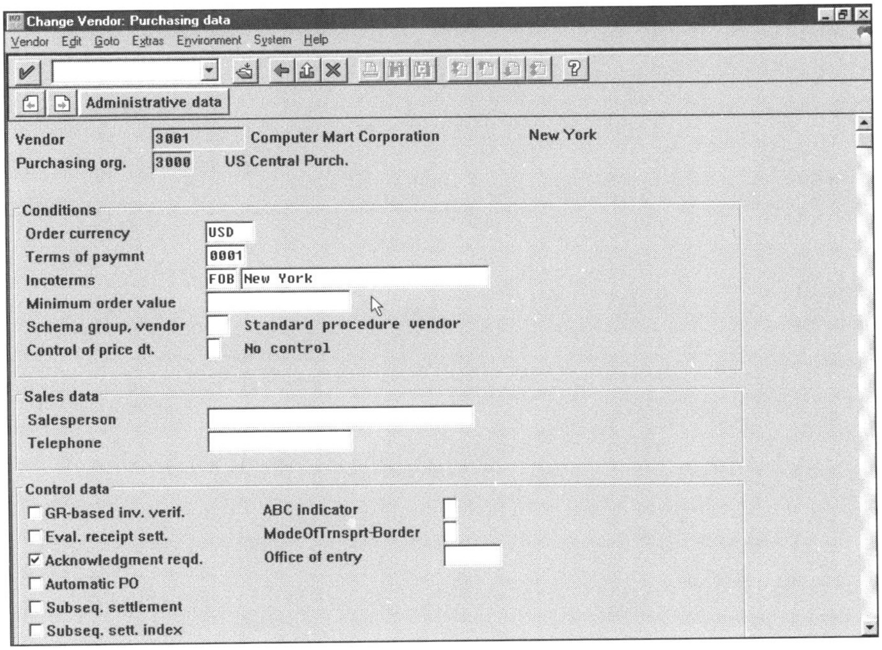

FIGURE 14-12

Vendor master—purchasing data view details

Purchasing Information Records

Transaction: ME11

Menu Path: Logistics, Materials Management, Purchasing, Master Data, Info Record, Create

A vendor material information record contains vendor-specific information about a material. For example, if you procure a particular material from three different vendors, each vendor may call it by a different name, the delivery times may be different, and the prices may vary. You store the vendor-specific information about a material in this table. Figure 14-13 shows that material DPC1020 in your system is identified as VEN1000 at your vendor Computer Mart Corporation. The fields in this table are required. You are not required to send the vendor's part number on an EDI transaction. It is the vendor's responsibility to convert the customer part number to the vendor's internal number.

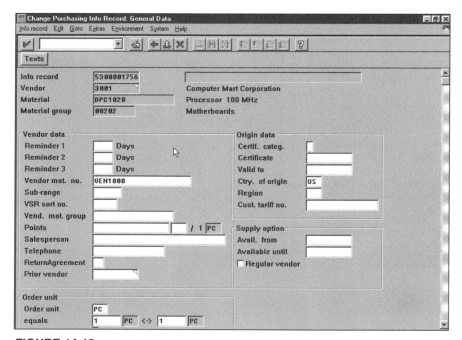

FIGURE 14-13

Purchasing information record details showing the relationship between your material and vendor material

The Testing Phase

After you have configured the system, it is ready for testing. Follow the unit testing technique discussed in Chapter 10, "Testing the EDI Interface." To begin, you can only carry out the sanity tests to make sure the configuration is correct. You can execute the process as described in the next section.

Executing the Process

Starting an outbound process via Message control is standard. You create the application document from its respective application process and then go to the output control screen to verify the outputs proposed by the system.

Create a purchase order using your vendor number, material, and a suitable quantity. Figure 14-14 shows an example of a purchase order entered for vendor Computer Mart Corporation to order 10 pieces of 100 MHz processors.

Transaction: ME21

Menu Path: Logistics, Materials Management, Purchasing, Purchase Order, Create

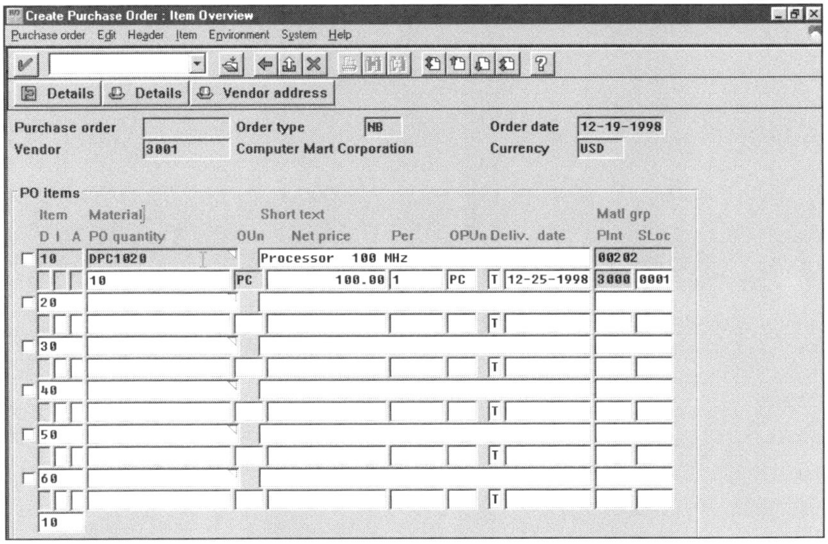

FIGURE 14-14

The purchase order detail screen for entering items to be ordered

To see the proposed output types, go to Header, Messages. Check your output type and make sure the medium and timing are correct, as shown in Figure 14-15. Save your document. IDoc processing should start.

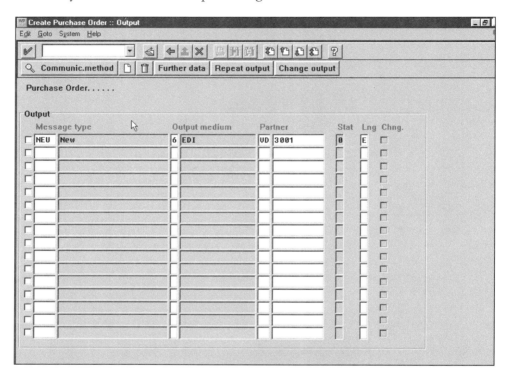

FIGURE 14-15

The output control screen showing the EDI output proposed for a purchase order

Verifying the Output

The procedure for verifying the output for messages generated via Message control is straightforward. Go to the output control screen and check the status of your output type. For a detailed log, check the processing log for the output type. The IDoc number generated for the output is logged in the processing log, as shown in Figure 14-16. You can use one of the IDoc display tools to see the data in the IDoc, as shown in Figure 14-17.

For the purchase order, go to the output control screen using Header, Messages, and check the status. Get the IDoc number from the processing log. Display the IDoc using WE05 and verify the data values.

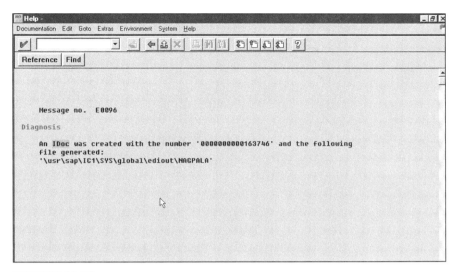

FIGURE 14-16

Determining the IDoc number from the processing log for the output type

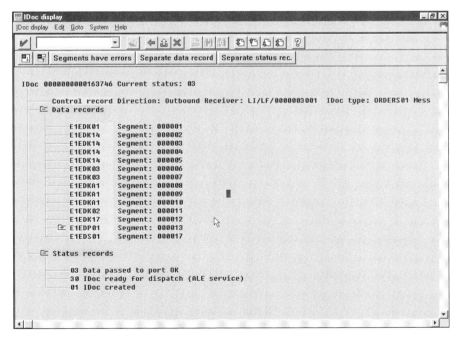

FIGURE 14-17

IDoc created for the purchase order document

If you experience problems in the process, use the troubleshooting guide in Chapter 12, "EDI Process Troubleshooting and Recovery" to determine the cause of the problem and restart the process.

Summary

The steps to configure an outbound process via Message control require a preparatory phase in which the necessary data for the transaction is gathered. In the next stage, various components are set up, including the EDI components and master data needed for the transaction. The setup phase is followed by a unit-testing phase in which all the components are given a sanity test. Next the process is executed to generate an IDoc. In the verification phase, the output is verified to ensure that all the fields are being generated as desired. These steps can be applied to any outbound EDI process that uses Message control.

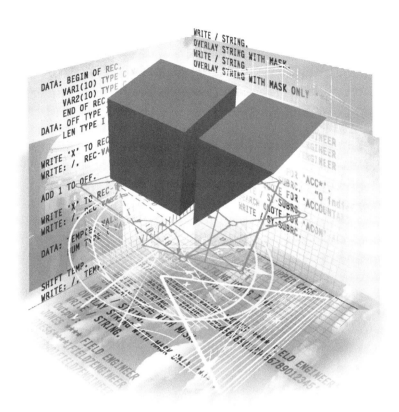

Chapter 15

Outbound without Message Control— Remittance Advice

This chapter uses an outbound remittance advice and payment order transaction to illustrate how an outbound process works without using message control. The remittance advice and payment order transactions are chosen because these are commonly deployed transactions in the FI module and are standard transactions in the system. These two transactions are generated from the same payment program.

This chapter describes how the process works from an EDI perspective and explains the steps you need to perform. You must have a basic understanding of the accounts payable process to be able to carry out this transaction, but the configuration of the accounts payable process is not the focus of this chapter. The concepts discussed here apply to all outbound EDI transactions that do not use message control.

Overview of Remittance Advice/Payment Order

The remittance advice/payment order (820 in ANSI X.12, PAYADV in EDIFACT) is a transaction that can be used in three cases:

◆ To advise a financial institution (a bank) to make payment to a payee on your behalf (payer).

◆ To report the completion of payment to a payee by a financial institution (a bank).

◆ To advise a payee about a payment that has been made to the payee's account either by a payment order or through other means (inbound).

When this transaction is sent to a bank, the transaction contains financial instructions (clearing information) that the bank uses to process the payment data. This information has no significance for a payee.

In the SAP system, this transaction is implemented in the FI module. Figure 15-1 shows the business partners involved in the process and the messages exchanged between them. The process begins with an invoice received in the system from a vendor for goods or services procured from the vendor. The invoice can be entered manually in the system or can be input via EDI. When the invoice is due, payment must be made.

In the SAP system, the payment is generated through a payment run program that is scheduled periodically to process outstanding invoices. This process selects entries that are due and creates a payment proposal. The payment proposal allows you to view and edit payments that will be made. After the proposal has been verified and changed (if necessary), the actual payment run can be scheduled. The payment run will create the necessary payment documents such as checks or payment advice to be sent to a bank and/or a vendor.

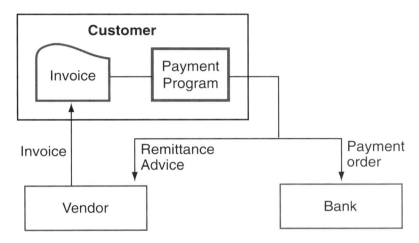

FIGURE 15-1

EDI messages exchanged in the remittance advice/payment order process

The methodology to create an IDoc from an outbound process without message control has six phases (analysis phase, preparation phase, setup phase, test phase, execution phase, verification phase), as described in Chapter 14, "Outbound with Message Control—Purchase Orders." The objectives of each phase are the same but the tasks under each phase vary in some cases. In the following sections you will find details specific to the remittance advice/payment order process only.

The Analysis Phase

The analysis phase consists of analyzing business requirements and comparing them with the standard functionality of SAP. The tasks in the analysis phase are described next.

Identifying Business Processes

The remittance advice transaction is part of the Accounts Payable application under the FI module. The transaction is F115 for starting the payment run program.

The payment run program is a two-step process. In the first step, called a proposal run, you'll create a proposal that allows you to view and edit the payments that will be generated. The proposal run can also create test IDocs that can be analyzed and verified before the actual IDocs are generated. The test IDocs are not transmitted to the bank or the vendor. In the second step, the actual payment run program is executed. At this time the program generates the actual output that is sent to your vendors and banks. Thus identifying a business process helps you understand your company's business rules and the SAP process.

 NOTE

To develop cross-reference sheets, refer to "Developing a Cross-Reference Sheet" in Chapter 14, "Outbound with Message Control—Purchase Orders," for details.

Identifying User Exits Available in the Process

The user exit for the outbound remittance advice process is FEDI0003 and FEDI0004. To see a list of all user exits and their purpose, execute transaction SMOD, enter the enhancement name (FEDI0003 or FEDI0004), click on the Documentation button, and select Display.

The Preparation Phase

In this phase you'll do all the groundwork and identify all the parameters needed for your transaction.

Identifying Business Partners

Identify the business partner (vendor, bank) to whom you are sending the business document. The vendor number is an entry from your vendor master data (Transaction: XK02). The partner number for the bank is stored under the EDI partner profiles section in the DME (Data Medium) view of the house bank master entry (Transaction: FI12). Consult with your accounts payable team for the setup of bank master information. As an EDI person, you are responsible for making sure there is a valid entry in the partner no field. If a value does not exist, you will not be able to create a partner profile. The other catch is that when you enter a value in the partner no field, you must create the partner profile by pressing the partner profile button next to the field. The system will not allow you to exit unless you maintain the partner profile.

Identifying IDoc and Message Types

Identify the IDoc type and the message type to support the process: PEXR2001 and PAYEXT & REMADV (from the reference chart in the appendix).

NOTE

Use the latest version of the IDoc type unless you specifically need the older version. The version is identified by the last two characters of the IDoc type. Thus if your system has IDoc type PEXR2002, use it instead of PEXR2001. Each IDoc type is thoroughly documented. Execute transaction WE60 to display the documentation for an IDoc type.

Identifying Workflow Parameters

In this step you'll identify the organization object (user ID, position, workcenter, and so on) that is responsible for handling errors associated with this EDI transaction. You can choose from several different types of organization objects. Refer to Chapter 9, "Configuring Workflow," for details on the different types of objects. To begin, you can use your user ID for this step.

The Setup Phase

After you identify the parameters, you'll set up the EDI components that are required for each transaction and the master data needed from an EDI perspective. The master data is required before you can do some of the EDI settings. For example, you cannot create a partner profile before you create the vendor master.

Master Data Requirements

The type of master data and the required fields from an EDI perspective in the master data vary for each transaction. Your task is not necessarily to maintain the entire master data, but you should be aware of the fields that are required from an EDI perspective. These fields may not be required fields otherwise in the master data.

The values in these fields populate critical information in the IDoc or are absolutely required fields in the EDI standards. For example, an Account at Vendor field in the vendor master populates the Sender field in the control record of the IDoc. The cross-reference sheet will help you identify the fields that must be filled for your business needs. The master data required for the remittance advice transaction to a bank and a vendor are described next.

TIP

A detailed description of the master data setup required is available in the documentation for the RFFOEDI1 and RFFOEDI2 programs. To view the documentation, execute transaction SE38, click on the Documentation button, and enter the program name.

Partner Settings for the House Bank

Transaction: FI12

Menu Path: From the IMG, choose Financial Accounting, General Ledger Accounting, Bank Related Accounting, Bank Accounts, Define House Banks.

A bank ID is created at a company code level for every bank that you have an account with. This ID uniquely identifies the bank and contains general information such as the contact person and bank address, as shown in Figure 15-2.

The DME (Data Medium) view in the bank master contains information about the data medium used to transfer funds. In the DME view, the EDI partner profile section identifies the partner number assigned to the bank for EDI purposes. This entry must be filled with a value that uniquely identifies the bank as an EDI business partner.

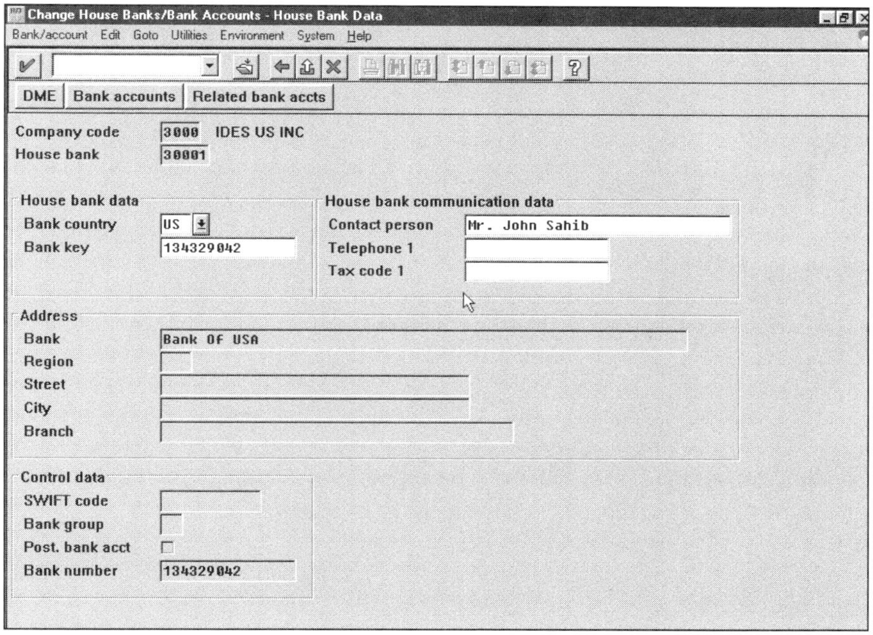

FIGURE 15-2

General information about your bank

TIP

If this entry does not exist and you want to add a value in this field, you must also click on the partner profile button to create the partner profile record. The system will not let you exit without a partner profile entry.

Make sure that an account exists in the bank, and that details such as G/L account and bank account number are filled out, as shown in Figure 15-3.

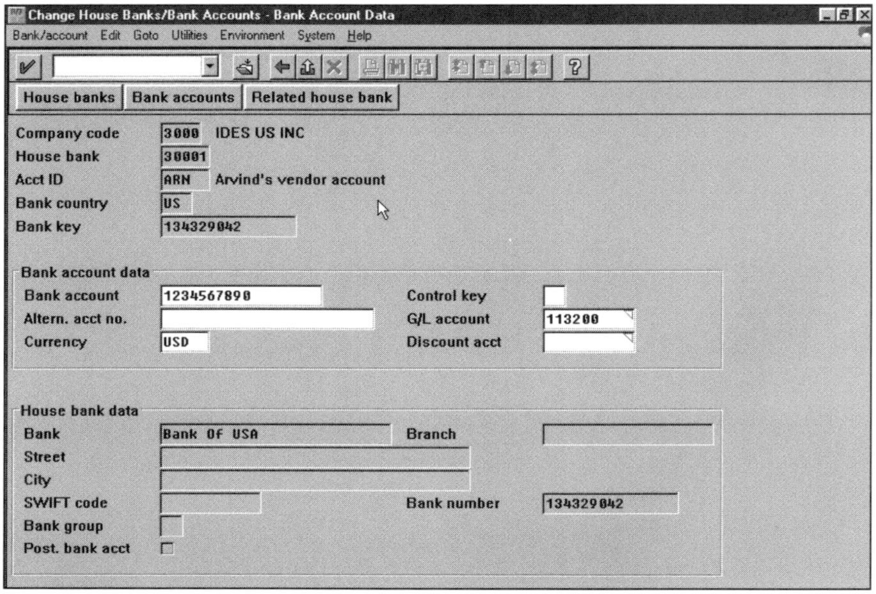

FIGURE 15-3

Bank account details from which payments are made

EDI Accompanying Sheet for the Paying Company

Transaction: FBZP

Menu Path: From the IMG, choose Financial Accounting, Accounts Receivables and Accounts Payables, Business Transactions, Outgoing Payments, Automatic Outgoing Payments, Payment Method/Bank Selection, Configure Payment Program.

Under Paying Company Codes, select the company code and view the details. You need to verify the settings in the EDI Accompanying Sheet Form field. A standard form, F110_EDI_01, is supplied in the standard system. This sheet prints the totals. The Form for the Payment Advice field should also be set appropriately.

Vendor Master Data

Transaction: XK01 and XK02

Menu Path: Logistics, Materials Management, Purchasing, Master Data, Vendor, Central, Create or Change

A vendor master is created for vendors from whom you procure material. You must maintain the vendor for each purchasing organization that can procure from this vendor. Required fields for EDI are listed in Chapter 14. You now need some additional Company Code Data fields in the vendor master record, as shown in Figure 15-4. The payment run program uses the following payment transaction fields:

- ◆ Payment Terms must be set
- ◆ Payment Method must be filled
- ◆ House Bank must be filled
- ◆ Pyt adv. by EDI must be checked

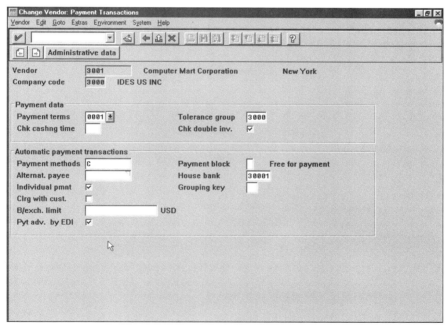

FIGURE 15-4

Vendor master—details of payment terms for paying invoices

EDI Configuration Components

The various EDI components to be set up are discussed in the next three sections.

Basic One-Time EDI Settings

This chapter assumes that you have already carried out the one-time EDI setting required by all EDI transactions (See Chapter 6, "Configuring Basic EDI Components," for details). The settings include basic IDoc settings and communication settings.

Partner Profile: Create Outbound View

A partner profile is created for every business partner that sends or receives EDI documents. In the partner profile, an outbound record is created for each outbound message.

Create a partner profile for your vendor and your bank. Add an outbound record for the outbound message: REMADV and PAYEXT, as shown in Figure 15-5 and Figure 15-6. The REMADV message is created for the vendor, and the PAYEXT message is created for the bank. Both messages use the IDoc type PEXR2001. Note that the partner Function field is blank.

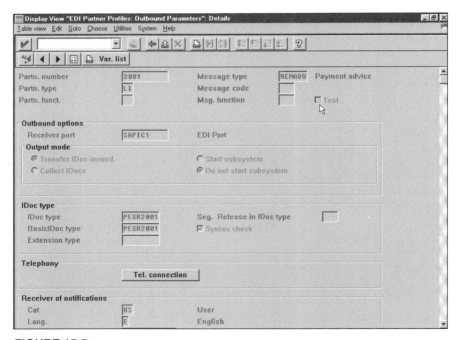

FIGURE 15-5

Partner profile for the vendor—outbound record for the remittance advice message

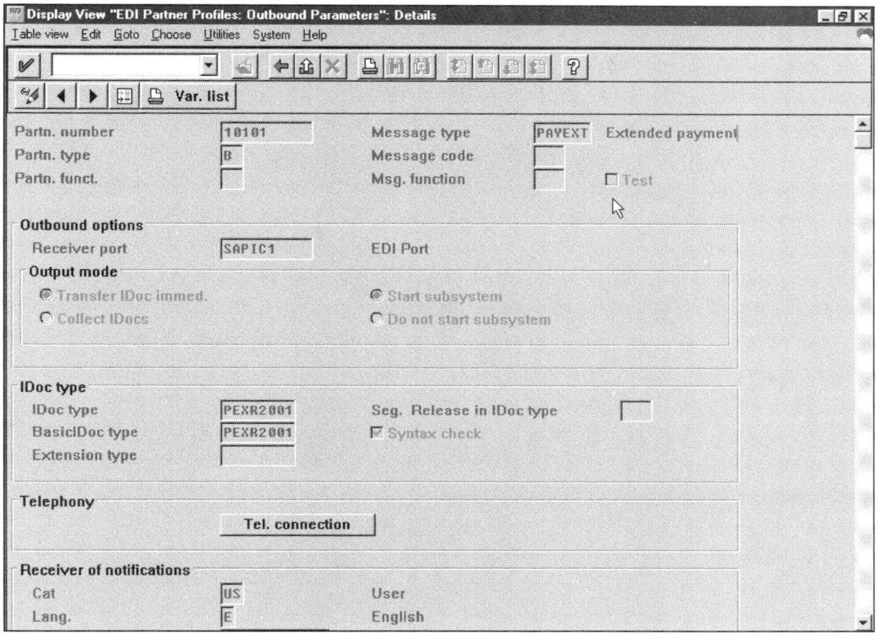

FIGURE 15-6

Partner profile for the bank—outbound record for the payment order message

The payment process allows you to create a test IDoc message at the time of the proposal run. To enable this text, you must create an additional entry for the test message in the partner profile. This entry looks exactly like the entry for the REMADV and the PAYEXT message except that now the test flag should be turned on. This optional step is recommended in the initial stage to test the process.

Workflow Settings: Create Task Profile

This chapter assumes that the Workflow configuration is complete. Please refer to the section "Setting Up Workflow for Exception Handling" in Chapter 9, "Configuring Workflow," for details. Outbound messages require the following Workflow settings:

◆ Basic Workflow settings

◆ Setting up the organization unit

◆ Task profile for the error tasks

The Testing Phase

After you have configured the system, you're ready for the testing phase. Follow the unit-testing technique discussed in Chapter 14. To begin, you can only carry out the sanity tests to make sure the configuration is correct. You can execute the process as described in the next section.

Executing the Process

In the execution phase, you generate payments for outstanding invoices. You can view a list of open invoices using transaction FBL1. If there are no outstanding invoices, then the payment run will not produce any output.

As mentioned earlier, the payment run process is a two-step process: proposal run and payment run. After you complete the proposal run, you can execute the IDoc generation program, RFFOEDI1. This step generates the test IDocs for verification. After you have verified the proposal run, you execute the payment run. After the payment run is finished, you execute the RFFOEDI1 program again to generate the actual IDocs that are to be sent to the bank and the vendor.

Another program, RFFOEDI2, resets the status of outbound EDI process. This program is useful if you have to retransmit an IDoc. RFFOEDI1 does not allow you to retransmit unless status has been set by RFFOEDI2.

Entering Invoices

Transaction: F-43 (Vendor Invoice), MRHR (Any Invoice)

Menu Path: Logistics, Materials Management, Invoice Verification, Invoice Verification, Enter Invoice

This step creates an invoice online. Invoices can also be created via EDI. Enter the vendor line item for charges from the vendor, as shown in Figure 15-7, in the invoice. Balance the payment by creating an entry for the G/L account against which the document will be posted. You can enter the same G/L account as entered in the bank account.

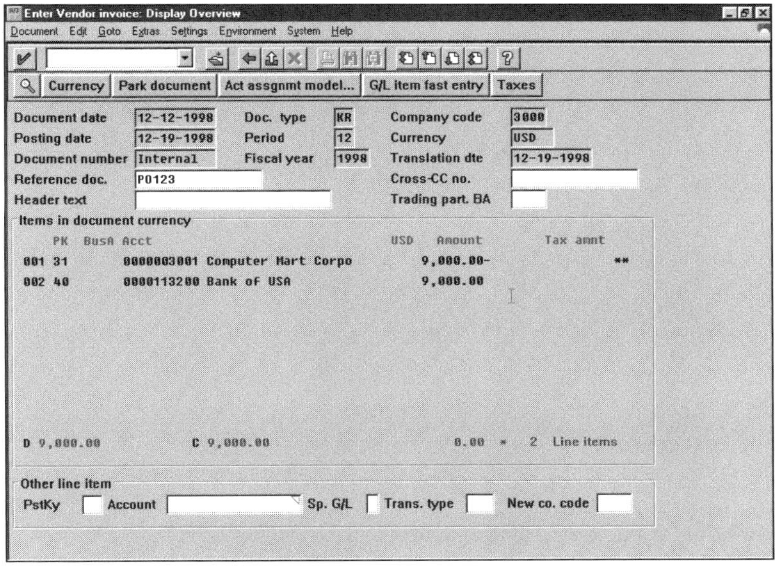

FIGURE 15-7

Entering an invoice for the vendor

The Payment Proposal Run

Transaction: F110

Menu Path: Accounting, Financial Accounting, Accounts Payable, Periodic Processing, Payment

The proposal run creates the payment proposal. Each run is given a unique ID, which is entered on the first screen. The proposal run has several steps.

Maintaining Parameters

You must specify the selection parameters for invoices that need to be paid, as shown in Figure 15-8. You can select the vendors, payment method, posting date, and so on. You should also specify the Additional Log parameters to log detailed information about the run, as shown in Figure 15-9.

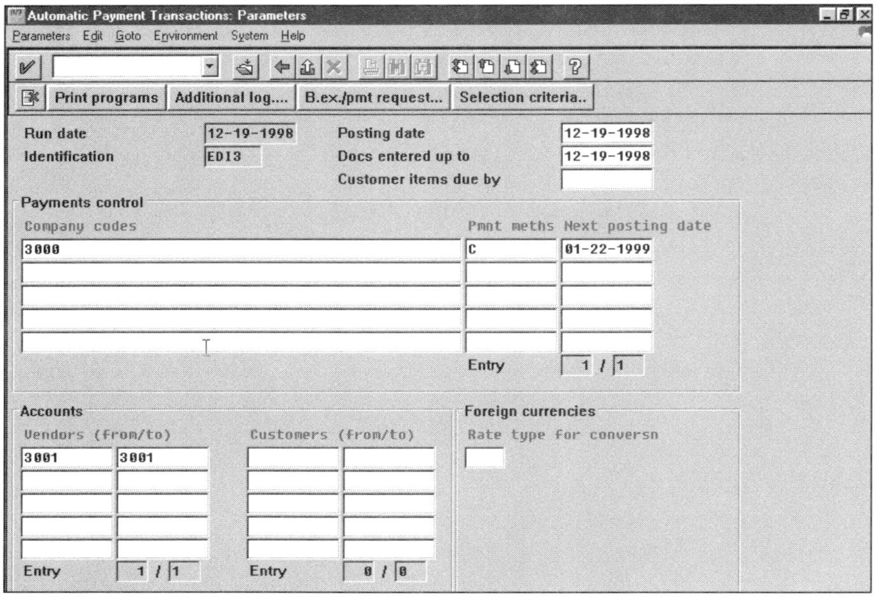

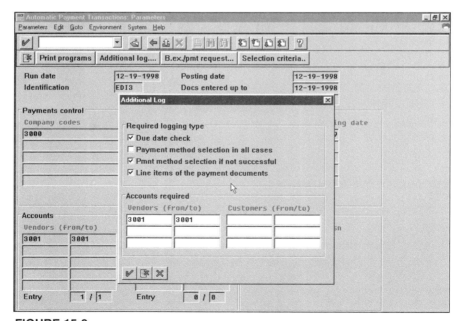

FIGURE 15-8

Selection screen to specify parameters for the payment run program

FIGURE 15-9

Specifying parameters for an additional log from the payment run program

After you save the parameters the screen displays the current status, as shown in Figure 15-10, indicating that parameters have been maintained.

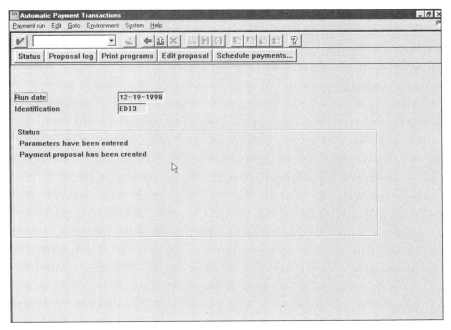

FIGURE 15-10

Status screen for the payment proposal run program

Scheduling the Proposal Run

You can schedule the proposal program to run immediately, or you can set a time. The system automatically creates the background job. For testing purposes you can elect to run the program immediately. The status is updated when you press Enter.

Viewing the Log

After the proposal program is complete, you can view the proposal log, which shows you the invoices selected by the proposal program and their status, as shown in Figure 15-11. At the end a total of all the invoices is shown. If problems occur in the run, the log contains comprehensive debugging details.

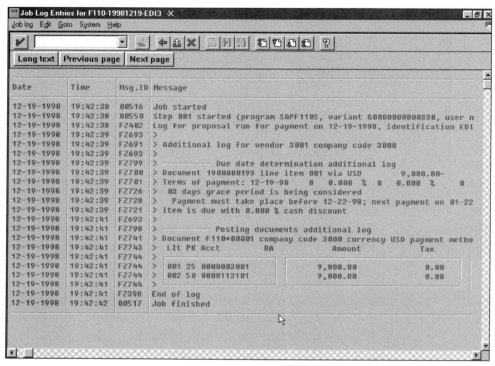

FIGURE 15-11

Output log for the payment proposal run program

Starting the IDoc Generation

If you are satisfied with the invoices selected in the proposal run and they did not have any errors, then you can create the IDocs from the output of the proposal run.

Execute program RFFOEDI1 to start the generation of IDocs. Select the proposal run using the ID that was used to start the proposal run. Click on the Proposal Run Only check box and any additional selection criteria that you may want to select, as shown in Figure 15-12. Click on the Execute button, and the proposal run program should create the test IDocs. The IDoc number is displayed on the screen. If there are errors, you can double-click to view the log.

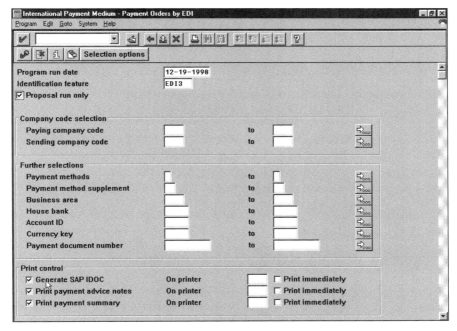

FIGURE 15-12

Selection parameter list for the RFFOEDI1 program

TIP

If you get a message that no records were selected, you may want to check the selection parameters. If everything looks fine, execute the RFFOEDI2 program to reset the status of the transmission.

Verifying the Output

You verify the results of processing by displaying the IDoc, using any of the IDoc display tools. Verify the data fields and values. The IDoc generated in this step is a test IDoc for verification purposes only. The system generates a test IDoc for remittance advice and payment order.

If you experience problems in the process, use the troubleshooting guide in Chapter 12, "EDI Process Troubleshooting and Recovery" to determine the cause of the problem and then restart the process as necessary.

The Payment Run

Transaction: F110

Menu Path: Accounting, Financial Accounting, Accounts Payable, Periodic Processing, Payment

The payment run is executed after you have edited the proposal run (if necessary) and are satisfied with the output. The payment run creates the actual payments that are sent to your business partner. The payment run goes through several steps.

Scheduling the Payment Run

You can schedule the payment program to run immediately, or you can set a start time. The system automatically creates a background job for you. The status is updated on the screen when you press Enter.

Viewing the Log

After the payment run is complete, you can view the payment log. The log displays the invoices selected by the payment program, their status, and a total of all the invoices, as shown in figure 15-13.

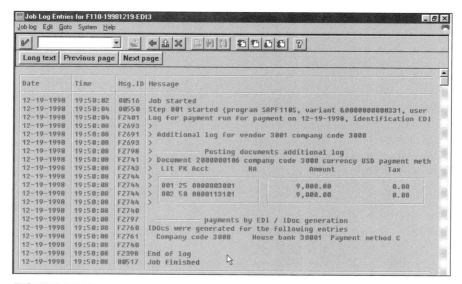

FIGURE 15-13

Output log for the payment run program

Start the IDoc Generation

If you're satisfied with the invoices selected in the payment run and they had no errors, then you can create the IDocs from the output of the payment run.

Execute program RFFOEDI1 to start the generation of IDocs. Select the payment run using the ID that was used to start the payment program. Select any field combination. Do not select the Proposal Run Only check box, as shown in Figure 15-14. Click on the Execute button, and the proposal run program should create the final IDocs. The IDoc number is displayed on the screen. If there are errors, you can double-click to view the log.

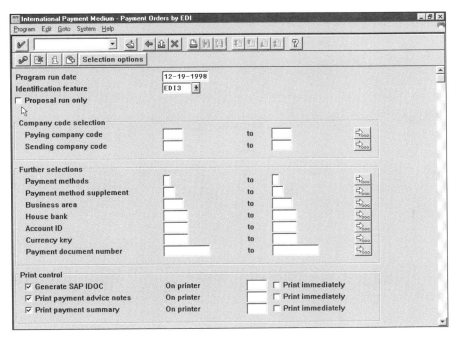

FIGURE 15-14

Selection parameter list for the RFFOEDI1 program

Verifying the Output

You can verify the results of processing (including data fields and values) by using any of the IDoc display tools to display the IDoc. An IDoc should be generated for the remittance advice (see Figure 15-15) and payment order (see Figure 15-16).

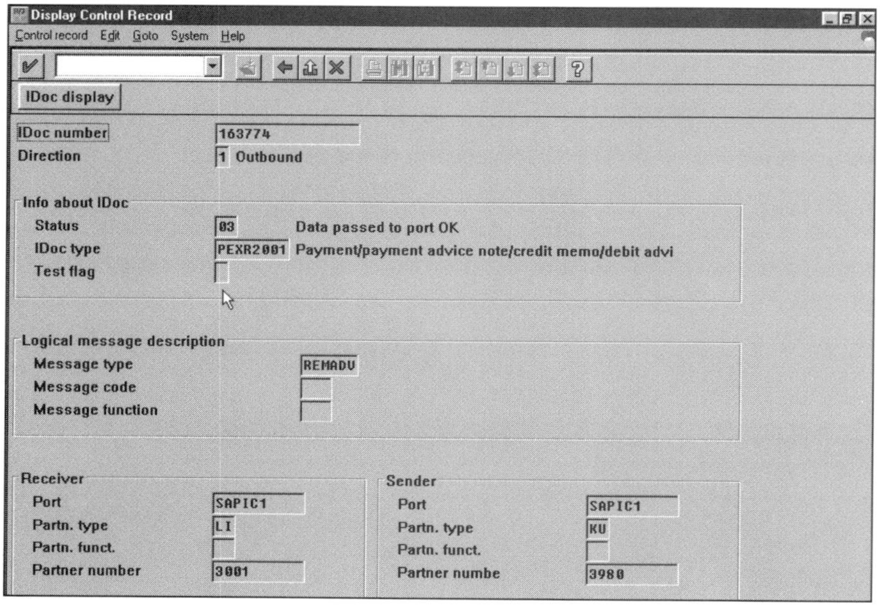

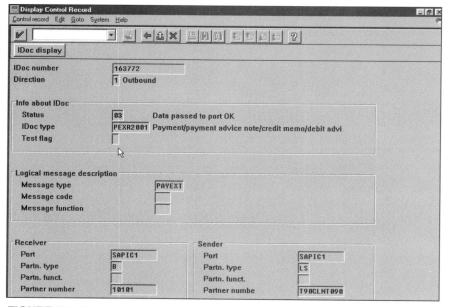

FIGURE 15-15

Final IDoc—remittance advice to the vendor

FIGURE 15-16

Final IDoc—payment order to the bank.

Summary

Configuring an outbound process without message control requires moving most of the selection criteria and business rules that were part of the message control component to the selection screen for the payment program and the RFOEDI1 program. The partner profile is also slightly different without message control than it is with it. There is no entry for the Message Control view. The processing program is now part of the core application logic itself; in contrast, with message control the processing program is disconnected from the application logic. The last difference is in the verification stage—in this case the output log is temporary, whereas with message control the output processing log is permanently maintained for each output type, so you can view the results at any time.

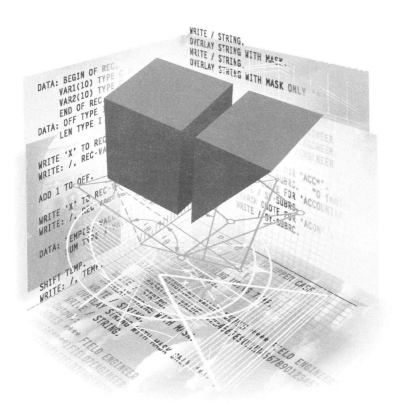

Chapter 16

Inbound with Function Module— Sales Orders

This chapter uses an inbound sales order transaction to illustrate how an inbound process works, using a direct path via a function module. The sales order process was chosen because you are probably familiar with sales documents and this is a commonly deployed transaction for the inbound process. This material should be viewed as a guide to help you get your transaction up and running, not as a tutorial. The text points out the important steps and issues that you need to consider in building this transaction.

This chapter describes the various phases in developing an inbound transaction. The tasks in each phase are also described. You need a good understanding of the sales order process to be able to carry out this transaction, but the configuration of the sales order process is not the focus of this chapter. The concepts covered in this chapter apply to all inbound EDI transactions that use direct posting via a function module.

Overview of the Sales Order Process

The sales order (850 in ANSI X.12, ORDER in EDIFACT) is a document that is received from a customer by a vendor to supply goods or services.

 NOTE

The formal definition of the ANSI X.12 850 transaction is as follows:

"This transaction set provides for customary and established business and industry practice relative to the placement of purchase orders for goods and services."

In the SAP system, this transaction is implemented in the Sales and Distribution module. The process begins with a sales order transaction received from a customer. The EDI document is converted to an IDoc, which is then used to post a sales order in the system (see Figure 16-1).

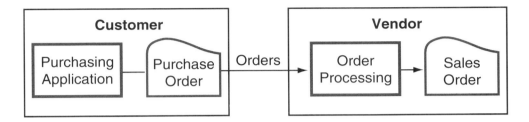

FIGURE 16-1

Messages exchanged in the sales order process

The methodology to create an application document from an incoming EDI document is simple. First you analyze the business requirements and compare them with what SAP provides (analysis phase). Then you identify various parameters used in the process (preparation phase). Next you configure the EDI components and build the necessary master data (setup phase), test the setup (test phase), execute the process (execution phase), verify the results (verification phase), and celebrate if they look good! In the following sections you will learn the objectives of each phase and tasks involved in each phase.

The Analysis Phase

The analysis phase consists of analyzing business requirements and comparing them with the standard functionality of SAP. A good understanding of the SAP business process can help you fill the gaps by customizing the system. If gaps cannot be filled via customizing, then you should explore the use of user exits to meet your business needs. Tasks in the analysis phase are described next.

Identifying Business Processes

Identify the SAP business process that supports the EDI transaction you're interested in. In some cases the lingo in SAP may be different from what you are used to. You can use online help to identify the SAP document that is created in this process.

In the case of inbound sales orders via EDI, a sales document is created. The EDI process uses the CALL Transaction method to post an incoming sales order IDoc. Thus a sales document created via EDI goes through checks similar to a regular sales order that is entered online. Knowledge of the sales order process—how it works, what causes a sales order to fail, how pricing is carried out, how you can support multiple ship-to locations, how the system performs ATP (Available To Promise) checks, and so on—will help you design your EDI process to meet your business needs. Work closely with the functional team to get a better understanding of the process.

Developing a Cross-Reference Sheet

Customers develop a cross-reference spreadsheet that maps the EDI fields received to the SAP data elements via IDoc data fields. The idea behind developing a cross-reference sheet is the same as with the outbound process. Refer to "Developing a Cross-Reference Sheet" in Chapter 14, "Outbound with Message Control—Purchase Orders" for details.

Identifying User Exits Available in the Process

Like the outbound process, user-exits have been provided at strategic points in the inbound process. Refer to "Locating User-Exits" in Chapter 32, "Programming in the IDoc Interface," for details on locating user exits for the IDoc processes.

The enhancement for the inbound sales order transaction is VEDA0001. To see a list of all the user exits in this enhancement, and their purposes, execute transaction SMOD, enter the enhancement name VEDA0001, click on the Documentation button, and click on Display.

Developing Conversion Lists

A tricky situation occurs with inbound processes. The SAP system has its own terminology for organization objects such as sales organizations, company codes, and purchasing organizations. These are used when you create documents in the SAP system. For example, company code is required when you create an invoice, and sales area is required when you create sales documents. There is no industry standard for these objects. Therefore, when an EDI document is received, it will not have these values. You need to have a lookup table that can provide a translation based on values from some field in the EDI document, or the values can be hard-coded in the EDI map if they are constant. For example, if you receive a sales order, the Vendor Number field on the incoming data can be used to deduce the sales area in SAP.

For the incoming sales order process, carry out the following conversions:

◆ When you create a sales order document, sales area you are required to provide information (sales organization, distribution channel, and division). This information is not available on an incoming EDI transmission. SAP provides a lookup table, EDSDC, to determine the sales area. The sales area can also be determined in a user exit of the IDoc process. If none of these techniques is acceptable the conversion can be done in the EDI subsystem. As part of the analysis phase, you'll make a decision about the best place to carry out such conversions. Although the general rule is to carry out most conversions on the EDI subsystem, some situations can be better accommodated in SAP owing to instant availability and the fact that the most recent data resides in the SAP system.

◆ Another common issue with inbound documents is the conversion of external representation to an internal representation. For example, a customer generally sends you its generic customer number, which does not map to a customer number in the SAP system. You'll need to design a solution in the EDI subsystem to do this conversion, as SAP has no standard way of handling this problem. Conversion of the customer's material number to an SAP material number is also required.

By identifying such information, you become aware of the issues that you need to address in processing an incoming document.

TIP

The best strategy is to offload conversions to the EDI subsystem, but this method may not always be acceptable to your EDI subsystem team.

The Preparation Phase

In the preparation phase, you'll do all the groundwork and identify the parameters needed for your transaction.

Identifying Business Partners

Identify the business partner (the customer) who is sending you the EDI document. An entry for that customer must exist in your customer master data. You can locate a customer in the system using transaction XD02.

Identifying IDoc and Message Types

Just as you had identified an IDoc type and Message type for an outbound process, you need to identify the IDoc type and the Message type to support the inbound process.

For a sales order, the IDoc type is ORDERS01 or ORDERS02, and the message type is ORDERS (from the reference chart in the appendix).

 NOTE

Notice that the IDoc type for the outbound purchase order and inbound sales order is the same.

Identifying Conversion Tables to Be Maintained

As mentioned in the analysis phase, you may need to convert some of the data in an incoming document. These conversions are best carried out in the EDI subsystem except for those conversions that point to data that is continuously changing, such as customer numbers and material numbers.

However, in some cases the responsibility may fall on the shoulders of the SAP EDI team. In this case you need to collect the data for your conversion tables. For example, in the sales order you may decide to maintain the determination of sales area (sales organization, distribution channel, and division) for an incoming sales order in the SAP system. If so, you need data values that you can use to deduce the sales area in SAP.

SAP provides conversion abilities for the following cases in the sales documents:

- ◆ Determination of sales area
- ◆ External number for a partner function (for example, customer's ship-to locations to internal SAP ship-to customer numbers)
- ◆ Customer's material number to the material number in the SAP system

Identifying Process Codes

A process code represents the function module that is used for the inbound process. The link between any process code and its corresponding function module can be seen by using transaction WE42. The process code for incoming sales order documents is ORDE.

TIP

An easy way to determine the process code is to locate the function module. Function module names are based on message type.

Identifying Workflow Parameters

You'll need to identify two elements: organization object and workflow task. This step is slightly different from an outbound process, where you do not have a workflow task specific to a message type.

The organization object (user ID, position, workcenter, and so on) is responsible for handling errors associated with the EDI transaction. You can choose from several types of organization objects. Refer to Chapter 9, "Configuring Workflow," for details on the different types of objects. To begin, you can use your user ID for this step.

The workflow task handles application errors. The tasks for standard SAP messages are named <message type>_Error. For sales orders the task is Orders_Error (TS00008046).

The Setup Phase

After you identify the parameters, you will set up the master data needed from an EDI perspective, conversion tables, and the EDI components that are required for each transaction. The master data is required before you can make some of the EDI settings. For example, you cannot create a partner profile before you create the customer master. The components to be set up vary with each transaction.

Master Data Requirements

The type of master data and the required fields from an EDI perspective in the master data vary for each transaction. Your task is not necessarily to maintain the entire master data, but you should be aware of the fields that are "required" from an EDI perspective and how the master data is used in EDI. These fields may not otherwise be required fields in the master data.

The cross-reference sheet can help you identify the fields that must be filled in the IDoc for your business needs. A discussion of the master data for an incoming sales order document follows.

Customer Master Data

Transaction: XD02

Menu Path: Logistics, Sales and Distribution, Master Data, Business Partners, Sold to Party, Change, Change Centrally

A customer master is needed for each customer with whom you exchange business documents via EDI. A customer can be of several kinds: sold to, ship to, bill to, and so on. The sold-to customer is used for incoming sales orders. In SAP, a ship-to customer can be different than the sold-to customer. For example, if Wal-Mart (sold-to customer) orders computers from IBM, it request that the shipment be sent to SAM'S Club (ship-to customer).

A sales area view is needed for each sales organization that deals with the customer. For example, if a sales area (Sales Organization: 3000, Distribution Channel: 01, and Division: 05) will be accepting sales orders from a customer, then you'll need to make sure that the customer is defined in the sales area.

Material Master

Transaction: MM02

Menu Path: Logistics, Materials Management, Material Master, Material,
Change, Immediately

A material master is needed for materials that you sell to your customers. Like any other master data, the material must also be defined for the sales organization and distribution channel that will accept the sales orders.

Maintaining Conversion Tables

The conversion tables convert an external representation to an internal representation or provide a lookup mechanism to deduce information that is not supplied by your business partner.

Some of the conversions can be done in the EDI subsystem or in the SAP system. Based on your decision in the analysis phase, you may choose to use any of the optional conversions in the SAP system, as discussed in the following sections.

Customer Material Information Records

Transaction: VD51

Menu Path: Logistics, Sales and Distribution, Master Data, Agreements, Cust.material Info, Create

The system uses a customer material information record to convert the material number of the customer to a material number in the SAP system. For example, in Figure 16-2 the customer material number CUST-MAT-01 is converted to your material number DPC1020 in the SAP system.

Partner Conversion Table (EDPAR)

Transaction: VOED (Partner, Application, Conversion)

Menu Path: From the IMG, Sales and Distribution, EDI messages, Configure EDI Partners

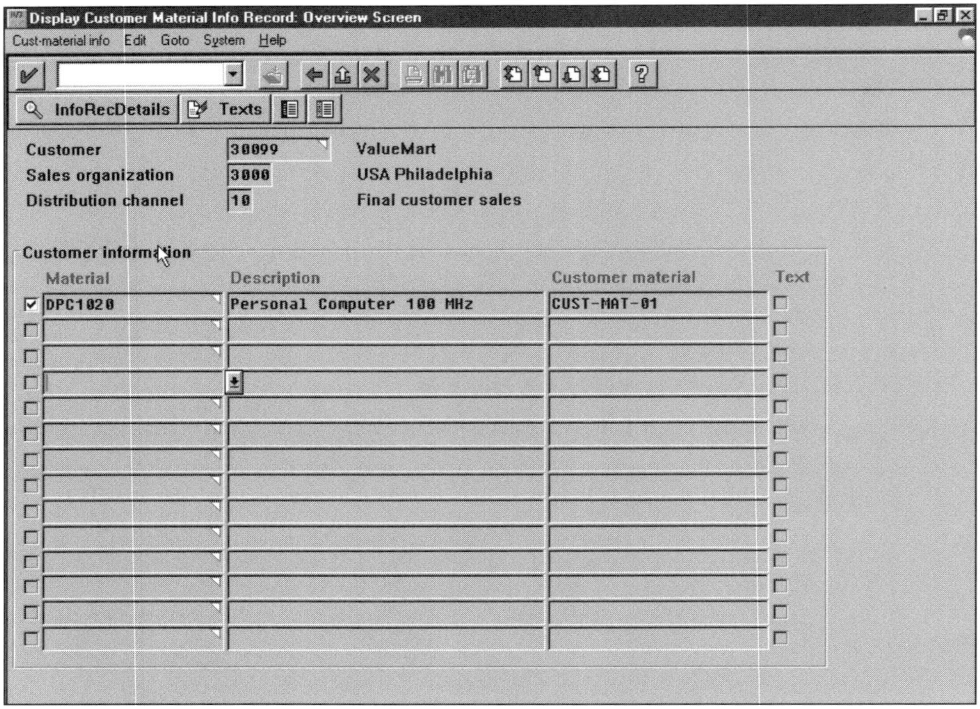

FIGURE 16-2

Material information record

The partner conversion table is used to convert an external representation of a partner function number (ship to, bill to, and so on) to an internal representation. This table can be used for all incoming and outgoing SD transactions via EDI. This table is used for entries in the E1EDKA1 segment of the IDoc.

For example, you can accept a sales order from a customer (say, 30099) and ship the products to the customer's warehouse location A or warehouse location B. These two warehouses are represented by two ship-to customers in SAP (say, 3980 and 3000) and are tied to the customer master in the partner functions screen. When you accept a sales order via EDI, the customer will not send you the ship-to numbers as represented in the SAP system. The customer will send its terminology (say, WH-A for warehouse A and WH-B for warehouse B). The partner conversion table will convert the WH-A to your SAP number 3980 and WH-B to your SAP number 3000, as shown in Figure 16-3.

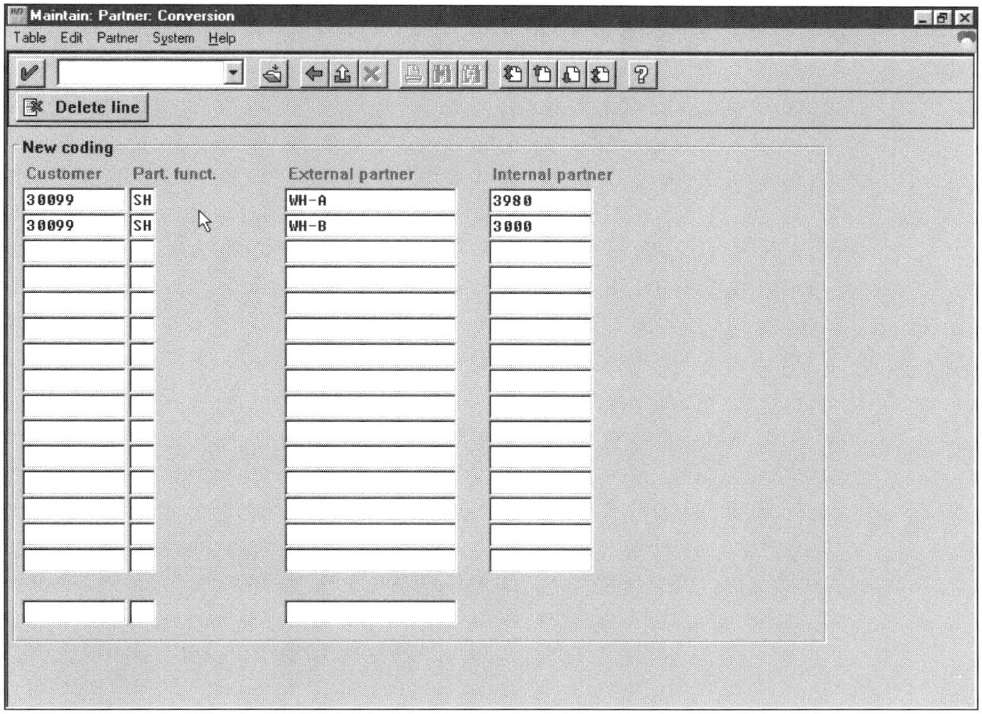

FIGURE 16-3

Conversion of external partner function number to an internal number

The first column (Customer) contains the customer number. The second column
(Part. Func.) is the partner function that you want to convert. The third column
(External Partner) is the external representation of your partner. The fourth column
(Internal partner) is the internal representation of the business partner in SAP.

TIP

Some customers have tweaked the system into using this table to convert
external representation of the sold-to to an internal sold-to number by maintaining
the table directly via SM31. This approach is not recommended; SAP does not
officially document this feature, and you could be in trouble down the road.

CAUTION

If the external representation is a number, then you have to prefix it with leading zeros if the number in the IDoc is prefixed with leading zeros.

Determining the Sales Area for the Sales Order

Transaction: VOED (Partner, Application, Customer/Supplier)

Menu Path: From the IMG, choose Sales and Distribution, EDI messages, Configure EDI Partners.

A sales area is required when entering a sales order in the system. The system first checks the E1EDK14 segment for the sales area values. If the system doesn't find the data, then it uses the sales area lookup table (EDSDC) to deduce the sales area information. Entries in the EDSDC table map a vendor number supplied in the E1EDKA1 segment to a sales area in SAP, as shown in Figure 16-4. In the example, when a customer who recognizes you as VENDOR-01 orders goods, then sales area (Sales Organization: 3000, Distribution Channel: 10, and Division: 00) is used for the sales order.

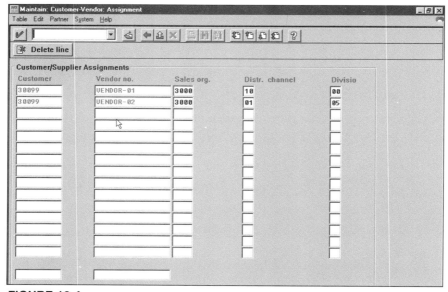

FIGURE 16-4

Determining the sales area for an order

The first column is the customer number for the customer sending the order. The second column is the vendor number from the LIFNR field of the E1EDKA1 segment. The next three columns represent the sales area.

 CAUTION

If the LIFNR field in the E1EDKA1 segment has leading zeros, then the values entered in the Vendor Number field must also have leading zeros.

 TIP

You can write a BDC (Batch Data Communication) program to load this table if you already have this information in a legacy system.

 NOTE

You can also use the user exit number 07 from the enhancement VEDA0001 to deduce the sales area. If you use the user exit, you do not need to maintain this table. However, you will have to design your program logic to return the appropriate values.

Maintaining Pricing

Transaction: V/08

Menu Path: From the IMG, choose Sales and Distribution, Basic Functions, Pricing, Pricing Control, Define and Assign Pricing Procedures.

If an order entry clerk enters a sales order online, then pricing is not a major issue. The order entry clerk can communicate any price variance that exists between the customer's expected price and the price calculated by the system. However, the pricing issue is always important when incoming documents are being entered automatically in the system, as in the case of EDI. The system provides two condition types for incoming EDI orders: EDI1 and EDI2. These must be included in the pricing procedure adopted by your organization, as shown in Figure 16-5.

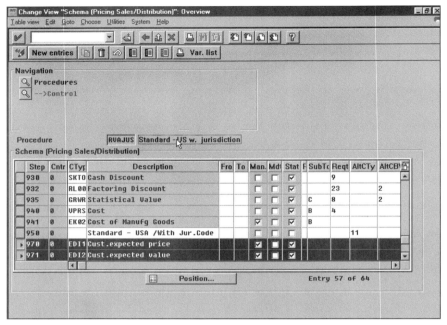

FIGURE 16-5

Including pricing conditions in the pricing procedure

The condition type EDI1 represents customer expected price. The customer requested price from the E1EDP01-VPREI field in the IDoc is used to calculate the customer expected price. This value is compared with the actual price calculated by the system. You can specify any formula for comparing the price when including this condition type in the pricing procedure. In the standard system, the system provides a formula 9 to check the difference of a single unit of the currency. For example, if the price difference in the United States is greater than $1, then the order is flagged as incomplete due to pricing issues.

The condition type EDI2 represents customer expected value. The customer requested value from the E1EDP01-NETWR field in the IDoc is used to calculate the customer expected value. This value is compared with the actual value calculated by the system. You can specify any formula for comparing the value when including this condition type in the pricing procedure. In the standard system, the system provides a formula 8 to check the difference of greater than 5 percent. If the value difference is greater than 5 percent, then the order will be flagged as incomplete due to pricing issues.

Your responsibility as an EDI member is to make sure the pricing procedures include these two conditions. The configuration of the pricing module is another issue.

EDI Configuration Components

You should have already carried out the one-time EDI setting required by all EDI transactions. The settings include:

◆ Basic Settings for IDocs
◆ Communication Settings

Refer to Chapter 6, "Configuring Basic EDI Components," for step-by-step details on performing the setup.

Partner Profile: Create Inbound View

A partner profile is created for every business partner with whom you exchange business documents via EDI. In the partner profile, an inbound record is created for each inbound message.

Create a partner profile for your customer if it doesn't already exist. Add an inbound record for the sales order message using the values identified in the preparation phase, as shown in Figure 16-6.

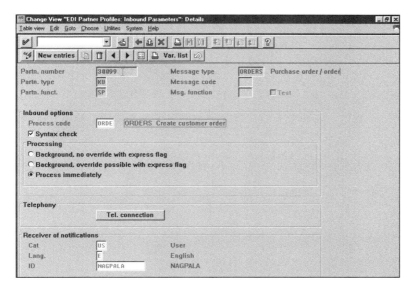

FIGURE 16-6

*Partner profile—
inbound record for
sales order*

Workflow Settings: Create Task Profile

In this step you verify the one-time setting of workflow components for EDI and create a task profile for the incoming EDI message. This section assumes that the workflow configuration has been done. Please refer to "Setting Up Workflow for Exception Handling" in Chapter 9, "Configuring Workflow," for details. The following workflow settings are necessary:

◆ Basic workflow settings
◆ Setting up the organization unit
◆ Task profile for the error tasks

In addition to the one-time settings, you need to assign a task profile to the Orders_Error task. To begin, you can also make the task a General Task, which allows everyone to handle this task.

The Testing Phase

After you configure the system, you're ready for the testing phase. Follow the unit-testing technique described in Chapter 10, "Testing the EDI Interface." To begin, you can only carry out the sanity tests to make sure the configuration is correct. You can execute the process as described in the next section.

Executing Processes

To execute the process, you first create an IDoc and then pass it to the ALE/EDI interface layer for processing. To create an IDoc for the inbound process, use any of the tools discussed in "Testing Utilities to Start the Inbound Process" in Chapter 10, "Testing the EDI Interface," for creating IDocs. The most common tool (transaction WE19) used to copy an existing IDoc and start the inbound process is shown in Figure 16-7.

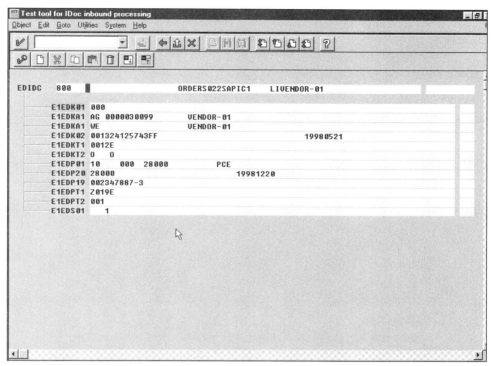

FIGURE 16-7

Copying an existing IDoc to create a new IDoc

Verifying Output

The process of verifying an inbound process via a function module is straightforward. First you verify the results of processing by displaying the IDoc, using any of the IDoc display tools. The status record with a status code of 53 indicates success and logs the application document number generated using the IDoc. You can then display the application document.

For the sales order, go to the IDoc display and check the status records in the IDoc. Get the sales order number from the status record with a status code of 53, as shown in Figure 16-8. Display the sales order using VA03, confirm the values, and make sure the document is complete. You can check for incompleteness by selecting Edit, Incomplete Log from the sales order display screen.

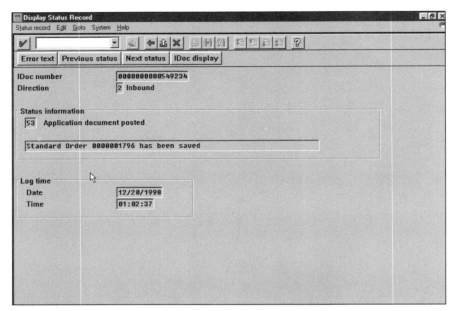

FIGURE 16-8

IDoc status record showing the sales order number created from an incoming IDoc

If you experience problems in the process, use the troubleshooting guide in Chapter 12, "EDI Process Troubleshooting and Recovery," to determine the cause of the problem and then restart the process as necessary.

Summary

The steps to configure an inbound process via a function module are categorized into phases. In the analysis phase, you'll develop an understanding of the SAP business process that supports the EDI transaction and then develop a cross-reference sheet to identify gaps between your business needs and standard SAP functionality. The inbound process requires several conversions, which can be done in the EDI subsystem or in the SAP system by using standard conversion tables provided for the process or through user exits. In the preparation phase, you identify various parameters that are used in the setup phase to configure the system. Next comes the testing phase, followed by the execution phase, in which you run the process. Finally, the results are verified in the IDoc and in the application document created in the process.

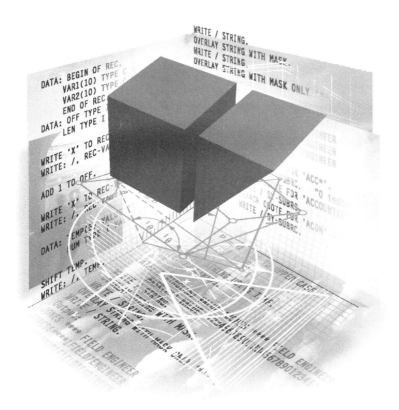

Chapter 17

Inbound via Workflow—Sales Order Changes

This chapter uses an inbound sales order change transaction to illustrate how an inbound process works using a workflow task. It points out the important steps and issues that you need to consider in building this transaction. The sales order change was chosen because it makes the most sense if you were going to implement an inbound via workflow. The concepts covered here apply to all inbound EDI transactions that use workflow. This chapter should be viewed as a guide to help you get your process up and running, not as a tutorial.

 CAUTION

EDI transactions that use workflow are not a standard scenario in the system.

Overview of the Sales Order Change

The sales order change (860 in ANSI X.12) is a document that a customer sends to a vendor to inform them of changes to a previous sales order (refer to Figure 16-1).

 NOTE

The formal definition of the ANSI X.12 860 transaction follows:

"This transaction set provides the information required for the customary and established business and industry practice relative to the purchase order change."

In the SAP system this transaction is implemented in the Sales and Distribution module. The process begins with a sales order change transaction that the vendor receives from a customer. The default processing is to create an IDoc and post the order change IDoc directly into the system without any human intervention, but this approach can be a problem for many companies. You really shouldn't process an order change without knowing what will be changed. The scenario in this chapter uses workflow to notify a person of the changes being requested.

The methodology is slightly different from that described in the previous chapter. A new development and design phase has been introduced. The steps in the setup phase are also different because of the nature of the process.

The Analysis Phase

The analysis phase consists of analyzing business requirements and comparing them with the standard functionality of SAP. In the case of a sales order change process, the sales document that was created earlier as part of the incoming sales order transaction is changed. The process does not restrict the type of changes being made to the sales order. Thus, if an original order was for 1,700 pieces and the production has already started, you might receive a sales order change that reduces the quantity to 5 pieces.

NOTE

Developing Cross-Reference Sheets is similar to the step described in Chapter 16, "Inbound with Function Module—Sales Orders."

The Design and Development Phase

The gaps identified in the process may require you to enhance the existing process or to develop the process from scratch. The "SAP rule" is to use standard components whenever and wherever possible. In this phase you'll design and develop the enhancements.

The scenario described in this chapter assumes that automatic changes are unacceptable and that you want to involve a person to review the changes being requested, as shown in Figure 17-1. Refer to Figure 4-3 in Chapter 4 for details on the process flow.

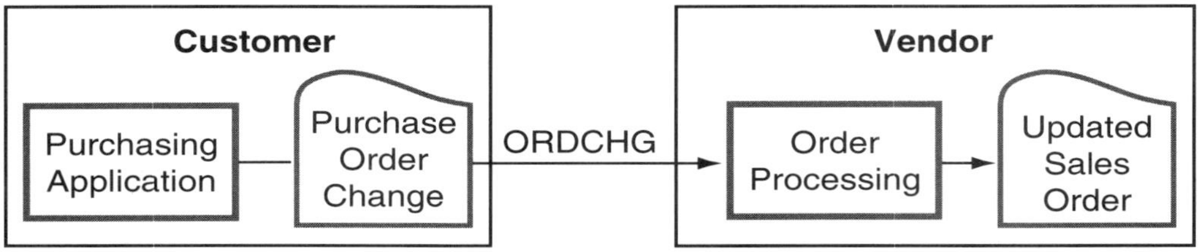

FIGURE 17-1

Enhanced sales order change process via workflow

The inbound sales order change process can be implemented to simulate the following process:

1. An incoming EDI document is converted to an IDoc. (This step is the same as the corresponding step in the standard scenario.)

2. The IDoc is routed to a person responsible for verifying the changes. (This step is different from the normal process of posting the IDoc.)

3. The responsible person gets a workitem in their SAP Inbox, informing them of the order change IDoc. They execute the workitem, which automatically displays the IDoc.

4. If the changes are acceptable, they are manually implemented in the sales order document.

5. If changes are not acceptable, then the IDoc will not be posted.

The enhanced scenario is implemented as a simple process that explains the concept very clearly. It uses existing workflow components and does not involve any programming. Your business scenario may require additional development. You may use a multistep workflow, rather than a single-step task. workflow development and design skills are necessary for a sophisticated workflow to be used in the process.

A standard task, named Display (TS30200088), exists in the system to display any IDoc. It will be used to display the sales order change IDoc data. The name for the process code chosen is ZOCH.

The Preparation Phase

In the preparation phase you'll do all the groundwork and identify the parameters needed for your transaction.

Identifying IDoc and Message Types

Identify the IDoc type and the message type to support the process. For a sales order change, the IDoc type is ORDERS01 or ORDERS02, and the message type is ORDCHG (from the reference chart).

NOTE

Identifying the business partners is similar to the step described in Chapter 16, "Inbound with Function Module—Sales Orders."

Identifying Workflow Tasks and Process Codes for Inbound Processes

The workflow task to be started is represented by a process code. You'll need to identify that task and establish a process code for it. The process code should start with the letter Z. In this scenario you can use a standard system task to display an IDoc. The task name is Display (TS30200088), and the name chosen for the process code is ZOCH.

NOTE

Identifying the workflow parameters for error handling is identical to the step discussed in Chapter 16, "Inbound with Function Module—Sales Orders."

The Setup Phase

After you identify the parameters, you'll set up the master data needed from an EDI perspective, the necessary conversion tables, and the EDI components that are required for each transaction. The master data is required before you can enter some of the EDI settings. For example, you cannot create a partner profile before you create the customer master. The components to be set up depend on the transaction.

 NOTE

The master data requirements are identical to those described in Chapter 16, "Inbound with Function Module—Sales Orders."

EDI Configuration Components

You should have already carried out the one-time EDI setting required by all EDI transactions. The settings include:

◆ Basic Settings for IDocs

◆ Communication Settings

Refer to Chapter 6, "Configuring Basic EDI Components," for step-by-step details on performing the setup.

Process Code Settings

Transaction: WE42

Menu Path: From the Area menu of EDI, choose Control, Inb. Process Code, Inbound with ALE service, Processing by Task.

In this step you link the process code to the single-step task. Create an entry with process code ZOCH and task TS30200088, as shown in Figure 17-2.

Partner Profile: Creating the Inbound View

A partner profile is created for every business partner with whom you exchange business documents via EDI. In the partner profile, an inbound record is created for each inbound message.

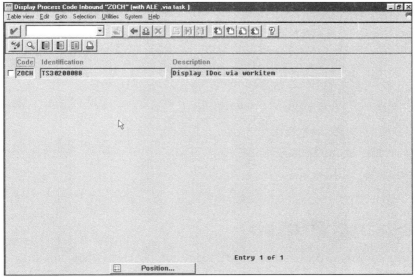

FIGURE 17-2

Process code pointing to a single-step task for an inbound process

Add an inbound record for the sales order change message using the values identified in the preparation phase (see Figure 17-3).

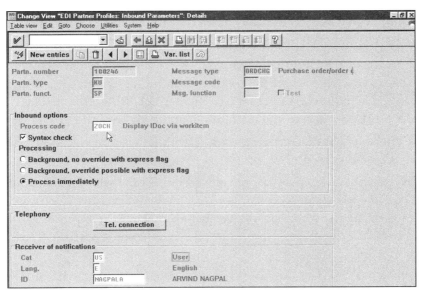

FIGURE 17-3

Partner profile—inbound record for the sales order change message

Workflow Settings

In this step you verify the one-time setting of workflow components for EDI and create a task profile for the incoming EDI message. This section assumes that the workflow configuration is complete. Please refer to "Setting Up workflow for Exception Handling" in Chapter 9, "Configuring workflow," for details. The following workflow settings are necessary:

- ◆ Basic workflow settings
- ◆ Setting up the organization unit
- ◆ Task profile for the error tasks

The Testing Phase

After you configure the system, you're ready for testing. Follow the unit-testing technique discussed in Chapter 10, "Testing the EDI Interface." To begin, you can only carry out the sanity tests to make sure the configuration is correct. You can execute the process as described in the next section.

Executing the Process

To execute the process, you first create an IDoc and then pass it to the ALE/EDI interface layer for processing. Follow these steps:

1. To create an IDoc for the inbound process, use any of the tools discussed in "Testing Utilities to Start the Inbound Process" in Chapter 10, for creating IDocs. The most common tool (transaction WE19) used to copy an existing IDoc and start the inbound process is shown in Figure 17-4.

2. Once the inbound process is started, a workitem is placed in your SAP Inbox (see Figure 17-5).

3. Execute the workitem. This step should display the sales order change IDoc. The last status record of the IDoc indicates that the IDoc was passed to a task and the workitem was generated, as shown in Figure 17-6. You can view the data fields. Look at the PO number in the BELNR field of the E1EDK01 segment.

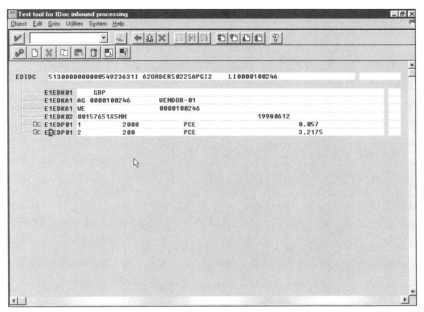

FIGURE 17-4

Copying an existing IDoc to create a new IDoc and start the inbound processing

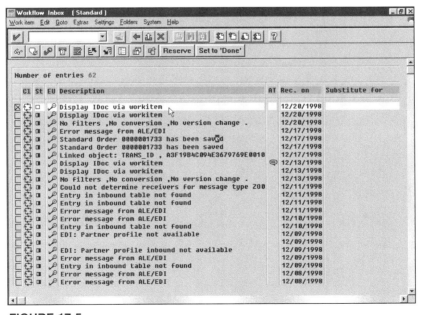

FIGURE 17-5

A work item in the Inbox

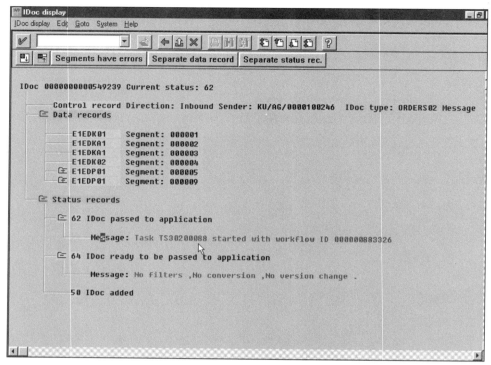

FIGURE 17-6

An IDoc displayed via the work item

4. Use this PO number to locate the sales order that was created in the system.

5. For each sales order item, compare the quantity field in the sales order to the value in the MENGE field in the E1EDP09 segment. If the values are acceptable, go to the sales order change transaction and manually apply those changes.

6. If any changes are unacceptable, delete the IDoc, as shown in Figure 17-7.

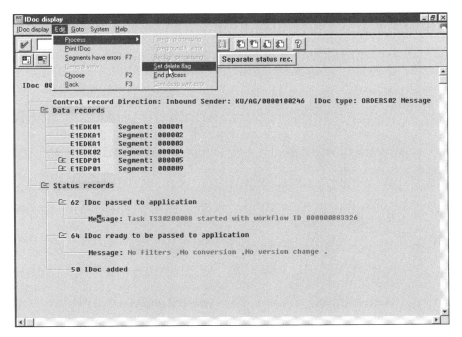

FIGURE 17-7

Rejecting an inbound sales order change IDoc for further processing.

Verifying the Output

Verifying an inbound process via workflow occurs when a work item appears in the Inbox of the responsible user. You can additionally verify the IDoc contents by using any of the IDoc display tools. The status record with a status code of 62 indicates success. If you experience problems in the process, use the troubleshooting guide in Chapter 12, "EDI Process Troubleshooting and Recovery," to determine the cause of the problem and then restart the process as necessary.

Summary

An inbound process via workflow incorporates human intervention. This approach is useful for incoming transactions that can have a negative effect on your business logistics.

Implementation of the process via workflow requires the same methodology as other transactions. Additionally, this type of inbound process involves a design and development phase in which you develop a single-step task or a multistep workflow that replaces the posting module. The inbound IDoc is transferred to the workflow. This step creates a work item that is transferred to a responsible agent, who then executes it and displays the results. If satisfied, the agent can continue with the processing; if not satisfied, they can purge the process.

SAP does not provide standard workflows for the inbound EDI process. You can, however, use some of the tasks that exist for other processes to model yours. The workflow environment is like a programming environment, and you can develop very sophisticated workflow processes for your incoming IDocs.

SECTION II

ALE

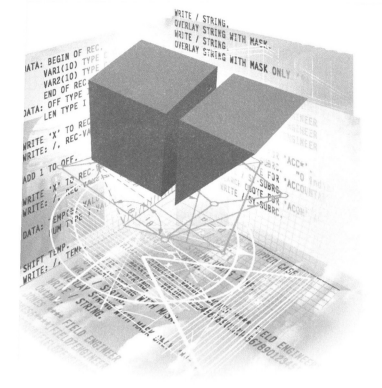

PART

6

ALE Basics

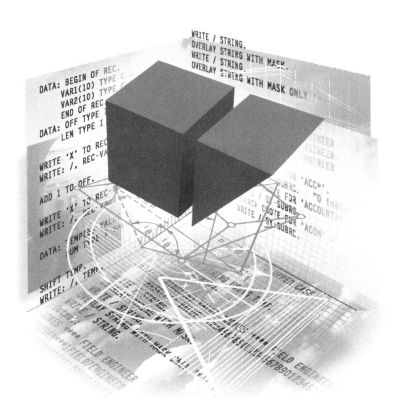

Chapter 18

**Introduction to
Distributed
Systems**

ALE (Application Link and Enabling) is SAP's technology to support distributed yet integrated processes across several SAP systems. In this chapter you'll learn what a distributed process is, why there is a need for distributed processing, why some of the existing technologies do not suffice, and how SAP provides a distributed environment. Distributed systems is a highly technical topic in computer science, but this chapter covers the concept from a business standpoint.

Introduction to the Distributed Process

A distributed process is one in which part of a business process is carried out on one system and part on another. For example, consider the sales and distribution process in SAP. The sales process that performs all of the sales-related activities, such as storing a sales order, calculating delivery dates, checking for availability, performing credit checks, and calculating price could be carried out on one SAP system. The shipping process that performs shipping-related activities such as determining the shipping point, creating deliveries, picking goods, calculating the shortest route, determining the cheapest mode of transportation, and performing goods issue could be carried out on another SAP system.

The two systems exchange data with each other at appropriate points to stay synchronized. SAP provides several tools to keep the systems synchronized at the technical level. In addition, business procedures are required in many cases to keep the systems synchronized.

Reasons for Distributing Processes

Why not stay with an integrated system? Distributing a process does not enhance any application functionality; in fact, it reduces functionality in many cases. So, why distribute?

Geographical Location

The first wave of companies that implemented SAP were large corporations with operations in several parts of the world. Typically, manufacturing units are strategically located to take advantage of cheap labor or to provide local distribution. These units tend to operate autonomously and don't like to be dependent on a distant central system. Time differences and cultural differences intensify the problems. If a manufacturing unit is located in Japan, the time difference requires round-the-clock support from the United States. In the real world, cultural and language differences are also issues.

In addition to business issues, technical considerations such as network availability and bandwidth also play a major role in distributing SAP systems. High network availability, which is no longer an issue for developed countries, cannot be guaranteed in developing countries, where network outages are frequent. It is not uncommon for a dedicated link to be down for half a day. The bandwidth required to support an enterprise application over a wide area network is also a concern; because several applications use the same network, the response time for a simple transaction can be slow. Therefore, it becomes a necessity to have a dedicated system for each geographical area in which a company does business.

Consolidation

A company could have several business units that share some common resources. For example, a company with several sales operations could share a common warehouse and shipping system. In such a case, the warehouse and distribution application could reside on one SAP system and sales applications could reside on another.

System Capacity

System capacity such as database size, memory requirements, number of concurrent users, and network bandwidth may force you to split a system regardless of geography. Although major improvements in speed and database capacity have been achieved, system capacity remains an issue for large corporations that have very high transaction volumes.

Mission-Critical Applications

Mission-critical applications such as manufacturing and distribution cannot afford frequent downtime due to system maintenance activities. If all business functions reside on one system, the number of such outages and activities might increase. In these situations deploying such mission-critical applications on a separate system becomes a necessity.

Upgrading a Module Separately

With SAP delivering new modules and enhanced functionality in every release, some business units may require the latest release of the SAP system while others continue to work with an older release. For example, assume a company has gone live with all modules in release 3.1G. The sales and marketing division is interested in the customer service module available in release 4.0. However, that division cannot use the functionality until the next implementation when the entire company moves to release 4.0, which requires complete verification and testing of the system before it can be deployed. In such situations the ability to upgrade a module without worrying about compatibility issues with other modules is highly desirable.

Data Security

If your organization is involved in a sensitive project for the government, you may be required to separate the classified information from the unclassified. Companies often choose to create a separate instance that is linked to the unclassified instance via ALE.

Political and Business Reasons

Other reasons, such as autonomy of a business unit and subsidiaries, completely different business models, corporate culture, and politics, may cause a company to split a system. Such non-technical factors are the most common reasons for businesses to deploy distributed systems.

Existing Technologies for Data Distribution

By now you should be convinced that businesses have legitimate non-technical needs for distributing processes. In this section you will learn about some of the data distribution capabilities offered by major database vendors and why they may not be sufficient. The various technologies or techniques offered by database vendors are based on the structure of data and not the business meaning or semantics of the data. The following sections describe common data replication techniques.

Disk Mirroring

Disk mirroring is like a disk copy. Changes occurring in a database are simultaneously propagated to another disk that maintains a mirror image of the main disk's contents. This purely technical copy can be used for creating a repository for a DSS (Decision Support System), which requires the most recent data for evaluation. This technique has a severe effect on the OLTP (Online Transaction Processing) system and cannot encapsulate business rules for copying only specific data for an organization.

Online Distribution Using Two-Phase-Commit Protocol

Online distribution allows you to maintain a distributed database in which enterprise data is managed across multiple database servers connected via a network. The database design dictates where a table resides, and the database management system manages queries and updates to these tables. The two-phase-commit protocol guarantees that related tables across systems are updated in one logical unit of work. This process is useful to circumvent problems with database size. However, the technique cannot be used to split tables. For example, you cannot specify that a material master for your Asian subsidiary should be created on system B, whereas a material master for the U.S. unit should be created on system A. Segregation based on the semantics of data is not possible.

Distributed Updates to Replicas

In this technique the system allows you to maintain redundant data across multiple systems. An owner of the data is defined, and data can be updated by the owner or the holder of a copy. If changes are made to a copy, then changes are first propagated to the owner, from whence they again flow down to the replicas. Conflicts can occur because of simultaneous updates to the owner and replica copies, and other issues—such as the need for a homogeneous data model (the database structure is required to be the same), network load, managing deadlocks, synchronization in case of network failure, and long query processing times—can arise. This technique also requires the same version of database and operating system components on the systems involved in the process.

Distributed SAP Systems

Now you're convinced that it's important to have distributed systems, and you know that the techniques offered by database management systems have limitations. What's next? In this section, you'll learn how SAP faced the challenge of developing a distributed environment and what solutions the SAP environment provides.

SAP's Challenge for a Distributed Environment

The challenge was to develop a solution to meet the following requirements:

◆ A system that would understand the syntax and semantics of the data. It was important from the very beginning to base the distribution of data on business rules and not on database replication techniques.

◆ Distributed systems that could maintain their autonomy while being integrated as one logical SAP system. The systems would be able to operate independently and support local processing of transactions and data.

◆ Distributed systems that could handle different data models. A local implementation should be able to customize the system to meet its local needs.

◆ Receiving systems that could handle their own problems and not tie up the sending system, and vice versa.

◆ Systems that could maintain continued operation in spite of network failure. Changes made to either system should be synchronized after the network connection is restored.

◆ A sound technology and methodology that could be used in all distribution scenarios.

SAP's Answer for a Distributed Environment

SAP introduced ALE as its initiative to support a distributed yet integrated environment. ALE allows for efficient and reliable communication between distributed processes across physically separate SAP systems to achieve a distributed, yet integrated logical SAP system.

ALE is not based on any database replication techniques. It is based on application-to-application integration using messaging architecture; a message defines data that is exchanged between two processes. IDocs are containers that hold data exchanged between the two systems. IDocs constitute a major component of the ALE process.

ALE provides a distributed environment with the benefits described in the following sections.

Integration with Non-SAP Systems

ALE architecture is independent of the participating systems, allowing SAP to use the techniques used for SAP-to-SAP communication to communicate with non-SAP systems. This breakthrough is a major advantage for ALE. In fact, you will find more third-party applications integrated with SAP using ALE than distributed SAP systems.

Reliable Distribution

The ALE technology supports guaranteed delivery, which means an application sending a message does not have to worry about network problems or connection failures. The application can concentrate on the business logic. After the application generates a message and a correct receiver is determined, the message will be delivered to the recipient. If there are network problems, the message is buffered, and when the network is restored, buffered messages are delivered. The system also guarantees that a message is not delivered twice.

Release Upgrade

Any of the distributed systems can be upgraded to a newer release of the SAP system without affecting the existing functionality. The ALE layer ensures backward compatibility of messages exchanged between systems. Thus in the sample scenario mentioned earlier, the sales system can be upgraded without requiring an upgrade of the shipping system.

Autonomy

SAP systems connected via ALE are loosely coupled, but they provide a high level of business integration. The systems can operate independently if network problems or maintenance on one of the systems disrupts the connection. Each system maintains its own data and applications. The systems are administered separately, and various maintenance tasks can be carried out on an independent basis without affecting the partner system.

CAUTION

It is important to understand that keeping the systems synchronized is not an easy task. It's a challenge, and companies have developed numerous procedures to keep the systems synchronized. Maintaining a poorly designed distributed system can be a nightmare.

Provisions of the Standard System

Out of the box, the standard system provides several preconfigured distribution scenarios and master data that are enabled for distribution.

Preconfigured Distributed Process Scenarios

SAP provides several preconfigured scenarios, based on the most commonly deployed distributed applications, in the various application modules. SAP has already identified process boundaries, optimized these scenarios, and defined various IDocs that must be exchanged to keep the distributed systems integrated. Examples of these include a distributed sales and shipping system, central contracts and distributed purchasing, distributed accounting, distributed cost center accounting, and profit center accounting.

Preconfigured Distributed Application Scenarios

When it comes to distributed applications, SAP also permits third-party applications to be integrated with SAP, using ALE and IDocs. SAP provides a predefined IDoc interface that defines "what" and "when" for the IDocs exchanged between the applications. Several standard interfaces exist in the system; for example, the PP-POI (Production Planning—Production Optimization Interface) is used to interface with third-party production-planning optimization software products.

Preconfigured Master Data Scenarios

To support various scenarios, several master data objects in the SAP system have been enabled for ALE, including customer master, vendor master, material master, profit centers, cost centers, and G/L accounts. Master data is critical information that is shared across several applications in a company. Companies deploy different strategies for the maintenance and distribution of such information.

Summary

Businesses need a distributed environment for a variety of business and technical reasons, such as autonomy of business, geographical location, and network availability. Database vendors provide a means for distributing data across several systems. The drawback to these solutions is that they understand the structure of the data, but not the semantics. ALE was designed to provide a distributed yet integrated environment that does not suffer from problems associated with database distribution.

SAP ALE provides standard scenarios for distributing processes across multiple SAP systems, distributed application scenarios to interface with third party products, and distributed master data scenarios to support distributed processes and distributed applications.

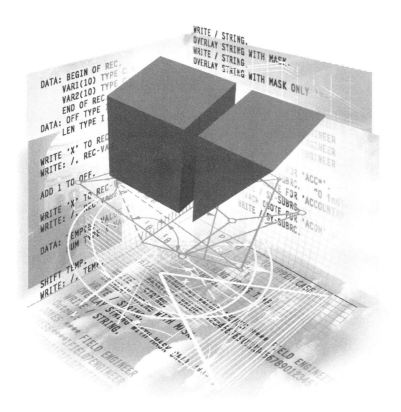

Chapter 19

Introduction to ALE Technology

In the previous chapter, you learned about distributed systems and how ALE is the basis for distributing processes in SAP. ALE technology supports all technical aspects of distributed processes, starting from the generation of IDocs in the sending system to the posting of IDocs in the destination system. This chapter looks at ALE technology, its various components, and its architecture; provides a brief overview of IDocs; and examines various system tools that support distributed processing.

ALE Architecture

Examine the process flow used to exchange data between distributed systems in ALE architecture. It consists of an outbound process, an inbound process, and an exception-handling process.

The Outbound Process

The outbound ALE process in SAP (see Figure 19-1) sends data to one or more SAP systems. At a very high level, an outbound process involves four steps.

1. **Identify the need for sending an IDoc.** This moment could be immediately upon creating an application document, related to a change to a master data object, user initiated, or simply a point in a process that necessitates the exchange of data. The outbound ALE process for the IDoc data is started. For example, when a material master is created, it consults the ALE layer to determine whether any system is interested in the data. If so, the ALE layer starts the process to send material master data to the interested party.

2. **Generate the master IDoc.** The document or master data to be sent is read from the database and formatted into an IDoc format. This IDoc is called a master IDoc. At this point think of IDoc as yet another format in which a document can be represented. You know how a date can be stored in different formats, so imagine date as a document with three components: day, month, and year. In one case you may represent the date as MM/DD/YYYY, the standard American way. But to make the information meaningful to a German business partner, you may have to represent the date as DD.MM.YY. IDocs are based on a similar concept of representing one set of data in various ways. The data in the application document format is suitable for application modules, screens, and internal programs. The same data in an IDoc format is suitable for exchange with external systems.

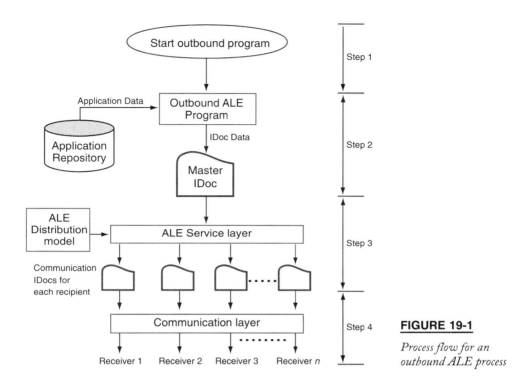

FIGURE 19-1

Process flow for an outbound ALE process

3.   **Generate the communication IDoc.** The ALE service layer generates a separate IDoc from the master IDoc for each recipient who is interested in the data. Separate IDocs are generated because each recipient might demand a different version or a subset of the master IDoc. These recipient-specific IDocs are called communication IDocs and are stored in the database. The recipients are determined from a customer distribution model that maintains a list of messages exchanged between two systems and their direction of flow.

 NOTE

Communication IDocs are stored in the database, but the master IDoc is not. The master IDoc is kept in memory buffers until communication IDocs are generated.

4. **Deliver the communication IDoc.** This step delivers IDocs to the appropriate recipients using an asynchronous communication method, allowing the sending system to continue its processing without having to wait for the destination system to receive or process the IDoc.

The Inbound Process

The inbound process receives an IDoc and creates a document in the system. At a very high level, the inbound process can be seen as the sequence of steps, as shown in Figure 19-2.

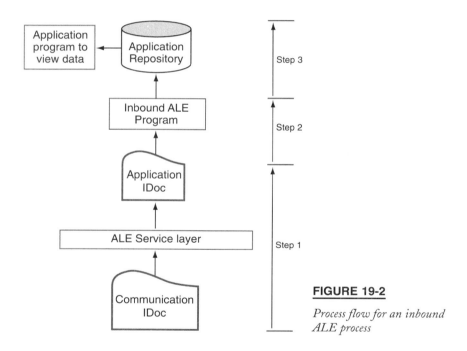

FIGURE 19-2

Process flow for an inbound ALE process

1. **Store the IDoc in the database.** First, an IDoc is received in the system and stored in the database. Then the IDoc goes through a basic integrity check and a syntax check. If everything is fine, the next step is performed.

2. **Invoke the posting module.** The control information in the IDoc and configuration tables are read to determine the posting program. The IDoc is then transferred to its posting program.

3. **Create the document.** The posting program reads the IDoc data and then creates a document in the system. The results are logged in the IDoc.

Exception Handling via Workflow

The preceding steps describe a success path. Exceptions can occur at any point in the outbound or the inbound process. These exceptions can be of different types (such as network problems or data problems), depending on where they occur. The type of error determines who is responsible for handling it. Workflow provides the flexibility to determine the correct person(s) at run time and to inform them in a timely manner.

Each person responsible gets a work item that can be executed to display the error and diagnose the problem. Errors are fixed outside workflow. When the problem is fixed, the process can be restarted from the point of failure.

Overview of IDocs

An IDoc is a container that is used to exchange data between any two processes. The document represented in an IDoc is independent of the complex structure that SAP uses to store application data. This type of flexibility enables SAP to rearrange its internal structure without affecting the existing interfaces.

The word IDoc is used very loosely in the IDoc interface. An IDoc represents an IDoc type and/or IDoc data depending on the context in which the word IDoc is used. An IDoc type represents the definition component of the IDoc, which defines the structure and the format of the data that is being exchanged. IDoc data can be seen as an instance of an IDoc type.

IDoc Type

IDocs were originally designed for the EDI interface, but now they are used in several applications, including ALE. An IDoc type structure can consist of several segments, and each segment can consist of several data fields. The IDoc structure defines the syntax of the data by specifying a list of permitted segments, arrangement of the segments, and any mandatory segments. Segments define a set of fields and their format.

Instantiated IDocs

An IDoc is an instance of an IDoc type. An IDoc consists of three types of records, as shown in Figure 19-3.

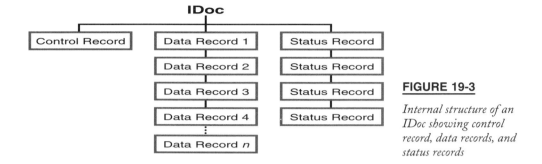

FIGURE 19-3

Internal structure of an IDoc showing control record, data records, and status records

One control record. Each IDoc has only one control record. The control record contains all the control information about an IDoc: the IDoc number, sender and recipient information, and other information like the message type it represents and IDoc type. The structure of the control record is the same for all IDocs and is defined by SAP. The field values can be different.

One or many data records. An IDoc can have multiple data records as defined by the IDoc structure. Segments translate into data records, which store the application data such as purchase order header information and purchase order detail lines.

One or many status records. In most cases multiple status records exist in an IDoc. When status records are processed, they are attached to an IDoc as the IDoc achieves different milestones. At every milestone a status code, date, and time are assigned. Status records help you determine whether an IDoc is in error or not. Several tools are available to view the IDocs and their status records.

 NOTE

For more on IDocs, see Chapter 29, "IDocs from the Outside," and Chapter 30, "IDocs on the Inside."

Multiple Messages per IDoc Concept

A message represents a specific type of document that is transmitted between two partners. Orders, order response, material master, and customer master are examples of messages. In SAP an IDoc may be used to represent several messages or several business documents. Of course, the messages must be logically related. For example, the orders IDoc (ORDERS02) is used for several messages, including order (ORDERS), order response (ORDRSP) and order change (ORDCHG).

Or consider an example in which an IDoc type exists to represent all possible information about an employee, as shown in Figure 19-4. This IDoc is being used to send separate messages to two separate applications. One message is Employee Salary Information, and the other message is Employee Security Profile. The difference between the messages is the set of segments used.

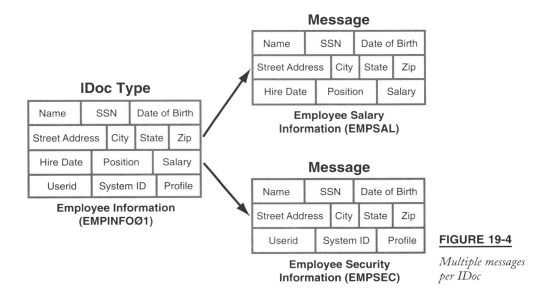

FIGURE 19-4

Multiple messages per IDoc

Special Features of Data Distribution

ALE technology includes special features for managing data that is exchanged between two systems. These features provide a functionally rich interface for distributing data:

◆ **Reduced IDocs.** In standard scenarios, a data object such as material master is exchanged between two systems to its full extent. In your implementation you may not be interested in distributing the full set. You can reduce an IDoc so that it contains only the desired information.

This process is called reducing an IDoc type. For example, the material master IDoc (MATMAS02) is delivered with information on all possible views of a material master. If one of the business units in your company does not implement production planning, at definition time you can create a subset of the IDoc type to eliminate the production-planning information. This step helps to reduce the size of the IDoc.

♦ **Filtering.** The filtering technique creates a subset of data at run time. Filtering can remove certain segments from an IDoc or a complete IDoc for distribution to a specific system.

♦ **Conversion.** The conversion technique converts data in certain fields of the IDoc (for example, Company Code) from their local meaning to a global meaning for distribution.

♦ **Version change.** IDocs and segments are version controlled. The system can be configured to distribute a specific version of an IDoc or a segment to a destination system. For example, if you've upgraded the sales system from version 30A to 31G but the shipping system continues to operate on 30A, you can configure the system to generate version 30A segments for the shipping system.

 NOTE

The filtering, conversion, and version changes can also be done by a receiving system.

Tools

To support a distributed environment, the SAP provides several tools to configure, test, and monitor distributed systems. SAP also provides development tools to either enhance a scenario or create a new scenario from scratch.

Configuration Tools

Configuration tools are provided to set up communication links and to model distribution scenarios between the distributed systems. See Part 8, "Configuring the ALE Interface," for complete details on the various options and how to carry out the configuration process.

◆ **Modeling a distribution scenario.** A distribution scenario is represented in a customer distribution model. It identifies the various systems involved, the list of messages exchanged between the systems, and the owner of specific data.

◆ **Communication link.** A communication link and the mode in which data will be exchanged needs to be established between the systems involved in the process. This communication link is accomplished by creating RFC (Remote Function Call) destinations, port definitions, and partner profiles. Configuration tools are also used for custom scenarios to make the components known to the system.

Testing Tools

Several tools are available to test individual component processes such as creating and posting IDocs, checking the validity of communication links, and handling exceptions. These are discussed in Chapter 26, "Testing the ALE Interface."

Monitoring Tools

When you start executing any ALE process, IDocs will be generated in the system. IDocs serve as a focal point for the logging of information. Several tools enable you to view IDocs in different ways and to display the logged information. The status of processing in the receiving system can also be monitored from the sending system. These tools are discussed in Chapter 11, "Monitoring the Interface."

Development Tools

If you decide to create custom ALE scenarios, you'll need several tools at different stages of your development:

◆ **Business analysis tool.** SAP provides the business navigator tool, which is used to analyze existing business processes in SAP. You can use the business analysis tool to study the process flow or component view of a process.

◆ **IDoc development tool.** Soon after you are done with your analysis and have identified data that is to be exchanged, you will create IDocs for custom scenarios. SAP provides the IDoc editor, which you can use to extend existing IDocs or to develop new IDocs.

◆ **Process extension.** To enable your process for ALE, you need to program it using ALE services. The ALE service layer provides several function modules that act as an interface for using the ALE services. These tools are discussed in Section III, "IDocs."

Documentation Tools

IDoc structures are thoroughly documented; you can view the documentation of IDoc structures in a report format. These reports can be printed or downloaded to a file and can be used to understand the functionality of an IDoc. The use of segments and their fields is clearly documented. These tools are discussed in Chapter 30, "IDocs on the Inside."

Summary

ALE technology is at the heart of distributed processing in SAP. ALE technology encapsulates all the tools and components required to support distributed processing. IDocs are a major component of ALE technology, and they define the structure and format of the data that is exchanged between two systems. Several tools are available for administrative and development functions in a distributed environment.

An IDoc generally has two programs associated with it: the IDoc generation program and the IDoc processing program. These programs are written to understand the syntax and semantics of data in IDocs.

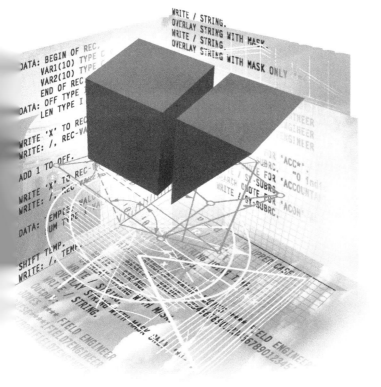

PART

The SAP ALE Interface

7

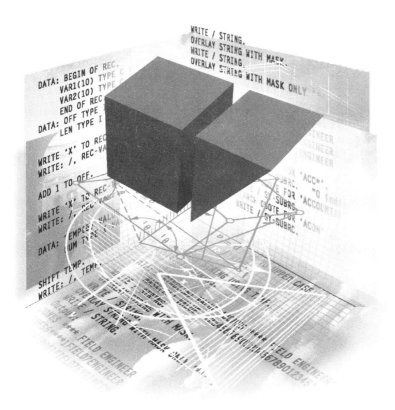

Chapter 20

The Outbound ALE Process

This chapter describes the functional and technical details of the process flow for outbound processes. The chapter begins with an overview of the various components used in the outbound process. Distributed SAP systems exchange three types of data for achieving a distributed yet integrated environment:

- ◆ **Transactional Data:** Sales orders, purchase orders, contracts, invoices, G/L postings
- ◆ **Master Data:** Material master, customer master, vendor master, employee master
- ◆ **Control Data:** Company codes, business areas, plants, sales organizations, distribution channels, divisions

Transactional and master data are distributed using the ALE interface layer. Control data is transferred using the regular CTS (Correction and Transport System) process.

Overview of Components Used in the Outbound Process

An outbound process uses the following components to generate an IDoc: customer model, IDoc structure, selection programs, filter objects, conversion rules, port definition, RFC destination, partner profile, service programs, and configuration tables. Some of these components—for example, filter objects and conversion rules—are optional, and some of the components—for example, RFC destinations and partner profiles—are configurable. A detailed description of the various configuration options within these components is included in Part 8, "Configuring the ALE Interface." This chapter focuses on the process flow and its components.

Customer Model

A customer model is used to model a distribution scenario. In a customer model, you identify the systems involved in a distribution scenario and the messages exchanged between the systems. See Chapter 23, "Distributing Master Data," for details on how to set up a model.

Message Control

Message control is a cross-application technology used in pricing, account determination, material determination, and output determination. The output determination technique of message control triggers the ALE and EDI outputs for a business document. Message control separates the logic of generating IDocs from the application logic. Refer to Chapter 8, "Configuring Message Control," for complete details on message control.

Change Pointers

The change pointers technique is based on the change document technique, which tracks changes made to key documents in SAP, such as material master, customer master, and sales orders. Changes made to a document are recorded in the change document header table CDHDR, and additional change pointers are written in the BDCP table for changes that are relevant for ALE. See "Distributing Changes" in Chapter 23, "Distributing Master Data," for details on how to set up change pointers.

IDoc Structure

A message is defined for data that is exchanged between two systems. The message type is based on one or more IDoc structures. For example, if you're going to send material master information to another system, a message type MATMAS is already defined in the system. This message is based on MATMAS01 and MATMAS02. IDocs form a major component of the ALE and EDI interfaces.

 NOTE

A basic overview of IDocs was presented in Chapter 19. Complete details about IDocs are provided in Section III, "IDocs."

Selection Programs

Selection programs, which are typically implemented as function modules, are designed to extract application data and create a master IDoc. A selection program exists for each message type. The design of a selection program depends on the triggering mechanism used in the process. See Chapter 32, "Programming in the IDoc Interface," for complete details on the structure and flow of these programs.

Filter Objects

In a distributed environment, each recipient of data may have different requirements for the data being distributed. Filter objects remove unwanted data for each recipient of data.

Port Definition

A port is used in an outbound process to define the medium in which documents are transferred to the destination system. ALE uses a tRFC (transactional Remote Function Call) port, which transfers data in memory buffers.

 NOTE

The EDI process uses file ports to transfer data to the subsystem in a standard text file format.

RFC Destination

The RFC (Remote Function Call) destination is a logical name used to define the characteristics of a communication link to a remote system on which a function needs to be executed. In ALE, the RFC specifies information required to log on to the remote SAP system to which an IDoc is being sent.

 NOTE

The EDI process uses an RFC destination to specify parameters for the communication link to an EDI subsystem.

Partner Profile

A partner profile specifies the various components used in an outbound process (logical name of the remote SAP system, IDoc type, message type, tRFC port), the packet size for an IDoc, the mode in which the process sends an IDoc (batch versus immediate), and the person to be notified in case of errors.

A partner profile is created for each SAP system that you communicate with, and a record exists for each message sent and received from a system. For example, if you are sending two outbound messages, purchase order (ORDERS) and material master (MATMAS), to the SHIPPING system, then a partner profile will exist for the SHIPPING system and two outbound records in the partner profile—one for each message type (ORDERS and MATMAS)—will exist in the partner profile.

Service Programs and Configuration Tables

The outbound process, being asynchronous, is essentially a sequence of several processes that work together. SAP provides service programs and configuration tables to link these programs and provide various customizing options for an outbound process.

Process Flow for Distributing Transactional Data

Transactional data is distributed using two techniques: with message control and without message control. The technique that a process uses greatly depends on the application area. The core logic of the selection programs remains the same. The SD (Sales and Distribution) and MM (Materials Management) applications use message control to trigger the ALE process. For example, programs for generating IDocs for sales order responses or purchase orders start via message control. Applications in other areas such as FI (Financials), PP (Production Planning), and HR (Human Resources) do not use message control for transactional data. The core logic of generating IDocs is part of the application logic itself.

NOTE

There is no documented reason to explain why these applications do not use message control. The informal reason is that message control technology is very complex, yet generic by nature.

The EDI process is used to exchange business documents such as purchase orders, invoices, and remittance advice with a business partner. It uses both techniques (message control or no message control) to send data. ALE uses the same process. In the case of ALE, the remote SAP system is configured as a business partner. The architecture of ALE/EDI processes allows them to be shared. The application logic is separate from the distribution and communication logic.

NOTE

Refer to Chapter 3, "The Outbound EDI Process," for complete details on the process flow for transactional data.

The difference between ALE and EDI process flows occurs at the communication level. The EDI process transmits IDocs to an EDI subsystem using flat file format. The ALE process transmits IDocs to an SAP system via memory using asynchronous communication. There is no need for an intermediate EDI subsystem because both the sending and receiving SAP systems understand the IDoc format. These minor differences at the communication layer can be understood by referencing the master data distribution, described next. The core program logic for generating IDocs for transactional data and master data is the same.

Process Flow for Distributing Master Data

Master data between SAP systems is distributed using two techniques: stand-alone programs and change pointers. The process flows are the same for these two processes except for the triggering mechanism that starts the IDoc selection programs. Figure 20-1 shows what occurs at each layer in the process. The technical flow shown in Figure 20-2 will help you understand the technical components such as service programs, table entries, and parameter values that are used.

NOTE

The process flow in ALE has certain similarities with EDI processes used for distributing transactional data without the message control technique.

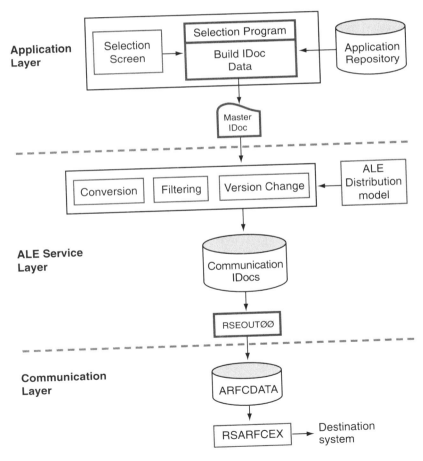

FIGURE 20-1

Process flow for an outbound process for master data

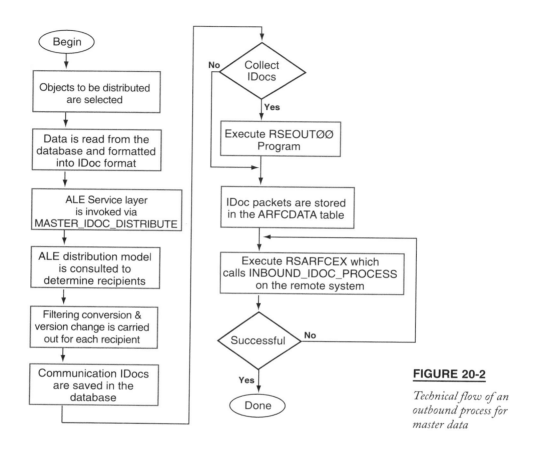

FIGURE 20-2

Technical flow of an outbound process for master data

Triggering the Outbound Process via Stand-Alone Programs

Stand-alone programs are started explicitly by a user to transmit data from one SAP system to another. Standard programs for several master data objects exist in SAP. For example, the material master data can be transferred by using the RBDSEMAT program or transaction BD10.

 NOTE

Stand-alone programs for the master data objects are grouped under the master data transaction screen, which can be reached by using transaction BALE.

The stand-alone programs provide a selection screen to specify the objects that need to be transferred and the receiving system. The selection screen for the material master object is shown in Figure 20-3. After the stand-alone program is executed, it calls the IDoc selection program with the specified parameters. The call to the IDoc selection programs is hard-coded in the stand-alone programs. The IDoc selection program may be implemented as a separate function module, but is still physically embedded in the stand-alone program.

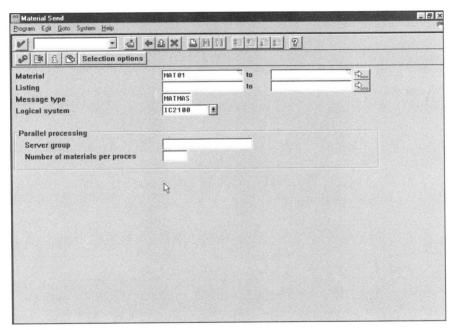

FIGURE 20-3

Selection screen for distributing material master data

Triggering the Outbound Process via Change Pointers

The change pointer technique is used to automatically initiate the outbound process when master data is created or changed. For example, if a user changes the basic description of a material master or creates a new material, then the system automatically generates an IDoc for the material and sends it to the destination system.

A standard program RBDMIDOC is scheduled to run on a periodic basis to evaluate the change pointers for a message type and start the ALE process for distributing the master data to the appropriate destination. The RBDMIDOC program reads the TBDME table to determine the IDoc selection program for a message type. Entries in this table also link a message type to the change pointer table. The IDoc selection program is started.

 NOTE

Entries in the TBDME table are maintained using transaction BD60.

Processing in the Application Layer

The customer distribution model is consulted to make sure that a receiver has been defined for the message to be transmitted. If not, processing ends. If at least one receiver exists, then the IDoc selection program reads the master data object from the database and creates a master IDoc from it. The master IDoc is stored in memory. The program then calls the ALE service layer by using function module MASTER_IDOC_DISTRIBUTE, passing it the master IDoc and the receiver information, if known.

 NOTE

The program structure and the logic of IDoc selection programs for the two triggering mechanisms are described using sample programs in Section III, "IDocs."

Processing in the ALE Interface Layer

Processing in the ALE layer consists of the following substeps:

> **Receiver determination.** If the receivers are not known, they are determined from the customer distribution model. If a receiver are not found, processing ends; for each receiver identified in this step, the following substeps are executed.

> **IDoc filtering.** If an IDoc filter is specified in the distribution model for a receiver, values in the filter are compared against the values in the IDoc data records. If a data record does not meet the filter criteria, it is dropped.

Segment filtering. For each sender and receiver combination, a set of segments that are not required can be filtered out.

Field conversion. Field values in data records are converted by using the conversion rules specified for the segment. Values can be converted to global values or converted to specific values for the receiver. For example, storage location 0001 may correspond to storage location 1000 in the receiving system. The rules specified here are also available in the EIS (Executive Information System) module.

Version change for segments. Segments are version controlled. A new version of a segment always contains fields from the previous version and additional fields that are added for the new version. Thus the segment can communicate with a back-level system by blanking out the new fields. The version specified in the Seg. Release in IDoc Type field of the partner profile is read to determine the version of the segment to be generated.

Version change for IDocs. IDocs, like the segments, are also version controlled. A new version of an IDoc always contains segments of the previous version and any additional segments that were added in the new version. Thus the IDoc can communicate with a back-level system by deleting segments that do not exist in the version specified. The version is determined from the BasicIDocType field of the partner profile.

Communication IDocs are generated. The final IDoc generated for a receiver after all the conversions and filtering operations is the communication IDoc. One master IDoc can have multiple communication IDocs, depending on the number of receivers identified and the filter operations performed. Communication IDocs are saved in the SAP database. At this point a tangible IDoc that can be viewed by using various monitoring tools has been created in the system. The IDoc gets a status record with a status code of 01 (IDoc created).

Syntax check is performed. The IDoc goes through a syntax check and data integrity validation. If errors are found, the IDoc gets a status code of 26 (Error during syntax check of IDoc—outbound); if no errors are found, the IDoc gets a status code of 30 (IDoc ready for dispatch—ALE service).

IDocs are dispatched to the communication layer. In the ALE process, IDocs are dispatched using the asynchronous RFC method, which means the sending system does not wait for data to be received or processed on the destination system. The setting in the Output Mode field of the partner profile is read to determine the timing of the dispatch. If the mode is set to Transfer IDoc Immed., IDocs are immediately transferred to the communication layer; if not, they are buffered until the next run of dispatch program RSEOUT00. After IDocs have been transferred to the communication layer, they get a status code of 03 (Data passed to port OK). This status does not necessarily mean that IDocs have been dispatched to the destination system.

NOTE

The dispatch timing of IDocs to the communication layer is important from a performance standpoint. Refer to Chapter 28, "Managing ALE Process Performance and Throughput," for details.

Processing in the Communication Layer

To dispatch an IDoc to a destination system, the system reads the port definition specified in the partner profile to determine the destination system, which is then used to read the RFC destination. The RFC destination contains communication settings to log on to the remote SAP system. The sending system calls the INBOUND_IDOC_PROCESS function module asynchronously on the destination system and passes the IDoc data via the memory buffers.

Asynchronous communication means that data to be transferred (IDocs in this case) and function modules to be invoked are temporarily stored in tables ARFCSSTATE and ARFCSDATA. A separate function module ARFC_DEST_SHIP transports the data to the target system, and function module ARFC_EXECUTE executes the stored function module. If a communication problem occurs, then the program RSARFCSE is automatically scheduled to run on a periodic basis to process the specific entry. You can turn this automatic option on/off in the tRFC parameters in the RFC destination. If transmission is successful, then entries from the ARFCSSTATE and ARFCSDATA tables are deleted. This strategy helps in decoupling the application from the communication process and assures delivery. If the automatic option is turned off, then you can process failed entries on a mass basis using program RSARFCEX.

Exception Handling in the Outbound Process

The process flow described previously represents the success path. The system can experience problems at any stage of the process. Workflow is integrated in the outbound process to handle exceptions. If an error occurs at any stage, a designated user is notified.

The system uses the Person to Be Notified field in the partner profile to send the error notification. If an error occurs before an IDoc has been created, or because the partner profile cannot be read, the EDI administrator specified in EDIADMIN is notified. You can find a complete description of workflow in Chapter 9, "Configuring Workflow."

Summary

The outbound process flow for distributing master data is similar to the outbound process for messages dispatched without message control (see Chapter 3, "The Outbound EDI Process"). The first step is to identify a master data object to be transferred. The master data object to be transferred is made from an explicit request from a user to transfer an object or from changes made to an object for which change pointers have been configured. The IDoc selection program formats the object into an IDoc format, which is called a master IDoc. The IDoc is then passed to the ALE service layer for filtering, conversion, and version change, which creates a communication IDoc for each recipient identified in the customer distribution model. The communication IDocs are then dispatched to the remote SAP system via an RFC. If errors occur at any point in the process, a person responsible for handling the errors is notified via workflow.

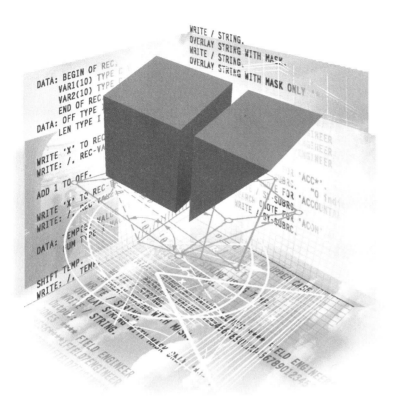

Chapter 21

**The Inbound
ALE Process**

This chapter describes the functional and technical details of the process flow for inbound processes. Like the outbound process, the inbound process must handle three types of data: transactional data, master data, and control data. Transactional and master data are received via the ALE interface layer. Control data is received via the CTS process. The inbound process for any kind of transactional or master data has two distinct paths for posting the documents from the IDocs:

◆ Via a function module
◆ Via workflow

Overview of Components Used in an Inbound Process

An inbound process uses IDoc structure, posting programs, filter objects, conversion rules, partner profile, service programs, and configuration tables to post an application document from an IDoc. The concept behind some of these components is the same as for the outbound process discussed in Chapter 20, "The Outbound ALE Process."

Posting Programs

Posting programs, which are implemented as function modules, read data from an IDoc and create an application document from it. A posting program exists for each message.

A process code is assigned to each posting program. You have the flexibility of assigning two processing options to a process code. A process code can point to a function module or a workflow. In the standard system, process codes always point to a function module. The option of assigning a workflow to a process code is discussed in Chapter 9, "Configuring Workflow."

For example, the posting program for message type MATMAS is IDOC_INPUT_MATMAS. A four-character process code MATM has been assigned to this function module.

Workflow

A workflow represents a sequence of customized steps (dialog and background) to be carried out for a process. The workflow management system is used to model the sequence, identify information required to carry out the various steps, and identify the person responsible for the dialog steps.

Partner Profile

A partner profile specifies the various components used in an inbound process (partner number, message type, process code), the mode in which IDocs are processed (batch versus immediate), and the person to be notified in case of errors.

A partner profile is created for each SAP system that you communicate with, and a record exists for each inbound message received from a remote SAP system. For example, if two inbound messages, purchase order (ORDERS) and material master (MATMAS), are received from the SALES system, then a partner profile exists for the SALES system, and two inbound records—one for each message type (ORDERS and MATMAS)—exist in the partner profile.

Process Flow for the Inbound Process via a Function Module

In this process IDocs are received from another system and passed to the posting function modules directly. Figure 21-1 shows the processing that occurs in each layer of the inbound process. The technical flow shown in Figure 21-2 explains the technical components such as programs, table entries, and parameter values used.

NOTE

The process flow in this case is very similar to the inbound process for EDI, except for the mode in which IDoc data is transferred to the ALE/EDI layer. In the case of EDI, IDoc data is transferred using files, whereas in ALE the IDoc is transferred using memory.

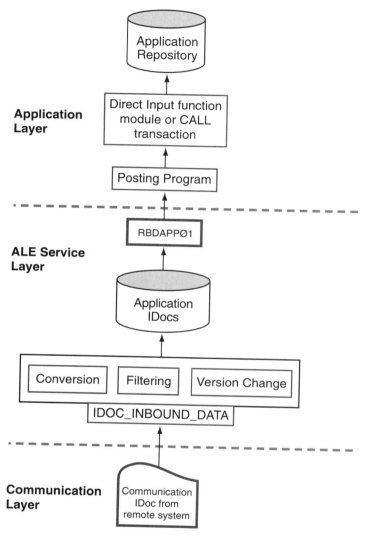

FIGURE 21-1

The inbound process using a direct function module

Processing in the Communication Layer

The INBOUND_IDOC_PROCESS program, triggered as a result of an RFC from the sending system, acts as the entry point for all inbound ALE processes. The IDoc to be processed is passed as an input parameter. Control is transferred to the ALE/EDI layer.

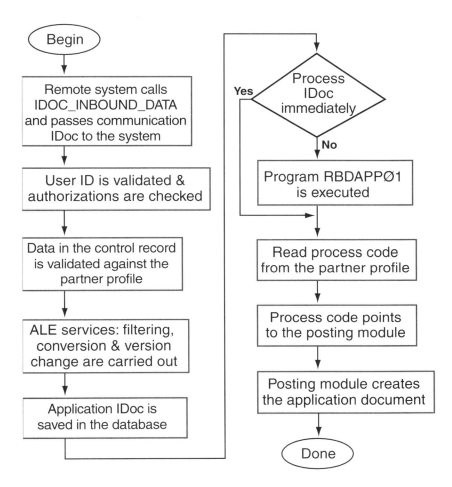

FIGURE 21-2

The technical flow of the inbound process using a direct function module

Processing in the ALE/EDI Interface Layer

The processing in this layer is as follows:

> **Basic integrity check.** A basic integrity check is performed on the control record data such as direction, message type, and IDoc type. The user ID used to start the process is validated to make sure it has appropriate authorizations.

Segment filtering and conversion. Unwanted segments can be filtered out at this stage, and any required conversion of field values can be carried out.

Application IDoc is created. The application IDoc is stored in the database and a syntax check is performed on it. If it fails the syntax check, it gets a status code of 60 (Error during syntax check of IDoc—inbound). At this point a tangible IDoc, which can be monitored via one of the monitoring transactions, is created in the system. The IDoc gets a status code of 50 (IDoc added).

The IDoc is marked ready for dispatch. After some housekeeping in SAP, the IDoc is marked ready for processing. It gets a status code of 64 (IDoc ready to be passed to application), signifying that the follow-on process can continue.

The IDoc is passed to the posting program. The partner profile table is read. If the value of the Processing field is set to Process Immediately, the IDoc is passed to the posting program immediately using the program RBDAPP01. If the field is set to Background Processing, the IDoc is buffered in the system until RBDAPP01 is executed explicitly. RBDAPP01 is usually scheduled to run on a regular basis when IDocs are buffered.

Processing in the Posting Module

The process code in the partner profile points to a posting module for the specific message in the IDoc. The posting program, implemented as a function module, either calls a standard SAP transaction by using the Call Transaction command for posting the document or invokes a direct input function module.

 NOTE

Direct input function modules are preferred over the call transaction approach because of the inherent problems of screen sequence associated with call transaction (the screen sequence may change with every release). In Chapter 27, "ALE Process Troubleshooting and Recovery," you'll see that it's easier to debug inbound processes that use the call transaction approach than debug those that use the direct input function module approach.

TIP

To see whether a standard inbound process uses call transaction or direct input, you can execute transaction BD51 and inspect the entries in table TBD51. Entries with value 1 or 2 in the Input Type column use the call transaction method, whereas entries with value 0 use a direct input function module.

The results of execution are passed back via the function module's output parameters. If the posting is successful, an application document is created. The IDoc gets a status code of 53 (Application document posted). If the IDoc contains errors, it gets a status of 51 (Error: Application document not posted).

Process Flow for the Inbound Process via Workflow

In the inbound process using workflow, the IDocs are passed to a single-step task or multistep workflow instead of to a posting function module.

Workflow allows human intervention in the process to review data before posting it in the system. In ALE, processing an incoming IDoc via workflow doesn't offer much value; doing so in EDI processes can be useful because data comes from an outside source.

NOTE

In the standard system, the inbound processes use the function module method for posting documents. No process uses workflow. However, you can customize the interface to start workflow.

The process flow in this case is very similar to the inbound process described in the EDI section, except for the mode in which IDoc data is transferred to the ALE/EDI layer. In EDI, data is transferred using files, whereas in ALE it is transferred using memory. Refer to "Inbound Process via Workflow" in Chapter 4, "The Inbound EDI Process," for more information on the process flow.

Exception Handling in the Inbound Process

The process flows described previously represent the success path. The system can experience problems at any stage of the process. The inbound process offers more chance for error than the outbound process does because the data originates outside the SAP system. Therefore, SAP validates the data by using the same business rules as if it were entered online.

The workflow system uses the Person to Be Notified field in the partner profile to send the error notification. If an error occurs before an IDoc has been created or because the partner profile cannot be read, the EDI administrator specified in EDIADMIN is notified. See Chapter 9, "Configuring Workflow," for more detail on workflow.

Summary

In this chapter you learned how an inbound process posts an application document from an IDoc. The inbound process is triggered from the remote system via an RFC. The IDoc data is transferred to the receiving system in memory buffers. It goes through basic checks, filtering, and conversion to create an application IDoc. The IDoc is then passed to the posting module, which can be a function module or workflow.

In the standard system, the posting module is always a function module. The posting module then creates the application document, using either the standard call transaction method or a direct input function module. If errors occur at any point in the process, a person responsible for handling the errors is notified via workflow.

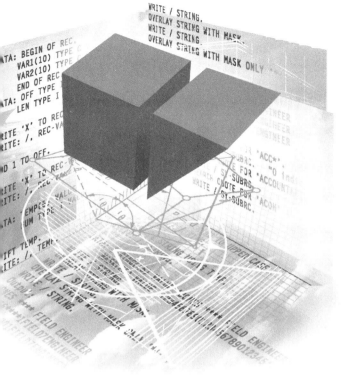

PART

8

Configuring the ALE Interface

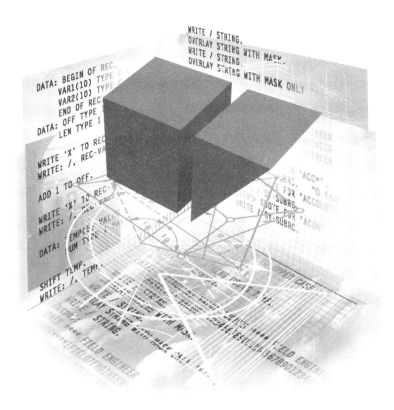

Chapter 22

Configuring the
ALE Infrastructure

ALE-enabled processes and master data objects have to be configured to implement a distributed system. SAP doesn't know how you want to distribute your processes and data, how many systems are involved, and what data you want to exchange between systems. The first task in configuring any ALE scenario is to have the basic ALE infrastructure in place. Setting up the basic infrastructure is like building a bridge. You must connect the ends before traffic can move over it. The bridge is built once and remains the same regardless of the type of traffic. You are simply providing the basic infrastructure for two systems to recognize each other and communicate with each other, including logical system names, an RFC destination, and a port definition.

In this chapter you'll learn how to establish ALE communication links between two SAP systems. You'll start with some basic settings for IDocs that are used for housekeeping and administrative purposes, and then you'll learn about the communication components. The end of the chapter covers two advanced settings for monitoring the system.

NOTE

Some of these settings are common with the EDI process because the ALE and EDI processes share the IDoc interface. Therefore, you may notice some repetition as you read.

Making the Configuration Settings

The various configuration settings for ALE processes are made in the IMG (Implementation Guide) under Cross-Application Components, Distribution (ALE). The following text refers to this path as ALE customizing in the IMG when describing the configuration options.

TIP

The ALE settings can also be reached directly by executing transaction SALE. This method saves you several keystrokes. You will be spending quite a bit of time in this area, so it is a good idea to explore the various options and read the IMG help.

ALE processes also require the basic settings of the IDoc interface, which are carried out from the IMG under Cross-Application Components, IDoc Interface/Electronic Data Interchange, IDoc Interface—Basis. The following text refers to this path as basic settings for IDocs in the IMG when describing the configuration options.

Basic Settings for IDocs

The basic settings for the IDoc interface need to be maintained once on each system involved in distributed processing that is not subject to frequent changes. If you have already maintained these settings for the EDI process, you can skip this material.

NOTE

The ALE process uses fewer settings in IDoc customizing than the EDI process uses.

EDIADMIN Table

Transaction: WE46

Path: From the basic settings for IDocs in the IMG, choose Setup IDoc Administration.

The EDIADMIN table assigns values to some of the global variables used in the IDoc process. The table consists of two columns. The first column represents the parameter name, and the second column represents the value assigned to that parameter, as shown in Figure 22-1.

CAUTION

The system does not validate the parameter name. If someone types the name incorrectly, the error won't be caught until very late in the process. Be extra careful when entering these values.

NOTE

The screen to maintain global parameters has changed in release 4.0. Please see the appendix.

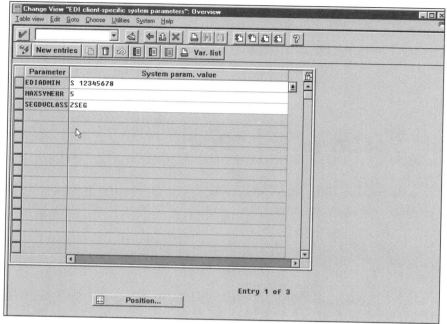

FIGURE 22-1

Relevant ALE parameters in the EDIADMIN table

The EDIADMIN parameter specifies the administrator for the IDoc interface at run time. The administrator has overall responsibility for the integrity of the IDoc interface. The workflow system uses the EDIADMIN parameter when a technical error occurs in the ALE interface layer, such as an error in reading the partner profile for an incoming IDoc.

The format for the value assigned to this field is XXCCCCCCCC. The two-character ID (XX) represents the object type. If the object type is a single character, it must be followed by a space. CCCCCCCC is the eight-character object identifier. See Chapter 9, "Configuring Workflow," for details on the types of objects that you can specify here. For example, if a position with position number 12345678 is assigned as the administrator, then the value of the parameter EDIADMIN is S 12345678. If the IDoc administrator has user ID AN000001, then the value of the parameter in the EDIADMIN field is USAN000001.

TIP

Avoid using a user ID in the EDIADMIN field. You should use a more abstract object type such as position, job, or organization unit. Doing so will save you the headache of changing the entry whenever a user leaves the company or changes jobs. Positions, jobs, and organization units tend to be more stable than

The MAXSYNERR parameter sets the maximum limit on the number of status records created for syntax errors. A good recommendation is to set the limit at five. If your IDoc gets more than five syntax errors in a production environment, something is terribly wrong. Setting the status record limit higher usually does not help you in debugging the problem. You need to investigate the process more deeply at the source of data. The SEGDVCLASS parameter is the development class used for developing new segments.

NOTE

The ALE process involves fewer settings in the EDIADMIN table than the EDI process does.

Communication Settings

This section describes the ALE settings for linking two SAP systems involved in distributed processing. These settings are done once for each system and are independent of the distribution scenario.

NOTE

A separate system does not have to be physically separate. Two clients on the same physical box can be set up to use ALE processes to exchange data.

Maintaining a Logical System

Path: From the ALE customizing in IMG, choose Basic Configuration, Setup Logical System, Maintain Logical Systems.

The systems involved in distributed processing are assigned a logical name, which uniquely identifies a system in a distributed environment, as shown in Figure 22-2. The name can have up to 10 alphanumeric characters. These names must be known to all the systems in the distributed network.

Adopt a naming standard for the logical names of the systems so that they are easily identifiable. Some common naming standards used by companies are:

◆ **Simple approach.** You can concatenate the SAP instance name with the client number. This simple yet elegant approach uniquely identifies a logical system.

◆ **Function-based.** You can choose names based on the functions carried out on a system, such as SALES or SHIPPING.

◆ **Fancy convention.** You can choose names intelligently that can identify the type of system (legacy or SAP); owning geography (US, ASIA, EUROPE); and function. This naming standard is a hybrid of the simple and functional approaches.

Allocating Logical Systems to the Client

Path: From the ALE customizing in IMG, choose Basic Configuration, Setup Logical System, Allocate Logical System to the Client.

In this step the logical name of the local system is linked to a client of the SAP system, as shown in Figure 22-3. The link basically establishes a logical name for an SAP client in the distribution process. A one-to-one relationship exists between a logical system and a client. Again, this setting is required on every system involved in the process.

CAUTION

The authority to maintain this setting must be held by one person only. The setting should never be changed, because some of the documents created in the FI module record the name of the logical system on which they are created. When you retrieve those documents, the system checks for the logical system

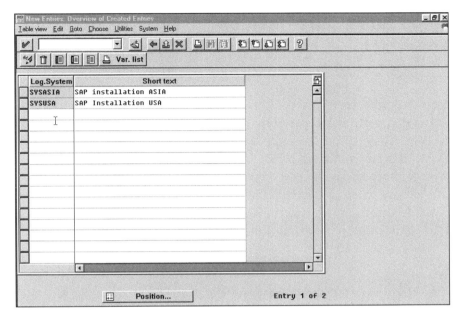

FIGURE 22-2

Maintaining logical names for systems involved in the ALE process

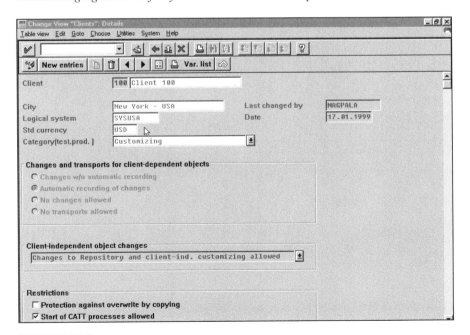

FIGURE 22-3

Allocating a logical system to a client

Setting Up an RFC Destination

Transaction: SM59

Path: From the ALE customizing in IMG, choose Communication, Define RFC Destination.

In this step you'll create an RFC destination on the local system for each remote SAP system with which you want to communicate. In the RFC destination, you'll specify all the necessary information required to log on to the remote system to execute functions remotely: the host name, user ID, password, client, system number, and additional communication settings. Figure 22-4 shows the RFC settings made in the SYSUSA system to log on to SYSASIA system. A similar RFC setting will exist on the SYSASIA system with SYSUSA as the RFC destination. A basic prerequisite for the RFC destination is that the systems should be accessible to each other via TCP/IP or one of the supported network protocols.

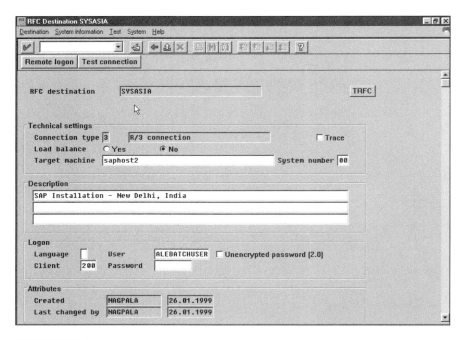

FIGURE 22-4

RFC destination settings to log on to the remote SAP system

Several types of RFC destinations are available. ALE uses type R/3 connections for communicating with a remote SAP system. Click on the create button to enter attributes for a new RFC destination. The attributes and their meanings are described in the following list:

CAUTION

RFC destinations are not transported. You must maintain them on each system manually.

- ◆ **RFC destination.** This entry is a unique name for your RFC destination. You should use the logical name defined for the remote system.
- ◆ **Connection type.** Use type 3 to indicate R/3 connections. The ALE process uses type R/3 connections to communicate with a remote SAP system, whereas the EDI process uses type TCP/IP connections to communicate with the EDI subsystem.

TIP

Press Enter after you have entered the type and description of your RFC destination. This step enables the fields necessary for connection type TCP/IP.

- ◆ **Load balance.** This item is useful if you are going to log on to a message server instead of an application server. The message server will then decide which application server is least loaded and dispatch the request to the application server. To start, you can select No.
- ◆ **Target machine.** This item is the TCP/IP host name of the remote system. The target machine could be any application server on your remote system. If you have an account on the remote system, you can find the list of application servers by executing transaction SM51 and looking in the second column under Host.
- ◆ **System number.** This entry is the system number assigned to the remote SAP system. Your Basis staff can help you with this value. If you have an account on the remote system, log on to the remote system and execute transaction SM51. Under the Server Name column, look at the last two

characters of the entry pertaining to your application server. These two digits are your system number for the remote system. You can also determine this value from the SAP logon pad.

◆ **Logon parameters.** Enter the client number, user ID, and password to log on to the remote system. The user ID must have been defined on the remote system.

CAUTION

This user ID must have all authorizations and should be configured as a background user.

Save your entries and then test the connection to make sure the system is accessible. If you get an error, check one of the parameters and make sure the systems are linked via TCP/IP.

Advanced Settings in the RFC Destination

In addition to the basic settings previously described, you can optionally specify the tRFC options for this RFC destination. The tRFC options control the retry logic when communication errors occur. Refer to "Processing in the Communication Layer" in Chapter 20, "The Outbound ALE Process," for details on the retry mechanism. Choose Destination, TRFC Options from the menu (see Figure 22-5).

◆ **Suppress background job if conn.** If this field is blank, the system automatically retries the failed tRFC individually by submitting a background job. Keep in mind that leaving this field blank can severely affect performance of the system when many messages are exchanged and there is a connection problem. Therefore, you should select this flag so the system does not attempt to retry failed connections automatically.

◆ **Connection attempts up to task.** This field specifies the number of attempts the system makes to connect to the remote system before giving up. Using one of the three options just specified then processes the entries.

◆ **Time betw. 2 tries [mins].** This field specifies the amount of time to wait between attempts.

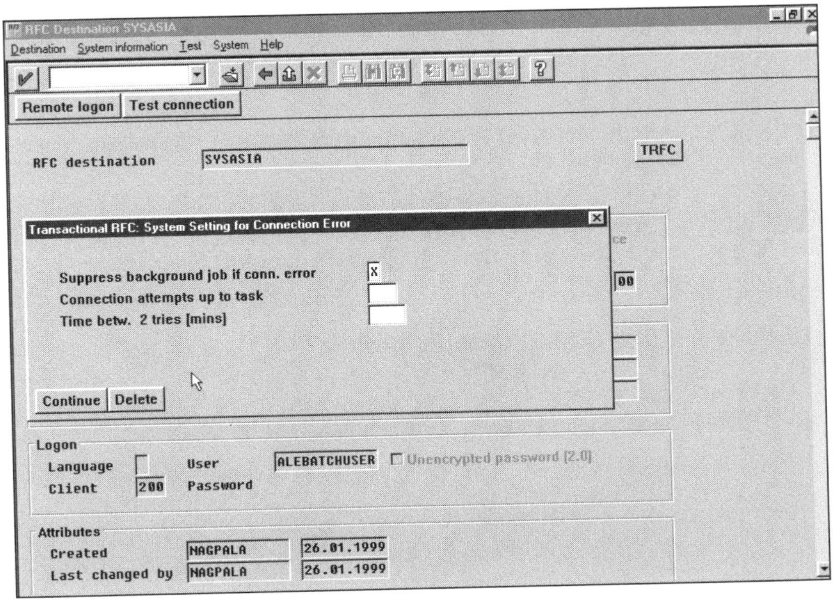

FIGURE 22-5

tRFC settings for handling connection errors

NOTE

If you choose to select the Suppress background job if conn. field in the tRFC
options described above, you can choose one of the following options to process
failed tRFC connections:

◆ Schedule program RSARFCCP in the background for a
destination system. This setting retries all failed tRFC calls
for the specific destination.

◆ Execute transaction SM58, and you can manually process
one or multiple entries. This setting is mainly used for
debugging.

◆ Execute program RSARFCEX and selectively execute
failed tRFCs.

Port Definition

Transaction: WE21

Path: From the ALE customizing in IMG, choose Communication, Manual Maintenance of Partner Profiles, Define Port.

A port defines the medium in which data is exchanged between the two systems. In the ALE process, IDocs are transferred via memory. As of release 4.0, four types of ports are available:

- ◆ tRFC ports used for ALE communication
- ◆ File ports used by EDI
- ◆ R/2 system ports used to communicate with R/2 systems
- ◆ Internet ports used to connect with Internet applications.

Port definitions are client-independent objects. The tRFC port used in the ALE process can be generated automatically when you generate partner profiles, or it can be maintained manually.

CAUTION

The RFC destination name must be the same as the logical system name for port definitions to be generated automatically.

Port definition is maintained for each remote system with which your system communicates. Figure 22-6 shows the Port definition maintained on the SYSUSA system for the SYSASIA system.

- ◆ **Port name.** This attribute is any meaningful name to uniquely identify the port. During automatic generation, SAP assigns it using sequential numbers prefixed with A.
- ◆ **Description.** Any meaningful description of the port. This attribute is for documentation only.
- ◆ **Logical destination.** This attribute is the RFC destination maintained in "Setting Up an RFC Destination."

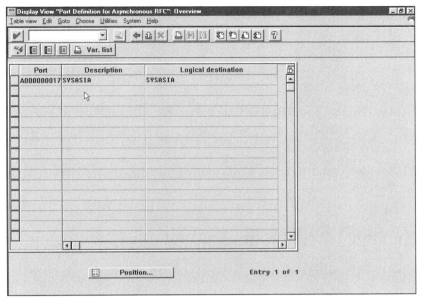

FIGURE 22-6

Attributes in the Port definition for a remote system

Advanced Settings

This section describes advanced settings that provide an end-to-end view of the state of the system. If you are an ALE novice, you can skip this section; doing so won't have any effect on the ALE process flows. These settings are mainly for getting information about the state of the process that is not available with standard settings.

Setting Up Transactional RFC Reporting

Transactional RFC is an asynchronous communication process, meaning that when an IDoc is dispatched, the sender does not wait for the IDoc to be received on the destination system. Control returns as soon as the IDoc is successfully transferred to the communication layer. The IDoc gets a status code of 03 (Data passed to port OK). The communication layer must make sure the IDoc is successfully transferred to the destination system. Thus by looking at an IDoc that has a status code of 03, you cannot say for sure that the IDoc was actually received on the destination system.

A standard program RBDMOIND is scheduled or executed online to determine whether the communication was successful. If the IDoc has been dispatched to the destination system, RBDMOIND updates the status of the IDoc to 12 (Dispatch OK); otherwise, the IDoc stays in status 03. The selection screen has the following parameters:

◆ **IDoc creation date (from).** This parameter contains the date from which you want to update the status. It selects all IDocs dispatched from this date to the current date.

◆ **IDocs per commit work.** This parameter specifies the number of IDocs to be checked before a commit is performed. Stick with default values.

Setting Up Audit Reporting

In the default behavior, after an IDoc is dispatched to a destination system, the sender does not know the state of the process on the destination system. You can configure the system, however, for cross-system reporting. You need to model the ALEAUD message between the systems. In the next chapter, you learn how to set up various messages exchanged between the systems in the customer distribution model.

Two programs enable cross-system reporting:

◆ RBDSTATE. This program is scheduled to run periodically on the destination system. RBDSTATE reports the status of incoming IDocs to the sending system, using the ALEAUD message and ALEAUD01 IDoc. This status information is recorded separately from IDoc status information in the audit logs.

◆ RBDAUD01. This program is executed on the sending system. It analyzes the audit log and displays the output as a report.

 CAUTION

This report is a performance hog and should be scheduled only if you absolutely must have cross-system reporting. The best approach is to log on to the destination system and view the state of the process on the destination system.

Summary

The basic IDoc settings for the ALE process establish administrative information for the IDoc interface. The communication settings for the ALE process establish links between two SAP systems so they can execute any function on each other. These configuration settings are one-time settings that must be done at the beginning of the project. The Basis group is likely to carry out some of these settings because doing so involves setting up communication components that they typically manage.

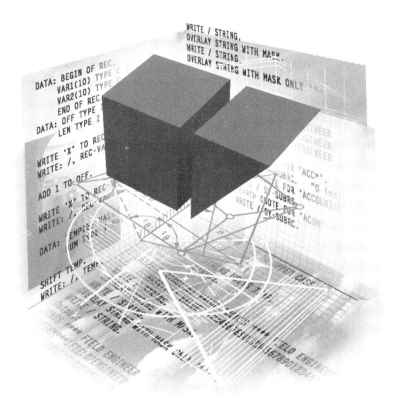

Chapter 23

*Distributing
Master Data*

A major use of ALE in an implementation is for the distribution of master data. Companies start with this approach to build very loosely connected distributed SAP systems. This chapter covers distributing master data from one system to another, using the material master object as an example (because of its rich functionality and common use). You'll learn to configure the different techniques of distributing master data, and at the end of the chapter you will find some answers to frequently asked questions about master data distribution.

Overview of Distributing Master Data

This section shows you why there is a need for distributing data, what is supported in the standard system, and what techniques are used to distribute master data.

Why Distribute Master Data?

Business units require master data objects such as material master, vendor master, customer master, cost center, G/L master data, and pricing. In a distributed SAP environment, you need to exchange master data with other SAP systems. Companies usually deploy a central SAP system to maintain all the master data in one place and then use ALE to distribute the data to other SAP systems. You may also need to exchange master data with legacy applications. For example, if you continue to run the production planning operations on a legacy system, you will exchange several master data objects such as the material master and material bill between your SAP system and legacy system. Thus, distributing master data is necessary in any distributed environment.

ALE is a useful means to distribute data in the following cases:

◆ **Transferring data from conversion clients to production systems.** Some companies maintain a separate conversion client where data from legacy systems is converted into SAP format. When data is ready, it is used for initial data load into the production systems. ALE can be a useful utility because it requires very minimal setup for distributing master data objects.

◆ **Transferring master data from production systems to test systems.** After companies go live with SAP, they have most recent data on the production system. It is often necessary to transfer data using ALE to test development systems or legacy systems.

◆ **Transferring configuration data.** Configuration data is usually transported using the CTS process. As a special case for cost center grouping, SAP recommends using ALE instead of CTS because it has superior error handling and checks.

Which Master Data Can Be Distributed?

A master data object to be distributed has to be ALE-enabled, which means it has an outbound process to generate IDocs and an inbound process to read those IDocs and create master data on the receiving system. Table 23-1 contains a list of commonly distributed master data with descriptions of each message type.

Table 23-1 Commonly Used Master Data in ALE

Message type	Description
COACTV	Activity price of cost center and cost element combination
COAMAS	Activity type
COGRP5	Activity type group
BOMMAT	Bill of material (materials)
BOMDAT	Bill of material (documents)
CLSMAS	Classes
CHRMAS	Characteristics
CLFMAS	Classification
COSMAS	Cost center
COGRP1	Cost center group
COGRP2	Cost element group
COELEM	Cost element
DEBMAS	Customer master
GLMAST	G/L account
HRMD_A	HR master and PD-ORG data
MATMAS	Material master
PRCMAS	Profit center
COGRP6	Profit center group
INFREC	Purchasing info record
SRVMAS	Services master
SRCLIST	Source list
CREMAS	Vendor master

If your master data is not supported, then you should check with SAP to see whether it is planned for future release. If there are no plans, then you can develop your own distribution scenario by using sample code provided in Section III, "IDocs."

How Is Data Distributed?

There are three ways to exchange master data between systems:

◆ **Push Original Copy.** Master data is sent explicitly from one system to another using stand-alone programs. The selection screen allows you to specify object values, destination system, and message type. For example, BD10 is used for sending material master data to another system.

◆ **Push Changes.** This is an automated process in which changes made to certain fields of a master data object trigger the process of distributing the object to remote systems. You can customize the fields for which changes are to be recorded. This allows you to distribute only the necessary changes. This method provides an automatic and efficient means of keeping the master data synchronized between the systems.

◆ **Pull Master Data.** A system sends a request for a specific master object to be transferred to the requesting system. The request is asynchronous, so the system does not wait for the object to be transferred. The request is delivered to the sending system, which initiates the process of sending the master data to the requesting system.

Strategies for Distributing Master Data

Master data is critical information that is shared across several applications. It is important to have a good strategy to allow centralized control yet distributed use. The system offers infinite combinations of ways in which you can maintain and distribute master data for your organization. The following sections explain two popular strategies, central maintenance and distributed use, and distributed maintenance and distributed use.

Assume a company has four plants, PL01–PL04. Material master is to be created for the entire company to provide purchasing information and accounting information. The following describes how to implement this scenario using these two strategies.

Central Maintenance and Distributed Use

In this case master data is maintained centrally on one system and then distributed to other systems where it is used for local processes. This simple approach accommodates the needs of most companies. Data flow is shown in Figure 23-1.

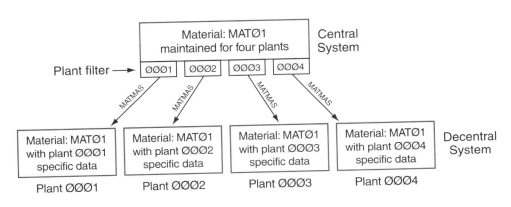

FIGURE 23-1

Centralized maintenance of master data

Users who are responsible for maintaining master data are assigned an account on the central system, for which they maintain the values. Purchasing views for four plants (PL01-PL04) and Accounting views are maintained for material MAT01 in the central system. When maintenance is complete, material MAT01 is distributed to all four plants, but each plant only gets a view for its specific plant.

This plant-specific distribution is achieved by setting filters (plant filter) at the IDoc level in the customer model. The advantages of this simple approach are that there is no unnecessary network load (only the required master data is distributed) and that there are fewer operational and maintenance issues (errors can be monitored and resolved from one system). The disadvantages of this approach are that the ownership of data is not clearly defined, the maintenance activities between various groups must be coordinated, and users need to log on to a central system.

Distributed Maintenance and Distributed Use

In this case, master data is initially created on the central system with the minimum amount of information, and then maintained on one or more systems where specific information is added. It is then consolidated in a central reference system from which it is distributed to the various receiving systems (see Figure 23-2).

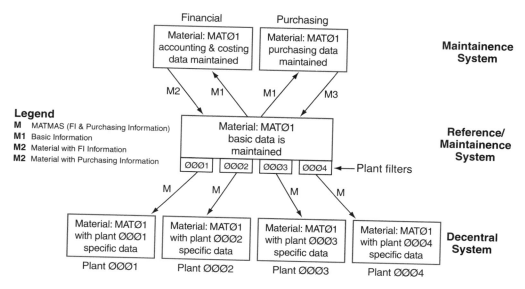

FIGURE 23-2

Decentralized maintenance of master data

The data flow steps are as follows:

1. A material MAT01 is created in the reference system with basic views and is distributed to the Financial and purchasing systems.

2. Users maintain master data on their local systems for the specific functions. The FI system maintains accounting views for material MAT01, and the purchasing system maintains purchasing views for all plants (PL01–PL04).

3. After maintenance is complete, material MAT01 is sent back to the central system where additional data can be maintained. Data is then distributed to all four plants, but each plant only gets a view for that specific plant using plant filters.

The advantages of this approach are that users are grouped by functions and do not need to sign on to a central system, systems are autonomous, and the ownership of data is clearly defined. The disadvantages of this approach are that the network can overload (if too much data is transmitted across the systems), there can be more points of failure, and many operational issues need to be considered (errors need to be monitored in several places).

Basic Configuration for Distributing Data

Before you can distribute any data between the systems via ALE, the basic infrastructure described in Chapter 22, "Configuring the ALE Infrastructure," must be in place and the following steps must be executed:

1. Maintain customer model
2. Generate partner profile
3. Distribute customer model
4. Maintain workflow settings

Two systems, whose logical names are SYSUSA and SYSASIA, are used in the following example. The SYSUSA system sends customer master data to SYSASIA, and SYSASIA sends material master data to SYSUSA. A customer distribution model named MASTERDATA will be created on SYSUSA and distributed to SYSASIA.

Maintaining the Customer Model

Transaction: BD64

Path: From the ALE customizing in IMG, choose Distribution Customer Model, Maintain Customer Distribution Model Directly.

A customer model is used to model a distributed environment in which you specify various messages exchanged between sending and receiving systems. You must also identify a system that will be the owner of the model. This owner is responsible for maintaining the model and distributing it to various systems. Other systems are prohibited from making changes to the customer model. In the sample scenario, a model, MASTERDATA, is created on SYSUSA, which automatically assigns SYSUSA as the owner of the model.

NOTE

The owning system can be a system other than the sending or receiving systems. The only requirement is that sender and receiver must each have a copy of the model.

Figure 23-3 shows the first screen for the customer model, which contains the following fields:

◆ **Maintain logical system.** In this field you enter the name of the sending system. For the sample scenario, SYSASIA is the sending system for material master and SYSUSA is the sending system for customer master.

TIP

You only need to maintain outgoing messages. The inbound messages are implied.

◆ **Customer model.** This field contains the name of your distribution model. It can be any meaningful name that represents the distribution scenario that you are implementing.

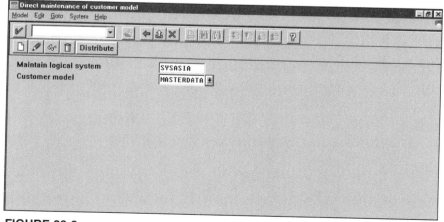

FIGURE 23-3

Initial screen for the customer model

Enter the values and click on the Create or Change button as appropriate. On the next screen you see a list of systems in a tree format, as shown in Figure 23-4. The sending system is listed first, and then various receiving systems are listed. Select the receiving system and click on the Create Message Type button. The system allows you to pick any message including custom-developed messages. This step establishes the sending system, receiving system, and the message exchanged between them. Figure 23-4 shows that material master (MATMAS) is sent from SYSASIA to SYSUSA.

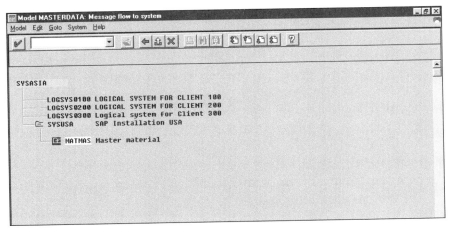

FIGURE 23-4

Maintaining the customer model

You can continue to add messages between the sender and receiver. Repeat this step with SYSUSA as the sending system and model the message DEBMAS (customer master) going to the SYSASIA system using the same model (MASTERDATA).

Here are some important points to keep in mind about the customer model:

◆ A customer model is maintained on only one system. It is distributed to other systems for use.

◆ Two models cannot distribute the same message between the same set of senders and receivers.

◆ By default, the client on which you create a model becomes the owner of the model. This approach prevents the model from being changed on another client or system.

Generating Partner Profiles

Transaction: BD82

Path: From the ALE customizing in IMG, choose Communication, Generate Partner Profiles.

Partner profiles can be generated automatically for your partner systems using transaction BD82. Figure 23-5 shows the selection screen for generating partner profiles. The customer distribution model and settings in the ALE tables TBD52, EDIFCT are read to generate partner profiles and port definitions. The partner profiles generated using this utility get you started quickly. However, you will need to fine-tune partner profile parameters later for production purposes because the utility assigns the same values for parameters like person to be notified, packet size, and distribution mode. This process generates a partner profile for each system that your system communicates with. Outbound records are created in the partner profile for each outgoing message and inbound records for each incoming message. You can execute transaction WE20 to view the partner profiles generated by this transaction. Refer to Chapter 7, "Configuring Partner Profiles," for details on each field in the outbound and inbound records of a partner profile. A good understanding of the partner profile will be very beneficial in analyzing problems later in the execution time.

CAUTION

This utility does not generate partner profiles for messages based on extended IDocs. Complete details on maintaining partner profiles manually are presented in Chapter 7, "Configuring Partner Profiles."

This step is to be carried out on all the systems involved in the process. In the example this step is performed on the SYSUSA system and the SYSASIA system. However, before you execute this program on the SYSASIA system, the SYSASIA system needs to have a copy of the model.

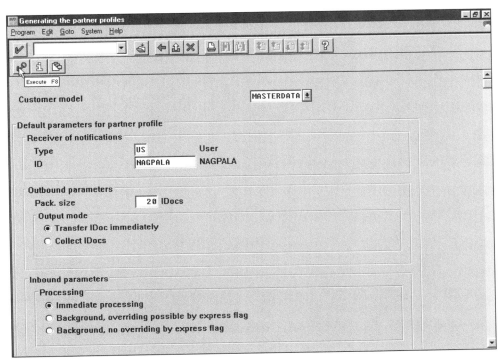

FIGURE 23-5

Selection screen for generating partner profiles automatically

Distributing the Customer Model

Transaction: BD64

Path: From the ALE customizing in IMG, choose Distribution Customer Model, Maintain Customer Distribution Model Directly.

When the maintenance of a customer model is complete, you can distribute the model to the various systems involved in the distributed process. In the example (see Figure 23-6), the model will be distributed from SYSUSA to SYSASIA.

FIGURE 23-6

Distributing the customer model

Maintaining Workflow Settings

Workflow is used for sending a work item to the person responsible for errors in the distribution process. The person to be notified is determined from the partner profile. Complete details on how to set up workflow for error notification are discussed in Chapter 9, "Configuring Workflow." This step is to be carried out on all the systems involved in the process. In the example this step is performed on the SYSUSA and SYSASIA systems.

Techniques for Distributing Master Data

This section covers the three techniques for exchanging master data between systems: push master data, distribute changes, and pull master data.

Push Approach

For the push approach, data is transferred explicitly from one system to another. This approach does not require any additional configuration settings, so you are ready to test and execute the process.

Testing the Configuration

Once you have done all the necessary configuration settings, you should carry out sanity tests and process flow tests for the inbound and outbound process, as described in Chapter 26, "Testing the ALE Interface." The tests will help you pinpoint any problems in the configuration.

Executing the Process

Transaction: BALE

Path: From the main menu, choose Logistics, Central Functions, Distribution.

SAP provides standard programs for distributing master data. The BALE transaction is the main transaction to access all the ALE functions for distributing master data.

To distribute the material master, choose Master Data, Materials, Send. The system displays the selection screen (see Figure 23-7) where you can specify different parameters for distributing material master data. The fields have the following purposes:

◆ **Material.** This field is the material master that you want to send. You can select a single value or select multiple values by using the range button (arrow) on the far right of the field.

◆ **Listing.** This field is an advanced option that allows you to send materials based on classification and is discussed later in this chapter. You can leave the Listing field blank for the moment.

◆ **Message type.** This field is the message type associated with the material master object. The standard message type is MATMAS.

◆ **Logical system.** This field is the system to which you want to send the material master data. If you leave this field blank, the system searches all customer models and determines the receivers for the message.

◆ **Server group.** This field is also an advanced option, used to control the throughput of the process by executing the process in parallel. This option is discussed in Chapter 28, "Managing ALE Process Performance and Throughput," but for the current example you can leave this field blank.

◆ **Number of materials per process.** This field is also an advanced option, used to control throughput by specifying the number of materials processed during parallel processing. This option is also discussed in Chapter 28, but for the current example you can leave this field blank.

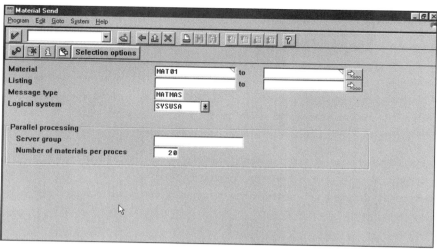

FIGURE 23-7

Selection screen for distributing material master data

Enter the desired values and click on the Execute button. The system starts executing the IDoc generation process. At the end it displays the number of communication IDocs generated. If errors occur in the process, refer to Chapter 27, "ALE Process Troubleshooting and Recovery," for a troubleshooting guide to quickly find the cause of the problem and fix it.

CAUTION

If you leave the Material field blank on the screen, the system assumes you want to send all the materials. You should enter specific values for the materials unless you really want to transfer every single material.

Viewing IDocs

IDocs can be displayed by using the IDoc monitoring tools (transaction WE02 or WE05). Refer to Chapter 11, "Monitoring the Interface," for details on how to interpret the information displayed in the IDocs. The IDoc contains the material master data to be transferred to the receiving system. You should check the IDoc status to determine the state of the IDoc. If everything works successfully, the IDoc will be in status 03 (Data passed to port OK). If your IDoc is not in status 03, you should refer to Chapter 27, "ALE Process Troubleshooting and Recovery," for a troubleshooting guide to quickly find the cause of the problem and fix it. You should also log on to the receiving system and verify that an IDoc was created on the receiving system as well. Execute transaction MM03 to view material master data on the receiving system.

Distributing Changes

In this section you learn about the change pointer technique for distributing master data. First you learn how the process works, and then you learn the steps to configure the system.

The Change Pointer Technique

Figure 23-8 shows the process for distributing master data using change pointers, which follows.

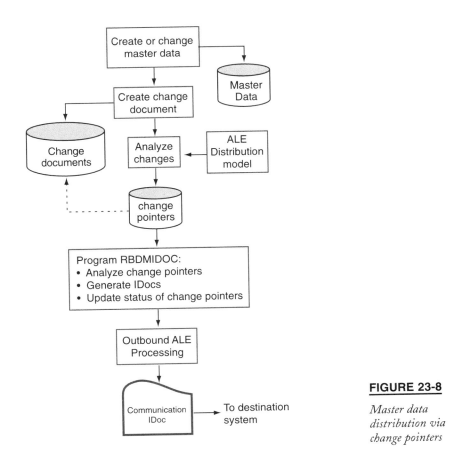

FIGURE 23-8

Master data distribution via change pointers

◆ **Application writes change documents.** SAP maintains change documents for several objects in the system, such as materials, customers, invoices, and bank data, to provide an audit trail for changes made to an object. A change document object represents a set of tables for which changes are recorded. For example, the change document for material master is named MATERIAL and contains the various tables of the material master object, such as MARA, MARC. When an application transaction makes changes to an object, the application writes change documents, which are stored in the CDHDR and CDPOS tables for each change made to an object.

TIP

Execute transaction SCDO to see a list of change document objects and their tables.

◆ **Shared Master Data (SMD) tool writes change pointers.** When changes are made to an object, the SMD tool checks ALE settings and consults the ALE distribution model to determine whether a receiver is interested in the object that was changed. If the system finds an appropriate receiver, the system creates change pointers in the BDCP table that point to change documents in the CDHDR table.

◆ **ALE programs analyze change pointers and generate IDocs.** SAP provides standard function modules that read the change pointer table and generate IDocs for the objects that were changed. These programs are designed to ignore multiple changes and create only one IDoc. For example, if a material is changed four times before the function module is invoked, only one IDoc with the latest data from the material master data is created. The various function modules are invoked by a standard report RBDMIDOC. The selection parameters of this report allow you to specify the message type for which change pointers are to be analyzed.

Configuration

Besides the basic infrastructure described in Chapter 22, "Configuring the ALE Infrastructure," and the steps described earlier in "Basic Configuration for Distributing Data," you need to carry out the following configuration steps to enable master data distribution based on changes to the object.

Enable Change Pointers Globally

Transaction: BD61

Path: From the ALE customizing in IMG, choose Distribution Scenarios, Global Organizational Units, Master Data Distribution, Activate Change Pointer, Activate Change Pointer (Generally).

This option enables the change pointer process globally. Make sure the flag is checked.

Enable Change Pointers for a Message Type

Transaction: BD50

Path: From the ALE customizing in IMG, choose Distribution Scenarios, Global Organizational Units, Master Data Distribution, Activate Change Pointer, Activate Change Pointer for Message Types.

This setting is required for activating change pointers for a specific message type. On this setting screen (see Figure 23-9), make sure the Active flag is checked for your message type.

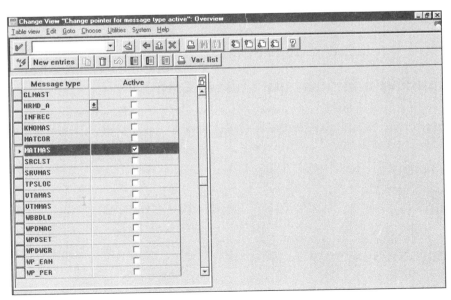

FIGURE 23-9

Enabling change pointers for material master

Specify Fields for Which Change Pointers Are to Be Written

Transaction: BD52

Path: From the ALE customizing in IMG, choose Extensions, Master Data Distribution, Activate Change Pointer per Change Document Item.

For the standard master data objects such as material, customer, and vendor, SAP already provides a list of fields for which change pointers are written. If you are satisfied with the standard set of fields, you can skip this step. But if you want to add new fields, then you must add entries for the required fields; or if you are not interested in IDocs being generated for changes to a particular field, then you can remove it from the list. For example, if you do not want to distribute material master for changes made to the Catalog Profile (RBNRM) field, then you can delete this entry from the table.

Testing and Executing the Configuration

Once you have done all the necessary configuration settings, you should carry out sanity tests and process flow tests for the inbound and outbound process, as described in Chapter 26, "Testing the ALE Interface." The tests will help you pinpoint any problems in the configuration or with missing elements. You are now ready to execute the process, which involves changing a material master and verifying that an IDoc is generated.

Changing a Field in the Master Data

Change a field in the master data object for which the change pointer is enabled. For example, if you change the net weight of a material in the material master data, a change pointer is written.

TIP

You can verify a change document and change pointer by viewing entries in the table CDHDR and BDCP, respectively.

Executing Program RBDMIDOC to Process Change Pointers

Execute program RBDMIDOC to initiate the process of generating an IDoc. On the selection screen specify the message type. In this example you will specify MATMAS. Once you execute the process, it displays the number of entries processed. If you experience problems, use the troubleshooting guide in Chapter 27, "ALE Process Troubleshooting and Recovery," for details on how to locate the problem and fix it.

NOTE

Normally you schedule this program to run frequently and start IDoc generation for different message types.

TIP

To view the IDocs, follow the instructions as listed under "Viewing the IDocs" earlier in "Push Approach." To view changes on the receiving system, see the changes made to the material master on the sending system.

Fetch Master Data

The fetch technique is not available for all master data objects. To determine whether a master data object supports a fetch process, execute transaction BALE; then from the menu option Master Data, select any object and see whether the fetch option exists. For example, it is provided for the material master, customer master, G/L master, and vendor master objects.

The Fetch Process

Figure 23-10 shows the fetch process. A fetch request originates from the requesting system in the form of a message (MATFET). This fetch request contains a list of materials to be transferred. The reference system that contains the materials processes the request and generates material master IDocs. These IDocs are then transferred to the requesting system using the standard MATMAS message.

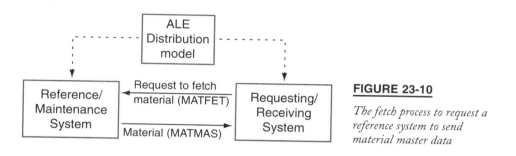

FIGURE 23-10

The fetch process to request a reference system to send material master data

Configuration and Testing

Besides the basic infrastructure discussed in Chapter 22 "Configuring the ALE Infrastructure," and the steps described in "Basic Configuration for Distributing Data" earlier in this chapter, you need to make sure the message type to fetch master data is modeled in the customer model. In this case the requesting system is the sender of the fetch request. For example, if system SYSUSA can request material master data from system SYSASIA, then the MATFET message type should be included in the model with SYSUSA as the sender and SYSASIA as the receiver, as shown in Figure 23-11. After you change the model, it must be distributed; partner profiles also need to be generated on every system involved in the process.

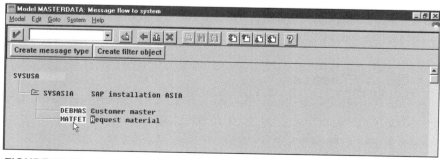

FIGURE 23-11

Modeling the MATFET message to request material master data from the SYSASIA system

Once you have done all the necessary configuration settings, you should carry out sanity tests for the inbound and outbound process as described in Chapter 26, "Testing the ALE Interface." The tests will help you pinpoint any problems in the configuration or missing elements.

Executing the Process

Transaction: BALE

Path: From the main menu, choose Logistics, Central Functions, Distribution.

To fetch material master, choose Master Data, Materials, Fetch. On the next screen, the system displays the selection screen to specify different values for requesting material master data, as shown in Figure 23-12. The various fields have the following meaning:

- ◆ **Material.** This field is the material master that you wish to fetch. You can select a single value or multiple values using the range button (arrow) on the far right of the field.

- ◆ **Listing.** This field is an advanced option. You can leave it blank for the moment. The Listing field allows you to fetch materials based on classification. This field is discussed in "Advanced Distribution Option via Classification," later in this chapter.

- ◆ **Message type.** This field is the message type associated with the material master object. The standard message type is MATMAS.

 NOTE

You will notice there is no option to specify the system that has the material master data. The system that processes the fetch request is determined from the customer model.

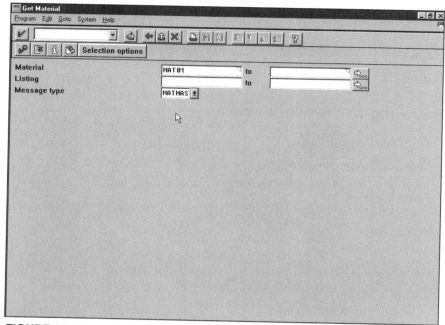

FIGURE 23-12

Selection screen to specify material master data to be fetched

Enter the desired values and press the execute button. The system sends the MATFET request to the appropriate system. The entire process is asynchronous; therefore, the time when the material master objects are received depends on the settings in the partner profile.

Viewing the IDocs and Material Documents

IDocs can be displayed using the IDoc monitoring tools (Transaction WE02 or WE05). There will be IDocs based on the MATFET message. You should also log on to the system that sends the material master to determine the state of the request.

If everything works successfully, the material master should be created on the requesting system. You can use transaction MM03 to view the material documents.

Advanced Distribution Option via Classification

This section explains the details of distributing master data by using the classification system. First a business scenario is described in which you can use the classification approach; then the various steps to configure the process are explained.

Business Scenario

Assume that material master data is maintained on a central system for the entire company and there are roughly 20,000 materials. Of these 20,000 materials, approximately 5,000 are to be distributed to SYSUSA, which is the sales system, and the rest go to another SAP system SYSASIA, which is the production-planning system.

You have two choices in the standard system:

◆ Execute transaction BD10 and specify each material to be transferred in the material field, saving the variant for future use. This process can be tedious and not very practical because every time a material is added or deleted in the system, you will have to update the variant.

◆ Use the classification system to categorize materials based on criteria that allow you to distinguish materials for a specific system. For example, you can classify a material as a sales material, a production material, or both.

How the Classification System Works

In the classification system, you set up a class type that is enabled for distribution. Then you create classes based on this class type, such as sales materials class and production materials class. Each material master object would be classified to belong to one or both classes. Then you can distribute materials based on the class.

 NOTE

This option is available for material master, customer master, and vendor master objects only.

Create a Class Type

Transaction: O02D

Path: From the ALE customizing in IMG, choose Communication, Distribution Scenarios, Master Data Distribution, Distribution via Listings, Maintain Class Types.

In this step (see Figure 23-13), you create a class type for the object that is to be used in the ALE process. In the example you create a class type for the material object MARA. Enter a name (beginning with a Z) for the class type and select the Distrib. Class Type and Multiple Classification Allowed check boxes.

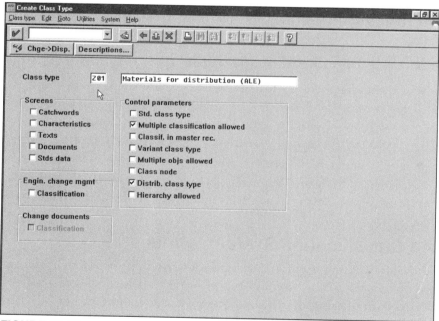

FIGURE 23-13

Create a class type for material master data

 NOTE

Only one class type per object can be configured as Distrib. Class Type.

Maintain Status for the Class Type

Transaction: O02F

Path: From the ALE customizing in IMG, choose Communication, Distribution
Scenarios, Master Data Distribution, Distribution via Listings, Maintain Status for
the Class Type.

Maintaining status for the class type is an administrative step for the class type
you created earlier. You can assign various status values to your class type and
control what can and cannot be done in each state. For ALE purposes, create a
Status 1 named Ready for distribution and select all four options for the class
type, as shown in Figure 23-14.

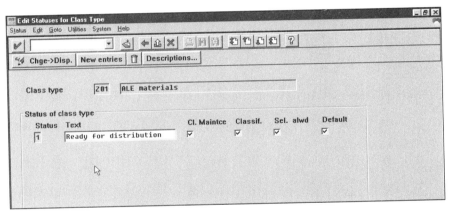

FIGURE 23-14

Maintain status for the class type

Maintain Classification Status

Transaction: O02I

Path: From the ALE customizing in IMG, choose Communication, Distribution
Scenarios, Master Data Distribution, Distribution via Listings, Maintain
Classification Statuses.

Maintaining classification statuses is also an administrative step for the status you
created earlier. For ALE purposes, select the Incomplete—System flag, as shown
in Figure 23-15.

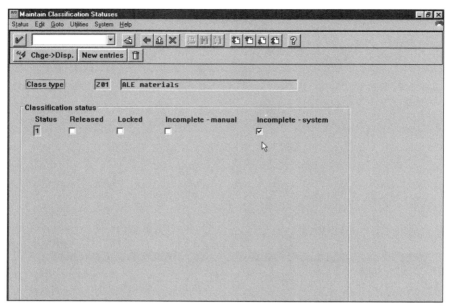

FIGURE 23-15

Additional status maintenance for the class type

Maintain Lists

Transaction: CL01

Path: From the ALE customizing in IMG, choose Communication, Distribution Scenarios, Master Data Distribution, Distribution via Listings, Maintain Lists.

Figure 23-16 shows where you specify the various classes to be used for your object. The example contains two classes, sales materials and production materials.

To maintain lists, follow these steps:

1. Execute transaction CL01 and assign a name to your class by entering SALES in the Class field and press Enter.

2. Assign a short description to your class and save it.

3. Repeat steps 1 and 2 for all the classes.

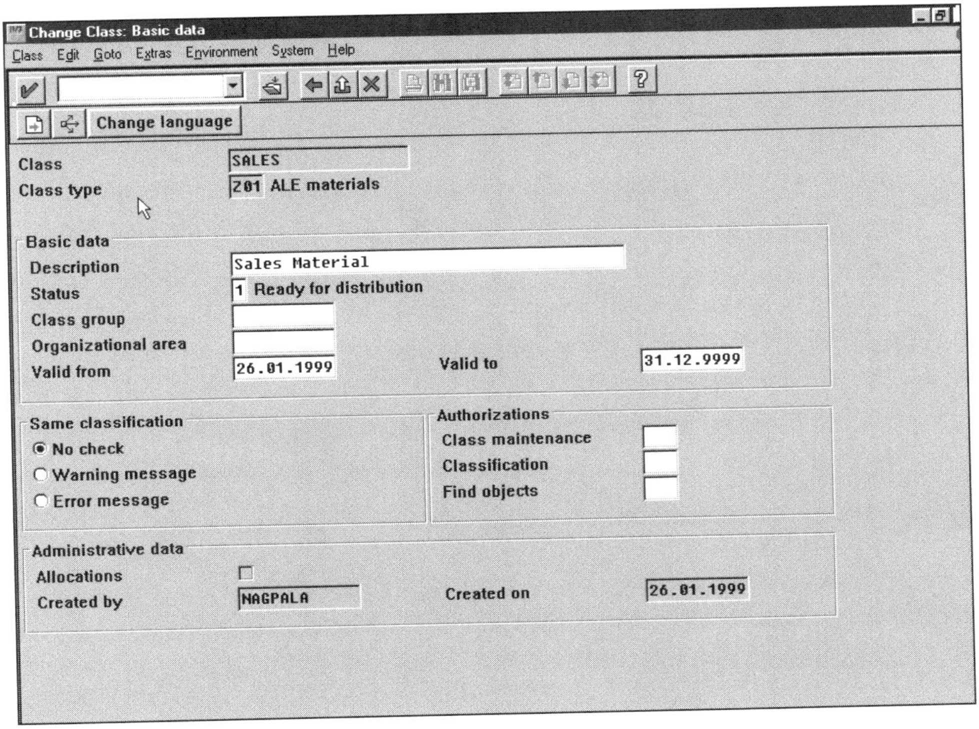

FIGURE 23-16

Create a class for sales material

Allocate Listings to the Logical System

Transaction: BD68

Path: From the ALE customizing in IMG, Communication, Distribution Scenarios, Master Data Distribution, Distribution via Listings, Allocate Listings to Logical System.

In this step, you assign the class you created earlier to the logical system that will receive data based on the class. Figure 23-17 shows that SALES class is assigned to the SYSUSA system.

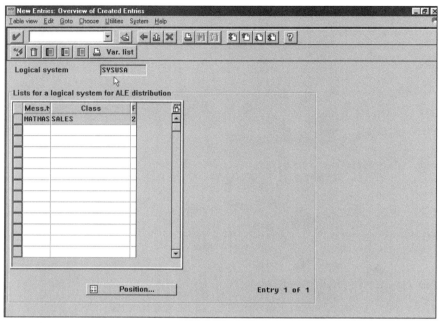

FIGURE 23-17

Allocate the class to a logical system

Assign the Object to One of the Classes

In this step you classify your object into one of the classes created above. In the example the material is classified as sales material or production material. The steps are as follows:

1. Execute transaction MM02. Enter the material to be classified and press Enter. On the dialog box, select the classification check box and press Enter.

2. On this screen the system allows you to specify the various classes you created earlier. Pull down the options for classes and select the appropriate class. You can select more than one class for your material; thus if a part is both a sales part and a production part, you can classify it twice.

Execute the Process

After you classify your objects, you can select the class on which you want to carry out the distribution process. This example uses BD10 to distribute the material master. In the Listing field, press F4 and select the class on which you want to distribute your materials.

Advanced Formatting Scenarios

The preceding section introduced various techniques for distributing master data. SAP distributes a full-blown maximum IDoc for every message that contains all possible views and data for that object. In the real world, companies often have peculiar situations for which the standard scenarios do not suffice; alternatively, transmitting a complete set of data might not be efficient. Each receiving system may demand a slightly different flavor of the same data. For example, system A may require an older version of data, while system B may require data specific to its area of operation only. You can use various customizing options to meet those specific needs of your company. The system generates one master IDoc, which is massaged to suit the needs of each receiver, to generate one communication IDoc per receiver. The various options to customize the distribution of master data are described next. First you examine a business situation in which the customizing option is used, and then you learn the concept and steps to configure the system.

> **NOTE**
>
> Refer to "Processing in the ALE Interface Layer" in Chapter 20, "The Outbound ALE Process," for a discussion of master IDocs and communication IDocs.

Filtering at the IDoc Level

Filtering at the IDoc level creates a communication IDoc in which views of an object are filtered out based on the filters specified in the customer distribution model. The following sections describe a business scenario in which you use IDoc filtering and set up filters for the material master object.

Business Scenario

Consider a company that has 10 plants in which a material MAT01 is manufactured. Each plant operates independently on its own SAP system. The material master data is maintained in a central SAP system for all 10 plants and then distributed to the various facilities. The material MAT01 has an MRP view for each plant. If you distribute this material to the various plants using the standard scenario, each plant gets the material with MRP views, including the ones for other plants. When the number of materials exchanged between the systems is large and very frequent, this approach can be an unnecessary waste of network resources and may not be desirable from a business point of view.

The technique of filtering at the IDoc level enables you to send a subset of data that is relevant for a receiving system. The system provides several filter objects for each message type to filter data. You will choose the appropriate filter for your business needs and add it to your customer model. In the business scenario described previously, plant is a suitable filter. Several other filters such as company code and sales areas are also provided.

How Filtering at the IDoc Level Works

When a master IDoc is created, the IDoc consults the distribution model and determines whether any filter objects are specified for a receiver. If so, the value in the filter object is compared to values in the data records of the master IDoc. If the values do not match, then the data record is dropped.

 NOTE

This setting can also be carried out on the receiving system; that is, you can receive a full-blown IDoc and filter it to eliminate unwanted data at the receiving end.

Configuration

The steps to configure filtering at the IDoc level follow.

1. **Identify the Filter Object**

   Transaction: BD59

   Path: From the ALE customizing in IMG, choose Extensions, ALE Object Maintenance, Maintain Object Types (for Separate Message Types).

   A filter object represents a field of an IDoc segment whose values are compared at runtime to determine whether a data record is relevant for a receiving system. You will need to identify the filter object from the list displayed using transaction BD59. For example, to filter MRP views for a plant, the filter object is WERKS under E1MARCM segment. You can also create a new custom filter object (if none of the existing filters meets your requirements) by adding an entry to this list.

2. **Modify the Customer Distribution Model.** In the customer distribution model, you can add filter objects and assign values to be checked. Assume SYSASIA is the central system for material master data, and SYSUSA is one of the systems that requires data for plants 0001 and 0002 (see Figure 23-18).

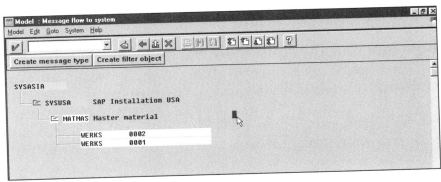

FIGURE 23-18

IDoc filters configured in the customer distribution model

Segment Filtering

Segment filtering creates a communication IDoc in which segments of a particular type are completely removed from the IDoc. The following sections describe a business scenario in which you use segment filtering and then set up segment filters for the material master object.

Business Scenario

Consider a company that has distributed operations based on business functions in the company. System A is the sales system where all the sales activities are carried out, and system B is the production-planning system where production-related activities are carried out. A central system C maintains master data information, which is then distributed to systems A and B. The sales system is not interested in the MRP views, and similarly, the production-planning system is not interested in the sales views. Therefore, when the material is distributed, each system requires a subset with a limited number of segments.

The segment filtering technique is used in this type of situation to send a subset of data that is relevant for a receiving system.

Notice the difference between segment filtering and IDoc filtering. In the IDoc filtering, segments that do not contain relevant data for a receiving system are filtered out. In the segment filtering, a segment of particular type is completely removed from the IDoc. For example, consider that a master IDoc for material MAT01 contains 10 data records (segment type E1MARCM—MRP view) pertaining to 10 plants. In IDoc filtering, each plant only gets one data record that is relevant for that plant. In segment filtering all 10 records are dropped.

How Segment Filtering Works

For each specific sender/receiver combination, you can specify a set of segments to remove from a message. In the standard delivered system, all segments of an IDoc are distributed. You will learn how to customize a message to filter out segments in the configuration steps. When a master IDoc is created, it consults the segment filters and removes any unwanted segments to create the communication IDoc for a receiver. The advantage of this technique is that it determines the segments to be filtered out at run time, and therefore the standard message can be used.

 NOTE

This setting can also be carried out on the receiving system—you can receive a full-blown IDoc and filter the unwanted segments at the receiving end—but filtering at the receiving end doesn't make much sense because you have already used the network resources for transferring a full-blown IDoc.

Configuration

Configuring the segment filtering technique is a one-step process. All you need to do is specify the segments to be filtered.

Transaction: BD56

Path: From the ALE customizing in IMG, choose Functions for the IDoc Processing, Settings for Filtering.

Identify the IDoc segment that corresponds to the data that you do not want to distribute. The segment names and documentation of the IDoc should help you identify the correct segment. For example, if SYSUSA is not interested in MRP-related data in a material master IDoc, you can filter out the E1MARCM segment, as shown in Figure 23-19. Similarly, if a system is not interested in sales-related data, the E1MVKEM segment can be filtered out.

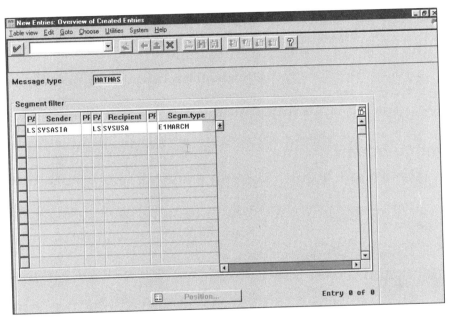

FIGURE 23-19

Filtering out MRP-related information from a material master

Reduced IDoc Type

Reduced IDoc type technique allows you to get down to the field level and specify the fields that are not needed by a receiving system. The system still sends the fields, but it has no affect on the receiving system because it has a null value, represented with a '/' in the field. The following sections describe a business scenario in which you reduce a standard IDoc type using the MATMAS02 IDoc type as an example.

Business Scenario

In the preceding scenario, you saw how you could filter out unwanted segments at run time. Consider the following situation. The two systems (SYSUSA and

SYSASIA) decide to maintain the standard price for material master data locally on their systems and do not want it to be wiped out every time the material master is loaded from the central system, where most of the material master information is maintained. This time you want certain fields of the segment to be filtered out (or not affect) the receiving system. You can use the reduced IDoc technique to filter out fields that are not to be wiped out.

How the Reduced IDoc Type Works

You create a reduced IDoc from a standard IDoc type at definition time by enabling or disabling segments or even specific fields within a segment. Of course, you cannot disable mandatory segments. This reduced IDoc gets a new message type, which is then used in the partner profile to indicate that the reduced IDoc, rather than the complete IDoc, is wanted.

Configuration

1. **Data analysis.** You first identify the master data fields that you want to protect from being overwritten. Then you identify their corresponding fields in the IDoc segments. If you determine that you do not want any of the fields in a segment, then you can remove the complete segment.

 NOTE

Keep in mind that you cannot remove mandatory segments.

You will find the IDoc structure and the documentation of IDocs useful in your analysis. Execute transaction WE60 to view the documentation of an IDoc type.

2. **Reduce the IDoc type.**

   Transaction: BD53

   Path: From the ALE customizing in IMG, choose Distribution Scenarios, Master Data Distribution, Reduce IDoc Types for Master Data.

   Follow these steps to reduce IDoc type:

   1. On the first screen (see Figure 23-20), enter the message type to be assigned to the reduced IDoc type. This name must

start with a Z. It is generally recommended that you give the new message type a name that is similar to the original message type. For example, the reduced message type for MATMAS could be ZMATMS.

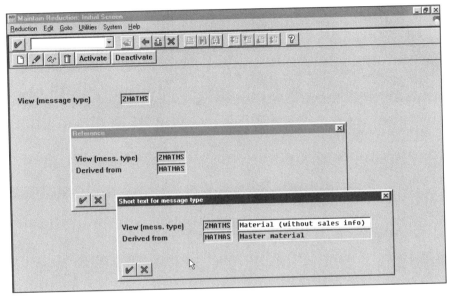

FIGURE 23-20

Initial screen to reduce a message type

2.   Click on the Create button and enter the name of the standard message type. Move down and enter a short description of the new message type.

3.   The system copies the latest version of the IDoc associated with the message type (see Figure 23-21). By default, only the mandatory (green) segments are activated. You must activate additional segments that you want to include in your reduced IDoc. Click on the segment that you want to activate and then click on the Select button (the color of the segment turns from red to white). Repeat this step for all the segments you want to activate.

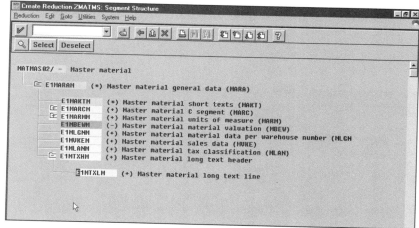

FIGURE 23-21

Activation at the segment level for material master

4. Activate the fields in the active segments. Double-click on any active segment, including the mandatory segments. The system displays a list of fields in the segment, as shown in Figure 23-22. Mandatory fields are in green and are automatically activated. To activate additional fields, click on the check box next to the field and click on the Select button. Core fields change from purple to blue when activated, and normal fields change from red to white. Repeat this step for all segments that you have activated.

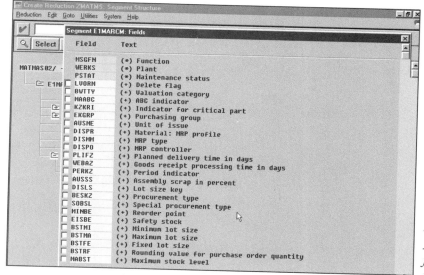

FIGURE 23-22

Activation at the field level for material master

5.   Save your changes and then from the initial screen activate the reduced IDoc type.

3.   **Change the Partner Profile to Use New Message Type.** You need to add a new entry in the partner profile with the message type created for the reduced IDoc.

4.   **Change the Distribution Model.** The distribution model also needs to be modified to use the message type assigned to the reduced IDoc type. During execution, the system allows you to select the reduced message type as one of the possible message types for distribution. For the example scenario, when you execute BD10, the system will have the ZMATMS message type as one of the possible choices for the Message type field.

Version Change for Segments and IDocs

The version change technique allows you to exchange IDocs with back level systems. The following sections describe a business scenario to enable version change for an IDoc.

Assume that the SYSUSA and SYSASIA systems are on version 3.0F of SAP and now, to get enhanced functionality, the 3.1I version is being installed on SYSASIA. But the SYSUSA system will continue to operate on version 3.0F because it's running mission-critical applications. You must determine how to support the version 3.0F IDocs when you transfer the material master IDoc from the SYSASIA system to the SYSUSA system. For example, the material master data that was being exchanged in version 3.0F used the MATMAS01 IDoc and the MATMAS message. In version 3.1G the system has a newer IDoc—MATMAS02—and segments in the IDoc have additional fields that the receiving system cannot interpret.

The ALE service layer reads the partner profile to determine the IDoc version and segment version to be generated. Configuring version change requires just one step: modifying the partner profile. On the sending system, SYSASIA, enter the desired segment version in the Seg. Release in IDoc Type field and enter the IDoc version in the IDoc Type field of the outbound record of the partner profile for the receiving system (SYSUSA), as shown in Figure 23-23.

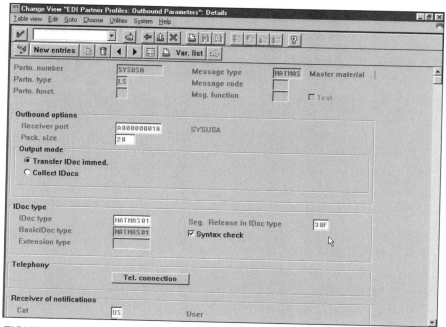

FIGURE 23-23

Settings in the partner profile to generate back-level IDocs and segments

Extending IDocs

So far you have learned how to reduce or otherwise modify the information that is sent to the receiving system. In addition, you will be required to extend the data that is exchanged between two systems. Extending an IDoc requires several steps. Refer to Section III for details on how to extend IDocs, program the extensions, and configure the system to recognize the extensions.

Frequently Asked Questions on Master Data

What if a field in the master data is required on the receiving system but is not a required field on the sending system?

In this case you need to change the configuration on the sending system to make the field mandatory or use the user exits to add default values.

What if a field is maintained locally and you do not want it to get wiped out when master data is copied?

You can customize the standard IDocs to prevent certain fields from being overwritten by using reduced IDoc type technique. Refer to "Reduced IDoc Type" in this chapter for details.

What if the receiving system is upgraded to a newer version?

The sending system will continue to provide the message as usual. The receiving system will be able to process an IDoc from a previous version without any modifications. SAP guarantees backward compatibility. You will not be able to take advantage of the latest upgraded functionality, but the system will work.

What if the sending system is upgraded to a newer version?

The sending system will have to be configured to generate a back-level IDoc for the receiving system via the partner profile. See "Version Change for Segments and IDocs."

What if I have 10,000 materials and I want to distribute a set of materials to system A and the rest to system B?

You have four choices. The first two choices are standard in the system but can limit you in certain cases. The last two choices are custom techniques provided to make your task easy. Readers with less experience may prefer to skip the last two:

◆ On the selection screen for distributing materials (transaction BD10), you can specify the material numbers. Save the specification as a variant for later use. This approach is useful when you can easily distinguish the necessary set based on the material numbers but may not be practical for large quantities or systems where new materials are added frequently.

◆ Use the classification system. In this approach you can classify materials using particular characteristics. See "Advanced Distribution Option via Classification" for details. This choice is only available for customer master, material master, and vendor master objects because they can be classified.

◆ Create a custom program that allows you to specify or select materials based on your criteria and then call the RSBDEMAT (transaction BD10) program with the selected materials. For example, to select all materials that belong to a specific plant, you can write a simple program. In the program you have a select statement that determines all materials that have an entry in the MARC table with your desired plant and then calls the RSBDEMAT program with selected materials.

◆ Create a new customer segment with a field whose value can be used to distinguish the destination system. Attach it to the top-level segment E1MARAM and then populate the values in this field in the customer exit for the IDoc. Create a filter based on this custom field and add the filter to your customer model. For example, if you want to distribute materials that belong to a plant, then create a segment Z1MARAM with a plant field and use this segment to extend the E1MARAM segment. In the customer exit, you can fill the value of the plant in this field. Create a filter using this new field and add it to the customer model.

What if I have created purchasing views in the material master for all the plants in our company, but I do not want each plant to get views for other plants?

You can use filters in the customer model to filter objects for specific plants.

What if I have separate systems for sales activities and FI activities, and the FI system does not care about the sales views at all?

You have two options:

◆ Create a reduced message type for your FI system without the sales segments. The system assigns it a new message type. Use this new message type for distribution.

◆ Filter out segments at run time using segment filtering.

Summary

Master data is a critical piece of information that is shared across multiple applications in an organization. Most companies develop a strategy to maintain the integrity of the master data while supporting a distributed environment. SAP provides the ALE process for distributing and controlling master data distribution.

Several customizing options are available to tailor the system to suit your needs, such as filtering, version management, and classification. The overall functionality of the master data is very rich. The system offers a nearly infinite combination of ways to design your distribution strategy.

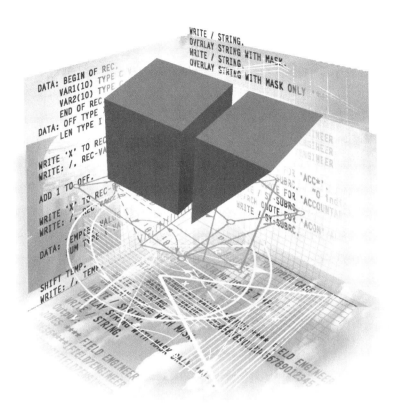

Chapter 24

Implementing Distributed Business Processes

ALE was invented to support distributed processing across multiple SAP systems. This chapter covers the implementation of a distributed system and examines the issues and strategies involved in keeping distributed systems synchronized. This chapter uses the distributed contracts scenario, a standard SAP-delivered scenario, to illustrate the various steps in implementing a distributed system.

Introduction to Distributed Processing

As the term suggests, in distributed processing part of the business process is carried out on one system and part on another. This segregation of business processes is based on the principle of executing a business process on the system best suited for the process. Consider the purchasing process in a company that has several subsidiaries. Each subsidiary procures certain common materials for local use, for which it negotiates rates with its own selected vendors. However, if the purchasing requirements could be reported to a central corporate system that negotiates rates with vendors based on the collective requirement, the company might receive better rates, quality, and delivery times. The purchasing process, however, can continue to operate on individual systems to provide autonomy of operations. This example shows how distributed business processes can provide a competitive advantage.

 NOTE

Chapter 18, "Introduction to Distributed Systems," provides full details of the various technical and business reasons for distributing processes.

In order to transform an integrated business process to a distributed business process, you need to re-engineer the business process and enhance the technology component to support distributed processing, as described below:

- ◆ **Reengineered business processes.** Business processes that are typically carried out on stand-alone systems are re-engineered to support distributed yet integrated processing. Process chains are split at appropriate process boundaries. Processing to achieve a distributed yet integrated system is an art. A process chain split at the wrong boundaries can mean unnecessary data exchanges and difficulties keeping the systems in synch. On the other hand, an optimal distributed process provides an independent operating unit with minimal dependence on the other system, resulting in minimal network load.

◆ **Technology to support distributed processes.** Programs that were once used in integrated processes are enhanced so that they are "ALE—enabled," which means they understand the syntax and semantics of IDocs that are used to exchange data between distributed processes. The two systems exchange data with each other at appropriate points to stay synchronized. To make optimal use of network resources and to maintain autonomy, only necessary data is shared between the systems.

Data Types Exchanged

In a distributed scenario, three types of data are exchanged:

◆ **Transactional data.** Transactional data represents day-to-day business transactions carried out in the system, such as purchase orders, sales orders, and invoices. The ability to exchange transactional data between distributed systems achieves the highest business benefits.

◆ **Master data.** Master data is required to support the creation and interpretation of transactional data across systems. Examples of master data include vendor master, customer master, and material master data. Master data does not change very frequently. This data is exchanged via the ALE process when a scenario is first deployed and on a timely basis if the master data is changed or new relevant master data is created.

◆ **Customizing data.** A set of customizing data must also be the same on the distributed systems. ALE calls this type of data control data. Examples include purchase organization, sales organization, and business areas. Because customizing data does not change very frequently, this data is exchanged via the existing CTS (Correction and Transport System) process. ALE controls who owns the data and what can be exchanged but does not carry out the actual transfer.

Implementing a Distributed Scenario

SAP provides a set of standard preconfigured scenarios in various application areas based on the commonly distributed applications and processes. It has optimally distributed the processes to provide a distributed yet integrated environment.

NOTE

A complete list is available in the online help for ALE under Application Scenarios.

It is impossible to provide general directions for implementing a distributed scenario; each scenario is unique and presents different options, although at the technical level you will find several similarities. This chapter uses the distributed contracts scenario to illustrate the various steps in implementing a distributed business process. You can use this example as a guideline for other scenarios.

The methodology used to implement a distributed scenario is similar to that used in the EDI process to configure a transaction. In the analysis phase, you analyze the business requirements and compare them with what SAP provides. In the preparation phase, you identify the various parameters used in the interface. The setup phase involves configuring the application components and ALE components. You test the setup in the testing phase and then execute the process. The results are ultimately verified in the verification phase. Finally, in the support phase you monitor the system and troubleshoot if the system experiences any problems.

The Analysis Phase

In the analysis phase you study the integrated process, identify process boundaries, identify data flows, study system limitations, and make decisions on customer enhancements.

Studying the Integrated Process

It is important to study the integrated process before you begin analyzing the distributed process. You can use the online help, implementation guide, and reference model to understand the business process. The online help provides a detailed description of a business process, the implementation guide points out the customizing options available in the process, and the reference model can help with process flows and component descriptions.

The distributed contracts scenario in the example is part of the Materials Management module. A purchasing contract or outline agreement is a long-term agreement with your vendor. It describes the total quantity or purchase value that you agree to procure from the vendor. It does not contain specific quantities or delivery dates. Those items are specified in individual purchase orders that are released against the contract.

Identifying Process Boundaries in the Distributed System

Process boundaries define the business functions that take place on each system.

In the example, a contract is created in a central system, and purchase orders against the contract are created in one or more decentral systems where local operations are carried out, as shown in Figure 24-1.

TIP

A distributed scenario is documented in the ALE consultant's guide, and the various settings are discussed in the IMG. The documentation should provide a clear picture of the process boundaries.

Identifying Data Flows

Integration between the systems is achieved by timely and controlled exchange of transactional and master data. Each system maintains a redundant copy of the data needed to execute business processes on the local system. The systems are responsible for the integrity and maintenance of their local data only. One of the systems is assigned as the owner of the data that multiple systems share and is thus responsible for creating, maintaining, and distributing it to the other system(s). Data flows help you to understand the information exchanged between the systems. From the data flows, you should be able to identify the various transactional and master data exchanged between the systems (see Figure 24-1).

1. A purchasing contract is created centrally without any plant information and distributed to one or more decentral systems. The contract contains vendor number, material, and quantity or value of goods to be procured over a period of time. Any changes made to the contract are also distributed. Changes can only be made in the central system.

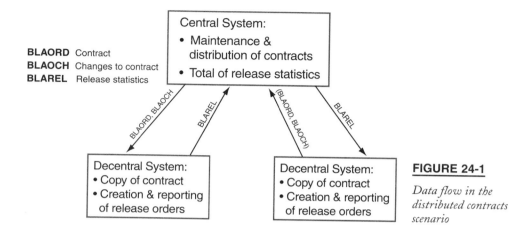

BLAORD Contract
BLAOCH Changes to contract
BLAREL Release statistics

FIGURE 24-1

Data flow in the distributed contracts scenario

2. Purchase orders are entered in the decentral systems against the purchasing contract, and release statistics indicating quantity and values used in the purchase order are communicated to the central system and updated locally.

3. The central system maintains the total value and quantity used up so far. The decentral systems do not have access into the statistics on the central system. If the value or quantity exceeds the total value or quantity of the contract, it can be blocked, which results in a change to the contract. The blocked contract is distributed to various decentral systems, which prevents them from entering additional purchase orders against the contract.

Studying System Limitations

A distributed scenario certainly provides business benefits, but in most cases the application functionality is reduced because the systems are distributed. In a single integrated system, data and processes are readily available, and therefore execution time is mainly based on the processing time. In a distributed environment, the execution time is based on the processing time and the network distribution time. Waiting that long may not always be practical. For example, if a sales order is being entered in a single integrated system, the system calculates the delivery dates and carries out credit checks instantaneously. If, however, the systems are distributed, a real-time availability check performed in another system may not be supported.

The distributed contracts scenario is inferior to an integrated process because the decentral systems can continue to release purchase orders against a purchasing contract that's near its maximum value until they receive a blocked contract from the central system. Such a situation can result in purchase orders exceeding the maximum value set in a contract.

Deciding on Customer Enhancements

As part of the analysis process, you may have discovered gaps between your business needs and the standard SAP functionality. If gaps cannot be filled with one of the customizing options, you can use a user exit instead. In any IDoc process, one of the common enhancements is to extend IDocs and use the user exits to populate data in the extensions. User exits have been provided at strategic points in the process to formally add customized code to an existing SAP process; they are supported during an upgrade. Refer to "Locating User Exits" in Chapter 32, "Programming in the IDoc Interface," for details on locating user exits for the IDoc processes.

The following user exits are available for the messages exchanged in the distributed contracts scenario:

- For message type BLAOCH/BLAORD:

    MM06E001 (EXIT_SAPLEINM_001). This user exit can modify the control record information of the outbound IDocs.

    MM06E001 (EXIT_SAPLEINM_002). This user exit can populate IDoc extensions for outbound IDocs.

    MM06E002 (EXIT_SAPLEINN_001, EXIT_SAPLEINN_002, EXIT_SAPLEINN_003). These user exits process incoming data in extended IDocs.

- For message type BLAREL:

    MM06E001 (EXIT_SAPLEINM_001). This user exit can modify the control record information of the outbound IDocs.

    MM06E001 (EXIT_SAPLEINM_003). This user exit can populate IDoc extensions for outbound IDocs.

    MM06E002 (EXIT_SAPLEINM_004). This user exit can process incoming data in extended IDocs.

The Preparation Phase

In the preparation phase, the basic objective is to identify the various elements that will be used in the configuration process.

Identifying the Central and Decentral Systems

Identify the SAP systems involved in the process. The scenario allows one central and multiple decentral systems. A logical name is assigned to each system involved in the process. For this scenario the central system is SYSUSA, and the decentral system is SYSASIA.

Identifying Lists of IDocs and Messages

At the technical level, master data and transactional data exchanged between the systems are implemented via IDocs. A list of IDocs and messages should be identified for each type of data exchanged between the systems.

For the sample scenario, the data flow described in Figure 24-1 depicts the transactional data exchanged between the systems. Besides the transactional data, material master and vendor master must also be kept in sync between the two systems. Table 24-1 lists the IDocs and messages for data exchanged between the systems.

Table 24-1 Messages Exchanged in the Distributed Contracts Scenario

Message	IDoc Type	Description
BLAORD	BLAORD02	Purchasing contract
BLAOCH	BLAORD02	Changes to the purchasing contract
BLAREL	BLAREL02	Release statistics
MATMAS	MATMAS02	Material master
CREMAS	CREMAS01	Vendor master

Identifying Workflow Parameters

You must also identify the organizational object (user ID, position, workcenter, and so on) responsible for handling errors associated with this process and the standard tasks associated with each message exchanged. You can choose from several different types of organizational objects. Refer to Chapter 9, "Configuring Workflow," for details on the workflow component.

To begin, you can use your user ID as the person to be notified in case of errors. The standard tasks for error handling are shown in Table 24-2.

Table 24-2 Standard Tasks for Error Handling

Workflow Task	Task ID
BLAOCH_Error	TS00007975
BLAORD_Error	TS00007974
BLAREL_Error	TS00007979

Identifying Lists of Control Data Objects

To make semantic sense of data that is exchanged, the systems must have the same values for several customizing objects such as company codes, plants, and sales areas.

Table 24-3 shows the customizing objects that must be known to all the systems in the sample scenario. The IDocs exchanged between the systems refer to these values, and it is important that these values are known to the systems before IDocs are exchanged.

Table 24-3 Customizing Objects for the Distributed Contracts Scenario

Description	Customizing Object
Company code	V_T001
Purchasing organization	V_T024E
Purchasing group	V_024
Contract type	OMEF
Incoterms	V_INC
Terms of payment	V_T052
Shipping instructions	V027A
Tax indicator	FTXP

The Setup Phase

In the setup phase you'll carry out the various steps to configure the system using the information identified in the preparation phase. The setup phase consists of application configuration and ALE configuration.

Configuring Application Components

These settings are specific to the scenario being implemented and must be carried out in the context of the business process. The settings are then distributed to the various systems involved in the distribution process via the CTS process. Because each system involved in the process is an independently operating SAP system, companies have different strategies for distributing the customizing data. Control data distribution is explained separately toward the end of this chapter.

 CAUTION

Some of the customizing tables are marked type A, which means they are treated as master data; therefore, either they must be transported manually or the customizing steps must be repeated in all the systems. If you make a setting in the IMG and the system does not prompt you for a change request, then it is very likely that the setting is treated as master data.

Maintaining General Application Settings

The various customizing objects for the sample scenario were identified in the preparation phase. The settings for company code, purchasing organization, purchasing group, incoterms, terms of payment, shipping instructions, and tax indicator are part of the overall setup of the purchasing module and outside the scope of this book. You will work with team members in the functional area to make sure the necessary application settings are maintained and distributed to the various systems.

Number Range for Contracts

Transaction: OMH6

Menu Path: From the IMG (SPRO), choose Materials Management, Purchasing, Contract, Define Number Range

The document type for distributed contracts has an internal and external number range associated with it. The internal number range is used on the central system for assigning unique numbers to the distributed contracts. The external number range is used on the decentral systems when contracts are received from the central system. Therefore, the external number assignment in the document type on the decentral system must contain the range used in the central system, as shown in Figure 24-2.

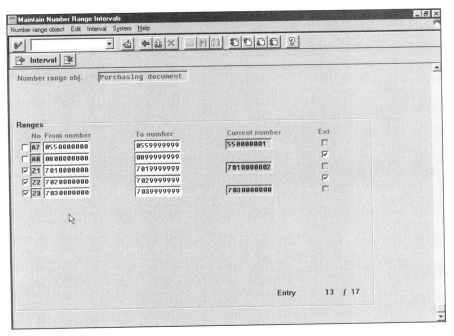

FIGURE 24-2

Number ranges (external and internal)

Contract Type for Distributed Contracts

Transaction: OMEF

Menu Path: From the IMG (SPRO), choose Materials Management, Purchasing, Contract, Define Document Types

A new document type (see Figure 24-3) is required to distinguish distributed contracts from regular contracts that are created in the integrated system. This document type must exist on the central and decentral systems.

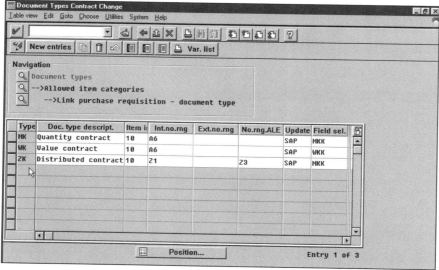

FIGURE 24-3

Document type for distributed contracts

Message Control Settings to Propose ALE Output

Transaction: MN07

Menu Path: Logistics, Materials Management, Purchasing, Master Data, Messages, Outline Agreement, Create

The outbound IDoc for contracts is triggered via message control. A condition type VNEU exists to distribute contracts via ALE. In the default setting, this condition type is not proposed automatically. Condition records (see Figure 24-4) can be created to have the output proposed automatically for the document type used for distributed contracts.

NOTE

For complete details on the concepts and use of message control, refer to Chapter 8, "Configuring Message Control."

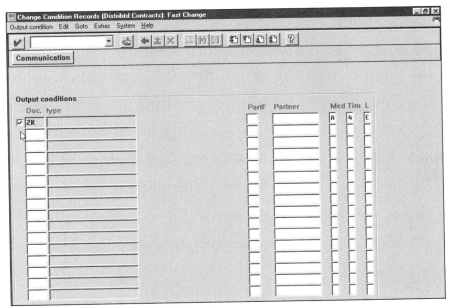

FIGURE 24-4

Condition records for output type VNEU

Configuring ALE Components

The technical implementation has similarities across several scenarios. The following ALE settings are carried out. Details of these five steps were covered in Chapter 22, "Configuring the ALE Infrastructure" and Chapter 23, "Distributing Master Data" so only a brief description is provided here.

1. **Maintain basic ALE infrastructure.** The basic ALE infrastructure, as discussed in Chapter 22, "Configuring the ALE Infrastructure" allows the systems involved in distribution to recognize each other.

2. **Maintain customer distribution model.** A customer model (see Figure 24-5) depicts various messages (master data, transactional data) exchanged between the systems and establishes a sender and receiver of data.

TIP

If a message has been included in another model for the same set of senders and receivers, the system will not allow you to create another entry. Therefore, a good technique is to maintain one model for all master data distribution. That way several scenarios can use the same master data model and one model specific to the transactional data for the distribution scenario.

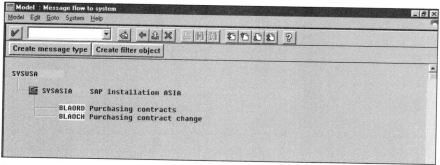

FIGURE 24-5

Customer distribution model for the distributed contracts scenario

3. **Distribute the customer model.** A customer model is always maintained on any system for the entire distributed network of SAP systems, and therefore it must be distributed to various systems in the distributed network.

4. **Generate the partner profile.** After the model has been successfully distributed, partner profiles can be generated automatically in each individual system. On every system, a partner profile exists for each system that it communicates with, and a record exists for each outbound message and each incoming message.

 NOTE

Complete details on various parameters in a partner profile are explained in Chapter 7, "Configuring Partner Profiles."

5. **Make workflow settings.** Workflow is used for sending a work item to the person responsible for errors in the distribution process. The person to be notified is determined from the partner profile. This step is also carried out on every system involved in the process.

 NOTE

Chapter 9 discusses how to set up workflow for error notification.

Advanced ALE Settings

The preceding sections describe the basic setup without any enhancements or extensions to the process. Depending on your business needs, you can utilize the following options to tailor the process.

◆ **Customer enhancements.** If enhancements such as extended IDocs and user exits are utilized, then you will have to transport those objects to the various systems.

 NOTE

See Section III, "IDocs," for complete details on how to extend IDocs and develop user exits.

◆ **Advanced formatting options.** The various advanced formatting options for an IDoc, such as filtering and version control, are discussed Chapter 23, "Distributing Master Data." They can be utilized as necessary.

Testing Phase

Before you execute the process, you can carry out a basic sanity test of the configuration. The system provides standard tools to test the various components. You can test the ALE settings, control data settings, and application settings.

 NOTE

Complete details on how to test the components are presented in Chapter 26, "Testing the ALE Interface."

Execution and Verification Phase

After completing the configuration, you are ready to execute the process. The steps to execute a scenario are specific to the scenario. You work in the context of the business process to carry out the various steps. For the distributed contracts scenario, do the following:

1. **Synchronize the master data.** Vendors and materials that are used in the scenario must be known to the central and decentral systems. Any changes to the master data must also be replicated between the systems. Various techniques of distributing master data are discussed in Chapter 23, "Distributing Master Data."

2. **Create a contract in the central system.**

    Transaction: ME31

    Menu Path: Logistics, Materials Management, Purchasing, Outline Agreement, Create

    Enter material, quantity or value of the contract, and validity date, as shown in Figure 24-6. Check the messages proposed on the output control screen via Header, Messages. Output type VNEU should be proposed automatically with medium A (ALE) as shown in Figure 24-7. Save the contract and note the number. When the document is saved, the IDoc processing begins.

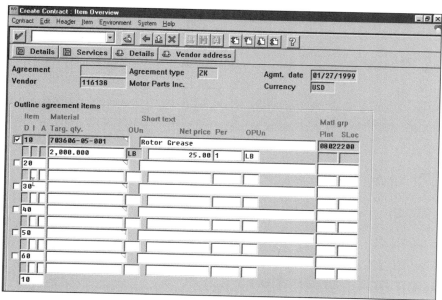

FIGURE 24-6

Creating a contract in the central system

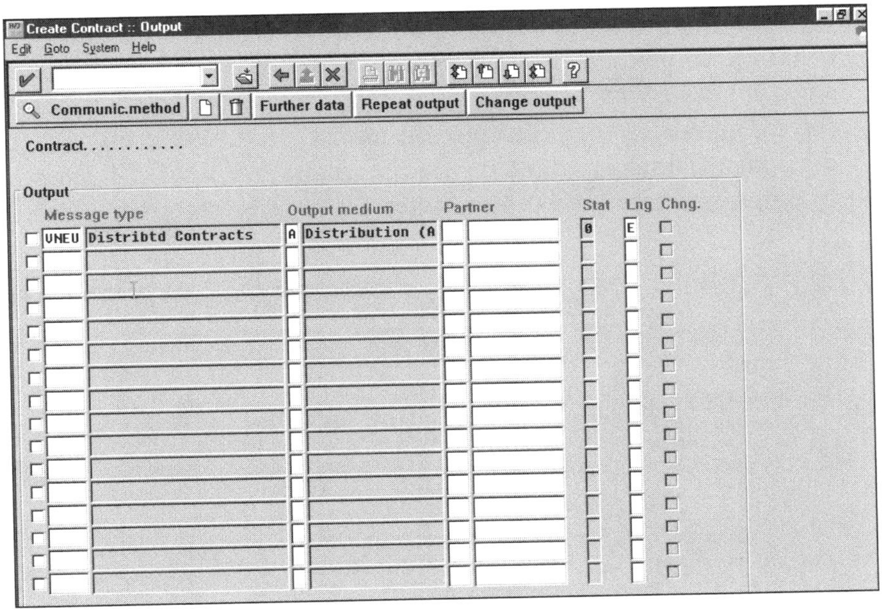

FIGURE 24-7

Output type ALE proposed for the distributed contract

On the central system, you can do the following:

◆ Display the results in the output control screen to make sure the message was processed successfully.

◆ Check the IDoc and make sure it was passed to port successfully.

On the decentral system, you can do the following:

◆ Check the IDoc to make sure it was posted successfully.

◆ View the local copy of the contract in the system.

3. **Create a purchase order against the contract.**

   Transaction: ME21

   Menu Path: Logistics, Materials Management, Purchasing, Purchase Order , Create, Vendor Known

   On the decentral system, create a purchase order using the contract as a reference. To select a contract as a reference, choose Purchase Order, Create w. Reference, To Contract from the menu. The system prompts you to enter the contract number. Enter the number, and you can copy the material information. Copy the line and enter the desired quantity, delivery date, and plant information as shown in Figure 24-8. Save the purchase order. The system recognizes that the purchase order is against a distributed contract and automatically generates the BLAREL (release statistics) message to the central system.

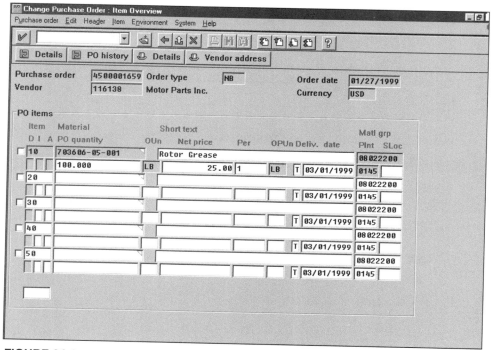

FIGURE 24-8

Entering a purchase order in the decentral system against the distributed contract

4. **Verify release statistics in the decentral system.** You can check the release statistics on the local system, which will show the quantity consumed. In addition, you can check the release statistics IDoc (BLAREL) sent from the decentral system to the central system, as shown in Figure 24-9.

CCode	Plnt	Purch.ord.	Item	Order date	Order qty. Un	Order value Currenc
0048	0145	4500001659	00010	01/27/1999	100.000 LB	2,500.00 USD
0048	0145	Qty. released to date			100.000 LB	2,500.00 USD
0048	****	Qty. released to date			100.000 LB	2,500.00 USD
****	****	Qty. released to date			100.000 LB	2,500.00 USD
		Tgt. qty.			2,000.000 LB	
		Open target qty.			1,900.000 LB	

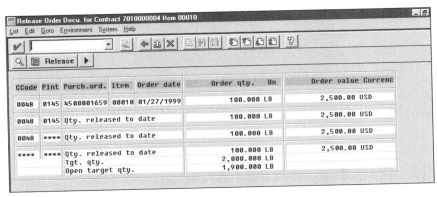

FIGURE 24-9

Release statistics on the local system

5. **Verify Release Statistics in the Central System.** You can check the release statistics on the central system, where it shows the total quantity consumed based on release orders from the decentral systems, as shown in Figure 24-10.

CCode	Plnt	Purch.ord.	Item	Order date	Order qty. Un	Order value Currenc
0048	0145	4500001659	00010	01/27/1999	100.000 LB	2,500.00 USD
0048	0145	Qty. released to date			100.000 LB	2,500.00 USD
0048	****	Qty. released to date			100.000 LB	2,500.00 USD
****	****	Qty. released to date			100.000 LB	2,500.00 USD
		Tgt. qty.			2,000.000 LB	
		Open target qty.			1,900.000 LB	

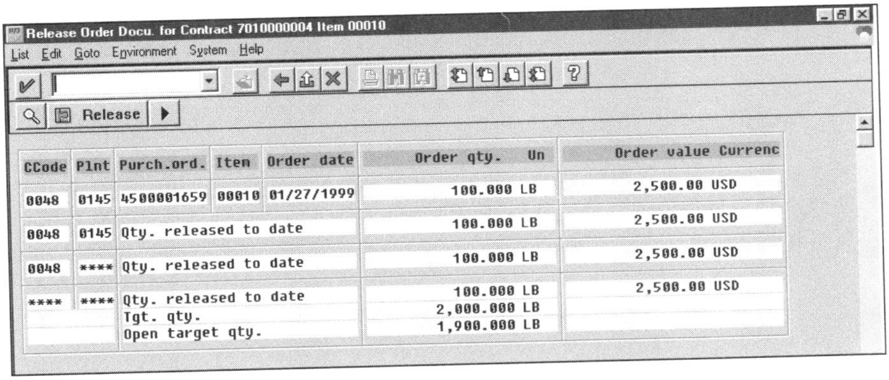

FIGURE 24-10

Release statistics on the central system

Support Phase

In the support phase you monitor the system on an ongoing basis and identify problems if they occur.

It may be necessary to monitor the state of the system at any time. You may be interested in the number of contracts distributed between the systems. IDocs serve as a focal point to monitor the state of the system. You can view the number of IDocs created in the system and drill down to get more detailed information. Several monitoring tools are described in Chapter 11, "Monitoring the Interface."

The system can fail at any point. It will be necessary to find the problem, fix it, and restart the system. Complete details are provided in the troubleshooting guide in Chapter 27, "ALE Process Troubleshooting and Recovery."

Distributing Control Data

The biggest challenge in a distributed SAP environment is keeping the customizing data synchronized among the various SAP systems. The challenges faced here are similar to those faced with master data, but master data has much richer functionality to maintain backward compatibility, version management, filtering, reduction, and so on. These options are currently not available for control data.

Strategies in Distributing Control Data

 NOTE

In the ALE user conferences, several customers have voiced their concern over making the task of maintaining control data across distributed systems easier to manage and easier to comprehend.

The most common approach to manage control data is the centralized approach, as shown in Figure 24-11. In this approach, one of the systems is set up as the global configuration system. Any changes to customizing objects are made in this system and then transported to the various distributed systems. A control data model is maintained on this system to identify the owner of various control data objects and recipients. This locks the recipient systems from making changes to the customizing objects.

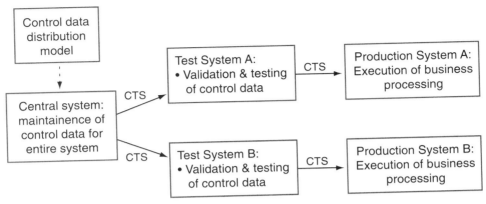

FIGURE 24-11

Centralized maintenance of control data

The biggest advantage of this approach is the control over configuration data. Changes are made on one system and any conflicts are tested immediately. The disadvantage is that systems have customizing data that they don't need and it takes away the autonomy of the distributed systems to customize processes for their local needs without having to worry about the impact on other systems. It also requires procedures and rules to make global changes. SAP plans on delivering better tools to manage customizing data for master data distribution.

Managing Control Data

The following guidelines are offered until a better system is available for controlling configuration across distributed systems:

◆ Start with the distributed scenarios concept from the very beginning without physically splitting the systems. Later this will help you in splitting the systems easily. It is easier to separate an integrated system than merge two systems that have drifted apart.

◆ Develop procedures and rules to restrict users from making local changes. You can use the control data model to restrict such changes.

Maintaining the Control Data Model

The system provides a standard CONTROLDATA model. You can maintain this model directly (similar to the customer distribution model) or using a standard utility that simplifies maintenance of the control data model for first-time users.

Maintaining the Control Data Model Directly

This is very similar to maintaining the customer model for transactional data and master data objects. Assume that you want to control the maintenance of purchasing organization and company codes in system SYSUSA and lock other systems from making changes to these customizing objects.

Determine the Object ID for the Customizing Object

The object ID is determined from the IMG. For example, to see the customizing object for the purchasing organization, go to the area in the IMG where the purchasing organization is maintained, click on the line and select Goto, Document attributes, Display from the menu. In the pop-up menu that appears, click on the Objects button. The object ID is displayed in the far left corner on the top. For the purchasing organization, it is V_T024E. Similarly, the object ID for a company code is V_T001.

Enter Values in the Control Data Model

Transaction: BD64

Path: From the ALE customizing in IMG, choose Distribution customer model, Maintain customer distribution model directly

In this step you enter values in the control data model. The following fields are available on the first screen:

- Maintain Logical System—In this field you enter the name of the system that owns the control data.
- CONTROLDATA in this field.

Enter values and press the create or change button as appropriate. On the next screen, you see a list of systems in a tree format. The owning system is listed first and then various receiving systems are listed. Select the desired receiving system and press the Create message type button. Type CONDAT and press Enter. Next, click on the line containing CONDAT and press the Create filter object' button. On the pop-up window, enter OBJECT in the object type field and enter the object ID determined in the previous step in the object field.

Repeat these steps for the company code object and you should have a model that looks like Figure 24-12 for the distributed contracts scenario.

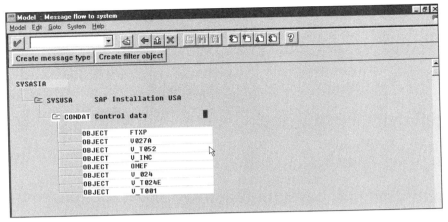

FIGURE 24-12

Control data model for the distributed contracts scenario

Distribute the Model

Transaction: BD71

Path: From the ALE customizing in IMG, choose Distribution customer model, Distribute customer model

Enter the name of the model and the receiving logical system name. The model is distributed synchronously. You must have the RFC destinations maintained between the systems.

Maintaining the Control Data Model Automatically

Transaction: BD89

Path: From the ALE customizing in IMG, Distribution scenarios, Control data distribution, Maintain control data model

This utility carries out a consistency check for the messages exchanged between the systems. In the process it determines the various customizing objects referred to in the IDoc message. The results are shown on the output. You can then select a customizing object and assign the owner. This automatically creates an entry in the control data model.

1. Execute transaction BD89. The system displays a list of all messages maintained in the various models.

2. Click on any message and press the Control data adj. button. The system outputs a list in tree format of customizing objects applicable for the message. Expand the tree until you reach an object. Click on the object and select Edit, Details from the menu. The system displays a message for the object if it has not been maintained in the control data model. Double-click on this line, the system prompts you to enter the owning system if it is not defined. Enter the logical name of the owning system and press the Update model button. The system automatically updates the model for you. Once you have the model, you can distribute it as described earlier.

NOTE

The list of customizing objects displayed in the output report of transaction BD89 is very comprehensive. You may or may not want to enter every single customizing object.

Summary

In this chapter you learned how distributed processes are implemented. In a distributed system three types of data (transactional, master, and customizing) are exchanged between the systems. Each system maintains a local copy of the data needed for the business processes. It is thus responsible for the integrity and maintenance of local data only. Data that is shared between the systems is assigned an owner who is then responsible for maintaining and distributing the data to other systems. A well-designed distributed system requires minimum dependency on the other system and operates independently with optimal use of network resources.

True benefits of a distributed system are achieved with a timely and controlled exchange of transactional and master data between the systems. Various messages exchanged between the systems are modeled in a customer distribution model. The ALE process is used for exchanging master and transactional data. Customizing data must be consistent across systems to make semantic sense of master and transactional data. Maintaining and customizing data consistently across various systems is a challenge. A control data model is used to model the customizing objects. It defines an owner for the data and keeps other systems from modifying the data.

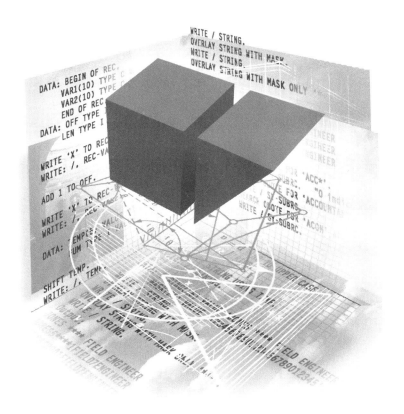

Chapter 25

SAP to Non-SAP Communication

In this chapter you'll learn why companies have embraced the ALE/IDoc technology for SAP to non-SAP communication. The various technical and business reasons are discussed, and configuration steps to set up the exchange of IDocs between SAP and non-SAP systems are presented. This chapter assumes you are familiar with the ALE or EDI process.

The technical architecture of ALE technology makes it suitable for communication with external systems. The ALE architecture consists of three layers:

◆ **Application services.** The application services layer is responsible for the application logic. This layer is where all the business rules are encapsulated and IDocs are processed.

◆ **Distribution services.** The distribution services layer is responsible for determining recipients and formatting data according to the requirements of each recipient.

◆ **Communication services.** The communication services layer is responsible for actually delivering data to the recipients. The settings in this layer determine the medium in which data is to be transferred. This layer allows SAP to communicate with any external system by simply changing the communication settings.

ALE/IDoc Interface Applications

Two of the most commonly used applications of ALE/IDoc technology outside the SAP to SAP realm are SAP to third-party products and SAP to legacy systems.

SAP to Third-Party Products

SAP interfaces with several bolt-on products—for example, the production-planning optimizers, shipping optimizers, and warehouse management system—through the ALE/IDoc interface. The use of bolt-ons has been a strategic step in SAP's growth. SAP concentrated on the core business processes and applications while the bolt-on products provided functionality in specific areas in which SAP was either not interested or needed more time to build. An IDoc interface exists for several application areas. The interface defines the what and the when for the IDocs that must be exchanged between SAP and the bolt-on. SAP certifies products for compatibility with a specific interface.

CAUTION

SAP certification provides an assurance of connectivity only. Evaluating the functionality of the product is up to the customer.

The implementation methodology of these scenarios is very similar to the distributed SAP processes discussed in the previous chapter. Technical differences at the communication layer require settings that are different from those for SAP to SAP transfer. These settings are discussed later in the chapter.

SAP to Legacy Systems

At some point all SAP implementations need to interface with legacy systems for a smooth transition to the SAP environment. Any of the IDoc interfaces developed for EDI, SAP to SAP, and SAP to third-party products can be deployed for integration with legacy systems without any modification to the SAP programs. Several companies have realized the benefits offered by this interface and use it as a standard architecture for all of their interfacing needs. Data between SAP and legacy systems is usually exchanged via files.

Why Is ALE/IDoc a Better Approach?

Before the availability of the ALE technology, the BDC (Batch Data Communication) technique was the main choice for developing interfaces between external systems and SAP. Although simple to develop, the BDC approach poses several problems, such as differences in screen sequences in batch versus online mode, lack of a standard error-handling process, and complicated management during upgrades. The following list summarizes the reasons that ALE is better suited for the job. These features have been discussed in the context of ALE and EDI processes throughout the book, and therefore the technical details are omitted here.

◆ **Several standard scenarios.** The standard ALE, EDI, and SAP to non-SAP scenarios can be used without any modification to interface with legacy systems.

◆ **Future support.** The ALE/IDoc technology is the basis for SAP's business framework architecture. The number of IDocs has grown considerably, and this technology is definitely here to stay.

◆ **Use of IDoc structures.** One of the major tasks for integration with external systems is the definition of business rules for data structures. IDocs can be used to represent very complex structures. You can accommodate several business rules within the IDoc structure—such as mandatory versus optional data records, order of data, and arrangement of data—without having to write additional code. These structures are self-documenting as long as the data fields have been documented. You can use standard reports to view, download, and print IDoc documentation.

◆ **Development tools.** Interfaces with legacy systems require quite a bit of development because of proprietary structure and content of the data. SAP provides a complete development environment for new ALE scenarios and IDocs. Custom scenarios blend with standard scenarios to take full advantage of the ALE interface layer tools and utilities.

◆ **Superior error handling.** A major chunk of the program logic for an interface program is devoted to error handling. With ALE you can focus on the business logic because error handling is built into the ALE interface layer. It logs information in the IDocs and utilizes workflow, which offers several benefits for notification and resolution of problems. Thus development time and size of code are reduced considerably.

◆ **Restart and recovery options.** A major operational concern is the restart and recovery procedure. Companies develop procedures that are typically unique for each interface. This environment poses several problems in training and maintenance of procedures. With ALE the restart and recovery mechanism is similar across the board.

Legacy Interface Development Issues

Although the ALE interface should be an obvious choice, true benefits are achieved if you keep the following points in mind while developing legacy interfaces:

- **Learning curve.** The ALE technology has a steeper learning curve than other techniques, and people with ALE, EDI, and IDoc skills are in short supply. It's advisable to develop templates for inbound and outbound programs to make the development easier and consistent.

- **Acceptability of the IDoc format.** In some companies development on legacy systems is frozen in order to phase them out. Interface with legacy applications may have already been defined, and IDoc format may not be an acceptable format. You'll require a subsystem (ALE converter) to convert data from IDoc format to the legacy format.

- **Reuse of IDocs and processes.** Reuse the standard IDocs and processes as much as possible. Companies often develop new IDocs using new segments without researching the existing repository of IDocs and segments.

- **Size of data files.** Data exchanged with legacy applications can grow very large. It's not uncommon to see data files in the range of 200MB. Although technically the IDoc interface does not have any restriction, it is advisable to break a data file into smaller independent units. For example, you could dump the entire material master data into one single IDoc, but this would take up too many resources, take too long to display, be difficult to manage, and possibly halt a system without enough memory. A good approach is to break the data being transferred into units that can be used independently.

TIP

IDocs up to 2MB do not affect performance. A few large IDocs don't matter, but if you consistently exchange IDocs along the order of 100MB, you should rethink your design approach.

- **Distribution of changes.** A common tendency is to distribute entire sets of data. At one site a complete load of employee information was being distributed to an external system on a periodic basis to keep the systems in sync. This process caused unnecessary performance hits on the system. SAP provides the change document concept for several objects, allowing you to distribute only those objects that have been modified in some way. This approach can reduce the number and size of IDocs considerably. See Chapter 23, "Distributing Master Data," for details on distributing changes.

Interfacing with Non-SAP Systems

To interface with external systems, you can either employ the direct approach or use converters.

The Direct Approach

In the direct approach (see Figure 25-1), the IDoc file format is sent to an external system without any conversion. The external system is responsible for stripping the control records and administrative information out of the IDoc data records. For data being sent to SAP, the external system is also responsible for appending this information.

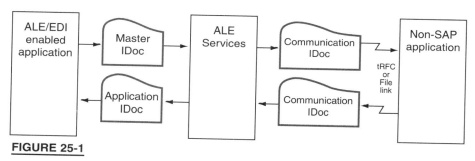

FIGURE 25-1

Interfacing with an external system directly

 NOTE

In one interesting situation, I saw legacy files brought into the SAP system and converted into an IDoc format using ABAP/4 programs, written out to the operating system as IDoc files, and then brought in through the normal IDoc channel.

Using Converters

Another way to interface with external systems is to use converters. In this approach a middleware product called an ALE converter handles the transformation between the IDoc format and legacy format, as shown in Figure 25-2. SAP certifies several ALE converters; a list can be obtained from SAP's Web site. These converters are based on the same principle as the EDI subsystems that convert IDoc data to EDI standards, and vice versa. The difference lies in how data is exchanged between SAP and the converter. EDI subsystems use a file interface, whereas ALE converters use memory-to-memory transfer. In fact, most products that were certified as EDI subsystems have been enhanced to be certified as ALE converters. If you've already deployed an EDI subsystem for your EDI project, check with your vendor about its ALE certification. You can use a system that is not certified, but certification provides an assurance of connectivity. Several companies that aren't very concerned with memory-to-memory transfer have used their EDI subsystem to perform the conversion process.

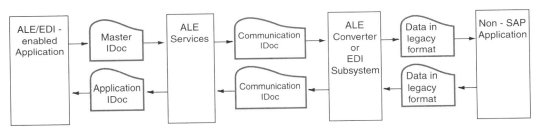

FIGURE 25-2

Interfacing with an external system via an ALE converter

The advantage of using the memory-to-memory transfer option is not having to deal with file permissions and file management. The advantage of using a file interface is apparent when you're dealing with large data packets. For example, if you are going to transfer files from 50MB to 60 MB, then a file interface is more suitable because the entire file is not loaded into the memory.

Configuration Requirements

To interface with an external system using standard ALE and EDI scenarios, you use components from both the ALE interface and the EDI interface. This section does not cover any new settings, but you'll need to know which components are used from the ALE and EDI processes. Check the EDI and ALE chapters suggested below for details on how to set up specific components. The configuration settings required are as follows:

1. **Maintain the logical system.** Assign a logical name to the external system (ALE converter, EDI subsystem, or legacy system). The logical name must be unique across the distributed network. This setting is similar to those for

SAP to SAP communication. See Chapter 22, "Configuring the ALE Infrastructure," for details on how to set up logical names for systems. This step was not required for EDI processes.

2. **Create the RFC destination.** Identify the technical parameters for the SAP system to communicate with the external system. You'll want to create an RFC destination of type T. This setting is the same as the setting in the EDI configuration. See Chapter 6, "Configuring Basic EDI Components."

3. **Maintain the customer distribution model.** A sending system uses the customer distribution model to determine the recipients for a message. You will maintain a customer distribution model for outgoing messages from SAP to the external system. You do not need to model incoming messages from the legacy system to SAP because the distribution model is an SAP concept and does not exist outside SAP. The steps to maintain the customer distribution model are described for ALE processes in Chapter 23, "Distributing Master Data."

4. **Create a port definition.** A port definition controls the medium of communication. If your external system uses files to exchange data, then you need to create a file port in which the attributes for directory names and file names are specified. If the external system uses memory-to-memory transfer, then you need to create a Transactional RFC port. File ports are described in Section I, "EDI." See Chapter 6, "Configuring Basic EDI Components" for complete details on maintaining file ports. Transactional RFC ports are described in the context of ALE in Chapter 22, "Configuring the ALE Infrastructure."

5. **Create partner profiles.** Create one partner profile for the logical system name identified in step 1. An outbound record will exist for each outgoing message and an inbound record will exist for each incoming message. Refer to Chapter 7, "Configuring Partner Profiles" for complete details on establishing and maintaining partner profiles.

 TIP

You can maintain incoming messages in a distribution model to depict the distribution scenarios and use it for automatically generating partner profiles, but the model has no business functionality.

6.   **Set up the inbound trigger.** The inbound trigger depends on the communication medium used to exchange data with the external system. If IDoc data is exchanged via files, then the inbound trigger as explained in the EDI section is used. If IDoc data is exchanged via memory buffers, then settings for inbound triggers are done on the external system. Because the inbound trigger is specific to the product being used, you have to rely on documentation from the vendor for details.

TIP

See Chapter 6, "Configuring Basic EDI Components" for complete details on inbound triggering via files.

Testing

The testing tools described in the EDI process will be more useful than the testing tools described in Section II, "ALE," for two reasons:

◆ The EDI process is used for SAP to non-SAP communication.

◆ During initial development, a great deal of testing is carried out using IDoc files, and therefore the testing described in the EDI process is more appropriate.

Monitoring, Troubleshooting, and Performance

Monitoring, troubleshooting, and performance depend on the communication method being used to exchange data. If you are using the file mechanism, refer to Chapter 13, "Managing EDI Process Performance and Throughput" for details; otherwise, for memory to memory transfer, refer to Chapter 28, "Managing ALE Process Performance and Throughput" for details.

Enhancements and Custom Development

A great deal of custom programming and IDoc development is carried out for interfaces with legacy systems. These programs are independent of the communication method, and they focus on business logic. Section III, "IDocs," includes complete coverage of extending IDocs, creating new IDocs, programming, and customizing the IDoc interface for customer enhancements.

Summary

The various components needed to configure SAP to interface with non-SAP systems via the IDoc interface have been borrowed from the ALE and EDI process. Because of the segregation of the communication layer in the ALE/EDI process, you can easily adapt ALE and EDI processes to communicate with an external system. Data can be exchanged via files or memory buffers, depending on the capabilities of the external system.

PART

9

Operating and Administering the ALE Interface

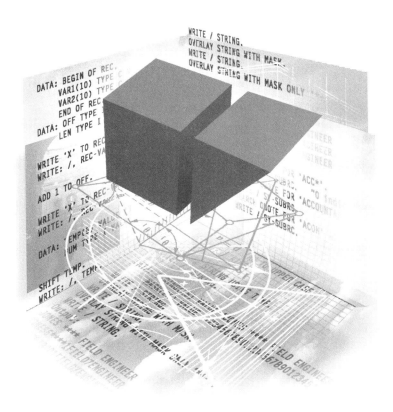

Chapter 26

Testing the ALE Interface

After you configure the ALE interface, you need to test each component to make sure the configuration settings work as desired. You may have developed some components of the ALE interface from scratch, such as message control, IDoc structure, and IDoc programs, to meet your business needs. In this case it becomes all the more important to test each individual piece thoroughly before deploying it in production.

This chapter introduces various utilities and techniques for testing inbound and outbound ALE processes. New tools appear in every release, and existing tools are enhanced to better support the testing utilities. Some of the inbound tools mentioned here may not be available in your current release.

For each test, the following items are mentioned:

◆ Steps to carry out the task
◆ Where to look for errors
◆ Possible causes of errors (to help debug)
◆ How to verify the successful execution of the test

The focus of this chapter is on testing methods and techniques. On several occasions you'll need to refer to Chapter 11, "Monitoring the Interface" and Chapter 27, "ALE Process Troubleshooting and Recovery."

Testing Outbound Processes

The outbound process is relatively simple to test and requires the least simulation because the process originates in SAP, and all the major components reside in SAP. The best approach for testing an outbound process is to test each component and then the whole process. The following sections describe the utilities available for testing, and explain how to test each component.

SAP provides two types of test utilities:

◆ Utilities for a sanity test
◆ Utilities to test the process

The first type of utility performs a basic sanity test on the configuration of ALE objects such as customer model, partner profile, and RFC destination parameters. A sanity test allows you to test a component without executing the actual process. These utilities are accessed from within the maintenance screens of the objects. The second type of utility tests the process. The outbound process is tested with the actual components that are involved in the process.

Prerequisites for Testing Outbound Processes

The outbound process is composed of various programs that are linked to run one after another. To test each component separately, you'll have to disconnect them. In the outbound record of the partner profile for your message, set the Collect IDocs flag. The flag prevents the RSEOUT00 program from running immediately after an IDoc is created in the system.

 NOTE

The process flow described in Chapter 20, "The Outbound ALE Process," should be used as a reference.

Performing Sanity Tests

This section describes the basic sanity tests available for each individual object, such as partner profile, customer model, and RFC destination. These tests check the validity of various attributes in the objects without executing the process. Although you may have carried out some of these tests while configuring particular components, the tests are mentioned here in complete detail.

Testing Partner Profiles

Partner profiles can be checked to make sure the parameters specified are still correct. The following checks are carried out:

◆ Process code

◆ User to be notified

◆ Message control consistency with outbound parameters

You can execute the program RSECHK07 to check the consistency of partner profiles. You can execute this program via transaction SE38 or from the menus of the initial partner profile screen. The output is a color-coded report that contains details about any problems that occur.

Although a check is carried out when the partners are created, some parameters can become invalid over time. For example, if a user ID that no longer exists was specified in the partner profile, this report flags the invalid user ID as an error.

Testing the RFC Destination

This test confirms the connectivity between the SAP systems. Execute transaction SM59. Click on the RFC destination being used in the process—typically the logical system name assigned to the remote SAP system. You can confirm your RFC destination by viewing the details of your port definition that will be used for outbound processes. Click on the Test button. If the results are positive, then the connectivity is okay. In addition, you should test the logon process to make sure logon parameters are correct. Click on the Remote Logon button.

If the test connection returns negative results, the message should indicate the problem. If the message is not self-explanatory, then you can turn on RFC trace to log every step in the RFC test process. This log is slightly cryptic, and knowledge of CPIC (Common Programming Interface Communication) is necessary to interpret the trace information.

If the remote logon test is successful and the user ID is a background user, the system does not display a response. If a problem occurs, the system creates a session for the remote system and prompts you to enter a user ID and password.

The connectivity between the two SAP systems is at fault. The possible causes of errors are:

♦ The TCP/IP host name for the SAP system specified in the Target Machine field may have been misspelled.

TIP

If the problem persists, you can try to use the IP address of the host on which the EDI subsystem is or will be installed. If this method works, then the problem lies in the TCP/IP configuration. Check with your Basis staff.

♦ The value entered in the System Number field may be incorrect. Log on to the remote system and use transaction SM51 to display the application servers. The last two digits in the application server name provide the value for the system number.

♦ The user ID, password, or client number may be incorrect, or the password may have expired.

◆ The physical links and network links may not be working (this is rare). You can execute the ping command at the OS level to make sure that the link is up.

Testing Distribution Model Consistency

This test (see Figure 26-1) checks three areas for the messages modeled in a customer model:

◆ **Technical consistency.** This test validates that partner profiles exist for various messages modeled in the system.

◆ **Consistency of application.** This test validates the application settings for a message type. For example, for message type BLAOCH, the test checks the number range specification, message control objects, item categories, and so on. This test is available for BLAORD, BLAOCH, FIROLL, CODCMT, and ORDERS message types only.

◆ **Consistency of control data.** This test determines and validates various customizing objects such as plants and company codes for a message type to make sure an owner has been defined for those objects in the control data model.

TIP

By default, this test does a cross-system check, but you can limit it to your local system by clicking on the Cross-System On/Off button.

Execute transaction BDM5. Select any one of the areas and drill down until you get to the right message and destination system. Click on the message and choose Edit, Check from the menu. The system carries out the checks and changes the color of the message type, depending on the results. Red means error, yellow means warning, and white signifies a successful test.

If the tests result in a warning or an error, you can select the line and choose Edit, Details from the menu. The system displays the cause of the problem. Double-clicking on the problem may transfer you directly to the area where you can fix the problem.

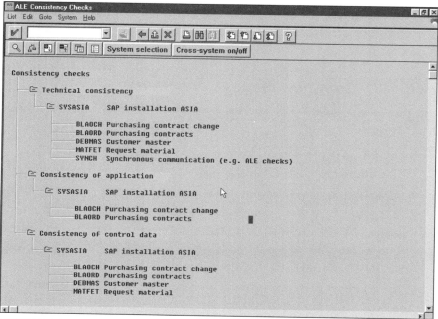

FIGURE 26-1

Consistency test of the distribution model

Errors in the technical consistency check are due to missing partner profiles. Errors in the application checks are specific to each application area. Check the output report log to determine the cause and fix the problem. The main cause of errors in the control data is that an owner has not been defined for the customizing objects. You can ignore errors in the consistency check of control data because control data does not affect the execution of the process. Making sure that a system has ownership of the customizing data is an administrative function, and other systems are prohibited from changing the customizing data.

Testing Outbound Processes

Message control, change pointers, or stand-alone programs can trigger an outbound ALE process. The outbound process is essentially a sequence of several subprocesses that link together to form the total process. This section describes the testing procedure for each subprocess.

The testing of the message control process is discussed in Chapter 10, "Testing the EDI Interface." The four subprocesses that are tested in the outbound process for stand-alone programs and the change pointer process are as follows:

◆ Successful triggering from change pointers

◆ Successful triggering from the stand-alone program

◆ Generation of IDocs

◆ Successful dispatch of IDocs to a remote SAP system

Verifying Successful Triggering from Change Pointers

In this test you want to make sure that change pointers are written when an application document is changed. To test this process, change the application document for which you want to test the change pointers. For example, to test change pointers for material master, execute transaction MM02 and make appropriate changes.

This process does not have a formal log for failure. However, you can check the BDCP and BDCPS tables. An entry is created in these tables for every change made to a document enabled for change pointers. If an entry is missing, you have a problem.

The change pointer process does not work in the following situations:

◆ Changes are probably not recorded for the object you are working with. Execute transaction SCDO and verify that a change document object exists for your object. The names of the change document objects are sometimes cryptic, so you may need to view complete details such as the tables included in the change document to locate the right change document object.

◆ Changes to only certain data elements are recorded. Determine the data element for the field that you are trying to change. Use transaction SE11 and verify that the Change Document field is selected for the data element. If this field is not turned on, the change document will not be written.

◆ The IDoc message type for the object has not been maintained in the customer model. Thus if you are trying to generate IDocs for the material master, MATMAS should exist in a customer model.

◆ Change pointers are not globally active. Execute transaction BD61 to verify this condition.

◆ Change pointers have not been activated for the message type. Execute transaction BD50 to verify this condition.

♦ The fields for which ALE change pointers are written do not include the field that you are modifying. Execute transaction BD52 to verify this condition.

If this step is successful, an entry should appear in the BDCP table (see Figure 26-2) for the change. Use transaction SE16 or SE17 to view entries in this table. If everything looks good, you should execute program RBDMIDOC to start the IDoc generation process from change pointers.

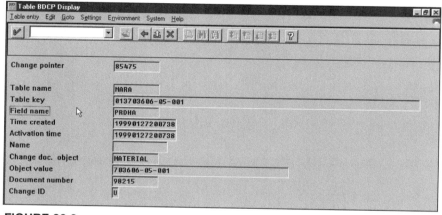

FIGURE 26-2

Entries in the BDCP table for changes made to the material master object

Verifying Successful Execution of Stand-Alone Programs

This test is applicable if you are using a stand-alone program to generate IDocs. In this test you want to make sure that your program is executed successfully.

A program exists for each master data object that is enabled for ALE. Execute transaction BALE and select the appropriate master data to be distributed from the Master Data menu option. For example, BD10 to send material master data.

Because this program is executed online, the results are displayed on the screen. If the number of master IDocs or communication IDocs is zero, you probably have a problem. Following is a list of places to check, depending on the type of error that's occurring:

♦ If the number of master IDocs processed is zero, check the parameters entered on the selection screen of the stand-alone program.

◆ Make sure the message type has been modeled in the customer distribution model and the customer distribution model is available on the sending system.

◆ If you have developed a custom program or an IDoc type, check the configuration settings for message type and IDoc type. Refer to Chapter 33, "Customizing the Interface for New or Extended IDocs" for details on how to configure the ALE process for custom IDocs.

If this step is successful, you should get a message indicating the number of communication IDocs generated.

Verifying Generation of IDocs

This step verifies the program logic that generates the IDocs. If you have extended the IDoc selection program via user exits, modified the program, or created a new one, you will be particularly interested in this step. This step is simply an extension of the previous step and doesn't require any new programs or transactions.

There are several possibilities for errors in this step, and if they occur, the status record of the IDoc indicates the problem. You can use transaction WE02 or WE05 to display the IDoc and its status records.

If you are testing a standard SAP-supplied program, then errors at this stage are rarely due to program logic. The main cause of errors is a missing or incorrect partner profile. (The sanity tests you carried out earlier should have caught this error.) If you have done custom development, then either of the following factors can cause errors:

◆ The partner profile is missing or incorrect

◆ The IDoc structure or program logic is incorrect

TIP

If you cannot figure out the problem, start the debugger and begin debugging the program.

If this step works correctly, then the IDoc must be in status 30 (IDoc ready for dispatch).

Verifying Dispatch of IDocs to Remote SAP Systems

In this step you test the process to dispatch IDocs from one SAP system to another. One of the major culprits in this process is the RFC destination setting for the remote SAP system. You will experience the most problems with this setting because parameters in the RFC destination pertain to another SAP system. If you successfully carried out the sanity test for RFC destination as described earlier, the chance of error here is minimal.

Transaction: WE14

Path: From the Area menu of ALE (BALE), choose Periodic Processing, ALE Outbound IDocs.

The IDoc must be in status 30 (IDoc ready for dispatch) to be passed to the communication layer. A standard program—RSEOUT00—handles this operation. Execute program RSEOUT00 via transaction SE38 or execute WE14. The selection screen (see Figure 26-3) allows you to select IDocs based on various criteria. You can enter the IDoc number generated in the previous test, "Verifying Generation of IDocs." If the process executes successfully, you should then execute program RBDMOIND for completeness. The RBDMOIND program updates the IDoc status to 12 (Dispatch OK) when the IDoc is received on the remote system. Refer to "Setting Up Transactional RFC Reporting" in Chapter 22, "Configuring the ALE Infrastructure" for details on the significance of the RBDMOIND program.

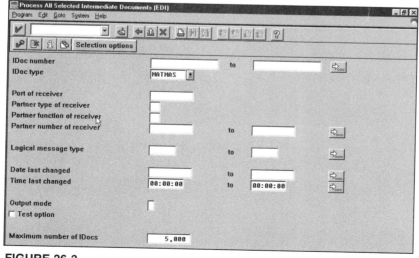

FIGURE 26-3

Selection screen for the RSEOUT00 program

Check the last status record of the IDoc and the tRFC log (SM58) for errors. See the errors explained in the sanity test for RFC destination section, "Testing the RFC Destination," earlier in this chapter. This step is verified by checking the last status code of the IDoc. The status should be 12 (Dispatch OK).

CAUTION

The IDoc status 03 (Data passed to port OK) does not guarantee that the IDoc has been received on the other system.

Testing Inbound Processes

The inbound process is different from the outbound in that the former originates outside the local SAP system. The sending system may not always be available, or you simply may not want to start the outbound process from scratch every time you test the inbound process. When you test the inbound process, you can use several utilities to simulate the start of the process. The actual processing is carried out by the real components. The best strategy for testing an inbound process is to test each component separately.

As it does for the outbound process, SAP provides two types of test utilities for the inbound process:

- ◆ Utilities for the sanity test
- ◆ Utilities to test the process

Prerequisites for Testing an Inbound Process

The inbound process is composed of various programs that are linked to run one after another. To test each component separately, enable the Background, No Override with Express flag in the partner profile. This setting disconnects the components from each other and prevents them from starting the next process immediately. You can use the process flow described in Chapter 21 as a reference.

Performing Sanity Tests

You can use standard system tools to test the configuration components defined for the inbound process. These tools help do a basic sanity test of the configuration settings without executing the process.

Testing Partner Profiles

Partner profiles can be checked to make sure the parameters specified are still correct. The test is the same as the corresponding test defined in the outbound process.

Testing Inbound Settings

The ALE system provides a tool to test the consistency of inbound parameters for error handling. You can use this tool to test all the process codes or one process code at a time. The output is a color-coded report that displays the possible cause of any problem.

You can run this report for all process codes by using program RBDMOINF via transaction SE38. However, if you are only interested in testing one process code, you can run program RBDMOINC to test an individual code. Test results are displayed on the output screen in a color-coded report. Double-click any problem to get additional details. Errors in this test can be due to the following reasons:

◆ The link between process code and function module is not defined.

◆ The object type for the IDoc of this message is missing. If an object is present, it checks for the presence of a triggering event (INPUTERROROCCURED) and a terminating event (INPUTFINISHED). This error is more likely to occur for the custom-developed processes.

◆ The object type for IDoc packets for this message is missing. If an object is present, it checks for a terminating event named MASSINPUTFINISHED.

◆ The task for error handling has not been defined.

◆ The linkage between the task and triggering events is inactive or undefined.

◆ The linkage for the terminating events is undefined or inactive.

◆ The roles for the task are undefined.

Most of these settings are related to workflow settings for a new process. SAP already provides these objects for standard messages. This test is useful for custom-developed processes. Refer to Chapter 33, "Customizing the Interface for New or Extended IDocs" for details on configuring new inbound processes.

Testing Inbound Processes

An inbound ALE process is essentially a sequence of several subprocesses that link together to form the total process. This section describes the testing procedure for the three subprocesses listed:

◆ Inbound triggering process

◆ Successful creation of IDocs in the database

◆ Posting of the application document

One of the major components for the inbound process is the IDoc itself. If the sending system is not available or you want to quickly start the inbound process repeatedly, you need a way to create an IDoc and start the inbound process. The following section describes a tool you can use to generate an IDoc and start the inbound process and then explains how to test the subprocesses.

Using the Test Tool

Transaction: WE19

Path: From the Area menu of EDI (WEDI), choose Test, Test Tool, Inbound.

The test tool is a two-step process. In the first step, you'll create an IDoc by using one of the following four options:

◆ Copy an existing IDoc

◆ Create an IDoc based on an IDoc type

◆ Create an IDoc based on a message type

◆ Create an IDoc with no template

The option you choose depends on your tastes and program requirements. The first option is most commonly used because it allows you to modify an existing IDoc (inbound or outbound) to suit your needs (see Figures 26-4, 26-5, and 26-6).

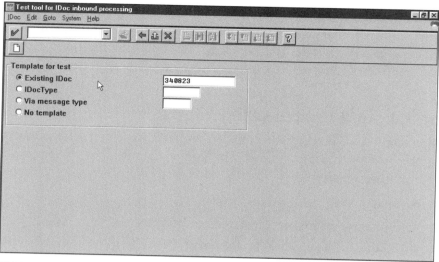

FIGURE 26-4

Options to create an IDoc

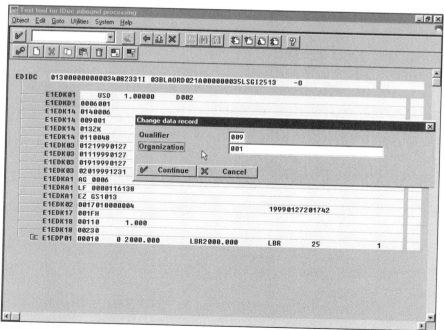

FIGURE 26-5

Screen to modify the contents of a copied IDoc

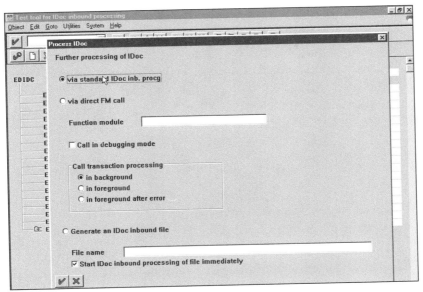

FIGURE 26-6

Options to select a method to start the inbound process

In the second step, the IDoc created above is passed to the inbound process. You have several options to select the method of starting the inbound process (see Figure 26-6):

◆ **Start the inbound processing via the standard path.** This method uses all inbound components.

◆ **Call the inbound function module directly.** In this case the system bypasses the checks for partner profile and hands the IDoc data to your inbound function module directly. This method is useful for testing an inbound process without having to maintain any inbound configuration. You can also start the function module in debug mode and select the processing option for your posting module.

◆ **Save the IDoc in a file and start the inbound process.** This method is similar to the first method except that here you also create an IDoc file at the operating system. This method is mainly used for EDI processes.

Verifying the Creation of Successful IDocs

This step uses the information in the control record of the IDoc to verify that a partner profile is found and that the IDoc is created without any structural errors. This step is useful for checking the structural accuracy of incoming custom-developed IDocs.

Start the inbound process using any of the utilities described earlier. The results are logged in the status records of the IDoc. The status records can be displayed by using the IDoc display utilities. If an error occurs, the IDoc gets a status code of 56 (IDoc with errors added) and an error workflow is started. The person notified in this case depends on whether a partner profile could be read or not. If a partner profile was found, then workflow is sent to the responsible person specified in the partner profile. If a partner profile entry could not be read, then the message is sent to the EDI administrator specified in the EDIADMIN table.

Common problems in this step are related to data in the control record and syntax errors in the IDoc:

◆ You need to make sure the parameters in the control record match the key of the partner profile record for that inbound message.

◆ Various factors cause syntax errors (see "Syntax Rules for an IDoc" in Chapter 30 for more information). The status records should pinpoint the problems.

If this step is successful, you should see an IDoc that has a status code of 64 (IDoc ready to be passed to application).

Verifying the Logic of the Inbound Function Module

Transaction: BD87

Verifying the logic of the inbound function module is the most important step for custom-developed function modules. You must verify that the posting function module is working correctly. You must also verify the logic and the interface of the function module. If problems exist, you may want to debug the process one step at a time.

The IDoc created in the previous test, "Verifying the Creation of Successful IDocs," is used to test this process. SAP provides a standard program—RBDAPP01—to start the processing of IDocs in status 64. Figure 26-7 shows the selection screen for this program where you can specify various parameters. Enter your IDoc number and start the process.

Errors in this step are mainly related to data errors and are logged in the status records of the IDoc. You can use the IDoc display utilities to display the relevant status records. The IDoc gets a status code of 51 (IDoc with errors added). Detailed information about a specific error is also logged in the status record. An error workflow is started to notify the person responsible for handling the error.

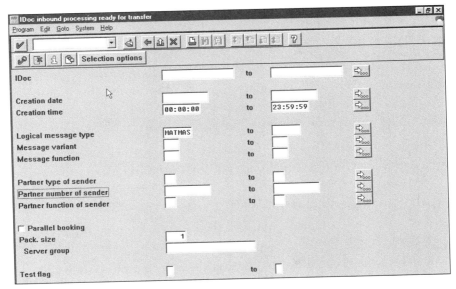

FIGURE 26-7

Selection screen to pass an IDoc to the posting program

If your posting program uses the call transaction to post the document, then you can step through every screen to determine the exact location of the error. The most common problems in this step are related to data or are in the application configuration. Make sure the data values are correct in the various fields of the data record. Also check your program logic for any errors. If this step is successful, you'll see an application document successfully created and the IDoc will get a status code of 53 (Application document posted).

Testing the Workflow Exception Process

After you test the inbound and outbound processes, you can specifically test the workflow component to test the exception-handling process. One obvious test method is to create an error in the process and check for a workitem in the Inbox of the responsible user. However, doing so requires you to build error data, which may be difficult. You can test just the workflow component by using the simple procedure listed below. This procedure applies to all error workflows for outbound as well as inbound processes.

Transaction: SWUS

Menu Path: From the Area menu of workflow, choose Runtime Tools, Start Workflow

In this step your aim is to test the exception-handling process to make sure the right person is notified when an error occurs. You can use this tool to start the error process manually without introducing a real error. In an actual process, the system starts the error process based on the type of error. The steps are as follows:

1. Identify the workflow task that is started for a particular exception. Refer to Chapter 9, "Configuring Workflow," for a list of error tasks. For example, the error task for application errors in posting a material master IDoc is MATMAS_Error (TS00007947).

2. Enter the task number in the Task field and click on the Input Data button. Press F4 on the next screen and enter an IDoc number.

3. Click on the back arrow and click on the Start button as shown in Figure 26-8. This step should start a workflow process.

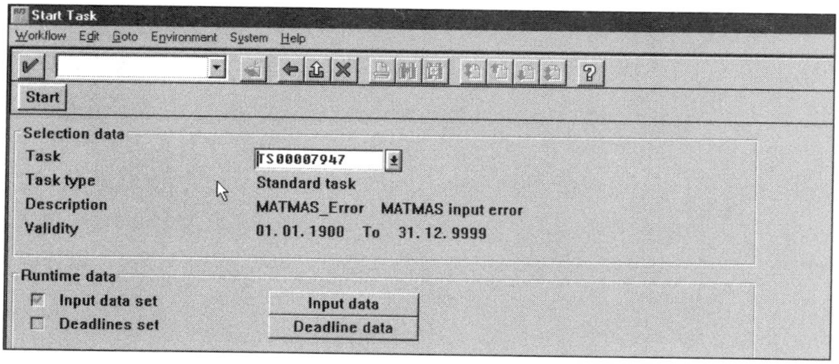

FIGURE 26-8

Testing a workflow error task

Errors in this step are communicated in the status bar. You can click on the message to get additional details. The common problems in this step are related to workflow configuration. If the system reports that you are not one of the possible agents, the task profile has not been maintained or a problem exists with your PD-ORG setup. Refer to Chapter 9 to see how to set up the task profile for workflow tasks. If this step is successful, the responsible person for the task should get a workitem in their Inbox.

Summary

The tools and techniques for testing an outbound process and an inbound process are similar. The tests involve doing a sanity test in which the components are tested without executing the actual process. The sanity tests expose problems in configuration settings. Another set of tests involve testing the process one step at a time. For testing inbound processes, a test tool allows you to create test IDocs on-the-fly. After you create an IDoc, you conduct a three-step test on each component of the inbound process. The results of each step are verified before proceeding to the next step.

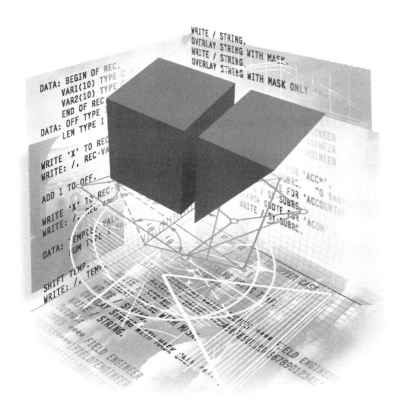

Chapter 27

ALE Process Troubleshooting and Recovery

Even if you carry out all of the configuration steps exactly as detailed in the configuration section and test all the components thoroughly, any system will experience problems at some point. In this chapter you learn what is considered successful process execution, how to troubleshoot the system when it fails, and how to restart the system from the point of failure.

Where you view the problem depends on where it occurred. This section helps you logically navigate to the point where an error has occurred or a problem exists. In Chapter 11, "Monitoring the Interface," several tools to monitor the system were mentioned—this chapter explains which one to use under particular conditions.

NOTE

The troubleshooting process for ALE is similar to its counterpart for the EDI process. The main difference lies in troubleshooting errors in the communication process. The restart points are also slightly different because of differences in architecture at the communication level.

How to Troubleshoot

The best approach to troubleshoot any process is to first understand the process, identify the possible points of failure, and determine how the system reports problems. This discussion assumes that you have a good grasp of the technical concepts of outbound and inbound processes discussed in Chapter 20, "The Outbound ALE Process," and Chapter 21, "The Inbound ALE Process."

Follow this simple approach to troubleshoot:

1. Determine whether a failure has occurred or not.
2. For a given symptom, use the troubleshooting chart (presented later in the chapter) as your guide to quickly get to the root of the problem.
3. Use the appropriate monitoring tools described in Chapter 11, "Monitoring the Interface" to read and interpret the appropriate log. Use the information in the log to help you analyze the problem.
4. Fix the cause of the problem.
5. Determine the point of restart. Depending on the problem, you may be able to restart the process from the point of failure, or you may have to restart from the very beginning.

6. Use the technique most suitable for restarting the process. You can restart the process from within workflow (if applicable) or use one of the ALE/EDI tools for restarting the process.

Troubleshooting the Outbound Process

An outbound ALE process is triggered in three ways: by message control, change pointers, or stand-alone programs. Troubleshooting an outbound process started via message control was discussed in Chapter 12, "EDI Process Troubleshooting and Recovery." Here you learn how to troubleshoot outbound ALE processes started either from the change pointer process or from stand-alone programs.

Points of Failure in the Outbound Process

The outbound process is essentially a sequence of asynchronous processes. Failure can occur within any process. The points of failure on an outbound process are as follows:

◆ Error in the change pointer process

◆ Error in the stand-alone program

◆ Error in the ALE/EDI interface layer

◆ Error in the IDoc structure (syntax error, conversion problem, and so on)

◆ Error in sending the IDoc to a remote SAP system

How the System Reports Problems

When problems occur in the outbound process, the system uses the technique most suitable at that point to report the problem. The main technique used is the workflow component, but workflow is not started while you are interacting with the system in a dialog mode. After control passes to the SAP system for processing, the system logs any problems and reports them via workflow. An explanation of the outbound process in the context of the error process follows.

1. When the outbound process is triggered, any problems at that point are reported to the user immediately and thus workflow is unnecessary. This occurs when you execute transaction BD10 to transfer material master. If

communication IDocs cannot be generated, a workflow is not necessary because the system has already informed you of the results.

2. If step 1 finds no problems, an IDoc is created in the system. The system performs some basic integrity checks on the IDoc, and a syntax check is done. If an error is found, then the IDoc gets a status code of 26 (Error during syntax check of IDoc outbound). A workflow message is sent to the person responsible, as identified in the partner profile.

3. The system then looks for an outbound record in the partner profile. If the outbound record is missing, then the IDoc gets a status code of 29 (Error in ALE service) and a workflow message is sent to the person identified in the general view of the partner profile. If the partner profile is completely missing, then the EDI administrator is notified via workflow.

4. If step 3 is successful, the IDoc is passed to the communication layer for dispatch. If errors occur during dispatch, workflow is not started. The system maintains information about failed transmissions in the tRFC logs. Refer to "Restarting Failed tRFCs" later in this chapter for details.

CAUTION

If the TRFC options have been left at their default values in the RFC destination and there are communication problems, then outbound ALE processes have a tendency to take up all the free background processes. In this situation, non-ALE processes will start erroring out and entries will be logged in the system log, but you will not be notified directly.

How to Determine the Success of an Outbound Process

An outbound ALE process is considered successful if the IDoc gets a status code of 03 (Data passed to port OK) and there are no entries in error in the tRFC log (SM58).

TIP

The tRFC log is a common log for all tRFC errors. Sometimes it may be loaded with errors from other applications. In such situations it is best to execute program RBDMOIND (BD75). This program updates the status of IDocs that have been successfully transmitted to 12 (Dispatch OK); otherwise, it leaves them at status 03.

Troubleshooting Guide for Outbound Errors

For an outbound process, the best approach is to check the IDoc status and then the SAP Inbox. The flowchart in Figures 27-1 through 27-6 depicts the troubleshooting process as a logical sequence of steps. The troubleshooting chart also tells you which log to monitor and identifies the point of restart. Figure 27-1 helps you analyze problems that occur during the initial process to start the generation of IDocs. Figure 27-2 navigates you to the next process in the analysis process. If an IDoc is not present, it indicates a severe error, but if an IDoc was created, most of the error analysis is done based on the IDoc status. If your IDoc is in status 03, it is usually considered a success unless you have problems depicted in Figure 27-3. Figure 27-4 helps you analyze IDocs that have syntax errors. Figure 27-5 is useful in analyzing problems with IDocs that have an error in the ALE service layer. The main reason is an incorrect partner profile, but additional reasons are also possible, as shown in Figure 27-5. Figure 27-6 helps you analyze reasons for IDocs stuck in status 30. IDocs in status 30 are usually due to the settings in the partner profile, but sometimes it results due to locking problems.

NOTE

The set of Figures 27-1 through 27-6 should be viewed as one logical figure. But like any other flowchart, you will find suitable connectors that allow you to navigate from one figure to another.

Restart Points for Outbound Errors

A failed process can be restarted from the very beginning or from the point of failure. This section explains the various restart points proposed in the troubleshooting chart in Figures 27-1 through 27-6.

Restarting from the SAP Inbox

Transaction: SO01

Menu Path: Office, Inbox

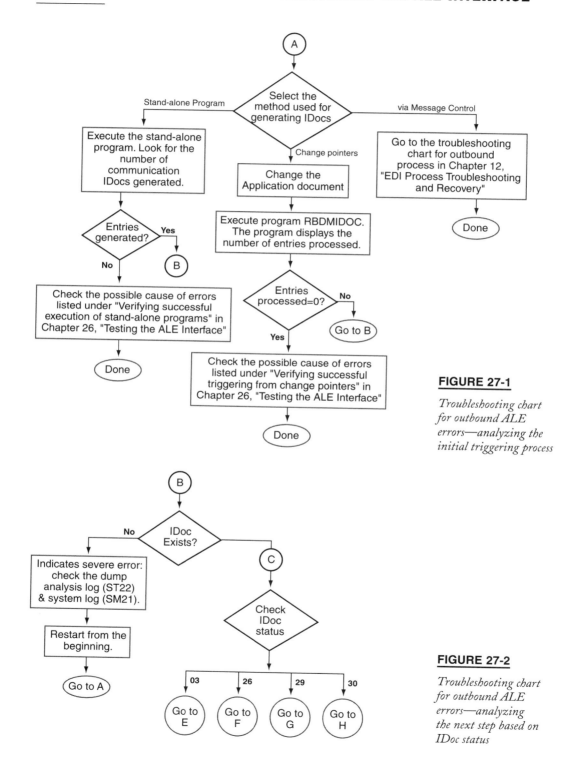

FIGURE 27-1

Troubleshooting chart for outbound ALE errors—analyzing the initial triggering process

FIGURE 27-2

Troubleshooting chart for outbound ALE errors—analyzing the next step based on IDoc status

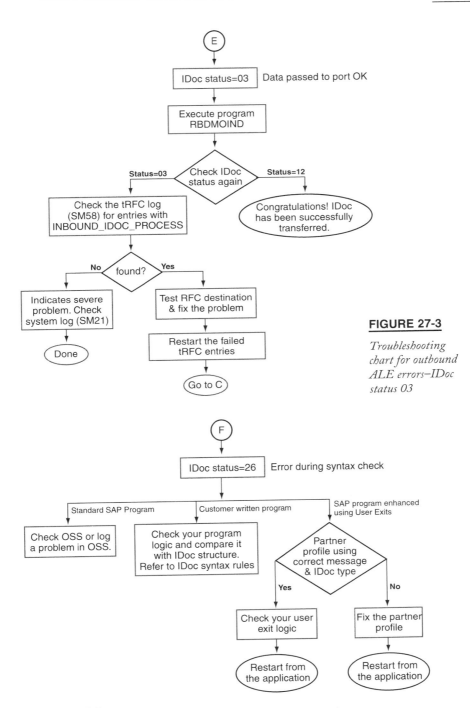

FIGURE 27-3

Troubleshooting chart for outbound ALE errors—IDoc status 03

FIGURE 27-4

Troubleshooting chart for outbound ALE errors—IDoc status 26

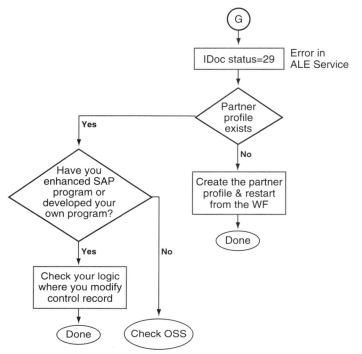

FIGURE 27-5

Troubleshooting chart for outbound ALE errors— IDoc status 29

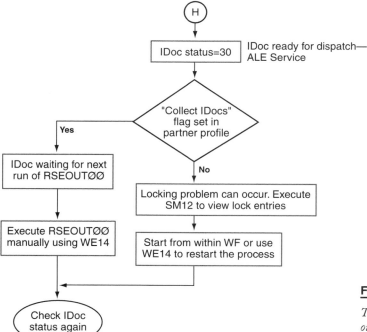

FIGURE 27-6

Troubleshooting chart for outbound ALE errors— IDoc status 30

If a workflow message was generated for the error then you have the option of restarting the process from within workflow. Restarting from the SAP Inbox saves you the trouble of remembering the application transaction and data values. Remember, workflow brings the right task with the right information to the right person at the right time in the right sequence. You can simply execute the work item to start the process. See Chapter 11, "Monitoring the Interface" for details on how to display and execute work items.

If the error was such that several IDocs failed for the same reason, then it is convenient to start the process using one of the ALE/EDI tools described in the next section. In my experience, most ALE errors occur in mass numbers, so the SAP Inbox is rarely used for restarting failed ALE processes. In EDI it is quite common to use the SAP Inbox to restart failed processes.

Restarting with ALE Tools

Transaction: BD88

Menu Path: Logistics, Central Functions, Distribution, Periodic Processing, ALE Outbound IDocs

This method is an alternative to restarting the process from the SAP Inbox. This method is commonly deployed for mass errors, but you can also use it for single errors. There are merits to using this tool instead of the workflow tool in certain cases. For example, assume you started the ALE process to transfer 10,000 materials, but you forgot to generate partner profiles. The system will generate 10,000 work items. It is very cumbersome to execute each work item individually when the cause of error is the same for all errors. After you fix the problem, you can use the outbound ALE tool to restart all failed IDocs in one step. This tool allows you to process the IDocs from the point of failure without having to restart the process from the beginning. The steps are as follows:

1. Execute Transaction BD88.

2. From the screen displayed (see Figure 27-7), select the appropriate radio button, based on the status of your IDoc.

3. On the next screen, you can restrict the number of IDocs to be processed. Enter the desired parameters and click on the Execute button to start the processing. If you have too many failed IDocs (in the hundreds), processing them all in one run can cause the system to slow down considerably. Refer to "Managing Performance of Inbound Processes" in Chapter 28, "Managing ALE Process Performance and Throughput" for details on how

you can utilize packet size and the server group field to restrict the number of dialog processes consumed.

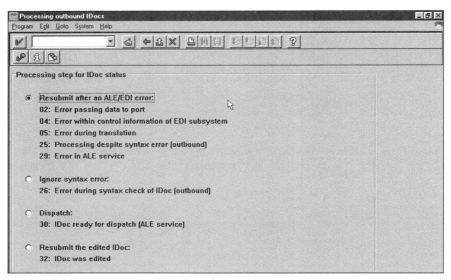

FIGURE 27-7

Selection screen for restarting outbound IDocs

Restarting Failed tRFCs

If several tRFCs have failed, you can either restart each one individually or restart them all together. The second option is useful if several entries failed for the same reason.

To restart failed tRFCs individually, execute transaction SM58 and display all the failed tRFCs. Click on the desired entry and choose Edit, Execute Funct. Mod. from the menu. This step restarts the particular entry. If successful, the entry is removed from the log.

 TIP

Failures at the tRFC level are frequent. Refer to "Advanced Settings in the RFC Destination" in Chapter 22, "Configuring the ALE Infrastructure" on how to automate the reprocessing of failed tRFCs.

To restart several failed entries together, execute transaction BDA1 or choose Periodic Processing, Transactional RFC from the Area menu of ALE (transaction BALE). The selection screen shown in Figure 27-8 allows you to select entries based on their status, date, time, user, and destination. The status values have the following meaning:

◆ **Communication error.** These errors are related to network problems.

◆ **Not yet processed.** Entries in this status were awaiting dispatch when the system was shut down.

◆ **Termination (dump, E/A msg).** These entries caused a severe error or a dump error on the receiving system. Errors in user ID and password for remote logon are also classified in this category.

◆ **Currently being processed.** These entries are being sent. You should never select this status unless an entry is hung for an extended period. If you select this entry, then the IDoc is dispatched again.

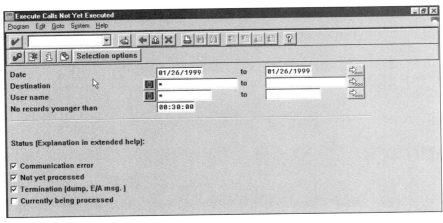

FIGURE 27-8

Selection screen for restarting failed tRFCs

Purging the Outbound Process

In certain situations you may not be able to fix a problem because the data in the IDoc is incorrect, and therefore the process has to be restarted from scratch. If the process in error has created an IDoc, you do not want to leave the IDoc in limbo. You must purge it to prevent it from being processed accidentally.

An IDoc in error can be purged from the work item that was generated as a result of this error. Execute the work item and look for the Delete button. When you press the Delete button, the IDoc is marked for deletion and gets a status code of

31 (Error—no further processing). This status prevents any of the EDI or ALE tools from accidentally processing the IDoc.

Troubleshooting the Inbound Process

The troubleshooting process for inbound ALE errors is very similar to the troubleshooting process for the inbound process described in Chapter 12, "EDI Process Troubleshooting and Recovery." The only difference lies in how the inbound process is triggered in ALE versus EDI. In ALE, it is triggered from the remote system with a tRFC call and IDoc data is passed to the inbound process in memory. In EDI, the process is triggered using the startrfc command and the IDoc data is passed as a file. Once the process is started, it does not matter how it was triggered and therefore the troubleshooting process is exactly the same from that point on. Errors that can occur in the inbound triggering process are actually part of the troubleshooting process for outbound because an outbound process is the one that triggers the inbound process. An outbound ALE process is not considered successful until an IDoc is created successfully on the receiving system.

The points of failure, points of restart, and method to purge incoming IDocs are all the same. Refer to "Troubleshooting the Inbound Process in EDI" in Chapter 12, "EDI Process Troubleshooting and Recovery" for complete details.

Summary

Errors are possible at various steps in the outbound and inbound processes. SAP provides extensive log information at various points. Until an IDoc is generated, SAP logs the error in the application initiating the process. After an IDoc is generated, the IDoc becomes the main vehicle for any log information, and errors are routed via workflow to the responsible person.

Because errors are possible at various points, knowing where to start troubleshooting can reduce the time required to fix a problem. The troubleshooting process follows a simple approach. First, determine whether an error has occurred or not. Then use the troubleshooting chart to track down the problem. When you find the cause of the problem, fix it and then restart the process from the point of failure if possible. If not, then you must restart the process from the very beginning. In some cases you may opt to restart the process from the beginning instead of from the point of failure because the data is corrupt. In these situations you must be sure to purge the items in error.

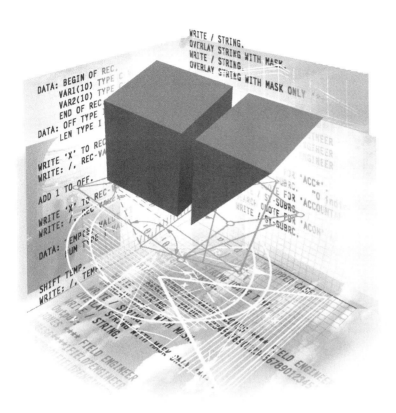

Chapter 28

Managing ALE Process Performance and Throughput

The performance of a system is usually measured by the response time of a user transaction. When a user creates a document or runs a report, the time it takes for the process to complete becomes a starting measure to improve the performance. ALE processes are asynchronous, which means users do not wait online for the IDocs to reach the destination system, or post in the destination system. However, ALE processes consume lots of system cycles in the process of creating IDocs and dispatching them to the destination system. For example, it is not uncommon to see 50,000 materials being transferred via ALE. These huge data transfers via ALE can hamper the performance of the system for other users. One option would be to serialize the process, but it would impact the rate at which data transfer occurs. Moving 50,000 materials could take forever.

On the flip side, if you allow ALE processes to run uncontrolled, they have a tendency to use up all dialog and background processes, which in most cases requires the system to be shut down. Therefore, managing performance is an important issue for the overall health of the system.

In this chapter you learn how to manage the performance of ALE processes by controlling their timing, packet size, and parallel-processing options. In addition this chapter points out general strategies that you can adopt to keep your system in good shape, such as data archiving and performance-tuning procedures used for ABAP/4 programs and databases. Those procedures are part of an overall performance-tuning strategy that applies to all modules.

 NOTE

This chapter requires a good understanding of the technical details of the outbound and inbound process. Refer to Chapter 20, "The Outbound ALE Process" and Chapter 21, "The Inbound ALE Process" for details. Pay special attention to the buffering options available and the processing that occurs in the communication layer.

Methods for Performance Management

You can use three methods to manage the performance and throughput of ALE processes:

- ◆ **Controlling process timing.** This method enables you to control the timing of the ALE process at four stages: creation of IDocs, dispatch of IDocs to the communication layer, retry of failed transmissions, and posting of IDocs on the receiving system. This approach allows you to select a time that is most appropriate for a process. For example, instead of creating an IDoc every time an object is changed, you can wait to send one IDoc at the end of the day for all changes.

◆ **Controlling packet size.** This method enables you to specify the number of IDocs that are bundled together in a packet used for communication and for posting of documents. The IDocs in a packet are processed one at a time on the receiving end. This method allows you to make optimal use of network resources, memory buffers, and the number of dialog processes used on the sending system and receiving system. This method is useful when you are constrained by the amount of resources you can use. If you increase the packet size, you get good performance but bad throughput.

◆ **Controlling multiprocessing.** With this method you can specify parallel processing for the generation of IDocs and posting of IDocs. I call this approach "let the ALE system run wild but restricted by the number of processes it can consume." This method allows you to make the most of resources allocated to your process. If you increase the number of parallel processes, you increase the throughput, but you degrade the performance of other processes.

A good strategy is one that strikes a good balance among these three methods. The definition of a good strategy is, however, subjective, and attempting to design a common strategy that will work for all companies would be a futile effort. Performance management is an iterative and ongoing exercise in which the goal is to achieve a system that optimally uses its resources. Such a system is subject to change, so you're never truly free of the performance management challenge.

The three options discussed above are explained below in the context of the inbound and outbound process. You will learn where to make the settings and discuss the benefits and drawbacks of each option.

Managing Performance of Outbound Processes

This part of the chapter covers outbound processes that use change pointers or stand-alone programs. Performance of outbound processes that use message control is described in Chapter 13, "Managing Performance and Throughput," in the EDI section.

Although every company has different needs, you can classify the various outgoing messages into two broad categories:

- ◆ Those requiring near-real-time operation
- ◆ Those that can be operated in batch mode

You do not have any way to control the performance of messages that require near-real-time operation, but such processes exist, and you need to account for system cycles consumed by such processes. For outgoing messages that can be operated in batch mode, you can implement the various methods described earlier.

Near-Real-Time Outbound Messages

In near-real-time mode, an IDoc can be generated and passed to the communication layer immediately. From there the IDoc is dispatched to the destination system in a very short period of time. The actual time lag depends on the load in the system. This technique gives the near-real-time feel, which is useful for critical ALE transactions. For example, if you are interfacing with an external warehouse management system and you create a transfer order in SAP, you want the transfer order sent to the warehouse management system immediately.

CAUTION

Criticality is a relative term and has a different meaning for each organization. Changes to master data are less likely to be critical than changes to transactional data. This option should not be used for high volume and noncritical transactions, as it causes performance problems.

The configuration options allow you to control real-time behavior at a very granular level. For example, you can enable all messages going to a system for real-time mode or limit that mode to specific messages only. The following settings achieve the near real-time behavior for a message:

- ◆ For processes triggered from change pointers, schedule the RBDMI-DOC program to execute more frequently (every five minutes) for critical messages.
- ◆ In the partner profile for the outbound message, set the outbound mode to Transfer IDoc Immediately.

Batch Mode Outbound Messages

Batch mode is used for noncritical and high-volume transactions. This mode provides the most control from a performance perspective. The choices are:

◆ **Controlling timing.** The timing for an outbound process has two points of control, depending on the needs of the company.

The first point of control is at the change-pointer level. When master data is changed, the process to analyze change pointers (RBDMIDOC) can be delayed. This type of control achieves the highest performance benefits because there is no load on the system from an ALE perspective. The process can be scheduled to run when the system is not loaded (at night, for example). The only drawback with this approach is that any errors in the outbound process are not discovered until the process is executed.

The second point of control is when IDocs are transferred to the communication layer. This type of control is achieved by setting the output mode in the partner profile to Collect IDocs. The biggest advantage of buffering IDocs at this stage is that they have been generated; thus any errors in the IDoc process should have been discovered. The RSEOUT00 program is then used to transfer buffered IDocs in the database to the communication layer. This program must be scheduled on an as-needed basis. Several instances of this program can be scheduled, each with a different variant and different timing to send the buffered IDocs to the OS layer.

◆ **Controlling error handling.** If errors occur during communication, the system by default creates a background job for each communication failure. This background job retries the process in 5-minute intervals. In a large volume transaction, the system can exhaust all the background jobs in a very short interval and thus prevent other processes from submitting background jobs. The error-handling process in the communication layer is explained in Chapter 20, "The Outbound Process." To avoid this avalanche, the tRFC options in the RFC destination should be set to suppress the automatic start of background jobs. Refer to "Advanced Settings in the RFC Destination" in Chapter 22, "Configuring Basic ALE Components" for details on how to set up tRFC options and programs required to retry failed transmissions.

◆ **Controlling packet size.** The packet size for a message depends on the number of IDocs and the number of data records in each IDoc. You cannot control the number of data records in an IDoc, but you can control the number of IDocs in a packet. The latter, of course, will be small if the number of data records per IDoc is large. The packet size is specified in the outbound record of the partner profile in the Pack Size field.

TIP

An average packet size of 2MB to 3MB uses network resources optimally. Each data record occupies roughly 1K (Kilobyte) and thus you can calculate the number of IDocs in a packet depending on the number of typical data records in your IDoc.

◆ **Controlling parallel processing.** You can specify parallel processing for stand-alone programs that transfer master data, for example, BD10 for material master. On the selection screen for these programs, you can specify the server group and maximum number of objects for each process.

CAUTION

If you have many objects to be transferred and have not configured a separate server group for parallel processing, then you will exhaust all the available processes. The system will slow down considerably and eventually come to a halt.

To specify server group, use transaction RZ12. This option limits the number of processes that are available for parallel processing. Transaction RZ12 is a system-level setting for which you may not have authorization. You will have to work with your Basis staff for this configuration.

Managing Performance of Inbound Processes

As with the outbound process, you can classify the various incoming messages into two broad categories:

◆ Those requiring near-real-time operation

◆ Those that can be posted in batch mode

In the first option, you cannot control performance, but such processes exist, and you need to account for system cycles consumed by such processes. In the second option, you can implement the various methods described earlier.

Near-Real-Time Inbound Messages

In near-real-time mode, when an IDoc is received, it is posted immediately. Although the process is asynchronous, the system feels like a real-time system. This mode is useful for critical ALE processes as described earlier for the outbound process.

 CAUTION

This option should not be used for high volume and noncritical transactions because it will cause performance problems.

The configuration options allow you to control the near-real-time behavior at a very granular level. For example, you can enable all messages from a system to be processed in near-real-time mode, or you can limit the near-real-time mode to specific messages from that system. In the partner profile for the inbound message, select the Process Immediately flag to enable this option.

Batch Mode Inbound Messages

Batch mode is used for noncritical and high-volume transactions. This mode is useful from a performance perspective. The choices to control performance are as follows:

◆ **Controlling timing.** A document is not posted as soon as an IDoc is received. It is batched to run when the system is not busy (such as at night) to pass it to the posting programs. The Processing Option field in the inbound record of the partner profile should be set to Background, No Override with Express Flag.

The RBDAPP01 program passes buffered IDocs in the database to the posting program. This program must be scheduled on an as-needed basis. Several instances of RBDAPP01 can be scheduled to send the buffered IDocs to the posting program based on the IDoc type. Each instance can be scheduled with a different variant. As an example, suppose that inbound sales orders and material master data are buffered. You want to process sales orders once every hour, whereas the material master can wait until the end of the day. Therefore, you need to schedule two instances of RBDAPP01. The first instance runs every hour to process sales orders; the second instance runs, for example, at 10:00 p.m. to process the material master.

◆ **Controlling packet size.** When scheduling the RBDAPP01 program, you can specify the packet size, which defines the number of IDocs that are bundled together for processing in the inbound function module. This approach improves the performance by using one LUW (Logical Unit of Work) for several documents. This option is available for a limited set of inbound function modules.

 TIP

Execute transaction BD51. Entries with a 0 in the Input Type field allow mass processing.

◆ **Controlling parallel processing.** Batched IDocs can be passed to the posting program in a single-threaded or multithreaded mode. In single-threaded mode, the system passes one IDoc packet and waits for the process to finish before the next IDoc packet is sent. In multithreaded mode the IDoc packets are passed to the inbound process simultaneously. If there are several IDoc packets, then the system keeps dispatching until it runs out of packets or the number of processes is exhausted.

You enable this option on the selection screen of the RBDAPP01 program by selecting the Parallel Booking field and specifying the Server Group. Refer to the "Batch Mode Outbound Messages" section earlier in this chapter for details on setting up server groups.

General Strategies

In addition to the various options described earlier to improve the performance of inbound and outbound ALE processes, you should also consider the following items which can help you further improve performance.

◆ **Data Archiving.** Over time the number of IDocs will grow in the system. A large number of IDocs in the database means longer access times and update times. It is best to archive IDocs on a periodic basis to keep the IDoc database under control. The work item log also tends to grow very quickly. The work item log should also be cleaned up on a periodic basis. Refer to Chapter 34, "Archiving IDocs and Deleting Work Items," for details on deleting IDocs and work items.

◆ **Reorganizing change pointers.** The change pointer table can also become very large. SAP provides a program RBDCPCLR to reorganize change pointer tables. This program should also be run periodically to clean up the change pointer tables.

◆ **Performance of ABAP/4 Programs.** IDoc programs have a fairly large amount of executable code. Some sections of the code may not be optimized for batch input, thereby causing long processing times. Several notes in the OSS system discuss how to improve the performance of individual IDoc programs. These patches can be applied to improve the efficiency of the programs.

◆ **Database Performance.** You can significantly improve database operations such as selecting data for IDocs and posting data for IDocs by creating indexes for fields commonly used to access information from the database. This procedure is part of the overall performance-tuning task for the entire system.

Summary

ALE processes are asynchronous, but they consume a lot of system cycles, thus causing performance problems for other processes in the system. Three methods are available for managing performance: (1) controlling the timing of IDoc creation, dispatch of IDocs, and posting of IDocs; (2) controlling the packet size of communication packets and number of IDocs processed by a posting module; and (3) controlling the parallel processing option by creating IDocs in parallel, dispatching IDocs in parallel, and posting IDocs in parallel. In addition, you can configure the error-handling process for failed communications to suppress the automatic start of background jobs for each failed transmission. Apart from these methods, other methods such as archiving IDocs, reorganizing change pointers, program tuning, and database tuning can yield additional performance benefits.

SECTION III

IDocs

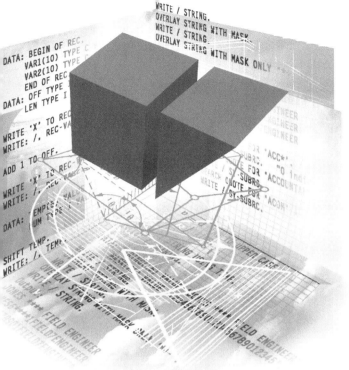

PART 10

IDoc Basics

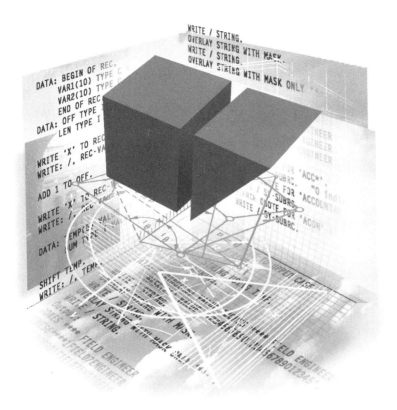

Chapter 29

IDocs from
the Outside

This chapter introduces the concept of IDocs without going into any technical details, starting with the basics of an IDoc from an end user's perspective. Next you'll learn various applications and benefits of the IDoc interface.

What Is an IDoc?

You have probably heard the term IDoc many times. This section should help you understand exactly what an IDoc is, and what it does.

◆ IDoc is not a process. The term IDoc stands for "Intermediate DOCument." An IDoc is simply a data container that is used to exchange information between any two processes that can understand the syntax and semantics of the data. An IDoc is created as a result of execution of an outbound ALE or EDI process. In an inbound ALE or EDI processes, an IDoc serves as an input to create application document.

◆ IDocs are stored in the database. In the SAP system, IDocs are stored in database tables. Several utilities are available to display the information contained in an IDoc and present it in different ways. Refer to "Displaying Information in IDoc Tables", in Chapter 11, "Monitoring the Interface" for details.

◆ Every IDoc has a unique number. When an IDoc is generated in the system, a unique number is assigned to it. This number is unique within a client.

◆ IDocs are independent of the sending and receiving systems. They can be used for SAP to SAP and SAP to non-SAP process communication as long as the participating processes can understand the syntax and semantics of the data.

◆ IDocs are based on EDI standards (ANSI X.12 and EDIFACT). They are closer to the EDIFACT standards than they are to ANSI X.12. The size and format of data elements in an IDoc type are derived from these standards wherever applicable. For example, if a material number is represented by 20 characters in an EDIFACT message, then the corresponding data element in the IDoc is also 20 characters. If there is a conflict in data size between standards, the one with bigger length is adopted. This approach ensures compatibility with most standards.

◆ IDocs are independent of the direction of data exchange. An IDoc can be used by an inbound as well as an outbound process. For example, the

ORDERS01 IDoc is used by the purchasing module to send a purchase order and is also used by the sales and distribution module to accept a sales order. Using this technique avoids creating redundant IDoc types for the same information.

◆ IDocs can be viewed in a text editor and do not contain any binary data. Data is stored in character format in an IDoc. When IDocs are transferred to the operating system, they are stored in a file in text format and can be viewed using a regular text editor. However, the contents make sense only if you understand the structure and format of the data in that IDoc. An example of an IDoc file is provided in the appendix.

IDoc Applications

This section describes various uses of IDocs. Several SAP applications use the robust IDoc interface. The robustness of the interface has been proven since release 2.2, when IDocs were initially used in the EDI process. The following sections describe the various applications of the IDoc interface. In all of these applications, IDocs serve the basic purpose of transferring data from one application to another.

EDI Integration

EDI is the electronic exchange of business documents between trading partners in a common industry standard format such as ANSI X.12 or EDIFACT.

Several applications (purchasing, sales, or shipping) in SAP are enabled for EDI. To use EDI, an application first creates an application document such as a purchase order. Then the EDI interface layer converts the application document (the purchase order) into an IDoc, which is transferred to an EDI subsystem. The EDI subsystem translates the IDoc into an industry-standard format and then transfers it to a business partner over a network.

ALE Integration

ALE (Application Link and Enabling) enables the exchange of data between two SAP systems. This system allows SAP business processes and applications to be distributed across multiple SAP systems. ALE ensures integration in a distributed

SAP environment. The IDoc acts as the data container. The introduction and ever-increasing use of ALE technology has made the IDoc a popular component in SAP.

Legacy System Integration

IDocs are independent of the sending and receiving applications. Hence ALE technology can be used to exchange data between the SAP system and the legacy system. For example, if a legacy application needs to send data to SAP, first the application exports the desired data. This data can be exported in an IDoc format or a proprietary format. Data that is exported in a proprietary format can be converted into an IDoc format using a third-party translator tool. The IDoc data can be passed to the SAP system using the standard ALE/EDI interface layer. This approach allows the use of a functionally rich interface technology to integrate SAP with legacy systems.

Third-Party Product Integration

The products of several CSPs (Complementary Software Partners) use the IDoc interface to communicate with the SAP system. A standard IDoc interface has been defined for numerous applications, such as a warehouse management system, a production planning optimizer, and transportation planning optimizer. This interface describes various IDocs and the sequence in which these IDocs must be communicated to and from the SAP system. CSPs can get their products certified as long as they can support those IDocs in the prescribed sequence. The use of IDocs for integration with third-party products has been the widest implementation of IDocs outside the SAP system.

Workflow Integration

Workflow is used to control and coordinate the sequence of steps in a business process. Workflow uses IDocs in two situations:

- ◆ To enable the form interface
- ◆ To enable data exchange between workflows in a distributed SAP environment

The form interface in workflow enables novice or infrequent users of the SAP system to carry out a task in SAP without logging on to the SAP system. This approach shields users who are less familiar with SAP from the complexities of the SAP system.

The form, which can be developed using a product such as Visual Basic, acts as the front end to the SAP system. When a form is executed, the data from the form is saved in IDoc format. The IDoc is then passed to the SAP system, where it finds a corresponding workflow task that should be started. The data in the IDoc is bound to the workflow process, which then can take necessary action.

The second workflow-related use of IDocs is to support the cross-system exchange of workflows in a distributed SAP environment. If a workflow process is started in one system and one of the steps of this workflow is to be executed in another system, then the data required to execute the step in the second system is made available via IDocs. This strategy is important to support SAP's Business Framework architecture.

SAP R/2 Integration

Starting with release 5.0 of SAP R/2, IDocs have been supported for data transfers. Hence organizations that have part of the business running on R/2 can communicate seamlessly with R/3.

Internet Integration

Web-based applications can be easily integrated into the SAP business process by capturing the data on the Internet through an interface such as a Web browser. The data collected from the Web in HTTP format is converted to IDoc format. The IDoc data can then be passed to SAP applications via the IDoc interface.

OCR Application Integration

OCR (Optical Character Recognition) is a technology that scans and interprets printed matter using pattern recognition. You can integrate an OCR application with SAP via IDocs. Documents in a standard format can be scanned to generate IDocs, which then can be transferred to the SAP system for processing.

ICR Application Integration

A barcode system is an example of ICR (Intelligent Character Recognition) technology. Data encoded using barcodes can be captured and stored as an IDoc, which then can be passed to SAP for further processing.

IDoc Interface Benefits

IDoc benefits are especially important if you are considering using the ALE/IDoc interface for integration with legacy systems. The advantage of using the IDoc interface is that you can use existing tools and utilities for custom IDocs as well.

Independence from Applications

The biggest advantage of using the IDoc interface is that it's an open interface. It's independent of the internal structure used by SAP to store data and independent of the sending and receiving applications. Any application that can understand the syntax and semantics of the data can use the IDoc interface.

For example, one of the published IDoc interfaces integrates SAP with third-party transportation-optimization systems. The transportation interface allows third-party products to optimize the mode of transportation and the best route to transport goods. This interface describes the IDocs that are to be exchanged and the order in which they are exchanged. Any vendor of transportation-optimization application software can use this interface as long as the application can send and receive the specified IDocs in the specified sequence. It does not matter whether the source of the IDoc is an internal application, Internet application, or manually created IDoc.

Communication with Back-Level IDocs

The standard IDocs and the segments within the IDoc have a version associated with them. Each time a standard IDoc or a segment is enhanced, the system assigns it a newer version. Partner applications that were developed using a previous version of the IDocs are fully supported. SAP can generate and process back-level IDocs. This technology ensures backward compatibility, which offers a major advantage over other interfacing techniques that are available in SAP.

For example, assume you have used the standard MATMAS01 IDoc to exchange material master information with your legacy system in version 3.1G. Now you have upgraded to version 3.1H in which the MATMAS01 IDoc has been enhanced. You can continue to use the old version and then decide to switch to the enhanced IDoc later.

Exception Handling via Workflow

Handling exceptions is always tricky and tedious. If you have designed sophisticated applications in the past, you can no doubt relate to the agony of designing a consistent means of logging errors and exceptions across the board, and then developing tools to display that information. In my opinion, about 40 percent of application code is related to error handling in some way.

The standard IDoc interface provides comprehensive log information about the processing of IDocs. Several tools are available to display the logged information. SAP uses the workflow technology to intelligently route an error to the right person. By using the IDoc interface you automatically take advantage of the exception-handling process for your custom IDocs. This feature helps explain the continued growth in the use of the IDoc interface for legacy integration.

Ability to Create and Enhance IDocs

Using standard tools (IDoc editor and Segment editor), you can either enhance standard SAP IDocs or create new IDocs in the system to support custom interfaces. This feature has been the basis for exchanging data with legacy systems using ALE and IDoc technology. The newly developed IDocs integrate seamlessly into the standard EDI interface because they are developed using standard tools provided by the system. IDocs developed in this manner become available in the standard list of SAP IDocs and can take advantage of all the tools that are designed for standard IDocs, such as IDoc monitoring, error handling, and archiving. Custom IDocs are distinguished from SAP IDocs by their names, as they start with Z. You learn about enhancing IDocs in Chapter 31, "Extending and Developing a Basic IDoc Type."

Standard Monitoring Tools

Several tools are available to monitor the state of the system. They range from simple IDoc display to IDoc statistics. These tools provide an overview of the system from which you can repeatedly drill down to view more details. Refer to "Displaying Information in the IDoc Tables," in Chapter 11, "Monitoring the Interface" for details.

Standard Testing Tools

Several tools are available in the system to help with the testing of the IDoc interface. Refer to Chapter 10, "Testing the EDI Interface" for details on various tools available in the system.

IDoc Type Documentation

Each IDoc in the system is thoroughly documented. The usage is detailed down to the field level with possible values for each field and how it affects the process. Because the entire documentation of the ORDERS02 IDoc cannot fit on one screen, a snapshot of the documentation is shown in Figure 29-1. You can obtain complete documentation on any IDoc by using transaction WE60. The report can also be executed to save the output in HTML format or in a format suitable for C programming.

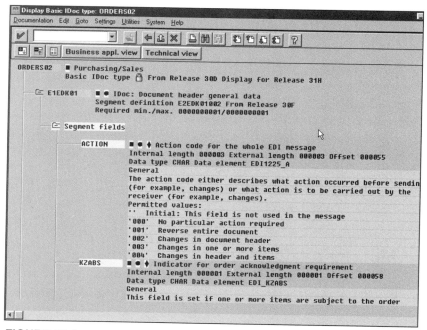

FIGURE 29-1

A snapshot of the documentation for the ORDERS02 IDoc

Reports for the Subsystem

The system generates output from an IDoc structure for the EDI subsystem. You can use this report to load the IDoc structure into the EDI subsystem for the mapping process. A snapshot of the report for the ORDERS02 IDoc is shown in Figure 29-2.

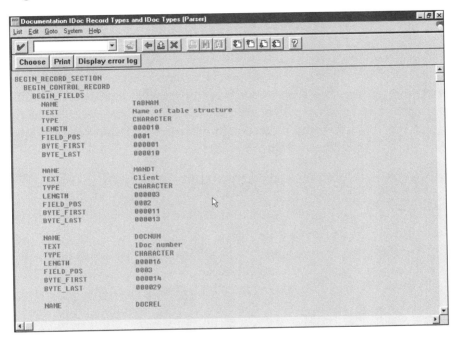

FIGURE 29-2

A snapshot of an IDoc report generated for the subsystem

Restart and Recovery Tools

Restart and recovery from errors are integral parts of the IDoc interface. Again, several tools are provided to restart the process from the point of failure. Refer to Chapter 12, "EDI Process Troubleshooting and Recovery" and Chapter 27, "ALE Process Troubleshooting and Recovery" for details.

Reading IDoc Data

Function modules are available to read and manipulate data in the IDocs. You can use the standard function modules contained in the function group EDI1 to develop custom utilities.

Archiving Tools

Tools are available for miscellaneous tasks such as archiving, data cleanup, and restoring information back into SAP. Chapter 34, "Archiving IDocs and Deleting Workitems" describes the archiving process in detail.

Future IDoc Applications

SAP has endorsed IDoc technology in several areas. It is the communication vehicle for SAP's Business Framework architecture that enables plug-and-play capabilities to integrate applications from different SAP releases and different legacy systems to work together as one logical system. SAP will continue to add functionality, such as better monitoring tools, improved ease of use, and greater robustness, to the standard IDoc interface.

Summary

IDocs act as a container for data that is exchanged between two applications. The IDoc interface is functionally rich and is used in various applications. It provides a robust environment for interfacing SAP with SAP and with external applications. Using the IDoc interface for integrating external applications with the SAP system offers several benefits such as a thoroughly documented interface, independence of the application product, numerous testing and troubleshooting tools, and sophisticated means of error handling via workflow.

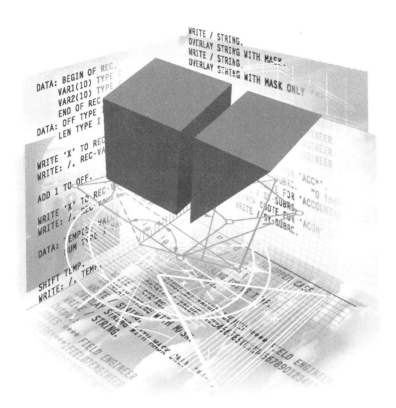

Chapter 30

IDocs on the Inside

By now you should have a good idea of what the IDoc is, what it's used for, and its benefits. It's now time to explore the architecture of an IDoc. The architecture can be best explained by looking at an IDoc's definition and run-time components.

NOTE

Prepare to encounter some technical jargon in this chapter. By its end, you'll be able to converse with any IDoc geek.

Comparing Flat File Structure to IDoc Structure

The best way to explain the IDoc architecture is to compare your legacy world to how SAP implements the same concept in IDoc lingo. An example of a file structure is used for comparative analysis (see Figure 30-1).

Last Name (10)	First Name (10)	Social Security Number (11)	Date of Birth (8)	**Employee Header** (occurs once, required)		
Week Number (1)	Hours Worked (3)	Hourly Rate (3)	Client Site (20)	Work Description (40)	**Weekly Details** (multiple)	
Total Hours (3)	Total Amount (10)	**Summary** (occurs once)				

FIGURE 30-1

A flat file structure for a typical monthly report

Assume that you have an application that records an employee's weekly hours. At the end of the month, a file containing the monthly report data for each employee is sent to an external system. This application has been replaced by the SAP system, and a standard IDoc has been developed to support the process. Following are some properties of the file:

◆ It has three types of records: employee header information, weekly details, and monthly summaries.

◆ Each record type has certain properties, such as whether it's optional or mandatory, number of times it can be repeated, field names, data type for each field, and length of each field.

◆ The client site and work description in the weekly details are not
   always available.

The information in Figures 30-2, 30-3, and 30-4 forms the basis of the
following explanation of how the flat file information matches up with the IDoc
version at definition time and run time.

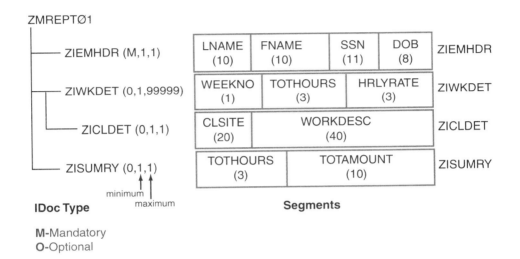

IDoc Type   **Segments**

M-Mandatory
O-Optional

FIGURE 30-2

The IDoc type representation of the flat file structure shown in Figure 30-1

Smith	John	123-45-6789	102668	
1	30	40	Houston Brewery	Beer Testing
2	30	40	Network Computers	High Level Consulting
3	30	50	Network Computers	Programming
4	50	60	DSP Systems	EDI Programming
140			6900	

FIGURE 30-3

An example of the monthly report file for one particular employee

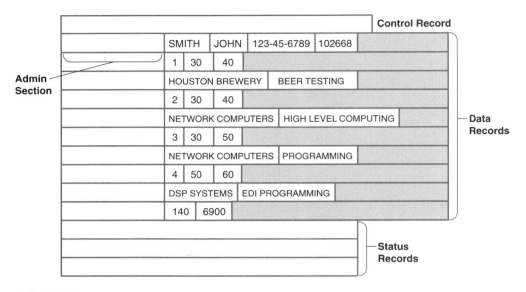

FIGURE 30-4

The IDoc representation of the employee report shown in Figure 30–3

IDoc Definition Components

Each of the following sections begins with a formal definition of the component and then compares the file lingo and the IDoc lingo.

Basic IDoc Type

Basic IDoc type defines the structure and format of the business document that is to be exchanged between two systems. Basic IDoc type is commonly referred to as IDoc type, although there is a technical difference between a basic IDoc type and an IDoc type. The difference is important only when you are dealing with extending an IDoc. A basic IDoc type can refer to an SAP-provided basic IDoc type or a customer-developed basic IDoc type. Therefore, concepts discussed in this chapter with a simple customer-defined basic IDoc type should apply to SAP-provided basic IDoc types also. The basic IDoc type for the monthly report example is shown in Figure 30-5.

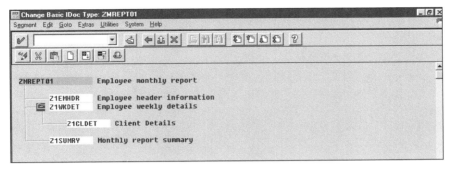

FIGURE 30-5

The basic IDoc type for ZMREPT01

A basic IDoc type has the following characteristics:

◆ **Name.** A basic IDoc type can be assigned up to a thirty-character name in release 4.0 onwards. To encompass all releases, I am using an eight-character name; for example, ZMREPT01 represents the monthly report IDoc type in this example. Custom IDoc types always start with a Z. The last two characters are the version number. After a basic IDoc type is released and you move to a newer version of the SAP system, any changes to the structure of the basic IDoc type will create a new basic IDoc type. In general, the version number is incremented by one. Thus, ZMREPT02 represents an enhanced version of this IDoc. Segments of a previous version are never deleted. This approach is necessary to maintain backward compatibility. In the standard list of IDocs, you will see ORDERS01, ORDERS02, ORDERS03, and so on.

◆ **List of permitted segments.** These segments make up the IDoc structure. The current example has four segments: Z1EMHDR, Z1WKDET, Z1CLDET, and Z1SUMRY.

◆ **Arrangement of segments.** Arrangement specifies the physical sequence and any parent-child relationship in the segments. A parent-child relationship signifies that the child segment cannot exist without the parent and is commonly used for text segments. It gives an IDoc type a hierarchical structure.

NOTE

In the example, the Client Site and Work Description fields were separated out as another segment. The purpose of this design is to present the concept of parent-child relationship; this design should not be used as a guide to break up segments. Candidates for parent-child relationships are discussed in the "Design Guidelines" in the next chapter, "Extending and Developing a Basic IDoc Type."

◆ **Mandatory versus Optional segment.** When used in an IDoc type, each segment has an attribute that defines whether the segment is optional or mandatory. In the example, Z1EMHDR is a mandatory segment because the monthly report will not make sense without the employee's basic information (see Figure 30-6).

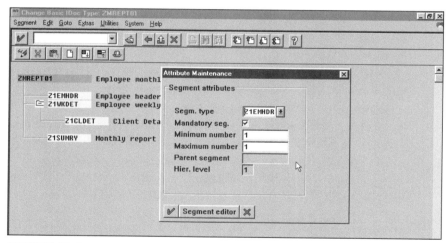

FIGURE 30-6

Attributes of a segment when used in an IDoc type

◆ **Minimum/maximum range for each segment.** When used in an IDoc type, each segment has an attribute that defines the minimum and the maximum number of times a data record corresponding to a segment can exist in an IDoc. In the example, data records corresponding to the Z1WKDET segment can occur multiple times.

An extension type is a customer-defined object that serves as an extension to a basic IDoc type. Extension types are covered in Chapter 31, "Extending and Developing a Basic IDoc Type," where you'll learn how to extend a basic IDoc type.

An IDoc type represents a basic IDoc type combined with an extension type. Again, developing IDoc type is covered in Chapter 31, "Extending and Developing a Basic IDoc Type."

Segments

A segment defines the format and structure of a data record. Segments are reusable components, which means they can be used in more than one IDoc type. A segment consists of various fields that represent data in a data record. Data elements can be of two types: positional or based on qualifiers.

A positional data field occupies a fixed position in an IDoc. In the example, the Z1WKDET segment has fixed fields such as week number and weekly hours. These fields always occur in the same position shown in the diagram.

A field can also be based on a qualifier, in which case the value represented in a field is tied to the qualifier. For example, assume a segment has a date field for three dates: the delivery date, the goods issue date, and the order creation date. Instead of creating three separate fields and assigning a fixed position to each one, the three fields can be represented using two fields, a qualifier field and a date field. The qualifier field identifies the type of date, and the date field contains the date.

Segment Components

A segment in the SAP system is technically implemented as three physically separate pieces, as shown in Figure 30-7:

- Segment type
- Segment definition
- Segment documentation

Segment type is the version independent name of the segment. SAP-provided segment types begin with E1, whereas custom-defined segment types begin with Z1. In the example, Z1EMPHDR and Z1WKDET are segment types. Segment definition is the version-dependent definition of a segment where you specify the fields that belong to the segment.

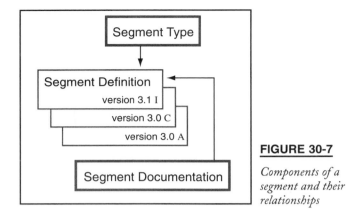

FIGURE 30-7

Components of a segment and their relationships

Segment definitions can be no more than 1,000 bytes. SAP segment definitions start with E2, whereas customer segment definitions start with Z2. The name of a segment definition is 10 characters long and is automatically assigned by the system from the name of the segment type. The last three characters represent the version of the segment. For example, the segment definition for the segment type E1EDKA1 is E2EDKA1.

After a segment is released and a new version of SAP is installed, any change to the segment definition creates a new segment definition, as depicted in Figure 30-8. An example of a standard SAP segment E1EDKA1 with two definitions is shown in Figure 30-9. You will note the last three characters are incremented by one to reflect the new definition. Thus, a segment can have multiple segment definitions. The first segment definition has spaces in the last three characters.

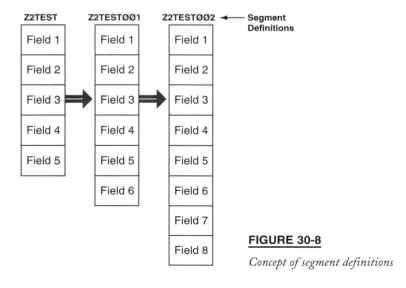

FIGURE 30-8

Concept of segment definitions

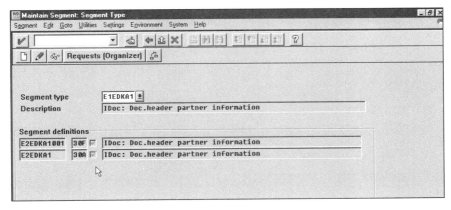

FIGURE 30-9

Segment definitions of SAP segment E1EDKA1

TIP

A field from a previous segment definition cannot be deleted. This prohibition is necessary to maintain backward compatibility.

Segment documentation represents the data dictionary documentation for each field in the segment definition. Segment documentation of SAP-provided segments begins with E3, whereas the segment documentation of customer-defined segment types begins with Z3. There is only one segment documentation per segment.

TIP

When using segments in SAP (for example, in IDoc types and in ABAP/4 programs), you always work with segment types. By default, the type points to the latest segment definition. When you work with segments outside the SAP system, you always use segment definitions. You may have noticed that an IDoc type at the operating system level has data records that begin with E2 instead of the segment types E1.

Data Fields

A data field represents a single data item that is used in a segment. All data field values must be alphanumeric values. The valid data types for a field are CHAR, CLNT, CUKY, DATS, LANG, and NUMC.

IDoc Run-Time Components

An IDoc is an instance of an IDoc type. An IDoc has a record-oriented structure, which is very much like the record structure in a file (refer to Figure 30-4). At run time the following events occur:

- A unique IDoc number is allocated.
- One control record is attached to the IDoc.
- Segments translate into data records.
- Status records are attached.
- Syntax rules are checked. The run time is compared with the definition. Syntax rules checked for IDocs are defined at the end of this chapter.

Although there are several records in an IDoc, they are still classified as one of the three record types. Figure 30-10 shows an IDoc as viewed using the IDoc display tool (transaction WE02 or WE05):

- Control record
- Data record
- Status record

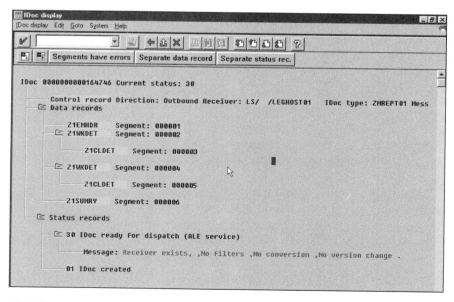

FIGURE 30-10

An IDoc with control record, data records, and status records

NOTE

The IDoc number is the element that ties the control records, data records, and status records together.

Control Record

As the name suggests, the control record contains all of the control information about an IDoc; this information basically includes the IDoc number, sender and receiver information, and information such as the message type it represents and the IDoc type, as shown in Figure 30-11. Think of the control record as the envelope of a letter. By looking at the envelope, you can identify the sender and the recipient.

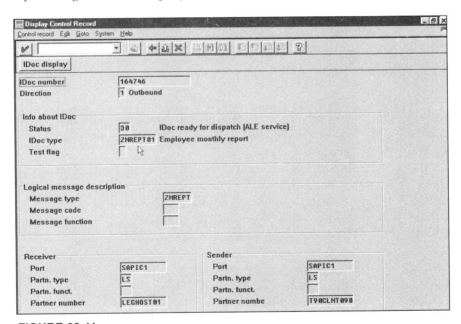

FIGURE 30-11

Control record of an IDoc as viewed using IDoc display tools

 TIP

If you look at an IDoc file in a text editor at the operating system level, the control record is always the first record.

A control record has the following characteristics:

◆ There is one and only one control record per IDoc.

◆ The structure of the control record is the same for all the IDocs and is defined by SAP. Of course, the field values are different.

◆ The control record is stored in the EDIDC table. The key to this table is the IDoc number.

The structure of the EDIDC table is shown in Table 30-1.

Table 30-1 Fields of the Control Record Table

Field Name	Description	Length
MANDT	Client	3
DOCNUM	IDoc number	16
DOCREL	SAP Release of IDoc	4
STATUS	Status of IDoc	2
DOCTYP	IDoc type	8
DIRECT	Direction	1
RCVPOR	Receiver port (SAP System, EDI subsystem)	10
RCVPRT	Partner type of receiver	2
RCVPRN	Partner number of receiver	10
RCVSAD	Receiver address (SADR)	10
RCVSMN	SADR client (receiver)	3
RCVSNA	SADR flag for international receiver address	1
RCVSCA	Communication method (SADR) of the receiver	3
RCVSDF	SADR default flag for the receiver address	1
RCVSLF	Sequential number of the receiver address (SADR)	3
RCVLAD	Logical address of receiver	70
STD	EDI standard	1
STDVRS	Version of EDI standard	6
STDMES	EDI message type	6
MESCOD	Logical message code	3
MESFCT	Logical message function	3
OUTMOD	Output mode	1
TEST	Test flag	1
SNDPOR	Sender port (SAP System, EDI subsystem)	10
SNDPRT	Partner type of sender	2
SNDPRN	Partner number of sender	10

SNDSAD	Sender address (SADR)	10
SNDSMN	SADR client (sender)	3
SNDSNA	SADR flag for international sender address	1
SNDSCA	Communication method (SADR) of sender	3
SNDSDF	SADR default flag for the sender address	1
SNDSLF	Sequential number of the sender address (SADR)	3
SNDLAD	Logical address of sender	70
REFINT	Reference to interchange file	14
REFGRP	Reference to message group	14
REFMES	Reference to message	14
ARCKEY	EDI archive key	70
CREDAT	Date IDoc was created	8
CRETIM	Time IDoc was created	6
MESTYP	Logical message type	6
IDOCTP	Name of basic IDoc type	8
CIMTYP	Name of extension type	8
RCVPFC	Partner function of receiver	2
SNDPFC	Partner function of sender	2
SERIAL	EDI/ALE: Serialization field	20
EXPRSS	Overriding in inbound processing	1
UPDDAT	Date changed: Control record	8
UPDTIM	Time changed: Control record	6

The complete documentation of the control record can be viewed online by using transaction WE61.

Data Records

In an IDoc, data records contain the application data (see Figure 30-4). The employee header information, weekly details, client details, and summary information reside in data records. Figure 30-12 shows a data record viewed using one of the IDoc display tools. A data record has two parts: an administrative section and a data section, as shown in Figure 30-13.

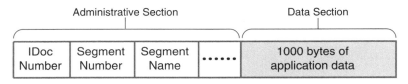

FIGURE 30-12

Details of a data record viewed using the IDoc display tool

FIGURE 30-13

Administrative and data sections in a data record

◆ The administrative section contains the segment name, segment number, and hierarchy level as shown in Figure 30-12.

◆ The data section of a data record is a stream of 1,000 bytes where the actual data resides. The data section is mapped to a segment type, as defined in the administrative section, to interpret the meaning of various data values in a record. For example, the Z1EMHDR segment translates to a data record at run time. The administrative section of this data record contains the segment type Z1EMHDR. The SDATA field of the data record is mapped to Z1EMHDR to interpret the values in the SDATA field.

Data records are stored in the EDID2 table. Table 30-2 lists the fields in the EDID2 table. The complete documentation of the data record can be viewed online by using transaction WE61.

Table 30-2 Fields in the Data Record Table

Field Name	Description	Length
DOCNUM	IDoc number	16
SEGNUM	Number of SAP segment	6
SEGNAM	Name of SAP segment	10
PSGNUM	Number of the hierarchically higher SAP segment	6
HLEVEL	Hierarchy level	2
DTINT2	Length of VARC field	2
SDATA	Application data	1000

Status Records

Status records are attached to an IDoc throughout the process as the IDoc achieves different milestones. At every milestone a status code, date, and time are assigned. The latest status code is also maintained in the control record. Figure 30-14 shows a status record viewed using one of the IDoc display tools.

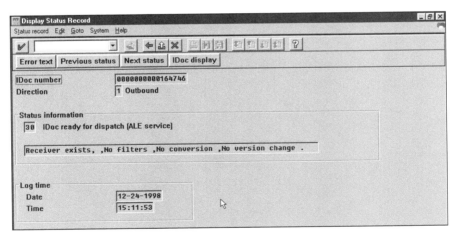

FIGURE 30-14

Details of a status record as viewed using the IDoc display tool

Status records have the following characteristics:

◆ Multiple status records are usually attached to an IDoc.

◆ In outbound processes, after the IDoc is passed from SAP to the subsystem, the subsystem generates the status records and passes them to SAP. For inbound processes, SAP generates the status records.

◆ The system defines numerous status codes. Status codes 01 to 49 are reserved for outbound processes, and those at and above 50 are reserved for inbound processes. A status code has several attributes, as shown in Figure 30-15:

- ◆ A description of the status code
- ◆ Whether it is inbound or outbound
- ◆ A process level that indicates the point in the process at which status code is attached
- ◆ Whether a workflow is to be started (if the status code represents an error)
- ◆ Status group for statistical reporting
- ◆ Whether or not an IDoc is suitable for archiving

A list of status codes and their details can be seen by executing transaction WE47.

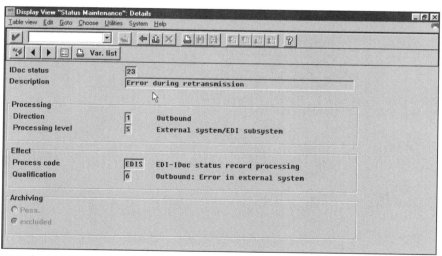

FIGURE 30-15

Details of a status code

Fields in a Status Record

The format of the status record is supplied by SAP, and they are stored in the EDIDS table. The key for this table is the IDoc number, date and time a message was logged, and a status counter. Table 30-3 shows a complete list of fields in the status record.

Table 30-3 Fields in the Status Record Table

Field Name	Description	Length
MANDT	Client	3
DOCNUM	IDoc number	16
LOGDAT	Date of status information	8
LOGTIM	Time of status information	6
COUNTR	EDI status counter	16
CREDAT	Date status record was created	8
CRETIM	Time status record was created	6
STATUS	Status of IDoc	2
UNAME	User name	12
REPID	Program name	8
ROUTID	Name of subroutine (routine, function module)	30
STACOD	Status code	8
STATXT	Text for status code	70
SEGNUM	Number of SAP segment	6
SEGFLD	Field name in SAP segment	10
STAPA1	Parameter 1	20
STAPA2	Parameter 2	20
STAPA3	Parameter 3	20
STAPA4	Parameter 4	20
STATYP	EDI: Type of system error message (A, W, E, S, I)	1

The complete documentation of the status records can be viewed online by using transaction WE61.

Syntax Rules for an IDoc

When any IDoc is created, it goes through a syntax check to ensure its integrity. The syntax of an IDoc is governed by the definition of its IDoc type. The syntax rules checked for an IDoc are as follows:

◆ Only valid segments as defined in the IDoc type are allowed.

◆ Segments specified as mandatory must exist.

◆ A data record cannot exceed the maximum number of repetitions defined for the segment type.

◆ Segments must occur in the same physical sequence defined in the
IDoc structure.

◆ A child segment cannot exist without its parent segment. A parent
segment, however, can exist without a child segment.

Summary

An IDoc type represents the definition component of an IDoc. An IDoc type
is a version-controlled object that defines a list of permitted segments for an
IDoc and the hierarchical arrangement of those segments. A segment consists
of a version-independent segment type, several version-dependent segment
definitions, and a version-independent segment documentation. The IDoc
type effectively defines the syntax of an IDoc.

An IDoc is the run-time instance of an IDoc type. An IDoc consists of a
control record, several data records, and a list of growing status records. The
control record defines control information such as sender and receiver
information. The data records contain the application data that is to be
transferred via IDocs. The status records contain status information (success
or failure) recorded at each milestone in the process. A status record that
represents an error code can contain additional details such as the segment
in error.

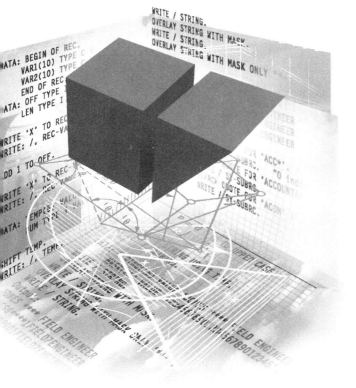

PART

11

Customer Modifications to the IDoc Interface

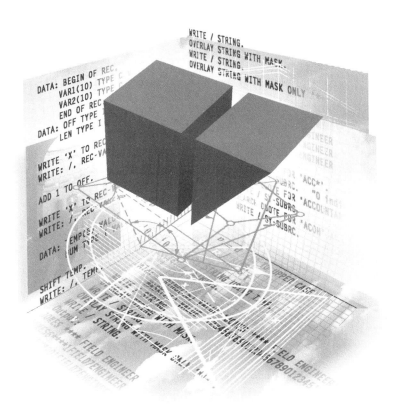

Chapter 31

**Extending and
Developing a
Basic IDoc Type**

Understanding the IDoc development process and knowing how to program IDocs are among the most important skills needed to support an SAP ALE/EDI implementation. IDoc development is a three-step process. First you create a new IDoc or extend an existing IDoc. Then you create programs for the new and/or extended IDocs. Finally, you customize the ALE/EDI interface layer to recognize the IDocs and their programs. The monthly report IDoc introduced in the previous chapter is used to explain the various concepts.

This chapter covers IDoc enhancements. The first step here is deciding whether to extend an existing IDoc or create one from scratch. This decision is not difficult, but sometimes it is fuzzy. The sample scenarios that follow are designed to help you with this decision. In this chapter you walk through the steps to extend and create an IDoc. You learn various design tips to create functionally rich IDocs that make optimum use of segments, thus saving memory and disk space at run time.

Note the distinction between the terms basic IDoc type and IDoc type. Basic IDoc type is for standard SAP IDoc types and customer-developed IDoc types. When basic IDoc types are extended, they are called IDoc types.

Extending versus Developing New IDocs

After careful analysis of the IDoc process and its documentation, you may conclude that the standard basic IDoc type meets most of your requirements. In this case you can simply extend the basic IDoc type. If it does not meet your requirements at all, then you create a new basic IDoc type from scratch.

TIP

Always remember that if you create a basic IDoc from scratch, it is considered a modification and is not supported on an upgrade; on the other hand, extending an IDoc is an enhancement and is supported on an upgrade.

Extending IDocs

You extend a basic IDoc type when it meets most of your requirements. Following are some examples:

◆ You have extended the SAP screens to include custom fields, such as in the material master and customer master. The master data is to be distributed across several SAP systems using ALE. This situation is a perfect candidate and obvious choice for IDoc extension.

◆ Your business partner sends you additional information or expects additional information on an EDI document. For example, your customers may expect an invoice number and date on an advance shipment notice transaction.

◆ You are interfacing with legacy systems using IDocs. One of the basic IDoc types fits your needs except for some elements that are specific to your business environment. For example, if you are sending sales orders to your legacy system and it requires engineering information for the materials ordered, you can extend the sales order IDoc to include engineering information.

Creating IDocs

You create a new basic IDoc type when the standard basic IDoc types do not meet your business needs as is or by extending them. Consider the following situations:

◆ New basic IDoc types are developed especially for interfaces to legacy systems or third-party products using ALE. Data to be exchanged with legacy systems is usually in a proprietary format and does not map one to one with a standard SAP business process.

◆ A basic IDoc type is created when an existing IDoc cannot be mapped to an EDI transaction that you want to exchange with your business partner. For example, to exchange EDI transaction 863 (Report of test results, which is not supported in SAP) with your business partner, you would have to create an IDoc.

◆ You want to synchronize master data between two SAP systems, and this master data is not supported in the standard system. For example, to exchange condition record data, which is not supported in the system, you would create an IDoc from scratch.

 TIP

The number of basic IDoc types has increased with every new version of SAP. You should check with SAP to see whether an IDoc is under construction for a future release. If so, examine your requirements for an alternative (possibly interim) solution. It is always advisable to use a standard process whenever and wherever applicable.

> **CAUTION**
>
> Because developing new IDocs is considered a modification—and therefore not supported on upgrade—you have to review and test your process again after you upgrade.

Creating a New IDoc Type

The process of creating IDocs is presented first because it involves more concepts. Some of the details presented here are also applicable to the IDoc extension process discussed later in the chapter.

To develop a new basic IDoc type from scratch, you need to understand various IDoc design issues. You need to be aware of what is and what is not permitted in the system. You can map your business data into an IDoc in several ways. The first step is to analyze the requirements to determine the best possible way to group data into an IDoc. The next section presents several design tips to help you get started. Then the steps to create an IDoc are described. They guide you through the complete process, addressing important issues as they arise.

The process of creating a new basic IDoc type is the same for EDI, ALE, or an external process such as legacy or third-party applications.

Design Guidelines

Here are some design guidelines to help you during the creation of a basic IDoc type:

- ◆ Develop an IDoc type for a function, not for a specific application. For example, the ORDERS02 IDoc is designed for the order process and not specifically for the sales order entry application. This IDoc is used for several documents such as purchase order, sales order, order response, and order change. You should follow a similar strategy when creating a new basic IDoc type.

- ◆ Use industry standards whenever possible for your data elements. If you are designing an IDoc for a business document, consult the EDI standards for appropriate length and data types. Use ISO (International Standards Organization) codes for fields such as measurement units and currencies.

◆ Organize the document to contain header information, detail information, and summary information. This technique is commonly used for SAP documents.

◆ Do not repeat a segment type in an IDoc definition. For example, consider the monthly report basic IDoc type (ZMREPT01) from the previous chapter. If you were asked to also add the client information (Z1CLDET) of the last client to the summary information, your instincts would be to attach the Z1CLDET segment to the summary segment (Z1SUMRY). SAP does not permit placing a segment type more than once in the definition of an IDoc type. Because you cannot use the same segment type more than once in an IDoc definition, the only alternative is to create a new segment type with the same information. This requirement may seem like a limitation, but it really is not. You can alter your design a little bit or use the approach suggested above. The fact that SAP has designed its IDocs with the same limitation suggests that it is not a problem.

CAUTION

Repeating a segment type should not be confused with the Maximum Number field in the attributes for the segment type. The Maximum Number field specifies how many data records for a segment type are permitted at run time.

◆ Use the parent-child relationship when you are going to permit several entries of the same type in one IDoc. For example, the current design of the ZMREPT01 IDoc allows only one employee per IDoc, as shown in Figure 31-1. If you want to support multiple employees per IDoc to improve performance or because it makes sense for your business, then the IDoc design would use the parent-child relationship, as shown in Figure 31-2.

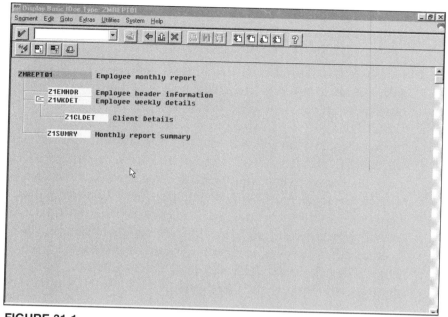

FIGURE 31-1

Structure of the monthly report basic IDoc type for single employee

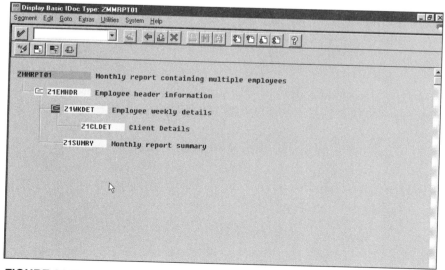

FIGURE 31-2

Structure of the monthly report basic IDoc type to support multiple employees

◆ Avoid having too many mandatory segments. A segment should be "truly" mandatory and not used because the person giving you the requirements thinks it is necessary. Having extra mandatory segments reduces the reusability of the IDoc. If a segment is mandatory, then every process that uses the IDoc must supply the segment. For example, in the monthly report IDoc, the weekly details segment (Z1WKDET) seems to be mandatory. Consider another process that could make use of this IDoc to send just employee header information and summary information. If the weekly segment were mandatory, then the IDoc would not be reusable in that way. By contrast, the employee header information is truly mandatory because this sort of data will not make sense without knowing who it belongs to.

◆ Do not make segments larger than 1,000 bytes. Try to split the segments into functionally separate segments when a segment definition exceeds 1,000 bytes. If not, then split the segment into two segments.

◆ Combine IDoc segments that are functionally similar into one segment whenever possible. Remember, each data record occupies 1,000 bytes at run time. It does not matter if the record has 1 field or 50 fields. Do not overdo it, though—leave enough room for expansion.

◆ Create segments that can be reused by other IDocs.

◆ Avoid qualifiers. They are difficult to document and manage. They do not necessarily save any space unless a field has too many variations of the same type. For example, assume a segment has several G/L account fields for each type of account in a company (for example, credit account, debit account, vendor account, asset account, reconciliation account). You could certainly have a separate field for each type of account but in this scenario it makes sense to use a qualifier. A qualifier can represent the type of G/L account, and a field can be assigned for the G/L account number.

Formatting Guidelines

The following guidelines are useful when you are creating segments and when you are programming for your IDocs:

◆ Data fields in a segment can contain only alphanumeric values. Table 31-1 contains the allowed data types for fields in a segment definition.

Table 31-1 Allowed Data Types for Segment Fields

Data Type	Description
CHAR	Character strings
CLNT	Client
CUKY	Currency key, referenced by CURR fields
DATS	Date field (YYYYMMDD) stored as char(8)
LANG	Language key
NUMC	Character field with only digits
TIMS	Time field (HHMMSS), stored as char(6)

◆ Fields should be left-aligned. Character fields are automatically left-aligned, but number values when assigned to a character field are padded with spaces on the left. These spaces must be removed from the fields programmatically using the condense command.

◆ Dates are represented as YYYYMMDD.

◆ Data is not case sensitive.

◆ Negative numbers are represented with a dash symbol at the end. Thus −123 is written as 123-.

◆ Numbers with fractional values use a period to represent the decimal point. Thus 123.45 represents 123 dollars and 45 cents.

◆ Floating point numbers also use a period to represent the decimal point. Thus 123.45 is written as 1.2345E+02.

◆ No formatting is used to separate values in the thousands. For example, 29,000.00 will be written as 29000.00 without the comma.

Creating a New Basic IDoc Type

The six steps to create a basic IDoc type follow.

Step 1: Data Analysis

In this stage you analyze data that needs to be exchanged between the two processes. Using the guidelines mentioned earlier in the chapter, develop a conceptual picture of the IDoc on a piece of paper.

Follow a top-down approach if you are starting at a business-document level. Break the document into segments and group the segments that belong together into a segment group. Identify fields in a segment and their data type. Identify any parent-child relationships.

Follow a bottom-up approach if you are starting at the field level. You have been given a document that contains various values that must be exchanged between two systems. Group fields that are functionally related into segments. Group those segments into segment groups and arrange them in an IDoc type. Identify any parent-child relationship. After you complete the analysis, you are ready to build your basic IDoc type.

TIP

You can use standard SAP segments in your custom IDocs, so feel free to have a mix of custom segments and SAP segments. You can use the search tool (transaction WE32) for a list of matching segments and IDoc types for a given field.

Step 2: Create Data Elements

The second step is to create data elements for the segment definition. The need to create new data elements is minimal because if you are extracting data from SAP to put into an IDoc, the data already exists in the database and is represented by a data element. You need to create new data elements in the following cases only:

◆ A data element in SAP does not use one of the allowed data types for IDoc segments. For example, the Future Price field (ZKPRS) in the E1MBEWM segment of the MATMAS02 basic IDoc type uses data type CHAR12, instead of ZKPRS. The reason is that the data type for ZKPRS is CURR (Currency) which is not allowed in a segment definition.

◆ A field in SAP is smaller in length than the industry standard (this occurrence is rare).

Follow these steps to create new data elements:

1.   Execute transaction SE11. Enter a data element name in the Object Name field and click on the Create button.

2. Enter the various attributes (see Figure 31-3). The domain should be based on one of the allowed data types, as shown in Table 31-1.

3. Save your entry and generate the data element.

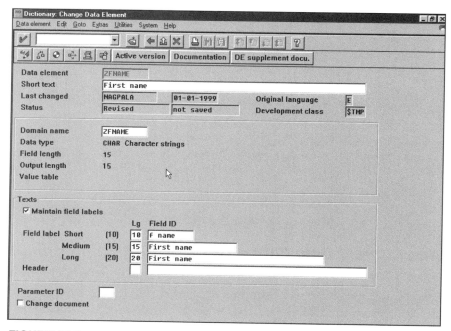

FIGURE 31-3

Specify values for a data element to be used in a segment.

Step 3: Create Segments

Segments are created by using the Segment Editor tool. This tool can be started by executing transaction WE31 (from the Area menu for EDI, choose Development, IDoc Segments). This tool is very similar to the screen for creating a table or a structure. However, you should not attempt to use the create table or change table transaction to change or create segment structures.

Follow these steps to create a segment:

1. Execute transaction WE31. Enter the name for your segment type (it must start with Z1) and click on the Create icon. The system prompts you with the name of the development class it uses for the segment. The development class is derived from the SEGDVCLASS entry in the EDIADMIN table, but you can override the default value.

2.   Enter the values in the various fields. You are now maintaining the first segment definition. The system automatically assigns a name to the segment definition based on the segment type. Figure 31-4 shows the segment definition Z2WKDET, which is based on segment type Z1WKDET.

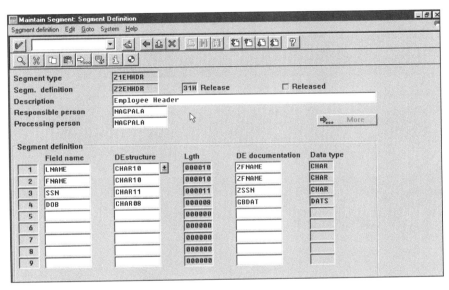

FIGURE 31-4

Maintain segment definition in the segment editor.

 NOTE

An additional column, DE Documentation, appears in the documentation of the data field. You normally enter the same value here as you entered in the DE Structure column. The DE Documentation entry is different only if you want to assign documentation based on a different data element. For example, if you created a new data element as described in "Step 2: Create Data Elements," then the two values could be different.

3.   Save your values and generate the segment definition. Once you save your segment, return to the previous screen and enter a description for your segment type, as shown in Figure 31-5. Click on the Save icon, and you are done. Use the same procedure to create other segments for your IDoc type.

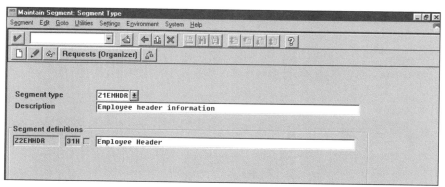

FIGURE 31-5

The segment editor, showing the segment definition for the segment type

 TIP

After saving your entry, you can click on the Check button to test the integrity of your segment. If one of your data elements is not generated or active, the system will report problems.

Step 4: Create Basic IDoc Type

Once you have developed all the needed segment types, you are ready to create the basic IDoc type. You use the IDoc editor, which is started with transaction WE30 (from the Area menu for EDI, choose Development, IDoc type), to create a basic IDoc type.

Follow these steps to create a basic IDoc type:

1. Execute transaction WE30. Enter the name for your basic IDoc type (it must start with a Z), select the Basic IDoc Type radio button, and click on the Create icon.

2. On the next screen, select the Create New option and enter a description for your basic IDoc type, as shown in Figure 31-6. Press Enter.

3. Click on the IDoc name and click on the Create icon. The system prompts you to enter a segment type and its attributes (see Figure 31-7). Choose the appropriate values and press Enter. The system transfers the name of the segment type to the IDoc editor.

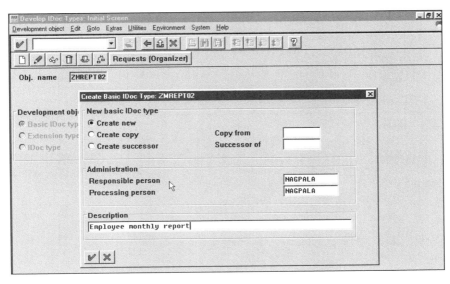

FIGURE 31-6

Specify the method of creation and description for your IDoc type.

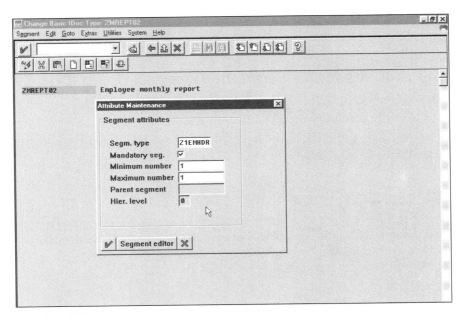

FIGURE 31-7

IDoc editor—specify segment attributes for a segment used in the IDoc type.

4. To add additional segments, click on the segment created in step 3 and repeat the procedure described in step 3. Note that after you create the first segment, the system prompts you for the level (same level or child) at which you want to create the next new segment.

TIP

The IDoc editor has cut and paste features. If you create a segment at the wrong level or in a wrong sequence, you can cut and paste the segments to position them correctly.

5. Save your basic IDoc type.

TIP

From the initial screen, you can click on the Check button to test the integrity of your IDoc. The system reports any problems that it may find. You can ignore the warnings due to segments not being released, but you should investigate any other problems that are reported.

Step 5: Release the Segment Type and Basic IDoc Type

When you are satisfied with your IDoc structure and segments, you can release them formally to signify their completion and make them available for transport to the test and production systems. First you release segments, and then you release the basic IDoc type.

CAUTION

The system checks the release authorizations as you enter the editor. If you do not have authorization, the system grays out the release options. The authorization object checked is S_IDOCDEFT and activity 43.

To release a segment, execute transaction WE31. Enter the segment type and choose Goto, Release. The system enables a check box in the segment definitions block. You can select the check box and save your entry.

To release a basic IDoc type, execute transaction WE30. Enter the basic IDoc type in the Obj. Name field and choose Extras, Release Type. The system informs you that it is about to release the object. Confirm the entry, and the basic IDoc type is released. This step prevents further modifications to the basic IDoc type.

TIP

As long as you are on the same release of the SAP system in which the segments or basic IDoc type were originally created, you can always cancel the release of a basic IDoc type or a segment type. Canceling a released object allows you to modify it. The steps to cancel a release for a segment type are same as the release procedure. Uncheck the Release check box.

CAUTION

If you are in the process of developing new segments and basic IDoc types and you upgrade to a new version of SAP, the segments are assumed released and you cannot delete any fields when you are on the new version of SAP. Any changes you make to a segment from this point on will give it a new segment definition. Therefore, you must make sure that segments have the correct fields before you upgrade.

Step 6: Transport Segments and Basic IDoc Types

Changes to basic IDoc types and segments are automatically recorded in a change request. After you transport the objects, you can also manually retransport them from the segment editor and IDoc editor screens by choosing Segment, Transport and Development Object, Transport, respectively. Transporting a segment transports all the segment definitions and documentation, but transporting an IDoc does not automatically transport all the segments.

CAUTION

If you release a basic IDoc type without releasing its segments and then transport the basic IDoc type, the segments are not transported.

Extending a Basic IDoc Type

To extend a basic IDoc type, you also need to understand what is permitted and what is not. The concept of extending a basic IDoc type means adding one or more custom segments to one or more existing SAP segments of a basic IDoc type, as shown in Figure 31-8. I have seen situations in which users have misinterpreted the IDoc extension process to mean extending the segment tables using the "append structure" concept. This technique is not permitted (see the appendix).

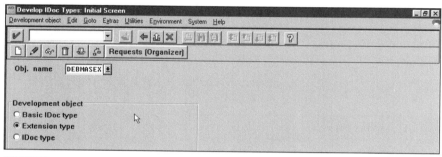

FIGURE 31-8

A basic IDoc type combined with an IDoc extension yields an IDoc type.

The formal procedure of extending a basic IDoc type is as follows:

1. Start with data analysis. Identify a segment in the basic IDoc type that needs to be extended.

2. Create a custom segment with your fields.

3. Create an IDoc extension that ties the custom segment to the SAP segment which is to be extended.

4. Tie the extension to a basic IDoc type to create an IDoc type. Pay attention to the careful difference in terminology, which was discussed earlier.

The design and formatting guidelines presented earlier in the IDoc creation process apply to the extension process as well. The steps, however, are different.

 NOTE

The process of extending a basic IDoc type is the same for EDI, ALE, or an external process such as legacy or third-party applications.

Assume that you have extended the customer master screen to include additional sales data information about your customer. This includes two custom fields: delivery priority and customer ranking. In order to distribute customer master data between two SAP systems, you need to also distribute information in the two custom fields. The steps described below walk you through the process of extending the basic IDoc type for customer master (DEBMAS01).

Step 1: Data Analysis

In this step you analyze the basic IDoc type and identify segments that need to be extended. In this example, the standard SAP segment E1KNVVM contains the sales data information and Z1KNVVM is a custom segment that contains user-defined fields. Thus DEBMAS01 is extended by extending the E1KNVVM segment. The segment to be extended is called the reference segment.

Step 2: Create Custom Segments

In this step you create the custom segment Z1KNVVM. The Z1KNVVM segment contains two fields: ZZDELPRTY (Delivery priority) and ZZRANK (Customer Rank). Refer to "Step 3: Create Segments" under "Steps to Create a New Basic IDoc Type" earlier in the chapter for details. Before you create your custom segment you will also need to create data elements for the two fields ZZDELPRTY and ZZRANK. Refer to "Step 2: Create Data Elements" under "Steps to Create a New Basic IDoc Type" earlier in the chapter for details.

Step 3: Create an IDoc Extension

You use the IDoc editor, which is started with transaction WE30 (from the Area menu for EDI, choose Development, IDoc type) to create an IDoc extension.

Follow these steps to create an IDoc extension:

1. Start the IDoc editor. Enter the name for your IDoc extension in the Obj. Name field. This entry can be any meaningful name and does not have to start with a Z. Click on the Extension Type radio button and then click on the Create icon.

2. On the next screen (see Figure 31-9), click on the Create New button and enter a description for your extension. Press Enter.

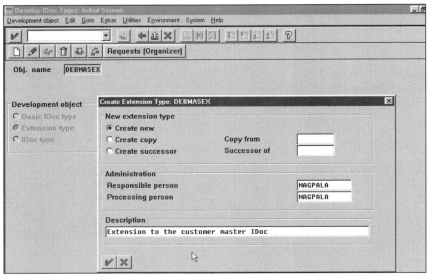

FIGURE 31-9

Specify the creation method and enter an appropriate description of the extension here.

3. Click on the extension type name and then click on the Create icon. The system prompts you to enter a reference segment type. This item is the segment that you want to extend. In the example, you will enter the E1KNVVM as the reference segment, as shown in Figure 31-10. You can repeat this step for additional reference segments that you want to include in this extension.

 NOTE

The reference segment is usually an SAP segment. Theoretically, you could extend custom-defined segments, but extending your own segments doesn't make much sense.

4. Now you tie the custom segment to the reference segment identified in the previous step. Click on the reference segment and then click on the Create icon. The system informs you that the segment is added as a child segment. Confirm the entry, and the system prompts you with a dialog box to enter the name of the custom segment and various attributes such as maximum number and mandatory versus optional, as shown in Figure 31-11. Enter the appropriate values and press Enter. Repeat this step for any additional segments that you may have in your extension.

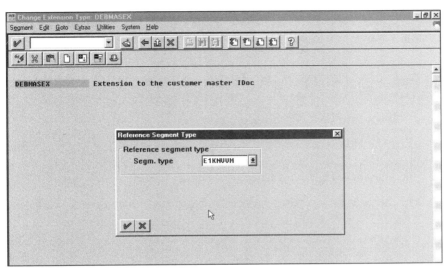

FIGURE 31-10

Specify the reference segment in the IDoc extension.

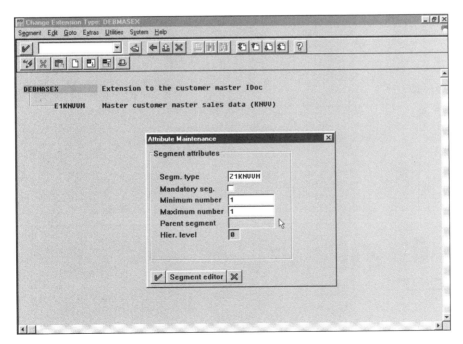

FIGURE 31-11

Specify attributes for the custom segment used to extend a reference segment.

5. Save your extension. The system may prompt you for a change request if the Changes to Repository Objects option is turned on.

Step 4: Create the IDoc Type

Now you will create the IDoc type, which is basically a sum of the basic IDoc type and the extension. Follow these simple steps:

1. Start the IDoc editor. Enter the name for your IDoc type in the Obj. Name field. This entry can be any meaningful name that starts with a Z. Click on the IDoc Type button and then click on the Create icon.

2. On the next screen (see Figure 31-12), the system prompts you to enter the basic IDoc type and the extension type. Enter appropriate values. The extension type was created in "Step 4: Create an IDoc Extension." The system now checks to make sure that the reference segments in the extension type are present in the basic IDoc type.

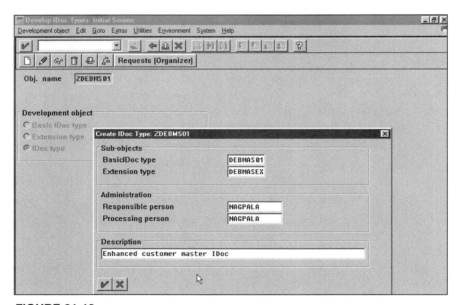

FIGURE 31-12

Specify the basic IDoc type and extension type to create an extended IDoc type.

3. Press Enter, and the system displays the extended IDoc type (see Figure 31-13). You can expand the reference segment. The system shows the custom segment as a child of the reference segment. It is displayed in white background to distinguish it from the SAP segments.

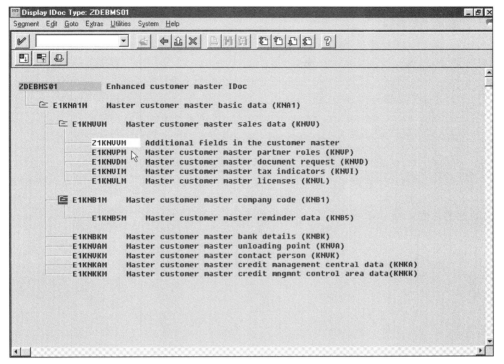

FIGURE 31-13

Custom segment included in the extended IDoc type

Step 5: Release the Custom Segment and IDoc Extension

IDoc extensions and customer segments are to be released, but the IDoc types are not designed to be released. An IDoc type is merely a combination of the basic IDoc type and the extension type. The steps are the same as defined in step five in "Create a New Basic IDoc Type" earlier in the chapter.

Step 6: Transporting Segments, IDoc Definition, and IDoc Type

It is necessary to transport the IDoc extension and IDoc type to make them available on the production system. The steps are the same as defined in step six in "Creating a New Basic IDoc Type" earlier in the chapter.

Summary

The IDoc interface allows you to extend basic IDoc types or create new basic IDoc types to meet your business needs. Extending existing IDocs is preferable to creating new IDoc types because extended IDocs are supported during an upgrade. IDocs are extended mainly to accommodate additional functionality in the business process, such as custom fields in the material master data. New IDocs are mainly created for integration with legacy systems or third-party products.

A functionally rich IDoc requires a good amount of analysis and design. After the analysis, segments are created using the segment editor, and IDocs are created and extended using the IDoc editor. After segments and IDoc objects are created and tested, they are released to prevent further modifications. Then they are ready for transport to the production environment.

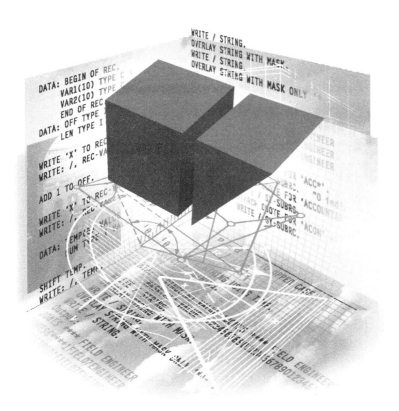

Chapter 32

Programming in the IDoc Interface

This chapter covers the various situations in which you may have to program in the IDoc interface. Program structure varies depending on the type of process (inbound or outbound) and techniques used in the process to generate and process the IDocs such as user exits, message control, and change pointers. Although a major programming task is populating and processing the IDoc data, programs can also be written to customize existing process flow and add custom checks. This chapter not only shows you how to write the programs but also discusses the important issues that you need to consider when designing your programs such as strategic location of user exits and steps to locate user exits. Sample programs are provided for reference.

Writing ABAP/4 Programs

The programming tasks in the IDoc interface can be categorized as follows:

◆ **Programs for custom IDocs.** These programs are specifically written for new basic IDoc types developed for your process. A separate program is written for the outbound process and the inbound process. The design and program logic of these programs mimics the standard SAP programs for the outbound and inbound processes.

◆ **Programs for IDoc extensions.** These programs are written specifically for extended IDocs. Standard user-exits are available in the outbound IDoc process for populating data in the extended segments. Similarly, user-exits are available in the inbound IDoc process for reading data in the extended segments and posting the data.

◆ **Programs to enhance the process.** These programs are written to enhance the process flow for existing IDocs and add custom checks to the IDoc interface. These programs also utilize the user-exits to implement these checks.

Programs for Custom Basic IDoc Types

Programs for Custom IDocs are considered modifications to the SAP system. They are written just like the standard SAP programs for the basic IDoc types. Therefore, the best approach is to copy an existing program of a similar scenario and modify it to suit your needs. The following sections describe various types of outbound and inbound programs written for basic IDoc types.

Outbound Programs for Custom Basic IDoc Types

Outbound programs are also referred to as IDoc generation programs. In this section you learn how these programs are designed to extract data from an SAP document and create an IDoc. The outbound programs that generate IDocs come in three flavors based on the triggering mechanism used for the IDoc generation program: outbound IDocs from message control, outbound IDocs from stand-alone programs, and outbound IDocs from change pointers.

In these programs, the basic principle or core logic for building the IDoc data is the same; the interface of these programs is different. These programs use the monthly report IDoc type (ZMREPT01) developed in the preceding chapter as the IDoc to be generated. The three variations of the outbound programs are described next.

Here's a brief rundown:

◆ **Outbound IDocs from message control.** These programs are implemented as function modules and are specifically designed for applications that make use of the message control component to generate IDocs. The interface for these programs is preset by SAP. The message control component is mainly used by EDI processes for transactional data, though ALE can also make use of the message control for distributing transactional data. For example, the purchase order process uses message control to generate an IDoc for a purchase order going out via EDI. Purchase orders can also be transferred to an external system via ALE.

◆ **Outbound IDocs from stand-alone programs.** These programs are developed as stand-alone programs with their own interface. They can be implemented as reports or separate function modules that can be called from another program. These programs are mainly used for master data distribution in ALE. For example, the process to transfer material master data from one SAP system to another uses this technique to create IDocs.

Some EDI processes also use this technique. For example, the FI transactions use this technique to generate IDocs for the remittance advice and payment order transactions.

◆ **Outbound programs from change pointers.** These programs are specifically designed for generating IDocs from change pointers. The programs are implemented as function modules and their interface is set by SAP. These programs are mainly used for master data distribution based on changes made to the master data. For example, you can generate an IDoc when a material master is changed or customer master is changed.

An Outbound Program Triggered from Message Control

This technique is mainly used for creating IDocs for transactional data. EDI-enabled applications use it to generate IDocs for business documents such as purchase orders and sales orders. This technique is also used in some ALE scenarios to distribute transactional data between different SAP systems. Figure 32-1 depicts how the IDoc generation logic is implemented as a separate piece and invoked from an outbound process that uses Message control to generate an IDoc.

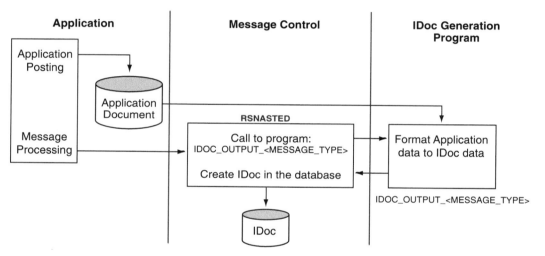

FIGURE 32-1

IDoc generation program invoked from the Message control component

In the message control, the RSNASTED program is used to process outbound ALE and EDI messages. The RSNASTED program calls the appropriate IDoc generation program (implemented as, function module) for a message. The key of the application document to be extracted is passed in the NAST entry, which is one of the parameters of the function module. The function module builds the IDoc control record and the data records. The results are passed back to the RSNASTED program, which creates a physical IDoc in the SAP system.

The function modules are generally named IDOC_OUTPUT_<message_type> for SAP messages and Z_IDOC_OUTPUT_<message_type> for customer messages. This is a guideline and not a rule.

Interface for the Function Modules

The interface for the function modules follows. You can see the interface at work in the corresponding sample code.

- ◆ **IMPORTING Parameters.** The following parameters are passed to the function module by the message control component:

  OBJECT. This parameter is the NAST entry that contains the key of the document to be extracted. In the example, an IDoc is to be generated for John Smith. The NAST entry contains the key to identify John's record, which is his Social Security number, in the system.

  CONTROL_RECORD_IN. This parameter is the control record information that is prefilled with information that is known to the calling program, including sender system, receiving partner, and IDoc type.

- ◆ **EXPORTING Parameters.** The following parameters are returned by your function module to the calling program:

  OBJECT_TYPE. This parameter represents the business object name assigned to the application document. This parameter is used to create a link between the IDoc and the application document.

  CONTROL_RECORD_OUT. This parameter is the control record with all the information filled out, including message type, IDoc type, direction, and receiver.

- ◆ **TABLES Parameter.** The following internal table is passed into and out of a function module: **INT_EDIDD.** This parameter is the internal table for data records that are filled by the function module. Data records are filled in the same physical sequence as they are defined in the IDoc type.

- ◆ **EXCEPTIONS.** Exceptions convey any problems to the calling program. The system starts a workflow for these exceptions.

Program Flow

The program logic contains the following blocks:

1. Copy incoming control record information to the outgoing control record.
2. Populate remaining fields in the control record.
3. Select application data from the database using the object key passed in the NAST record.
4. Populate the internal table of data records (int_edidd) with the various segments.

TIP

Before you start developing your program, copy an existing program and make use of its interface.

5.   Return control to the calling program. When the control comes back to the message control component, an IDoc is created in the database.

The program in Listing 32-1 generates the monthly report IDoc ZMREPT01 from message control.

Listing 32-1

```
FUNCTION Z_IDOC_OUTPUT_ZMREPT.
*"----------------------------------------------------------------
*"*"Local interface:
*"      IMPORTING
*"             VALUE(CONTROL_RECORD_IN) LIKE  EDIDC STRUCTURE   EDIDC
*"             VALUE(OBJECT) LIKE  NAST STRUCTURE   NAST
*"      EXPORTING
*"             VALUE(OBJECT_TYPE) LIKE  WFAS1-ASGTP
*"             VALUE(CONTROL_RECORD_OUT) LIKE  EDIDC STRUCTURE   EDIDC
*"      TABLES
*"             INT_EDIDD STRUCTURE   EDIDD
*"      EXCEPTIONS
*"             ERROR_MESSAGE_RECEIVED
*"----------------------------------------------------------------


*----------------------------------------------------------------
* Constants
*----------------------------------------------------------------

DATA:
*      segment names
       C_HEADER_SEGMENT            LIKE EDIDD-SEGNAM VALUE 'Z1EMHDR',
       C_WEEKLY_DETAILS_SEGMENT    LIKE EDIDD-SEGNAM VALUE 'Z1WKDET',
       C_CLIENT_DETAILS_SEGMENT    LIKE EDIDD-SEGNAM VALUE 'Z1CLDET',
       C_SUMMARY_SEGMENT           LIKE EDIDD-SEGNAM VALUE 'Z1SUMRY',
*      idoc type
```

```
        C_MONTHLY_REPORT_IDOC_TYPE LIKE EDIDC-IDOCTP VALUE 'ZMREPT01',
*     message type
        C_MONTHLY_REPORT_MESSAGE    LIKE EDIDC-MESTYP VALUE 'ZMREPT'.


*-----------------------------------------------------------------------
* Data declarations
*-----------------------------------------------------------------------
* field string for the data records
DATA: FS_INT_EDIDD LIKE EDIDD.
* employee header data
DATA: FS_EMPHDR_DATA LIKE Z1EMHDR.
* employee weekly details data
DATA: FS_WEEKDET_DATA LIKE Z1WKDET.
* client details data
DATA: FS_CLIENTDET_DATA LIKE Z1CLDET.
* employee monthly summary data
DATA: FS_SUMMARY_DATA LIKE Z1SUMRY.
* total hours and amount for the summary segment
DATA: TOTAL_HRS_MONTH TYPE I,
      TOTAL_AMT_MONTH TYPE I.
* object key (Social security number for the employee)
DATA: P_SSN LIKE ZEMPDETAIL-SSN.
*-----------------------------------------------------------------------
* Database Tables
*-----------------------------------------------------------------------
* Application data tables
tables: zempdetail, zempwkdet.


*-----------------------------------------------------------------------
* Internal tables
*-----------------------------------------------------------------------
DATA:
*     weekly details - appplication data
      IT_WKDET LIKE ZEMPWKDET OCCURS 0 WITH HEADER LINE.
*-----------------------------------------------------------------------
* Program logic
*-----------------------------------------------------------------------


*********************Select Application Data***************************

* determine the object key from the NAST entry
P_SSN = OBJECT-OBJKY.   " employees social security number
```

```
SELECT SINGLE * FROM ZEMPDETAIL WHERE SSN = P_SSN.
SELECT * FROM ZEMPWKDET INTO TABLE IT_WKDET WHERE SSN = P_SSN.


*********************Build Control Record******************************

CLEAR CONTROL_RECORD_OUT.
* copy control record from the input parameters to the output parameters
MOVE CONTROL_RECORD_IN TO CONTROL_RECORD_OUT.
* Fill control record information
CONTROL_RECORD_OUT-DIRECT = '1'.
control_record_out-mestyp = c_monthly_report_message.
control_record_out-idoctp = c_monthly_report_idoc_type.
control_record_out-rcvprt = 'LS'.
CONTROL_RECORD_OUT-RCVPRN = 'LEGHOST01'.


*********************Build Data Records******************************

*----------------Employee header------------------------------------

* fill the employee header information
FS_EMPHDR_DATA-LNAME = ZEMPDETAIL-LNAME.
FS_EMPHDR_DATA-FNAME = ZEMPDETAIL-FNAME.
FS_EMPHDR_DATA-SSN   = ZEMPDETAIL-SSN.
FS_EMPHDR_DATA-DOB   = ZEMPDETAIL-DOB.


* fill the administrative section of the data record
FS_INT_EDIDD-SEGNAM = C_HEADER_SEGMENT.
FS_INT_EDIDD-SDATA = FS_EMPHDR_DATA.


* append the employee header data record to the IDoc data
APPEND FS_INT_EDIDD TO INT_EDIDD.


*----------------Employee weekly details----------------------------
LOOP AT IT_WKDET.
* fill the weekly details for each week
  FS_WEEKDET_DATA-WEEKNO = IT_WKDET-WEEKNO.
  FS_WEEKDET_DATA-TOTHOURS = IT_WKDET-TOTHOURS.
  FS_WEEKDET_DATA-HRLYRATE = IT_WKDET-HRLYRATE.

* add administrative information to the data record
  FS_INT_EDIDD-SEGNAM = C_WEEKLY_DETAILS_SEGMENT.
  FS_INT_EDIDD-SDATA = FS_WEEKDET_DATA.
```

```
* append the data for the week to the IDoc data
  APPEND FS_INT_EDIDD TO INT_EDIDD.


* Client details of each week
  FS_CLIENTDET_DATA-CLSITE = IT_WKDET-CLSITE.
  FS_CLIENTDET_DATA-WORKDESC = IT_WKDET-WORKDESC.


* add administrative information to the data record
  FS_INT_EDIDD-SEGNAM = C_CLIENT_DETAILS_SEGMENT.
  FS_INT_EDIDD-SDATA = FS_CLIENTDET_DATA.


* append the client details for the week to the IDoc data
  APPEND FS_INT_EDIDD TO INT_EDIDD.


ENDLOOP.
*-----------------Employee monthly summary--------------------------
* compute total hours and amount for the month
LOOP AT IT_WKDET.
  TOTAL_HRS_MONTH = TOTAL_HRS_MONTH + IT_WKDET-TOTHOURS.
  TOTAL_AMT_MONTH = TOTAL_AMT_MONTH + ( IT_WKDET-TOTHOURS *
                                        IT_WKDET-HRLYRATE ).
ENDLOOP.


* fill the summary information
FS_SUMMARY_DATA-TOTHRS = TOTAL_HRS_MONTH.
FS_SUMMARY_DATA-TOTAMT = TOTAL_AMT_MONTH.


* condense the summary record fields to remove spaces
CONDENSE FS_SUMMARY_DATA-TOTHRS.
CONDENSE FS_SUMMARY_DATA-TOTAMT.


* add administrative information to the data record
FS_INT_EDIDD-SEGNAM = C_SUMMARY_SEGMENT.
FS_INT_EDIDD-SDATA = FS_SUMMARY_DATA.


* append summary data to the IDoc data
APPEND FS_INT_EDIDD TO INT_EDIDD.



ENDFUNCTION.
```

A Stand-Alone Program to Generate IDocs

ALE processes for distributing master data are implemented as stand-alone report programs. For example, the RBDSEMAT report program generates material master IDocs. A stand-alone program can embed the IDoc generation logic in any manner it chooses; in contrast, the message control component must place the IDoc generation logic in a function module. The program logic is quite similar except for a call to the ALE layer for creating a physical IDoc in the system. Figure 32-2 depicts how the IDoc generation logic is part of the standalone program itself.

Selection Screen

The selection screen in the stand-alone programs allows the user to specify the objects for which IDocs are to be generated. Although the selection screen has not been standardized because of varying needs of the application programs, the ALE programs for master distribution have some similarities. At a minimum they allow a user to select one or more objects, a receiving system, and the message to be generated. Refer to the selection screen for distributing the material master (Transaction BD10).

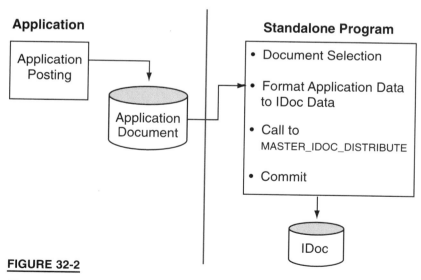

FIGURE 32-2

IDocs created from a stand-alone program

Program Flow

The program logic contains the following blocks:

1. Provide a selection screen to allow a user to specify the various objects for which IDocs are to be generated.

2. Determine the key of the application document from the object specified in step 1.

3. Select application data from the database using the object key identified in step 2.

4. Populate control record information.

5. Populate an internal table of type EDIDD with data records for the various segments.

6. Call the ALE service layer (MASTER_IDOC_DISTRIBUTE) to create the IDocs in the database.

7. Commit work.

The program in Listing 32-2 generates the monthly report IDoc ZMREPT01, which illustrates a stand-alone outbound process.

Listing 32-2

```
REPORT ZARNEDI1 MESSAGE-ID ZE.


*-----------------------------------------------------------------
* Parameters
*-----------------------------------------------------------------
* object key (Social security number for the employee)
PARAMETERS: P_SSN LIKE ZEMPDETAIL-SSN.
* message type
PARAMETERS: P_MESTYP LIKE EDMSG-MSGTYP OBLIGATORY.
* destination system
PARAMETERS: P_LOGSYS LIKE TBDLST-LOGSYS.


*-----------------------------------------------------------------
* Constants
*-----------------------------------------------------------------
```

```
DATA:
*      segment names
       C_HEADER_SEGMENT            LIKE EDIDD-SEGNAM VALUE 'Z1EMHDR',
       C_WEEKLY_DETAILS_SEGMENT    LIKE EDIDD-SEGNAM VALUE 'Z1WKDET',
       C_CLIENT_DETAILS_SEGMENT    LIKE EDIDD-SEGNAM VALUE 'Z1CLDET',
       C_SUMMARY_SEGMENT           LIKE EDIDD-SEGNAM VALUE 'Z1SUMRY',
*      idoc type
       C_MONTHLY_REPORT_IDOC_TYPE LIKE EDIDC-IDOCTP VALUE 'ZMREPT01'.
*-----------------------------------------------------------------------
* Data declarations
*-----------------------------------------------------------------------
* idoc control record
data: control_record_out like edidc.
* employee header data
DATA: FS_EMPHDR_DATA LIKE Z1EMHDR.
* employee weekly details data
DATA: FS_WEEKDET_DATA LIKE Z1WKDET.
* client details data
DATA: FS_CLIENTDET_DATA LIKE Z1CLDET.
* employee monthly summary data
DATA: FS_SUMMARY_DATA LIKE Z1SUMRY.
* total hours and amount for the summary segment
DATA: TOTAL_HRS_MONTH TYPE I,
      TOTAL_AMT_MONTH TYPE I.
*-----------------------------------------------------------------------
* Database Tables
*-----------------------------------------------------------------------
* Application data tables
TABLES: ZEMPDETAIL, ZEMPWKDET.


*-----------------------------------------------------------------------
* Internal tables
*-----------------------------------------------------------------------
DATA:

*      weekly details - appplication data
       IT_WKDET LIKE ZEMPWKDET OCCURS 0 WITH HEADER LINE,
*      data records
       INT_EDIDD LIKE EDIDD OCCURS 0 WITH HEADER LINE,
*      communication idocs geneerated
```

```
        IT_COMM_IDOCS LIKE EDIDC OCCURS 0 WITH HEADER LINE.


*------------------------------------------------------------------------
* Program logic
*------------------------------------------------------------------------


**********************Select Application Data***************************
SELECT SINGLE * FROM ZEMPDETAIL WHERE SSN = P_SSN.
IF SY-SUBRC NE 0.
   MESSAGE E001 WITH P_SSN.
   EXIT.
ENDIF.

SELECT * FROM ZEMPWKDET INTO TABLE IT_WKDET WHERE SSN = P_SSN.
IF SY-SUBRC NE 0.
   MESSAGE E002 WITH P_SSN.
   EXIT.
ENDIF.


**********************Build Control Record****************************

* Fill control record information
CONTROL_RECORD_OUT-MESTYP = P_MESTYP.
control_record_out-idoctp = c_monthly_report_idoc_type.
control_record_out-rcvprt = 'LS'.
control_record_out-rcvprn = p_logsys.


**********************Build Data Records******************************

*----------------Employee header---------------------------------

* fill the employee header information
FS_EMPHDR_DATA-LNAME = ZEMPDETAIL-LNAME.
FS_EMPHDR_DATA-FNAME = ZEMPDETAIL-FNAME.
FS_EMPHDR_DATA-SSN   = ZEMPDETAIL-SSN.
FS_EMPHDR_DATA-DOB   = ZEMPDETAIL-DOB.

* fill the administrative section of the data record
INT_EDIDD-SEGNAM = C_HEADER_SEGMENT.
INT_EDIDD-SDATA = FS_EMPHDR_DATA.
```

```
* append the employee header data record to the IDoc data
APPEND INT_EDIDD.


*------------------Employee weekly details---------------------------
LOOP AT IT_WKDET.
* fill the weekly details for each week
  FS_WEEKDET_DATA-WEEKNO = IT_WKDET-WEEKNO.
  FS_WEEKDET_DATA-TOTHOURS = IT_WKDET-TOTHOURS.
  FS_WEEKDET_DATA-HRLYRATE = IT_WKDET-HRLYRATE.


* add administrative information to the data record
  INT_EDIDD-SEGNAM = C_WEEKLY_DETAILS_SEGMENT.
  INT_EDIDD-SDATA = FS_WEEKDET_DATA.


* append the data for the week to the IDoc data
  APPEND INT_EDIDD.


* Client details of each week
  FS_CLIENTDET_DATA-CLSITE = IT_WKDET-CLSITE.
  FS_CLIENTDET_DATA-WORKDESC = IT_WKDET-WORKDESC.


* add administrative information to the data record
  INT_EDIDD-SEGNAM = C_CLIENT_DETAILS_SEGMENT.
  INT_EDIDD-SDATA = FS_CLIENTDET_DATA.


* append the client details for the week to the IDoc data
  APPEND INT_EDIDD.


ENDLOOP.
*------------------Employee monthly summary--------------------------
* compute total hours and amount for the month
LOOP AT IT_WKDET.
  TOTAL_HRS_MONTH = TOTAL_HRS_MONTH + IT_WKDET-TOTHOURS.
  TOTAL_AMT_MONTH = TOTAL_AMT_MONTH + ( IT_WKDET-TOTHOURS *
                                        IT_WKDET-HRLYRATE ).
ENDLOOP.


* fill the summary information
FS_SUMMARY_DATA-TOTHRS = TOTAL_HRS_MONTH.
FS_SUMMARY_DATA-TOTAMT = TOTAL_AMT_MONTH.
```

```
* condense the summary record fields to remove spaces
CONDENSE FS_SUMMARY_DATA-TOTHRS.
CONDENSE FS_SUMMARY_DATA-TOTAMT.

* add administrative information to the data record
INT_EDIDD-SEGNAM = C_SUMMARY_SEGMENT.
INT_EDIDD-SDATA = FS_SUMMARY_DATA.

* append summary data to the IDoc data
APPEND INT_EDIDD.

**************Pass control to the ALE layer****************************
CALL FUNCTION 'MASTER_IDOC_DISTRIBUTE'
     EXPORTING
          master_idoc_control              = control_record_out
     TABLES
          COMMUNICATION_IDOC_CONTROL    = IT_COMM_IDOCS
          MASTER_IDOC_DATA              = INT_EDIDD
     EXCEPTIONS
          ERROR_IN_IDOC_CONTROL         = 1
          ERROR_WRITING_IDOC_STATUS     = 2
          ERROR_IN_IDOC_DATA            = 3
          SENDING_LOGICAL_SYSTEM_UNKNOWN = 4
          OTHERS                         = 5.

IF SY-SUBRC NE 0.
   MESSAGE E003 WITH P_SSN.
ELSE.
   LOOP AT IT_COMM_IDOCS.
     WRITE: / 'IDoc generated', IT_COMM_IDOCS-DOCNUM.
   ENDLOOP.
   COMMIT WORK.
ENDIF.
```

An Outbound Program Triggered from Change Pointers

When important master data such as customer master or material master are changed, the system writes change documents for each document to track changes. Change pointers can be written in response to change documents. A standard report RBDMIDOC can be executed to process entries in the change pointer table. This program calls a function module, specific to each message, to generate the IDocs. This technique is used in ALE processes to keep master data synchronized across multiple SAP systems. Figure 32-3 depicts how the IDoc generation logic is implemented as a separate piece in case of outbound processes that use the change pointer technique.

The IDoc generation logic is quite similar to the stand-alone programs except for additional logic to analyze change pointers.

The function modules are generally named MASTERIDOC_CREATE_SMD_<message type> for SAP messages and Z_MASTERIDOC_SMD_<message type> for customer messages.

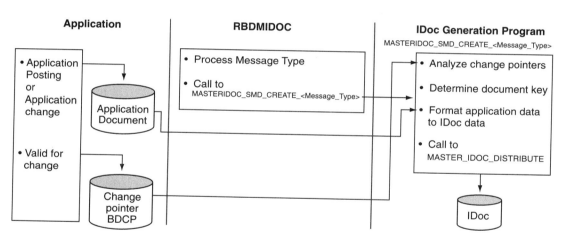

FIGURE 32-3

IDoc creation triggered from a change pointer

The interface for these function modules is very simple. It has only one input parameter: MESSAGE_TYPE. This parameter is the message type for which change pointers are to be analyzed for creating IDocs.

The program logic contains the following blocks:

1. Read change pointers using the CHANGE_POINTERS_READ function module.

2. Analyze change pointers to determine which documents are valid.

3. Determine the key of the application document from step 2.

4. Select application data from the database using the object key identified in step 3.

5. Populate control record information.

6. Populate an internal table of type EDIDD with data records for the various segments.

7. Call the ALE service layer (MASTER_IDOC_DISTRIBUTE) to create the IDocs in the database.

8. Update change pointer status.

9. Commit work.

The program in Listing 32-3 generates the monthly report IDoc (ZMREPT01) based on change pointers.

Listing 32-3

```
FUNCTION Z_IDOC_CHGPTR.
*"----------------------------------------------------------------
*"*"Local interface:
*"      IMPORTING
*"             VALUE(MESSAGE_TYPE) LIKE   TBDME-MESTYP
*"----------------------------------------------------------------


*----------------------------------------------------------------
* Data declarations
*----------------------------------------------------------------
  DATA:
    SSN                   LIKE ZEMP-SSN,        "employee's social security
    CREATED_C_IDOCS       LIKE SY-TABIX,        "no. of created IDoc
    CREATED_M_IDOCS       LIKE SY-TABIX,        "no of processed chg.pointer
    CREATED_COMM_IDOCS    LIKE SY-TABIX,        "IDocs of one document
    DONE_SINCE_COMMIT     LIKE SY-TABIX,        "no of IDocs since last com.
    C_MARK(1)             TYPE C VALUE 'X',     "mark for a checkbox
    C_IDOCS_BEFORE_COMMIT LIKE SY-TABIX         "commit after 50 IDocs
                          VALUE 50.
```

```
* key structure of changepointer
 DATA:
*   employee key
   BEGIN OF EMP_KEY,
     MANDT LIKE ZEMP-MANDT,
     SSN   LIKE ZEMPDETAIL-SSN,
   END OF EMP_KEY.


* Changepointer (standard structure for any object)
 DATA: BEGIN OF T_CHGPTRS OCCURS 0.
         INCLUDE STRUCTURE BDCP.
 DATA: END OF T_CHGPTRS.


* Changepointer (employee structure)
 DATA:
   BEGIN OF T_CHGPTRS_EMP OCCURS 0,
     SSN     LIKE ZEMP-SSN,
     CPIDENT LIKE BDCP-CPIDENT,
   END OF T_CHGPTRS_EMP.


* written changepointers
 DATA:
   BEGIN OF T_CPIDENT OCCURS 0,
     CPIDENT LIKE BDCP-CPIDENT,
   END OF T_CPIDENT.



*--------------------------------------------------------------------
* Program logic
*--------------------------------------------------------------------
* read all not processed changepointers
 CALL FUNCTION 'CHANGE_POINTERS_READ'
     EXPORTING
         MESSAGE_TYPE                 = MESSAGE_TYPE
         READ_NOT_PROCESSED_POINTERS = C_MARK           " = 'X'
     TABLES
         CHANGE_POINTERS              = T_CHGPTRS.
* create IDocs for all change pointers
 CLEAR:
   CREATED_C_IDOCS,
   CREATED_M_IDOCS,
   DONE_SINCE_COMMIT.
```

```
    REFRESH: T_CHGPTRS_EMP,
             T_CPIDENT.
* copy standard change pointers into employee change pointer format
  LOOP AT T_CHGPTRS.
*    extract key information from the standard structure (has client)
     EMP_KEY = T_CHGPTRS-TABKEY.
     MOVE-CORRESPONDING EMP_KEY TO T_CHGPTRS_EMP.
     T_CHGPTRS_EMP-CPIDENT = T_CHGPTRS-CPIDENT.
     APPEND T_CHGPTRS_EMP.
  ENDLOOP.
* sort by employee's ssn
  SORT T_CHGPTRS_EMP BY SSN.

  CLEAR SSN.
  LOOP AT T_CHGPTRS_EMP.
*    if IDoc already created, append CPIDENT (list of same documents)
     IF T_CHGPTRS_EMP-SSN EQ SSN.
       T_CPIDENT-CPIDENT = T_CHGPTRS_EMP-CPIDENT.
       APPEND T_CPIDENT.
       CONTINUE.
     ENDIF.
     SSN = T_CHGPTRS_EMP-SSN.

     CALL FUNCTION 'Z_MASTERIDOC_CREATE_ZMREPT'
          EXPORTING
               SSN               = SSN
               MESSAGE_TYPE      = MESSAGE_TYPE
          IMPORTING
               CREATED_COMM_IDOCS = CREATED_M_IDOCS
          EXCEPTIONS
               OTHERS            = 1.

*    create IDocs for the document
     CREATED_M_IDOCS = CREATED_M_IDOCS + 1.
     CREATED_C_IDOCS = CREATED_C_IDOCS + CREATED_COMM_IDOCS.
     DONE_SINCE_COMMIT = DONE_SINCE_COMMIT + 1.
     T_CPIDENT-CPIDENT = T_CHGPTRS_EMP-CPIDENT.
     APPEND T_CPIDENT.
*    initialize counter variables for created idocs
     IF DONE_SINCE_COMMIT GE C_IDOCS_BEFORE_COMMIT.
       DONE_SINCE_COMMIT = 0.
```

```
*      write status of all processed pointers
       CALL FUNCTION 'CHANGE_POINTERS_STATUS_WRITE'
             EXPORTING
                   MESSAGE_TYPE              = MESSAGE_TYPE
             TABLES
                   CHANGE_POINTERS_IDENTS = T_CPIDENT.
       REFRESH: T_CPIDENT.
       COMMIT WORK.
       CALL FUNCTION 'DEQUEUE_ALL'.
     ENDIF.
   ENDLOOP.   " AT t_chgptrs_emp
* commit if necassary
  IF DONE_SINCE_COMMIT GT 0.
* write status of all processed pointers
     CALL FUNCTION 'CHANGE_POINTERS_STATUS_WRITE'
             EXPORTING
                   MESSAGE_TYPE              = MESSAGE_TYPE
             TABLES
                   CHANGE_POINTERS_IDENTS = T_CPIDENT.
     COMMIT WORK.
     CALL FUNCTION 'DEQUEUE_ALL'.
   ENDIF.
* Number of master idocs created
  MESSAGE ID 'ZE' TYPE 'I' NUMBER '004'
          WITH CREATED_M_IDOCS MESSAGE_TYPE.
* Number of communication IDocs
  MESSAGE ID 'ZE' TYPE 'I' NUMBER '005'
          WITH CREATED_C_IDOCS MESSAGE_TYPE.
ENDFUNCTION.


FUNCTION Z_MASTERIDOC_CREATE_ZMREPT.
*"----------------------------------------------------------------------
*"*"Local interface:
*"       IMPORTING
*"             VALUE(SSN) LIKE   ZEMPDETAIL-SSN
*"             VALUE(RCVPFC) LIKE   BDALEDC-RCVPFC OPTIONAL
*"             VALUE(RCVPRN) LIKE   BDALEDC-RCVPRN OPTIONAL
*"             VALUE(RCVPRT) LIKE   BDALEDC-RCVPRT OPTIONAL
*"             VALUE(SNDPFC) LIKE   BDALEDC-SNDPFC OPTIONAL
*"             VALUE(SNDPRN) LIKE   BDALEDC-SNDPRN OPTIONAL
*"             VALUE(SNDPRT) LIKE   BDALEDC-SNDPRT
```

```
*"            VALUE(MESSAGE_TYPE) LIKE   TBDME-MESTYP
*"       EXPORTING
*"            VALUE(CREATED_COMM_IDOCS) LIKE   SY-TABIX
*"-----------------------------------------------------------------
*-------------------------------------------------------------------
* Constants
*-------------------------------------------------------------------


DATA:
*     segment names
      C_HEADER_SEGMENT             LIKE EDIDD-SEGNAM VALUE 'Z1EMHDR',
      C_WEEKLY_DETAILS_SEGMENT     LIKE EDIDD-SEGNAM VALUE 'Z1WKDET',
      C_CLIENT_DETAILS_SEGMENT     LIKE EDIDD-SEGNAM VALUE 'Z1CLDET',
      C_SUMMARY_SEGMENT            LIKE EDIDD-SEGNAM VALUE 'Z1SUMRY',
*     idoc type
      C_MONTHLY_REPORT_IDOC_TYPE LIKE EDIDC-IDOCTP VALUE 'ZMREPT01'.
*-------------------------------------------------------------------
* Data declarations
*-------------------------------------------------------------------
* idoc control record
data: control_record_out like edidc.
* employee header data
DATA: FS_EMPHDR_DATA LIKE Z1EMHDR.
* employee weekly details data
DATA: FS_WEEKDET_DATA LIKE Z1WKDET.
* client details data
DATA: FS_CLIENTDET_DATA LIKE Z1CLDET.
* employee monthly summary data
DATA: FS_SUMMARY_DATA LIKE Z1SUMRY.
* total hours and amount for the summary segment
DATA: TOTAL_HRS_MONTH TYPE I,
      TOTAL_AMT_MONTH TYPE I.
*-------------------------------------------------------------------
* Database Tables
*-------------------------------------------------------------------
* Application data tables
*tables: zempdetail, zempwkdet.


*-------------------------------------------------------------------
* Internal tables
*-------------------------------------------------------------------
```

```
DATA:

*       weekly details - appplication data
        IT_WKDET LIKE ZEMPWKDET OCCURS 0 WITH HEADER LINE,
*       data records
        INT_EDIDD LIKE EDIDD OCCURS 0 WITH HEADER LINE,
*       communication idocs geneerated
        IT_COMM_IDOCS LIKE EDIDC OCCURS 0 WITH HEADER LINE.


*-------------------------------------------------------------------
* Program logic
*-------------------------------------------------------------------


*********************Select Application Data***************************
SELECT SINGLE * FROM ZEMPDETAIL WHERE SSN = SSN.
IF SY-SUBRC NE 0.
* Employee & not found
   MESSAGE E001(ZE) WITH SSN.
   EXIT.
ENDIF.

SELECT * FROM ZEMPWKDET INTO TABLE IT_WKDET WHERE SSN = SSN.
IF SY-SUBRC NE 0.
* weekly information missing for employee &
   MESSAGE E002(ZE) WITH SSN.
   EXIT.
ENDIF.


*********************Build Control Record*****************************

* Fill control record information
CONTROL_RECORD_OUT-MESTYP = MESSAGE_TYPE.
control_record_out-idoctp = c_monthly_report_idoc_type.
*control_record_out-rcvprt = 'LS'.
*control_record_out-rcvprn = p_logsys.


*********************Build Data Records******************************

*----------------Employee header-------------------------------------

* fill the employee header information
```

```
FS_EMPHDR_DATA-LNAME = ZEMPDETAIL-LNAME.
FS_EMPHDR_DATA-FNAME = ZEMPDETAIL-FNAME.
FS_EMPHDR_DATA-SSN   = ZEMPDETAIL-SSN.
FS_EMPHDR_DATA-DOB   = ZEMPDETAIL-DOB.


* fill the administrative section of the data record
INT_EDIDD-SEGNAM = C_HEADER_SEGMENT.
INT_EDIDD-SDATA = FS_EMPHDR_DATA.


* append the employee header data record to the IDoc data
APPEND INT_EDIDD.


*-----------------Employee weekly details----------------------------
LOOP AT IT_WKDET.
* fill the weekly details for each week
  FS_WEEKDET_DATA-WEEKNO = IT_WKDET-WEEKNO.
  FS_WEEKDET_DATA-TOTHOURS = IT_WKDET-TOTHOURS.
  FS_WEEKDET_DATA-HRLYRATE = IT_WKDET-HRLYRATE.


* add administrative information to the data record
  INT_EDIDD-SEGNAM = C_WEEKLY_DETAILS_SEGMENT.
  INT_EDIDD-SDATA = FS_WEEKDET_DATA.


* append the data for the week to the IDoc data
  APPEND INT_EDIDD.


* Client details of each week
  FS_CLIENTDET_DATA-CLSITE = IT_WKDET-CLSITE.
  FS_CLIENTDET_DATA-WORKDESC = IT_WKDET-WORKDESC.


* add administrative information to the data record
  INT_EDIDD-SEGNAM = C_CLIENT_DETAILS_SEGMENT.
  INT_EDIDD-SDATA = FS_CLIENTDET_DATA.


* append the client details for the week to the IDoc data
  APPEND INT_EDIDD.


ENDLOOP.
*-----------------Employee monthly summary---------------------------
* compute total hours and amount for the month
LOOP AT IT_WKDET.
```

```
        TOTAL_HRS_MONTH = TOTAL_HRS_MONTH + IT_WKDET-TOTHOURS.
        TOTAL_AMT_MONTH = TOTAL_AMT_MONTH + ( IT_WKDET-TOTHOURS *
                                              IT_WKDET-HRLYRATE ).
    ENDLOOP.

    * fill the summary information
    FS_SUMMARY_DATA-TOTHRS = TOTAL_HRS_MONTH.
    FS_SUMMARY_DATA-TOTAMT = TOTAL_AMT_MONTH.

    * condense the summary record fields to remove spaces
    CONDENSE FS_SUMMARY_DATA-TOTHRS.
    CONDENSE FS_SUMMARY_DATA-TOTAMT.

    * add administrative information to the data record
    INT_EDIDD-SEGNAM = C_SUMMARY_SEGMENT.
    INT_EDIDD-SDATA = FS_SUMMARY_DATA.

    * append summary data to the IDoc data
    APPEND INT_EDIDD.

    **************Pass control to the ALE layer****************************
    CALL FUNCTION 'MASTER_IDOC_DISTRIBUTE'
        EXPORTING
            master_idoc_control              = control_record_out
        TABLES
            COMMUNICATION_IDOC_CONTROL       = IT_COMM_IDOCS
            MASTER_IDOC_DATA                 = INT_EDIDD
        EXCEPTIONS
            ERROR_IN_IDOC_CONTROL            = 1
            ERROR_WRITING_IDOC_STATUS        = 2
            ERROR_IN_IDOC_DATA               = 3
            SENDING_LOGICAL_SYSTEM_UNKNOWN   = 4
            OTHERS                           = 5.

    * get number of created IDocs
      DESCRIBE TABLE IT_COMM_IDOCS LINES CREATED_COMM_IDOCS.
    ENDFUNCTION.
```

Inbound Program for Custom Basic IDoc Types

Inbound programs are also called posting programs. This section explains how these programs are designed to read IDoc data and post application documents.

You start with the basic design of these programs in which a single IDoc is passed to the posting programs.

♦ **Basic Scenario.** The ALE layer calls the posting program and passes IDoc data to it. Posting programs are implemented as function modules and are designed to read IDoc data and create an application document. The programs can use one of the two methods available for posting an application document: a direct input function module or a call transaction. In a direct input function module, the database tables are updated directly; in call transaction mode, the system simulates data for each screen to post a document. The results of posting are passed back to the ALE layer, which then updates the status records.

♦ **Advanced Scenarios.** In addition to the basic scenario, the function modules can be designed for advanced scenarios such as mass processing, serialization checks, advanced workflow programming, and enabling an existing transaction for ALE. In case of mass processing, the function module is designed to handle several IDocs at the same time. This approach is useful in improving the throughput of the system. Serialization check is used in cases when the sequence in which IDocs are posted is important. For example, if two order change IDocs are waiting to be posted and the first changes the current order quantity to 100 while the second changes the quantity to 20, the sequence in which these are posted is important. You want to post them in the sequence in which they were received. This sequence can be implemented by using serialization check. The advanced workflow scenario is used for raising application-specific events after a successful posting. Finally, enabling a transaction for ALE is useful when you cannot afford to post the same document twice even in the worst possible case of a system failure. In the standard system, only the IDOC_INPUT_INVOICE_MM function module to process incoming invoices is designed with this approach.

The scenarios most commonly implemented for the inbound process are the single IDoc and multiple IDoc scenarios. Serialization check, advanced workflow programming, and ALE enabling are not commonly deployed. The posting programs are implemented as function modules and are generally named IDOC_INPUT_<message_type> for SAP messages and Z_IDOC_INPUT_<message_type> for customer messages. This is a guideline and not a rule. Figure 32-4 depicts how the inbound posting program logic is implemented as a separate piece and invoked from the inbound IDoc process.

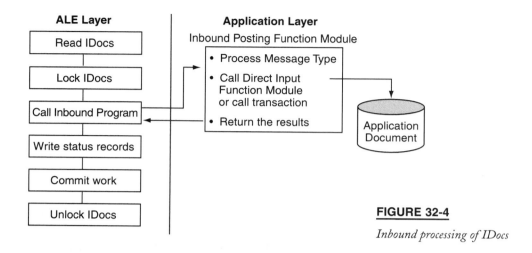

FIGURE 32-4

Inbound processing of IDocs

Interface for the Function Module

The interface for the function module is preset by SAP and is the same for all inbound scenarios described above. This situation of using the same interface for all possible scenarios makes the interface more involved in comparison to the outbound programs, where the interface is different for each type of program. The various parameters in the interface are described below using the mass processing scenario as an example.

◆ **IMPORTING Parameters.** The following parameters are passed to the function module by the ALE interface layer:

INPUT_METHOD. This parameter specifies the mode in which the posting program is to be executed and is valid only for programs that use the call transaction method. The various values are A (show all screens), E (show error screen only) and space (background mode).

MASS_PROCESSING. This parameter is used for the advanced workflow programming scenario only. The default value is space.

◆ **EXPORTING Parameters.** The following parameters are returned from the posting program to the ALE layer to provide information on the results of posting:

WORKFLOW_RESULT. This parameter indicates whether the posting was successful or not. Workflow is started for the error condition. The value of 0 indicates success and 99999 indicates failure (workflow is started).

APPLICATION_VARIABLE. This parameter is used in advanced workflow programming only. Leave it blank.

IN_UPDATE_TASK. This parameter indicates how the piece of code that updates the database tables was invoked in the posting program. The value of ' ' indicates that the update task was not used, and 'X' indicates that the update task was used. This value delays the posting until a commit is done.

CALL_TRANSACTION_DONE. This parameter should be blank unless you are using an ALE-enabled transaction. An ALE-enabled transaction has been modified to update the IDoc status in its code rather than in the ALE layer. The ALE layer does not update the status information for ALE-enabled transactions.

 CAUTION

Don't let the parameter name Call_Transaction_Done mislead you. It does not represent whether your posting program uses call transaction or not.

◆ **TABLES Parameters.** These parameters are internal tables used to pass multiple data values to and receive multiple values from the function module. The following entries are used in the posting program:

IDOC_CONTRL. This parameter contains control records of the IDocs to be processed and is passed as an input parameter.

IDOC_DATA. This parameter contains data records of the IDocs to be processed and is also passed as an input parameter.

IDOC_STATUS. This parameter contains status records for each IDoc processed in the posting program and is an output parameter. Therefore, IDOC-_STATUS is populated by the posting program. The various fields that can be filled in the program can be seen in the structure BDIDOCSTAT, using transaction SE11. The structure mainly consists of IDoc number, status code, message ID, and variables.

For example, assume three IDocs (100, 101, and 102) were passed to the posting program. The first and third IDoc successfully posted and created application documents. The IDoc number 101 failed to post the document. The error was in segment number 3 in the

HRLYRATE field, and the error message is represented by error code 15 in the message class ZE. Table 32-1 shows how the IDOC_STATUS table can be populated:

Table 32-1 Values in the IDOC_STATUS Table

DOCNUM	STATUS	MSGTY	MSGID	MSGNO	SEGNUM	SEGFLD
100	53					
101	51	E	ZE	015	03	HRLYRATE
102	53					

RETURN_VARIABLES. This parameter is also an output parameter that contains additional processing results for each IDoc. The ALE layer uses RETURN_VARIABLES for workflow processing. This internal table is based on structure BDWFRETVAR, which has two fields: WF_PARM and DOC_NUMBER. The WF_PARM qualifies the document number specified in the DOC_NUM field. The DOC_NUMBER can contain the IDoc number or the document number of the application document created. The various values for the WF_PARM field are Processed_IDOCs, Error_IDOCs, and Appl_Objects.

These values are case-sensitive and must be spelled out exactly as shown. For example, assume three IDocs (100, 101, and 102) were passed to the posting program. The first and third IDoc successfully posted and created application documents 9000 and 9001. The IDoc number 101 failed to post the document successfully. The RETURN_VARIABLES table will be populated, as shown in Table 32-2.

Table 32-2 Values in the RETURN_VARIABLES Table

WFPARM	DOCNUMBER
Processed_IDOCs	100
Appl_Objects	9001
Error_IDOCs	101
Processed_IDOCs	102
Appl_Objects	9002

SERIALIZATION_INFO. This parameter is also an export parameter and is relevant only if you are using the serialization object.

◆ **Exceptions.** Exceptions convey problems with control record information, such as incorrect message type.

Program Flow

The program logic contains the following blocks:

1. Read control record information. Verify control information (message type). If the message type is incorrect, then raise the exception.

2. Read the IDoc data for an IDoc. Remember that several IDocs can be passed together.

3. Parse through each data record. If using the call transaction, then build the BDC data table; if not, build internal tables as required by the direct posting function module

4. Call the posting program and capture the results.

5. Populate return parameters.

6. If more IDocs are present, return to step 2; if not, go to step 7.

7. Return from the function module. The results of execution are passed to the ALE layer.

CAUTION

Do not perform commit work in your posting program. The ALE layer is responsible for the COMMIT command to ensure data integrity between the results of IDoc posting and status table update.

The monthly report IDoc (ZMREPT01) developed in the preceding chapter is used here to illustrate the logic of inbound programs for mass processing. The same program automatically works for a single IDoc. The program code is shown in Listing 32-4.

TIP

The MBDCONWF program contains various constants used in an inbound program. You should include this program in your inbound program for consistent use of the constant values

Listing 32-4

```
FUNCTION Z_IDOC_INPUT_ZMREPT.
*"----------------------------------------------------------------
*"*"Local interface:
*"        IMPORTING
*"              VALUE(INPUT_METHOD) LIKE  BDWFAP_PAR-INPUTMETHD
*"              VALUE(MASS_PROCESSING) LIKE  BDWFAP_PAR-MASS_PROC
*"        EXPORTING
*"              VALUE(WORKFLOW_RESULT) LIKE  BDWFAP_PAR-RESULT
*"              VALUE(APPLICATION_VARIABLE) LIKE  BDWFAP_PAR-APPL_VAR
*"              VALUE(IN_UPDATE_TASK) LIKE  BDWFAP_PAR-UPDATETASK
*"              VALUE(CALL_TRANSACTION_DONE) LIKE  BDWFAP_PAR-CALLTRANS
*"        TABLES
*"               IDOC_CONTRL STRUCTURE  EDIDC
*"               IDOC_DATA STRUCTURE  EDIDD
*"               IDOC_STATUS STRUCTURE  BDIDOCSTAT
*"               RETURN_VARIABLES STRUCTURE  BDWFRETVAR
*"               SERIALIZATION_INFO STRUCTURE  BDI_SER
*"        EXCEPTIONS
*"               WRONG_FUNCTION_CALLED
*"----------------------------------------------------------------
   INCLUDE MBDCONWF.


*----------------------------------------------------------------
* Database Tables
*----------------------------------------------------------------
* Application data tables (Defined in global data)
*tables: zempdetail, zempwkdet.


*----------------------------------------------------------------
* Data declarations
*----------------------------------------------------------------
* employee details - IDoc
```

```
      DATA: FS_EMPHDR_DATA LIKE Z1EMHDR.
* employee weekly details data - IDoc
      DATA: FS_WEEKDET_DATA LIKE Z1WKDET.
* client details data - IDoc
      DATA: FS_CLIENTDET_DATA LIKE Z1CLDET.
* employee monthly summary data - IDoc
      DATA: FS_SUMMARY_DATA LIKE Z1SUMRY.


* total hours and amount
      DATA: TOTAL_HRS_MONTH TYPE I,
            TOTAL_AMT_MONTH TYPE I.


* employee details - application data
      DATA:  FS_APP_EMPDET LIKE ZEMPDETAIL.


* weekly details - appplication data
      DATA:  IT_APP_WKDET LIKE ZEMPWKDET OCCURS 0 WITH HEADER LINE.


*------------------------------------------------------------------------
* Program logic
*------------------------------------------------------------------------
* initialize workflow result
      WORKFLOW_RESULT = C_WF_RESULT_OK.

      LOOP AT IDOC_CONTRL.

*    make sure we have the correct message passed to us
      IF IDOC_CONTRL-MESTYP NE 'ZMREPT'.
        RAISE WRONG_FUNCTION_CALLED.
      ENDIF.

*    clear application buffers before reading new employee
      CLEAR: IT_APP_WKDET, FS_APP_EMPDET.
      REFRESH IT_APP_WKDET.

*    process all data records in an IDoc and transfer them to
*    application buffers
      LOOP AT IDOC_DATA WHERE DOCNUM EQ IDOC_CONTRL-DOCNUM.

        CASE IDOC_DATA-SEGNAM.

          WHEN 'Z1EMHDR'.                    " employee header
```

```
            FS_EMPHDR_DATA = IDOC_DATA-SDATA.
            MOVE-CORRESPONDING FS_EMPHDR_DATA TO FS_APP_EMPDET.

        WHEN 'Z1WKDET'.                 " employee weekly details
            FS_WEEKDET_DATA = IDOC_DATA-SDATA.
            MOVE-CORRESPONDING FS_WEEKDET_DATA TO IT_APP_WKDET.

        WHEN 'Z1CLDET'.                 " client details
            FS_CLIENTDET_DATA = IDOC_DATA-SDATA.
            MOVE-CORRESPONDING FS_CLIENTDET_DATA TO IT_APP_WKDET.
            MOVE FS_APP_EMPDET-SSN TO IT_APP_WKDET-SSN.
            APPEND IT_APP_WKDET.            " append weekly details

        WHEN 'Z1SUMRY'.                 " summary data
            FS_SUMMARY_DATA = IDOC_DATA-SDATA.
      ENDCASE.

    ENDLOOP.


* verify totals in the data records against the summary record
    CLEAR: TOTAL_HRS_MONTH, TOTAL_AMT_MONTH.
*   compute total hours and amount for the month from weekly details
    LOOP AT IT_APP_WKDET.
        TOTAL_HRS_MONTH = TOTAL_HRS_MONTH + IT_APP_WKDET-TOTHOURS.
        TOTAL_AMT_MONTH = TOTAL_AMT_MONTH + ( IT_APP_WKDET-TOTHOURS *
                                             IT_APP_WKDET-HRLYRATE ).
    ENDLOOP.


* compare the values with values in the summary record
    IF TOTAL_HRS_MONTH NE FS_SUMMARY_DATA-TOTHRS OR
       TOTAL_AMT_MONTH NE FS_SUMMARY_DATA-TOTAMT.

*       totals in the summary record do not match with weekly details
*       fill IDOC_Status
        IDOC_STATUS-DOCNUM = IDOC_CONTRL-DOCNUM.
        IDOC_STATUS-STATUS = '51'.
        IDOC_STATUS-MSGTY  = 'E'.
        IDOC_STATUS-MSGID  = 'ZE'.
        IDOC_STATUS-MSGNO  = '005'.
        IDOC_STATUS-MSGV1  = FS_APP_EMPDET-SSN.
        APPEND IDOC_STATUS.
```

```
            WORKFLOW_RESULT = C_WF_RESULT_ERROR.
            RETURN_VARIABLES-WF_PARAM = 'Error_IDOCs'.
            RETURN_VARIABLES-DOC_NUMBER = IDOC_CONTRL-DOCNUM.
            APPEND RETURN_VARIABLES.
        ELSE.

*       Data looks good. Create weekly report if it does not already exist
*       If wekly report exists then simply update the records
            SELECT SINGLE * FROM ZEMPDETAIL WHERE SSN EQ FS_APP_EMPDET-SSN.
            IF SY-SUBRC NE 0.
              INSERT INTO ZEMPDETAIL VALUES FS_APP_EMPDET.
              INSERT ZEMPWKDET FROM TABLE IT_APP_WKDET.
            ELSE.
              UPDATE ZEMPDETAIL FROM FS_APP_EMPDET.
              UPDATE ZEMPWKDET FROM TABLE IT_APP_WKDET.
            ENDIF.

            IF SY-SUBRC EQ 0.
*             poulate return variables for success
              RETURN_VARIABLES-WF_PARAM = 'Processed_IDOCs'.
              RETURN_VARIABLES-DOC_NUMBER = IDOC_CONTRL-DOCNUM.
              RETURN_VARIABLES-WF_PARAM = 'Appl_Objects'.
              RETURN_VARIABLES-DOC_NUMBER = FS_APP_EMPDET-SSN.
              APPEND RETURN_VARIABLES.

*             add status record indicating success
              IDOC_STATUS-DOCNUM = IDOC_CONTRL-DOCNUM.
              IDOC_STATUS-STATUS = '53'.
              IDOC_STATUS-MSGTY  = 'I'.
              IDOC_STATUS-MSGID  = 'ZE'.
              IDOC_STATUS-MSGNO  = '006'.
              IDOC_STATUS-MSGV1  = FS_APP_EMPDET-SSN.
              APPEND IDOC_STATUS.
            ELSE.
*             poulate return variables indicating error
              WORKFLOW_RESULT = C_WF_RESULT_ERROR.
              RETURN_VARIABLES-WF_PARAM = 'Error_IDOCs'.
              RETURN_VARIABLES-DOC_NUMBER = IDOC_CONTRL-DOCNUM.
              APPEND RETURN_VARIABLES.

*             add status record indicating failure in updating
              IDOC_STATUS-DOCNUM = IDOC_CONTRL-DOCNUM.
```

```
        IDOC_STATUS-STATUS = '51'.
        IDOC_STATUS-MSGTY  = 'E'.
        IDOC_STATUS-MSGID  = 'ZE'.
        IDOC_STATUS-MSGNO  = '007'.
        IDOC_STATUS-MSGV1  = FS_APP_EMPDET-SSN.
        APPEND IDOC_STATUS.
      ENDIF.
    ENDIF.
  ENDLOOP.                              "End loop at idoc_contrl.


ENDFUNCTION.
```

Programs for IDoc Extensions

In the previous section you learned about programs that are developed for Basic IDoc types. In this section you learn about programs that are written in the user exits of the SAP programs for extended IDocs. The customer master IDoc that was extended in the previous chapter is used in this section to illustrate the process of writing user-exit programs for extended IDocs. The programs written in the user-exits are considered enhancements to the SAP system and are supported on an upgrade. User exits have been provided at strategic locations in the IDoc programs. SAP provides a formal method to develop programs for the various user exits. Here you learn about various types of user exits, strategic locations of user exits, how to locate them in the standard SAP programs, and how to use the formal process of developing user exits. Sample programs are provided for reference.

Types of User Exits

It is important to understand the types of user exits available in the system. SAP provides two types of user exits:

- ◆ Old method—perform USEREXIT_xxxx
- ◆ New method—CALL CUSTOMER FUNCTION

In the first type, SAP provides hard-coded user exits in its program logic. There is no formal method of documenting these user exits, and the only way to find them is to search for the string literal USEREXIT in the programs. This process is considered a modification to the SAP code. You have to use the corrections procedure to implement these user exits. Most of the SD applications use this form of user exits. Although SAP is moving toward the new method as described next, several applications still have the old style of user exits. For example, the user exit in the SD module for incoming orders is implemented in the old style in the program LVEDAF0U. These exits are now replaced with the new method.

The second type formally documents and implements user exits without having to go through SAP's correction procedures. These user exits are implemented as function modules that are called from SAP programs. The calling program identifies the user exits with a number. For example, the code in Listing 32-5 is taken from the inbound program that processes a customer master IDoc. This code calls user-exit number 001.

Listing 32-5

```
call customer-function '001'
     exporting
            idoc_control     = f_idoc_control
            input_method     = input_method
     importing
            workflow_result  = v_workflow_result
     tables
            idoc_data        = t_idoc_data
            idoc_status      = t_idoc_status
            return_variables = t_return_variables.
```

In the actual implementation, this user exit equates to a function module with the following naming convention: EXIT_<program name>_<exit number>. Thus exit number 001 implemented in the SAPLVV02 program will be named EXIT_SAPLVV02_001. The user exit function modules contain an include program that starts with a Z. You write your user exit programs in these include modules. The formal procedure for programming in the user exits is described later in the chapter.

Strategic Location of User Exits

User exits are available at strategic points in the IDoc programs to handle customer extensions. SAP controls these locations, and they are guaranteed to exist with the same functionality on an upgrade. An explanation of the commonly used user exits for outbound as well as inbound processing follows. Note that some of these may not be available for every process and some processes may have additional user exits.

Outbound IDoc Processing

◆ A user exit is available after each segment is populated. This exit allows you to add custom logic for any of your extended segments. Technically, the same user exit is invoked after every segment is filled. Therefore, in your user exit program you must check the name of the current segment being processed.

◆ A user exit is also available after the system populates the control record information. This exit allows you to modify any control information that may be necessary. For example, if you have extended an IDoc, you will populate the IDoc type using this user exit. This user exit lends itself to creativity. For example, you can use it to create a variant of your message type to allow special processing or to determine recipients dynamically.

◆ A user exit is also available after the system has completely filled out the control record and data records. This exit allows you to make any final adjustments to the data being sent out.

Inbound IDoc Processing

◆ A user exit is available when a customer segment is encountered. This exit allows you to add custom logic for any of your extended segments.

◆ A user exit is also available after the system populates the status records and is about to return control back to the ALE layer. This exit allows you to modify any status records or add additional status records.

Common Process

◆ A user exit is located in the routine that creates a physical IDoc in the system. Technically, the exit is called in the EDI_DOCUMENT_OPEN_FOR_CREATE function module, which creates a control record. This user exit is invoked for inbound as well as outbound IDocs. It can be used to modify control record information in the IDoc. This exit is typically used to make global changes to your IDocs. For example, you could modify the control record on outbound IDocs for any specific information desired by your EDI subsystem. This user exit (EXIT_SAPLEDI1_001) is implemented in enhancement SIDOC001.

◆ Another user exit is available in the ALE service layer during version change of incoming and outgoing IDocs. The exit is not especially valuable on outbound, because the system takes care of the version change. On the other hand, on inbound, for example, if you are on 3.0F and you are receiving IDocs from a back-level system 3.0A, then you could modify the segment to include additional fields that may be required in the application for 3.0F. This user exit (EXIT_SAPLBD11_001) is implemented in enhancement ALE00001.

Steps to Locate User Exits

The first and foremost task before you can start programming is to identify the specific user exit that you should use. User exits in the system are grouped under enhancements. Refer to the appendix for a list of enhancements for the commonly used IDoc programs. If you do not know the enhancement, the steps are listed later in "Determining SAP Enhancements." After you identify the correct enhancement, finding the appropriate user exit is very simple, as described in the following steps:

1. Execute transaction SMOD.
2. Enter your enhancement name and click on the Components button.
3. Click on Display to see the various components that are effectively user exits. Click on any one and then click on the Documentation button to view the documentation. If no documentation is available, then you are at the mercy of documentation in the SAP code to determine the intent behind the user exit.

Steps to Determine SAP Enhancements

The most commonly used approach to locate an enhancement for an IDoc program is explained here, using the customer master IDoc program as an example.

1. Identify the program in which you want to locate a user exit. The IDoc programs follow a naming convention for outbound and inbound function modules. Follow these guidelines to identify program names. Unfortunately, program names are not enforced, and therefore you will notice some inconsistency.

    Outbound programs via message control are generally named as IDOC_OUTPUT_<message_type>.

Outbound programs via change pointers are generally named as MASTERIDOC_CREATE_SMD_<message_type>.

For stand-alone outbound programs, the IDoc logic is generally coded in MASTERIDOC_CREATE_<message_type> function modules.

Inbound programs are generally named IDOC_INPUT_<message type>.

The program name for outbound customer master is SAPLVV01 (MASTERIDOC_CREATE_REQ_DEBMAS).

2. Determine the development class for this program, using the administration attributes of the program via transaction SE37. For the customer master, the development class is VSV.

3. Execute transaction SMOD. You can list enhancements by development class. Press F4 on the Enhancement field. The next screen allows you to enter a development class. Click on the Execute button for a list of all enhancements available in a development class. You can list the various components for each enhancement by clicking on the Components+/- button. The one that matches your program name is the enhancement for you. In the case of customer master, the program name is SAPLVV01, and thus the enhancement for the customer master is VSV00001.

Process for Developing User Exits

After you identify an appropriate user exit for your process, you can start building the programs by creating a project. A project defines one or more enhancements carried out for a module. For example, if you are enhancing the customer master process, one project can encapsulate all developments associated with the process, including the programs for IDoc extension. Follow these steps to create a project and develop programs:

1. Execute transaction CMOD. Enter a project name on the initial screen (see Figure 32-5). The name does not need to start with Z. Click on the Create icon.

2. On the next screen, enter a short description of your project, save your project, and then click on the SAP Enhancements button.

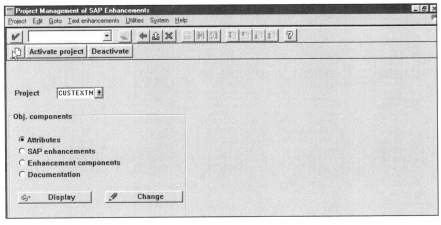

FIGURE 32-5

Initial customer–modification screen

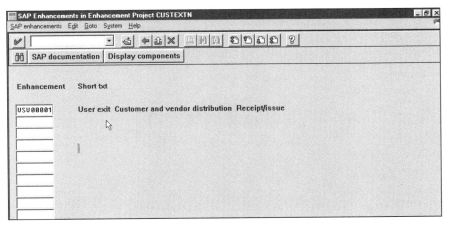

FIGURE 32-6

Enhancement included in a project

3. On the next screen (see Figure 32-6), enter the enhancement name as identified earlier. If you've forgotten it, press F4. Save your project again and use the green arrow to return to the main screen of CMOD.

4. Select the Enhancement Components option and click on the Change button.

5. On the next screen (see Figure 32-7), click on the user exit that you are interested in and then click on the Edit Component button.

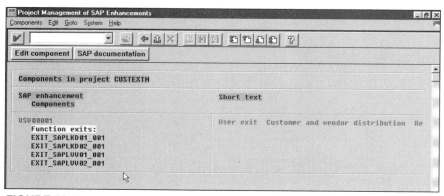

FIGURE 32-7

User exits in an enhancement

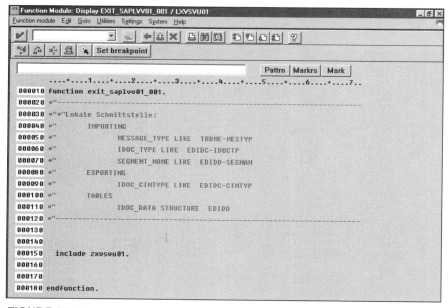

FIGURE 32-8

A user exit program to enter custom code

6. The next screen (see Figure 32-8) shows you the function module; it has an include program that starts with a Z.

7. Double-click on this program. The system will tell you that it will create the program. Accept the message, and you are in the ABAP editor, where you can write the necessary code for the user exit.

8. After completing the program and saving it, go back to the main screen for CMOD transaction and activate your project. This step automatically activates the function module in which you coded your program logic.

9. Test your code by running the process that invokes the user exit. Test until you drop!

10. Transport the project to your production system when you are satisfied with the enhancement.

Outbound Programs for Extended IDocs

These programs are written specifically to populate data in the extended segments of the IDoc. The interface of the user exit function module is not fixed. It varies for each process and user exit. Some of the typical parameters supplied in a user exit for the outbound programs are described next.

Interface for the User Exits

The interface for the user exits typically contains the parameters shown here.

◆ **IMPORTING Parameters.** These parameters are provided as input parameters to your user exit:

MESSAGE_TYPE. This parameter represents the message type being processed. Some user exits are shared across several messages, and therefore checking for the correct message type is important.

IDOC_TYPE. This parameter represents the basic IDoc type in process. You need to know the IDOC_TYPE because a message can be based on multiple IDoc types.

SEGMENT_NAME. This parameter represents the last segment filled by the system before it calls the user exit. Because the same user exit is called for all the segments, you want to make sure that your code gets executed after the segment that you have extended.

◆ **EXPORTING Parameter.** This parameter is returned by your user exit to the calling program:

IDOC_CIMTYPE. This parameter is the name of your IDoc extension. IDOC_CIMTYPE allows the system to perform a syntax check according to the enhanced definition of the basic IDoc type.

◆ **Tables.** The following table acts as a two-way parameter for input as well as output:

> **IDOC_DATA.** This parameter represents the IDoc data records that have been populated so far by the system. The IDOC_DATA table is where you will append your data records and pass them back to the caller. This table is always provided as an input parameter.

Program Flow

The program logic typically contains the following blocks:

1. Determine the key of the object for which an IDoc is being generated. If you are writing the user exit for an extended segment in a customer master, you want to know which customer master is being processed. If the key is not available through one of the interface parameters, you can loop through the existing segments that are filled to locate the key.

2. Write whatever code or logic you have to implement. The following sample program extracts user-defined data stored in the customer master table.

3. Create one or more data records for the custom segment.

4. Append it to the internal table of data records supplied in the parameters. You're done!

The program shown in Listing 32-6 populates an extended segment (Z1KNVVM) of the customer master IDoc (DEBMAS01). Data for the extended segment is available in the user-extended customer master tables. See "Extending a Basic IDoc Type" in Chapter 31, "Extending and Developing a Basic IDoc Type" as a reference when reading the program code.

Listing 32-6

```
*----------------------------------------------------------------*
*    INCLUDE ZXVSVU01                                          *
*----------------------------------------------------------------*
* In this scenario, the E1KNVVM segment has been extended to accomodate
* user-defined fields in the customer master table KNVV. The name of
* the extended segment is Z1KNVVM. There are two custom
* fields ZZDELPRTY (Delivery priority) and ZZRANK (Customer Rank)
*----------------------------------------------------------------*
```

```
* Make sure you are processing correct message type
CHECK MESSAGE_TYPE EQ 'DEBMAS'.

*  Make sure data is added after the correct segmnent
CHECK SEGMENT_NAME EQ 'E1KNVVM'.

* since customer number is not passed in this user exit, you need
* to go through the data records to find the customer number and the
* sales organization, distribution channel, division.
LOOP AT IDOC_DATA.
  CASE IDOC_DATA-SEGNAM.
    WHEN 'E1KNA1M'.                     " has customer number in it
       MOVE IDOC_DATA-SDATA TO KNA1M.
    WHEN 'E1KNVVM'.          " has sales org, dist ch and division
       MOVE IDOC_DATA-SDATA TO KNVVM.
  endcase.
endloop.

* Select data from the user defined fields in KNVV
SELECT SINGLE * FROM KNVV WHERE KUNNR = kna1m-KUNNR
                        AND    VKORG = KNVVm-VKORG
                        AND    VTWEG = KNVVm-VTWEG
                        AND    SPART = KNVVm-SPART.

* set the IDoc extension name for control record
IDOC_CIMTYPE = 'DEBMASEX'.

* clear and fill extended segment with user defined fields in KNVV
CLEAR Z1KNVVM.

* copy custom fields from KNVV to the extended segment.
MOVE-CORRESPONDING KNVV TO Z1KNVVM.     "field names must be same

*    condense all fields of extended segment
CONDENSE: Z1KNVVM-ZZDELPRTY,
          Z1KNVVM-ZZRANK.

* populate segment name in the data record, copy data contents into
* it, and append the data record to existing data records
```

```
MOVE 'Z1KNVVM' TO IDOC_DATA-SEGNAM.
MOVE Z1KNVVM   TO IDOC_DATA-SDATA.
APPEND IDOC_DATA.
```

Inbound Programs for Extended IDocs

These programs are written specifically to process data in the extended segments
of the IDoc. The point in the processing when a user exit is invoked is different
for each process. A user exit may be invoked after the end of posting or before
posting the document. With customer master, the user exit is called after data has
already been posted. In the case of material master, the user exit is called before
the data is posted. The point at which the user exit is called makes a difference in
how you code your logic. The interface of the user exit function module varies for
each process and user exit.

Interface for User Exits

◆ **IMPORTING Parameter.** This parameter is provided as an input parameter to your user exit:

  IDOC_CONTROL. This parameter is the control record for the IDoc.

◆ **EXPORTING Parameter.** This parameter is returned by your user exit
  to the calling program:

  WORKFLOW_RESULT. This parameter conveys any problems discovered in the user exit for which you want to end the inbound processing. The system creates a status record and starts workflow.

◆ **Tables.** The following tables act as two-way parameters for input as well
  as output:

  IDOC_DATA. This table is the data record for the IDoc. You can
  loop through it to locate your extended segment.

  RETURN_VARIABLES. This table represents return variables as
  required in inbound programs. You can append values to this table
  in the user exit. This table is optional.

  IDOC_STATUS. This table is for you to provide any status
  records that you want to have created.

Program Flow

The program logic typically contains the following blocks:

1. Read data in your custom segment, typically by looping through the data records unless the system explicitly provides you the custom segment as an input parameter.

2. Determine when this user exit is called. If it is called after the document is posted, you must find the key of the document that was posted. This information is usually available in the data records. You can then update tables per your requirement. In the case of a customer master, for example, the user exit is invoked after the data is posted.

3. If the user exit is invoked before the document is posted, you can move data from the custom segment to one of the tables that may be passed as a parameter. For example, the user exit for the material master IDoc allows you to append data in the customer segment to the extended fields in the material master table before posting.

The wide variety of scenarios makes it impossible to describe every scenario, but the essence is to know when your user exit is invoked and how to process your data.

Sample Program

The program in Listing 32-7 reads an extended segment of a customer master IDoc. This data is then posted to the user-defined fields in the customer master table.

Listing 32-7

```
*----------------------------------------------------------------*
*    INCLUDE ZXVSVU02                                            *
*----------------------------------------------------------------*
* In this scenario, data in the Z1KNVVM segment is read and processed.
* This user exit is called after the system has already updated the
* customer master. Therefore data is updated in the SAP tables directly
*----------------------------------------------------------------*


TABLES: KNVV.

DATA: KNVVM LIKE E1KNVVM,
      KNA1M LIKE E1KNA1M,
```

```
            Z1KNVVM LIKE Z1KNVVM.

   LOOP AT IDOC_DATA.                          " loop through all data records

      CASE IDOC_DATA-SEGNAM.
         WHEN 'E1KNA1M'.                        " has customer number in it
            KNA1M = IDOC_DATA-SDATA.

         WHEN 'E1KNVVM'.                  " has sales org dist ch and division
            KNVVM = IDOC_DATA-SDATA.

         WHEN 'Z1KNVVM'.                        " has custom data
            Z1KNVVM = IDOC_DATA-SDATA.

   *        Always a good idea to make sure we have a valid customer number
            SELECT SINGLE * FROM KNVV WHERE KUNNR = KNA1M-KUNNR
                                   AND    VKORG = KNVVM-VKORG
                                   AND    VTWEG = KNVVM-VTWEG
                                   AND    SPART = KNVVM-SPART.
            IF SY-SUBRC EQ 0.                   "customer was found
               UPDATE KNVV SET
               ZZDELPRTY    = Z1KNVVM-ZZDELPRTY
               ZZRANK       = Z1KNVVM-ZZRANK
               WHERE KUNNR = KNA1M-KUNNR AND
                     VKORG = KNVVM-VKORG AND
                     VTWEG = KNVVM-VTWEG AND
                     SPART = KNVVM-SPART.
            ELSE.
   * The following lines of code will create a status record
   * with status 51, and a workflow is started
               IDOC_STATUS-DOCNUM = IDOC_CONTRL-DOCNUM.
               IDOC_STATUS-STATUS = '51'.
               IDOC_STATUS-MSGTY  = 'E'.
               IDOC_STATUS-MSGID  = 'ZE'.
               IDOC_STATUS-MSGNO  = '005'.
               IDOC_STATUS-MSGV1  = KNA1M-KUNNR.
               APPEND IDOC_STATUS.

               WORKFLOW_RESULT = C_WF_RESULT_ERROR.
               RETURN_VARIABLES-WF_PARAM = 'Error_IDOCs'.
```

```
          RETURN_VARIABLES-DOC_NUMBER = IDOC_CONTRL-DOCNUM.
          APPEND RETURN_VARIABLES.


      ENDCASE.
    ENDLOOP.
```

Programs to Enhance the Process

This section describes how user exits can be utilized for tasks other than IDoc extensions. A wide variety of scenarios can be implemented in user exits. Combining your knowledge of the location of exits in the process with a little creativity will enable you to solve many common problems. An example of generating the trading partner for the EDI subsystem is presented here.

Generating the Trading Partner of the EDI Subsystem

You can implement the code shown in Listing 32-8 in the user exit EXIT_SAPLEDI1_001 of enhancement SIDOC001 to generate the trading partner of the EDI subsystem for an outbound IDoc.

Program Flow

Here are the necessary blocks:

1. Make sure the IDoc is an outbound IDoc.

2. Concatenate the SAP trading partner and value stored in the EDI Message Type field of the partner profile to the Receiver Address field (RCVSAD) in the control record.

3. Copy the incoming control record to the outgoing control record.

Listing 32-8

```
*-----------------------------------------------------------------*
*    INCLUDE ZXEDIU01                                             *
*-----------------------------------------------------------------*
* This exit is used to build a trading partner id for the EDI
* subsystem. The partner number in SAP and the EDI message type
```

```
* fields in the partner profile are being used to build a trading
* partner id for the EDI subsystem
*----------------------------------------------------------------*
   IF CONTROL_IN-DIRECT = '1'.              " needed for outbound only

      CONCATENATE CONTROL_IN-RCVPRN,
                  CONTROL_IN-STDMES
              INTO CONTROL_IN-RCVSAD.

   ENDIF.


   CONTROL_OUT = CONTROL_IN.
```

Summary

Programming in the IDoc interface is carried out to enhance the interface to meet various business needs. Programs are written for custom-developed basic IDoc types in which outbound programs are written to populate IDocs with data from application documents. Although the core logic for the IDoc generation programs is always the same, there can be different flavors of these programs depending on the triggering mechanism used in the process, such as message control, stand-alone programs, and change pointers. Each program has a different interface. Similarly, inbound programs are written to read IDoc data and post application documents from it. All inbound programs use a common interface, but the internal implementation of the inbound programs depends on the scenario, such as, single IDoc processing, mass processing, serialized IDocs, and ALE-enabled transactions.

Apart from programs for the custom IDoc types, programs are also developed for extended IDocs. These programs are implemented in the user exits that provide a formal method of enhancing the system and are supported on a future upgrade. These programs populate and process data in the extension.

User exits are available at strategic locations in the IDoc interface. Programs are written to carry out additional checks and customize the flow to meet business needs.

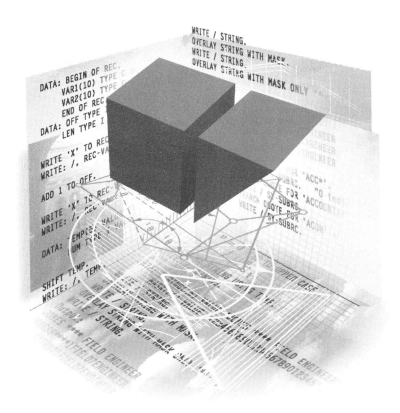

Chapter 33

**Customizing the
Interface for New or
Extended IDocs**

After you extend or develop an IDoc type and the necessary programs, you need to configure the system to make these components known to the ALE/EDI interface layer. This chapter shows you how to configure the system to recognize new components created for the outbound and the inbound process. These settings can be made in the IMG. Some of the settings are also available from the Area menu of EDI (Transaction: WEDI). These settings are not required if you are using standard SAP processes and have not made any changes to IDocs or programs.

This chapter contains two major sections: configuring the system for new IDocs and configuring the system for extended IDocs. In each section you learn about configuring the outbound and the inbound process. You should read this chapter as a reference. First you should identify the section that describes your scenario and then branch directly to the steps that pertain to the scenario you are trying to configure.

Configuring the System for New IDocs

This section explains how to make a custom basic IDoc type and its programs known to the ALE/EDI interface layer.

Configuring an Outbound Process for New IDocs

The steps in configuring an outbound process depend on the type of program that you have developed for the outbound IDoc. Three types of outbound programs were discussed in the preceding chapter: IDocs via message control, IDocs from stand-alone programs, and IDocs from change pointers. Each requires a slightly different setup. The monthly report IDoc and its programs are used as an example to describe the procedure.

Configuring an Outbound Process That Uses Message Control

The steps listed here are carried out if your outbound process uses Message control and you have replaced a standard SAP provided function module with your custom function module to generate custom IDocs. The steps below describe how you configure the system so that message control invokes your custom programs and generates custom IDocs:

1. Create a new message type.
2. Link the IDoc type to the message type.

3. Create a new process code.

4. Create or change a partner profile to add a message control record and an outbound record.

Create a New Message Type

Transaction: WE81

Menu Path: From the Area menu of EDI, choose Development, IDoc types, Environment, Message Types.

In this step you assign a message type to the data contents transferred in the IDoc and give it a short description. Customer-defined messages begin with Z. This should be the same name used in your IDoc programs. For the monthly report IDoc, message type ZMREPT is chosen.

Link the IDoc Type to the Message Type

Transaction: WE82

Menu Path: From the Area menu of EDI, choose Development, IDoc types, Environment, IDoc type/Message

This step assigns the message type created above to the IDoc type, as shown in Figure 33-1. This step not only serves to document which message is based on which IDoc type but also checks this link in the process when IDocs are generated.

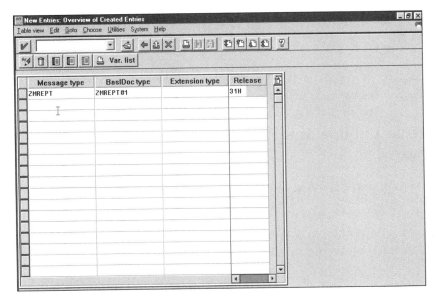

FIGURE 33-1

Linking the IDoc type and message type

Create a New Process Code

Transaction: WE41

Menu Path: From the Area menu of EDI, choose Control, Outb. Process Code, Outbound with ALE Service, With function Module Version 3

This step assigns a process code to the function module created for the outbound process, as shown in Figure 33-2. The process code is an indirect means of identifying the function modules.

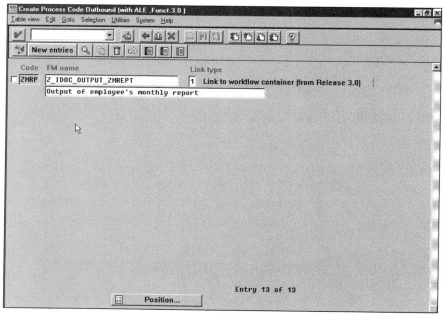

FIGURE 33-2

The process code assigned to the function module that generates the monthly report IDoc

Create or Change the Partner Profile

Transaction: WE20

Menu Path: From the Area menu of EDI, choose IDoc, Partner Profile

A partner profile is created for every partner system that sends or receives IDocs. In the partner profile, a message control record and an outbound record are created for each outbound message that operates under message control.

Create a partner profile if it does not exist. Add the message control record (see Figure 33-3) and outbound record (see Figure 33-4) for your message. This step assumes that Message control components such as the Application and Output type have already been configured. Refer to "Creating a New Condition Component" in Chapter 8, "Configuring Message Control" for details on how to create output types and tie them to Message control applications.

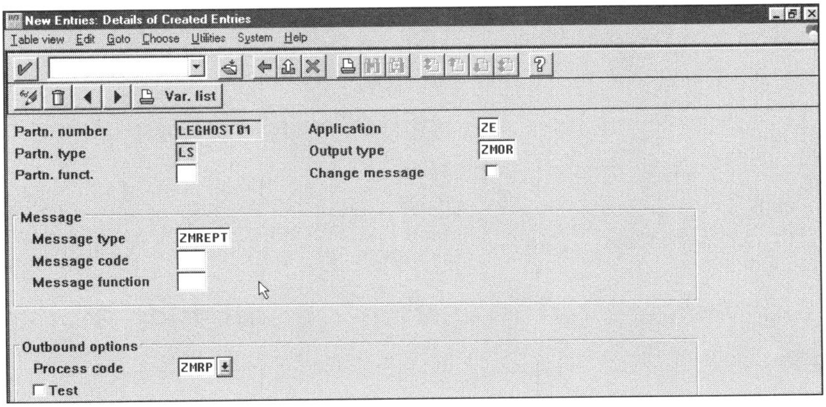

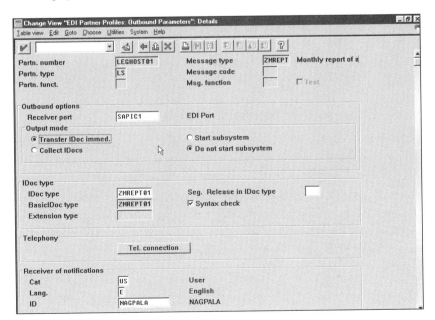

FIGURE 33-3

Partner profile—Message control parameters

FIGURE 33-4

Partner profile—outbound parameters

Configuring an Outbound Process for Stand-Alone Programs

The steps listed here are carried out if your outbound program is developed as a stand-alone program to generate IDocs. These programs are mainly designed for master data distribution in ALE and interfaces with legacy systems. Here are the configuration steps:

1. Create a new message type.
2. Link the IDoc type to the message type.
3. Add the message to the ALE distribution model (optional).
4. Create or change the partner profile.

Steps 1 and 2 are the same as described earlier in "Configuring an Outbound Process That Uses Message Control." Step 3 is new and step 4 is slightly different.

Add the Message to the Customer Distribution Model

Transaction: BD64

Menu Path: From the ALE configuration in the IMG (SALE) Area menu of EDI, choose Distribution Customer Model, Maintain Customer Distribution Model Directly

Here you add your message to the distribution model. Figure 33-5 shows how a message type ZMREPT that is sent to legacy system LEGHOST01 is created in the customer distribution model. This step is necessary only if you have not specified the receiving partner in the control record within your program (see Chapter 23).

Create or Change the Partner Profile

Transaction: WE20

Menu Path: From the Area menu of EDI, choose IDoc, Partner Profile

In the partner profile, an outbound record is created for each outbound message generated from stand-alone programs. Note that the message control record is not created in this case because stand-alone programs do not use the message control component. Refer to Figure 33-4 for attributes specified in the outbound record of a partner profile.

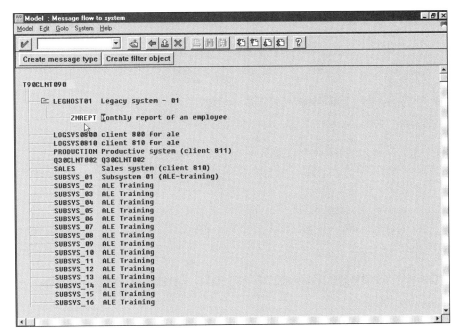

FIGURE 33-5

Adding your message to the customer distribution model

Configuring Change Pointers for an Outbound Process

The steps below describe how you configure the system so that RBDMIDOC calls your custom program. The steps are carried out if you have developed an IDoc generation program using change pointers. These programs are designed to generate IDocs based on changes to a document or master data. The RBDMIDOC program reads configuration tables to determine the appropriate IDoc generation program for a particular message type. The settings for those configuration tables are as follows:

1. Create a new message type.
2. Link the IDoc type to the message type.
3. Make sure change pointers are globally activated.
4. Activate change pointers for your message type.
5. Link message type to function module.
6. Add the message to the ALE distribution model (optional).
7. Create the partner profile.

Steps 1 and 2 are the same as those described in the "Configuring an Outbound Process That Uses Message Control" section earlier in the chapter. Steps 3,4, and 5 regarding change pointers are new. Steps 6 and 7 are the same as steps 3 and 4 of "Configuring an Outbound Process for Stand-Alone Programs."

Verify Global Activation of Change Pointers

Transaction: BD61

Menu Path: From the ALE configuration in the IMG (SALE), choose Distribution Scenarios, Master Data Distribution, Activate Change Pointer, Activate Change Pointer (generally).

In this step you want to make sure that the change pointer process is active. Execute transaction BD61 and activate the change pointer process if it's not already active.

Activate Change Pointers for the Custom Message

Transaction: BD50

Menu Path: From the ALE configuration in the IMG (SALE), choose Distribution Scenarios, Master Data Distribution, Activate Change Pointer, Activate Change Pointer for Message Types.

Change pointers also need to be activated for each individual message. Execute transaction BD50 and add an entry for your custom message.

Link Message Type to Function Module

Transaction: BD60

The message type also needs to be linked to the function module developed for analyzing the change pointers. Execute transaction BD60 and add an entry for your custom message, as shown in Figure 33-6.

Configuring an Inbound Process for New IDocs

As mentioned in the previous chapter, the inbound IDoc process is the same no matter what outbound process is used to generate an IDoc. The inbound configuration for a new process can be divided into two parts: process configuration and workflow configuration for exception handling. The steps for process configuration require some of the components defined in the workflow configuration, so it is necessary to maintain the workflow configuration before maintaining the process configuration.

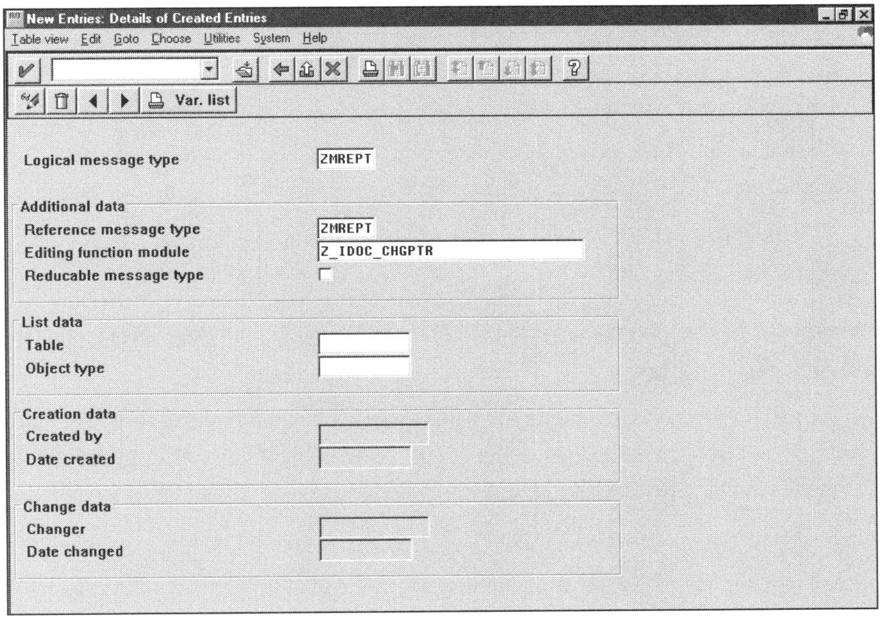

FIGURE 33-6

Link the custom message to the function module to change pointers

Workflow Configuration

Workflow configuration is necessary for exception handling in the inbound process. The various elements used in the exception handling process can be understood by looking at the process flow:

◆ When an application error occurs, an event is raised. This event is called a triggering event. The triggering event is part of the IDoc application object. For standard messages, the triggering event is named INPUTERROROCCURRED.

◆ The triggering event is linked to a workflow error task. The task gets started and a work item appears in a user's inbox.

◆ The user processes the work item. At the end, the system raises a terminating event to mark the completion of the work item. The terminating event is also part of the IDoc application object. For standard messages, the terminating events are named INPUTFINISHED.

From the above process, you will see that the system needs to know the IDoc application object, triggering event, terminating event, task, and linkage between the triggering event and task.

The steps to make the above components known to the system are as follows:

1. Create a new IDoc application object in the business object repository with triggering and terminating events.

2. Create a new task based on the application IDoc object.

3. Create the event linkage.

4. Create a new IDoc packet object in the business object repository (optional).

Create a New Application IDoc Object in the Business Object Repository

Your objective is to create an IDoc application object for your message. The best option is to copy an existing IDoc application object and change the necessary settings. Follow these simple steps:

1. Execute transaction SWLD (Area menu for workflow).

2. Click on the Object Repository button. This step should take you to the business object repository. Click on the Find icon (it looks like a pair of binoculars) and enter IDOCAPPL in the Object Type field. Make sure you click on the Position in Tree button at the bottom and then press Enter.

3. Expand the object list under IDOCAPPL as shown in Figure 33-7.

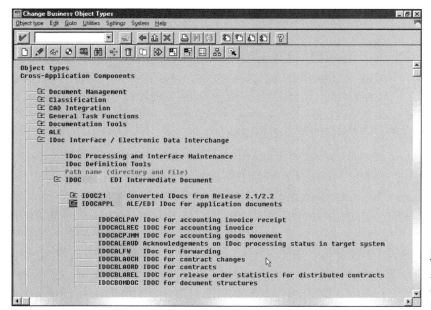

FIGURE 33-7

IDoc application objects for IDoc messages

4.   Click on any object and click on the Copy icon from the application toolbar.

 NOTE

Make sure the object being copied has the INPUTERROROCCURED and INPUTFINISHED events. You can confirm this by double-clicking the object and then verifying the event list.

5.   Assign a name for the object type and the program. The names must start with a Z. Click on the Copy button. When prompted, enter the development class. This step should create an entry in the object list at the bottom.

6.   Double-click on the newly created entry. Click on the Header icon (it looks like a hat). Press the Display->Change icon in the application toolbar, and if the system prompts you for several interfaces, simply cancel out of the dialog box. Change the short text and description to match your IDoc. See Figure 33-8 for values entered for the monthly report IDoc. Generate your object type. You can also release the object type.

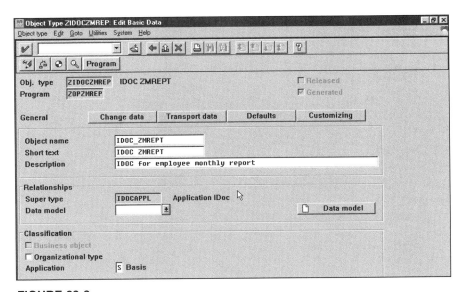

FIGURE 33-8

Object type for a custom message and its attributes

Create a New Task Based on the Application IDoc Object

A workflow task defines the attributes of a task that need to be carried out when an application error occurs. You need to create a task for your inbound process. A task points to an object method to be executed, and the triggering event that starts the task. The best option is to copy an existing task such as Orders_error (TS00008046). Follow these simple steps:

1. Execute transaction SWLD (Area menu for workflow).

2. Click on the Tasks button. Enter the task number for Orders_Error (TS00008046). Press the Copy icon.

3. Enter an abbreviation and name for the task. Make sure the Customer Task radio button is selected. Press Enter. This should copy the task. Note the number.

4. You should be back on the task screen with the task number filled out. If not, enter the number you saw in step 3 and click on the Change icon.

5. Replace the object type field with the IDoc application object you created earlier in "Creating a New Application IDoc Object in the Business Object Repository." See Figure 33-9 for task attributes defined for the monthly report IDoc.

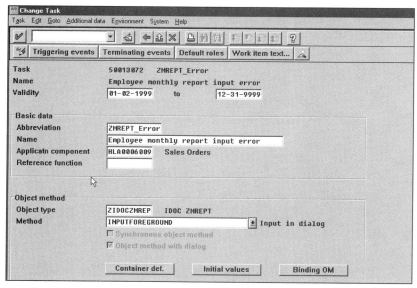

FIGURE 33-9

Task attributes for the customer task for the monthly report IDoc

6. Now you will change the triggering event. Click on the Triggering Event button to go to the triggering event screen. Delete the existing event and then create another event based on your object type. Click on the Insert Event button. Enter your object type and the INPUTERROROCCURRED event. Figure 33-10 shows the triggering event defined for the customer task for the monthly report IDoc.

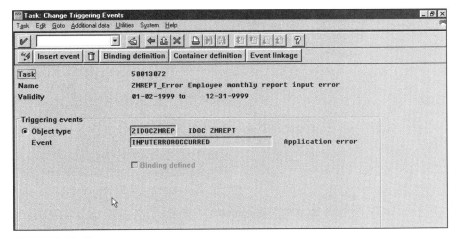

FIGURE 33-10

Triggering event for the customer task

7. Now you are ready to define the binding of data between triggering the event and the task. A binding between two elements is basically saying a=b in a programming language. Click on the Binding Definition button. In the right column, press F4 and select the default entry (it's highlighted in green). Perform the same operation for the Exception field. See Figure 33-11 for the binding definition between the triggering event and the task for the monthly report IDoc. You can also click on the Check button for testing the consistency in binding. Click on the Green arrow to go back to the triggering event screen.

8. Now you will activate the linkage between your task and triggering event. Click on the Event Linkage button. On the next screen, scroll to the right and double-click on the text that says Deactivated. This step should activate your linkage, as shown in Figure 33-12. Press Enter and click on the green arrow to return to the task screen.

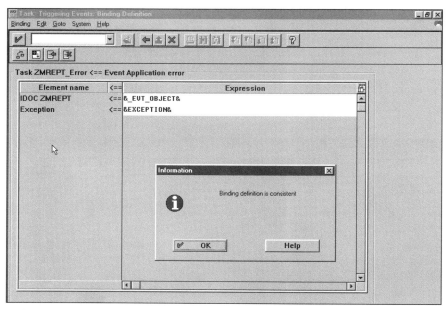

FIGURE 33-11

Binding definition between the triggering event and task

 NOTE

Step 8 has taken care of the third requirement for maintaining workflow configuration for the inbound process for a new IDoc, creating the event linkage. Now that you've established this link between the event and the workflow task, the workflow system uses this link to start the task whenever the event is raised.

9. Now you can define the terminating event. Click on the Terminating Event button. Delete the entry that exists from the copy operation. Next click on the Insert Event button and enter the values for Object Type, Event (this should be the terminating event INPUTFINISHED), and Element; press F4; and select the only entry. See Figure 33-13 for the terminating event defined for the customer task for the monthly report IDoc. Press Enter and click on the green arrow icon in the application toolbar to go back.

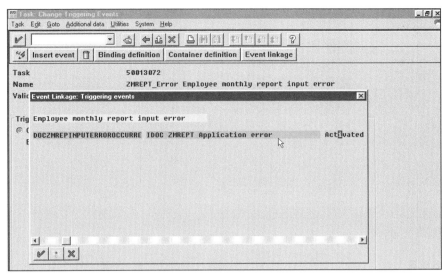

FIGURE 33-12

Event linkage for the triggering event

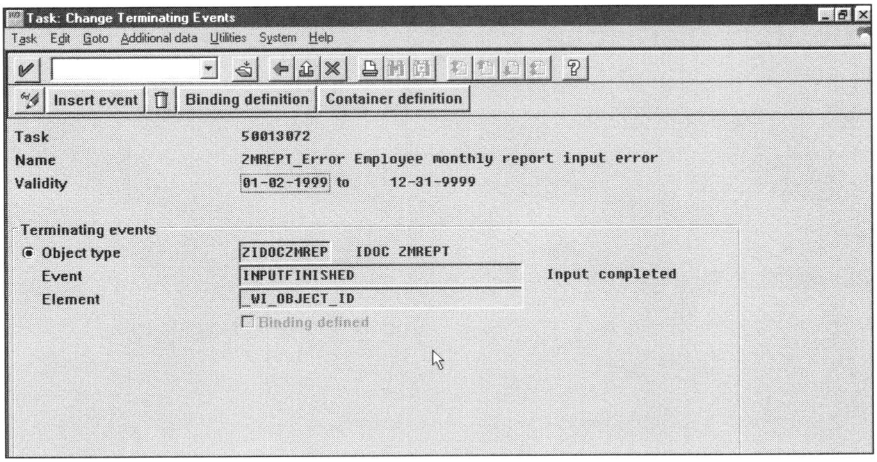

FIGURE 33-13

The terminating event for the customer task

10. Make your task a General Task so that anyone can execute it. Choose
    Additional Data, Agent Assignment, Maintain. Click on the General Task
    button and select the General Task check box (see Figure 33-14). Press
    Enter and click on the green arrow icon in the application toolbar to back.

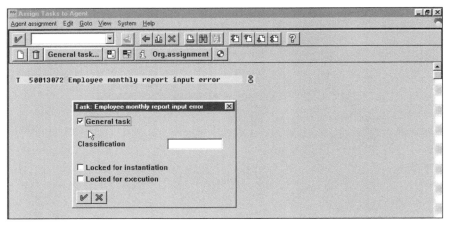

FIGURE 33-14

Making the customer task a General Task

11. Save your task.

Create a New IDoc Packet Object in the Business Object Repository (Optional)

This object is used for processes that are capable of processing many IDocs. Follow the steps outlined in the "Create a New Application IDoc Object in the Business Object Repository" section earlier in the chapter, but this time use IDOCPACKET instead of IDOCAPPL as the starting point.

Process Configuration

After you create the necessary workflow configuration, you can carry out the steps for process configuration:

1. Create a new message type.

2. Link the message type to the IDoc type.

3. Allocate the function module to the logical message type.

4. Define attributes for the inbound function module.

5. Create a new process code.

6. Create a partner profile.

Create a New Message Type

Transaction: WE81

Menu Path: From the Area menu of EDI, choose Development, IDoc types, Environment, Message Types

Just like the outbound process, the inbound process also requires a message type assigned to the data contents transferred in the IDoc. Customer-defined messages begin with Z. The name of the message type should be the same name used in your IDoc programs. For the monthly report IDoc, message type ZMREPT is chosen. If you have already created this entry in your system for the outbound process, you can ignore this step.

Link IDoc Type to Message Type

Transaction: WE82

Menu Path: From the Area menu of EDI, choose Development, IDoc types, Environment, IDoc Type/Message

This step assigns the new message type to the IDoc type. This step is also similar to the outbound process. Figure 33-15 shows the linkage between a message and IDoc type for the monthly report IDoc.

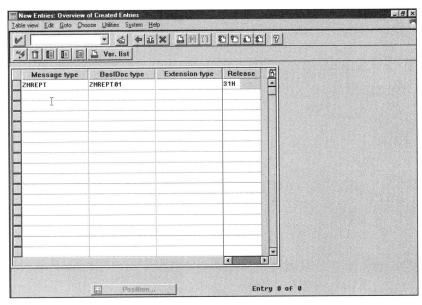

FIGURE 33-15

Linking IDoc type and message type

Allocate the Function Module to the Logical Message

Transaction: WE57

Menu Path: From the ALE configuration in the IMG (Transaction: SALE), choose Extensions, Inbound, Allocate Function Module to Logical Message

This configuration establishes a link between the function module; message variant (message type, message function, message code); IDoc type; and business object created by the function module. The Business Object field is optional. Figure 33-16 shows the allocation of the function module to the logical message for the monthly report IDoc.

 NOTE

In the case of outbound messages, this link is established in the partner profile. For inbound messages, there is no entry for an IDoc type in the partner profile, and therefore this entry is used to establish a valid IDoc type, message, and business object for a function module.

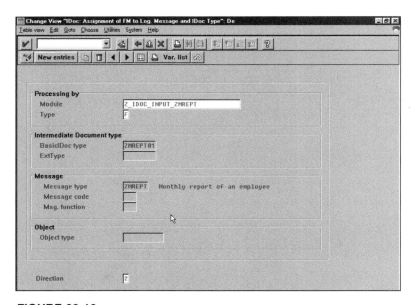

FIGURE 33-16

Linking IDoc type, message type, and business object

Define Settings for the Inbound Function Module

Menu Path: From the ALE configuration in the IMG (Transaction: SALE), choose
Extensions, Inbound, Define Settings for Input Modules.

This configuration step tells the ALE system how your function module has been
implemented. The ALE layer uses these settings to invoke the function module
with correct parameters. Figure 33-17 shows the settings for the function module
written for the monthly report IDoc.

In the Input Type field, the possible values are

> **Mass processing (0).** This option is for function modules that use a
> direct input method to create an application document. The ALE layer
> can pass multiple IDocs to the function module at the same time.

> **Individual input (1).** This option is for function modules that use the
> call transaction method to post an application document.

> **Individual input with IDoc lock in CALL TRANSACTION (2).** This
> option is for function modules that use ALE-enabled transactions to
> post an application document.

The Dialog All field indicates whether or not the IDoc can be posted in a dialog
mode after an error. If this option is turned on, then the user can watch each
screen during input processing.

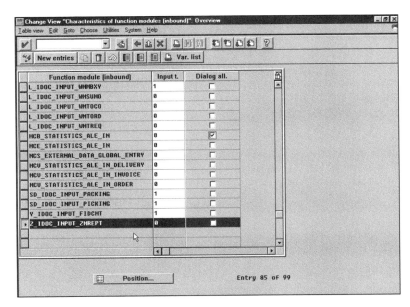

FIGURE 33-17

*Attributes of the
input function
module*

Create a New Process Code

Transaction: WE42

Menu Path: From the ALE configuration in the IMG (Transaction: SALE), choose Extensions, Inbound, Maintaining Process Codes (Inbound), Inbound with ALE Service, Processing by Function Module

This step defines a process code that points to the function module developed for the inbound process. Process codes provide an indirect means of determining the process (in this case, function module). Using process codes allows you to change the process without affecting other configurations.

The process code must start with a Z. Assign a short description and then save your entry as shown in Figure 33-18. The system prompts you with the following message: Please maintain codes added in 'ALE entry methods.' Accept the message by pressing Enter, and you are taken to a screen that shows the existing links between process codes and function modules.

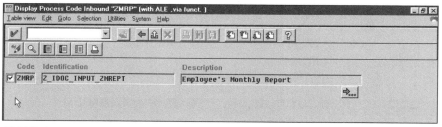

FIGURE 33-18

Process code pointing to a function module

Assign Input Methods

Transaction: BD67

Menu Path: From the ALE configuration in the IMG (Transaction: SALE), choose Extensions, Inbound, Assign Input Methods

This step creates a link between the process code defined above and the function module. This screen also contains additional parameters that the workflow component uses for error handling as well as for advanced workflow programming.

You enter the process code, function module, and various workflow components developed earlier in "Workflow Configuration."

You can leave the Application Event field blank for the monthly report scenario. This field is used to specify the application event that should be raised after the application document has been posted successfully. The inbound function module has to be coded using the Advanced workflow programming technique to take advantage of this field (see Figure 33-19). You should refer to the ALE programming guide in the online help of SAP for details.

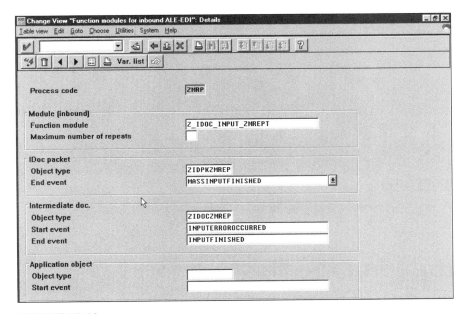

FIGURE 33-19

Process code details for an inbound function module

Create or Change the Partner Profile

Transaction: WE20

Menu Path: From the Area menu of EDI, choose IDoc, Partner Profile

A partner profile is created for every partner system with which you exchange IDocs. In the partner profile, a record is created for every incoming message.

Create a partner profile if it does not exist. Add a record for your incoming message. Figure 33-20 shows the inbound parameters in the partner profile for the monthly report IDoc.

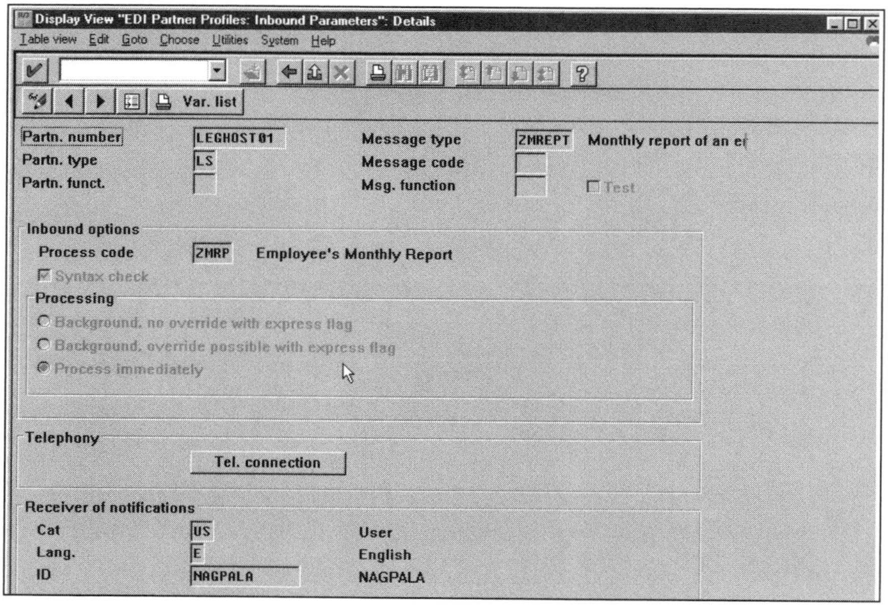

FIGURE 33-20

Partner profile—inbound parameters for an incoming message

Configuring the System for Extended IDocs

In this section you learn how to make IDoc extensions known to the ALE/EDI interface layer. The programs for IDoc extensions are already known to the ALE/EDI interface because these programs are written in the user-exits that are part of the standard SAP programs. Therefore the only requirement is to make the extended IDoc known to the system.

Configuring an Outbound Process for Extended IDocs

The outbound process requires only the two configuration settings: establishing a link between message type, IDoc type, and IDoc extension; and partner profile: outbound parameters.

Establishing a Link between Message Type, IDoc Type, and IDoc Extension

Transaction: WE82

Menu Path: From the Area menu of EDI, choose Development, IDoc Type, Environment, IDoc Type/Message

This step links the standard SAP message to your new extended IDoc while maintaining the original settings of the SAP basic IDoc type. This arrangement is possible because SAP permits a message type to be based on different versions of the IDocs. Figure 33-21 shows the settings for the IDoc extension created for the customer master data in Chapter 31, "Extending and Developing a Basic IDoc Type."

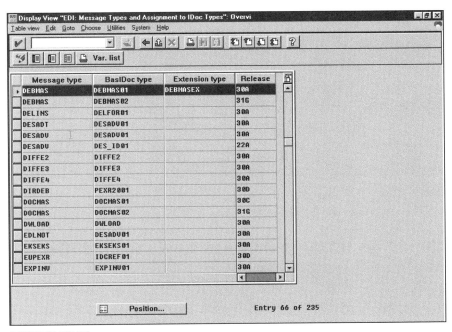

FIGURE 33-21

Link between message type, IDoc type, and IDoc extension

Partner Profile: Outbound Parameters

Transaction: WE20

Menu Path: From the Area menu of EDI, choose IDoc, Partner Profile

Here you specify the message and IDoc type that you want to use for the outbound process, as shown in Figure 33-22. Notice that when you enter the IDoc type, the system automatically fills the Basic IDoc type field and the Extension type field. The system knows the link when you created the IDoc extension.

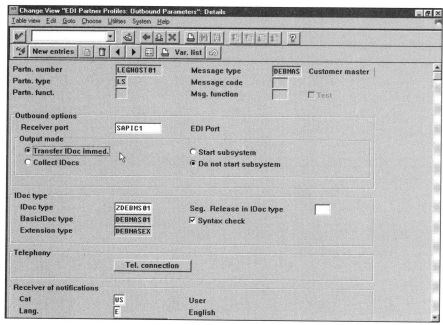

FIGURE 33-22

Specifying the extended IDoc in the partner profile

Configuring an Inbound Process for Extended IDocs

The inbound process needs only one configuration setting to make the IDoc extension known to the system, as described in the following sections. Notice that you do not need to make any change to the inbound record of the partner profile because the inbound view does not have any mention of the IDoc type.

Establishing a Link between Message Type, IDoc Type, and IDoc Extension

Transaction: WE57

Menu Path: From the ALE configuration in the IMG (Transaction: SALE), choose Extensions, Inbound, Allocate Function Module to Logical Message

This step links the standard SAP message to your new extended IDoc while maintaining the original settings of the SAP basic IDoc type, as shown in Figure 33-23. This arrangement is possible because SAP permits a message type to be based on different versions of the IDocs. Notice that the transaction for the inbound process is different than what you used for the outbound process earlier.

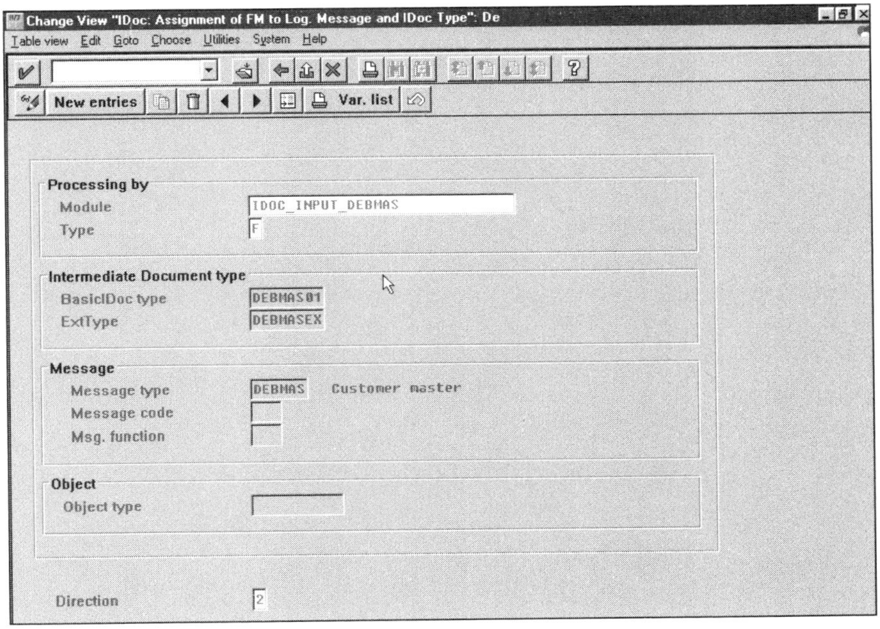

FIGURE 33-23

Link between message type, IDoc type, and IDoc extension

Summary

Newly created or extended IDocs and programs blend into SAP's existing IDocs and programs repository through various configuration options. This approach allows you to use the EDI interface for custom IDocs and thereby take advantage of the benefits of the infrastructure such as superior error handling, flexibility of process control, and documentation. Configuration for a newly created inbound process is slightly more involved because it requires additional workflow components for exception handling. The rest of the settings, however, are fairly simple.

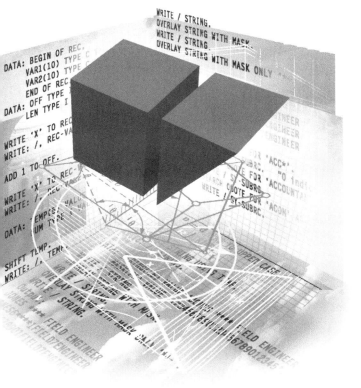

PART

12

Archiving in the IDoc Interface

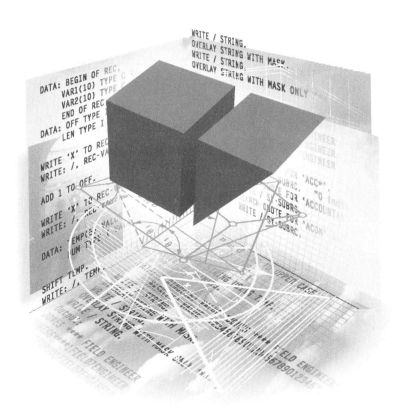

Chapter 34

**Archiving IDocs
and Deleting
Work Items**

When your system is operational and in production, the number of IDocs and workflow run-time logs can grow quickly. A workflow log is maintained for every work item generated for any exception in the IDoc interface. If your transaction volume is high, you need a strategy to clean up IDocs and completed work items from the system. SAP provides archiving programs and deletion programs for several documents in the system. This chapter shows you how to archive IDocs and delete work items along with work item history.

The major reason to archive is to improve performance, but archiving also helps to reclaim disk space that otherwise would be taken up by obsolete documents (IDocs and work items in this case).

Archiving is a process in which you offload data in SAP documents to a file at the operating system layer for later retrieval, and optionally delete the documents from the SAP system. The important point here is later retrieval. SAP provides a workbench for archiving objects and later retrieving objects from the archives.

Deleting is a process in which you permanently remove data from SAP with no provision to restore data. There are two choices for deleting data: either use the archiving programs or special deletion programs. In the case of IDocs, there is no special deletion program, so the archiving process is used to delete them. For work items, in contrast, you can use a special deletion program, in addition to the deletion program that is part of the archiving program's suite for work items.

You must start the archiving/deleting process soon after you go live on SAP to avoid falling behind. The archiving programs can take a long time to run depending on the load and amount of data in the system. In some situations the rate at which documents are created in the system may be greater than the rate at which they can be removed, which means that the archiving/deleting process will never be able to catch up. Hence the system performance deteriorates over time, and the system eventually comes to a halt. Therefore, it is important to start the archiving process soon after you go live with SAP.

Overview of the Archiving Module

Before you dig into the archiving process, it is important to understand the SAP lingo used in the archiving module. The archiving module is best understood by looking at the various functions provided in the system, how the system implements these functions, and how the process is executed.

Functions of the Archiving Module

The functions of the SAP archiving process are as follows:

◆ **Archiving Data.** The ability to archive data is certainly the most important function of the archiving module. Archiving is implemented as a two-step process. First, documents such as IDocs, work items, and purchase orders are offloaded to an archive file at the OS layer. Second, the archive file is read and objects are deleted from the system. This failsafe mechanism ensures that an object does not get deleted until it has been successfully archived to a file. Archiving in SAP is different from database archiving. Database archiving is based on data rules such as referential integrity rules. Archiving in SAP is implemented at the business level. A document must fulfill certain business rules before it can be archived. For example, an IDoc cannot be deleted if the status is 51 (Application error).

◆ **Analyzing Data Stored in Archives.** After data has been archived to a file, you can analyze the archived data and get details on the objects stored in an archive file.

◆ **Reloading Data.** Data from archives can be reloaded into the SAP system. This function is usually not required, but if a situation demands that data be reloaded, it is possible.

Implementing the Archiving Module

The following items explain how the system implements the above functions using archiving objects, archiving programs, and platform-independent file names. Then you learn about the interface of the archiving module with external archiving systems.

Archiving Object

Each business document that is to be archived is assigned an archiving object name. This name is used in various operations carried out as part of the archiving process. The name assigned to IDocs is IDOC, and the name assigned to work items is WORKITEM.

Archiving Programs

The various functions discussed earlier are achieved through programs that are part of the archiving object. An archiving object is comprised of four programs: the archiving program, deletion program, analysis program, and reload program.

 NOTE

Not all archiving objects support all four programs.

- ◆ **Archiving program.** This program selects documents that satisfy business conditions established for the object and then writes those documents to a file. The documents are still present in SAP.
- ◆ **Deletion program.** This program takes as input an archive file created by the archiving program and reads the various documents in the archive file. Those documents are then deleted from the SAP system.
- ◆ **Analysis program.** This program takes as input an archive file, analyzes data stored in the archives, and displays the results in a report format.
- ◆ **Reload program.** This program takes as input an archive file and allows you to reload one or more objects from the archive back into SAP database tables.

Platform-Independent File Names

Archive files are named using the platform-independent naming concept in SAP. As the name suggests, archive files are independent of the hardware platform. They also provide the capability of dynamic file names such as naming the file based on the date and time the archive process was started. Complete details on maintaining platform-independent file names are provided later in the chapter.

Interface with an External Archive Management System

Managing archive files is another nightmare. SAP integrates with third-party archive-management systems via the archivelink interface, which offloads the management of files to an external system. SAP certifies third-party vendor software for compatibility with the archivelink interface.

Maintaining Platform-Independent File Names

The archiving process starts by first establishing names for the archive files. Platform-independent file names can be maintained for the archive files via transaction FILE. First you define a path name, and then you define a file name in which you include the path name. Several paths and file names are already set up in the system, based on the standard SAP directory structure. You can elect to use those or copy them and modify them to suit your needs. The file names can be dynamic, and they support substitution parameters for file names. Several parameters, such as day, month, system ID, and client, have been defined in the system for substitution.

In the following example, a platform-independent file name is created for IDocs, using the naming convention IDOC_<date in MMDDYY format>. This file is located in the /usr/sap/archive/ directory.

Maintaining Logical Path Names

The steps to create a logical path for the archive file are as follows:

1. Execute transaction FILE. The first screen for this procedure, shown in Figure 34-1, displays the paths that exist in the system.

2. Assign a logical name for the path. Click on the New Entries button and give a name starting with Z, to represent the path, and a short, but meaningful description. For the IDoc example, call the file Z_IDOC_PATH. Save your entry.

3. Assign a true physical path to your logical path. Select your logical file path and press the magnifying glass next to Assignment of Physical Paths to Logical Path. Accept the system's information message, and on the next screen enter the platform on which you are working. For the example, UNIX is chosen, but of course, you should choose whatever is appropriate for you. Enter the physical path and end it with <FILENAME> as shown in Figure 34-2. This entry is a placeholder for the file name that will be attached to the file. Save your entry and click twice on the green arrow icon in the application toolbar to return to the first screen of file maintenance.

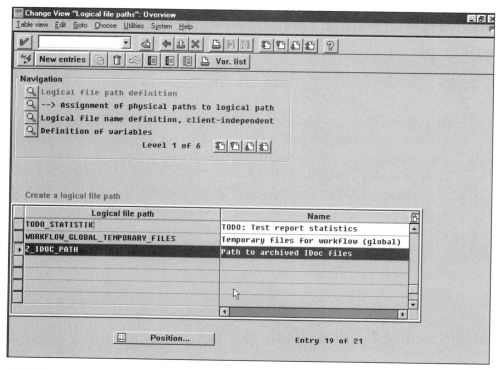

FIGURE 34-1

Initial screen for platform-independent file names.

Maintaining File Names

Once you have maintained the logical path name for the archive file, you need to maintain a logical name for the archive file.

Click on the magnifying glass next to Logical File Name Definition, Client-Independent to see a list of existing logical file names. Click on the New Entries button. Enter values in the various fields as shown in Figure 34-3. The file name contains substitution parameters, which are represented with angle brackets. Several standard substitution parameters can be used. Table 34-1 lists the commonly used substitution parameters in the file names.

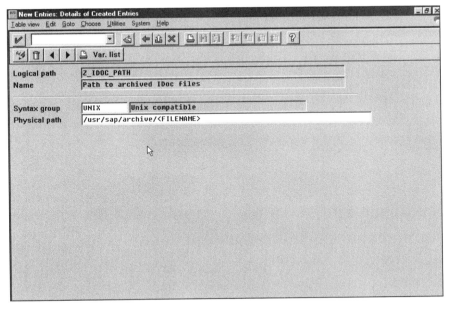

FIGURE 34-2

Assigning a logical path to a physical path for UNIX

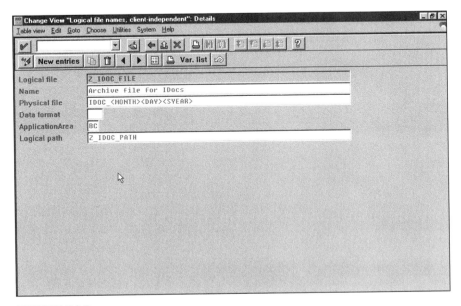

FIGURE 34-3

Maintaining platform–independent file names

Table 34-1 Substitution Parameters for File Names

Parameter Name	Description
<SYSID>	R/3 application name in SY-SYSID
<SAPRL>	R/3 release in SY-SAPRL
<HOST>	Host name in SY-HOST
<CLIENT>	Client in SY-MANDT
<DATE>	Date in SY-DATUM
<YEAR>	Year in SY-DATUM, four characters
<SYEAR>	Year in SY-DATUM, two characters
<MONTH>	Month in SY-DATUM
<DAY>	Day in SY-DATUM
<WEEKDAY>	Day of the week in SY-FDAYW
<TIME>	Time in SY-UZEIT
<STIME>	Hour and minute in SY-UZEIT
<HOUR>	Hour in SY-UZEIT
<MINUTE>	Minute in SY-UZEIT
<SECOND>	Seconds in SY-UZEIT

Archiving IDocs

Once you have maintained the archive file names, you are ready for the actual archiving process. IDocs can be archived for later retrieval or for permanent deletion. There is not much value in archiving IDocs generated in ALE as a result of SAP-to-SAP transfer, because the sending and receiving systems belong to your own company. It is best to delete these IDocs. For EDI-generated IDocs, it is usually best to leave the archiving function up to the EDI subsystem because it has the document in original form, as sent and received from business partners. EDI documents are legal bindings, so it is necessary to preserve the documents in the form that was exchanged with the business partner.

However, some companies require archiving at the source of the data, and therefore it may become necessary to archive IDocs in SAP. Otherwise, IDocs can usually be deleted. The deletion process builds out of the archiving process; therefore the following steps apply to both procedures.

Determining Which IDocs Can Be Archived

You cannot arbitrarily archive IDocs. IDocs must be in a state that makes sense for archiving. The status code of an IDoc governs whether or not the IDoc is suitable for archiving. Table 34-2 lists the status codes in the standard system that allow an IDoc to be archived. For example, it is perfectly OK to archive IDocs that have been successfully posted (status code 53), but it does not make sense to archive IDocs that have not been processed yet (status 64). However, in certain situations you may want to archive IDocs that were created accidentally, or for some reason you want to get rid of certain IDocs. You can change the settings of a status code to enable archiving (if not already permitted) as follows: Execute transaction WE47 and select the status code for which you want to make archiving possible. Click on the Detail icon (magnifying glass), select the Poss. field in the archiving block, and save your changes.

Table 34-2 IDoc Status Codes that Permit Archiving

Status Code	Description
03	Data passed to port OK
18	Triggering EDI subsystem OK
19	Data transfer for test OK
21	Error passing data for test
31	Error—no further processing
33	Original of an IDoc which was edited
38	IDoc archived
40	Application document not created in target system
41	Application document created in target system
53	Application document posted
57	Test IDoc: Error during application check
68	Error—no further processing
70	Original of an IDoc which was edited
73	IDoc archived

Archiving Programs Used in IDocs

The following programs are utilized in archiving IDocs:

♦ RSEXARCA and RSEXARCB are archiving programs. RSEXARCB is similar to RSEXARCA except for the selection screen. The selection options for RSEXARCB are designed for periodic scheduling.

- ◆ RSEXARCD is a deletion program.
- ◆ RSEXARCR reads from the archive.
- ◆ RSEXARCL reloads from archive.

These programs are documented thoroughly. You can read their documentation from the archiving transaction SARA or you can use transaction SE38 to view the documentation.

Customizing

Before you can start archiving, you need to tell the system which file name to use and how big the file can be. Customizing for archiving objects is carried out from transaction SARA. Enter IDOC in the Object Name field and click on the Customizing button. In the customizing options screen (see Figure 34-4), specify the following attributes:

- ◆ **Log. File Name.** This field contains the logical file name you created earlier.
- ◆ **Size in MB.** This field contains the maximum size of the archive file in MB. The system checks the current file size before opening the archive file. If the file size exceeds the limit specified here, the system opens another file in which to put the IDocs.
- ◆ **Max. number of data objects.** This field specifies the maximum number of IDocs allowed in an archive file. Before adding an IDoc to the archive file, the system checks the number of IDocs in the file against the number specified in the field. If there are too many IDocs, it creates a new archive file.
- ◆ **Commit counter.** The commit counter field specifies the number of IDocs to be deleted before the commit is performed. You can tune this parameter to improve performance.
- ◆ **Start automat. field under Settings for delete program.** This field specifies whether to start the deletion program automatically or not. Set this option to on; otherwise, you have to manually schedule the deletion program.

Archiving IDocs

To this point you have maintained all the necessary settings and now you are ready to carry out the actual archiving process.

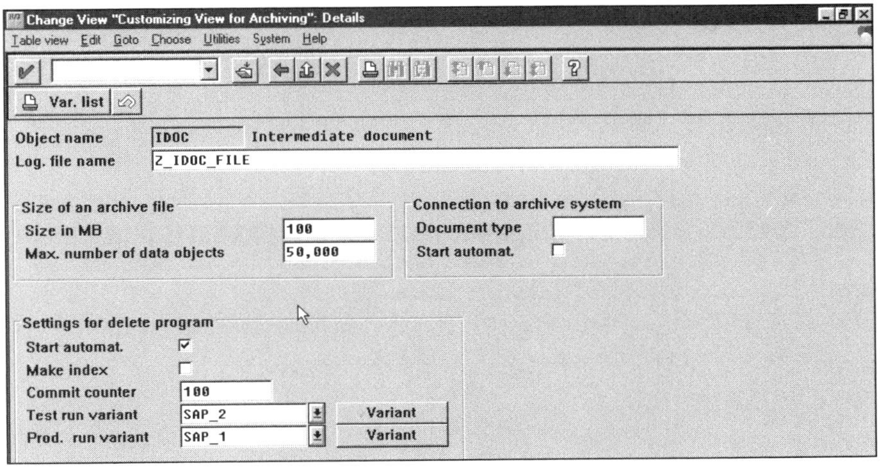

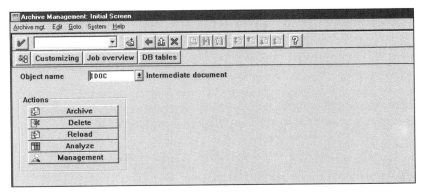

FIGURE 34-4

Settings to customize the IDoc archiving process

Start the Main Transaction for Archiving

Execute transaction SARA, enter IDOC in the Object Name field, and press
Enter. This process should enable all the options available for the object, as shown
in Figure 34-5.

FIGURE 34-5

The main screen for archiving IDocs

Maintain Variants for the Archiving Program

This step sets up a variant for the archiving program. Click on the Archive button.
Choose an existing variant or enter a variant name and then click on the maintain

button. Create your variant as desired. You can select the IDocs to be archived based on date, message type, message code, message function, direction, and IDoc number range, as shown in Figure 34-6. For example, if you want to delete all the material master IDocs, you can enter MATMAS in the message type field. Save your variant and go back to the main screen.

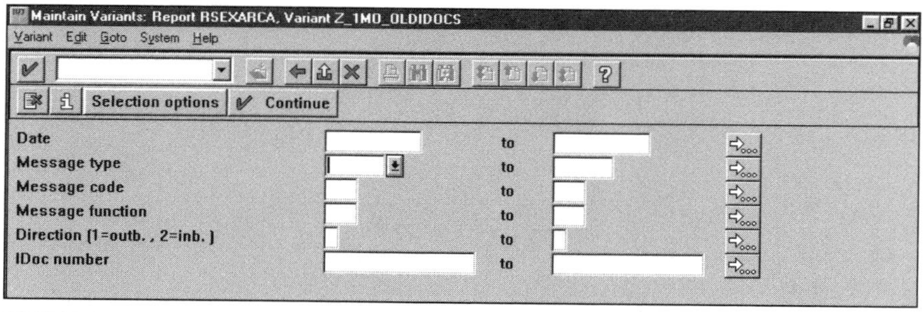

FIGURE 34-6

Selection parameters for archiving IDocs

Now you can specify the start time and spool parameters for the archiving program. Click on the Start Time button and enter the appropriate values. You can also elect to run the program immediately. After you specify the start time, you can specify the spool parameters that determine where to send the output of the program.

CAUTION

In the spool parameters, make sure the Print Immediately flag is turned off; otherwise, you may end up killing several trees unnecessarily.

Execute the Archive and Deletion Program

Click on the Execute button, and the system should begin archiving the objects. The archiving program is submitted as a background job. For security reasons the system does not permit two background jobs in the system with the same variant. Therefore, you must delete any previous instances of the archiving job before you execute the program. You must have authorization to execute the archiving programs— S_ARCHALL authorization is recommended.

TIP

Archiving jobs are scheduled with a priority class C (the lowest priority). On some application servers, class C jobs are restricted—in that case you will not be able to run archiving programs. Ask your Basis staff to turn on class C jobs on the application server where you will be executing these jobs.

Check the Results

You can check the results by clicking on the Job Overview button. First check the job log to make sure the program ran successfully. If so, display the spool list for the IDocs that were archived.

TIP

If there is a problem in the job log, you can try to execute the RSEXARCA program online by using transaction SE38.

Execute transaction WE05 and make sure the IDocs have been deleted. If you forgot to check the Start automat. checkbox when you customized earlier, the deletion program is not automatically started after the archiving process is completed. In this situation, you need to manually run the deletion program from transaction SARA. The steps to execute the deletion program are quite similar to the steps you followed to execute the Archiving program. First you maintain input parameters for the deletion program which in this case means specifying the archive file. Next you maintain the start time and spool parameters. Once all the necessary parameters have been maintained, you can execute the deletion program and verify the results.

Deleting Work Items

As mentioned earlier, the workflow management system maintains an extensive log for work items. It maintains a complete history of various actions that were carried out on a work item and maintains work items even after they have been completed. Work items can be archived or deleted. If work items are archived, they can be retrieved later. From an ALE/EDI perspective, there is no reason to archive work items.

NOTE

If you are interested in archiving work items, you can follow the steps presented earlier for the IDoc object. The archiving object to be used is WORKITEM. The archiving program for work items is RSWWARCA, and the deletion program is RSWWARCD. These programs are also thoroughly documented. You can view the documentation either using SARA or through SE38.

The following programs are utilized for deleting work items:

- ◆ RSWWWIDE, which deletes work items
- ◆ RSWWHIDE, which deletes work item history

You can use these programs to delete any work item regardless of its current state. For example, you can delete work items that are still in process. In contrast, archiving deletes completed work items only. Therefore, you must use extreme caution when executing these programs; as a workflow developer at SAP once said, "If you don't, you stand a good chance of losing lots of friends!" If you have a workflow development team, leave the task of deleting work items in their hands. Refer to "Work Item Status" in Chapter 11, "Monitoring the Interface," for a list of status values for a work item. Users often ask whether they can delete work items from their Inbox. In response, it is important to understand that work items are not treated like e-mail messages, which a specific user owns. A specific user owns a work item only when he or she has executed it at least once. Until then a work item does not have an established owner. Work items appear in your Inbox because you are designated a responsible user. They cannot be deleted based on a specific responsible user ID.

The RSWWWIDE and RSWWHIDE programs clean up the work item log and history. You can also use these programs to clean up work items from a user's Inbox that are not required anymore. You must execute RSWWWIDE before you execute RSWWHIDE.

Entering Selection Parameters for RSWWWIDE

Start RSWWWIDE by using transaction SE38. Some fields on the selection parameters screen for the program (see Figure 34-7) are self-explanatory, but the following fields need important consideration:

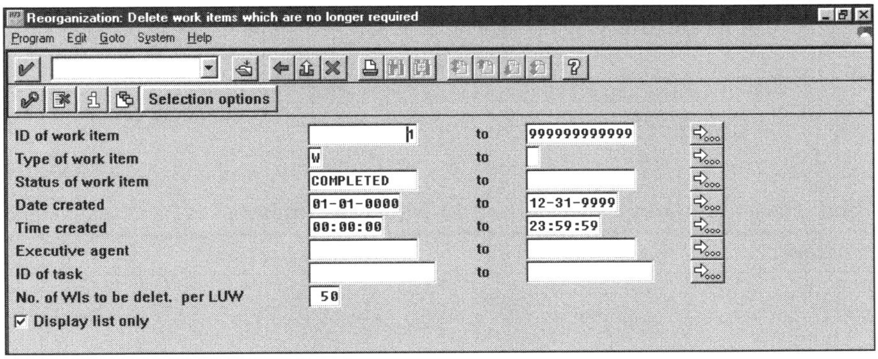

FIGURE 34-7

Selection parameters for the RSWWWIDE program

Display list only. If this field is checked, the program runs in a simulation mode and work items are not actually deleted. This setting is useful for initial tests to make sure the system deletes the desired work items only. When you are satisfied, you need to turn off this flag and rerun the program for the work items to be actually deleted from the system.

ID of work item. This field represents the range of work items that need to be processed. You can choose the default unless you want to delete a specific work item.

Type of work item. This field represents the type of work items to be deleted. In the ALE/EDI process, only type W is used.

Status of work item. This field defaults to Completed. With this setting the program deletes only work items that are in a completed state. Work items that are still visible in the Inbox are not completed; therefore, if you want to clean up work items that have been sitting in the Inbox for a long time, you should leave this field blank.

Executive agent. In this field enter the user ID of the person whose work items you want to delete. If you leave it blank, then the program selects work items for all users. If you enter a user ID, then the program deletes only the work items for which a user has been established. Work items that have not been executed at least once will not be selected. Therefore, if you want to clean up the Inbox, leave this field blank.

ID of task. You can use this field to restrict the work items to a specific task or a set of tasks. It is recommended that you restrict them to ALE/EDI tasks only. Table 34-3 contains a list of ALE/EDI tasks.

Table 34-3 Workflow tasks related to ALE/EDI Process

Process Code	Task Number	Description
EDIM	TS00007988	No IDoc created yet
EDIO	TS00007989	Error in the Outbound process
EDIX	TS00008070	Syntax error—Outbound
EDII	TS00008068	Error in the inbound process
EDIY	TS00008074	Syntax error—Inbound
EDIS	TS30000078	Error in the subsystem

In addition to these tasks, you need to include application-specific tasks that exist for each IDoc message. For example, the task name for errors in the DEBMAS message is DEBMAS_Error. The task ID is TS00008039. You can determine the task ID by using transaction PFTC. In the task type, enter TS; in the task, enter the task name; and then press Enter. The system looks up the task number and returns it in the task field.

TIP

If you maintain a variant for this program, you won't have to enter the values every time.

CAUTION

The variant shown in Figure 34-8 deletes all work items from the system regardless of user and work item state. Do not perform this procedure in the production system unless you know what you are doing or don't care about being fired. In the development and testing systems, it is not uncommon to execute the RSWWWIDE program in the "deadly" mode.

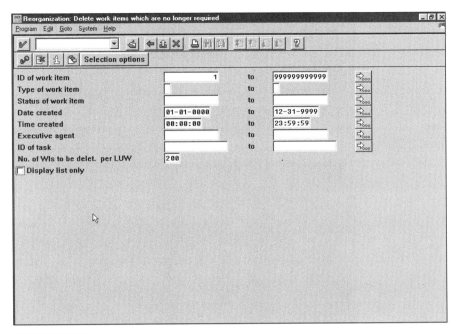

FIGURE 34-8

Selection parameters for the RSWWWIDE program to delete all work items regardless of their state

After you enter the necessary parameters, you can click on the Execute button to start the execution. In the production system, it is recommended that you execute this program in the background mode.

The deleted work items are displayed on the screen. You can also check the Inbox of the user who had ALE/EDI-related work items in their Inbox prior to executing the deletion programs.

Executing the RSWWHIDE Program

After you delete the work items, you can delete the history by executing the RSWWHIDE program. As with RSWWWIDE, the selection parameters for RSWWHIDE allow you to run the program in simulation mode, which you can do until you are satisfied with the results. When you are satisfied, you can execute the RSWWHIDE program in real mode to actually clean up the history log.

Summary

IDocs and work items created in the ALE/EDI process tend to build up in a system and cause performance problems. Thus on a regular basis it is necessary to get rid of unwanted IDocs and work items. You can choose to either archive those items or delete them permanently. Archiving and deleting are two separate processes. Archiving is useful if you need to retrieve archived data in the future. Deleting is useful for removing data you never need again. In some cases the deletion programs of the archive module are used to clean up the documents.

From an ALE/EDI perspective, archiving IDocs or work items is not very useful; rather it is best to delete them permanently. IDocs are deleted using archiving programs, and work items are deleted using special deletion programs provided by SAP. IDocs must be in a state that allows deletion, but you can customize this option. Work item deletion programs do not carry out any checks, so you need to be extra careful in the selection parameters specified for these programs.

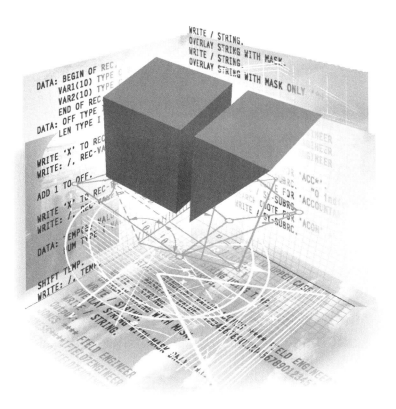

Appendix

FAQs, User Exits, and Miscellaneous Resources

Frequently Asked Questions

This appendix provides answers to many of the most frequently asked questions on the EDI listserver and in training classes.

1. Where can I get a list of the various status codes in the system?

Execute transaction WE47 to get a list of the various status codes. For each status code, you can also check additional details such as status text, direction, and whether archiving is possible.

2. How do I remove IDocs from my system?

SAP provides standard programs (RSEXARCA, RSEXARCB) to archive IDocs and then delete (RSEXARCD) them from the system. See Chapter 34, "Archiving IDocs and Deleting Work Items" for details.

3. I created an IDoc in the system that is in status 30 (IDoc ready for dispatch [ALE service]). I do not want to send this particular IDoc to our business partner. How can I prevent the system from accidentally processing the IDoc?

Create a status file for the IDoc with a status code of 31 (Error—no further processing). Use WE17 to import this file. This IDoc can also be archived. A sample status file is shown in Chapter 10, "Testing the EDI Interface" under "Verifying Status Reporting by the Subsystem."

4. How can I temporarily suspend EDI transmissions to a business partner?

Set the status of that partner in the General view of the partner profile to Inactive. This setting works for EDI partners (customers and vendors). It does not work for logical systems as used in ALE.

5. How can I temporarily stop sending purchase orders to a trading partner?

It depends on whether you have used a generic business rule (condition table) or a very specific one to propose EDI output. If you have used a very specific rule down to the vendor level, you can delete the condition record for that vendor. This action eliminates the automatic proposal and stops any EDI output for that vendor.

6. I created a purchase order but the Sender field in the control record is empty. What am I missing?

It is populated from the "Account at vendor" field in the vendor master. Refer to Chapter 14, "Outbound with Message Control—Purchase Orders" for all the required fields from an EDI perspective.

7. A workflow task was started due to an error in the IDoc processing. How can I tell who got the work item?

The person to be notified is determined from the outbound or inbound record of the partner profile, depending on the direction of the process. If not found, the general view of the partner profile is used to determine the person responsible. If a partner profile cannot be read at all, the EDI administrator as specified in the EDIADMIN table is notified. To bypass this lengthy process, you can execute transaction SWI1, enter W in the type field, and specify the approximate date and time when the process had the error. Locate the work item and go to its detail by double-clicking on the work item. Choose Goto, Agent, Selected Agents. This will reveal the user who has the work item.

8. Can I delete work items for a specific user?

You can only delete work items based on a user ID, provided the user has been established as the "owner" of the work item. Until a user executes a work item at least once or specifically reserves a work item, a work item does not have an established owner. You can delete work items based on task, work item ID, date, time, and several other parameters.

9. How do I delete old work items?

SAP provides standard archiving and deletion programs to clean up work items. You can delete work items regardless of their status by using the RSWWWIDE and RSWWHIDE programs. The various parameters for these programs are discussed in Chapter 34, "Archiving IDocs and Deleting Work Items."

10. How can I tell how many IDocs are in error?

There are several ways to determine the number of IDocs in error. The IDoc statistics tool (WE07) provides a comprehensive picture of the state of the IDocs in the system. Read Chapter 11, "Monitoring the Interface," for details on the various monitoring tools.

11. How can I determine the IDoc number generated for a purchase order?

Go to the output control screen of the purchase order (Header, Messages). Click on the output type and choose Processing Log from the menu. The log should display the IDoc number.

12. How can I determine the purchase order number from an IDoc?

The purchase order number in an IDoc is stored in the E1EDK01 segment in the BELNR field.

13. I see two IDoc types that look similar, such as ORDERS01 and ORDERS02. What is the difference?

The last two digits in an IDoc type represent the IDoc version. ORDERS02 is a newer version that supports configurable materials.

14. I see segments with names starting with E1, E2, and E3, such as E1EDK01, E2EDK01, and E3EDK01. What is their significance?

A name starting with E1 is the version-independent name of a segment type. By default, it points to the latest segment definition. A name starting with E2 is the version-dependent segment definition, and a name starting with E3 is a version-independent segment documentation.

15. Can I assign multiple message types to an IDoc type?

Of course. In fact, SAP uses this technique for maintaining backward compatibility. For example, message type ORDERS is assigned to ORDERS01 and ORDERS02.

16. Can I use the append structure option to extend an SAP segment?

No, you are not permitted to use the "append structure" option to extend a segment. You should use the formal method of IDoc extension to first create custom segments and then include the custom segment in the extended IDoc type.

17. A user who has nothing to do with ALE/EDI process has several EDI-related work items in their Inbox. What's wrong?

This scenario is typically the result of assigning ALE/EDI error tasks as General Tasks and incorrect configuration for the EDI administrator in the EDIADMIN table. See Chapter 6, "Configuring Basic EDI Components" for details on maintaining this table.

18. Why can't I set certain work items in my Inbox to "Done" and get rid of them?

Those work items probably require a terminating event to mark their completion. See Chapter 11, "Monitoring the Interface" for details on how to determine whether a work item requires a terminating event. Work items generated for application errors (status 51) in the IDoc require a terminating event.

19. Can someone else execute the work items if the user who handles errors with ALE/EDI processes is on vacation?

This problem has several solutions:

◆ Assign more than one user to the position that handles errors. This approach allows more than one user to receive work items, yet only one user can execute a work item at a time.

◆ Set up backups in the HR module.

◆ Set up Inbox views using evaluation paths.

These options are described in detail in Chapter 9, "Configuring Workflow."

20. Why does data transfer using ALE causes the receiving systems to hang?

When an ALE process transfers an IDoc to the receiving system, the IDoc takes up a dialog session on the receiving system. If numerous objects are being transferred and partner profiles have not been set to collect the IDocs, ALE processes may well have exhausted the dialog sessions currently available in the system. This condition causes a considerable slowdown and eventually halts the system. See Chapter 28, "Managing ALE Process Performance and Throughput" for details on the settings required to control ALE processes.

21. Why do I sometimes get a pop-up message saying that an update task was terminated?

In several outbound processes (especially the ones that use Message control), the task of generating IDocs is detached from the application processing. The IDocs are generated in an update task. SAP uses this method to speed up the update process. If one of the updates has an abnormal termination (usually the result of syntax errors in programs), then SAP sends the update terminated message. Execute transaction SM13 to examine the details.

22. I have written a user-exit for the L_IDOC_CREATE_WMTOID01 program which is called upon in the asynchronous update task. Is there a way to debug IDoc programs that are called upon in the asynchronous update task?

Use transaction SM66. You must have authorization to execute this transaction and debug the programs. You don't have much time between when you create a transfer order and when the system executes the IDoc generation program. The best option is to utilize one of the user exits and add some code to insert the delay in the IDoc processing. This will give you a chance to see an entry in transaction SM66 and then allow you to debug.

23. Why does data transfer using ALE cause background jobs to fail on the sending systems?

When an ALE process transfers an IDoc to the receiving system and encounters an error, the default behavior is to create a background job to retry the transmission later. If many objects are being transferred, the system will exhaust all the background jobs. This problem occurs due to the default settings on the tRFC options in the RFC destination. See Chapter 22, "Configuring the ALE Infrastructure" for details on how to set up the tRFC options in an RFC destination.

24. Can I get my work items in my e-mail client?

Yes, SAPLABS provides a MAPI connector that allows a MAPI-compatible client, such as Microsoft Outlook or Exchange, to view and execute work items in the SAP Inbox. Check out the SAP Labs Web site at **www.saplabs.com**.

25. Why doesn't the system archive certain IDocs?

Whether an IDoc can be archived or not depends on the status of the IDoc. You can execute transaction WE47 and change the default settings of the archiving flag for a status value to allow archiving. See Chapter 34, "Archiving IDocs and Deleting Work Items" for details on how to carry out archiving.

26. My organization has hundreds of vendors and customers. How can I build partner profiles without entering them manually?

You can either write BDC programs or use function modules specifically provided for creating partner profiles. See Chapter 7, "Configuring Partner Profiles" for details.

27. When processing inbound IDocs that are in error, why is the Process in Foreground button grayed out for some messages?

The inbound function modules for posting an incoming IDoc are programmed using either the call transaction method or a direct input function module. The system enables the Process in Foreground button for function modules that use the call transaction method. The button is grayed out in other cases because there is no provision to step through the screens.

28. How can I tell whether an inbound process uses call transaction or direct input?

Execute transaction BD51. Entries that have 1 or 2 in the Input T. field and a check in the Dialog All. field use the call transaction method. Entries with a value of 0 use the direct input method.

29. How do I communicate with back-level versions?

You can specify the IDoc version and the segment version in the partner profile.

30. If I have more questions, who can help me?

Drop me an e-mail at anagpal@bacusa.com. I look forward to hearing from you.

Transaction Codes

Transaction codes provide a shortcut to the function without navigating through the menus. The following transaction codes are frequently used in the areas indicated.

Main Menus

WEDI	Main menu for EDI-related activities
BALE	Main menu for ALE-related activities
SWLD	Main menu for workflow-related activities
SALE	Main area for ALE configuration
NACE	Main menu for Message control configuration

IDoc Definition

SE11	Data dictionary
WE31	Segment editor
WE30	IDoc editor to create and extend IDoc type
BD53	Reduce IDoc types for master data
WE60	IDoc documentation (IDoc structure and segment definition)
WE61	IDoc documentation (control record, data record, and status record)

IDoc Monitoring

WE02	IDoc display
WE05	IDoc list
WE07	IDoc statistics

Configuration (Basic Infrastructure for ALE and EDI)

WE20	Maintain partner profile manually
BD82	Generate partner profiles automatically
WE21	Port definitions
SM59	RFC destination
BD64	Maintain customer model
BD71	Distribute customer model

Workflow (Definition)

SWU3	Basic workflow settings
PPOC	Maintain organization structure
PFTC	Task definition
SWE2	Event linkage table

Workflow (Run Time)

SO01	SAP Inbox
SWEL	Event log
SWI1	Workflow log
SWI2	Work item analysis
SWI5	Workload analysis

Message Control

NACE	Maintain condition records for various applications
VOK2	Message control components for sales and distribution
VOK3	Message control components for purchasing
VOFM	Maintain requirements for message control
V/86	Field catalog for condition tables

Testing

WE19	Test tool for IDocs
WE12	Convert an outbound IDoc to an inbound IDoc
WE16	Process an incoming IDoc file
WE17	Process an incoming status file

Reprocessing IDocs

BD88	Process outbound IDocs
BD87	Process inbound IDocs

System Monitoring

SM12	Locked entries
SM13	Asynchronous update log
ST22	Dump analysis
SM21	System log
SM66	Debug asynchronous update tasks

Miscellaneous

XD02	Maintain customer master
XK02	Maintain vendor master
MM02	Maintain material master
VA01	Create sales order
ME21	Create purchase order
ME11	Create purchasing info records

Enhancement

SMOD	Search and locate user exits
CMOD	Maintain projects to code user exits

Configuration of New Components

WE81	Create new message type
WE82	Link IDoc type and message type
WE41	Create outbound process code
WE42	Create inbound process code
BD64	Maintain ALE distribution model
WE57	Allocate inbound function module to message type
BD51	Define settings for inbound function module
BD67	Assign input methods for a process code (inbound)
WE57	Link IDoc to message and function module (inbound)

Programs

The following programs are scheduled to run on a periodic basis for processing at different layers of ALE and EDI processes. One or more instances of each program are scheduled on an as-needed basis.

◆ **RSNAST00.** This program processes buffered entries in the NAST table and is used for applications that use message control to process IDoc output. The use of RSNAST00 in the process flow is described in Chapter 3, "The Outbound EDI Process." Steps to execute the RSNAST00 program are listed in Chapter 10, "Testing the EDI Interface."

- ◆ **RBDMIDOC.** This program generates IDocs by processing change pointers that have been logged for changes made to master data objects. The significance of change pointers and the use of the RBDMIDOC program is described in Chapter 20, "The Outbound ALE Process." Steps to execute the program are listed in Chapter 26, "Testing the ALE Interface."

- ◆ **RSEOUT00.** This program processes outbound IDocs (status 30) that have been buffered to support mass processing. The use of RSEOUT00 in the process flow is described in Chapter 3, "The Outbound EDI Process." Steps to execute the RSEOUT00 program are listed in Chapter 10, "Testing the EDI Interface."

- ◆ **RBDAPP01.** This program processes inbound IDocs (status 64) that have been buffered to support mass processing. The use of RBDAPP01 in the process flow is described in Chapter 4, "The Inbound EDI Process." Steps to execute the RBDAPP01 program are listed in Chapter 10, "Testing the EDI Interface."

- ◆ **RBDMANIN.** This program reprocesses inbound IDocs that failed because of application errors (status 51). This program can be executed directly using transaction SE38, but in most cases this program is invoked from the ALE tool to process incoming IDocs (transaction BD88). Steps to execute the BD88 transaction are listed in Chapter 12, "EDI Process Troubleshooting and Recovery" under "Troubleshooting Guide for Inbound Errors."

- ◆ **RBDMOIND.** This program updates the status of IDocs that have been successfully dispatched to a receiving SAP system. The use of RBDMOIND in the process flow is described in Chapter 20, "The Outbound ALE Process." Steps to execute the RBDMOIND program are listed in Chapter 26, "Testing the ALE Interface."

- ◆ **RSEIDOCM.** This program can be scheduled to run as a monitoring program. This program starts workflow when the state of the system crosses a predefined threshold. Configuration of this program is described in Chapter 9, "Configuring Workflow."

User-Exits in the IDoc Programs

User exits are an important aspect of enhancing the IDoc interface to accommodate extended IDocs. A list of the user-exits is provided in Table A-1 for quick reference. Because this list is always growing, you can refer to "Locating User Exits" in Chapter 32, "Programming in the IDoc Interface," for step-by-step instructions. The list in Table A-2 shows a cross-reference between SAP messages, ANSI X.12 EDI messages, and EDIFACT messages.

Table A-1 User exits in the IDoc interface

IDoc Message	Description	Direction	Enhancement
BLAOCH	Contracts change	I/O	MM06E002
BLAORD	Contracts	I/O	MM06E002
BLAREL	Contract release	I/O	MM06E002
COND_A	Pricing Conditions	O	VKOE0001
COND_A	Pricing Conditions	I	VKOI0001
CREMAS	Vendor master	I/O	VSV00001
DEBMAS	Customer master	I/O	VSV00001
DELINS	Scheduling Agreement	O	MM06E001
DESADV	Advanve Shipment notice	I	MM06E001
FIDCMT	Distributed General Ledger	I/O	F050S001
INFREC	Purchasing information record	O	MMAL0003
INFREC	Purchasing information record	I	MMAL0004
INVOIC	Invoices	O	LVEDF001
INVOIC	FI Invoices	I	FEDI0001
MATMAS	Material master	I/O	MGV00001
ORDCHG	Purchase Order Change	O	MM06E001
ORDCHG	Sales order change	I	VEDB0001
ORDERS	Purchase Orders	O	MM06E001
ORDERS	Sales Orders	I	VEDA0001
ORDRSP	Order confirmation	O	SDEDI001
ORDRSP	Order response for a purchase order	I	MM06E001
PAYEXT	Payment Order	I	FEDI0002
PAYEXT	Payment Order	O	FEDI0003
REMADV	Remittance Advice	I	FEDI0002
REMADV	Remittance Advice	O	FEDI0003

REQOTE	Incoming request for quote	I	VEDQ0001
SDPACK	Error handling for input IDoc	I	VMDE0001
SDPACK	Packing	I	VMDE0004
SDPICK	Error handling for input IDoc	I	VMDE0001
SDPICK	Picking	O	VMDE0002
SDPICK	Picking	I	VMDE0003
SRCLST	Source List	O	MMAL0001
SRCLST	Source List	I	MMAL0002
SRVMAS	Serveice master	O	BASO0001
SRVMAS	Service master	I	BASI0001
WMBBIN	Error handling for input IDoc	I	MWMIDI01
WMBBIN	Block storage type	I	MWMIDI04
WMCATO	Error handling for input IDoc	I	MWMIDI01
WMCATO	Cancel Request Transfer Order	I	MWMIDI03
WMCATO	Cancel Request Transfer Order	O	MWMIDO02
WMINVE	Error handling for input IDocs	I	MWMIDO07
WMINVE	Count Data Inventory	I	MWMIDO09
WMINVE	Count Data Inventory	O	MWMIDO04
WMMBXY	Error handling for input IDocs	I	MWMIDO07
WMMBXY	Goods movement	I	MWMIDO08
WMRREF	Release reference number	O	MWMIDO03
WMSUMO	Error handling for input IDoc	I	MWMIDI01
WMSUMO	Move storage unit	I	MWMIDI06
WMTOCO	Error handling for input IDoc	I	MWMIDI01
WMTOCO	Confirm Transfer Order	I	MWMIDI02
WMTORD	Error handling for input IDocs	I	MWMIDO07
WMTORD	Create Transfer Order	I	MWMIDO10
WMTORD	Create Transfer Order	O	MWMIDO01
WMTREQ	Error handling for input IDoc	I	MWMIDI01
WMTREQ	Create Transfer Request	I	MWMIDI05

Message	Description	Direction	User exit Program
ORDERS	Sales Order	I	LVEDAF0U
ORDCHG	Sales Order Change	I	LVEDBF0U
DESADV	Advance Shipment Notice	O	LVED2FZZ

Table A-2 Cross-referencing between SAP messages, ANSI X.12 messages, and EDIFACT messages

IDoc Type	Message	Description	ANSI X.12	EDIFACT	Inbound	Outbound
PEXR2001, PEXR2002	CREADV	Credit memo display	812	CREADV	X	X
PEXR2001, PEXR2002	DEBADV	Debit display	812	DEBADV	X	X
DELFOR01	DELINS	Delivery schedule	830	DELFOR	X	X
DELFOR01	DELINS	JIT delivery schedule	862	DELJIT	X	X
DELVRY01 (previously , DESADV01) DELVRY02	DESADV	Shipping notification	856	DESADV	X	X
FINSTA01	FINSTA	Financial statement of an account message		FINSTA	X	
GSVERF01	GSVERF	Cred. memo procedure	861		X	X
INVOIC01	INVOIC	Invoice / Billing document	810	INVOIC	X	X
INVOIC01	INVOIC	Invoice / Billing document	880	INVOIC	X	X
FINSTA01	LOCKBX	Lockbox	823		X	
ORDERS01, ORDERS02, ORDERS03, ORDERS04	ORDCHG	Purchase order/ order changeᵭ	860	ORDCHG	X	X
ORDCHG ORDERS01, ORDERS02, ORDERS03, ORDERS04		Purchase order/order change	876	ORDCHG	X	X
ORDERS01, ORDERS02, ORDERS03, ORDERS04	ORDERS	Purchase order / order	850	ORDERS	X	X
ORDERS01, ORDERS02, ORDERS03, ORDERS04	ORDERS	Purchase order / order	875	ORDERS	X	X

ORDERS01, ORDERS02, ORDERS03, ORDERS04	ORDRSP	Purchase order / order confirmation	855	ORDRSP	X	X
ORDERS01, ORDERS02, ORDERS03, ORDERS04	ORDRSP	Purchase order / order confirmation	865	ORDRSP	X	X
PEXR2001	PAYEXT	Extended payment order		PAYEXT		X
PRICAT01	PRICAT	Price catalog	832	PRICAT		X
PRICAT01	PRICAT	Price catalog	879	PRICAT		X
PRICAT01	PRICAT	Price catalog	888	PRICAT		X
PRICAT01	PRICAT	Price catalog	889	PRICAT		X
PROACT01	PROACT	Stock and sale data	852			
ORDERS01, ORDERS02, ORDERS03, ORDERS04	QUOTES	Quotation	843			X
PEXR2001, PEXR2002	REMADV	Payment advice	820	REMADV	X	X
ORDERS01, ORDERS02, ORDERS03, ORDERS04	REQOTE	Inquiry	840	REQOTE	X	X
DELVRY01	SHPCON	Shipping confirmation	945		X	
SHPMNT01, SHPMNT02, SHPMNT03	SHPMNT	Shipping outbound	856	IFTMIN		X
SHPMNT03	SHPMNT	Shipping outbound	204	IFTMIN		
DELVRY01	SHPORD	Shipping order	940			X
TXTRAW01	TXTRAW	Message for free text in SAPoffice format 'RAW'	864		X	
DELVRY01	WHSCON	Stock confirmation	945		X	
DELVRY01	WHSORD	Stock order	940			X

An IDoc File Example

Listing A-1 contains a dump of an orders IDoc (ORDERS02) to a file. This was generated using transaction WE19. As you can see, everything in an IDoc is character-based. The first record is the control record, followed by several data records. Data records start with E2.

Listing A-1

```
EDI_DC                                   68ORDERS022              LIVENDOR0001
CORHDR          SAPEDIPORTKUCUSTOMER01
64
199903101438250RDERS               LFAG


E2EDK01002                      000001E2EDK01002000000000 000 USD

E2EDKA1001                      000002E2EDKA1001000000000 AG 1000000009
VENDOR000001

E2EDKA1001                      000003E2EDKA1001000000000 WE
1000000009

E2EDK02                         000004E2EDK02     000000000 001BP3333377
19990302

E2EDP01002                      000005E2EDP01002000000000 010             100
PCE100             PCE     2.002           1000

E2EDP20                         000006E2EDP20     000000000 100
19990308

E2EDP19                         000007E2EDP19     000000000 001MATERIAL00001

E2EDPT1                         000008E2EDPT1     000000000 Z019E

E2EDPT2                         000009E2EDPT2     000000000 LONG TEXT
```

IDoc Status Codes

The status codes in Table A-3 have been defined for the IDocs.

Table A-3 IDoc status codes

Status Code	Description
0	"Not used, only R/2"
1	IDoc created
2	Error passing data to port
3	Data passed to port OK
4	Error within control information of EDI subsystem
5	Error during translation
6	Translation OK
7	Error during syntax check
8	Syntax check OK
9	Error during interchange handling
10	Interchange handling OK
11	Error during dispatch
12	Dispatch OK
13	Retransmission OK
14	Interchange Acknowledgment positive
15	Interchange Acknowledgment negative
16	Functional Acknowledgment positive
17	Functional Acknowledgment negative
18	Triggering EDI subsystem OK
19	Data transfer for test OK
20	Error triggering EDI subsystem
21	Error passing data for test
22	"Dispatch OK, acknowledgment still due"
23	Error during retransmission
24	Control information of EDI subsystem OK
25	Processing despite syntax error (outbound)
26	Error during syntax check of IDoc (outbound)
27	Error in dispatch level (ALE service)
28	Not used
29	Error in ALE service
30	IDoc ready for dispatch (ALE service)
31	Error--no further processing
32	IDoc was edited

33	Original of an IDoc which was edited
34	Error in control record of IDoc
35	IDoc reloaded from archive
36	Electronic signature not performed (timeout)
37	IDoc added incorrectly
38	IDoc archived
39	Receipt confirmed by target system
40	Application document not created in target system
41	Application document created in target system
50	IDoc added
51	Error: Application document not posted
52	Application document not fully posted
53	Application document posted
54	Error during formal application check
55	Formal application check OK
56	IDoc with errors added
57	Test IDoc: Error during application check
58	Not used
59	Not used
60	Error during syntax check of IDoc (inbound)
61	Processing despite syntax error (inbound)
62	IDoc passed to application
63	Error passing IDoc to application
64	IDoc ready to be passed to application
65	Error in ALE service
66	Not used
67	Not used
68	Error—no further processing
69	IDoc was edited
70	Original of an IDoc which was edited
71	IDoc reloaded from archive
72	"Not used, only R/2"
73	IDoc archived

Release 4.x versus 3.x

You may be wondering what is different between the 3.x and 4.x systems. The basic concepts covered in this book have not changed between the 3.x system and the 4.x system. However, there have been some changes at the internal implementation level that may have some impact on you as the user of the ALE/EDI Interface. In addition, some new tools have been added to ease the task of maintaining partner profiles. IDoc extensions are now more intuitive. And, as always, there are cosmetic changes. Menu options have been regrouped to make it simpler and easier to navigate to the various functions. Throughout this book wherever applicable, the changes between 4.x and 3.x have been noted.

File Name Changes

The space for object names in the IDoc interface has been increased from 4 and 8 characters to 30 characters. For example, IDoc type, Segment type, Segment definition, Process code, and Message type names can be up to thirty characters.

This increase in space impacts the structure of IDoc files used in the inbound EDI process. If you have upgraded to release 4.x and you want to take advantage of the extended space, you will have to modify the IDoc files as per the new format. You can use the IDoc documentation (transaction WE61) tool to look at the new structure of the control record and data record. Another option is to use the IDoc tool (transaction WE19) to copy an existing IDoc and save the IDoc to a file. Then you can do some cut paste exercises to build your IDocs.

 NOTE

You can continue to use the old format provided you do not want to use the extended name space. To support backward compatibility, SAP will accept an IDoc file which is in 3.x format.

Because of the increase in name space, you can run into problems when communicating with systems that are at a release level of less than 4.0. SAP provides a conversion table to map long names to short names for Basic IDoc types (transaction WE70), IDoc extensions (transaction WE71), IDoc types (transaction WE72), and Message types (transaction WE73). To access the conversion tables, go to the IDoc editor (transaction WE30) and choose Environment, Conversion. You can select the appropriate conversion table. Figure A-1 shows the conversion table for an IDoc type monthly report from its long name to a short name. The monthly report was an example Basic IDoc type used throughout Section III, "IDocs."

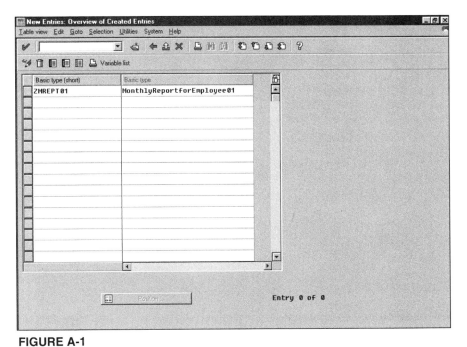

FIGURE A-1

Conversion between long names and short names for basic IDoc types

New Tools to Maintain Partner Profiles

As mentioned in Chapter 7, "Maintaining Partner Profiles," the task of maintaining partner profiles is a nightmare, especially for large EDI shops where you can have hundreds of trading partners. In release 4.0, you can maintain default parameters for the message types, which can be used later during the maintenance of partner profiles. This saves you a great deal of typing effort. The steps are as follows:

1. **Maintain default parameters for the message type.** In the IMG, choose Cross-Application Components, IDoc Interface/Electronic Data Interchange, IDoc interface—Basis, Set proposal values for partner profiles. From this path, you can select the object for which you want to maintain the default parameters. Figure A-2 shows the default values for the outbound message DESADV (Shipment notice) to a customer.

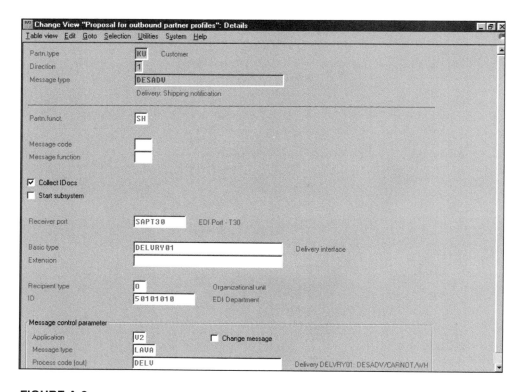

FIGURE A-2

Default parameters maintained for outbound message DESADV to customers

2. **Maintain partner profile.** Execute transaction WE20 and enter your partner number and partner type. Select Partner, Fast Entry from the menu. The system prompts you to select whether you want to maintain inbound or outbound parameters. Then a list of messages for which defaults were maintained in the previous step are displayed. You can select the appropriate message type, and the system automatically copies the values for you. Figure A-3 shows the values copied in the outbound record for DESADV. You then have the option of modifying any attributes that you may wish.

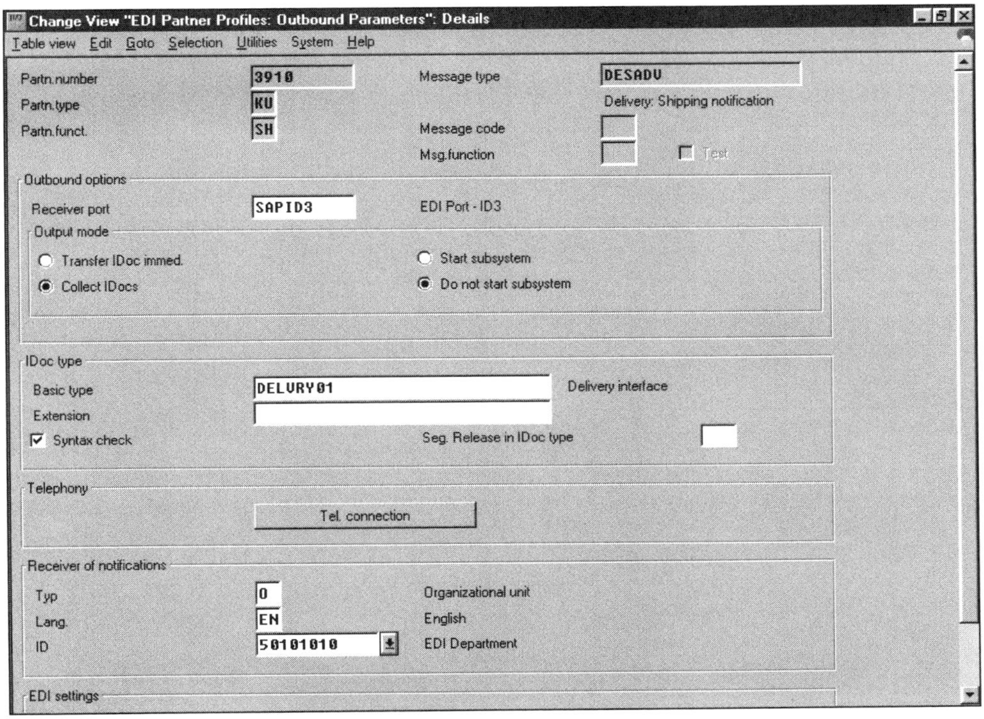

FIGURE A-3

Outbound record (DESADV) in the partner profile created using defaults maintained for message type

---

 NOTE

Similar to partner profile, you can also maintain default parameters for the port definitions.

Creating IDoc Extensions

The IDoc extension process as described in Chapter 31, "Extending and Developing a Basic IDoc Type," shows the two-step process to extend a Basic IDoc type. First you create an IDoc extension and then apply the extension to a

Basic IDoc type to get an IDoc type. This two-step process has been simplified in 4.0 and entails only one step—to create an IDoc extension. You maintain a customer segment and tie the customer segment to an SAP segment as a child segment. The steps are listed below using the same example used in Chapter 31, "Extending and Developing a Basic IDoc Type" to explain the two-step process:

1. Start the IDoc editor using transaction WE30. You will notice the IDoc editor screen compared to 3.x systems has one less option because of the simplified process. Enter the IDoc extension name and press the create button. The system prompts you to enter the basic IDoc type and other related information, as shown in Figure A-4.

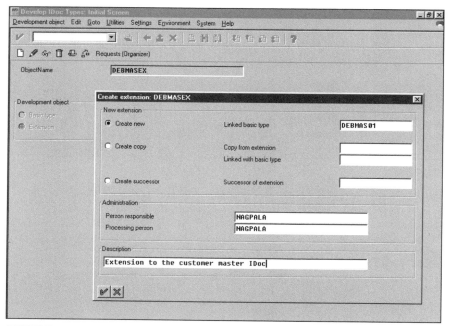

FIGURE A-4

Extending a Basic IDoc type to add a custom segment

2. On the next screen, the system displays the structure of the Basic IDoc type. Select the reference segment that you wish to extend and press the create button. The system informs you that the segment will be added as a child segment. On the next screen the system prompts you to enter the custom segment name, as shown in Figure A-5. Once you enter the custom segment name, the segment is inserted as a child segment to the Basic IDoc type.

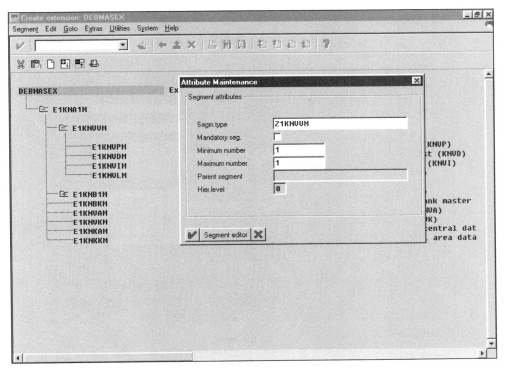

FIGURE A-5

Specifying attributes of custom segment to be inserted in the Basic IDoc type

The IDoc test tool (transaction WE19) has been enhanced to support outbound processing as well. In 3.x, the IDoc test tools support inbound processing only. This allows you to send IDocs in bursts to test performance issues.

Cosmetic Changes

There are several cosmetic changes in 4.x, and they are all very intuitive. The new interface is much more user-friendly. Following is a summary of some of the important cosmetic changes:

◆ **The segment editor has a better look.** On the first screen you can tell the various segment definitions associated with a segment type. The display has been improved to make it look more like a segment editor than a table maintenance screen (see Figure A-6).

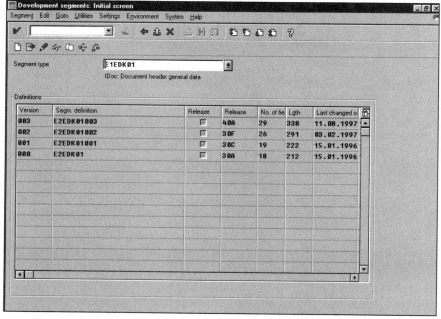

FIGURE A-6

The segment editor displays various segment definitions

◆ **The general settings for IDocs are easier to maintain and comprehend.** In Chapter 6, "Configuring Basic EDI Components," and Chapter 22, "Configuring the ALE Infrastructure," the Basic IDoc settings are discussed. In 4.x, the procedure is fairly simple. Execute transaction WE46, the system displays the various settings that can be maintained. Select the Global parameters checkbox and click on the change button. The Basic settings for IDocs and additional fields can be maintained here, as shown in Figure A-7.

◆ **Configuring the ALE/EDI Interface for new processes is easier.** The steps to configure the ALE/EDI interface to recognize custom IDocs and processes has not changed, but the steps can now be easily accessed from the area menu of ALE (transaction BALE) by choosing Goto, ALE development. In 3.x, the steps are partially distributed between the area menu of EDI and IMG, as described in Chapter 33, "Customizing the Interface for New or Extended IDocs." I find this cosmetic change to be the most useful.

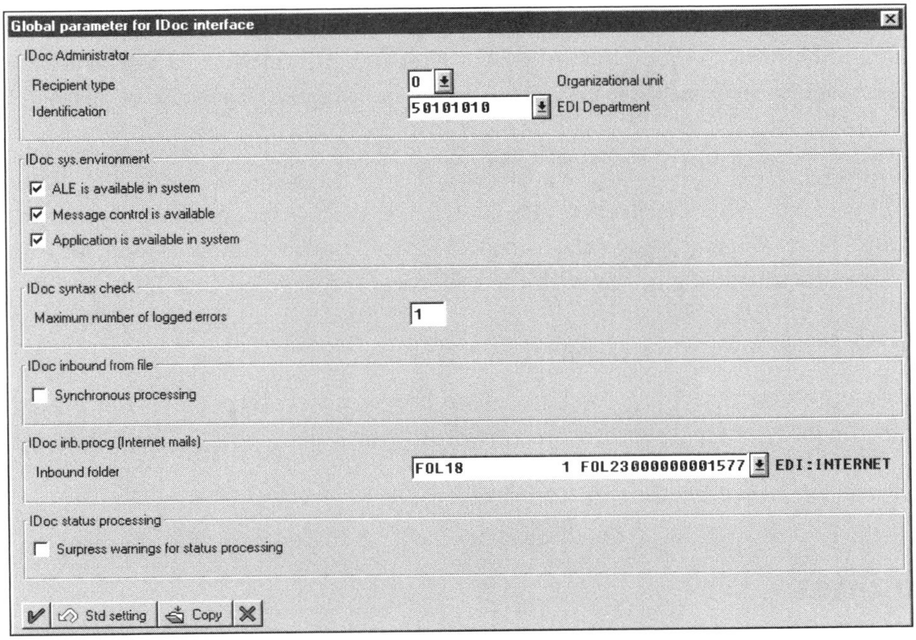

FIGURE A-7

Global parameters for the IDoc interface

Internet Resources

A great deal of supplementary information on ALE and EDI topics is available on the Internet.

Internet Discussion Groups

The following listservers are useful resources for interacting with your peers. As with any listserver, you will find some very useful tips and advice, but the timing is unpredictable.

The SAP FAQ EDI Discussion List is a free, e-mail-based forum for the discussion of EDI-related topics of interest to those involved with SAP. To subscribe, send an e-mail message to **md@ichat.gen.com** with the following command in the body of your message:

```
subscribe SAPFAQ-EDI
```

The SAP EDI Special Interest Group provides a forum for discussion of EDI-related questions of interest to SAP users. To subscribe to the list, send an e-mail message to **listproc@listserver.com** with the following message on a single line:

```
subscribe sap-edi-sig <firstname lastname>
```

The SAP MIT Listserver (SAP-R3-L) is for technical and nontechnical discussion on any topic related to SAP. For complete details send an e-mail to **listserv@mitvma.mit.edu** with the following message on first line:

```
INFO SAP-R3-L
```

To subscribe to the list, send an e-mail message to **listserv@mitvma.mit.edu** and in the body of the message enter the following line:

```
subscribe sap-r3-l <lastname firstname>
```

Web Sites

You are encouraged to explore the following Web sites for additional information on various topics discussed in this book.

The SAP home page (**www.sap.com**) contains a wealth of information on the products and services offered by SAP. Among other things, you can find a complete list of third-party products certified for ALE and EDI.

The SAP Intranet (**sapnet.sap-ag.de**) site contains a wealth of technical literature and white papers on various products and services offered by SAP. This site is restricted to SAP customers and partners. You'll need OSS ID to access this site.

SAP Labs (**www.saplabs.com**) is a completely owned subsidiary of SAP. This site has useful information on products from SAP Labs that make SAP implementation easier.

Also called ASUG, the SAP Americas User Group (**www.asug.com**) organization is dedicated to communicating the needs of the user community to SAP. This site is for member companies only. A group within the ASUG focuses on EDI-related activities.

The SAP Technical Journal (**www.saptechjournal.com**) is the official technical journal from SAP and a great resource for technical advice. You can also contribute to this journal.

The SAP Fans Club (www.sapfans.com) is a great site for anyone interested in conversing with other SAP professionals in a particular area of interest.

Other Resources

The following sources of information on ALE, EDI, and IDocs are available directly from SAP.

Online Help CD

ALE-related information is available under R/3 Library, Cross Applications, ALE.

IDoc-related information is available under R/3 Library, Cross Application, The IDoc Interface for EDI.

Message control information is available under R/3 Library, Cross Application, Message Control.

Workflow information is available under R/3 Library, Basis Components, Business Engineering Workbench, SAP Business Workflow.

Training Courses

The following training courses pertain to the material in this book and might be of interest to you. These courses are offered at SAP training centers throughout the world. Check SAP's Web site at **www.sap.com** for the course schedule and location.

CA210	EDI Interface
CA910	ALE
BC600	SAP Business Workflow Introduction
BC601	Build and Use SAP Business Workflow
BC620	SAP IDoc Interface Technology
BC621	SAP IDoc Interface Development
BC615	Archiving Technology

Index

A

X

Z

SAP
TECHNICAL JOURNAL

FREE SUBSCRIPTION FORM

To receive a FREE *SAP Technical Journal*, complete and return this form.

Please answer all questions, sign and date the card.

❑ **YES!** I wish to receive my FREE subscription to *SAP Technical Journal*.

❑ NO, I don't wish to subscribe

Signature (required)_____

Date (required)_____

Name_____

Title_____

Company_____

Address_____

City_____ State/Province_____

Country_____ Zip/Postal Code_____

Telephone_____ Fax_____

E-mail Address_____

1 What is your relationship to SAP? (check only one)
01 ❑ Customer
02 ❑ Third-Party vendor
03 ❑ Development partner
04 ❑ Consulting partner
05 ❑ Hardware partner
06 ❑ SAP Employee
07 ❑ Other_____

2 If a customer, is your R/3 System live?

Currently	Within the next 6 months
08 ❑ Yes	10 ❑ Yes
09 ❑ No	11 ❑ No

3 How many years have you been working with SAP products? (check only one)
12 ❑ Less than 1 year
13 ❑ 1 - 2 years
14 ❑ 2 - 5 years
15 ❑ Over five years

4 What is your current job function? (check only one)
16 ❑ Analyst/Program Analyst
17 ❑ Application Consultant
18 ❑ Application Developer
19 ❑ Basis Consultant
20 ❑ Basis Developer
21 ❑ Business Operations Manager
22 ❑ Design/Development or R&D Engineer
23 ❑ Network Engineer
24 ❑ Process Engineer
25 ❑ Product Manager
26 ❑ Quality/Reliability Manager
27 ❑ Software Engineer
28 ❑ Test Engineer
29 ❑ Web/Internet Professional
30 ❑ Other_____

5 Which SAP release(s) do you currently work with? (check ALL that apply)
31 ❑ R/2   32 ❑ R/3 3.x
32 ❑ R/3 2.x   34 ❑ R/3 4.x

6 Do you have Internet/intranet applications connected to SAP R/3?

Currently	Within the next 6 months
35 ❑ Yes	37 ❑ Yes
36 ❑ No	38 ❑ No

7 What SAP R/3 functionality do you use? (check all that apply)
39 ❑ Financial Accounting (FI)
40 ❑ Controlling (CO)
41 ❑ Asset Managment (AM)
42 ❑ Project System (PS)
43 ❑ Workflow (WF)
44 ❑ Industry Solutions (IS)
45 ❑ Human Resources (HR)
46 ❑ Plant Maintenance (PM)
47 ❑ Quality Management (QM)
48 ❑ Production Planning (PP)
49 ❑ Materials Management (MM)
50 ❑ Sales and Distribution (SD)

8 Which best describes your industry? (check only one)
51 ❑ Aerospace & Defense
52 ❑ Automotive
53 ❑ Banking/Insurance
54 ❑ Chemicals
55 ❑ Consumer Products
56 ❑ Consulting & Professional Services (please specify)_____
57 ❑ Computer Dealer (Reseller/Vendor)
58 ❑ Data Processing
59 ❑ Education
60 ❑ Entertainment/Tourism
61 ❑ Engineering & Construction
62 ❑ Healthcare
63 ❑ High Tech & Electronics
64 ❑ Media
65 ❑ Oil & Gas
66 ❑ Pharmaceuticals
67 ❑ Public Sector
68 ❑ Real Estate
69 ❑ Retail (not computers)
70 ❑ System House-Integrator or VAR/Systems/Integrators
71 ❑ Transportation
72 ❑ Telecommunications
73 ❑ Utilities
74 ❑ Other_____

9 What SAP R/3 infrastructure do you work with? (check ALL that apply)
75 ❑ OS/390   77 ❑ Windows NT
76 ❑ OS/400   78 ❑ UNIX

10 Which tools/languages do you use for SAP R/3 and SAP R/3-integrated solutions? (check ALL that apply)
79 ❑ ABAP
80 ❑ Active X
81 ❑ ALE
82 ❑ Batch
83 ❑ C/C ++
84 ❑ Cobol
85 ❑ COM/DCOM
86 ❑ CORBA
87 ❑ Delphi
88 ❑ DHTML
89 ❑ EDI
90 ❑ HTML
91 ❑ Java
92 ❑ JavaScript
93 ❑ PERL
94 ❑ PowerBuilder
95 ❑ SQL
96 ❑ Visual Basic
97 ❑ Other_____
98 ❑ None of the Above

FAX TO:
1-615-377-0525 or
SUBSCRIBE ONLINE
www.saptechjournal.com

11 What tools/topics are you interested in? (check ALL that apply)

099 ❑ Archiving
100 ❑ Application development tools
101 ❑ Application Link Enabling
102 ❑ Enterprise Management
103 ❑ Information Management
104 ❑ Internet/intranet
105 ❑ Middleware
106 ❑ Modeling
107 ❑ Performance Management
108 ❑ Reporting
109 ❑ Systems Management
110 ❑ Testing
111 ❑ Workflow
112 ❑ Other_____

12 How many total employees does your company have?

113 ❑ Under 100
114 ❑ 100 to 249
115 ❑ 250 to 499
116 ❑ 500 to 999
117 ❑ 1,000 to 4,999
118 ❑ 5,000 to 9,999
119 ❑ 10,000 or more

13 What is your company's total sales volume?

120 ❑ Under $10 million
121 ❑ $10 - $50 million
122 ❑ $50 - $250 million
123 ❑ $250 - $500 million
124 ❑ $500 million - $1 billion
125 ❑ $1 billion - $5 billion
126 ❑ Over $5 billion

PLEASE MAKE SURE YOU'VE:

☞ **Signed and dated the form**

☞ **Filled out the form completely**

☞ **Applied postage**

☞ **Folded form in half and taped closed (do not staple)**

FOLD HERE FOR MAILING

CIRCULATION DEPARTMENT
55 HAWTHORNE ST STE 600
SAN FRANCISCO CA 94105-3912

PLACE
STAMP
HERE